Belluno

Udine

Pordenone

Gorizia

Treviso

Trieste

enice

enna

Marino

Pesaro

Urbino

Ancona

Macerata

Perugia

Ascoli Piceno

Teramo

Terni

Rieti

L'Aquila

Pescara

Chieti

Rome

Frosinone

Campobasso

Latina

Foggia

GUIDE
TO ARTISTIC
ITALY

GUIDE TO ARTISTIC ITALY

by Giuliano Dogo

Electa

Translated from the Italian
by Daphne Newton

Printed in Italy
© Copyright 1981
by Electa, Milano
fourth edition 1989

INTRODUCTION

The aim of this Artistic Guide is to provide visitors to Italy with handy and reliable information concerning any item of artistic interest they may wish to know about. Far from replacing existing guides, it is intended to supplement them, enabling visitors to use the time and money they have spent discovering Italy to the best advantage.

What immediately strikes the eye, however, is the original use made of illustrations. This is not merely an "illustrated" book, but one where the pictures serve as a natural complement to the information supplied under the individual headings. They will help visitors to memorize what they have seen and pay special attention to details the casual observer might easily overlook.

Each entry begins with a brief description of the main geographical features of the place concerned, and goes on to provide a simple and impartial account of the monuments and works of art to be seen there. We have made no attempt to influence the visitor, leaving the works to speak for themselves. But in order to place each item in perspective, the essential dates regarding the birth and death, or known limits of the artist's activity are given beside the name.

The limited space at our disposal has prevented any lengthy or detailed description of the large cities. Only essential information has been given concerning the chief monuments, just enough to attract the reader's attention, and therefore leaving more specific descriptions to the various specialized guides.

Here we come to the second new characteristic and true function of this volume. Without neglecting the major works of art we have tried to bring to the visitor's notice the lesser known works which, being hidden away or off the beaten track, are often overlooked. These are an important part of Italy's artistic wealth, and with this in mind we would like to add that the Guide is intended to help visitors become familiar with an artistic patrimony which has been sadly neglected through not being included on the normal tourist itineraries. This book has the advantage of concentrating in only one volume essential information on the exciting discoveries the traveller may make by bus, by car or on foot.

The strict alphabetical order of each locality makes consultation easier, and to avoid excessive fragmentation isolated monuments have been included in the entries relating to the town in question.

For visitors less keen on discovering an Italy of "minor" though no less important interest, the name of each locality is preceded by one, two or three asterisks, depending on the number of monuments to be visited and importance of the place itself. An index can be found at the end of the book listing individual entries according to province.

We hope that we have provided a new means of getting to know a country which, perhaps more than any other, possesses records and masterpieces of incredible artistic and historical wealth.

We wish to thank all those who have contributed to its compilation.

* **ABANO TERME** (Padua). Spa and health resort, starting point for pleasant excursions into the Euganean Hills. The 10th cent. church of *San Lorenzo*, rebuilt several times in later centuries, contains some remarkable works of art, including a Via Crucis by Carl Henrici (1737-1823), two statues depicting Faith and Charity by Tommaso Allio (lived in the 17th cent.), and three paintings by Pietro della Vecchia, called Pietro Muttoni (1605-1678). Nearby can be found the 15th cent. *Santuario di Monte Ortone*: the main altar is a fine piece of Renaissance work, and the chancel contains important frescoes by Iacopo Parisati, called Iacopo da Montagnana (1440-1499).

* **ABBADIA SAN SALVATORE** (Siena). The community grew up around the famous abbey in the 8th cent. *Abbadia di San Salvatore* or *del Monte Amiata*, probably founded in the 8th cent. by Rachis, Duke of Friuli and King of the Longobards, was long the most splendid abbey in Tuscany. It belonged first to the Benedictines, then to the Cistercians, and used to contain a precious 8th cent. Bible, now in the Biblioteca Laurenziana in Florence. Inside the church is a fresco depicting the Martyrdom of St. Bartholomew by Giuseppe Nasini (1664-1736), a large wooden crucifix which, according to legend, was carved as a result of a vision of Rachis, and Leggenda di Rachis,

a series of frescoes by Francesco Nasini (17th cent.). The crypt was a church in the 8th cent., and has thirty pillars, much admired for the variety of the capitals. The *Borgo Medioevale* is a typical example of a hillside castle.

* **ABBASANTA** (Cagliari). Not far from the town is the *Nuraghe di Losa* interesting for its complex structure and enormous girth. The pre-1000 B.C. keep, the trilobed section (8th cent.-7th cent. B.C.) and the 6th cent. B.C. rampart are still recognisable. Inside, notice the circular ground-floor cell, with fillet vault, passages, traces of embrasures, etc. Excursion to the *Diga del Tirso*, known as the Santa Chiara an imposing many-arched dam, completed in 1923.

* **ABBIATEGRASSO** (Milan). Important agricultural and industrial centre. The *Castello*, built in 1382 by Gian Galeazzo Visconti and later spoilt by alterations, still reveals some interesting parts of the original construction on the outside. In the *Basilica di Santa Maria Nuova* the finest element is the gracious four-arched portico. Renaissance in style, it is decorated with terracottas and busts. Against the facade is a harmonious Renaissance arcade (1497) by Bramante. The basilica contains 15th cent. sgraffito decoration. A short walk away is the *Chiesa Abbaziale di Santa Maria di Morimondo*, built between 1186 and 1292. Cistercian-Gothic in style, the interior is composed of a nave and two aisles divided by heavy pillars. There is a 14th cent. holy-water stoup, surmounted by a statue of the Virgin and Child, probably by Bonino da Campione, whose work belongs to the second half of the 14th cent.

Abbadia San Salvatore, Abbey Church, crypt.

Abbiategrasso, Santa Maria Nova, facade.

* ACERENZA (Potenza). Magnificently situated in a commanding position on a rock of calcareous tufa. The ancient *Cattedrale* was possibly rebuilt in the second half of the 11th, and again in the late 13th cent. It is one of the finest in Basilicata. The exterior is interesting, even though it has been disfigured by clumsy alterations. The interior, with a nave and two aisles, is in the shape of a Latin cross. Artistic works include a panel depicting the Madonna of the Rosary and Saints Dominic and Thomas (second half of the 16th cent.), another 16th cent. panel depicting the Pietà, a 15th cent. triptych showing Christ enthroned, and, in the crypt, the fine 16th cent. marble tomb of Ferrillo and his wife.

* ACERRA (Naples). One of the most densely populated areas around Naples. The *Duomo*, consecrated to the Assunta, stands on the spot where, according to tradition, there used to be a temple dedicated to Hercules. Construction began in 1791. The interior contains an Assumption by Giacinto Diana (1730-1803); a marble bas-relief of the Assumption belonging to the 16th cent., and a marble Bishop's Throne of Renaissance design. In the tiny church of *Corpus Domini* there is a Pietà painted by Massimo Stanzione (1585-1656) and an 18th cent. painting representing the Marriage at Cana and the Last Supper. In a chapel in the Baroque-domed church of the *Annunciata* is an impressive wooden crucifix, Franco-Spanish in style (second half of the 12th cent.) and a 14th cent. panel of the Annunciation. Also worthy of note is the Baroque *Chiesa del Purgatorio*, and the *Castello*, which was formerly the residence of the Cardenas family, last feudal lords of the city. Excursion to the *Rovine di Suessula*, ruins of a city of Auruncan or Ausonian origin. There is a necropolis with tombs and related material dating from the 8th to the 4th cent. B.C. and great mass of "opus reticulatum".

** ACIREALE (Catania). Situated on a flat expanse of lava which plunges into the Ionian Sea. A popular tourist resort for its mild climate and enchanting surroundings, with mineral springs renowned since ancient times. The *Duomo*, dedicated to the Annunciation and St. Venera, was built at the turn of the 17th cent., and altered in the 18th. Its characteristic facade stands between two bell-towers. It has a lovely Baroque doorway in the gable of which are statues of the Virgin of the Annunciation and Saints Venera and Tecla, by Placido Blandamonte. The inside is in the shape of a Latin cross, with a nave and two aisles, and contains frescoes by Pietro Paolo Vasta (1697-1760) and the 17th cent. Chapel of St. Venera, patron saint of the city, with altarpiece and frescoes by Antonio Filocamo (1699-1743), and an exquisite holy-water stoup, probably by Antonello Gagini (1478-

1536). Lively Baroque flourishes can be seen in the *Palazzo Comunale* (1659). In one room is the well-known Madonna and Child entitled "I am the Light of the World" by Giuseppe Sciuti (1834-1911). In the *Biblioteca e Pinacoteca Zelantea*, founded in 1671, are 200,000 books including many incunabula or fifteeners, historical archives containing documents dating from 1450, archeological and Renaissance material, and a painting of the Holy Family, probably by Peter Paul Rubens (1577-1640). The *Chiesa dei Crociferi* is dedicated to St. Camillo, and has a frescoed vault by the mystic Pietro Paolo Vasta, who also carried out the Madonna delle Grazie above the high altar. The sacristy contains a painting of St. Joseph by William Borremans (1670-1744). In the *Chiesa del Suffragio* there are some important frescoes by Pietro Paolo Vasta. The church of *San Sebastiano* (first half of the 17th cent.) has a lively Baroque facade, and contains works by Vasta and his school as well as frescoes by Alessandro d'Anna (second half of the 18th cent.). The *Gabinetto Numismatico* consists of a rich collection of Greco-Sicilian coins. Walks to the *Scogli dei Ciclopi*, rocks which, according to legend, were hurled by the Cyclops at Ulysses.

* ACQUAPENDENTE (Viterbo). Built on a natural terrace; on the north side a steep descent leads into the valley of the river Paglia. The *Cattedrale*, dedicated to the Holy Sepulchre is a Benedictine basilica restored around the middle of the 18th century. The solemn facade is flanked by two bell-towers; the majestic interior contains two bas-reliefs by Agostino di Duccio (1418-c. 1481), depicting St. Michael defeating the Dragon and The Archangel Raphael leading Tobias on his Journey, a bust of Pope Innocent X by Alessandro Algardi (1595-1654), and a panel of the Pietà by Girolamo di Benevento (1470-1524). The 9th cent. crypt should be visited; it has nine aisles and contains frescoes belonging to the 13th century. The church of *Santa Maria*, also dedicated to St. Francis, is of Gothic origin. The interior consists of a single nave and contains a painting of San Bernardino by Sano di Pietro (1406-1481), and 17th and 18th cent. frescoes.

Acquapendente, Cathedral, crypt.

* **ACQUASPARTA** (Terni). Mineral-spring resort, surrounded by medieval walls. The imposing *Palazzo Cesi* was built in the second half of the 16th century to a design by Giovanni Domenico Bianchi. It has a loggia-style courtyard and interesting frescoes in the rooms, which now house the Municipal collection, with Roman stone fragments, 15th cent. carvings, gold ornaments, etc. The church of *San Francesco* (1290) contains an important 15th cent. wooden Crucifix; beside the church stand the remains of an attractive cloister. The church of *Santa Cecilia* was built in 1581, in accordance with the wishes of Isabella Liviani. It contains the tomb of Prince Federico Cesi, some 16th and 17th cent. reliquaries, and precious vestments.

* **ACQUAVIVA DELLE FONTI** (Bari). A pretty little town in the heart of the Murge. The *Cattedrale* was begun in the 12th cent. but underwent alterations in Lombard Renaissance style in the 16th. It is one of the four Palatine basilicas in the region. The facade is surmounted by a vast triangular gable, and the interior, consisting of a nave and two aisles, is much admired for its central altar with silver-leaf frontal (1699) and another notable silver frontal, dated 1753.

Acquasparta, Palazzo Cesi, facade.
Acquaviva delle Fonti, Cathedral.

* **ACQUI TERME** (Alessandria). The most remarkable town in southern Montferrat, on the banks of the river Bormida. The Romanesque *Duomo* was built in 1067, and extensively altered in later centuries. The interior is in the shape of a Latin cross, with a nave and four aisles. There are some noteworthy Renaissance reliefs on the main altar and pulpit, and underneath the chancel there is a vast, awe-inspiring crypt. The Cathedral is flanked by a mullioned Romanesque bell-tower (the upper part belonging to the 13th cent.) and the Bishop's Palace (15th cent.).
The *Antiche Terme* are among the most renowned ancient thermal baths in Italy. Little is left, however, of the ancient aqueduct, the Augustan-age *Acquedotto romano*.

* **ACRI** (Cosenza). Situated in the Sila, surrounded by little valleys and mountain streams. The *Chiesa Matrice di Santa Maria Maggore* stands on remains of a pagan temple. Romanesque in origin, it was completely restyled in the 18th cent. It contains an important painting of the Assumption of the Virgin, by an unknown 18th cent. artist. In the *Palazzo dei Sanseverino*, Time and Eternity, a fresco by Federico and Taddeo Zuccari (16th cent.). The 16th cent. church of *San Francesco di Paola*, spoilt by renovation work in the 18th cent., contains an 18th cent. wooden bust of St. Francis, and a fine canvas belonging to the Neapolitan school. The *Chiesa dei Cappuccini* has an 18th cent. alabaster group depicting the Deposition from the Cross. In the church of *San Domenico*, coloured stucco frontal.

* **ADRANO** (Catania). Situated on a lava terrace which juts out towards the valley of the river Simeto. The square-sided *Castello Normanno* is of the 11th cent. It houses an archeological museum containing material from the Neolithic and early Bronze ages, funeral urns of the pre-Castelluccian and Castelluccian age, from 2000 to 1500 B.C., various specimens of pottery and ornaments, excavated from areas inhabited in the Castelluccio age, etc. The *Chiesa Madre*, dedicated to the Assunta, was practically rebuilt in the middle of the 17th cent. The interior is divided into a nave and two aisles, and contains various works of art such as the Magdalen and the Apparition of

Acqui Terme, remains of the Roman aqueduct.

Christ, by Giuseppe Guzzardi and Angelo La Naia (both active in the first half of the present cent.). Remains of Greek walls *(Cinta di Mura)* of the 4th cent. B.C. Excursions can be made to the *Rovine della Contrada Mendolito* and to the Saracens' Bridge *(Ponte dei Saraceni)* which probably dates back to the 14th cent.

* ADRIA (Rovigo). Large agricultural and commercial town in the Polesine, it stands on the Canal Bianco which links it directly with the Adriatic. The *Cattedrale Nuova*, rebuilt at the beginning of the last cent., contains several works of art. It leads straight into the *Cattedrale Vecchia*, the crypt of which contains remains of 8th cent. Byzantine frescoes, unfortunately damaged by floods in 1951. The church of *Santa Maria Assunta della Tomba*, last restored in the early 18th cent., contains several works of art including the Sleeping Virgin (Dormitio Virginis), a high-relief in terracotta, probably by Michele da Firenze (recorded 1433-1438). The important *Museo Archeologico* contains material excavated in the surrounding area, such as an iron chariot from a Gallic warrior's tomb (4th cent. B.C.). The *Bacino di Canalbianco* provides a uniquely Venetian setting. It is overlooked by the Municipal Theatre, designed by Giovan Battista Scarpari (active in the present cent.). The *Biblioteca Civica* (public library) contains the painting: Blind Man of Adria by Jacopo Robusti, called Tintoretto (1518-1594).

* AEOLIAN ISLANDS, see Eolie.

* AFRAGOLA (Naples). The largest town in the Naples hinterland. The *Chiesa del Rosario* contains paintings by Giovanni Lanfranco (1582-1647) and Angelo Mozzillo (lived in the 18-19th cent.). There is an interesting *Castello*, built in 1380 for Queen Giovanna I, and the parish church of *San Giorgio* (14th cent.), commissioned by the same queen. The sanctuary of *Sant'Antonio da Padova* (first half of the 17th cent.) has always attracted pilgrims. Annexed to it is the Collegio Serafico, with library containing many ancient books including fifteeners and incunabula.

* AGIRA (Enna). Picturesquely set on a hillside. In the church of *San Filippo* or *Santa Maria Latina*, rebuilt in Rococo style in the 18th cent., are paintings by Olivio Sozzi (1696-1765) and Giuseppe Velasquez (1750-1827), and the crypt contains a statue of St. Philip, by Giambattista Amendola (1848-1887). In the mid-16th cent. church of *Sant'Antonio da Padova*, with Baroque facade, there is a fine polychrome-wood statue of St. Sylvester, by an unknown 16th cent. artist. The church of *Santa Margherita* has a vast 18th cent. interior; one chapel contains a statue of the Immacolata, by Giuseppe Picano (active in the second half of the 18th cent.); the chancel has

a fine engraved-wood choir, and in the left transept is a remarkable painting of Christ Crucified, possibly 16th cent. The mid-14th cent. church of *San Salvatore* has a mid-16th cent. Baroque facade. There are some good paintings inside and, in the Treasury, a precious mitre, as well as a rare abbey cross staff in Sienese style, all dating from the 15th cent. In the church of *Sant'Antonio Abate*, 16th cent. in origin, but with a modern facade, there is a Cross probably by Pietro Ruzzolone (recorded 1484-1526), and fourteen much-admired little 17th cent. paintings belonging to the Venetian school, depicting the Redeemer, Apostles and an Angel.

* AGLIATE (Town of Carate Brianza, province of Milan). The *Basilica di San Pietro* is one of the prime examples of Romanesque architecture in Lombardy. Dating from the 9th or 10th cent., it has a simple facade flanked by a mullioned bell-tower; the truss-roofed interior is divided into a nave and two aisles; the chancel stands above an interesting crypt. Next to the Basilica is the polygonal *Battistero*, belonging to the same period.

Agliate, Basilica of San Pietro and Baptistery.
Agliate, Basilica of San Pietro, interior.

* **AGNONE** (Campobasso). Pretty town on a hill overlooking the left bank of the Verrino. The church of *Sant'Emidio* has a Romanesque doorway, and contains a baptismal font and various sculptures: an Our Lady of Sorrows and a Risen Christ by the sculptress Amalia Dupré (1845-1928), a Dead Christ and a St. Francis of Assisi by Giovanni Dupré (1817-1882), a Crucified Christ by Giulio Monteverde (1837-1917). In the adjacent library, the Biblioteca Emidiana, are incunabula.

* **AGORDO** (Belluno). Main town in the Cordevole valley, surrounded by wooded hills, beyond which rise the lofty peaks of the Dolomites. The parish church (*Parrocchiale*), built to a design by Giuseppe Segusini (1801-1876), has two altarpieces by Palma il Giovane (1544-1628) and pictures by Paris Bordone (1500-1571). In the *Palazzo Crotta*, now de Manzoni, various architectural tastes are mingled, dating from the early 17th cent. to the late 18th. The *Museo Mineralogico* is worth a visit.

*** **AGRIGENTO.** Situated between two hills surrounded by ravines formed by the Drago and San Biagio streams. On one side it faces the Valley of the Temples, on the other, the sea. The 13th cent. church of *Santo Spirito* has a facade with a Gothic doorway. The interior was rebuilt in the 18th cent. and contains rich stuccoes by Giacomo Serpotta (1656-1732); to the right of the church is the monastery known as the Badia Grande, built in 1290. The *Museo Civico* consists of an art gallery containing works by Vincenzo degli Azani, called Vincenzo da Pavia (recorded 1519-1557), and Luca Giordano (1632-1705); and the Sinatra Gallery, with paintings by Francesco Lojacono (1841-1915), Francesco Camarda (active in the present cent.), Salvatore Marchesi (1852-1926), and Mario Mirabella (1870-1931). The church of *Santa Maria dei Greci*, a Greek cathedral in ancient times, was built on remains of a 5th cent. B.C. Doric temple.

The small courtyard contains drums of columns; a 13th cent. Gothic doorway leads into the interior, which has a nave and two aisles, and contains a fine early-16th cent. statue of the Madonna and Child. The *Cattedrale*, dedicated to San Gerlando, was rebuilt in the 13th and 14th cent. It was restyled and a sturdy bell-tower was added in the 15th cent. It contains several works of art, including the lavish shrine of San Gerlando, by Michele Ricca (working in the first half of the 17th cent.), a statue of the Madonna by Stefano di Martino (recorded 1475-1495), and a Madonna and Child, perhaps by Guido Reni (1575-1642). In the ancient, more interesting part of Agrigento, is the *Museo Nazionale Archeologico*, the most important museum in central-southern Sicily. It is divided into two sections: one devoted to Agrigento, the other to the surrounding areas; the most outstanding works are the gigantic Telamon (7.75 metres) and the Ephebus (perhaps carried out in 470 B.C.). The 13th cent. Romanesque-Gothic church of *San Nicola* has a simple unfinished facade, and its single-naved interior contains a fine marble sarcophagus of Phaedra, produced by a Roman workshop in the 2nd cent., after 5th cent. B.C. Greek models. The *Temple of Juno Lacinia* in its present state has twenty-five columns; those on the northern side still with architraves; hexastyle peripteral in form, the architecture, covered with the patina of thousands of years, seems to blend with the colours of the surrounding countryside, producing one of the most enchanting sights in the whole Mediterranean. The serenely majestic *Temple of Concord* is an excellent example of Doric architecture; the hexastyle peripteral was erected in the 5th cent. B.C.; it is the best-preserved monument in the Valley of Temples, mainly because it was turned into a Christian church in the 6th cent. A.D., consecrated to Saints Peter and Paul. The *Temple of Hercules* is a hexastyle peripteral, of the 6th cent. B.C.; eight of its columns still stand, four of them with capitals. The colossal *Temple of Olympian*

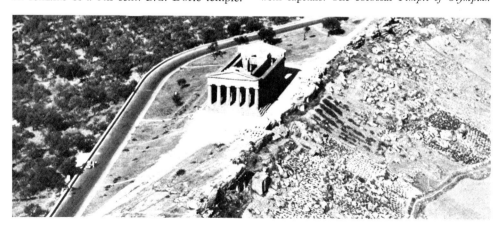

Agrigento, Temple of Concord.

Jupiter commemorates the victory of Gelo over Hamilcar in 480 B.C. Desecrated by man and earthquakes, today not a single column remains intact. Nevertheless, this vast expanse of ruins is an awe-inspiring sight; characteristic of the Temple are the telamones, gigantic human figures that were both decorative and functional in purpose. The *Sanctuary* of the Underworld Deities (*Divinità Ctonie*), brought to light in the present century, is dedicated to the goddesses Demeter and Persephone and is of great archeological interest. Erected in the 6th cent. B.C. it stands on a pre-historic base, remains of which have been excavated; in the favisse are large quantities of votive offerings. The smallish *Temple of Aesculapius* (probably 5th cent. B.C.) once held the famous statue of Apollo, masterpiece of the Greek sculptor Mirone (lived from c. 500 to 450 B.C.). The *Temple of Castor and Pollux* symbol of Agrigento, is fascinating for the colours of its marble and for its fine position. This beautiful building is seen to best advantage at sunset. It was erected in the 5th century B.C., and is a Doric hexastyle peripteral; the remains found here were finely recomposed in 1836 by the sculptor Valerio Villareale (1773-1854) and by the architect Francesco Saverio Cavallari (1809-1896). The *Quartiere Ellenistico Romano* (Greco-Roman district) has been recreated over an area of ten thousand square metres, from the original plan and layout (second half of the 4th cent. B.C.). It provides insight into the town planning of the age; several houses, such as those of the Gazelle, of the Swastika, of the Peristyle, and of the Abstractist Master, contain mosaics and geometric designs of the 1st and 2nd cent. Note, also, the bizarre 7th cent. B.C. sanctuary of Demeter (*Santuario Rupestre di Demetra*), the Greek walls (*Fortificazioni Greche*), the so-called *Tomba di Terone* and the *Oratorio di Falaride* (1st cent. B.C.), which is a real jewel of late-Hellenistic architecture.

* **AIROLA** (Benevento). On the west side of the Caudina valley with neat, broad streets. The church of *Annunciata* was built in the 16th century, and further elaborated in the 18th. Its facade is a fine piece of work by Luigi Vanvitelli (1700-1773). The large-domed interior has a Baroque ceiling and contains paintings by Paolo Domenico Finoglia (lived in the 17th cent.), an Assumption by Francesco Curia (1538-c. 1610), an Adoration of the Magi by Pietro Negroni called Zingarello (1503-1565), a fresco of the Assumption by Francesco De Mura (1696-1784), and a lavish Baroque high altar. The *Rovine del Castello* (castle ruins) are worth a visit.

* **ALA** (Trent). The main town in the lower Lagarina valley. The parish church of *Santa Maria Assunta* has a 17th cent. bell-tower. Inside the church are some remarkable paintings, including Madonna of the Rosary by Domenico Ricci called Brusasorci (1516-1567), Saint Lucy by Giambettino Cignaroli (1706-1770), and an Assumption and Saints by Giorgio Anselmi (1723-1797). Notice the *Palazzo Angelini* (18th cent.), the Baroque *Palazzo Pizzini* and *Palazzo Malfatti*, with frescoed doorways. The church of *San Giovanni* contains paintings by Alessandro Turchi called Orbetto (c. 1578-1650) and Giuseppe Craffonara (1790-1837).

* **ALASSIO** (Savona). Situated in the gently curved bay defined by Cape Santa Croce and Cape Mele, with picturesque houses facing the sea, and modern roads flanked by villas and gardens. The 11th cent. parish church of *Sant'Ambrogio* has a cusped bell-tower and Baroque interior. The *Torrione* is one of the few survivals of the characteristic constructions erected by the Ligurians to keep out the Turks. In the vicinity, the tiny church of *Santa Croce* and *Monumento Romano*.

* **ALATRI** (Frosinone). In the foothills of the Ernici mountains. The 4th cent. B.C. *Acropoli*, polygonal in shape, is the best preserved acropolis in Italy; the 4½ metre high Porta di Civita has a grand monolithic architrave; the Porta Minore and the lofty south-eastern corner of the Acropolis, with fourteen cyclopean rocks, are also worthy of attention. Visit the Romanesque-Gothic church of *Santa Maria Maggiore*: the facade has three doors with 15th cent. frescoes in the lunettes. A vestibule leads into the interior, where there is a group carved in wood by an unknown Romanesque artist of the late 13th cent. It represents the Madonna of Constantinople, and there is also a late-15th cent. polychrome-wood Madonna and Child. The *Duomo*, dedicated to St. Paul, has a 17th cent. facade marked by parastades. It contains the sepulchre of the canonized Pope Sixtus I, transferred to Alatri in 1132. The late-13th cent. church of *San Francesco* has a Gothic doorway. Inside are an important 15th cent. fresco of St. John the Baptist by an unknown artist, and a fragment of a 15th cent. fresco of the Madonna and Child with Saints, by a Master of the Madonna di Alvito. The *Palazzo Casegrandi* is a large Gothic building erected in the 13th cent. It houses the Civic Museum, which includes Roman epigraphs, a rare 14th cent. wooden Crucifix, and a small 15th cent. cusped tablet with folding panels, by Antonio da Alatri. *Piazza Santa Maria Maggiore*, the most characteristic square in the town, has a beautiful fountain in the centre, the Fonte Pia, erected in honour of Pope Pius IX.

* **ALBA** (Cuneo). Among vineyard-covered hills on the right bank of the Tanaro. It was already inhabited in pre-historic times, as is revealed by excavations begun in 1878, which resulted in the recovery of a large amount of material, including five hundred axes dated

from the Neolithic to the early Iron Age. It is called the "City of a Hundred Towers" on account of its many medieval towers, some of which still stand. The Gothic *Duomo di San Lorenzo*, begun in 1486 and restored several times, has a vast interior in the shape of a Latin cross and cruciform pillars supporting pointed arches and ogival vaults. The 14th cent. Gothic church of *San Domenico* has a facade with double-sloped roof, divided into three parts by pilaster strips, with deeply moulded portals; the interior consists of a nave and two aisles, in the form of a basilica. The Baroque church of *San Giovanni Battista* has interesting paintings by Macrino d'Alba (active 1494-c. 1528) and Barnaba da Modena (recorded 1361-1383). See also the church of *Santa Maddalena*, the *Civico Museo Archeologico*, and the *Palazzo Comunale*.

* ALBANO LAZIALE (Rome).

Situated south-west of the Lake of Albano, it is one of the most frequently visited of the "Castelli Romani". Impressive remains of the *Porta Pretoria*, leading into the "Castra Albana", the great military camp built by Septimius Severus (193-211), brought to light in 1944 after an air raid. Tomb of the *Horatii and Curiatii*, a parallelepiped sepulchre, begun in the last days of the Republican era. The *Cisternone* is a large subterranean cistern, formerly used by the Roman troops. The church of *Santa Maria della Rotonda* corresponds to the nymphaeum of a Roman villa; it has a 13th cent. portico, and is flanked by a Romanesque bell-tower, also 13th cent.

* ALBE (Town of Massa d'Albe, province of Aquila).

Small town in the Avezzano district. Standing on a low hill is the Romanesque church of *San Pietro*, built in the 11th cent. on the remains of a Roman temple; a portico dated 1526 stands in front of the facade; the interior consists of a nave and two aisles and contains a splendid marble pulpit with mosaic decoration, the work of Roman masters in the 12th and 13th cent. In the vicinity, recent excavations have brought to light the remains of the ancient *Alba Fucense*, ancient town of the Equi and then town hall in Roman times.

* ALBENGA (Savona).

Situated on the edge of the broadest plain in Liguria, in the delta formed by the rivers Aroscia, Neva and Lerrone. The remains of the Roman city lie three metres below ground level, and are visible in parts; the medieval city has survived almost intact. The *Museo Navale Romano*, unique of its type in Italy, includes among its treasures, a thousand amphoras, vases and ship's items, which show how advanced the ancient Romans were in nautical skill. The *Cattedrale di San Michele*, begun in the 11th cent., has been altered several times. It has a Baroque portal and interesting Baroque interior; in the sacristy

there is a collection of illuminated codices of the 15th and 16th cent., which are among the most valuable in Europe. The octagonal *Battistero* is the only Early-Christian monument still standing in Liguria; inside are two catacomb-type tombs and a large octagonal baptismal font of special interest. The Cathedral bell-tower, rebuilt in the late 14th cent. on an 11th cent. foundation, together with the Towers belonging to the Town Hall, form the most characteristic corner of this little town.

* ALBEROBELLO (Bari).

Considered the quaintest town in Italy, it consists almost entirely of "trulli". The *Zona Monumentale*.

Albenga, Museo Navale Romano. Ship's side and amphoras.

Albenga, Baptistery, Cathedral campanile and Town Hall tower.

formed by the Monti and Aia Piccola sections, is covered with "trulli" (over a thousand of them): these are simple, neatly whitewashed houses with conical roofs, made of superimposed drystone blocks. Even the modern church of *Sant'Antonio*, standing on a picturesque hilltop, is built in the form of a "trullo".

* **ALBINO** (Bergamo). In the Valle Seriana. The parish church of *San Giuliano*, entirely rebuilt in the 19th cent., contains paintings of St. Francis of Assisi by Alessandro Varotari, called Padovanino (1588-1648), the Holy Trinity by Giovanni Battista Moroni (c. 1525-1578), and Annunciation by Enea Talpino, called Salmeggia (c. 1550-1626). In the 15th cent. sanctuary of *Madonna del Pianto* are a Deposition from the Cross, by Salmeggia, and Christ carrying the Cross, by Giovanni Battista Moroni.

* **ALCAMO** (Trapani). Agricultural and industrial town, at the foot of Mount Bonifato. The 14th cent. *Chiesa Matrice*, rebuilt by Angelo Italia and Giuseppe Diamante in 1669, has a facade carried out in 1786 by Emanuele Cordova; inside are frescoes by William Borremans (1670-1744), a marble altar, with a Madonna delle Grazie by the sculptor Giovanni Battista Marino (recorded 1728-1765), and Death of the Virgin, a relief by Antonello Gagini (1478-1536). The church of *Sant'Oliva* designed by Giovanni Biagio Amico (1684-1754) contains stuccoes (1770) by Francesco and Giuseppe Rosso, and frescoes by Francesco D'Alessandro (lived in the 18th cent.). The interior of the *Badia Nuova* or *San Francesco di Paola*, planned by Giovanni Biagio Amico in the first half of the 18th cent., is extremely gracious; it contains stucco statues by Giacomo Serpotta (1656-1732). The church of *San Francesco d'Assisi*, first half of the 17th cent., contains two fine statues depicting St. Mark and Mary Magdalen, by Antonello Gagini. In the Baroque church of *Santi Paolo e Bartolomeo* are stuccoes by Vincenzo Messina (active at the turn of the 18th cent.), and Gabriele Messina, Vincenzo's son (active 1746-1757). Walk to the *Madonna dei Miracoli*, a sanctuary erected at the turn of the 17th cent., containing paintings by Giuseppe Patania (1780-1852) above the altars.

* **ALES** (Cagliari). Situated in a hollow, on the lower slopes of Mount Arci. The *Cattedrale* was rebuilt in the second half of the 17th cent. to a design by Domenico Spotorno (lived in the second half of the 17th cent.). It is flanked by two bell-towers and has a large dome; in the vast interior are stuccoes, works in marble, 17th cent. choirstalls, and a rich Treasury. *House of Antonio Gramsci* (1891-1937).

* **ALESSANDRIA**. Between the river Po and the Ligurian Appenines, on the right bank

of the Tanaro, it is an agricultural, commercial and industrial centre. The Gothic church of *Santa Maria di Castello* was built in the 14th and 15th cent. on the spot said to mark the origin of Alessandria; inside there is an important Baroque pulpit. The *Cattedrale* (1810) has an interesting neo-Classical facade; on the extreme left is a Romanesque sculpture probably depicting Gagliaudo. The porticoed *Palazzo Municipale* is surmounted by a most interesting clock with three faces. The *Museo Civico* contains: the Alessandria room, which documents the history of the city in the Risorgimento, the room devoted to archeology, the room of Pope Pius V, with thirty-seven chorales on parchment, and the room devoted to numismatics, with coins dating from the 2nd cent. B.C. to the 18th. cent. A.D.

* **ALFEDENA** (L'Aquila). Pretty little town at the bottom of the Sangritano valley, divided into two by the Torto stream. The ancient Aufidena was conquered by the Romans and became a Roman colony. Nowadays the town consists of a medieval and a modern quarter. In the Romanesque church of *Santi Pietro e Paolo*, there are some interesting frescoes, nearly all belonging to the 15th cent. In the *Museo Civico Aufidenate*, arranged in three rooms, there are numerous items excavated at Aufidena itself and in its necropolis, over one and a half thousand tombs of which have been explored. Walk to the *Avanzi di Aufidena* (remains of Aufidena).

* **ALGHERO** (Sassari). On a short promontory, dominating a vast roadstead, with interesting ancient centre, still partly enclosed by walls and bastions. The *Cattedrale*, built in the 14th cent., in late Gothic-Catalanese style, was largely rebuilt in the 18th and 19th. The interior contains pilasters with varied profiles, and in the left transept is the mausoleum of Maurizio Giuseppe di Savoia, Duke of Montferrat, by Felice Festa (recorded 1800-1826). The church of *San Francesco* was built in the

Alghero, San Francesco, interior.

16

14th cent. and later modified. Inside there are Gothic arches and a women's gallery. Other places worthy of attention in Alghero are the *Palazzo d'Albis*, now De Arcayne, with Aragonese traces; the church of *San Michele*, built in 1612, with majolica and polychrome dome; the *Torre di Porta*; the *Monumento a Giuseppe Manno*, a local historian, by Pietro Canonica (1869-1962), etc. In the neighbourhood, at Capo Caccia, one can visit the *Grotta Verde o dell'Altare* and the *Grotta di Nettuno*, which is the most attractive grotto in Sardinia. Heavy natural columns rise out of the water to support the roof. The Green or Altar Grotto is forty metres deep, and at the entrance there is an altar dedicated to St. Erasmus.

* **ALIFE** (Caserta). Surrounded by a square-sided Roman wall, with important ancient and medieval remains. The *Cattedrale*, dedicated to the Assunta and Pope Sixtus I, belongs to the 13th cent., but was completely rebuilt in the 17th. The interior, in the form of a Latin cross, contains the remains of a 13th cent. doorway, in the back wall of a chapel. The crypt has three apses and contains a large quantity of pillar fragments, perhaps taken from the Roman theatre of Allifae. The *Criptoportico Romano* is a rectangular gallery formed of two ambulatories, separated by a wall and intersected by thirty arches. Well-preserved Roman walls (*Mura della Cinta Romana*) of the first cent. B.C., with medieval extensions. *Mausoleo Romano* said to be of Acilius Glabrio: in spite of repeated alterations, the original, dome-covered cylindrical structure has remained almost intact.

* **ALMENNO SAN BARTOLOMEO** (Bergamo). On the slopes of Mount Albenza. In the *Parrocchiale*, built in the 18th and 19th cent.

Almenno San Bartolomeo, San Tomè.

are paintings by Giovanni Battista Moroni (c. 1525-1578), Bartolomeo Vivarini (c. 1432-1499) and Giovanni Carnovali called Piccio (1804-1873). In the surrounding district, the small 11th cent. church of *San Tomè* is the best-known construction. It is built in the round, and belongs to the Romanesque period in Lombardy.

* **ALMENNO SAN SALVATORE** (Bergamo). In the *Santuario della Madonna del Castello*, rising sharply above the Brembo, are frescoes and a small octagonal 16th cent. shrine. The ancient 11th cent. church has a crypt and contains an ancient stone ambo with symbols of the Evangelists. The parish church of *San Salvatore* contains a Madonna and Child, formerly attributed to Guercino, a Transfiguration, by Giampaolo Cavagna (1556-1627) and Holy Family, by Francesco Bassano (1540-1592). In the church of *San Nicola* or *della Consolazione*, dating back to the 15th cent., there is a Trinity and Saints, by Andrea Previtali (c. 1470-1528). The 12th cent. church of *San Giorgio* contains frescoes from the 13th to the 16th cent. by local artists.

* **ALPIGNANO** (Turin). On the river Dora Riparia. Crossing the *Ponte Vecchio* one reaches the parish church of *San Martino* beside which a characteristic, separate bell-tower can be admired.

** **ALSENO** (Piacenza). Market town. The 14th cent. parish church of *San Martino* – originally Gothic and later rebuilt – is a notable construction. In the surrounding district is the Abbey of *Chiaravalle della Colomba*. Construction began in 1135 through the efforts of St. Barnard of Chiaravalle; the abbey church has a tripartite brick facade and contains 14th cent. frescoes by several painters. There is a noteworthy Gothic cloister with open arcades on all four sides.

** **ALTAMURA** (Bari). Large agricultural and commercial centre in the Murge. The area was already inhabited in the Neolithic and Bronze ages, as archeological discoveries have proved, especially hundreds of specula belonging to tombs of the 8th cent. B.C. The present-day town stands on a Peucetic centre, of which nothing is known. The *Cattedrale*, dedicated to the Assunta, was begun in 1228 or 1232 by order of Frederick II. It is one of the four Palatine basilicas in Apulia; almost annihilated by an earthquake in 1316, it was rebuilt, but disfigured in later periods. The facade is surmounted by two 16th cent. bell-towers, with one, two and three-arched Baroque cuspidate openings of the first half of the 18th cent. It has a lovely 14th cent. rose-window, the fifteen rays ending in intricate arcs. The superb 14th cent. portal, the most magnificent in Apulia, is architraved, top-

Altamura, Cathedral.

ped by a double-arched lintel, and enriched by sculptures of rare artistic value (in the architrave, The Last Supper; in the lunette, Madonna and Child with two Angels; on the inner band of the arch, lush foliage, and on the outer one, Virgin of the Annunciation and the angel Gabriel; in the remaining part there are Gospel Stories). The basilican interior contains important paintings such as Saint Paul, by Domenico Morelli (1826-1901), Mary Magdalen, by Francesco Netti (1832-1894), Saint Thomas, by Saverio Altamura (1826-1897), and Presentation at the Temple, by Giuseppe Mancinelli (1813-1875), as well as an enormous picture of the Assumption, by Leonardo Castellani (16th cent. engraver). In the sacristy there is a fine picture of St. Jerome, (late-Renaissance panel by an unknown artist), and a St. Francis, probably by the Dutch painter, Gerard van Honthorst, known as Gherardo delle Notti (1590-1656). The Treasury contains precious sacred vestments of various periods, a silver statue of the Assunta (1698), a 17th cent. silver cross, etc. The church of *San Nicolò dei Greci*, named after the Greeks called here by Frederick II, has a simple and elegant facade; on the portal can be seen primitive but interesting bas-reliefs with stories from the Bible, and the single-naved interior contains carved and gilded-wood altars. The walls (*Mura*) were probably raised in the 5th cent. B.C. and a considerable stretch still stands, 5.50 metres wide at the base and 4 metres high. Native tombs have been found on the site. The *Palazzo degli Studi* contains a library with about forty thousand volumes, the Civic Museum, with important archeological discoveries from the Altamura area, and archives where historical papers are preserved. In the surrounding area, at Santeramo in Colle, is the early 18th cent. *Chiesa Matrice*, dedicated to St. Erasmus. The church contains the fragment of a lunette depicting the Madonna and Child, and, in the chancel, two pilasters with the Annunciation.

* **ALTOMONTE** (Cosenza). In an inaccessible area between the rivers Grondi and Fiumicello. The church of *Santa Maria della Consolazione* is considered the most important place of worship of the Angevin period in Calabria. It was built on the site of a small 11th cent. Norman church, dedicated to St. Mary of the Franks, and the present-day building was completed in 1380. The acute-arched portal has a lunette with a 14th cent. group in high relief representing the Madonna and Child. The interior, spoilt by restoration work in the 17th cent., contains some good works of art, including a 14th cent. unepigraphed warrior's tomb, a panel of the Madonna and Child (second half of the 15th cent.), Gothic altarpieces in alabaster, parchment choir books of the 15th, 16th and 17th cent., and fragments of frescoes belonging to the school of Giotto. On the right of the church is an ex-convent. The church of *San Giacomo* contains some exquisite wood carvings, and in the church of *San Francesco di Paola* there are marble statues of St. George and St. Michael the Archangel, belonging to the second half of the 16th cent.

* **ALTOPASCIO** (Lucca). On the Lake of Bientina. The church of *San Jacopo Maggiore*,

Altopascio, San Iacopo Maggiore, facade of the ancient church.

although restored last century, still preserves part of the ancient Lucca-style facade, with the figure of St. James in high relief. The crenellated bell-tower was built in 1280 and has a bell known as the "lost one" (la smarrita), cast in 1327.

* **ALVIANO** (Terni). Pleasant little town, surrounded by erosion-marked hills in the Tiber valley. The *Castello*, formerly known as the Doria-Pamphili, is a massive 15th cent. building with towers at the corners and an elegant Renaissance courtyard; the inner chapel contains a pleasing 17th cent. fresco. The 15th cent. *Parrocchiale* has a Madonna in Glory by Niccolò di Liberatore, called Alunno (1430-1502) and a precious fresco by Giovanni de' Sacchis, called Pordenone (1484-1539), depicting the Madonna, Saints Gregory and Jerome and a portrait of Pantasilea Baglioni. Walk to the *Eremo di Santa Illuminata*, a hermitage possibly founded in the 11th cent. by St. Romualdo, where St. Francis' Grotto can be seen.

* **ALZANO LOMBARDO** (Bergamo). Large commercial and industrial centre by the river Serio. The *Basilica di San Martino*, begun at the turn of the 11th cent., was completely rebuilt in 1659 to a design by Girolamo Qua-

Alzano Lombardo, Basilica of San Martino. Andrea Appiani, Rachel and Jacob.

drio (recorded 1650-1679). It contains a marble pulpit by Andrea Fantoni (1659-1734), a painting of the Madonna and St. Christopher, by Jacopo Robusti called Tintoretto (1518-1594) and Rachel and Jacob, by Andrea Appiani (1754-1817). The church of *San Pietro Martire*, Gothic in form, but with a Renaissance chancel, was designed by Pietro Isabello (c. 1480-1550).

** **AMALFI** (Salerno). Picturesque town, with sparkling white houses, at the entrance to the Valle dei Mulini. The *Duomo*, dedicated to St. Andrew, corresponds to an ancient basilica with a nave and two aisles, first recorded in the 9th cent. The squat, colourful facade was remade towards the end of the 19th cent., as the previous one collapsed in 1861. On its left stands the bell-tower, which is all that remains of the original construction. The entrance to the cathedral has a magnificent bronze door, cast in Constantinople around the middle of the 11th cent. The present-day interior is Baroque in form. It contains an early 16th cent. marble frontal with three Saints, a baptismal font in red Egyptian porphyry, and ancient monolithic pillars. In the crypt there is a huge bronze statue of St. Andrew, by Michelangelo Naccherino (1550-1622) and marble statues of Saints Stephen and Lawrence, by Pietro Bernini (1562-1629). From the Cathedral atrium one can enter the so-called Cloister of Paradise, a spectacular, Arabesque construction, built in the years 1266-1268 by order of Archbishop Filippo Augustariccio, to serve as Amalfi's Temple of Fame. The Arsenal of the Republic (*Arsenale della Repubblica*) has remains of two great pointed-arched naves; it was here that the greatest 11th cent. galleys were built. The former Capuchin Convent (*Ex Convento dei Cappuccini*), founded at the start of the 13th cent., still boasts its elegant cloister and a flowery loggia from where a sweeping view of Amalfi and its coastline can be obtained. Walk to the *Grotta di Smeraldo* (Emerald Grotto), five kilometres away from the town. Discovered in 1932, it is so called from the emerald sheen produced by the light as it is filtered through the seawater beneath the rocks.

* **AMANDOLA** (Ascoli Piceno). Panoramically situated on the left bank of the Tenna, at the foot of Mount Rotondo, facing the Sibilline Mountains. Three castles, Castelleone, Marrabbione and Agello were joined together in 1248 to form the present-day village. A fine portal leads into the 15th cent. church of *Sant'Agostino*, the work of Marino di Marco Cedrino (active from 1452 to 1476). In the church of *San Francesco* all that remains of the original Romanesque-Gothic construction is the doorway, dated 1423. The church contains 15th cent. frescoes, possibly by Panfilo da Spoleto (lived in the 15th cent.). Worthy of attention are the 15th cent. *Torrione del Cassero*

Maggiore and the *Torretta* (turret) of one of the Casseri, built in 1434 by Francesco Sforza in order to protect the village.

* AMANTEA (Cosenza). Situated partly on the plain and partly on the hillside, at the outlet of the wide gorge of the Catocastro. The facade of the 15th cent. church of *San Bernardino da Siena* is preceded by an ogival portico. The church contains an important marble group depicting the Madonna and Child, by Antonello Gagini (1478-1536); in the adjacent oratory of the Confraternity of the Nobles is a Nativity Scene in marble attributed to Rinaldo Bonanno (active from 1577 to 1591).

* AMATRICE (Rieti). In the upper valley of the river Tronto, surrounded by mountains. The late-14th cent. church of *San Francesco* is Romanesque-Gothic in form. It has a horizontally crowned facade, and a splendid portal. The severe interior, preceded by a three-arched Renaissance narthex, contains some good 15th cent. frescoes of the Marches school, a bust of Camillo Orsini, by Alessandro Leopardi (goldsmith, c. 1465-1523), an admirable Gothic reliquary, probably by Pietro di Vannini (died c. 1495), and an interesting Baroque pulpit, in carved wood. The church of *Sant'Agostino* also has a horizontally completed facade, and a rich cuspidate Gothic portal, dated 1428. It is overlooked by a rectangular bell-tower. The interior, renovated in the 18th cent., contains frescoes of the Annunciation and Madonna and Child with Angels (1492), by a "Master of the Madonna della Misericordia".

Amandola, Sant'Agostino, portal.

* AMELIA (Terni). Agricultural town on a steep hill to the right of the Fosso Grande, with remains of very ancient walls. The *Mura Poligonali* (Polygonal Walls) belong to the 6-4th cent. B.C., and consist of large blocks, standing as high as eight metres, and three and a half metres thick. The church of *Santi Filippo e Giacomo* or *San Francesco* (1287) has a sober facade and, inside, six tombs of the Geraldini family, one of which is the work of Agostino di Duccio (1418-1481). The *Duomo*, originally Romanesque but completely rebuilt in 1640, is flanked by a sturdy twelve-sided Romanesque campanile, dated 1050. The interior contains several works of art such as the tomb of Bishop Giovanni Geraldini, school of Agostino di Duccio, and paintings by Niccolò Circignani called Pomarancio and Giovanni Francesco Perini di Amelia (lived in the first half of the 16th cent.). The 14th cent. church of *Sant'Agostino* or *San Pancrazio* has a solemn, Romanesque-Gothic portal. The ceiling and dome are frescoed by Francesco Appiani (1704-1792).

* AMENO (Novara). Pleasantly situated near the Lake of Orta. The *Collegiata di Sant'Ambrogio* was originally Romanesque but subsequently almost entirely transformed. The interior contains an octagonal font (1317), and a six-panelled polyptych (1547), by Fermo Stella, depicting the Madonna and Child with Saints.

** ANAGNI (Frosinone). On a spur of the valley of the river Sacco, with typically medieval houses and streets. The *Duomo*, dedicated to St. Mary, is the most important building in the town and one of the most prominent in Latium. Romanesque in style, it was

Amelia, polygonal walls.

built at the turn of the 13th cent. and completed with Gothic elements. It has a lively facade with 12th cent. Romanesque campanile standing apart; the interior, with a nave and two aisles, is an impressive sight and contains an admirable Cosmatesque floor of the early 12th cent., the Gaetani chapel, containing the family tomb, another Cosmatesque work, a Romanesque ciborium on four pillars, and the bishop's chair, by Pietro Vassalletto (1154-1186). In the crypt, called the San Magno there is a Cosmatesque floor and, on the walls and ceiling, a magnificent cycle of frescoes by an unknown artist (active around the middle of the 13th cent.), representing episodes and characters from the Old Testament and Apocalypse, scientific teachings, Evangelists and Saints. From the crypt one enters the chapel of St. Thomas Becket, possibly built on the site of a Roman temple to Mithras with anonymous frescoes of the mid-13th cent., inferior in quality to the preceding ones. In the Treasury there is a collection of 13th cent. vestments, 12th and 13th cent. frontals, mitres of various periods, crosiers, ampullae and, most important of all, the reliquary of St. Thomas Becket, with Limoges enamel-work. The *Palazzo di Bonifacio VIII*, with majestic loggia, belongs to the second half of the 13th cent. The *Palazzo Comunale* is a plain, 13th cent. construction, well restored at the beginning of the present century. It has a broad, vaulted corridor divided in the middle by arches. The 14th cent. *Casa Barnekow* is a remarkable building. Romanesque in style, it has an external staircase. In the Romanesque church of *Sant'Andrea* are sections of the Redeemer triptych, the much-admired work of an unknown artist at the beginning of the 14th cent.

*** **ANCONA.** Attractive city, standing on a promontory, with ancient quarters of high artistic merit, and new ones characterized by straight, broad streets. The *Palazzo del Governo*, once known as the Town Hall, was built in the second half of the 14th cent. and later enlarged. The courtyard is austere and aristo-cratic in appearance, and the interior contains some good works of art. The church of *San Francesco delle Scale* or *Santa Maria Maggiore* was built in 1323, and largely remodelled in later centuries. It contains a magnificent Gothic-Venetian portal, with statues and reliefs by Giorgio Orsini (active from 1444 to 1475), one of the artistic gems of the Marches. The *Palazzo degli Anziani* was designed in 1270 by Margaritone d'Arezzo (1216-1290), and has a Baroque facade. It houses the faculties of Economics and Commerce of the University of Urbino, and the Town Art Gallery (the Podesti) which contains important, if comparatively few, works of art. They include a huge altarpiece, dated 1520, of the Madonna and Child in Glory, Saints Francis and Alvise and the Purchaser, the first work signed Tiziano Vecellio (1490-1576), Holy Conversation, by Lorenzo Lotto (c. 1480-1556), Madonna and Child by Carlo Crivelli (1430/35-1494), paintings by Andrea Lilli (1555-1610), a canvas depicting Santa Palazia, by Giovanni Francesco Barbieri called Guercino (1591-1666), and one by Giovanni Antonio Galli called Spadarino (c. 1595-1650). In the *Palazzo Ferretti*, designed in Baroque style probably by Pellegrino Tibaldi called Pellegrino Pellegrini (1527-1596), is the *Museo Nazionale delle Marche*, containing archeological collections of supreme interest, especially concerned with the Iron Age and Picenian, Greek, Gallic and Roman civilizations in the area. The *Duomo*, dedicated to St. Ciriaco, patron saint of the maritime Republic of Ancona, is an important medieval construction, erected between the 11th and 13th cent. Byzantine and Gothic influences are evident in its elegant appearance. The interior has been repeatedly damaged by earthquakes and human conflicts, and well restored last time after the destruction wreaked by the second world war. It contains some remarkable works of art, including the splendid altar of the Madonna, by Luigi Vanvitelli (1700-1773); also worthy of attention are the 14th and 15th cent. carinated painted ceiling, identical to the one in the Church of Santo Stefano in Venice. The annexed diocesan museum is worth a visit. Among the notable works of art on show are the 4th cent. tomb of Flavius Gorgonius, the 6th cent. tomb of San Dasio, Ravenna ambo of the 9th cent., 14th cent. tombstone of Bishop Nicholas of the Hungarians, two Vanvitelli cherubs, etc. The graceful *Arco di Traiano*, erected in honour of the Emperor Trajan in 115 A.D. probably by Apollodoro of Damascus, rises tall and slender, with a single barrel-vault. The church of *Santa Maria della Piazza* was built in the first half of the 13th cent. on remains of a previous early-Christian church. The basilican interior has a nave and two aisles, and contains some good works of art including a 16th cent. wooden Crucifix, remains of frescoes in three layers, executed from the 8th cent. onwards, and ancient mosaics. The *Loggia dei Mer-*

Ancona, Duomo.

canti was built by Giovanni Pace called Sodo (lived in the 15th cent.), and has a lively facade, work of Giorgio Orsini. In Ancona, other items of interest are the doorway to the former church of *Sant'Agostino*, in Venetian decorated-Gothic style, by Giorgio Orsini, the impressive *Porta Pia*, erected during the pontificate of Pius VI (1717-1779), the modern *Viale della Vittoria*, the *Mole Vanvitelliana* (Vanvitelli's Rock) or *Lazzaretto*, begun in 1733 by order of Pope Clement XII, and the church of *San Pellegrino* or *degli Scalzi* (second half of the 18th cent.).

** **ANDRIA** (Bari). On the southern slopes of the Murge. The *Duomo*, dedicated to the Assunta, was rebuilt in the 15th cent. and later modified. It has a facade with atrium and portico by Federico Santacroce (lived in the 19th cent.). Beside it stands a noble campanile, begun in 1118 A.D. The interior contains a half-bust Madonna and Child (panel dated 1275 by an unknown artist), the chapel of St. Richard, first Bishop of Andria, who came from England in 492 A.D., silver statues of St. Richard and the Madonna of Miracles. In the crypt there are the tombs of Iolanda di Brienne and Isabel of England, wives of Frederick II. The church of *San Francesco* was begun in the first half of the 13th cent. and completed in 1336 by Bonanno da Barletta. It has an ogival doorway with triangular tympanum in the facade, and is flanked by a slender Baroque campanile (mid-18th cent.). Inside there are some valuable 18th cent. paintings of the Neapolitan school, and in the apse a fine wooden choir, dated 1699. The church of *San Domenico*, begun early in the 14th cent., has a fine Renaissance doorway in the facade, dated 1510. The interior contains a 16th cent. wooden sculpture of the Madonna and Child, and in the sacristy there is an admirable bust of Francesco II del Balzo, Duke of Andria, by Francesco Laurana (c. 1430-c. 1502). The church of *Sant'Agostino*, erected by German knights in the 13th cent., has an impressive 14th cent. ogival doorway. The single-naved interior contains some important Baroque stuccoes. In the church of *Santa Maria Vetere* there is a Madonna and Child with Saints, by the Neapolitan painter Andrea Vaccaro (1598-1670). Walk to the *Basilica di Santa Maria dei Miracoli*, erected in the 16th cent. over a Byzantine grotto. It has a vast interior, consisting of a nave and two aisles, and is an impressive piece of pure Renaissance work, with numerous stuccoes and frescoes. In the crypt there is a 14th cent. fresco of the Madonna and Child. Walk to the *Crypt of the Holy Cross*, a remarkable 9th century Byzantine crypt, the walls of which are embellished with lively Byzantine-style frescoes.

* **ANGERA** (Varese). At the southernmost tip of Lake Maggiore, on the Lombard side, overlooked by the grandiose *Rocca*. The fort, founded by the Torriani on pre-existing Lombard fortifications, consists of a tall 13th cent. keep and castle, enlarged in later centuries. The inner rooms contain some original 14th and 15th cent. frescoes removed from the Borromeo Palace in Milan.

* **ANGHIARI** (Arezzo). On the spur of a hill, consisting of an ancient, walled settlement and modern part. Inside the 18th cent. *Collegiata di Santa Maria delle Grazie* are preserved a panel depicting The Last Supper, dated 1531, by Giovanni Antonio Sogliani (1462-1544) and a Deposition by Domenico Puligo (1492-post 1527), considered the best pupil of Ridolfo del Ghirlandaio (1483-1561). In the 13-14th cent. church of *Sant'Agostino* can be seen two valuable 15th cent. holy-water stoups in marble. The *Chiesa di Badia*, formerly of the Camaldolesi, contains an altar frontal in glazed terracotta, produced by the workshop of Andrea Della Robbia (1435-1525). In the surrounding area, *Santa Maria a Corsano*, with French-inspired campanile against the Romanesque facade. The interior contains some 15th cent. frescoes.

Angera, Borromei Fortress, Ottone Visconti entering Milan.

Anghiari, Oratory of Santa Maria a Corsano, the campanile.

Alatri, Santa Maria Maggiore, Madonna of Constantinople.

Anagni, Duomo, Bishop's Throne.
Ancona, Pinacoteca Civica. Carlo Crivelli, Madonna and Child, detail.

23

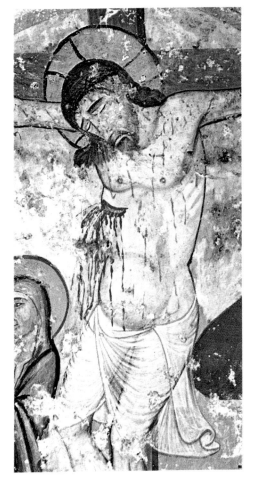

Ancona, Museo Nazionale delle Marche. Fragment of equestrian statue in gilt bronze (from Cartoceto di Pergola).
Andria, Crypt of Santa Croce, Crucifixion.

Aosta, Priorato di Sant'Orso, Story of St. George, detail.
Ardara, Santa Maria del Regno. Giovanni Muru, St. Gavino, predella of the retable.

* **ANGUILLARA SABAZIA** (Rome). On the shore of Lake Bracciano. In the 18th cent. *Collegiata dell'Assunta* is a painting of the Madonna of Roccamaggiore, 14th cent. in origin, but retouched at a later date. The village is overlooked by a well-preserved castle (*Castello Medievale*).

** **AOSTA.** At the point where the Buthier flows into the river Dora, with ancient town centre, surrounded by Roman walls, and the modern city spreading beyond them. The *Porta Praetoria*, 1st cent. B.C., is an impressive construction, consisting of a double gateway curtain of wall, in large square blocks. The *Teatro Romano* is visible over a vast surface, with rusticated buttresses, and partly-restored auditorium. The collegiate church of *Sant'Orso* was built in various stages and has a 5th cent. Gothic facade, with a single doorway, ending in a spire which goes up almost touching the roof. The interior, with a nave and two aisles, contains some remarkable works of art, including a late-15th cent. fresco of St. Sebastian, in Franco-Valdaostan style, a wonderful wooden Gothic choir, and the Treasury, with the statue-reliquary of Sant'Orso, Franco-Valdaostan style, the relic-chest of Sant'Orso, containing ancient cameos, jewel caskets, processional crosses, priory staffs, sacred vestments, etc. The collegiate church of Sant'Orso leads straight into the Romanesque *Chiostro*, built at the beginning of the 12th cent., with finely decorated capitals. In the small chapel of the *Priorato di Sant'Orso* are preserved late-15th cent. frescoes with Stories of St. George, Franco-Valdaostan in style. The *Arco di Augusto* was built when the city was founded, and is a clear example of the architectural skill of the Romans. The *Cattedrale*, dedicated to St. John the Baptist, must have been built before the 12th cent., but was modified and restored in later periods. The present, neo-

Classical facade, dates from 1848; the interior has a nave and three aisles, and contains some important Franco-Valdaostan frescoes, some of which are unfortunately in a dilapidated condition. The peribolus leads into a cloister, begun in 1442 by Pierre Berger of Chambéry and completed in 1460 by Marcello di Gherardo di San Marcello. The *Museo Archeologico* is worth a visit. It contains objects found in pre-Roman tombs, the *Cryptoportico*, which was probably a storehouse, and the *Torre Bramafam*, built at the end of the 11th cent. Interesting tour of the *Castelli Medievali* dotted around the Aosta area.

** **AQUILEIA** (Udine). Agricultural town, most important for its key position at the centre of an archeological area, full of remains of Early-Christian and medieval monuments. The *Basilica* is of unique artistic and historical importance. Modified in various periods, it is now a grandiose contruction dominated by the Romanesque style, and more or less as it was when consecrated by the Patriarch Poppone (11th cent.). It stands on the site of a place of worship where, in 381 A.D., the Council assembled to condemn the Arian heresy, with St. Ambrose present. The double-sloped facade is preceded by a partly-ruined early-9th cent. portico. The huge and solemn interior, in the form of a Latin cross, has a nave and two aisles. It boasts a mosaic floor, discovered at the beginning of the present century, the most extensive of its kind in Western Christendom. It consists of nine great squares, brightly coloured and richly decorated. In the right aisle there is a 16th cent. font with tegurio cover, 14th cent. polychrome group of the Madonna and Child, known as the Madonna del Latte or dell'Umiltà, and Gothic Chapel of St. Ambrose. In the right arm of the cross is the Chapel of St. Peter, containing a 15th cent. fresco of Christ enthroned with the Evangelists; in the chancel, Sacramental altar, by Bernardino da Bissone (active at the beginning of the 16th cent.), central tribune, most successful work of Bernardino da Bissone, and refined altar by Antonio and Sebastiano da Osteno (op. in the 15th cent.); in the apse, frescoes belonging to the age of the Patriarch Poppone, and inscription to commemorate the church's consecration. In the left arm of the cross, frescoes from the early 11th cent. onwards; in the left aisle, Rosary chapel, with Baroque altar and another, semicircular chapel, with a wooden Crucifix dated 1776. In the Excavation Crypt, a thousand square metres in size, are remains of three periods, from the beginning of the Empire to the end of the 4th cent. A.D. In the 9th cent. Church of the Pagans, once reserved for converts, there are some crumbling frescoes of the 13th and 14th cent. In the baptistery, six fragments of columns and remains of an ambulatory. They used to support

Aosta, Roman Theatre.

the pillars holding up the dome, which collapsed at the end of the 18th cent. The 73.35 metre-high campanile, set apart, may have been erected in Patriarch Poppone's times; behind it is the War Cemetery. The Basilica stands at the start of the *Via Sacra* where there are architectural remains, as far as the river port, which was used in the early days of the Empire and identified in 1925. In the heart of the town a 4th cent. Christian *Basilica* has been discovered, with contemporary mosaic floor. The Early-Christian Museum has been assembled here. It includes an impressive collection of archeological material, belonging to Early-Christian Aquileia. Remains of the *Foro Romano. Grande Mausoleo*, tomb of a Patrician family, beginning of the 1st cent. A.D. *Sepolcreto Romano*, a Roman burial-ground, in a perfect state of preservation. Remains of *Case Romane*, and of *Oratori Paleocristiani. Museo Archeologico*, with some of the most important collections of Roman antiquities in Italy; notice, in particular, the head-portrait of an old man, Republican age, and Deified Tiberius or Augustus (in the second room), cinerary urn (third room), Venus (fourth room) and Roman glass (ninth room). The Museum leads into the Lapidarium, with an important collection of architectonic and epigraphic material, as well as remains of mosaics and funeral altars.

* **AQUINO** (Frosinone). Medieval town, with some interesting monuments. The church of *Santa Maria della Libera* or *Vescovado* was begun in 1125, on remains of a temple to Hercules the Liberator. It has a finely decorated interior, which is entered through a spacious main doorway, with interesting architectonic elements. In the sacristy is a rare 12th cent. reliquary cross, in rock crystal. The medieval *Torre*, rhomboidal in plan, stands near remains of a church dedicated to St. Thomas. Walk to the *Rovine di Aquino*, the most important being the Roman Gate of St. Lawrence and the fairly well preserved Roman basilica.

* **ARCEVIA** (Ancona). Attractive walled town in the valley of the river Misa in an area already inhabited in prehistoric times. The Senone Gauls settled here, as is proved by the necropolis of Montefortino, which has been recently identified. The collegiate church of *San Medardo*, patron saint of Arcevia, was designed by Michele Buti (active from 1634 to 1655) and by Ascano Passari (lived in the 17th cent.). Inside there is a painting of the Madonna of the Rosary, by Claudio Ridolfi (c. 1570-1644), a scalloped table and polyptych by Luca Signorelli (c. 1445-1523), a fine altar by Giovanni della Robbia (1469-post 1529), a silver cross (1524-1526), by Cesarino del Roscetto, and a carved Gothic choir by Corrado Teutonico (op. from 1475 to 1490). Extensive and attractive *Giardino Leopardi*.

* **ARCIDOSSO** (Grosseto). Pleasantly situated, with a dark, picturesque ancient quarter and a modern part. The church of *San Leonardo*, built in the 12th cent. and modified in the 16th, has a Decollation, by the painter Francesco Vanni (1563-1610), and two interesting wooden statues representing St. Andrew and San Processo. The church of the *Madonna delle Grazie* was erected after the plague of 1348, and contains a Crowned Madonna, by Taddeo di Bartolo (c. 1363-1422). In the surrounding area, the 11th cent. *Pieve di Santa Maria ad Lamulas*, later restyled, still preserves its Romanesque apse and attractive interior. Excursion to Mount Labbro, 1187 metres high; on the peak there are the ruins of the church of *Davide Lazzaretti*, centre of the so-called Giurisdavidici religious sect, founded by Lazzaretti.

* **ARCO** (Trent). On the right bank of the Sarca, where the valley widens out towards Lake Garda, it is a holiday resort, with ancient houses and modern town centre. The first stone of the *Collegiata*, dedicated to the Assunta, was laid in 1613. It was built after the design of Giovanni Maria Filippi (recorded 1559-1616) and has an impressive facade. The interior contains a painting of the Madonna and Child, St. Michael and two Angels, by Domenico Ricci called Brusasorci (c. 1516-1567), and the Magdalen altar (1701) by Cristoforo and Sebastiano Benedetti. The crypt contains the tombs of Francesco II of Bourbon, last king of Naples (died 1894), and some of the Counts of Arco. The 16th cent. *Palazzo Marchetti* is noted for its attractive

Arco, Sant'Apollinare a Prabi, St. Martin.

fireplaces, and under the overhanging roof there is a remarkable frescoed frieze. On the outskirts is the ruined *Castello* and the church of *Sant'Apollinare* at Prabi, which has an apse decorated with early-15th cent. frescoes.

* ARDARA (Sassari). Farming village lying in a Miocene area and surrounded by basaltic plateaux. The 12th cent. Romanesque church of *Santa Maria del Regno* is the prototype of many other Sardinian churches. The facade is divided by delicate pilaster strips and there is an interesting mullion above the middle door. The basilican interior has a nave and two aisles and semicircular apse. It contains a 15-16th cent. pulpit, a fresco representing the Annunciation, by an unknown local artist in the 17th cent., and an impressive Gothic wooden altar-

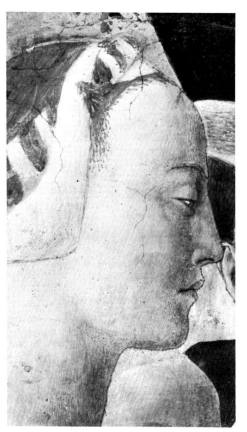

piece, made up of many sections containing about thirty pictures on a gold background, with Stories of Christ, the Virgin and Saints, by Giovanni Muru (mentioned in 1515), and by an anonymous artist, possibly the Majorcan Martin Torner, who worked here in the early 16th cent.

* ARDESIO (Bergamo). Holiday resort in the Valle Seriana. The church of *San Pietro* was erected in the 15-16th cent., and has a 17th cent. portico. Inside are seven polychrome-wood statues, in the style of Andrea Fantoni (1659-1734). In the *Parrocchiale*, dated 1747, is a painting of Saints Laurence and George, by Carlo Ceresa (1609-1679), and four marble statues by Andrea Fantoni. In the chapel of the *Santo Sepolcro* are 15th cent. frescoes. In the 17th cent. *Santuario della Madonna delle Grazie*, designed by Giovanni Maria Bettera (lived in the 16-17th cent.), are two huge paintings by Antonio Guadagnini (1817-1900).

*** AREZZO. Situated on a hillside, a leading agricultural and commercial centre. It is the ancient Arretium, which was originally the Etruscan Lucumon, then Umbrian city, and then Roman camp on the Via Cassia. The church of *San Francesco* was begun to the design of fra' Giovanni da Pistoia (1322). The Gothic interior is particularly rich in works of art; the

Ardara, Santa Maria del Regno.

Arezzo, San Francesco. Piero della Francesca, Retinue of the Queen of Sheba, detail.
Arezzo, Parish Church of Santa Maria, facade.

27

walls of the major chapel were frescoed between 1452 and 1466 by Piero della Francesca (1415-1492), with the Story of the Cross, suggested to him by Jacopo da Varagine's "Golden Legend", Arezzo's most precious painting and della Francesca's most successful artistic series. In front of the Captain's Palace or Mint, stands the parish church of *Santa Maria*, dating back to the 11th cent., but damaged and restored several times. The most characteristic part of the church is the Romanesque facade, which consists of a portico with five blind arches, and three rows of loggias above. At the right-hand side of the facade stands the sturdy campanile. Completed in 1330, it is a familiar landmark in the city. Inside there is a precious polyptych by Pietro Lorenzetti (recorded 1305-1348). The *Piazza Grande* is the most interesting square in Arezzo. Twice a year, in June and August, the Saracin's Joust takes place, an ancient game involving eight knights who represent former Arezzo districts. The huge Romanesque-Gothic *Duomo* stands at the top of a wide flight of steps. Construction began in 1277 and has only been completed this century; inside, are the Tomb of San Donato, the work of various artists, a fresco of Mary Magdalen, by Piero della Francesca, the impressive tomb of Bishop Guido Tarlati, a work executed in 1330 by Agostino di Giovanni and Angelo di Ventura da Siena, and the chapel of Our Lady of Comfort. In the Gothic church of *San Domenico*, built in 1275, there are two Saints by Piero della Francesca's school, the Dragonelli Chapel, a Crucifix believed to be by Cimabue (1240?-1302) and other important works of art. The *Chiesa di Badia*, dedicated to Saints Flora and Lucille, is a 13th cent. abbey, enlarged by Giorgio Vasari (1511-1574). Other places worth visiting in Arezzo are the *Palazzo della Fraternità*, the *Palazzo Pretorio*, the *Palazzo dei Priori* and the *Casa di Giorgio Vasari*, which Vasari bought while it was still under construction, and then frescoed. The *Museo* contains art treasures of inestimable worth, dating from Early-Christian times to the present day.

* ARIANO IRPINO (Avellino).

Set on three hills, on the watershed dividing the basins of the rivers Ufita and Cervaro. The area was already inhabited in aeneolithic times, as is revealed by archeological remains found in the Starza district. The *Cattedrale* was probably begun in the 11th cent. and later rebuilt several times following sackings and earthquakes. The sandstone facade has three large doors, surmounted by bas-reliefs and by three statues depicting Saint Otho, the Assunta, who gives her name to the church, and Sant'Eliziario. Inside, there are eight paintings of Apostles, by Severio Persico (lived in the 18th cent.) and a large font dated 1070. The interior of the church of *San Francesco* (16th cent.) is predominantly Baroque. In the Collegiate church of *San Michele*, rebuilt in the mid-18th cent., is an important abbot's chair (1563), belonging to the late Catalan period. In the church of *San Pietro Apostolo*, notice in particular the Gothic portals, executed in 1358 and inside, a late-15th cent. altar. The church of *Sant'Anna* has an elegant 14th cent. door. Standing on a rise are remains of the Norman *Castello*, trapezoid in shape, which collapsed during an earthquake in 1732.

* ARICCIA (Rome).

Village on the Via Appia. The centre is enhanced by the *Piazza della Repubblica*, an architectonic ensemble designed by Bernini in 1662-65. Facing it are the *Palazzo Chigi* and church of *Santa Maria dell'Assunzione*, built on a central plan; the interior contains a large fresco by Ambrogio da Fossano, called Bergognone (recorded 1481-1522). In the surrounding area can be found the *Santuario di Santa Maria di Galloro* (first half of the 17th cent.), with facade designed by Gian Lorenzo Bernini; inside is a painting of San Tommaso di Villanova, by Giacinto Gemignani (1611-1681).

* ARONA (Novara).

Presumed to have been a Roman resort, but not documented until the 10th cent., when Count Amizzone erected the Abbey of Saints Salvatore, Gratiniano and Felino. The *Collegiata dei Santi Gratiniano e Felino*, with Baroque facade and ogival, single-naved interior, contains some important paintings such as St. Charles by Jacopo Palma the Younger (1544-1628). The *Collegiata di Santa Maria*, begun in the 15th cent. and completed in the 17th cent. by Cardinal Federico Borromeo. The facade is Renaissance in style and in the lunette above the portal can be seen a 15th cent. bas-relief, depicting the Adoration of the Child.

* ARPINO (Frosinone).

In a hilly area, east of the Liri valley. The church of *San Michele* is believed to have been built on the site of a temple to the Muses. It has a Baroque interior and contains paintings of the Martyrdom of St. Peter of Verona, and St. Michael, and the Eternal, by Giuseppe Cesari called Cavalier d'Arpino (1568-1640). In the *Palazzo del Municipio* are ovals with busts, two of them possibly by Antonio Canova (1757-1822), representing Caius Marius and Cicero. In the church of *Sant'Andrea Apostolo*, begun in the 13th cent, is a painting by Cavalier d'Arpino depicting Saints Andrew and Benedict. Walk to the village of *Civitavecchia*, where one can see some important ruins of the megalithic walls of Arpinas or Arpinum.

* ARQUÀ PETRARCA (Padua).

Town with a medieval atmosphere, where the poet Petrarch lived and died (1304-1373). The *Tomba di Francesco Petrarca*, sarcophagus in red Verona marble, 1380. The 14th cent. *Casa del*

Petrarca is rich in Petrarchan relics. In the 11th cent. the church of *Santa Maria* are 13th and 14th cent. frescoes, and in the apse there is an Assumption by Jacopo Palma the Younger (1544-1628). The sacristy contains a painting of the Madonna of the Rosary, by Pietro Damiani (1591-1631). The 12th cent. *Oratorio della Trinità* has an altarpiece representing the Trinity and Saints Joseph, Margaret, Lucy and Francis, by Palma the Younger.

* **ARRONE** (Terni). Town perched on a rocky hill, on the left bank of the Nera, divided into an upper and lower, less ancient part. The parish church of *Santa Maria* has a remarkable 15th cent. doorway, and contains frescoes executed in 1516 by Vincenzo Tamagni (c. 1492-1530) and Jacopo Santori called Jacopo Siculo (died 1543 or 1544), and important 16th cent. terracottas. Interesting walk up to the ancient part of the town, known as *La Terra*, through a characteristic ogival gate.

* **ARZIGNANO** (Vicenza). Industrial town, at the entrance to the Chiampo Valley. The parish church of *Ognissanti* (first half of the 19th cent.) was designed by Francesco Antonio Baccari (1747-1835). Inside is a Deposition attributed to Francesco Bassano the Younger (1540-1592). *Villa Mattarello*, with deep-set portico and wide loggia, was built in the first half of the 18th cent. The *Rione Castello*, surrounded by black stone walls, was built in the 14th cent. by the Veronese and was later a Venetian stronghold. It has fourteen well-preserved towers.

* **ASCEA** (Salerno). In gently undulating countryside within sight of the Mediterranean. Marina di Ascea, along the sea front, is a popular seaside resort. One should visit the *Rovine di Velia*, a large town also known as Elea, founded in 540 B.C. The Ruins, in their present state of excavation, reveal parts of the walls and a road leading from the port to the acropolis. Also recognizable are the stereobate of a temple (second half of the 6th cent.), a Greco-Roman quarter, a Roman bath of the 2nd cent., an open-air sanctuary with cippus (4th cent. B.C.), with dedication to Poseidon Aspholeios, patron of sailors, and the porticoed agora.

* **ASCIANO** (Siena). A short way from the left bank of the upper reaches of the river Ombrone. The Romanesque *Collegiata di Santa Agata* contains a painting of the Pietà, by the school of Giovanni Antonio Bazzi called Sodoma (1479-1549). In the Romanesque-Gothic church of *San Francesco* are a 15th cent. holy-water stoup, a Sienese-school tabernacle in gilded wood of the same century, and other works of art. The *Museo d'Arte Sacra* has a collection of precious works of the Sienese School.

*** **ASCOLI PICENO**. Pleasant if austere-looking city, where the rivers Tronto and Castellano meet. It has a medieval town centre, turreted buildings and picturesque streets. The *Duomo*, dedicated to St. Emidio, was probably built in the 12th cent. It has a grandiose facade, designed by Nicola Filotesio called Cola dell'Amatrice (1489-1559) and a notable Renaissance doorway, with fine wooden doors decorated by Francesco di Giovanni (active from 1496 to 1501). The interior contains important works of art, including a polyptych depicting the Madonna and Child enthroned, Christ, the Ten Apostles and Saints, considered the masterpiece of Carlo Crivelli (c. 1430-c. 1495), a painting of the Epiphany, by Carlo Allegretti (lived in the 16-17th cent.), a majestic marble group representing St. Emidio baptising St. Polisia, by Lazzaro Giosafatti (1694-1781), and a Gothic choir in wood. The 12th cent. *Battistero*, is set apart, near the Cathedral, and is one of the finest baptisteries in Italy. Octagonal in shape, it stands on a square base, and has a semispheroid dome. It contains a 13th cent. font on a twisted column. The *Palazzo Comunale* is the result of the 17th cent. fusion of two medieval buildings. It houses a library containing 100,000 books, and the *Pinacoteca Comunale*, with hundreds of works, including a much-admired group of paintings by Cola dell'Amatrice. Other important works are the Grand Canal, by Bernardo Bellotto (1720-1780), a Deposition, by Vincenzo Pagani (c. 1490-1568), Christ in Captivity, by Francesco Giovanni Barbieri called Guercino (1591-1666), a triptych representing the Madonna and Child, and various Saints, by Carlo Crivelli, a pentaptych, depicting the Madonna and Child, and various Saints, by Pietro Alemanno (recorded 1475-1498), St. Jerome, by Alessandro Ma-

Asciano, Collegiata di Sant'Agata, tribune and apse.

gnasco (1667-1749), a Landscape, by the Dutch artist, Cornelius Decker (recorded 1640-1678), an Annunciation, by Guido Reni (1575-1642), a Madonna, by Giovanni Battista Salvi called Sassoferrato (1609-1685), Massacre of the Holy Innocents, by Jacques Callot (1592-1635), Holy Conversation by Paolo da Visso, and sculptures by Nicola Cantalamessa Papotti (1833-1910), a wonderful 13th cent. samite cope, by an unknown English artist. In the 16th cent. *Palazzo Vescovile*, which was probably designed by Cola dell'Amatrice, there is a rich museum with paintings by Cola dell'Amatrice, silverware including a crosier, probably by Giorgio Vasari (1511-1574), terracottas, carved ornaments, bronzes, enamelwork, etc. The 13th cent. *Palazzo del Popolo*, modified by Cola dell'Amatrice in 1520, has a facade recalling various styles. The grandiose doorway is dominated by a monument to Paul III, carried out in 1549, possibly by Cola dell'Amatrice himself. The 13th cent. church of *San Francesco*, with one side facing the vast Piazza del Popolo, busy centre of Ascoli Piceno, is a fine, harmonious, Gothic building. The dome was carried out in 1547-49 by Domenico di Antonio called Barotto and by Defendente di Antonio called Lupo, both Lombard architects.

Beside the church is the large cloister, constructed at the turn of the 17th cent., and the small cloister (14th cent.). The 11th cent. church of *Santi Vincenzo e Anastasio*, completed in the 14th cent., has an attractive facade divided into sixty-four squares: inside are various works of art. In the crypt there are some fine 14th cent. paintings on the vault representing Stories of San Silvestro among the Lepers. The 14th cent. Romanesque church of *San Pietro Martire* has a doorway executed in 1523 by Cola dell'Amatrice. The interior contains some works of art including a Madonna of the Rosary, by the French artist, Luigi Devò (active at the end of the 18th cent.), and altars by Giuseppe Giosafatti. The 13th cent. Romanesque church of *Santa Maria inter Vineas*, flanked by a ponderous bell-tower (second half of the 13th cent.), has a basilican interior, with interesting 13th and 14th cent. frescoes, a rare, 16th cent. wooden Crucifix, and funeral monument to Nicola Pizzuti (second half of the 15th cent.). The *Ponte di Solestà* or *di Porta Cappuccina* dates back to the early decades of the Roman Empire. It is a slender, graceful bridge boldly spanning the river Tronto. The 12th cent. *Torre Ercolani* is the most elegant of the noble towers still surviving in Ascoli

Ascoli Piceno, Santi Vincenzo e Anastasio, facade.

Piceno. The 12th cent. *Casa Longobarda*, in hewn stone, is a remarkably interesting building. The Romanesque-Gothic church of *San Giacomo* (13-14th cent.) has a sober facade with Romanesque doorway; in the lunette is a noteworthy 17th cent. fresco of the Madonna and Child with Saints. The Roman *Porta Gemina* was the entrance to Ascoli Piceno from the Via Salaria. The 13th cent. Romanesque church of *San Tommaso* has, on the main altar, an important sculptured group by Giuseppe Giosafatti and his son Lazzaro (1694-1781). The 13th cent. Romanesque-Gothic church of *Sant'Agostino*, with facade characterized by three oculi, contains works of art including a fresco of Christ bearing the Cross, by Cola dell'Amatrice, and a panel depicting the Translation of the Holy House of Loreto and four Saints, by Vincenzo Pagani (c. 1490-1568). Other places worthy of mention in Ascoli Piceno are the 13th cent. Romanesque church of *San Venanzo*, with stucco-decorated interior, by Giuseppe Giosafatti and his family; the church of *Santa Maria della Carità* or *della Scopa*, designed by Cola dell'Amatrice, with frescoes by Girolamo Buratti (lived in the 17th cent.); the *Colle dell'Annunziata*; the ex-*Convento dell'Annunziata*; the church of *Sant'Angelo Magno*, second half of the 13th cent.; the impressive *Palazzo Malaspina*, possibly designed by Cola dell'Amatrice; and *Palazzo Gallo*, by the architect Lazzaro Giosafatti.

* **ASCOLI SATRIANO** (Foggia). On three hills dominating the Carapelle valley. The *Duomo* was originally Romanesque, then modified in Renaissance style and finally altered to suit Baroque taste. Its simple facade is divided into three by pilaster strips. The interior contains a silver bust of San Potito (17th cent.), a wooden choir carved in 1643, and a Neapolitan-School painting of the Death of St. Joseph, (18th cent.). The Town Hall houses an archeological collection (*Raccolta Archeologica*), with ceramics and bronzes excavated from local necropoli, especially of the 4th and 3rd cent. B.C. In the neighbourhood are archeological remains (*avanzi archeologici*), including a Roman arch in brick, and an aqueduct.

* **ASIAGO** (Vicenza). In the middle of the Asiago plateau. The parish church of *San Matteo* has a large facade in red marble. Inside there is an altarpiece by Francesco Bassano the Elder (c. 1470-1540), depicting the Madonna and Child between Angels and Saints. The *Sacrario Militare* with niches containing the remains of tens of thousands of Italian and Austro-Hungarian soldiers killed in battle, many of them unknown. There is also a well-equipped *Osservatorio Astrofisico* founded in 1942, belonging to the University of Padua.

* **ASOLA** (Mantua). On the left bank of the river Chiese, it is built to a square plan, with straight streets. In the church of *Sant'Andrea*, built at the turn of the 16th cent., is an important pictorial cycle by Girolamo Romani called Romanino (c. 1484-1566). *Fontana d'Ercole*, dated 1596, in Piazza XX Settembre.

* **ASOLO** (Treviso). Pretty little town among picturesque hills, called "of the hundred horizons". The *Castello della Regina* was the official residence first of Queen Caterina Cornero Cornaro and subsequently of Venetian mayors; the Clock Tower, a squat tower, and the Audience Hall, are all that remain. The *Loggia del Capitano* houses the Civic Museum, which contains paleontological, archeological and medieval material found in the surrounding area; there are also paintings, manuscripts and other mementoes of Queen Caterina Cornero Cornaro, the sculptor Antonio Canova (1757-1822), and the English poet, Robert Browning. The *Duomo* is dedicated to Santa Maria di Breda. Reconstructed in the 18th and 19th cent., it still has a 15th cent. porch and contains important paintings including a St. Francis, probably by Bartolomeo Vivarini (c. 1432-1499), and the Madonna Assunta with Saints Basil and Anthony Abbot, by Lorenzo Lotto (1480-1556). The 18th cent. *Villa Scotti*, now called Pasini, is where Robert Browning lived. The *Rocca* is an attractive, polygonal structure dominating the town.

*** **ASSISI** (Perugia). On a spur of Monte Subasio. The *Basilica di San Francesco* has been defined "the most beautiful house of prayer in the world", a magnificent sacrarium where faith and art have blended and merged. It is uniquely formed by two super-imposed chur-

Assisi, Basilica Superiore di San Francesco.

ches, in all probability the brainchild of Brother Elias, at St. Francis' death. The facade (belonging to the upper church, as the lower one is partly carved out of the rock), has a twin-doorway and fine double rose-window, of Cosmatesque design. The lower church has a nave divided into five low-arched ogival bays; in it are the chapel of St. Sebastian, with a fresco depicting the Madonna della Salute, by Ceccolo di Giovanni (lived in the first half of the 15th cent.), chapel of St. Anthony Abbot, chapel of St. Catherine or The Crucifixion, crumbling frescoes narrating Stories of Christ, the crypt where the body of St. Francis was discovered in December 1818, having been concealed there by Bother Elias, the chapel of St. Ludovic or St. Stephen, chapel of St. Anthony of Padua, chapel of Mary Magdalen, with frescoes partly by Giotto di Bondone (1266-1337), the four famous vault-panels, frescoed by an unidentified follower of Giotto and called "Master of the vault-panels", chapel of St. Nicholas, chapel of St. John the Baptist, chapel of St. Martin, completely frescoed by Simone Martini between 1322 and 1326, and sacristies with reliquaries, etc. The upper church has a single nave, and radiates light and joy in contrast with the dark, sombre atmosphere of the lower church; in it are a splendid cycle of frescoes by Giovanni Cimabue (recorded 1272-1302), twenty-eight frescoes narrating the life of St. Francis, by Giotto di Bondone, etc. The Treasury, in spite of losses over the centuries, is still rich in works of art and precious objects. The *Temple of Minerva* is one of the best-preserved examples of the Roman world and was enlarged in 1539 to form the church of St. Mary above Minerva. The *Duomo*, dedicated to San Rufino, was erected in the 8th cent. and renovated in the second half of the 12th cent. It has a majestic facade and, inside, many works of art such as a painting by Dono Doni (died 1575), pictures possibly by Giovanni Andrea Carlone (1639-1697), the chapel of the Weeping Madonna, the Chapterhouse Museum, and the Roman Cistern. The *Rocca Maggiore*, with trapezoidal walls, is overlooked by the high square tower of the keep. The 13th cent. Gothic church of *Santa Chiara* reflects the style of the upper church of St. Francis. It has a sober facade and, inside, works of art partly inspired by Giotto and his school. The *Convento di San Damiano*, typical example of a 13th cent. monastery, was once an isolated oratory. The little church is preceded by a portico, and the single-naved interior is simple and rustic. The *Eremo delle Carceri*, in oak woods and surrounded by caves, where St. Francis and his first followers withdrew in prayer and meditation, is a most awe-inspiring sight: history and legend mingle here to produce an almost supernatural atmosphere. The *Basilica di Santa Maria degli Angeli*, begun in 1569 on the site of the Porziuncola chapel, is rich in Franciscan memories. The facade is 17th cent. in origin, but was noticeably modified later. Inside is the venerated chapel of the Porziuncola, dating back to the 10-11th cent. It was in this chapel that St. Francis founded the Franciscan Order in 1208. Also in the basilica of Santa Maria degli Angeli are the Cappella del Transito, where St. Francis breathed his last, lying on the bare ground; the famous rose-garden, with its thornless rose-bushes, and the Museum, with decorated Hall.

** **ASTI.** In the Tanaro valley, between northern and southern Montferrat. The Gothic *Collegiata di San Secondo*, dating from the 13th cent., has three entrance-doors finely decorated with high pointed arches. The interior, in the shape of a Latin cross, boasts many paintings and a silver coffin containing the body of San Secondo of Asti, patron saint of the city. The 13th cent. *Torre Troiana* or *dell'Orologio* has three storeys of Romanesque mullions with slender columns and Ghibelline crenellation. The *Cattedrale di Maria Assunta e San Gottardo*, is an impressive Gothic building, mainly erected in the first half of the 14th cent. The right side is the most interesting, and also worthy of note is a porch in decorated Gothic style (dated about 1470). The interior is exceptionally rich in frescoes and statues of high artistic value. The 12th cent. *Battistero di San Pietro*, called the Rotonda, is built on an octagonal plan, reinforced at the corners with buttresses, and is one of the most remarkable examples of the late-Romanesque tradition in northern Italy. The church of *San Pietro in Consavia* (1467), is a square-sided building, with two fine single-lighted windows and a round one in the facade. The *Pinacoteca Civica* contains art treasures of enormous value in its many rooms, and a museum devoted to the Risorgimento. The *Palazzo Alfieri*, rebuilt several times, is the birthplace of Vittorio Alfieri (1749-1803). On the first floor are a portrait, and a collection of manuscripts and antiques belonging to Vittorio Alfieri. The *Cripta di*

Asti, San Secondo, facade.

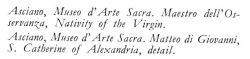

Asciano, Museo d'Arte Sacra. Maestro dell'Osservanza, Nativity of the Virgin.

Asciano, Museo d'Arte Sacra. Matteo di Giovanni,
S. Catherine of Alexandria, detail.

Ascoli Piceno, Pinacoteca Comunale. Paolo da
Visso, Holy Conversation, detail.

Assisi, Basilica Superiore di San Francesco. Giotto, St. Francis expelling the demons from Arezzo.

Assisi, Basilica Inferiore di San Francesco. Pietro Lorenzetti, Crucifixion, detail.

Assisi, Basilica Inferiore di San Francesco. Simone Martini, St. Martin's refusal, detail.

Atri, Duomo. Andrea Delitio, Mary Visiting Elizabeth, detail.

Sant'Anastasio, has slender columns and delicate capitals in Ravenna style. Interesting walks along the vie *Gioberti, Natta, Roero*, and *XX Settembre*.

* **ATRANI** (Salerno). One of the most characteristic villages along the Amalfi coast, at the entrance to the Valle del Dragone. The *Collegiata di Santa Maria Maddalena*, built in the second half of the 13th cent., has a dynamic Baroque facade, with majolic dome and a slender campanile, on a square plan. Inside is a panel depicting doubting St. Thomas, by Andrea da Salerno (c. 1490-1530), and paintings by Giovanni Angelo D'Amato (active in the second half of the 16th cent.). The church of *San Salvatore de' Bireto*, founded in 940 A.D., is so called because it was there that the newly-elected Doges received their Cap of Office. On the facade are two arches supporting the slender ribbed campanile. The 12th cent. entrance, with sculptured door-posts, has a fine bronze door, identical to the one in Amalfi Cathedral. Inside are some artistic pieces, such as a 12th cent. transenna with two peacocks facing each other with outspread tails.

** **ATRI** (Teramo). Set on a spur within sight of the Adriatic. The *Duomo*, dedicated to the Assunta, and begun in the 9th and 10th cent., is a solemn medieval structure, all in Bisenti stone. The appearance of the present-day building is the result of work carried out in the

second half of the 13th cent. The facade is sober and rectangular, divided into three parts by pilaster strips, with a perfect doorway by Rainaldo (lived in the 14th cent.). The lines of the Romanesque campanile were imitated by builders of bell-towers throughout the province. Inside are frescoes by Andrea Delitio (lived in the 15th cent.), a 15th cent. cross and reliquary in the shape of a little Gothic church, etc. In the archives are stamps, parchments, xylographs, illuminated codices, chorals and incunabula. The 14th cent. church of *Sant'Agostino* has a doorway revealing the transition from Flemish-Gothic to Renaissance style. The *Palazzo dei Duchi* was built in the 14th cent. by Antonio Acquaviva. Inside are three rooms, once elegantly frescoed by Giacomo Farelli (1624-1706) but now in a sadly dilapidated state, and largely indistinguishable.

** **AUGUSTA** (Syracuse). On an island joined to Sicily by two bridges, it is an important port and industrial centre. In the *Duomo*, dedicated to the Assunta and begun in 1644, are thirteen good paintings by an unknown artist, depicting Christ and the Apostles. The *Castello* (second half of the 13th cent.), was fortified with ramparts in the 16-17th cent. Impressive *Palazzo del Municipio* (1699). *Forte Avalos*, standing alone against the sea, was built in 1569 by command of Ferdinand Avalos de Aquino. Excursion to the ruins of *Megara Hyblaea*, founded possibly in 728 B.C. by the

Atri, Duomo.

Megarians, who flourished in the 6th cent. B.C. Razed to the ground by Gelo in the middle of the 5th cent., it was rebuilt and again destroyed, this time by the Romans, at the end of the 3rd cent. Archeologists have unearthed the centre of the ancient and Hellenistic city, and military works of the 3rd cent. B.C.

* AURONZO DI CADORE (Belluno). Holiday resort, surrounded by impressive mountains. At Villa Grande is the parish church of *Santa Giustina* (1772), with campanile of 1436, set apart. Inside are marble altars, frescoes and paintings by Giovanni De Min (1776-1859), a Holy Family by Tommaso Da Rin (1838-1922) and an altarpiece by Michelangelo Grigoletti (1801-1870), depicting Saints Nicholas and Sylvester.

** AVELLINO. Nestling among mountains, between two tributaries of the river Sabato. The 12th cent. *Duomo*, dedicated to the Assunta, has been rebuilt several times. Its facade, by Pasquale Cardolo (lived in the 19th cent.), is neo-Classical, as is the interior. It contains high-reliefs in stucco representing Saints Peter, Paul and two Angels, by Giuseppe Sorbilli (1824-1890), statues of the four Evangelists, also by Sorbilli, an admirable 16th cent. Epiphany, by an unknown artist, a tabernacle in relief-work, by Giovanni da Nola (1488-1558), and a carved-wood choir, possibly by the French artist Clemente Chierus (active in the second half of the 16th cent.). The *Museo Irpino* contains archeological material from prehistoric, Italic, and Roman Irpinia. Especially important are the marble altar of the 1st cent. A.D., from Abellinum, and remains found in the sanctuary of the goddess Mephitis, portraits, funeral reliefs, and inscriptions from Roman times. The *Palazzo della Dogana* is a rudimentary but characteristic building, decorated with ancient statues and busts of Nero, Caligula, Commodus, Apollo Citharoedus, and Prince Marino I Caracciolo, one of the last feudal lords of the city. Ruins of the medieval *Castello*, where Pope Innocent II, the Emperor Lothair, and Henry IV, numerous Neapolitan sovereigns, and Charles VIII of France all stayed at some time or other. To the north-east of the town is the *Collina dei Cappuccini*, with Capuchin monastery and church, inside which is a panel of the Deposition, by Silvestro Buono (active in the second half of the 16th cent.).

** AVERSA (Caserta). Agricultural centre, north of Naples in the Volturno plain. The *Duomo*, dedicated to St. Paul, was built in the 11th cent., and later modified and restored. Of the original construction, it still keeps the Arabic-Norman dome (characterized externally by 128 small columns) and the apse section. The interior contains a Renaissance altar (1563), a Romanesque ambulatory of the late 11th cent., a much-admired example of primitive Norman architecture, an 11th cent. doorway with bearded giants supported by dwarfs, a smaller sized reproduction of the Holy House of Loreto, dated 1630, a mid 13th cent. Catalan-art Crucifix, a Baroque monument to Cardinal Innico Caracciolo, and paintings by Angelillo Arcuccio (active from 1464 to 1492). The Baroque church of *Annunciata* is preceded by a slender portico. Inside are important paintings such as Madonna delle Grazie and St. John the Evangelist, by Angelillo Arcuccio, Deposition, by Marco da Siena called Marco Pino (c. 1525-c. 1587), Adoration of the Shepherds, by Francesco Solimena (1657-1747) and Massacre of the Innocents, by Giuseppe Simonelli (c. 1650-1710). In the small, 14th cent. church of *Santa Maria a Piazza* are 14th and 15th cent. frescoes by local masters. The 11th cent. church of *San Biagio* was rebuilt in the 18th cent. On the high altar there is a Martyrdom of St. Blaise, by Marco Pino. In the church of *San Francesco*, built in the 11th cent. and modified in the 17th and 19th, is an Adoration of the Shepherds, a mature painting by Pietro da Cortona (1596-1669). Other places worthy of mention in Aversa are: *Porta Napoli*, a solemn arch designed in the 17th cent. by Gentile di Aversa; the *Castello Angioino*, where Andrew of Hungary was strangled; the 13th cent. church of *Sant'Antonio*, containing the sarcophagus of Nardella Sanframondi (1382); the church of *Santa Maria Maddalena*, built in the 13th cent. and rebuilt in the early 18th cent., containing an ancon carved by Giovanni da Nola, called Mariliano, (1488-1558), and the church of *Santa Maria degli Angeli*, containing a painting depicting San Bonaventura receiving the Standard of the Holy Sepulchre from the Madonna, by Francesco Solimena.

* AVIGLIANA (Turin). At the entrance to the Susa valley, on the banks of the Dora Riparia, it dominates a vast morainic hollow containing the Lago Grande and the Lago Piccolo. Although a modern agricultural and industrial centre, it has kept its medieval appearance. From Avigliana (12.7 km.) one reaches the *Sacra di San Michele* or *Abbazia*

Avigliana, Sacra di San Michele, Abbey, Stairway of the Dead.

della Chiusa, a massive group of buildings and ruins incorporated into the peak of Mount Pirchiriano, a spur rising at the opening of the Val di Susa. The complex is important both for its originality (going from primitive Romanesque to Gothic in style), and for its eventful history, since the Sacra di San Michele was one of the most powerful fortified monasteries in the Middle Ages. The church of *San Michele*, perched on the summit of Mount Pirchiriano, was begun in Romanesque style and completed in Gothic. Passing through the late-Romanesque doorway one enters the basilican interior; in the right-hand apse is an altar once used in pagan rites.

* **BACENO** (Novara). Small centre in the Valle dell'Ossola, at the confluence of the Devero stream and the river Toce. The parish church of *San Gaudenzio* is perched on the brink of a chasm. It was erected in the early 14th cent. and enlarged, with two aisles, in the 16th. The gable facade is decorated with a rose-window and three Renaissance doorways. Inside, the walls and vaults are covered with frescoes of various periods; the apse contains a precious reredos in carved and gilded wood.

Baceno, San Gaudenzio, facade.

** **BACOLI** (Naples). Situated on the southwest extremity of the gulf of Pozzuoli. It preserves interesting remains from Roman times. The *Cento Camerelle* (Centum Cellae) are water reservoirs on two levels; the upper one contains a large cistern (1st cent. A.D.) and the lower one a system of cuniculi from the Republican period. The huge *Piscina mirabile* consists of five aisles divided by pillars and covered with vaults. In the *Parco archeologico* of *Baia* are preserved the remains of one of the most important thermal centres in Roman times (though it has been suggested that the buildings brought to light in the excavation area belonged to a large Imperial-age palace

rather than a thermal centre). Notice in particular the *Therma of Mercurius*, which is dominated by a circular, dome-covered room; the *Therma of Venus*, with a rectangular room and apse, and the *Therma of Sosandra*, consisting of three terraces on different levels. Outside the excavation area can be found the *Temple of Venus* with a round interior and polygonal exterior.

* **BADIA CALAVENA** (Verona). Agricultural centre and summer resort. The *Parrocchiale* contains a 16th cent. tabernacle and pictures by Alessandro Turchi, called Orbetto (lived c. 1582-1650) and Paolo Morando, called Cavazzola (1486-1522). Remains of the *Monastero dei Santi Pietro e Vito* (12th cent.), formerly held by the Benedictines. *Spigola* is a cave where paleontological material has been extracted.

* **BADIA POLESINE** (Rovigo). Agricultural and commercial town situated on the right bank of the Adige. It grew up in the 10th cent. around a monastery and a church dedicated to Santa Maria sull'Adige, later known as the *Abbazia della Vangadizza*. The Abbey was built in the 10th cent. by Almerico, Marquis of Mantua. On its site stands the Espagnac Palace, containing the ruins of the monastery: an irregular-shaped cloister, a 15th cent. refectory, the former church, with remains of three apses, the quadrilateral Chapel of Our Lady (1490), with stuccoes and frescoes attributed to Filippo Zaniberti (1585-1636). The 15th cent. *Palazzo degli Estensi* is in Gothic-Venetian style. The *Oratorio della Madonna della Salute* has a magnificent marble doorway (1715).

* **BAGHERIA** (Palermo). On the outskirts of Palermo, it is famous for its noble villas built in the 17th and 18th cent. Among the best known are *Villa Palagonia* and *Villa Valguarnera*, built respectively in 1715 and 1721 by Tommaso Maria Napoli. They are notable for their terraces, balconies, tenaille staircases and the flowing lines of the central part of the building.

Bagheria, Villa Valguarnera.

** **BAGNACAVALLO** (Ravenna). Small agricultural and industrial town situated on the left bank of the Naviglio Canal, with medieval quarters. The *Collegiata di San Michele*, designed by a Ravenna architect, who was inspired by the work of Bramante (1444-1514), contains a large number of important paintings including a Redeemer and Saints by Bartolomeo Ramenghi called Bagnacavallo (1484-1542). The *Istituto delle Opere Pie Raggruppate* contains an interesting art collection including a Madonna and Child enthroned and Four Saints, probably by Bagnacavallo. The church of *San Francesco* (1795), is neo-Classical in style. Inside is a 14th cent. panel of the Crucifixion by the Rimini school, and a Madonna and Child with Saints by Ferraù da Faenza (1562-1645). The *Pieve di San Pietro in Sylvis* was begun in the 8-9th cent. It contains a 15th cent. fresco of the Deposition, and other frescoes carried out during the first half of the 14th cent. by an unknown painter, after the style of Pietro da Rimini (active in the first half of the 14th cent.).

** BAGNAIA (Viterbo).

Attractive medieval town. *Villa Lante*, designed by Jacopo Barozzi, called Vignola (1507-1573) is an admirable example of late-Renaissance architecture. It was built during the period 1566 to 1578 by order of Cardinal Giovanni Francesco Gambara. In the geometrically designed Italian garden is the beautiful basin-shaped Fontana del Quadrato. The fountain has three circles of pools dominated by the group of the four Moors, by Taddeo Landini (c. 1550-1596). At the end of the garden are two small palaces. The one on the right is older and contains paintings and grotesques by Raffaellino da Reggio (1550-c. 1578) and frescoes by Antonio Tempesta (1555-1630). The palace on the left (built between 1583 and 1590 according to the wishes of Cardinal Alessandro Montalto) contains paintings by Agostino Tassi (1566-1644) and frescoes by Tassi and Giuseppe Cesari called Cavalier d'Arpino (1568-1640). Beyond the small palaces is the Lumini Fountain with seventy jets of water, grottoes of Venus and Neptune, with statues of these two deities; the Cardinal's Table, an enormous stone table for open-air banquets, and fountains of: the Giants, the Dolphins, the Flood, the Rain, and Pegasus.

** BAGNO A RIPOLI (Florence).

Named after a Roman bath on the Via Cassia, remains of which were discovered in 1687, it is pleasantly situated at the meeting point of several roads. The *Abbazia di Ripoli* was built in 790 for the Benedictine noons and handed over to the Vallombrosani monks in the 13th cent. In the 11th cent. church of *San Bartolomeo* are some fine 12th cent. paintings. The *Pieve di San Pietro a Ripoli* (8th cent.) was originally called the church of San Pietro a Quarto because it was built exactly 4 miles from Florence on the Via Cassia. Inside it is very bare and plain, but contains a graceful marble ciborium after the style of Benedetto da Rovezzano (1474-post 1552), valuable frescoes and canvases, and an imposing baptismal font on a Roman capital base. On the outskirts, at Villamagna,

is the *Pieve di San Donnino* with slender bell-tower.

* BAGNO DI ROMAGNA (Forlì).

Agricultural centre and spa, also summer holiday resort. The *Basilica di Santa Maria Assunta*, formerly belonging to the Camaldolites and built in the second half of the 11th cent., was rebuilt in the 15th. Inside are impressive paintings including a Crucifixion by Alessandro Gherardini (1655-1723), a triptych of the Assunta and Saints by Neri di Bicci (1419-1491), a fresco of San Romualdo with five monks by Andrea Sacchi (1599-1661), and an altarpiece representing the Madonna and Child with St. John the Baptist and St. John the Evangelist, after the style of Andrea del Sarto (1486-1531). The 16th cent. *Palazzo Pretorio* bears the coats-of-arms of the Captains of the Florentine Republic and standard-bearers. *Terme Sant'Agnese* and *Terme Giardino*.

* BAGNOLI IRPINO (Avellino).

Situated in a pleasant hilly district dominated by the ruins of a castle. In the 17th cent. parish church (*Parrocchiale*), dedicated to the Assunta, is a wooden choir consisting of nineteen stalls decorated with small statues and bas-reliefs depicting Stories from the New and Old Testaments, carved by local craftsmen in the 17th cent. There are also paintings by Andrea d'Aste (1673-1721) and wooden sculptures by Domenico Venuta (1687-1744). The church of *San Domenico*, rebuilt in the 16th cent., is flanked by an imposing medieval bell-tower in front

Bagno a Ripoli (surrounding district), Pieve di San Donnino at Villamagna, campanile and apse.

of which is a portico with columns belonging to the original building. Inside the church is the tomb of Alessandro Ronca, a captain adventurer from Bagnoli; and a large panel representing the Madonna of the Rosary and Saints, carried out by Marco Pino in 1576.

* **BARD** (Aosta). Picturesquely crammed together in a gorge of the river Dora, facing the Champorcher valley. It has 13th and 14th cent. houses with arches and mullioned and cross-shaped windows. The gorge is dominated by the *Forte di Bard*, which towers on a cliff, 467m. high. It was built in the 11th cent. for toll-collecting, and converted into a fortress in 1242 by Amedeo of Savoy. It was rebuilt in the 19th cent., when further fortifications were added. Nearby, along the old road, is a 221m. stretch of the ancient *Strada delle Gallie* (road to Gaul); sliced out of the mountainside, and still with its original paving, it has an arch and Roman column cut out of the rock.

* **BARDOLINO** (Verona). Attractive little town situated on the lower slopes of green hills at the eastern side of Lake Garda. In the Romanesque church of *San Severo*, built at the beginning of the 12th cent., are interesting frescoes which are now in poor condition, and a few unusual architectonic elements. Also worth seeing is the church of *San Zeno*, believed to date back to pre-Roman times. In the neighbourhood is the Camaldolite Hermitage (*Eremo dei Camaldolesi*), dating from the second half of the 17th cent., the church of which is dedicated to St. George and contains a painting of San Romualdo by Jacopo Palma the Younger (1544-1628).

* **BARGA** (Lucca). Small town in the Garfagnana area situated on a terrace on the left side of the Serchio valley. The ancient quarter is built on a hill and dominated by the massive Romanesque *Duomo*, built in successive stages (9th, 12th and 14th cent.), the apse being modified in the 16th and 18th cent. The facade is decorated with two orders of small arches and has a beautiful portico. The interior, consisting of a nave and two aisles, contains a large pulpit with reliefs, by a sculptor from Lucca (second half of the 12th cent.), terracottas by Della Robbia, a polychrome-wood statue of St. Christopher (12th cent.), and a rich Treasury.

*** **BARI.** Situated on the Adriatic, halfway down the Apulia coast, in a densely populated and fertile area. It is formed by the merging of an old city, rich in monuments and historic associations, with a new city, with roads arranged in chessboard design. In the old city is the late 11th cent. of *San Nicola*, prototype of Romanesque architecture in Apulia. The facade is plain and majestic (13th cent.). On the right stands the massive Catapano Tower, believed to be even older than the Basilica. Inside, the Basilica is divided into a nave and two aisles. It contains works

Bari, Cathedral, interior.

ot art including Stories of Nicholas and Paradise by Carlo Rosa (died 1678), a ciborium dating from 1150, the oldest in the region; a marble episcopal chair of the 11th or 12th cent.; 14th cent. frescoes, a triptych of the Madonna between St. Nicholas and St. John the Evangelist by Andrea Rico da Candia (lived in the 16th cent.), a panel dated 1476, by Bartolomeo Vivarini of Venice. In the crypt, consecrated in 1089, is the body of St. Nicholas. Beside the Basilica is a valuable library containing 12th cent. diplomas and parchments, the most valuable of which dates from 939 A.D. The Romanesque *Cattedrale*, built in the second half of the 12th cent. and dedicated to San Sabino, has a facade divided into three sections by pilaster strips, with three Baroque doorways which do not blend with the simplicity of the building. The interior is spectacular and imposing, and contains works of art including a valuable 12th cent. pulpit, a ciborium similar to the one in the Basilica of San Nicola, carried out in 1233 by Alfano da Termoli (recorded in the first half of the 13th cent.), and the tomb of Bishop Romualdo Grisone (beginning of the 14th cent.). In the crypt is a Byzantine-style ikon of the Virgin Mary stolen from Constantinople in 733 A.D., and 13th cent. frescoes. In the Exultet archives is a precious illuminated parchment scroll. The *Castello*, built in the first half of the 13th cent. by Frederick II on the foundations of a Norman fort, still has two of the original four corner towers. The large inner courtyard is trapezoidal in shape. The castle contains plaster casts of sculptures and architectonic and decorative fragments of the most famous Romanesque monuments of the region. It also houses a small museum of 16th cent. frescoes and an attractive painted wooden relief of the Madonna of the Veil. The church of *San Gregorio* (11th cent.) is another beautiful example of Romanesque architecture, the facade, divided into three by pilaster strips, is embellished with distinctive windows. In the Romanesque interior, with ancient elements, are finely carved capitals and pulvins. The *Museo Storico* contains a vast collection of relics and documents, especially of the 1st World War. In the old part of Bari it is also worth visiting the 12th cent. church of *San Marco*, built by Venetian merchants; the 14th cent. *Arco di San Nicola*; the 13th cent. *Portico dei Pellegrini*; and the *Colonna della Giustizia*, flanked by a stone lion which, in olden times, those guilty of bankruptcy had to mount and be mocked by the crowd. In the new city is the impressive *Palazzo Ateneo*, designed by the architect Giovanni Castelli (1848-1902); the *Museo Archeologico* containing the richest collection of archeological remains in Apulia, is of fundamental importance in the study of Apulian art; the *Teatro Petruzzelli*, designed by Angelo Messeni (lived in the 19-20th cent.; the *Pinacoteca Provinciale* with 15th, 16th, 17th

& 18th cent. works, amongst which a polyptych by Antonio Vivarini (c. 1432-1499), Holy Conversation by Paris Bordone (1500-1571), St. Roch by Domenico il Tintoretto (1560-1635), Virgin and Saints by Paolo Caliari called Veronese (c. 1528-1588), Christ carrying the Cross by Giorgio Vasari (1511-1574), a Pietà by Andrea Vaccaro (1598-1670), and Flight into Egypt by Domenico Zampieri called Domenichino (1581-1641). Finally, in the new city, there are three attractive and picturesque promenade walks: the *Lungomare Nazario Sauro*, the *Lungomare Imperatore Augusto* winding its way around the Old Port, and the *Lungomare Cristoforo Colombo*.

* **BARILE** (Potenza). Situated to the east of Monte Vulture. The 17th cent. *Chiesa del Carmine* is a notable construction. Visit the quaint characteristic quarter with *Casette Asismiche*, and the unusual *Rione di Cantine*, cellars dug out of the volcanic rock which in ancient times formed a chain of forts. In the San Pietro area are *Tombe a Camerette* (cell tombs) and *Grotte Trogloditiche* (Troglodyte caves).

** **BARLETTA** (Bari). On the Adriatic coast, south-east of the estuary of the river Ofanto. It is an important agricultural and business centre, and popular seaside resort. The medieval churches and a picture-gallery are interesting. The Basilica of *Santo Sepolcro* is perhaps the city's most interesting building; originally Romanesque, it was modified towards the end of the 13th cent. in Burgundian-Gothic style. It is flanked on the left by the celebrated Colossus, a 4th cent. bronze statue,

Barletta, detail of the Colosso.

4½ metres high, of an Emperor, possibly Valentinianus I; of noble and dignified aspect, it is believed that this statue, certainly oriental in origin, was stolen from a shipwreck. Inside the Basilica are 13th cent. frescoes, a baptismal font of the same period, a 15th cent. Venetian school panel of St. Blaise, and a Byzantine-style painting of the Madonna on wood. The Treasury contains a 12th cent. Limoges Eucharistic Dove, a valuable 13th cent. breviary relating tales of the Crusades from 1097 to 1202, and a Gothic monstrance. The *Museo* and the *Pinacoteca Comunale* are among the best in Apulia. In the entrance hall of the museum is a much-admired headless statue draped in a toga. The first room contains armoury, the second, fragments of a 3rd cent. relief, Roman amphoras, ancient pottery, Canosino-type plates, ciboriums with red designs on the lids, canthari, large ablution bowls, large bowls in ancient Southern Italian style, decorated with cloaked youths, dating from the 5th cent. B.C. In the third room are relics pertaining to the Challenge of Barletta (1503). In the Art Gallery are works by the local painters Giuseppe De Nittis (1846-1884), Giuseppe Gabbiani (19th cent.), and Raffaele Girondi (1873-1911). There are also sixteen paintings by Francesco De Mura (1696-1784) and others by Francesco Solimena (1657-1747), Sebastiano Ricci (1659-1734), Giovanni Battista Tiepolo (1696-1770), Giovanni Battista Piazzetta (1682-1754), Paolo De Matteis (1662-1728), Antonio Raffaele Mengs (1728-1779), Giuseppe Bonito (1707-1789), and Nicola Vaccaro (1634-1709). The *Duomo*, dedicated to Santa Maria Maggiore, was begun in 1150, in Romanesque-Apulian style. It has a round high facade with a large round window framed by five corbels, and three porticoes (the centre one was rebuilt in Renaissance style in the 16th cent.). The basilican interior, partly Romanesque in style, contains a valuable ciborium on the high altar; a Madonna and Child and Redeemer popularly called the "Madonna della Disfida" because it was carried by the priests to the 13 Italian knights who won the Challenge; a panel, painted on both sides, by Paolo Serafini (active in the mid-14th century), an Ecco Homo, also by Serafini; Dormitio Virginis and Madonna enthroned, valuable panels by an unknown 15th cent. Sicilian artist; and a beautiful baptismal font. The square-sided *Castello*, built by the Swabians on the site of a Norman fortress, was strengthened by the French architect Pierre d'Agincourt (recorded 1269-1324). It has four impressive lancet-style ramparts at the corners, possibly the work of the architect Evangelist Menga (lived in the 16th cent.). The church of *Sant'Andrea*, built in the 12th cent. on the ruins of a 6th cent. church, has a beautiful doorway. Inside is a Madonna of the Angels, probably by Mattia Preti (1613-1699), St. Anthony of Padua by Francesco di Gentile da Fabriano (lived in the 15-16th cent.), a Madonna and Child by Alvise Vivarini (c. 1445-c. 1505), two magnificent 18th cent. tombs belonging to the Fraggianni family, a choir carved by Francesco Ferrara of Naples in 1599, and an attractive 16th cent. Roman school panel of the Resurrection. The *Cantina della Disfida* (Room of the Challenge) is reassembled on the ground floor of a medieval palace. It has treasures of the period and, on the walls, shields with the coats-of-arms of the thirteen Italian knights; worthy of note is a plaster group depicting Ettore Fieramosca killing La Motte, by Achille Stocchi (lived in the 19th cent.). In the *Chiesa dei Gesuiti* (1630) are a Deposition by Cesare Fracanzano (c. 1600-c. 1653), and Miracle of St. Francis Xavier by Francesco De Mura. Also noteworthy are: the *Palazzo del Monte di Pietà*, an impressive Baroque building joined to the Jesuits' Church; the *Palazzo della Marra* (late 16th cent.); the church of *San Giacomo*, with architectonic remains of the 13th and 14th cent.; and the church of *Sant'Agostino*, built at the end of the 13th cent., containing a Madonna and Donors by Andrea da Salerno (c. 1490-1530).

* BARUMINI (Cagliari). Noted for the *Villaggio Nuragico*, where the foundations of about fifty hut-dwellings can be seen, most of which are circular in shape and date back to the 7-6th cent. B.C. The *Nuraghe su Nuraxi* is particularly interesting. Together with the Nuraghe Santu Antine, known locally as Sa Domu de Su Rei (the King's Palace), it provides the most important architectonic evidence of the early Sardinian megalithic civilization; from its position it appears to have been the main stronghold of a strategic system formed by other nuraghi grouped along the spurs near the ridge of the Giara di Gesturi. It is a poly-lobed construction, and has a graceful centre tower made of blocks of basalt and basaltic lava, with a ground floor and first floor, probably built between the 13th and 9th cent. B.C.

** BASSANO DEL GRAPPA (Vicenza). Attractively situated below Monte Grappa and the Plateau of the Sette Comuni. The *Torre*

Barumini, view of the nuraghe village.

di Ezzelino is all that remains of the medieval Castle of Bassano. The church of *San Giovanni Battista* was erected at the beginning of the 14th cent. and rebuilt by Giovanni Miazzi (1699-1797). Inside is the Baroque chapel of the Blessed Sacrament, containing valuable stucco work, statues and frescoes: Saint John the Baptist by Giovan Battista Piazzetta (1682-1754) and Teaching the Child Mary, by Francesco Maggiotto (1750-1805). The Romanesque-Gothic church of *San Francesco* (13th cent.) was enlarged in later periods. It contains a painted wooden Crucifix by Guariento di Arpo (recorded 1338-1370). In the art gallery of the *Museo Civico* are works by the artists da Ponte called Bassano (active in the 15-16th cent.), Martyrdom of Saint Apollonia by Antonio Vivarini (c. 1415-1484), Christ Blessing by Bartolomeo Vivarini (c. 1432-1499), Burial of a Friar, Bivouac and the Diners by Alessandro Magnasco (1667-1749). The museum also contains the Remondiniana collection of engravings and prints, plaster casts, paintings and drawings by Antonio Canova (1757-1822), and collections of stones, ceramics and coins. The characteristic bridge (*Ponte Coperto*) over the river Brenta was first mentioned at the beginning of the 13th cent.), and has been rebuilt several times since. There are 16th cent. marble arcades at each end of the bridge; under the arch at the beginning there is a fresco of the Madonna with Saints Francis and Anthony by Guido Cadorin (born 1892), while at the other end there is the Museum of the Alpine regiment known as the Ponte degli Alpini. The church of *San Donato* (early 13th cent.) has paintings of the Madonna and Child, St. Bassiano, St. Michele and Donor by Francesco Bassano the Elder (c. 1470-1540). *Palazzo Pretorio* (14-15th cent.).

The *Castello Superiore*, originating in the 10th cent., dominates the city. The *Duomo* is dedicated to Santa Maria in Colle, and dates back to the early 15th cent., though it has been modified several times since. It contains paintings of the Madonna and the Martyrdom of St. Stephen by Leandro Bassano (1557-1622). Walks to the 17th cent. *Ca' Rezzonico*, designed by Baldassarre Longhena (1598-1682), and to the *Villa Bianchi-Michiel*, (early 17th cent.), also in the style of Longhena.

* **BASTIA** (Perugia). A largely modern town, but with medieval streets and houses. The ancient church of *San Michele Arcangelo* was rebuilt in the 15th cent. It has a facade of red and white limestone taken from Monte Subasio. The Gothic interior contains detached frescoes belonging to the school of Bartolomeo Caporali (c. 1420-1503) and a beautiful triptych by Niccolò di Liberatore called Alunno (c. 1430-1502). There are some interesting remains of the fort (*Avanzi Medievali*) and 15th cent. houses.

* **BATTAGLIA TERME** (Padua). Spa and industrial centre. The church of *San Giacomo* (1332) was rebuilt at the beginning of the 18th cent. It has an 18th cent. interior containing a statue of the Madonna and Child by Giovanni Maria Morlaiter (1699-1781) and a painting of the Epiphany by Carlo Ridolfi (1612). On the hill of Sant'Elena stands the late-16th cent. *Villa Emo Capodilista*, formerly called *Selvatico*. It contains paintings by Luca Ferrari (1605-1654), Alessandro Varotari called Padovanino (1588-1648), and Daniel Van Dyck (1631-1658).

* **BAZZANO** (L'Aquila). Overlooked by the mountain of the same name. In ancient times it was called Offidio, probably because it stood on the site of a "vicus offidius" of the Vestini. The early-13th cent. church of *Santa Giusta* was built on the spot where the Christian martyr was slain. It has an interesting and original facade, and portal with beautifully carved doorposts and architrave. There are some valuable works of art inside, including a damaged fresco of Our Lady of Mercy (14th cent.) and a pulpit belonging to the same period as the church. The internal side of the

Bassano del Grappa, facade of San Francesco and Ezzelino tower.

Bassano del Grappa, wooden bridge over the Brenta.

lunette above the portal has a 13th cent. fresco of the Redeemer and two Saints. The crypt, a very ancient oratory, has a small cavity which was possibly the entrance to a catacomb.

* BELGIOIOSO (Pavia). Farming village, fortified in the 14th cent. by Galeazzo II Visconti. The Visconti castle (*Castello*) consists of an ancient part dating back to the middle of the 14th cent. and an 18th cent. residential one. The former *Chiesa dei Frati* (15-16th cent.) has a cusped bell-tower.

Bazzano, Santa Giusta, pulpit.
Belgioioso, Castle, east front.

* BELLAGIO (Como). On the tip of the promontory that separates the two branches of Lake Como. *Villa Melzi*, built by Giocondo Albertolli (1742-1839) between 1808 and 1815, is neo-Classical in style. It contains stucco work decorations, frescoes and valuable furnishings. *Villa Serbelloni* is particularly interesting for its fine park, which is the largest on the lake. The villa stands on the site of a medieval castle, where there may also have been a villa belonging to Pliny the Younger. In the park of the Villa Triulzi Gerli is the small Romanesque church of *Santa Maria di Loppia*, dating back to the last quarter of the 10th cent. It stands on an irregular plan, and has a single nave. The interior has been remodelled by recent restoration work.

** BELLUNO. Attractive city, the oldest part of which rises on a high spur at the confluence of the Ardo stream and the Piave. The 16th cent. *Duomo*, dedicated to Santa Maria Assunta, is flanked by a drystone bell-tower designed by Filippo Juvara (1676-1736). The solemn interior contains several works of art including paintings of the Martyrdom of St. Lawrence by Jacopo Bassano (c. 1515-1592) and Deposition from the Cross by Jacopo Palma the Younger (1544-1628). *Palazzo dei Rettori*, a lovely Renaissance building designed by Giovanni Candi (active in the second half of the 15th cent.) used to be the seat of the Venetian mayoralty. The *Museo Civico* is housed in the Palazzo dei Giuristi (1664) and contains collections of archeological and Roman remains, seals, medals, coins and paintings, some of which by Jacopo da Montagnana (1440-1499), Pomponio Amalteo (1505-1588), Palma the Younger, Luca Giordano (1632-1705), Sebastiano Ricci (1659-1734) and Marco Ricci (1676-1729). In the Gothic church of *Santo Stefano* (1486) are works of art including frescoes by Jacopo da Montagnana, and carvings and inlays by Andrea Brustolon (1662-1732). Beside the church is the sarcophagus of Caius Flavius Ostilius and his wife Domitia. The church of *San Rocco* (1530) contains a painting of St. Francis by Gaspare Diziani (1689-1767). In the church of *Santa Maria di Loreto* there is another painting of St. Francis, by Francesco Frigimelica (died 1621); the Tabernacle is by Andrea Brustolon. The church of *San Pietro* (1326) was rebuilt in the mid-18th cent. It contains an Annunciation by Andrea Meldolla called Schiavone (1522-1563) and, on the high altar, a Madonna and Child with St. Peter by Sebastiano Ricci. The picturesque market square (*Piazza del Mercato*) is overlooked by some fine Renaissance buildings.

** BENE VAGIENNA (Cuneo). Agricultural town on a low hill at the foot of the western heights of the Langhe, with medieval houses. Walk to the excavated remains of *Augusta Bagiennorum*, a Roman city of the first century B.C., founded to protect the Gallic road, included in the ninth Augustan region. It was abandoned in the 4th cent. A.D., to be reconstructed on a safer site, where the present-day Bene Vagienna now stands. The discovery of this town has presented scholars with a clear example of a Roman city-colony unspoilt by later additions. The foundations of some of the buildings are visible, as well as traces of the four corner towers, of a temple, a porticoed forum, a basilica, and a theatre estimated to have seated two thousand spectators, baths, the swimming pool, gymnasium, and even a workshop. The aqueduct has also been discovered, and communicating roads identified, proving the strategic importance of Augusta Bagiennorum.

*** **BENEVENTO.** Built on a hillside that slopes down to the confluence of the Sabato and Calore. Trajan's Arch (*Arco di Traiano*), known locally as the Golden Gate, is the best-preserved Roman triumphal arch in existence. An inscription on the base testifies that it was built in 114 A.D. to celebrate the opening of the Via Traiana. It is decorated with sculptures of great artistic value, though some of the symbolism is unknown. They depict Trajan's return to Rome from Germany in 99 A.D., the founding of veterans' colonies, Trajan's efforts to promote commerce, Trajan entering the Capitol, victory sacrifices, symbolic figures, possibly Virtus and Honor presenting the soldiers to Trajan, youths, deities, the conquest of Mesopotamia, and Trajan's sacrifice (on the inside of the arch). The *Duomo* was founded in the 7th cent. and later rebuilt and modified in the 18th cent. The bronze portal has some fine panels dating from the first half of the 13th cent. The church of *Santa Sofia*, a most important 8th cent. construction, was rebuilt after the earthquake in 1688. The interesting portal (dating from the second half of the 13th cent.) has a mosaic pattern in the lunette depicting Christ enthroned between Mary and San Mercurio, who is presenting an Abbot. The interior provides a most startling effect, being half circular and half star-shaped. In the two smaller apses are extensive remains of a cycle of 8th cent. frescoes narrating the story of Zaccariah. The attractive cloister (first half of the 12th cent.) has four groups of majestic four-lighted windows with horseshoe-shaped arches. The *Museo del Sannio* was founded in 1873 in accordance with the wishes of Theodor Mommsen (1817-1903). It consists of sections devoted to archeology, numismatics, modern and medieval art, and is rounded off by a picture gallery and collection of designs and prints. The history section is housed elsewhere, in the Rocca dei Rettori. The archeological section includes material from pre-historic and proto-historic times, Egyptian and neo-Egyptian sculptures from the Temple of Isis, Roman copies of Greek sculptures, Greco-Italiot and Italian ceramics of the 5-3rd cent. B.C., examples of Hellenistic-Roman sculpture including a mutilated Nike and a Roman inscribed stone. The collection of medals includes ancient, medieval

Benevento, Cathedral, bronze door, detail of the panel.

Benevento, Cathedral, bronze door, panel.

and modern coins. In the section devoted to medieval and modern art are examples of High medieval and Romanesque works, 14th cent. sculptures, including some by Nicola da Monteforte (lived in the 13-14th cent.), ceramics, etc. The art gallery contains valuable works of art by such famous artists as Andrea da Salerno (c. 1490-1530), Marco Pino (c. 1525-1588), Belisario Corenzio (c. 1560-post 1640), Donato Piperno (lived in the 16th cent.), Giovanni Battista Caracciolo (c. 1570-1637), Francesco De Rosa called Pacecco (1580-1654), Mattia Stomer (active in the first half of the 17th cent.), Andrea Vaccaro (1598-1670), Luca Giordano (1632-1705), Nicola Malinconico (1673-1721), Francesco De Mura (1696-1784), Nicolò de Simone (lived in the 17th cent.), Carlo Maratta (1625-1713), Giacomo Francesco Cipper called Todeschino (lived in the 18th cent.), Paolo De Matteis (1662-1728), Leonardo Coccorante (active in the first half of the 18th cent.), Gennaro Greco (1663-1714), Francesco Solimena (1657-1747), Giuseppe Castellano (died 1724), Giacinto Diana (1730-1803), Pierre Jacques Volaire (1729-1802), Antonio van Pitloo (1791-1837), Giacinto Gigante (1806-1876), Saverio Altamura (1826-1897), Gaetano De Martini (active about the middle of the 19th cent.), Mino Maccari (20th cent.), Renato Guttuso (active in the present cent.), Giovanni Omiccioli (active in the present cent.). The collection of designs and prints contains work by Jacopo da Empoli (1551-1640), Polidoro da Caravaggio (c. 1495-1546), Giovanni Francesco Barbieri called Guercino (1691-1766), and Luca Giordano. The *Rocca dei Rettori* overlooks the city. It is formed by the merging of two well-restored buildings (first half of the 14th cent.) which were constructed on the remains of a Longobard, and even earlier, Roman fortress. As mentioned above, it houses the history section of the Sannio museum, containing pre-15th cent. and Roman stonework. The history of Benevento from the 15th to the early 19th cent. is amply documented, and there is also some modern stonework. The Saletta, devoted to the Risorgimento period, is worth a visit. The *Teatro Romano* (Roman Theatre), parts of which still remain, was built in accordance with the wishes of the Emperor Hadrian and enlarged by the Emperor Caracalla at the beginning of the 3rd cent. Also worth visiting are the *Basilica di San Bartolomeo,* (first half of the 18th cent.), the church of *San Domenico* or *San Vincenzo,* a notable example of local Baroque architecture; the church of the *Annunziata* (completely rebuilt at the turn of the 18th cent.), with the spectacular Chapel of San Gennaro designed by Filippo Raguzzini (c. 1680-1771); the *Basilica della Madonna delle Grazie* (1839) designed by Vincenzo Coppola and containing a polychrome statue of Santa Maria delle Grazie, possibly by Giovanni Mariliano (1488-1558); and the *Ponte Leproso* over the river Sabato (probably of pre-Roman origin).

* **BERCETO** (Parma). Pretty little town in a green hollow. A Benedictine abbey was erected in the neighbourhood during the 8th cent., in accordance with the wishes of Liutprando, King of the Longobards. Owing to the crumbling nature of the ground, the abbey was later transferred to the church of San Remigio, and the town grew up around it. The *Duomo* is an important 14th cent. building, dedicated to San Moderanno da Rennes. The facade is crowned with small arches, and on the left side of the building are two interesting Romanesque sculptures. At the bottom end there is a square apse between two smaller semi-circular ones. The interior contains some interesting works in marble, and in the Treasury are preserved a Byzantine-style cope (11th cent.) and a precious niello-work chalice, dated 1517.

*** **BERGAMO.** City rich in art treasures, important commercial and industrial centre, on the extreme edge of the Bergamasque Prealps, and divided into the Città Alta (Upper City) and Città Bassa (Lower City). The church of *Sant'Alessandro in Colonna* was begun at the start of the 6th cent. A.D., and then rebuilt to a design by Marco Alessandri (1664-1719). It is rich in works of art, including a Deposition, painted by Lorenzo Lotto (c. 1480-1556). The church of *San Benedetto* is an important Renaissance building, renovated at the start of the 16th cent. by Pietro Isabello (c. 1490-1550). *Piazza Pontida* has 15th cent. porticoes on three sides. The *Sentierone* is a tree-lined walk characterized by porticoes on the left. It leads to the Teatro Donizetti (18th

Bergamo, Santa Maria Maggiore, apse.

cent.). The church of *San Bartolomeo*, (rebuilt in the first half of the 17th cent.) contains several works of art, including an altarpiece by Lorenzo Lotto depicting the Madonna and Child with Saints. The early-14th cent. church of *Santo Spirito* was rebuilt by Pietro Isabello. It has a basilica-type interior with important works of art, including a Madonna Enthroned with Saints and Angels, by Lorenzo Lotto, St. John the Baptist, and other Saints by Andrea Previtali (c. 1470-1528), and a magnificent polyptych with eight compartments, by Ambrogio da Fossano, called Bergognone (c. 1455-1522). The attractive little church of *San Fermo* was begun in the middle of the 12th cent. but rebuilt in the 15th. The late 16th cent. church of *San Bernardino in Pignolo* contains a Madonna and Child enthroned, Angels and Saints, by Lorenzo Lotto. Along *Via Pignolo*, as it climbs towards the Upper City, are a number of 16-18th cent. palaces. The church of *Sant'Alessandro della Croce* (first half of the 17th cent.), contains many works of art, including a magnificent altar by Andrea Fantoni (1659-1734), a painting of the Last Supper by Gabriele Cappellini (recorded 1500-1520) and others, including Christ taken down from the Cross, by Giambettino Cignaroli (1706-1770), an Assunta, by Jacopo Bassano (c. 1515-1592), the Holy Trinity by Lorenzo Lotto, Christ Bearing the Cross by Lorenzo Costa the Elder (c. 1450-1535), and Christ Crucified, by Andrea Previtali. The *Accademia Carrara* is one of the most important museums in Italy, with its ample representation of the Bergamasque School, from the 14th to the 19th cent., the Venetian

school (from the 15th to the 18th), and the Lombard school, (from the 15th to the 17th). It contains paintings by major Italian artists, including Jacopo Bellini (1400-1471), Antonio Vivarini (c. 1415-1484), Antonio Pisano, called Pisanello (c. 1395-1455), Giovanni Bellini, called Giambellino (c. 1430-1516), Andrea Mantegna (c. 1431-1506), Antonello da Messina (c. 1430-1479), Lorenzo Lotto, Lorenzo Costa the Elder, Vincenzo Foppa (c. 1427-1516), Ambrogio da Fossano called Bergognone, Cosmè Tura (1430-1495), Andrea Previtali, Giovanni Cariani called Busi (c. 1480-1547), Jacopo Palma the Elder (1480-1528), Tiziano Vecellio (1490-1576), Alessandro Bonvicino called Moretto da Brescia (1498-1554), Raffaello Sanzio (1483-1520), Giovanni Battista Moroni (1523-1578), Albrecht Dürer (1471-1528), Evaristo Baschenis (1617-1677), Bernardo Bellotto (1720-1780), Francesco Guardi (1712-1793), Giambattista Tiepolo (1696-1770), Giandomenico Tiepolo (1727-1804). An interesting group of buildings is the former *Convento dei Celestini*, begun in 1310, with its two attractive cloisters. In the Upper City are important monuments and groups of buildings, including the 15th cent. *Piazza Vecchia*, the late 12th cent. *Palazzo della Ragione*; the *Duomo*, probably of Longobard origin (inside, Martyrdom of St. John the Bishop, by Giambattista Tiepolo); the *Cappella Colleoni*, masterpiece of the Lombard Renaissance; inside, tomb of Colleoni, by Giovanni Antonio Amadeo (c. 1447-1522), Martyrdom of St. Bartholomew, Baptism of Christ and Charity, and John the Baptist Preaching and Justice, by Giambattista Tiepolo. The Romanesque Basilica of *Santa Maria Maggiore* has a porch by Giovanni da Campione (recorded 1340-1367). The *Rocca* (14th cent.), houses the Risorgimento and Resistance Museum. The church of *San Michele al Pozzo Bianco* dates from the 8th cent. The late-13th cent. *Ex Monastero di Sant'Agostino* has a 14th cent. church. *Porta di San Giacomo*, dated 1522. The *Mura* (walls) are impressive fortifications erected by the Venetians in the 16th cent. The *Casa dell'Arciprete*, formerly Fogaccia, is a fine Renaissance building, designed by Pietro Isabello. The *Museo Donizettiano*, is housed in the Palazzo della Misericordia, built between the 15th and 17th cent. *Piazza della Cittadella* with *Archeological Museum* and *Natural History Museum*. The 14th cent. *Chiesa del Carmine* (Carmelite Church) contains some important paintings including Assumption of the Virgin, by Francesco Bassano the Younger (1540-1592).

* **BETTONA** (Perugia). Set panoramically on an olive-covered hillside, with many 14th and 16th cent. houses. The 13th cent. church of *Santa Maria Maggiore* contains a standard, by a follower of Perugino (1445-1452), Pietà, by Niccolò Alunno (c. 1430-1502) and a fresco in the apse, depicting the Assunta and two Angels, painted in 1942 by Gerardo Dottori.

Bergamo, Santa Maria Maggiore, east porch and Colleoni Chapel.

In the apse of the 13th cent. church of *San Crispolto* is a remarkable picture of the Nativity by Dono Doni (died 1575). The Palazzo del Podestà houses a small art gallery, *Pinacoteca*, containing works by Perugino, Fiorenzo di Lorenzo (c. 1440-1520/25), Tiberio di Assisi (c. 1470-1524), sculptures by Della Robbia and archeological remains. The Etruscan Walls (*Mura Etrusche*), in square, sandstone blocks, are of great archeological importance.

** **BEVAGNA** (Perugia). Lying on a bend of the Timia, at the foot of green hills, with Roman and medieval remains. The church of *San Francesco* was built at the end of the 13th cent. It has a single-naved interior, with a fresco of the Pietà, painted in 1596 by Ascensidonio Spacca called Fantino (1557-1646). The Gothic *Palazzo dei Consoli*, erected in 1270, has a wide external staircase and heavy ground-floor loggia. On the right of the Palace is the church of *San Silvestro*, one of the gems of Romanesque architecture, built by Master Binello (12-13th cent.). It has a facade with classical-inspired motifs and a basilican interior, which was entirely remodelled after the last war. The church of *San Michele*, built at the turn of the 13th cent. by Masters Binello and Rodolfo, has a vast Romanesque facade, with a splendid doorway in the middle. Just outside Bevagna is a vast elliptical excavation area, called *Imbersato*, with remains of the amphitheatre of the Roman Mevania, the present-day Bevagna.

* **BIBBIENA** (Arezzo). Built on a hillside where the rivers Archiano and Arno meet. The church of *Santi Ippolito e Donato* dates from the beginning of the 12th cent. and contains a Madonna and Child and Angels by Arcangelo di Cola da Camerino (recorded 1416-1429). Walk to the church of *Santa Maria del Sasso*, first mentioned in 1204. It contains valuable works of art, including paintings by Jacopo Ligozzi (1547-1626), Fra Bartolomeo (1475-1517), and Bicci di Lorenzo (1373-1452).

** **BIELLA** (Vercelli). At the foot of the Biella Pre-Alps, it is an industrial town and international wool market. The *Duomo di Santa Maria Maggiore e Santo Stefano Nuovo*, begun

Bevagna, San Silvestro, facade and side of the Palazzo dei Consoli.

in 1042, has a nave and two aisles divided by cruciform pillars. It contains a remarkable carved-wood pulpit, remains of Gothic frescoes and a "Christ of the Artisans", depicting Christ deeply wounded by a pair of cloth shears. On the left of the Cathedral is the pre-Romanesque *Battistero*, a square-plan construction, with fragments of Roman buildings incorporated in the wall. The Renaissance church of *San Sebastiano* contains the tombs of the Lamarmora family; in the apse, note the wooden choirstalls and lectern. Inside *San Girolamo* (16th cent.) is a remarkable wooden choir with inlaid work by Defendente Ferrari. The *Museo Civico*, inaugurated in 1592, is rich in paintings and ancient frescoes transferred from churches in the neighbourhood, as well as precious porcelain from Sèvres, Capodimonte, China and Japan, ancient weapons and Murano glassware. By funicular railway, or up the Costa one climbs up to *Biella Piazzo*, where there are the house once belonging to Amedeo Avogadro, the church of *Sant'Anna*, and the small church of *San Giacomo*.

* **BISCEGLIE** (Bari). A small port on the Adriatic coast between Molfetta and Trani. The facade of the church of *Sant'Adoeno* (1074), has a small round window with five corbels on which are carved four lions and a statue of Sant'Adoeno. Inside is a valuable medieval baptismal font. The *Cattedrale* (begun in 1073 and only completed towards the end of the 13th cent.) has a 13th cent. facade with a fine doorway surmounted by a canopy held up by griffins on columns. The building has been partly spoilt by alterations, but the blind arches and the apse section still retain their original beauty. The interior of the basilica, unfortunately rebuilt in Baroque style, has a beautiful wooden choir and, in the sacristy, an ancient wooden panel by an unknown artist, depicting St. Benedict. The small Romanesque-Apulian church of *Santa Margherita* (1197) has a double-arched doorway. On the left side of the church are three important tombs (end of the 13th cent.), and inside there is a monolithic baptismal font.

* **BITETTO** (Bari). Agricultural town. The centre preserves much of its late medieval

Biella, San Sebastiano, interior.

character, with remains of the town walls, including towers and valuable doorways. It was a small Apulian town (tombs have been found from the 4th cent. B.C.). The 11th cent. *Cattedrale di San Michele* was restructured in the first half of the 14th cent. The facade is divided into three by pilaster-strips, and has a magnificent central doorway. The interior has been damaged at various times, but restored to its original Romanesque form by recent restoration work.

** **BITONTO** (Bari). Well-known agricultural centre. It was an ancient Apulian city of especial importance in the 4th cent. B.C. as can be seen from archeological remains. The *Cattedrale*, dedicated to St. Valentine, is the most famous example of Romanesque architecture in Apulia. Built between 1175 and 1200, its facade is divided into three by pilasters

Bitetto, Cathedral, facade.
Bitonto, Cathedral.

and has a beautiful rose window above which is an archway supported by animals on hanging columns. The centre doorway is the most attractive one and has a bas-relief on the architrave depicting the Annunciation, the Visitation, Epiphany, and the Presentation of Jesus at the Temple. To the right of the building is the Door of Excommunication or Holy Vault. The interior is in pure Romanesque style and contains Baroque tombs of the Barba bishops (18th cent.) and an impressive ambo dated 1229 signed "Nicolaus sacerdos et magister"; in the crypt are numerous columns with beautiful capitals. The 15th cent. *Palazzo Sylos Labini* has a well-preserved Gothic-Catalan style doorway. The church of *San Francesco d'Assisi* was built in 1286. The facade, with an ogee-arched doorway and large three-mullioned window, is all that remains of the original building. The interior contains interesting 16-17th cent. wood carvings, and Venetian and Neapolitan-style paintings. The 9th cent. *Abbazia di San Leo*, modified at various periods, has an interior consisting of a single nave lit by pointed-arched apertures. The apse is square-shaped and contains Byzantine-style frescoes of the 14th cent.

* **BOBBIO** (Piacenza). The most important commercial town in the valley of the Trebbia, and popular holiday resort. In 612 A.D. San Colombano founded the monastery of Bobbio. The Basilica of *San Colombano* (7th cent.) was rebuilt in the second half of the 15th cent. and restructured in the 17th. Inside, there is a painting by Bernardino Lanzani (recorded 1490-1526) and an interesting crypt. The *Museum of San Colombano* consists of four rooms with valuable works of art, including paintings by Bernardino Lanzani and Giulio Campi (c. 1500-1572). The *Duomo* (13th cent.) is dedicated to the Assunta. Romanesque in origin, it was lengthened in the apse section in the 15th cent. It contains several works of art, including Guardian Angel with kneeling Madonna, by a 17th cent. local painter. The town is overlooked by the *Castello* (1440). Inside there is a 17th cent. fresco of the Madonna and Child.

Bitonto, Cathedral, detail of the ambo.

Bergamo, Accademia Carrara. Evaristo Baschenis,
Musical instruments.

Bergamo, Accademia Carrara. Giovan Battista
Moroni, Portrait of Pace Rivola Spini.

Biella, San Girolamo. Defendente Ferrari, Nativity.

Bologna, Pinacoteca Nazionale. Guercino, Irene dressing St. Sebastian's wounds.

Bolzano, Chiesa dei Domenicani. St. John's Chapel, detail of the frescoes.

Brescia, Pinacoteca Civica Tosio Martinengo. Giovanni Gerolamo Savoldo, Adoration of the shepherds, detail.

*** **BOLOGNA.** Chief town of Emilia Romagna, it stands on the Via Emilia, at the foot of the Appenines, between the rivers Reno and Savena. The church of *San Pietro* or *Metropolitana* has been rebuilt several times on the original Romanesque plan. The 13th cent. church of *San Domenico* contains St. Dominic's tomb, carved by Nicola Pisano between 1265 and 1267. The church of *San Francesco* (also 13th cent.) is in French Gothic style. The church of *San Giovanni in Monte* dates from the mid-11th cent. and was rebuilt in 1200. *Chiese e Chiostri Riuniti di Santo Stefano*, an unusual group of sacred buildings of various periods. The church of *San Giacomo Maggiore* was built between the 13th and 15th cent. The Basilica of *San Petronio* is Bologna's largest church and one of the biggest in the world. It was begun on 7th June 1390 and not finished until 1659. The middle doorway of the facade is considered to be the masterpiece of Jacopo della Quercia (1367-1438). Inside, are works of art, of which only the frescoes by Giovanni da Modena (op. 1420-1451) are mentioned here. The 13th cent. *Palazzo Comunale* or *d'Accursio*, contains rich art collections. The *Palazzo del Podestà* was begun at the beginning of the 13th cent. *Palazzo di Re Enzo* (mid-13th cent.). *Palazzo dell'archiginnasio* (1562-1563), until 1803 the site of Bologna University. *Palazzo Bevilacqua*, a graceful building erected between 1474 and 1482, with a magnificent porticoed courtyard and loggia. The house and Museum: *Casa con Museo di Giosuè Carducci* and *della Garisenda* leaning towers, erected between 1109 and 1119, the former inclined 1.23 metres towards the west, and the latter 3.22 metres to the north-east. *Fontana del Net-*

Bologna, Museo Archeologico, Kouros.

Bologna, the Garisenda and Asinelli towers.

tuno by Tommaso Laureti (c. 1530-1602) and Jean Boulogne (1524-1608). Also worth visiting are the *Museo Civico, Museo Archeologico*, and *Pinacoteca* containing a rich collection of paintings by the greatest local masters: Guercino, Parmigianino, Francesco del Cossa, the Carracci family, etc., *Musei di Geologia e di Mineralogia*, as well as many other buildings and art galleries too numerous to be mentioned here. On the outskirts of the city are the 18th cent. *Santuario della Madonna di San Luca*, designed by Carlo Francesco Dotti (1670-1759), *Parchi e già Cenobi di San Michele in Bosco e dell'Osservanza*, and the large complex of the *Certosa*.

* **BOLSENA** (Viterbo). Situated by Lake Bolsena, it is a holiday resort and fishing centre with medieval houses on the hillside. The 11th cent. *Collegiata di Santa Cristina* has a facade divided into three by Tuscan-style pilaster strips. In the lunette of the middle doorway is a Della Robbia terracotta depicting the Madonna and Child and St. Christine and St. George. The left aisle leads straight into the famous Baroque Chapel of the Miracle (1693). Its name recalls the miracle of the Host oozing blood. The Miracle of the Corporal, by Francesco Trevisani (1656-1746), and an antiquarium containing Etruscan, Roman and Christian inscriptions are worth noticing. The Chapel leads into St. Christine's grotto, which is the entrance to the catacombs. One of them contains the altar of St. Christine or of the Four pillars. The *Castello*, built at the turn of the 14th cent., was sacked by the townspeople in 1815 to prevent it falling into the hands of Luciano Bonaparte; it houses the *Museo Comunale*, where Etruscan and Roman exhibits are arranged.

*** **BOLZANO.** On the banks of the Tàlvera, where it flows into the river Isarco, in a vast and attractive hollow. The Gothic *Duomo* (14th cent.) is dedicated to the Assunta. It has a Romanesque doorway with a porch in

its main facade, dated 1498, and a polychrome roof. On the left side there is a much-admired Gothic doorway. The whole building is dominated by a slender bell-tower, with perforated cusps. The top part is the work of Giovanni Lutz (active at the turn of the 16th cent.). The interior has a nave and two aisles, and contains frescoes (1424) by Corrado Erlin, a Gothic sandstone pulpit, with bas-reliefs by Giovanni Lutz, Chapel with venerated Crucifix (14th cent.), impressive high altar in Baroque style, by the marble-worker, Giovanni Battista Ranghieri (1646-1718), after the design of Andrea Pozzo (1624-1709), and Cappella delle Grazie, with frescoes by Carlo Henrici (1737-1823) and a late 12th cent. Madonna and Child, in painted marble. The late-13th cent. *Chiesa dei Domenicani* has a sober facade and contains frescoes salvaged from air-raids in the Second World War. They represent the Madonna enthroned, Saints George, Barbara, and Anthony, and a gentleman from Castelnuovo, by Giovanni Stocinger (lived in the 14-15th cent.), and valuable 15th cent. paintings. The chancel leads into the 14th cent. chapel of St. John, the walls of which are decorated with frescoes by the Giotto school. The 13th cent. cloister was restructured at the end of the 15th cent., and is decorated with frescoes, mainly carried out in 1496 by Federico Pacher (1474-1508). The foundation stone of the *Chiesa dei Francescani* was laid in 1221. The most attractive part of the church is the Chapel of the Virgin, with its carved-wood Gothic altarpiece, by Giovanni Klocker (recorded 1482-1498), and the mystic cloister with its 14th cent. frescoes and 15th cent. trilobe arches. In the *Museo dell'Alto Adige*, are prehistoric and Roman collections, Gothic statues and furniture, paintings by Tomaso da Villaco (active in the second half of the 15th cent.), by Leonardo da Bressanone (active in the second half of the 15th cent.), Carlo Henrici, Paolo Troger (1698-1763), Giuseppe Schöpf (1745-1822), Giovanni Battista Lampi the Elder (1751-1830), Francesco Haller (lived

Bologna, Sanctuary of Madonna di San Luca and porticoed roadway.

in the 18th cent.), and many other masters, especially from the Tyrol and Austria. The Baroque-style *Palazzo Mercantile*, was once the seat of the Mercantile Law Courts. The vast meeting hall is worth seeing, with its portraits of Austrian princes, and paintings by Antonio Balestra (1666-1740), Alessandro Marchesini (1664-1738), and Ulric Glantschnigg (1661-1722). The *Monumento della Vittoria* (1928), is by the architect Marcello Piacentini. In the crypt are allegorical frescoes by Guido Cadorin (born 1892). The *Parrocchiale di Nostra Signora*, contains a fine, carved Gothic altarpiece, by Michele Pacher (active from 1460 to 1498). In the area around Bolzano, there are ruins of the 16th cent. *Flavon (Haselburg) Castle*, the *Firmiano Castle (Schloss Sigmundskron)*, the *Sarentino Castle (Schloss Rafenstein)*, and the *Roncolo Castle (Schloss Runkelstein)*.

* **BOMARZO** (Viterbo). Farming centre, on a hill facing the Tiber valley. *Palazzo Orsini*,

Bolzano, Castel Roncolo. Detail of the frescoes.
Bomarzo, Sacred wood monster.

erected between 1525 and 1583, consists of two distinct buildings, complete with terraces and other architectural features. Inside are frescoes from the school of Pietro da Cortona (1596-1669). The *Parco dei Mostri* or *Bosco Sacro* is one of the most characteristic groups of monuments in the whole region. It consists of a series of terraces descending deep into the valley, and some of the blocks of rock scattered around have been carved into the form of gigantic figures, which peer out of lush, uncultivated vegetation. They include a war-elephant, a winged horse, a Neptune, a female figure, a fountain, a tortoise and a hemicycle nymphaeum.

* **BOMINACO** (Town of Caporiciano, province of L'Aquila). The church of *San Pellegrino*, rebuilt in 1263, has a facade preceded by a pronaus, and a rectangular apse. The interior is decorated with 13th cent. frescoes. The church of *Santa Maria* (12th cent.) is one of the most characteristic Romanesque churches in the region. The three apses, decorated with small arches on corbels, and the interior, with a nave and two aisles, are particularly interesting; notice the capitals, a candelabra to hold the Paschal candle, and the Abruzzi-type ambo.

* **BONORVA** (Sassari). On the edge of the plateau known as "su Monte". The *Parish Church*, is flanked by a polygonal bell-tower with cusp. The entrance-door is adorned with lilies, and the interior (restored in the 16th cent.) is in Gothic-Aragonese style. Walks to the *Nuraghe Tres Nuraghes*, with "domus de janas" (graves dug by the Proto-Sardinians)

nearby; and to the *Grotte di Sant'Andrea Priu*, 20-18th cent. B.C. "domus de janas": twenty intercommunicating tombs underground, with interesting similarities to contemporary underground tombs found in Malta and Etruscan burial chambers which were actually dug about ten centuries later. The building technique and ornamental elements are worthy of note.

* **BORGO SAN LORENZO** (Florence). Situated on the river Mugello in the basin of the river Sieve, tributary of the Arno. The *Oratorio del Santissimo Crocifisso dei Miracoli* was rebuilt after an earthquake in 1919. Inside are paintings of a Consoling Angel, by Giuseppe Bezzuoli (1784-1855), and the Baptism of Constantine, by Ignazio Hugford (1703-1778). The ancient parish church of *San Lorenzo*, built at the beginning of the 12th cent. during the transition period from Romanesque to Gothic, was badly damaged by an earth tremor in 1919. Inside is a painting of St. Sebastian between St. Macarius and St. Vincent, by the Perugino school (1445-1523).

* **BORMIO** (Sondrio). On a plain where the Frodolfo stream flows into the Adda. The *Collegiata*, dedicated to Saints Gervasio and Protasio was cited in 803 in a diploma of Charlemagne. Rebuilt by Gaspare Aprile (recorded 1628-1640), it contains a painting of the Glory of St. John Nepomuceno by Giuseppe Torricelli (1710-1808) and other paintings, by Giuseppe Prina (lived in the first half of the 18th cent.) and Euclide Trotti (lived in the second half of the 16th cent.). In the

Borgo San Lorenzo, Parish Church of San Lorenzo, interior.

Museo Civico are collections pertaining to art, history, and folklore. In the 14th cent. *Santuario del Crocifisso*, or St. Anthony's Sanctuary, restored in 1872, 16th cent. frescoes.

* **BOSA** (Nuoro). On the right of the Temo. Here, in medieval times, the Malaspina family built the *Castello di Serravalle*, which dominated the town from a hilltop. The walls and towers can still be seen. The small 15th cent. church of *Sant'Antonio*, is an interesting building that illustrates the local adaptation of Gothic-Aragonese style. Walk to the picturesquely situated church of *San Pietro extra muros*; the main body of the church dates back to the 11th cent.

* **BOSCO MARENGO** (Alessandria). Ancient little town near Alessandria. The impressive Renaissance church of *Santa Croce* contains a vast collection of valuable paintings; the building, begun in 1567 on the orders of Pius V, was designed by Ignazio Danti. Also near Alessandria, at Sezzadio, is the church of *Abbazia di Santa Giustina*, founded in the 8th cent. by Liutprando in honour of Justina the martyr. It has a brickwork facade divided by elegant pilaster strips, and an impressive interior rich in statues and valuable paintings.

* **BOVEGNO** (Brescia). Popular summer resort. In the parish church of *San Giorgio* (first half of the 18th cent.), are wooden altarpieces by the wood-carvers Pialorsi (active in the 17-18th cent.), the Immaculate Conception, by Antonio Paglia (1680-1747), and Madonna of the Rosary, by Antonio Gandini (c. 1565-1631).

* **BOVINO** (Foggia). The houses are dotted along the hillside separating the Cervaro and Biletra valleys. The *Duomo*, dedicated to Santa Maria Assunta, is Byzantine in origin. It was erected in the early 10th cent., rebuilt in Ro-

Bosa, San Pietro extra muros, facade.

manesque style in the latter half of the 11th, and repeatedly altered in later periods. The asymmetrical facade has three architraved entrance-doors. Inside is the black and white marble tomb of Bishop Angelo Giustiniani (1609) and a painting of St. Sebastian by Mattia Preti (1613-1699). In the *Palazzo degli Uffici*, there are some interesting Roman inscriptions of Vibinum, the Roman Bovino. The church of *San Pietro*, Romanesque in origin, was completely restructured in later periods. Above the high altar is an important Neapolitan-school Crucifixion of St. Peter, painted in the 17th cent.

* **BOVOLONE** (Verona). Large agricultural centre. The 15th cent. parish church of *San Biagio* is now Baroque in appearance. Inside is an altar by Adriano Cristofali (1717-1788), and paintings by Domenico Ricci called Brusasorci (c. 1516-1567). The church of *San Giusto* (early 19th cent.) is annexed to the pre-existing one. The *Palazzo Vescovile* (15th cent.) was enlarged in the 18th to a design by Adriano Cristofali.

* **BRA** (Cuneo). Situated on the left bank of the Tanaro, it is a commercial and industrial centre. The 17th cent. church of *San Giovanni* or *dei Battuti Neri*, contains a splendid high altar in marble. The single nave of the *Chiesa della Trinità* or *dei Battuti Bianchi*, dated 1624, is lavishly decorated with Baroque stuccoes framing large frescoes by Sebastiano Taricco (1645-1710). The church of *Santa Chiara* (1742) is one of the most successful works from the youthful period of Bernardo Vittone. The History of Art Museum (*Museo di Storia d'Arte*) contains remains from Pompei: of the Neolithic and Paleolithic ages, as well as Etruscan vases, Roman tiles, medieval remains, medallions, paintings, and so on. The Natural History Museum (*Museo di Storia Naturale Craveri*) contains specimens from America, tools and weapons from Brazilian tribes, rare birds, reptiles, miriapods and fossilized minerals. Five kilometres away from Bra is *Pallenzo*, deriving from the Roman Pollentia, founded in 170 B.C.

Underground there are traces of Roman times, including a theatre capable of holding six thousand spectators and an amphiteatre to hold seventeen thousand, which is considered the largest of its kind in northern Italy. Remains of the Roman city can be found in the park of the *Castello Reale* (1385). The lovely Gothic church of *San Vittore* stands in the square. It has some remarkable carved-wood choirstalls taken from the Abbey of Staffarda.

* **BRACCIANO** (Rome). Situated on a trachytic rise on the south-eastern shore of Lake Bracciano. The site was already inhabited in Etruscan times, as traces of a burial-ground reveal. The *Castello Orsini-Odescalchi*, built by the Orsini family in the latter half of the 14th cent., is a proud example of military architecture and noble residences. Built on a pentagonal plan, with stout cylindrical towers, it has a 16th cent. portal relieving the mass of the encircling wall. Inside is a huge fresco, probably carried out by Antoniazzo Romano (recorded 1435-1517). A fine external staircase, with columns, leads to the upper floor, and numerous rooms containing fairly good works of art. The 14th cent. church of *Santo Stefano* was rebuilt in the 17th cent. It has a simple Baroque facade, flanked by a 16th cent. bell-tower. The Baroque interior has a nave and two aisles, and contains some works of art, such as St. Jehoshaphat in the desert, by Francesco Trevisani (1656-1746), a triptych of the Saviour, signed "Graegorius et Donatus de Aretio me fecerunt anno Domini MCCCXV", Martyrdom of St. Stephen, by Giovanni Battista Wicar (1762-1834), and a crowded painting by Domenico Zampieri called Domenichino (1581-1641).

* **BRENO** (Brescia). Commercial and industrial centre within sight of the southern slopes of the Adamello. It is of very ancient origin, as is borne out by an Iron-age necro-

Bovino, Cathedral, facade.

Bra, Santa Chiara.

55

polis. The 17th cent. *Duomo* is dedicated to San Salvatore. It has a Baroque portal and contains works of art such as a panel depicting the Madonna and Saints, a youthful work by Girolamo Romani called Romanino (c. 1484-1566), a Flagellation and St. Sebastian by Callisto Piazza (c. 1500-1562), and a Transfiguration by Jacopo Palma the Elder (c. 1480-1528). In the Gothic church of *Sant'Antonio* (14th cent.) are Stories of Daniel and other Biblical episodes, by Romanino. Late-16th cent. church of *San Maurizio*, with portal dated 1607. The *Museo Cumano* preserves many paintings and sculptures from the 15th to the 20th cent.

*** **BRESCIA.** Situated in the southern foothills of the Lombard Prealps, it has an important historical centre and modern districts. Elegant buildings, some of them modern ones, face the *Piazza della Vittoria*, designed by Marcello Piacentini (1881-1960). *Piazza della Loggia*, the civic and historic centre of the city was created at the end of the 15th cent. It is overlooked by the Town Hall or Logge, which was erected at the turn of the 16th cent. to designs by renowned architects such as Jacopo Tatti called Sansovino (1486-1570), and Andrea Palladio (1508-1580), and by the

Monte di Pietà or Monte Vecchio, partly Venetian-Lombard Renaissance in style, by Antonio Zurlango (active in the 15th cent.). In the church of *San Giuseppe*, built between 1521 and 1578, are important paintings including a Redeemer and St. Margaret of Cortona and Catherine of Bologna, by Ferdinando del Cairo (c. 1671-1730). *Piazza del Duomo* has always been the religious and political centre of Brescia. On the east side stand the Old Cathedral or Rotonda, the New Cathedral, and the Broletto. In the 12th. cent. *Duomo Vecchio* are an Assumption, St. Luke, St. Mark, Elijah sleeping and Sacrifice of Isaac by Alessandro Bonvicino called Moretto da Brescia, (c. 1498-1554), and the Conveyance of the bodies of some Brescian Saints, by Francesco Maffei (c. 1600-1660). The *Duomo Nuovo* (17-18th cent.) contains the Renaissance-style Tomb of Saints Apollonio and Filastrio, and paintings by Moretto. The *Broletto* is overlooked by the Torre del Popolo (11th cent.) and is admired for its firm straight lines, its porticoes and courtyard, with 17th cent. fountain. The *Civica Biblioteca Queriniana*, opened in 1750, is an important library containing a thousand incunabula, five thousand autographs, a 5th cent. Bible, etc. The *Tempio Capitolino*, 73 A.D., houses the Civic Roman Museum, consisting

Brescia, Old Cathedral and New Cathedral.

of a lapidary and an archeological section. Especially interesting is the Winged Victory, 1st cent. A.D. In the ex-church of St. Julia is the *Museo Civico dell'Età Cristiana*, with rich medieval, Romanesque and Renaissance collection. The 9th cent. *Basilica di San Salvatore* stands on the site of a previous, 8th cent. building; the interior has a nave and two aisles, crypt and remains of 8th and 14th cent. frescoes and stuccoes. The 12th cent. *Oratorio di Santa Maria in Solario* is Romanesque in style. The *Civica Galleria d'Arte Moderna* contains a rich collection of modern art. The 15th cent. church of *San Clemente* has important paintings, including Christ Arisen and Saints Catherine and Augustine, by Girolamo Romani called Romanino (c. 1484-1566), Saints Cecilia, Lucy, Barbara, Agnes and Agatha, by Moretto, and many other of his works. The *Pinacoteca Civica Tosio Martinengo*, contains collections of works mainly by major Brescian artists. The ancient church of *Sant'Angela Merici*, formerly Santa Afra, was redesigned by Pier Maria Bagnadore (c. 1550-1619); inside are important paintings including the Baptism of Sant'Afra, by Francesco Bassano the Younger (1540-1592), St Francis and an admirer, by Paolo da Cailina the Younger (c. 1485-1545), and a Transfiguration, by Jacopo Robusti called Tintoretto (1518-1594). Elegant buildings look on to Via Moretto, including the 17th cent. Palazzo Avogadro, now Bettoni Cazzago, and Palazzo Martinengo Colleoni, designed by Alfonso Torreggiani (1682-1764). In the church of *Sant'Alessandro* there is an Annunciation and Stories of Mary, by Jacopo Bellini (1400-1471). The church of *Santa Maria dei Miracoli* has been rebuilt after its destruction in an air-raid on 2nd March 1945; inside are valuable paintings, mainly by local masters. The church of *Santi Nazzaro e Celso* contains paintings by Moretto, Giovanni Battista Pittoni (1687-1767) and, most important of all, Christ Arisen, Gabriel and the Annunziata and Saints, a youthful masterpiece by Titian (1490-1576). The 13th cent. church of *San Francesco* contains paintings by

Moretto and Romanino. *Via Cairoli* is flanked by a large number of ancient buildings, which were partly destroyed by air raids in the Second World War. The *Torre della Pallata* (mid-13th cent.) combines Roman and high medieval elements. In the 16th cent. church of *Madonna delle Grazie* are preserved important paintings, including some by Moretto and Francesco Maffei. The church of *San Giovanni Evangelista* dates back to the 4th cent. A.D. and contains paintings by Moretto and Romanino. Inside the 15th cent. church of *Madonna del Carmine* are frescoes by Vincenzo Foppa (c. 1427-c. 1515). The church of *Santi Faustino e Giovita* was rebuilt at the beginning of the 17th cent. Inside is a Nativity, one of the most successful works of Lattanzio Gambara (c. 1530-1574). The *Civico Museo delle Armi Luigi Marzoli* contains 1300 items, of great historic and artistic importance. The *Museo del Risorgimento* has antiques, paintings, prints, proclamations, arms, and uniforms, connected with Brescian history from the end of the 18th cent. onwards. In the church of *San Pietro in Oliveto* (first built in the 8th cent.) are important pictures, including St. Dominic and the German Heretics by Andrea Celesti (1637-1712).

** **BRESSANONE** (Bolzano). Nestling in a hollow among fertile hills, at the point where the Rienza flows into the Isarco. It is a small artistic capital in the Alto Adige. The 13th cent. *Duomo*, dedicated to the Assunta, was originally Romanesque but largely rebuilt in the latter half of the 18th cent. It is flanked by two bell-towers and has a vast interior in the form of a Latin cross, designed by Teodoro Benedetti (1697-1783). Notice paintings

Brescia, Capitoline Temple.

Bressanone, Cloister. Detail of the frescoes.

by Paolo Troger (1698-1763), Giuseppe Schöpf (1745-1822), Michelangelo Unterberger (1695-1758), and Cristoforo Unterberger (1732-1798). The *Chiesa della Beata Vergine* or *Nostra Signora in ambitu* stands beside the Cathedral. Originally the bishops' private chapel, it is embellished with important Romanesque frescoes and leads into the Romanesque cloister, dating from about 1200. The vaults and walls are decorated with beautiful frescoes, carried out from the 14th to early 16th cent. by Iacopo Sunter (active 1441-1474) and a large number of unknown artists. The walls of the 13th cent. church of *San Giovanni Battista* or *Battistero* are embellished with frescoes, partly from the 13th and 14th cent. The rich *Museo Diocesano* boasts a Nativity Room, with four thousand little crib figures by Agostino Luigi Probst (1758-1807), a fresco of the Crucifixion by Federico Pacher (recorded 1474-1508), the cope of St. Alboin (12th cent.), a gilt silver reliquary bust of St. Agnes by Valentino Schauer (recorded 1481-1490) and Cristoforo da Bressanone (recorded 1484-1500), 17th and 18th cent. paintings and sculptures, furniture, and engravings. The 13th cent. *Palazzo dei Principi Vescovi*, where Bishop Bruno took up residence in 1265, was modified in the Renaissance and Baroque periods. It has a vast courtyard, with porticoes enriched with terracotta statues representing Hapsburg personalities, and various other carved and architectonic motifs. Walk along the characteristic *Via Portici Maggiori*, at the end of which is a 16th cent. wooden statue called the Wild Man. The nearby *Convento di Novacella* should be visited. It consists of a group of buildings partly surrounded by walls, with turrets. St. Michael's Chapel (late 12th cent.) is in the same form as the Church of the Holy Sepulchre in Jerusalem. In the church of the *Madonna*, rebuilt in Baroque style in the 18th cent., are remarkable frescoes, polychrome stuccoes, and marbles, by Tyrolean and Austrian artists. At Velturno, in the neighbourhood, is the *Castle of Velturno* (Schloss Zienberg), once the summer residence of Bressanone bishops.

* **BRIGNANO GERA D'ADDA** (Bergamo). Agricultural and industrial village. The *Castello Visconteo* (16th cent.), transformed into Baroque style by Giovanni Ruggeri (lived in the 17-18th cent.), is its most distinguished monument. Inside are frescoes by Alessandro Magnasco (1667-1749) and Camillo Procaccini (c. 1551-1629) and one depicting an Episode from the Crusades, possibly by Giambattista Tiepolo (1696-1770). In the *Parrocchiale*, an insignificant 18th cent. building, there is a painting of the Last Supper, attributed to Pier Francesco Mazzucchelli called Morazzone (c. 1571-1626).

** **BRINDISI.** Important agricultural, commercial and industrial centre, spread out on a

promontory. It consists of small areas of ancient and medieval remains, and a vast expanse of modern districts. The *Duomo* is Romanesque in origin, but was rebuilt in 1746 after the earthquake of 1743. It is overlooked by an imposing Baroque bell-tower, dated 1780. The interior is undecorated but contains a few works of art such as a magnificent set of choirstalls in carved and inlaid wood, dating from the last decade of the 16th cent., and two canvases depicting Saints Pelino and Leucio, by Oronzo Tiso (1729-1800). In the archives are diplomas of Norman, Swabian, and Angevin kings and papal bulls. The *Museo Archeologico Provinciale Francesco Ribezzo* contains objects found in the area around Brindisi. In the entrance-hall are Norman altars, funerary inscriptions, architectonic fragments; in the first underground room, Roman inscriptions, eulogical and funerary Greek and Hebrew inscriptions; a torso of a Roman loricate statue, headless mantled statues; on the ground floor, large-scale plan of the city, with precise references to archeological findings, two composite capitals, male torso in marble, perhaps representing Hercules, "trozzella" vases, figured terracottas. On the first floor, archeological material from Brindisi, Messapian "trozzella" vases, Gnathia-style bowls. On the second floor there is a collection of Greek and Roman coins, antefixa and small clay statues, large clay disc with Heros on a four-horse chariot and signs of the zodiac. On the third floor is an immense Roman floor mosaic, representing the Labyrinth and struggle between Theseus and the Minotaur; in the show-cases, pre-historic findings, stones and mouldings of various origins. The Romanesque church of *San Giovanni al Sepolcro* (11th cent.) is built on a circular plan. It belonged first to the Templars then to the Knights of the Holy Sepulchre. It contains 14th cent. frescoes depicting Christ, the Madonna and Child, Saint Peter, St. John, and St. George. The church of *San Benedetto*, erected in the second half of the 11th cent. and clumsily modified in the 16th, is flanked by a sturdy Romanesque bell-tower with mullioned windows and small arches. There are some fair works of art inside, and a fine cloister annexed to it. The church of *Santa Lucia* or of *Santissima Trinità*, Romanesque in origin, but disfigured in later ages, contains an important polyptych repre-

Brindisi, Swabian Castle.

senting the Madonna and Child, Saints and Angels, by an unknown artist in the late 15th cent. or early 16th. The walls are decorated with Byzantine-style frescoes of the 12th, 13th and 14th cent. The *Chiesa del Cristo* or *del Crocifisso*, designed in 1230 by Brother Nicola Paglia, has a cusped facade enhanced by a large rose-window. Inside are Baroque altars and remarkable polychrome-wood sculptures of the 13th cent. The *Biblioteca Arcivescovile De Leo* (the library founded in 1798 by Archbishop Annibale De Leo) is housed in the Palazzo del Seminario which was designed between 1720 and 1744 by Mauro Manieri. It contains some rare manuscripts, such as the notes on the Prophet Isaiah by Alessandro di Hales, a precious 14th cent. illuminated codex, Decretum Gratiani, of the 13th cent., a Humanist codex, presumed to be unique, and Aldine editions (16th cent.). Also worth visiting are the *Due Colonne Romane*, the two Roman columns that probably marked the end of the Appian Way, the *Castello Svevo*, Swabian castle with square keep, erected in 1227 by Frederick II, the Roman baths, *Vasche Limarie*, so called because they absorbed the lime from the water distributed in the city, and the nearby church of *Santa Maria del Casale*, which is an interesting Romanesque-Gothic building.

* **BRISIGHELLA** (Ravenna). Pretty little town on the left bank of the Lamone. The early-16th cent. church of *Santa Maria degli Angeli* or *dell'Osservanza*, contains a panel depicting the Madonna and Child enthroned, Angels and Four Saints by Marco Palmezzano (1459/63-1539). The collegiate church of *Santi Michele e Giovanni Battista* was designed by Gherardo Silvani (1579-1675) and contains wooden statues depicting Saints by Ottavio Toselli (1695-1777). A clock-tower dated 1290 (*Torre dell'Orologio*) stands on a hill of selenite. Early 14th cent. *Rocca Chiesa del Monticino* (1758). Walk to the Romanesque parish church of *San Giovanni in Ottavo o del Thò* (1100 A.D.). Inside are some valuable paintings and interesting decorative elements.

* **BRONI** (Pavia). Wine-producing centre and industrial town. The *Collegiata* was designed by the brothers Bernardino and Angelo Lovati (lived in the 16th cent.), and contains a painting of the Martyrdom of St. Peter, by Panfilo Nuvolone (c. 1581-1651) as well as the Tomb of San Contardo d'Este (1664). The porticoed Town hall (*Palazzo Comunale*) was designed by Carlo Arienti (1801-1873).

** **BRUNICO** (Bolzano). Characteristic and ancient town in the Val Pusteria, divided into two by the river Rienza. The parish church of *Nostra Signora* was rebuilt in the mid-19th cent. and has altars by Michael Stolz (1820-1890) with paintings by Franz Hellweger (1812-1880). In the *Chiesa del Salvatore*, built on the

site of an early-15th cent. chapel, there are 16th cent. polychrome-wood statues. In the Baroque-style *Chiesa di Santo Spirito* are mid-18th cent. stuccoes, and paintings by Giovanni Giorgio Domenico Grasmair (1691-1751) and other local artists. In the midst of a fir-wood is an Austrian war cemetery (*Cimitero di Guerra Austriaco*).

* **BUDRIO** (Bologna). Agricultural centre in the Bologna plain. Ancient in origin, and fortified in the Middle Ages, it has been destroyed several times. The church of *San Lorenzo* was restructured in the 17th cent. It contains a painting of St. Peter receiving the Keys of Heaven, by Giovanni Andrea Donducci called Mastelletta (1575-1655), and St. Sebastian, by Alessandro Guardassoni (1819-1888). The *Pinacoteca Civica Inzaghi* contains a Madonna and Child with Saints Roch and Sebastian, by Giovanni Luteri called Dosso Dossi (c. 1479-1542), Holy Family, by Giuseppe Maria Crespi, called Spagnolo (1665-1747), and Portrait of a Lady, by Cesare Gennari (1637-1688). Annexed to the Gallery is an archeological collection containing, above all, Roman material.

* **BUONCONVENTO** (Siena). On the left bank of the Ombrone. A fine medieval gateway leads into the town, which is built on a rectangular plan and surrounded by Sienese-type walls. The parish church of *Santi Pietro e Paolo* was rebuilt early in the 18th cent. It contains a Madonna and Child with Saints by Matteo di Giovanni from Arezzo (1435-1495). Nearby is a small art gallery which includes some 15th cent. Sienese gold ornaments among its treasures.

** **BURGUSIO** (Town of Malles Venosta, province of Bolzano). On either side of the Adige. Not far away is the Benedictine *Abbazia di Monte Maria*, built in the middle of the 12th cent., but devastated by fire and later rebuilt. It is an immense group of buildings, the most important element being the 12th cent. church of Our Lady, which has almond-shaped frescoes in the crypt, representing the Redeemer among Cherubs, Angels and Saints Peter and Paul. They were carried out in the second half of the 12th cent., and are among the most interesting in the region.

* **BUSSETO** (Parma). Small town built on a rectangular plan. The church of *Santa Maria degli Angeli* was completed in the second half of the 15th cent.; inside there is a terracotta group representing the Pietà, by Guido Mazzoni (c. 1450-1518). The *Villa Pallavicino* was constructed after a design attributed to Jacopo Barozzi, called Vignola (1507-1573). The parish church of *San Bartolomeo*, rebuilt in 1436, has a Gothic facade and contains frescoes by Michelangelo Anselmi (c. 1491-1555). The *Rocca*, erected around the middle of the 13th cent.

and restructured in the 16th, houses the Verdi Theatre. *Casa natale di Giuseppe Verdi*, at Roncole Verdi, is the house where the composer was born on 10th October 1813.

* **CACCAMO** (Palermo). Between the rocky Mount San Calógero and the valley of the San Leonardo, with a sweeping view, taking in the Gulf of Termini Imerese to the north. The white *Castello*, with bettlements and turrets, was founded long ago, possibly in the 12th cent. The wall expanses are decorated with single and double-arched openings. Inside is the Hall of Conspiracy, where the rebel barons met in 1160 to plot against William the Bad. The late-11th cent. *Duomo*, dedicated to St. George, was later restructured. It has a late-Renaissance interior containing pictures by Francesco Quaresima (lived in the 16-17th cent.), Giuseppe Velasquez (1750-1827), Vito d'Anna (c. 1720-1769), Giacomo Lo Verde (active in the first half of the 17th cent.), and Vincenzo La Barbera (recorded 1605-1637), and reliefs attributed to Francesco Laurana (recorded 1458-1500). In the Treasury are 16-18th cent. gold ornaments and precious sacred vestments of the 17th and 18th cent. The church of the *Santissima Annunciata*, with Baroque facade and twin pilaster-strips, (1643) contains stuccoes by Serpotta, and an Annunciation, altarpiece by William Borremans (1670-1744). In the church of *Santa Maria degli Angeli* or *San Domenico*, begun in 1487, is a fine statue of the Madonna, by Antonello Gagini (1478-1536). In the church of *Sant'Agostino*, Miracle of St. Isidor, painted by Matthew Stomer (r. 1600-c. 1650). In the church of *San Francesco* is a wooden panel depicting Christ and Veronica, by Simon de Wobreck (recorded 1557-1585). The Renaissance church of *Sant' Antonio Abate* has a Madonna and Saints, painted by Giuseppe Spadafora (lived in the 16th cent.).

* **CAGLI** (Pesaro). Agricultural centre on the spur of a hill, where the Bosso and Burano meet. The original town hall (*Palazzo Comunale*) dates back to the second half of the 13th cent., and was rebuilt in the 15th with the collaboration of Francesco di Giorgio Martini (1439-1502). The entrance-hall contains a fresco

by Giovanni Santi (active 1484-1494). The *Duomo* was almost entirely rebuilt at the end of the 18th cent. following a disastrous earthquake. The facade shows traces of its Romanesque origin and the left side of it contains a noble Gothic doorway, carried out by Antonio di Cristoforo da Cagli in 1424. Inside are paintings by Gaetano Lapis (1706-1758), Sebastiano Conca (c. 1680-1764) and Giovanni Battista Salvi called Sassoferrato (1609-1685). The church of *San Francesco* is a bare solemn mass of stone in Romanesque-Gothic style; inside are remains of 14th cent. frescoes. The only part left of the ancient Fortress, erected in 1481 by Francesco di Giorgio Martini, is the *Torrione*. The church of *San Domenico* is Romanesque in origin and haⁿ a facade adorned with a Renaissance doorway. The interior includes works by Gaetano Lapis, Giovanni Santi, and Federico Baroccio.

** **CAGLIARI.** Closely packed on a solitary hill and spread out along the seashore, it is

Busseto, Villa Pallavicino.

Cagli, Fortress Tower.
Cagliari, Cathedral. Guglielmo's pulpit, detail.

the main political, economic and cultural centre in Sardinia. The porticoed *Via Roma*, Cagliari's favourite walk, is a wide, graceful street. The *Terrazza Umberto I*, called Bastion of St. Remy after the first Viceroy of Savoy, was built on the site of the ancient bastions of the Spanish castle. The *Torre dell'Elefante* was commissioned by the rulers of the Commune of Pisa, in 1307, and built to the design of the architect Giovanni Capula (recorded 1305-1307). The building is remarkably harmonious, especially in the arrangement of the hewn-limestone blocks. The *Cattedrale*, dedicated to St. Mary, was built at the turn of the 13th cent., and enlarged and restructured in later periods. The 13th cent. bell-tower is worthy of attention. Inside are two pulpits, forming a single ambo at first, and interesting works of art, including a silver lamp by the goldsmith Giovanni Mameli (recorded 1569-1602), recalling the lamps of Venetian galleys. Another interesting item in this place of worship is a Raphael-inspired polyptych depicting the Madonna and Child, Annunciation and Crucifixion with Saints Jerome and Bartholomew, by Michele Cavaro (lived in the 16th cent.). The *Torre di San Pancrazio* (St. Pancras' Tower) was built in 1305 by Giovanni Capula, and is the most stalwart piece of defensive work undertaken by the Pisans in Cagliari. The *Museo Archeologico Nazionale* is important for the light it sheds on the Proto-Sardinian, Nuragic, and Phoenician-Punic civilizations. The material collected here is extremely interesting. It was found during excavation work in Sardinia and helps to document the mysterious history of the island. The *Pinacoteca* contains a relatively small but important collection of paintings, illustrating, most of all, the history of art in the southern regions of Sardinia from the 14th to the 17th cent. There are some remarkable ancons and fragments of ancons, which were originally preserved in the church of St. Francis of Stampace, burnt down in 1872. The three rooms contain valuable works of art mainly by Sardinian painters, but by Tuscans and Umbrians too; the polyptych of the Porziuncola by an unknown Sardo-Valencian painter, called "Master of Castelsardo" is worthy of note. The *Amphitheatre* was built in the second cent. A.D., and is the most important Roman building in Sardinia. The church of *San Domenico* was built in 1593 after the design of Raffaello Fagnoni, on the site of an ancient church, also dedicated to St. Domenic, which was bombed in the Second World War. The adjacent cloister, important for its late Gothic structure, was miraculously saved during the bombing, apart from the north wing. The cloister leads to the lower part of the church and to the Rosary Chapel in the ancient church, built in 1254 by Fra Nicolò Fortiguerra da Siena, and restructured in the 15th and 16th cent. The church of *Santi Cosma e Damiano* or *San Saturnino*, the most ancient Christian monument in Sardinia, is one of the most outstanding examples of Early-Christian art in the Mediterranean area: practically destroyed by bombing in 1943, it has been rebuilt stone by stone, so that it can now be seen in its original shape and structure. The *Santuario di Bonaria*, built in the first half of the 14th cent., is one of the most frequently visited sanctuaries in the area.

* **CAIAZZO** (Caserta). Pleasant town on a hillside. The area was inhabited in pre-historic times, as is shown by archeological remains preserved in the Archeological Museum in Naples. The Longobard *Castello*, with its square keep, dominates the town and looks towards the Monte Maggiore chain of mountains. The *Cattedrale*, dedicated to the Assunta, was rebuilt in the second half of the 16th cent.; inside is the sepulchre of St. Stephen of Macerata, Bishop of Caiazzo and patron saint of the city, as well as silver statues representing Saints Stephen and Ferrante, by Matteo Treglia (active 1685-1714). The *Cappella Votiva ai Caduti*, a Memorial chapel to the Fallen, has an important Renaissance doorway (1491).

* **CALALZO DI CADORE** (Belluno). In a fine position on a moraine terrace, it is the most important town in the Cadore area. The parish church of *San Biagio* contains four panels by Orazio Vecellio (1525-1576) depicting the Annunciation, Nativity, Epiphany and Presentation at the Temple.

* **CALANGIANUS** (Sassari). It is one of the most picturesque and interesting towns in Gallura. In the Sacristy of the *Parrocchiale* (parish church) is an important altarpiece (unfortunately in a deteriorated state) depicting the Assumption, by Andrea Lusso (recorded 1593-1610). Walk to the *Nuraghe Laicheddu*.

* **CALASCIBETTA** (Enna). On a rugged slope with houses arranged as in an amphitheatre. The *Chiesa Matrice*, dedicated to St. Peter, was built around the middle of the 14th cent., and later rebuilt, with an 18th cent. facade. It contains a much-admired baptismal font in marble (second half of the 16th cent.), a 16th cent. marble ciborium, and a Treasury containing some rare pieces. Walk to the *Necropoli di Realmese*, dug in the rock, with about three hundred favisse and little grottoes, of the 9-7th cent. B.C.

* **CALCI** (Pisa). In the hollow called Valgraziosa, at the foot of Mount Pisano. In the centre of the village is the Romanesque *Pieve*, (parish church), Pisan in style (late 11th cent.), with facade decorated by a double archway and massive unfinished bell-tower. Not far from the village is the *Certosa di Pisa*, a large monastic group of buildings founded in 1366,

including a church, guest-rooms, cells and cloisters. The buildings were almost entirely reconstructed in the 17th and 18th cent. The small chapter cloister (15th cent.), the large cloister and the Baroque church are interesting.

* CALDIERO (Verona). Agricultural and industrial centre. The *Parrocchiale*, designed by Giuseppe Barbieri (1778-1838), contains a painting depicting the Consignment of the Keys by Felice Ricci called Brusasorci (1546-1605). The 14th cent. entrance-door to *Casa Fortini* should be noticed.

**CALTAGIRONE (Catania). On three hills overlooking the valleys of the Caltagirone and Maroglio, with narrow streets and irregular-shaped squares. Human settlement as far back as the 20th cent. B.C. is revealed by traces of hut-dwellings. The *Duomo*, dedicated to St. Julian, was almost completely rebuilt in the early 19th cent. It has a modern floral facade and contains pictures by Francesco Vaccaro (1808-1882) and Giuseppe Vaccaro (c. 1793-1866). The *Chiesa del Gesù* was begun in 1570. There are twelve 17th cent. statues on the facade, and inside, a panel of the Nativity and Annunciation by Polidoro da Caravaggio (c. 1495-1546). The *Chiesa del Salvatore*, designed by Giovanni Battista Marino (recorded 1728-1765), has a facade in two parts, designed by Natale Bonaiuto (recorded 1782-1812). Inside is the sacellum containing the mortal remains of don Luigi Sturzo, with architecture by Ugo Tarchi (working in the present cent.). The church of *Santa Maria del Monte*, the first construction of which dates back to the middle

of the 12th cent., has a solid, late 16th cent. facade, in contrast with the slender 18th cent. campanile, designed by Natale Bonaiuto; in the Treasury, precious goldwork. The church of *San Giacomo*, originally built in 1090 to commemorate the liberation of the city from Moslem dominion, and rebuilt in the 17th cent., contains the reliquary sarcophagus of St. James, in embossed and engraved silver, by Nibilio Gagini (recorded from 1583 to 1607) and Giuseppe Gagini (died in 1610). The *Museo della Ceramica* is the most important ceramics museum in Italy after that of Faenza (Caltagirone is nicknamed the "Sicilian Faenza"). It has a fine collection ranging from enoelithic-age vases to local products of the 18th cent. The most highly-prized item is a 5th cent. large bowl chalice. The church of *San Giorgio*, probably erected by the Genoese in 1030 after they had expelled the Moslems from the city, and later rebuilt, contains a much-admired Flemish-school painting of the Trinity, and paintings by Epifanio Rossi (lived in the 17th cent.). The *Scala* (1608) is a straight flight of steps, designed by the architect Giuseppe Giacolone.

** CALTANISSETTA. On a hill facing the Valle del Salso, with broad straight streets, in the middle of the mining area in Sicily. The *Cattedrale*, dedicated to Santa Maria la Nova and St. Michael, was erected in the late 16th cent. and early 17th ,and is the most important monument in the city. The facade is divided by pilaster-strips and flanked by two 19th cent. bell-towers. The interior has a nave and two aisles; it contains frescoes by William Borremans (1670-1744), which perhaps show him at his best. The church of *Sant'Agata* or *del Collegio*, begun in 1605, has an austere facade designed by Natale Masucci (recorded from c. 1560). The interior contains some good works of art, such as the impressive Madonna del Carmine altar with a precious frontal, altarpieces depicting the Martyrdom of St. Agatha by Agostino Scilla (1629-1700) and St. Francis Xavier by Matteo Cristadoro (lived

Calci, Parish Church. Baptismal font, detail.

Caltanissetta, Badia di Santo Spirito, apse.

Cagli, San Domenico. Giovanni Santi, frescoed shrine.

Cagliari, Pinacoteca. Juan Mates, St. Julian the hunter.

Cagliari, Museo Archeologico Nazionale. Nuraghiage bronze from Santa Vittoria.

Caltagirone, San Giorgio. Vrancke van der Stockt,
Holy Trinity and Throne of Grace.

Camerino, Pinacoteca Civica. Arcangelo di Cola,
Madonna and Child with two Angels.

Carpignano Salentino, Crypt of Saints Christine
and Marina, the Angel of the Annunciation.

Camerino, Pinacoteca Civica. Girolamo di Gio-
vanni, Our Lady of Mercy, detail.

in the 17th cent.), and a large marble altarpiece by Ignazio Marabitti (1719-1797). The church of *San Domenico*, reconstructed in the last years of the 18th cent., has a curvilinear Baroque facade. Inside is a Madonna of the Carmelite, considered to be the best painting by Filippo Paladino (c. 1544-1614), a Madonna of the Rosary, also by Paladino, and a St. Vincent Ferrer by William Borremans. The former church of *Santa Maria degli Angeli* has a Gothic doorway with a triple archivolt. The *Museo Civico* contains a large archeological section, and another section devoted to modern art. Walk to the Romanesque *Badia di Santo Spirito*, dating from the middle of the 12th cent.; notice the 14th cent. fresco of Christ Blessing, in the lunette above the entrance-door. Walk to the *Zona Archeologica di Sabucina*, an archeological area made even more interesting by the excavations currently in progress, which have brought to light remains of pre-historic huts, mostly circular in form.

* **CALVI RISORTA** (Caserta). The Calvi Vecchia district corresponds to the ancient Cales of the Aurunci, recorded in the war against Hannibal. In ancient times Calenian vases were renowned, being completely covered with shiny black varnish and with plastic decoration. The *Cattedrale*, erected in the 9th cent. and restructured in the 15th, still has three fine apses belonging to the original Romanesque construction. The basilican interior, altered to Baroque style in the 18th cent., contains the remains of a 12th cent. pulpit with mosaics and sculptures, a Bishop's Throne of the same period, and the 15th cent. tomb of Bishop Angelo Mazziotta. Walk to the *Rovine di Cales*, where there are identifiable remains of an oval-shaped amphitheatre, thermal buildings, the forum, foundations of the theatre, a temple, Roman sepulchres and the 5th cent. church of San Casto Vecchio. Another walk takes one to the *Grotta dei Santi*, inside which, painted in the tufa, are some attractive votive frescoes dating from the 10-11th cent. In the neighbourhood is the *Grotta delle Formelle*, a natural cave, though modified by man, containing attractive 10-11th cent. frescoes.

* **CAMAIORE** (Lucca). In a vast plain surrounded by hills. The Romanesque-style *Collegiata* was built towards the end of the 13th cent. In the choir is an Assumption with Saints Peter and Paul, by Benedetto Brandimarte (recorded towards the end of the 16th cent.). The *Museo* contains a famous Flemish tapestry, dated 1516, possibly done to the cartoons of Hugo van der Goes (lived in the 15th cent.), or Justus of Ghent, of the same period. The tapestry depicts the Last Supper, Washing the Feet, and the Capture in the Garden. In the neighbourhood is the *Badia di San Pietro*, part of an ancient Benedictine monastery founded in the 8th cent. and rebuilt in the 11th.

* **CAMALDOLI** (Town of Poppi, province of Arezzo). On the eastern side of the Casentine Apennines. St. Romualdo built a hermitage here whose fame spread throughout Christendom. The *Convento di Camaldoli* is a characteristic building, in a picturesque setting. Facing it is the *Chiesa*, which was rebuilt at the start of the 16th cent. It has a Baroque interior; the vault, frescoed with the Glory of St. Romualdo, is popularly known as "the cloud". The Nativity above the third altar on the left-hand side, is by Giorgio Vasari (1511-1574). The *Eremo di Camaldoli* (Hermitage) stands in the middle of the forest and is immersed in a silence broken only by the murmur of water and twittering of birds. Beside it is the *Chiesa del Salvatore*, built in 1027 and later remodelled. It has a Baroque facade and contains some remarkable works of art. There are twenty *Celle*, arranged in five rows: each cell is, in effect, a small rectangular house, with a porch and three tiny windows.

** **CAMERINO** (Macerata). An ancient cultural centre, in a panoramic setting. *Piazza Cavour*, in the heart of the town, is its finest square. In the middle stands the bronze statue of Sixtus V, a fine piece of work by Tiburzio Vergelli da Camerino (1555-1610). The *Duomo*, reconstructed after a disastrous earthquake in 1799, contains several works of art including a painting of St. Joseph's Dream, by Simone Cantarini (1612-1678), another depicting St. Ansovino distributing Alms, by Andrea Sacchi (1599-1661), a triptych by Girolamo di Giovanni (recorded 1449-1473), seven paintings by Emilio Savonanzi (1580-1660) and, in the crypt, the tomb of St. Ansovino, Bishop of Camerino in the 19th cent., with bizarre animals

Camaiore, Badia di San Pietro, interior.

carved around the base. The *Palazzo dell'Università* was built in three different periods, and Baccio Pontelli (c. 1450-1492) took part in the third stage. The University, with its important Law faculty, is housed here: the Aula Scialoia, the Valentiniana Library, containing two hundred incunabula, the archeological museum, the coin collection and the botanic garden are all worth visiting. The church of *San Venanzio*, was destroyed by earthquake in 1799, as were most of the monuments of Camerino, and rebuilt in the second half of the 19th cent. In the facade it has a Romanesque-Gothic doorway dating from the second half of the 14th cent. The interior contains several works of art including a painting of the Coronation of the Madonna with Saints Charles and Ubaldo, by Alessandro Turchi called Orbetto (1578-1649), and a 16th cent. tabernacle attributed to Rocco di Tommaso da Vicenza (active from 1494 to 1526). The 13th cent. church of *San Francesco*, in sandstone blocks is no longer used as a place of worship. It houses the Pinacoteca Civica containing works by local artists from the 15th and 16th cent. and by Girolamo di Giovanni in particular. The *Rocca*, the fortress built for Duke Valentino in 1503, after the design of Lodovico Clodio (recorded in the early 16th cent.) still has some impressive remains, such as the formidable keep.

* CAMOGLI-SAN FRUTTUOSO (Genoa).

Ancient little port, sheltered by Mounts Esole and Portofino, and characterized by tall houses. The parish church of *S. Maria Assunta* dates back to the 11th cent. The Torre di Castel Dragone is down by the harbour. One can reach San Fruttuoso either by footpath or by boat. It nestles in an inlet beneath the towering heights of Mount Portofino. In the 10th century, Benedictine-Cassino monks built a church and a monastery, which enjoyed great splendour in the 13th cent. (e.g. the falcon-hunting), but declined on account of repeated raids by the Saracens. The *Monastero di San Fruttuoso di Capodimonte* is down by the beach; it stands on low, sturdy arches which were rebuilt in the 13th cent. and later restored. The church behind it is a Romanesque-Lombard reconstruction, with traces of Byzantine influence. The small Romanesque cloister contains the *Tombe dei Doria* (1275-1305); it was the Doria family who took over the Abbey from the Church in 1550.

* CAMPELLO SUL CLITUNNO (Perugia).

Source of the Clitunno, an area rich in springs of pure fresh water, which form a shallow lake fringed with weeping-willows and poplars. In ancient times the site was sacred to the God Clitumnus, famous for his oracles, and there was a small temple dedicated to him, together with others named after lesser divinities. The *Tempietto del Clitunno*, or church

of San Salvatore, is an early-Christian building possibly dating from the 4th cent. A.D. on a rise overlooking the Clitunno.

* CAMPIONE D'ITALIA (Como).

In a lovely position on Lake Lugano. In the parish church of *San Zenone* are kept some local 15th cent. sculptures. The *Oratorio di San Pietro* is a small 14th cent. construction by the Masters of Campione. The 14th cent. church of *Santa Maria dei Ghirli*, was remodelled in the 18th. Below the portico, on the right side, is a Universal Judgment by Franco and Filippolo De' Veris (active in the 14-15th cent.) and a Lombard-school Adam and Eve (1514). Inside are frescoes with Stories of the Virgin and John the Baptist, and The Months, by a 14th cent. Lombard artist.

Campello sul Clitunno, Temple of Clitunno.
Campione d'Italia, Santa Maria dei Ghirli. Franco and Filippolo De Veris, Last Judgement, detail.

** CAMPOBASSO. Pleasant, busy town consisting of new and old parts. It rises on a hillside, dominated by the formidable and picturesque mass of the recently restored, Monforte Castle (15th. cent.). The *Museo Sannitico* contains a large quantity of antiquities from Samnium, coin collections, and a picture representing Peace between Crusaders and Trinitarians, by Giovanni Maria Felici (16th cent.). The church of *Sant'Antonio Abate* (1572) contains a painting of St. Benedict Exorcizing a Devil, possibly by Fabrizio Santafede (c. 1560-1625).

* CAMPOSAMPIERO (Padua). Large agricultural and commercial centre. Roman in origin, the town grew up around the castle which the founder of the Counts of Camposampiero dynasty, Cavalier Tiso, had built in the year 1013 A.D. In the church of *Santi Giovanni e Antonio* is the cell from which St. Antony of Padua asked to be transferred to Arcella when he was dying. The *Santuario del Noce*, built on the spot where St. Anthony preached under a walnut-tree, contains 16th cent. frescoes illustrating Stories of St. Anthony and Franciscan Martyrs, and St. Anthony Preaching, by Bonifacio De' Pitati called Bonifacio Veronese (1487-1553).

* CANICATTÌ (Agrigento). Set among vineyards and olive orchards, with houses arranged as in an amphitheatre. In the 18th cent. *Chiesa del Purgatorio* is a Sacred Heart statue by Nicolò Bagnasco (lived in the 18-19th cent.). In the *Chiesa del Carmelo* is a painting of the Holy Family with Saints Joachim and Anna, by Pietro d'Asaro called Monocolo (1597-1647), and in the 18th cent. *Chiesa Matrice*, dedicated to St. Pancras, an Our Lady of Sorrows by Olivio Sozzi (1696-1765).

* CANNE DELLA BATTAGLIA (Town of Barletta, province of Bari). Archeological area surrounded by olive orchards and vineyards on the right bank of the Ofanto. Here stood Cannae, famous as the site of Hannibal's victory over the Romans in the spring of 216 B.C. The *Antiquarium* is partly dedicated to the historical battle, and contains archeological collections from the 6th cent. B.C. onwards. The ancient city (*Cittadella di Canne*) lay on the lowest spur of the north-eastern Murge, and was already inhabited in pre-historic times; excavations have brought to light the foundations of the ancient dwellings. *Basiliche Cristiane* with interesting remains from early Christian and medieval times. *Sepolcreto e Villaggio Apollo*: burial ground and village where recent excavations have unearthed remains from the 6th cent. B.C. onwards, of remarkable scientific interest.

* CANNOBIO (Novara). Last town on the western shore of Lake Maggiore, already a flourishing community in the period of the Italian Communes. *Palazzo della Ragione*, the town hall, known as the Parrasio, was built by order of the podestà, Ugolino Mandello, in 1291. It contains medieval sepulchres and tombstones and, on the right side, a slender tower with pyramidal cusp. The *Santuario della Santissima Pietà* was enlarged by St. Charles Borromeo after 1571. It has an octagonal dome and contains a fine altarpiece by Gaudenzio Ferrari (c. 1470-1546), depicting Jesus meeting the three Maries; the predella contains a wonderful picture of the Pietà. Two and a half km. from Cannobio is the *Orrido di Sant'Anna*, a deep chasm cleft in the gneiss by the Cannobino stream.

** CANOSA DI PUGLIA (Bari). Large agricultural and commercial centre, at the northeastern tip of the Murge, set on a hill commading a sweeping view of the Tavoliere and Ofanto valley. The *Cattedrale*, dedicated to San Sabino, Bishop of Canosa in the 6th cent. A.D., was erected in the 11th cent., but largely rebuilt in the second half of the 17th. Inside is the Ancient Church, an example of early Romanesque architecture in Apulia; the early-11th cent. pulpit, by Acceptus, and the Bishop's throne, by Romualdo (recorded 1078-1089) are worthy of attention. Set against the transept wall is the chapel containing the tomb of Bohemond, son of Robert Guiscard. It is one of the most characteristic Romanesque constructions in Apulia, and boasts a magnificent bronze portal, with asymmetrical doors. In the *Museo Civico* is a large quantity of archeological material, excavated in the surrounding area, and medieval material also. The *Tre Ipogei Lagrasta* are among the finest examples of local architecture; the largest consists of nine rooms, with ceilings cut out of the rock in rafter fashion. The other two hypogea have the same characteristics; it was here in 1843 (year of the first exploration) that skeletons were found, lying on gilded bronze beds

Canossa di Puglia, Tomb of Bohemond.

adorned with ivory statuettes. The *Arco Romano*, also known as the Roman, or Varro, Gate after the Roman consul defeated by Hannibal at Cannae, was built of brick in the 2nd cent. A.D. Walk to the *Scavi di San Leucio*, excavation site where remains of the basilica of San Leucio were identified in 1937.

* **CAORLE** (Venice). Seaside resort and fishing port. The Romanesque *Cattedrale* perhaps dating back to 1048, has a tripartite facade divided by pilasters, and a magnificent cylindrical bell-tower standing apart. It contains some important works of art, including six 15th cent. panels depicting Apostles, and a gold altarpiece, composed of 12th and 13th cent. Byzantine panels. In the church of *Madonna dell'Angelo* (rebuilt in the mid-18th cent.) there is a wooden image of the Madonna and Child, placed here by the Archangel Michael, as legend has it.

* **CAPODIMONTE** (Viterbo). On a promontory on the shores of Lake Bolsena. The *Castello Farnese* is an imposing octagonal construction, built to the design of Antonio da Sangallo the Younger (1483-1546).

* **CAPO DI PONTE** (Brescia). On the river Oglio. Near Naquane is the *Parco Nazionale delle Incisioni Rupestri* (national park of rock carvings). There are over forty thousand of them scattered over the red and greyish rock surfaces, carried out over a period of about twenty-five centuries, from neolithic times to the Roman conquest. Scholars have divided them into four periods: as time goes on, the figures become more precise and finished. In the *Parrocchiale* are paintings by Francesco Paglia (1636-c. 1713), Sante Cattaneo (1739-1819) and Francesco Monti (1683-1768). In the adjacent priest's house there is a remarkable

painting by Giuseppe Nuvolone (1619-1703). Not far away is the parish church of *San Siro* (early 12th cent.). Built to an asymmetrical plan, it looks as if it is a natural part of the rock it stands on. Inside are 15th and 16th cent. frescoes. Also in the neighbourhood is the church of *San Salvatore*, known as the *Monastero*. It is all that remains of a lovely Romanesque Cluniac monastery, dating back to the 11th cent.

** **CAPRAROLA** (Viterbo). On a slope of the Monti Cimini. *Palazzo Farnese*, built between 1559 and 1575 for Cardinal Alessandro Farnese, was designed by Jacopo Barozzi called Vignola (1507-1573) and represents an important landmark in the history of Mannerism and late-16th cent. culture. It has two large forecourts and an immense entrance-hall decorated with coats-of-arms and views of fiefs held by the Farnese family. The ceilings of the rooms on the right-hand side were frescoed by Taddeo Zuccari (1529-1566). The great spiral staircase is supported by 30 pairs of Doric columns, the work of Vignola. It is decorated with grotesques and landscapes by Antonio Tempesta (1555-1630). The State Hall, or Fasti di Ercole, was frescoed by Federico Zuccari (c. 1540-1609). In the Round Chapel

Capo di Ponte, San Salvatore.

Caprarola, Farnese Palace, main front facade.
Caprarola, Farnese Palace, spiral staircase.

are more works by Federico Zuccari, and rich stuccoes; in the hall of the Fasti Farnesiani, frescoes by Taddeo Zuccari. The hall of the Council of Trent has corners decorated with imitation columns painted by Vignola, and pictures by Taddeo Zuccari. In the Summer Apartment are frescoes by Taddeo Zuccari and his assistants; in the Winter Apartment, there is a Pala della Penitenza, with pictures by Giacomo Zanguidi called Bertoia (1544-1574). The Sala degli Angeli is the most splendid hall in the entire palace. It contains pictures by Raffaellino Motta called Raffaellino da Reggio (c. 1550-1578) and Bertoia. The Sala del Mappamondo has geographical decorations. In the park are terraced gardens and the so-called Palazzina, a villa with double loggia designed by Vignola. The church of *Santa Teresa* is considered the masterpiece of Girolamo Rainaldi (1570-1655). The Serlian motif is repeated both in the dynamic facade and in the interior, where a painting of St. Anthony Abbot, by Alessandro Turchi called Orbetto (1578-1649) can be admired, as well as an altarpiece representing the Madonna del Carmine and Saints, probably by Guido Reni (1575-1642). The church of *Santa Maria della Consolazione* or *San Francesco* has a fine late-Renaissance doorway and sumptuous wooden ceiling, crowned with a fine Annunciation and Saints.

* **CAPRI** (Naples). Main centre on the Isle of Capri, which rises at the southernmost tip of the Bay of Naples. Piazza Umberto I is surrounded by the medieval, most attractive part of the town, and from it a flight of steps leads up to the parish church of *Santo Stefano*, rebuilt in the 17th cent. in a fanciful Baroque style. The *Certosa di San Giacomo* was built between 1371 and 1374, but devastated and remodelled on several occasions. The Church still has its original pointed-arched doorway and simple interior, with an aisleless nave, cross-vaults, and single and triple-lighted windows. In the Monastery there is an interesting Small Cloister (15th. cent.) and Large Cloister (16th cent.). Walk to *Villa Iovis* or Tiberius' Villa, where excavation work has unearthed the state rooms, cisterns, baths, servants' quarters, and imperial dwelling, with a stately loggia.

** **CAPUA** (Caserta). Triangular-shaped city, still with its walls, situated in a bend of the river Volturno. The most important monument is the *Duomo*, dedicated to Saints Stephen and Agatha. Begun in the middle of the 9th cent., it was rebuilt at the start of the 12th, again remodelled in 1724, modified in 1850, almost entirely destroyed by bombing on 8th September 1942, and restored to its original form and reconsecrated in 1957. Twenty columns with beautiful Corinthian capitals, of the 3rd cent. A.D., support the quadrilateral entrance. The impressive bell-tower, to the right, dates

back to the 9th cent., and has bas-reliefs set in it, brought from the Campanian Amphitheatre. The basilican interior is divided by two rows of monolithic columns and contains a 13th cent. panel on a gilt background representing the Madonna of the Rose, a 15th cent. Madonna of Purity in polychrome wood, a painting of the Madonna and Child with Saints Stephen and Lucy on a gilt background (1489), by Antoniazzo Romano, a 13th cent. candelabra for the Paschal Candle, an Assumption by Francesco Solimena (1657-1747), and important sarcophagi. In the crypt is a chapel enclosed in a peribolos of granite columns and containing a marble statue of the Dead Christ by Matteo Bottiglieri (active 1724-1754). In the Treasury are a precious gold rose, an illuminated "Exultet" of the 11th cent., Islamic cut crystal of the 11th and 12th cent., etc. The Palazzo Antignano, with remarkable 15th cent. doorway in Catalan-Moorish style, houses the *Museo Campano*, consisting of thirty-eight show-rooms and twelve store-rooms. In the two courtyards can be seen a lapidarium with a large collection of Roman epigraphs from the Agro Campano, cippi and sarcophagi. In rooms one to twenty-four there is a rich archeological collection, especially bronzes, mosaics, coins, proto-historic and proto-Corinthian bucaro vases, as well as fibulae, sword-belts, terracottas, etc. The other rooms contain paintings from the 15th to the 18th cent. including the Redeemer by Bartolomeo Vivarini (c. 1432-1499), polyptych of the Crucifixion by Cristoforo Scacco (lived in the 15-16th cent.) and Calling of Saint Andrew, by Giuseppe Marullo (died c. 1685). Also housed in the Museum is a well-stocked library which boasts some rare books. The late 13th cent. church of *Annunciata* was rebuilt in the 16th. It has a graceful dome designed

Capua, Museo Campano, the Faith of Capua.

by Domenico Fontana (1543-1607). The gilded and painted wooden ceiling inside was almost entirely destroyed during an air-raid in 1943; there are a few important paintings, such as the Madonna of Constantinople by Antonio Sarnelli (c. 1742-1793), and a Holy Family, by Alessio D'Elia (active in the second half of the 18th cent.). The *Palazzo dei Principi Normanni* or *Castello delle Pietre* (latter half of the 11th cent.) was built with huge blocks of stone taken from the Campanian Amphitheatre. In the small church of *San Salvatore Piccolo* are fine 14th cent. frescoes by an unknown artist. The church of *Santa Caterina* (latter half of the 14th cent.) has a lively 17th cent, facade, and contains remains of frescoes from the 14th cent. building. The cloister is late Renaissance in style. The church of *San Marcello Martire*, begun in 851 A.D. has a fine entrance-door, while the 10th cent. church of *San Salvatore Maggiore a Corte* is a rare example of Longobard architecture. An excursion to the Basilica of *Sant'Angelo in Formis* is recommended. It is a 10th cent. Romanesque church built over the remains of a temple dedicated to Diana Tifatina and rebuilt or restored several times in later periods. A five-arched portico precedes the facade. In the lunette of the main entrance-door is a white marble fresco of St. Michael (latter half of the 11th cent.) and, above the doorway, an early 12th cent. Madonna at Prayer. The basilican interior is divided by two series of columns; it contains frescoes of the latter half of the 11th cent., exquisite works of art by local artists. On the right of the church stands the campanile, proto-type for cathedrals throughout the region. Its base is formed of square blocks of stone taken from the Temple of Diana Tifatina.

* **CARAVAGGIO** (Bergamo). Large agricultural and industrial centre. *Santuario della Madonna di Caravaggio:* building began in 1575 to Pellegrini's design, but was only completed in the late 18th cent. The huge interior is embellished with paintings by Luigi Cavenaghi (1844-1918) and a Deposition, by Giacomo Cavedoni (1577-1660). The *Arcipretale dei Santi Fermo e Rustico*, built at the turn of the 15th

Caravaggio, Sanctuary.

cent., has a 17th cent. bell-tower and a basilican interior consisting of a nave and two aisles. It contains some remarkable works of art, including frescoes by Bernardino Campi (1552-1591), and Francesco Prata (1512-1562). In the choir is a painting of the Martyrdom of Saints Fermo and Rustico, by Giovanni Moriggia (1796-1878), and a Madonna and Saints by Camillo Procaccini (c. 1551-1629). The *Palazzo Comunale* was built in the 17th cent; the Council Room has some fine frescoes. In the late 15th cent. church of *San Bernardino* there are frescoes by Bernardino Butinone (lived from c. 1445-1507) and Bernardino Zenale (c. 1456-1526).

* **CARBONIA** (Cagliari). The most typical mining village in Italy, it stands on a wide shelf sloping downwards from the barren hills to the plain. It was founded through the auspices of Benito Mussolini in 1936, and is an important example of planned architecture in the thirties. Excursion to the *Campo Trincerato Cartaginese* (Carthaginian encampment) where some significant remains have been brought to light in recent years.

* **CARIGNANO** (Turin). The ancient Carnianum, as findings from Roman and barbarian times have revealed. The Cathedral of *San Giovanni Battista* was erected in the mid-18th cent. after the design of Benedetto Alfieri (1700-1767), and has an imposing brick facade in two parts. The interior is interesting for its semi-elliptic plan, and there is a remarkable cycle of paintings by Paolo Gaidano (1861-1916).

* **CARINOLA** (Caserta). Small town with interesting 15th cent. buildings in Gothic-Catalanese style. Carinulum is thought to have been founded in Longobard times, on the remains of the Roman Forum Popilii. The *Cattedrale* was built in the 11th cent., as an inscription on the main entrance-door reveals. It is preceded by a portico with three Romanesque arches. The interior is mainly Cistercian-ogival in style; it contains an important font and the tomb of the canonized Bishop Bernardo, founder of the cathedral. The *Casa Novelli* is much

Carignano, Cathedral of San Giovanni Battista, facade.

70

admired, with its Durazzo-inspired entrance-door and three harmonious 15th cent. windows on the first floor. The *Castle* or ex *Ducal Palace* is 15th cent. in origin; the front part is in a bad state of repair. There are some interesting remains of the walls of the ancient *Forum Popilii*. Excursion to Ventaroli, where there is the simple *Basilica di Santa Maria in Foro Claudio*, known also as the *Episcopio*. It has an elegant Renaissance portal and valuable frescoes in the basilican interior; of various periods, they are the work of such important artists as Nicola De Belarducci (lived in the 15th cent.), and Antonino da Carinola, another local artist of the 15th cent.

* CARPI (Modena). Agricultural, commercial and industrial centre, with historical connections. The *Cattedrale*, dedicated to the Assunta, was begun in the early 16th cent., and has a Baroque facade. The interior was designed by Baldassare Peruzzi (1481-1536); it contains some valuable pictures including Saints Nicholas and Bartholomew, by Giacomo Cavedoni (1577-1660), and St. Charles Borromeo by Sante Peranda (1566-1638). The *Castello dei Pio* is the result of the union of various buildings, dating from the 14th to the 17th cent. The exterior is enlivened by the Passerino Tower, the Galasso Tower, the Clock Tower, and the Birdcage. Inside are the Civic Museum, the Xylographical Museum, the Clock Room, the Archives, the Chapel frescoed by Bernardino Loschi (c. 1460-1540), and other interesting rooms. The parish church of *Santa Maria*, called *della Sagra*, was begun in 751 A.D. Inside there are a few works of art, a 14th cent. fresco of the Epiphany, and a large number of 15th cent. frescoes. The *Tempio di San Nicolò*, Renaissance in style, was built between 1493 and 1516. It contains some important paintings including an Annunciation by Bernardino Loschi.

* CARPIGNANO SALENTINO (Lecce). On the slopes of the Serre di Serrano, and Greek in origin. The *Cripta delle Sante Cristine e Marina*, also known as *Madonna delle Grazie* is carved out of the tufa. The interior has a vault supported by four pillars and contains frescoes of varying periods. The most important ones depict St. Theodore, St. Nicholas, and St. Christine (12th cent.). In two small apses are Images of Christ Enthroned, one dated 1020 and signed Eustathios, the other dated 959 and signed Theofilaktos. The *Parrocchiale* (latter half of the 16th cent.) has a font dated 1594, and altars carried out in 1670 by Placido Buffelli.

** CARRARA (Massa Carrara). Situated among the green foothills of the Apuan Alps, and crossed by the Carrione torrent. The 11th cent. Romanesque *Duomo* has a wonderful panelled square in the facade, with interlaced rhombi, and in the centre is one of the finest rose-windows in Italy. The Longobard-style interior contains some valuable 18th cent. paintings, and in the nearby oratory-cum-baptistery one can admire a large hexagonal marble font, finely decorated, and dated 1527. The *Accademia delle Belle Arti* is worth a visit. On the right of it stands the keep to the Fortress, built in the 13th cent. by Guglielmo Malaspina. A trip to the marble quarries is advised.

** CASALE MONFERRATO (Alessandria). Busy agricultural and industrial centre, on the right bank of the Po, and north-eastern extremity of the Montferrat hills. The *Duomo di Sant'Evasio* is an imposing and complex Romanesque-Lombard building, with a dynamic, gabled facade. The interior contains some interesting pictures and statues; an ambulatory runs around the chancel, with Romanesque sculptures on the walls. The Gothic church of *San Domenico* was built in 1469 for Guglielmo VIII Paleologo, with a Lombard-type facade in brick and heavily-accentuated buttresses. The interior, remodelled in the 19th cent., contains the tomb of Benvenuto San Giorgio, of the House of Biandrate, by Matteo Sanmicheli. The Baroque *Palazzo Gozzani di Treville*, seat of the Philharmonic Academy, is one of the greatest works of Giovanni Battista Scapitta (active in the first half of the 18th cent.). The vault in the entrance-hall is supported by double columns, and the majestic courtyard is full of statues. The *Palazzo di Anna di Alençon*, has a characteristic courtyard partly porticoed and part loggia. The panelled ceiling in one of the ground-floor halls is decorated with portraits of the Marquises of Montferrat. The church of *Santa Caterina* is another important work of Giovanni Battista Scapitta. Inside, the high altar with a marble group representing the Assumption of the Virgin, by Giovanni Battista Bernero (1780) should be noticed.

Casale Monferrato, Duomo, part of the vault.

* **CASAMARI** (Abbazia di), see Veroli.

* **CASARANO** (Lecce). Mainly agricultural town, grouped on a height in the Serre. The *Parrocchiale* (1712) is a large building. It contains a painting of the Blazing Furnace by Oronzo Tiso (1763), Souls in Purgatory by Giovanni Andrea Coppola (1597-c. 1659), and Baroque altars. The church of *Casaranello* or *Santa Maria della Croce* is the only survival of the ancient village, which ceased to exist in the 15th cent. It contains the only early-Christian-Byzantine mosaics in the region and a late 14th cent. fresco of Santa Maria della Croce.

* **CASCIA** (Perugia). Small town rich in works of art, it is also a summer and autumn holiday resort. In the Gothic church of *San Francesco* (1424) are frescoes by Bartolomeo di Tomaso da Foligno (lived in the first half of the 15th cent.), a Madonna and Child with two Saints, by Nicolò da Siena (recorded 1461-1463), and an important carved altar by Fiorenzo di Giuliano (recorded 1582-1602). In the Collegiate church of *Santa Maria*, erected in the 11-12th cent. and later remodelled, there are some remarkable works of art and a fine wooden tabernacle (1567) by Francesco Piergentili da Cascia. The pointed-arched doorway of the Gothic church of *Sant'Agostino* (1380) is much admired. Inside is a remarkable Umbrian-school fresco of the 15th cent. The famous *Santuario di Santa Rita* was built between 1937 and 1947 in a spurious Byzantine-Romanesque style, after the design of Spirito Maria Chiapetta; the facade, overlooked by two towers, is by Giuseppe Martinenghi. Inside are the Corpus Christi reliquary, St. Rita's Chapel, and the Chapel of Consolation.

* **CASCINA** (Pisa). On the left bank of the Arno, surrounded by medieval walls. The facade and right side of the 12th cent. *Oratorio di San Giovanni* are still intact. The oratory is Pisan in form, and has a basilican interior, with a nave and two aisles. It contains some 14th cent. frescoes, fine capitals and several sculp-

tures. The parish church of *Santa Maria* dates back to the 12th cent., and the original right side and facade are still in good condition. The basilican interior consists of a nave and two aisles.

** **CASERTA**. Situated in the plain at the foot of the gentle range of hills culminating in Monte Tifata (604 metres). The *Palazzo Reale*, a building of exceptional size, was erected between 1752 and 1774 to the design of Luigi Vanvitelli (1700-1773), for King Charles of Bourbon, whose ambition it was to create his own Versailles. Work proceeded rapidly, but was interrupted in 1764, when the finished parts were taken over by starving survivors of the plague. Luigi Vanvitelli was succeeded by his son Carlo (1739-1821). The building, one of the most splendid in Italy, was eventually finished in 1774, and decoration began on the interior. The palace is rectangular in plan (247 metres by 184), with four internal rectangular courtyards; it has five storeys and is 36 metres high. The main facade is enlivened with two hundred and forty-three windows and marked by three wide-arched entrances. The east and west sides are decorated with a long row of windows. The side facing the park has windows defined by fluted pilasters. The main entrance leads into an immense vestibule that runs round the whole palace, opening sidewise onto the four courtyards. The Grand Staircase has a

Casaranello, Santa Maria della Croce. Mosaic in the cross-vault, detail.

Cascina, Parish Church of St. Mary, facade.

Caserta, Park of the Royal Palace. Luigi Vanvitelli, Diana's Fountain.

Castelfranco Veneto, Duomo. Giorgione, Madonna
and Child with Saints Francis and Liberale, detail.

Castel Seprio, Santa Maria foris portas. Journey
to Bethlehem.

Castiglion Fiorentino, Collegiata. Segna di Bonaventura, Madonna and Saints, detail.
Castiglione Olona, Baptistery. Masolino da Panicale, Stories of John the Baptist, detail.

Cesena, Malatesta Library. Silver missorium, detail.

great central flight of stairs, which then divides into two parallel flights, and the double vault is frescoed with the Four Seasons and Palace of Apollo, by Girolamo Starace (recorded 1757-1783). In the apse of the Palatine Chapel is an Immaculate Conception by Giuseppe Bonito (1707-1789). In the Royal apartments, sumptuously decorated with marbles, stuccoes, paintings and period ornaments, there is the Hall of the Halberdiers; on the ceiling a picture of the Bourbon Arms supported by the Virtues, by Domenico Mondo (1732-1806). The Hall of the Guards contains twelve bas-reliefs representing events from ancient history by Gaetano Salomone (recorded 1781-1790), Paolo Persico (c. 1729-1780) and Tommaso Bucciano (lived in the 18-19th cent.). The Hall of Alexander has a vault embellished with a fresco representing the Marriage of Alexander and Roxana, by Mariano Rossi (1731-1807). The New Apartment (so called because it was the last to be built) consists of the Room of Mars, in Empire style, by Antonio De Simone, with twelve bas-reliefs illustrating episodes from the Iliad by Valerio Villareale (1773-1854), Claudio Monti (recorded 1805-1837), and Domenico Masucci (c. 1772-1818), as well as frescoes by Antonio Raffaele Calliano (1785-1824); the Room of Astrea, with gilt bas-reliefs by Valerio Villareale and Domenico Masucci; and the Throne Room, which is the largest (35 x 13 metres), carried out by Gaetano Genovese (1795-1860). The King's Apartment consists of: the Council Room, where Abraham Driving out Agar, by Raffaele Postiglione (1818-1897) and the Gipsy Prophesying Felice Peretti's succession to the Papacy, by Tommaso De Vivo (1787/90-1884) can be admired; Francis II's Bedroom, with Theseus and the Dead Minotaur painted on the ceiling, by Giuseppe Cammarano (1766-1850); a drawing-room, with frescoed ceiling depicting Minerva advising Telemachus to leave Ithaca, by Francis Hill; and the Bedroom of Joachim Murat, in Empire style. In the Old Apartment are frescoes by Antonio De Dominici (lived from c. 1730-1800), and Fedele Fischietti (1734-c. 1789), and paintings with Allegories and Mythological legends, by Domenico Mondo. In The Art Gallery are still-life paintings by Italian and Dutch painters of the early 19th cent. and pictures referring to events in the House of the Farnese. The Court Theatre is an admirable example of 18th cent. theatre architecture. Painted on the ceiling is an Apollo killing the Serpent, by Crescenzo della Gamba (recorded 1759-1779). The Park, also designed by Luigi Vanvitelli, is three km long, and famous for the Margherita or Canestro Fountain, the Cascade of the Dolphins or Canalone, the Fountain of Aeolus, the Fountain of Ceres or Zampilliera, the Fountain of Venus and Adonis, the Grand Cascade, with a fall of 78 metres, and the Carolino Aquaduct. The English Garden, carried out under the supervision of Carlo Vanvitelli, contains plane trees, Lebanon cedars, palm trees, pines and rare plants. Both the Park and the English Garden are dotted with statues and statuary groups, some good, others mediocre, which all go to show the artistic taste of the period.

** **CASERTA VECCHIA** (Caserta). Situated on the slopes of Monte Virgo (620 metres), it is a small medieval town clustered round the Cathedral and tiny church of the Annunziata. The *Cattedrale*, dedicated to St. Michael, and erected in the 12th cent., is in Sicilian-Moslem style, with reminiscences of Romanesque and Apulian architecture. The marble and tufa facade has three scalloped entrance-doors. The exterior of the slender dome has an octagonal drum with two orders of blind arches. The campanile, completed in 1234, reveals Gothic influence. The interior, in the form of a Latin cross, is divided into three by rows of monolithic columns, presumably taken from a temple dedicated to Jupiter Tifatinus, a refined holy-water stoup with Corinthian capital, medieval in origin, a 13th cent. pulpit with mosaic decorations, a 14th cent. fresco of the Madonna and Child, an admirable candelabra to hold the Paschal candle, on four legs, the tomb of Francesco II della Ratta, Count of Caserta, who died in 1359, with twisted and knotted columns, and a Renaissance-style tabernacle for Holy Oil. The simple *Chiesetta dell'Annunziata* is a sweet little Gothic church, dating from the late 13th cent. Three harmonious, single-lighted ogival openings, surmounted by a rose, mark the facade, which is preceded by an 18th cent. portico.

Caserta, Royal Palace, facade.

The aisleless interior is brightened by large single-lighted windows, and contains a valuable holy-water stoup, supported by a lion. Not far from the town can be seen abundant remains of the *Castello*, probably built in the 9th cent., with six towers, now lost, and a picturesque keep – a massive cylindrical block which has survived intact.

* CASSANO D'ADDA (Milan). Large village built on a rise, to the right of the river Adda. The *Castello Borromeo d'Adda*, whose origins are pre-1000 A.D., was rebuilt in later periods. It has an interesting inner courtyard with pointed-arched porticoes. The mid-18th cent. *Villa Borromeo* formerly d'Adda, was almost entirely remodelled in neo-Classical style in 1781 by Giuseppe Piermarini (1734-1808). The *Parrocchiale* (parish church) has a 14th cent. campanile. Inside is a polyptych by Bernardino di Lorenzo Fasolo (1489-post 1526).

Cassano d'Adda, Villa Borromeo d'Adda.

** CASSINO (Frosinone). Situated on the river Rapido, and dominated by the mountain where the famous abbey of Montecassino stands. The archeological area (*Zona Archeologica*) contains survivals of a Roman amphitheatre, (first cent. A.D.), the Crucifixion Chapel, a large cruciform building which was turned into a Christian church around 1000 A.D. and a semi-circular Theatre, with excavated auditorium and orchestra. Walk to the *Terme Monticello*, formerly known as the Varroniane. The *Abbazia di Montecassino* is 8½ km from the town and can be reached by road. Founded in the 6th cent. A.D., it is one of the most famous Christian monasteries in the world, and has been completely rebuilt after the devastation wreaked on it during the Second World War. In the year 529 St. Benedict arrived at Casinum. On the Acropolis, where there was a temple to Apollo, he built an oratory and monks' dwellings, and it was from these humble beginnings that the great Abbey emerged. In 581 Duke Zotone of the Longobards sacked the colony, and the monks fled to Rome. They were re-established at Montecassino in the first half of the 8th cent., and the Abbey became increasingly rich and powerful, asserting itself as one of the most important cultural centres in Europe. In 883 it was attacked by the Saracens, who set fire to the buildings and killed the monks. They

returned in 950, and in the latter half of the 11th cent. Desiderio, son of Landone, Prince of Benevento, rebuilt the ruined and crumbling buildings and erected others. The renovated Abbey was consecrated on 1st October 1071 by Pope Alexander I. On account of its importance and strategic position, it was involved in political struggles in the 13th and 14th cent. Largely destroyed by an earthquake on 9th September 1349, it took on a new lease of life in the early 15th cent., when the buildings were reconstructed or repaired. They stand on a roughly rectangular plan comprising three cloisters, the Church and the Monastery itself. The most attractive part is the Benefactors' Cloister, so called after the statues of benefactors to the Abbey which used to stand under the portico (designed by Antonio da Sangallo the Younger, 1483-1546). Unfortunately they were almost all destroyed during hostilities in 1943-44. The Church has three entrance-doors. The interior, mainly the work of the architects Cosimo Fanzago (1593-1678) and Giovanni Battista Contini (1641-1723), contains a few works of art, but very little in comparison with the treasures the church boasted prior to its destruction in the War. We can mention here: Abraham giving hospitality to the Angels, by Nicola Malinconico (1673-1721), Deborah the Prophetess, by the same painter, Last Communion of St. Benedict, by Sebastiano Conca (c. 1680-1764), Saints Benedict and Scholastica, by Giuseppe Cesari called Cavaliere d'Arpino (1568-1640), and part of the tomb of Pietro de' Medici, son and successor to Lorenzo il Magnifico.

* CASTEGGIO (Pavia). Agricultural and industrial centre, with ancient and modern parts. The *Oratorio di San Sebastiano*, built in the second half of the 18th cent. to a design by Lorenzo Cassani (1687-post 1766), contains choirstalls belonging to the same period. The ancient *Parrocchiale di San Pietro Martire* was rebuilt in 1817. It has a 14th cent. bell-tower with a cone-shaped cusp.

* CASTELBUONO (Palermo). Important village lying in a fertile hollow in the Madonie. It was founded on the ruins of the Byzantine Ypsigro in 1316, when Francesco Ventimiglia erected the sturdy castle which was to become his descendants' family seat. The mid-14th cent. *Matrice Vecchia* is dedicated to the Assunta, and is flanked by a robust bell-tower. The interior contains a few works of art such as an impressive late-15th cent. marble ciborium by Giorgio da Milano (recorded 1487-1496), and a huge polyptych in a Gothic frame, representing the Eternal, the Annunciation, the Madonna and Child, Saints, and an Ecce Homo and Apostles, by an unknown Sicilian artist (possibly working at the beginning of the 16th cent.). The early 17th cent. *Matrice Nuova* is dedicated to the Nativity of the Virgin. It

contains important altars and stuccoes, a triptych representing the Madonna and Child and Saints Anthony and Agatha, by an unknown 16th cent. artist, St. Peter receiving the Keys, by Giuseppe Velasquez (1750-1827), and a Gothic monstrance by Bartolomeo Tantillo (active in the first half of the 16th cent.). The *Castello*, a massive square-towered construction, contains the Chapel of St. Anne, which is entirely faced with Serpottiano stuccoes. In the late-medieval church of *San Francesco* there is a statue of the Madonna and Child, probably by Antonello Gagini (1478-1536).

** CASTEL DEL MONTE (Bari).

One of the architectonic wonders of southern Italy, in a position of unrivalled beauty, it is a constant tourist attraction. It is within easy reach of Ruvo, Andria and Corato. Begun before 1240, it was completed within a decade. It was disfigured on several occasions and restored last century and this. The architect whose genius created it is unknown, though tradition has it that the design was made by Frederick II himself. It stands on an octagonal plan and has eight octagonal towers on the corners. The ground floor consists of eight trapezoid-shaped rooms corresponding to the eight sides of the octagon, and intercommunicating. The octagonal plan is repeated in the courtyard;

Castelbuono, Castle Chapel, stuccoes.
Castel del Monte, exterior.

windows and doors of varying styles open onto it, without any precise symmetry. The upper floor also has eight trapezoidal rooms, identical to those on the ground floor, and brightened on the external side by two and three-lighted windows, with fine Gothic arching, and a marble ledge running along the walls to sit on. Of particular interest (eighth room, upper floor) is the exquisite carving of a fawn's head on a vault keystone. The castle affords a sweeping view of the Murge and Tavoliere right up to the Gargano and the Lucan Apennines, overlooked by Monte Vulture.

* CASTEL DI SANGRO (L'Aquila).

Attractive town with important medieval remains. The *Cattedrale dell'Assunta* is a fine building, the facade being the result of various attempts at remodelling, from the 13th cent. onwards. Inside, on the font, is a bronze group representing Christ's Baptism, probably by Amico di Bartolomeo da Castel di Sangro (lived in the 15th cent.). Other works of art include a precious altar-frontal in carved wood (15th cent.), a splendid Neapolitan bishop's throne (18th cent.), an Abruzzi-style chalice (15th cent.) and an 18th cent. processional cross.

* CASTELFIDARDO (Ancona).

In an attractive and panoramic setting. The *Monumento Commemorativo della Battaglia di Castelfidardo* is a bronze monument by Vito Pardo (1872-1933) to commemorate the decisive victory by the Piedmontese army over the papal troops on 18th September 1860. In the ancient *Palazzo Municipale*, restored in the latter half of the 18th cent., is a Coats-of-Arms Hall, where the emblems of the cities in the Marches are collected. The church of *San Francesco* has an important carved-wood choir, of the 17th cent. In the park (*Giardino Pubblico*), are interesting survivals of medieval walls.

* CASTELFIORENTINO (Florence).

Extending over a plain and low hill, to the right of the river Elsa. The church of *San Francesco*, begun in the early 13th cent., contains an admirable 14th cent. fresco depicting St. Francis handing the rules to monks and nuns with

Castel di Sangro, Cathedral of the Assunta.

Angels, and a panel representing the Pietà and Saints, attributed to a pupil of Filippino Lippi (c. 1457-1504). The 18th cent. church of *Santa Verdiana* has a lively Baroque facade, a slender campanile and, inside, paintings by Alessandro Gherardini (1655-1723) and Giovanni di Isidoro Baratta (1670-1747). An art gallery (*Pinacoteca*) is annexed to the church, containing works by 14-16th cent. Tuscan artists.

* **CASTELFRANCO EMILIA** (Modena). Agricultural and commercial centre, perhaps corresponding to the Roman Forum Gallorum. In the apse of the parish church of the *Assunta*, is an Assumption of the Virgin painted by Guido Reni (1575-1642). In the 17-18th cent. church of *San Giacomo* is a Virgin in Glory and Saints Rita, Sebastian and Rocco, painted by Alessandro Tiarini (1577-1642), and Our Lady of Loreto and Saints, by Elisabetta Sirani (1638-1665).

** **CASTELFRANCO VENETO** (Treviso). Pleasant little town on the left bank of the Musone. The Palladian-style *Duomo* was designed by Francesco Preti (1701-1774) and contains some important works of art including a masterpiece by Giorgio Barbarelli called Giorgione (1478-1510), depicting the Madonna and Child enthroned and Saints Francis and Liberale. There are also paintings by Jacopo Palma the Younger (1544-1628), Paolo Caliari called Veronese (1528-1588) and Francesco Maffei (1600-1660). The *Castello* was formerly a Treviso fortress, and has survived almost intact. The *Villa Revedin-Bolasco*, designed by Vincenzo Scamozzi (1552-1616), is an impressive construction. In the park there is an open-air theatre surrounded by statues from the workshop of Orazio Marinali (1643-1720).

* **CASTEL GANDOLFO** (Rome). On the west shore of Lake Albano. The central square of Liberty has a fountain by Gian Lorenzo Bernini (1598-1680) are the church of St. Thomas and the Pope's Palace. The *Palazzo Papale*, erected between 1624 and 1629 for Pope Urban VIII, to the design of Carlo Maderno, was later enlarged and remodelled. The church of *San Tommaso* is by Bernini (1661); the interior, in the form of a Greek cross, contains works by Pietro da Cortona (1596-1669), and Antonio Raggi (1624-1686).

* **CASTELLANA GROTTE** (Bari). Agricotural centre on the edge of a karst depression, in an area dotted with dolines, grottoes and chasms. The *Grotte di Castellana* are the must impressive underground caves in Italy. Discovered on 23rd January 1938 by Franco Anelli, they are the result of a group of solution cavities with few branches. The stalactite and stalagmite formations are most awe-inspiring. The huge caves have been given picturesque names such as White Grotto, Monument Ca-

vern, Angel Corridor, Owl Cavern, Grotto of the Crib, Snake Passage, Altar Cave, Precipice Cavern, Desert Passage, etc. In the area called the "kingdom of alabaster" are the Curtain Room and Milan Cathedral, so called since the pinnacles repeat the pattern of Milan's famous monument. The caves have not yet been explored completely. Having seen the ones that can be visited, climb up the tower to obtain a sweeping view of the countryside around Castellana, with its green olive-groves, vineyards and almond-trees.

* **CASTELLANETA** (Taranto). Unusual town almost entirely surrounded by a deep ravine, which is one of the most impressive erosion valleys in the Murge. The town consists of an ancient and a modern part, the ancient part being divided into two quarters: Sacco and Muricello, with houses huddled together on the sides of the promontory leading to the Cathedral. The *Cattedrale*, dedicated to the Assunta, was begun in the 13th cent., completed in the 14th, and rebuilt in the 18th. It has an undistinguished facade (1771) and on the left a crude 14th cent. bell-tower with large mullions. Inside, one can admire the splendid ceiling with gilded cornices enclosing paintings by Carlo Porta (1713-1763), three paintings by Domenico Carella (1721-1813), Trinity, Mary and St. Nicholas of Bari, a valuable painting by an unknown artist at the turn of the 16th cent. In the church of *Santa Maria del Rifugio* are two valuable 16th cent. holy-water stoups, in marble.

* **CASTELLARANO** (Reggio Emilia). First a lake-dwelling settlement on piles, then a Roman town, it is now an industrial centre. The parish church of *Santa Maria* preserves remains of a crypt with a 12th cent. lunette. The *Castello* used to be a remarkable building, but was seriously war-damaged in 1944. In the nearby district of San Valentino is a parish church (*Parrocchiale*) containing an important panel of the Madonna and Child with Saints Eleucadio and Stephen, by Benvenuto Tisi called Garofalo (1481-1559).

Castellana Grotte, the White Grotto.

* **CASTELL'ARQUATO** (Piacenza). Medieval in atmosphere, it stands on a hill rich in fossil shells. The Romanesque *Collegiata*, dedicated to the Assunta, dates back to the first half of the 12th cent. It houses the 15th cent. Gothic chapel of St. Catherine, with 15th cent. frescoes. In the Collegiate Museum are sacred vestments, lapidary material and a picture gallery. *Palazzo Pretorio* is a late-13th cent. palace, with a pentagonal tower. The massive *Rocca* has battlemented towers and was built in 1343 by the Piacentini. The *Palazzo del Duca* is the 12-14th cent. Ducal Palace; below is the fountain known as the "Fontanone del duca", dated 1292.

* **CASTELLEONE** (Cremona). Agricultural and cheese-making centre, with historical associations. The Renaissance church of *Santi Filippo e Giacomo* was designed by Agostino De Fonduti (lived in the 14-15th cent.). It contains a Madonna and Child with Saints, and an Assumption of the Virgin, by Luigi Miradori called Genovesino (recorded 1639-1654). In the neighbourhood is the *Santuario della Madonna della Misericordia*, also designed by Agostino De Fonduti, with Bramantesque tiburium. Inside are 16th cent. frescoes.

* **CASTEL RITALDI** (Perugia). In a picturesque setting, with well-preserved 13th cent. castle. It stands on the site of a Roman village. In the parish church of *Santa Marina* is an Our Lady of Mercy, by Lattanzio di Niccolò Alunno (recorded 1480-1527) and a beautiful fresco by Tiberio d'Assisi (c. 1470-1524). The church of *San Nicola* has a much-admired portal (1486) and a remarkable fresco of the school of Giovanni di Pietro called Spagna.

Castell'Arquato, Colleggiata, apse.

* **CASTEL SAN PIETRO TERME** (Bologna). On the left bank of the Sillaro. The parish church of *Santa Maria Maggiore* was first built in the 13th cent. and still has a 14th cent. campanile. It was restructured in the 15th cent. (see the lunette in the portal with terracottas from the school of Niccolò dell'Arca) and again in the 18th. The 17th cent. Church and Capuchin Convent (*Chiesa* and *Convento dei Cappuccini*) contain an important lapidary collection and paintings by Lucio Massari (c. 1568-1633), and Giuseppe Marchesi called Sansone (c. 1699-1771).

* **CASTELSARDO** (Sassari). Characteristic and attractive little town situated on a promontory formed by a sloping trachytic bank, with a magnificent view over the bay and mountains of the Asinara on one side and the Gallura mountains on the other. It has narrow, stepped streets and is still surrounded by the ancient walls. The late-Gothic, *Cattedrale* (16th cent.) stands high above the sea. It contains a valuable votive tablet depicting the Madonna and Child with Angels, by an unknown artist of the latter half of the 15th cent. The *Rocca*, perched on the very top of the heights, affords a wonderful view. Excursion to the tiny church of *Nostra Signora de Tergu*, probably built on the spot where there was first a proto-Sardinian and then a Roman temple. Not far away is the *Elefante*, a trachytic mass of rock with an uncanny resemblance to a crouching elephant.

* **CASTEL SEPRIO** (Varese). The *Rovine di "Sibrium"* are the ruins of an ancient castle (possibly 5-6th cent. A.D.) and village destroyed by the Visconti at the end of the 13th cent. Excavation work has unearthed traces of the walls, the bridge linking the lake to the castle, the basilica of St. John, its baptistery, a reservoir, and the church of St. Paul. The most interesting monument is the church of *Santa Maria foris portas*, mainly because of its rare Oriental-origin construction, (mid-8th cent.) and for a precious cycle of frescoes, probably dating back to the 8-9th cent.

Castel Seprio, Santa Maria foris portas.

* CASTELVETRANO (Trapani). Large agricultural centre. The 16th cent. *Chiesa Madre* is dedicated to the Assunta. It preserves some works of art such as an Assumption by Orazio Ferraro (recorded 1594-1622) and stuccoes by Antonio Ferraro (lived in the 16th cent.). In the 15th cent. church of *San Domenico* one can admire stuccoes and frescoes again by Antonino Ferraro. The church of *San Giovanni Battista*, rebuilt at the end of the 18th cent., contains a marble statue of the Baptist by Antonello Gagini (1478-1536). In the Town Hall can be found the famous *Efebo di Selinunte* a bronze statue of the first half of the 5th cent. B.C. In the neighbourhood is the *Tempietto della SS. Trinità di Delia*, a 12th cent. Norman construction. The interior, in the form of a Greek cross inscribed in a square, is surmounted by an Arab-style dome resting on four columns.

* CASTIGLIONE DEL LAGO (Perugia). Situated on an oval-shaped promontory, on the shores of Lake Trasimeno, it is surrounded by sturdy medieval walls and a powerful castle. Remains of tombs and other findings show that the site was already inhabited in Etruscan times. The castle was erected in the Middle Ages. The church of the *Maddalena* has a neo-Classical pronaos; the interior is in the shape of a Greek cross and contains stuccoes and modern paintings as well as a panel dated 1500, depicting a Madonna and Child, Saints Anthony Abbot and Mary Magdalen. In the ancient *Palazzo Ducale dei Della Corgna*, the present-day Town Hall, there are frescoes and paintings of mythological scenes, from the latter half of the 16th cent. The *Castello* is remarkable for its walls with square and cylindrical towers and tall triangular keep. Within easy reach of Castiglione del Lago is Panicale, a fascinating

Castelvetrano, Temple of the SS. Trinità di Delia, dome interior.

village, perched on the spur of a hill. It boasts some remarkable monuments, including the church of *San Sebastiano*, mentioned here because the wall above the high altar is decorated with a Martyrdom of St. Sebastian, considered to be one of the most successful works produced in his home territory by Pietro di Cristoforo Vannucci called Perugino (1445-1523).

* CASTIGLIONE DELLE STIVIERE (Mantua). Agricultural and industrial town, on the outer slope of the morainic amphitheatre of Lake Garda, it has a historical centre and rapidly-spreading modern districts. The *Santuario di San Luigi*, the foundation stone of which was laid in 1612 by order of Francesco Gonzaga, brother to Saint Louis Gonzaga, contains a Death and Glory of St. Louis by Giorgio Anselmi (1723-1797), and Madonna and Child with St. Louis by Antonio Balestra (1666-1740). The interior of the *Duomo* was decorated by Luigi Sicurtà (active in the latter half of the 18th cent.), and contains a Betrothal of the Virgin, attributed to Camillo Procaccini (c. 1551-1629). The Collegio delle Nobili Vergini (Young Ladies' College) houses the *Museo Storico Aloisiano*, with its collection of precious paintings including a Holy Scene by Federico Fiori called Baroccio (1535-1612) and Burial of Christ by Pieter Pourbus (c. 1510-1585).

* CASTIGLIONE DI GARFAGNANA (Lucca). The early 15th cent. church of *San Michele* contains a valuable Madonna and Child, the only work signed by Giuliano di Simone (1389). The church of *San Pietro*, built at the end of the 12th cent., preserves its original Romanesque facade. *Rocca* and picturesque 14th cent. fortifications. Walk to San Pellegrino in Alpe, where the *Santuario di San Pellegrino* stands. The Saint retired into these hills to meditate, and he is buried here, together with San Bianco.

* CASTIGLIONE D'ORCIA (Siena). Situated on the summit of a hill on the northern slopes of the Amiata. In the *Pieve* are preserved frescoes of the Sienese school and a Madonna and Child by Pietro Lorenzetti (1280-c. 1348). In the church of *Santa Maria Maddalena* there is a Madonna attributed to Lippo Memmi (recorded 1317-1356) and a deteriorated panel by Lorenzo di Pietro called Vecchietta (c. 1412-1480). In the neighbourhood is Rocca d'Orcia, with the church of *San Simeone* containing an Our Lady of Succour by Bartolo di Fredi (c. 1330-1410) and a Madonna and Child by Giovanni di Paolo (c. 1403-1482).

* CASTIGLION FIORENTINO (Arezzo). Picturesque village, on a particularly attractive hillside overlooking the Valdichiana. The Romanesque church of *San Francesco* reflects Gothic influence. It contains a St. Francis by Margaritone d'Arezzo (lived in the 13th cent.)

In the *Palazzo Comunale* is a gallery with works of art almost all from the church of St. Francis and Collegiate Church of St. Julian, including an Our Lady of Succour from the workshop of Luca Signorelli (c. 1441-1523), and a panel by Bartolomeo della Gatta (1448-1502), depicting St. Francis receiving the stigmata. The *Collegiata di San Giuliano* was rebuilt around the middle of the 19th cent. Inside can be found a valuable Della Robbia terracotta of St. Anthony Abbot, a Madonna and Child enthroned, with Saints Julian, Peter, Paul and Michael by Bartolomeo della Gatta, a Madonna and Saints by Segna di Bonaventura, and important carved-wood choirstalls (17th cent.). Walk to the *Castello di Montecchio Vesponi*.

* CASTIGLIONE OLONA (Varese). Situated in the Olona Valley. The name of the village is linked with Cardinal Branda Castiglioni, by whom it was almost entirely rebuilt between 1421 and 1441. The *Casa Castiglioni* is worthy of note, with its 15th cent. doorway and 14th cent. loggia. The *Chiesa di Villa*, built after the style of Brunelleschi between 1430 and 1441, contains the Castiglioni tomb, of the Amadeo school (1485). The *Collegiata* (1421) has frescoes by Masolino da Panicale (1383?-c.1440) and Lorenzo Vecchietta (c. 1412-1480). Beside it is the *Battistero* with a beautiful baptismal font and a valuable series of frescoes by Masolino, depicting scenes from the life of John the Baptist.

Castiglione Olona, Baptistery. Masolino da Panicale, Stories of John the Baptist.

* CASTROCARO TERME (Forlì). Popular spa in the foothills of the Apennines situated on the left bank of the Montone, with an ancient quarter. The parish church of *Santi Nicolò e Francesco* contains a beautiful panel of the Adoration of the Child, by Marco Palmezzano (1459-1539), a painting of the Visitation, by Francesco Longhi (c. 1544-1620) and a Madonna del Carmine attributed to Carlo Cignani (1628-1719). The church of *San Nicolò*, first built in the 11th cent., contains interesting 16th cent. frescoes.

* CASTROREALE (Messina). Situated in the attractive Longano valley in a fairly hilly area. The 15th cent. *Chiesa Matrice* is dedicated to the Assunta. It has a doorway dating from the first half of the 18th cent and contains a Pietà by Francesco Cardillo (lived in the 16-17th cent.), a Purifying of the Souls, by Filippo Iannelli (lived in the 17th cent.), an Our Lady of the Dying, also by Iannelli, and statues by Antonello Gagini (1478-1536). The church of *Santa Maria degli Angeli* contains a polyptych of the Nativity, possibly by Marco Pino (c. 1525-c. 1587). The church of *Candelora* has a wooden high altar with a group depicting the Presentation of Jesus, by Giovanni Siracusano (recorded 1583-1628). The small church of *Sant'Agata* contains an Annunciation by Antonello Gagini, statues of the same school, and another statue, of the Madonna and Child, by Michelangelo Naccherino (1550-1662). The *Torre di Federico II* is all that remains of the castle built in 1324 by Frederick II of Aragon. The church of *Santa Maria di Gesù* contains the tomb of Geronimo Rosso by Antonello Gagini.

* CASTROVILLARI (Cosenza). Situated on a rock between the rivers Coscile and Fiumicello. The ancient quarter is a maze of crooked little alleys, but interesting artistically. The modern part, on a plain, has wide straight roads. The square-shaped *Castello* was built at the end of the 15th cent. It has cylindrical

Castrovillari, Keep of the Aragonese Castle.

corner towers and a marble tablet with the Aragonese coat-of-arms over the doorway. The *Chiesa delle Pentite* contains a painting of the Madonna and Child by Giuseppe Marullo (probably died in 1685). The church of *Santa Maria del Castello* was erected towards the end of the 11th cent., rebuilt in the 14th and badly restored in the 18th. It has a facade with two doorways in the centre. Inside, on the high altar, is a panel depicting the Assumption (1560), and a Madonna and Child with Saints Barbara and Lawrence (1552), by Pietro Negrone.

*** CATANIA.

On the shores of the Ionian Sea, at the foot of Etna. It is Sicily's second city, after Palermo, as regards population and commercial importance. Destroyed again and again by earthquakes and volcanic eruptions, it has been rebuilt on each occasion, each time gaining in size and importance. Nowadays, inside the ancient city walls, are wide straight roads, and monuments mostly Baroque in style. The town already existed in 729 B.C., when it was taken over by the Calcidians. It was enlarged, and temples, gymnasiums, theatres and baths were added. In 263 B.C. it was conquered by the Romans, who restored the ancient monuments and built new ones, including the impressive amphitheatre. The *Duomo*, first built in 1092 and dedicated to St. Agatha, patroness of the city, was rebuilt at the beginning of the 18th cent. It has a fine facade with two orders of columns, by Giovanni Battista Vaccarini (1702-1768). Two sides are enclosed by a marble balustrade on which are nine statues of Catanian and other Sicilian saints. The spectacular interior contains paintings by William Borremans (1670-1744) and sculptures by Giovanni Battista Mazzola (recorded 1513-1550). Notice also the tomb of the composer Vincenzo Bellini, and a 3rd cent. Roman sarcophagus containing the remains of Ara-

gonese kings. The chapel of St. Agatha contains a marble triptych representing St. Agatha being crowned by Jesus, and Mary Magdalen with Saints Peter and Paul, by Antonello Freri (recorded 1479-1513), and the Treasury of St. Agatha. In the chancel are frescoes by Giovan Battista Corradini (recorded in the first half of the 17th cent.). The *Castello Ursino*, built for Frederick II of Swabia towards the middle of the 13th cent., was designed by Riccardo da Lentini (recorded 1239-1250). It is an impressive construction, one-time residence of kings and seat of parliament. The outermost parts were destroyed by lava during the eruption of Etna in 1669, but recent restoration work has given them back their ancient grandeur. The castle houses the *Museo Comunale*, which consists mainly of the collections of Ignazio Paternò Castello, Prince of Bíscari, works from the monastery of San Nicolò collected by the Benedictines, and those of Baron Asmundo Zappalà. The most important items are the bust of an Emperor, remains of a Roman statue which adorned a basilica in Catania now no longer in existence, and the head of a Grecian youth (4th cent. B.C.). There is also a large collection of paintings and sculptures, mostly by local artists, and various other objects of artistic interest. The *Museo Belliniano*, set up in the house where Vincenzo Bellini was born, contains a collection of Bellini souvenirs. *Via dei Crociferi* is the most characteristic 18th cent. street of Catania. Several buildings of great architectural importance stand on either side of it, such as the church of St. Benedict, (early 18th cent.) at the top of a long flight of steps, with barrel-vaults covered with frescoes by Giovanni Tuccari (1667-1743); the Jesuits' Church, with a facade designed by Angelo Italia (lived in the 18th cent.); and the church of St. Julian, a beautiful Baroque building by Giovanni Battista Vaccarini, containing a painting of the Madonna delle Grazie and Saints

Catania, Castello Ursino.

Julian and Benedict, by Olivio Sozzi (1696-1765). The *Teatro Romano*, built on the slopes where the original acropolis stood, has been partially unearthed by excavations begun in 1967. The semicircular *Odeon*, near the Roman Theatre, was used for choir rehearsals and competitions. On the *Via Etnea*, the most important road in the town, with Etna in the background, are the Palazzo dell'Università, with a dynamic facade designed by Antonino Battaglia (recorded in the first half of the 19th cent.), and the Collegiate Church dating from the beginning of the 18th cent. It was designed by Angelo Italia and contains a painting of the Glory of Sant'Apollonia by Olivio Sozzi, as well as paintings by Giuseppe Sciuti (1834-1911). The church of *San Nicolò*, the largest in Sicily, was designed by Giovanni Battista Contini (1641-1723). The interior consists of a nave and two aisles divided by heavy pillars, and is awe-inspiring in its size and simplicity. There are still some interesting remains of the 2nd cent. oval-shaped amphitheatre (*Anfiteatro*) which once seated 16,000 spectators. The church of the *Trinità* has a dynamic facade in two orders and contains paintings of the Baptism of Jesus, and St. Benedict and the Blessed Trinity, by Olivio Sozzi, and St. John the Evangelist and the Madonna, by Sebastiano Conca (c. 1680-1764). The church of *Sant'Agata*, believed to be the best work of Giovan Battista Vaccarini, with a concave-convex facade, contains a few artistic works such as simple stuccoes and small Rococò choirstalls. The church of *Sant'Agata la Vetere* was rebuilt in the 18th cent. on the ruins of an early Christian basilica. It contains a painting of the Apparition of the Angel and St. Peter to St. Agatha (1777) by Antonio Pennisi, and a Madonna and Child by Giuseppe Sciuti. The church of *Santa Maria di Gesù* was rebuilt at the beginning of the 18th cent. It contains the 16th cent. Paternò Chapel, which fortunately escaped serious damage in the earthquakes in the second half of the 17th cent. In the chapel is a panel of the Madonna in Glory with Saints Agatha and Catherine, by Angelo di Chirico (recorded 1513-1525). Worth a visit is the *Villa Bellini*, a beautiful public park with floral decorations, and century-old trees.

** CATANZARO.

Situated on a rugged hill, near the meeting-point of the Musofalo and Fiumarella. The aisleless church of *San Domenico* or *del Rosario* is in the form of a Latin cross. It contains a Martyrdom of St. Peter of Verona, inspired by Mattia Preti (1613-1699), a Madonna of Victory (16th cent.) a Neapolitan-school Madonna of the Rosary, dated 1615, and a 15th cent. statue of the Redeemer. The *Duomo*, dedicated to the Assunta and Saints Peter and Paul, is of remote origin, but was rebuilt not long ago, after a disastrous earthquake shock. The huge interior is in the shape of a Latin cross and contains a successful

marble group (late 16th cent.) depicting the Madonna and Child, and a Crib containing thirty figures from an 18th cent. Neapolitan workshop. In the *Museo Provinciale* is an important collection of stone items, dating from the bronze and early iron ages, Roman remains, local ceramics, Abruzzi majolica, and a few paintings including the Glorification of Mary, probably by Mattia Preti. In the park (*Giardino Pubblico*), popularly known as "Paradise", are the busts of famous Calabrians including the philosopher Francesco Fiorentino da Sambiase, carved by Francesco Ierace (1854-1937). In the *Chiesetta dell'Osservanza*, is a Madonna of the Broom Flower, an exquisite statue by Antonello Gagini (1478-1536). Catanzaro has some characteristic streets, such as Via Bellavista, which leads to a belvedere overlooking the Bay of Squillace. Not far away is Catanzaro Marina, a popular seaside resort, from where one can reach the so-called Roccelletta del Vescovo di Squillace. Apparently constructed in the 11th cent., it was once a great cathedral but now the only remains are parts of the walls of the nave, the left and central apse and the crypt.

** CAVA DE' TIRRENI (Salerno).

Neat-looking town, with textile industries, lying in a fertile hollow, where tobacco and fruit are cultivated. The church of *San Francesco* has a solemn 17th cent. portal, and inside a much-admired high altar, with marble inlays. In the ceiling of the Basilica of the *Madonna dell'Olmo* are 17th and 18th cent. paintings, and, on the high altar, four statues of Saints by Francesco Ierace (1854-1937). Walk to Corpo di Cava, an attractive village with church of *Santa Maria Maggiore*, the ceiling of which is embellished with paintings illustrating Stories of the Virgin by Gennaro Rebolino (lived in the 18th cent.). Here is the famous *Abbazia della Trinità della Cava*, in an attractive setting, perched above the deep Selano torrent. The church, consecrated in 1092 by Pope Urban II, was rebuilt in 1757. The Baroque facade, in volcanic rock, was designed in 1772 by Giovanni Del Gaizo, and is crossed by two orders of fluted pilasters. The interior contains an important altarpiece by Vincenzo Morani (1809-1870) depicting the Martyrdom of St. Felicity and her Seven Sons, a 16th cent. Florentine-school painting of the Madonna delle Grazie, St. Mawr by Achille Guerra (1832-1903), and a precious 13th cent. ambo. In the Baroque Chapel of the Holy Fathers or Blessed Sacrament are four important marble statues (three from the 16th cent. and the fourth from the 18th) by unknown artists. The door on the left side of the church leads into the Monastery, which contains important frescoes of the first half of the 17th cent., and a bas-relief of the Crucifixion by Tino di Camaino (1285-1337). The 12th cent. Crypt in the so-called Longobard cemetery has columns taken from a Roman construction of the 3rd cent. A.D., and the chapel of St.

Germano was probably frescoed by Andrea da Salerno (c. 1490-1530). In the Museum of the Abbey of the Trinità della Cava are archeological remains and a few works of art.

* **CAVALESE** (Trent). Situated at the beginning of the Valle di Gambis, on a fertile plateau. The parish church of the *Assunta*, erected in the first half of the 12th cent., but completely rebuilt in later periods, has an 18th cent. campanile by Giuseppe Alberti (1640-1716). It contains fourteen Patrons, a painting by Orazio Giovanelli (1580-c. 1636), and a Last Supper by Giuseppe Alberti. In the neo-Classical *Chiesa dell'Addolorata* (1830) are pictures by Antonio Longo (1742-1820). Above the portal of the church of *San Vigilio* is a fresco by Antonio Longo. The *Palazzo*, begun in the 14th cent., has a frescoed facade, with tympanum, and was one-time summer residence of the Bishops of Trent. It contains an important picture gallery, with works by the Unterberger (local artists working in the 18th cent.), Francesco Lampi (1782-1852), Paolo Troger (1698-1763), Valentino Rovisi (1710-1772), Giuseppe Alberti, etc. In the public Park, notice the historic *Banco della Reson*, the seat where the Bishop's Vicar administered justice twice a year.

* **CECIMA** (Pavia). Agricultural centre in the Po valley near Pavia. In the Gothic parish church of *Santi Martino e Lazzaro* (1479) there is an important fresco of the Madonna and Child by an unknown artist of the first half of the 16th cent. Excursion to the 11th cent. abbey of *Sant'Alberto di Butrio;* in the church of St. Anthony are frescoes dated 1484. The church of St. Albert contains some valuable 15th cent. frescoes.

** **CEFALÙ** (Palermo). Situated at the foot of a high rock, it is a popular seaside resort.

Cefalù, Cathedral. Mosaics of the apse and of the triumphal arch.

The *Duomo* is one of the most admired places of worship of the Norman period. The foundation stone was laid in 1131 by order of King Roger II. The facade, designed by Giovanni Panettera (lived in the 13th cent.) has a horizontal crown and is flanked by two robust towers with three orders of single and mullioned openings. It has two rows of small blind loggias and a single, magnificent doorway. The majestic interior is divided into a nave and two aisles by two rows of columns with partly Roman and partly Byzantine capitals. It contains some interesting works of art. In the right-hand aisle there is a monument to Bishop Castelli, carried out in 1788 by Leonardo Pennino; in the transept, two gigantic columns with figured capitals, supporting a prodigious arch, and in the chancel mosaics on a gilt background, with Greek and Latin inscriptions. The square cloister is an elegant construction; three sides are porticoed with twin columns and a large number of double capitals. In the *Museo Mandralisca* is an archeological section with pre-historic, proto-historic, Greek and Roman remains, especially from the 4th cent. B.C., and Arab funerary steles (the most precious item is a bell-shaped bowl from Lipari, with caricatured figure of a tunny seller, of Siceliot manufacture, 4th cent. B.C.). There is an enormous collection of coins. The art gallery contains two Views of Venice inspired by the style of Francesco Guardi (1712-1793), Old Woman with Amphora and Ham by Dirck Baburen (active in the first half of the 17th cent.), a Madonna and Child by Antonello De Saliba (c. 1466-c.1535), a Holy Family by Vincenzo Catena (c. 1470-1531), a Last Supper by a pupil of Pietro Ruzzolone (recorded 1484-1526), paintings by Pietro Novelli (1603-1647) and, above all, Portrait of a Man, the pride of the gallery and masterpiece of Antonello da Messina (c. 1430-1479). In the science section, there is a collection of shells, with twenty thousand specimens, representing five hundred species, from seas all over the world. Remains of ancient walls (*Fortificazioni arcaiche*). Excursion to the *Santuario di Gibilmanna*, in a magnificent setting. The sanctuary belongs to the late 17th and early 18th cent., and contains a gigantic Madonna and Child (1534) and St. Helen, by the sculptor Fazio Gagini (1520-c. 1567).

* **CELANO** (L'Aquila). Overlooked by a ruined, yet still impressive castle. The *Chiesa del Carmine* was built in the 13th cent. but has remains from classical times. The facade is Baroque in style. Nearby is a round tower, survival of the ancient city walls. The 15th cent. church of *San Francesco*, with rough stone facade, was well restored in 1935. It has a remarkable Romanesque portal. The *Castello* is a great mass of rock, and still preserves its ancient charm. It was built in 1392 by Count Pietro di Celano, but completed by Leonello

Acclozzamorra. The central part is on a rectangular plan, and it is surrounded by walls with towers, unfortunately damaged in the earthquake of 1915. The church of *Sant'Angelo*, completed in 1451 by Leonello Acclozzamorra, has a Romanesque portal in the facade.

* **CENTO** (Ferrara). Industrial city on the left bank of the Reno. The 17th cent. *Chiesa del Rosario*, with an aisleless interior, contains paintings by Francesco Barbieri called Guercino (1591-1666). The Monte di Pietà palace

Celano, Castle.
Cento, Pinacoteca Civica. Zalone, St. Matthew and the Angel.

houses the *Pinacoteca Civica*, which contains innumerable works of art including detached decorative frescoes by Guercino, an Adoration of the Shepherds, by Pellegrino Tibaldi (1527-1596), a St. Matthew and the Angel by Zalone, and still-life paintings by Candido Vitali (1680-1753). The *Casa Provenzali* has frescoes by Guercino. Nearby is the village by *Pieve di Cento;* the collegiate church still preserves the bell-tower from the original Romanesque-Gothic construction, and there is a small art gallery.

* **CERCINA** (Town of Sesto Fiorentino, province of Florence). The parish church of *Santo Andrea*, recorded as far back as the 11th cent., still preserves its original Romanesque structure. The top of the belfry juts out sharply. The interior contains a revered Madonna enthroned and Child (13th cent. polychrome-wood panel). In the small cloister are 15th cent. frescoes in a poor condition.

* **CERIGNOLA** (Foggia). Situated on a fertile plain between the rivers Ofanto and Carapelle, on the southern edge of the Tavoliere of Apulia. The *Duomo*, designed by Enrico Alvino (1810-1876), is an impressive building in ogival Tuscan style. The interior, in the form of a Latin cross, contains a Byzantine-type panel of the Madonna di Ripalta, patron saint of the town.

* **CERRETO DI SPOLETO** (Perugia). Situated on a high spur between the rivers Nera and Vigi. The 12th cent. *Chiesa del Castello* is in a poor state of repair. It contains interesting frescoes of the Perugian school. On the high altar of the church of *San Giacomo* is a Visitation by Camillo di Gaspare Angelucci (recorded 1540-1585). In the *Oratorio della Misericordia* is a painting of the Crucifixion, also by Angelucci. *Montesanto* has a parish church with interesting altarpieces, the most beautiful of which is one of the Sacred Family, probably by Domenico Beccafumi (c. 1486-1651).

* **CERRETO SANNITA** (Benevento). Built where the Turio and Cappuccino streams flow into the Titerno, on a rectangular plan with wide, straight roads. The *Cattedrale*, was built in the second half of the 18th cent. It contains frescoes by Francesco Palumbo (recorded in the second half of the 18th cent.). The church of *San Gennaro* is a fine example of Baroque building. In the church of *San Rocco* is a statue of the Madonna of Providence by Silvestro Jacobelli (lived in the 18-19th cent.). The church of *Congregazione* contains a Madonna of Constantinople by Silvestro Jacobelli. Notice also, the parish church of *San Martino* (1702).

* **CERTALDO** (Florence). Built at the confluence of the Agliena and the Elsa, with ancient and modern quarters, it grew up around the

castle of the Counts Alberti di Vérnio. *Casa del Boccaccio* is the house where the great writer, Giovanni Boccaccio lived and died; in one of the rooms is a fresco by Pietro Benvenuti, painted in 1826, depicting Boccaccio seated at his desk. The *Palazzo Pretorio* was rebuilt in the 15th cent. and contains remains of frescoes by Pier Francesco Fiorentino. Worth a visit is the Sentence Room and the Trial Room, with a fresco of the Pietà by the Beato Angelico school, dated 1484.

** CERTOSA DI PAVIA (Pavia).

The *Certosa* is an important monument which combines the various artistic Lombard styles of the 15th cent. and later ones too. Building began on 27th August 1396 on the orders of Gian Galeazzo Visconti, who intended it to be a family mausoleum. The architects Giovanni Solari (1410-1480), Guiniforte Solari (1429-1481), Cristoforo Lombardo (lived in the 16th cent.), Martino Bassi (1542-1591), and others, contributed to its design. Since 1968 the Certosa has been looked after by the Cistercians, who took it over from various other orders who had cared for it over the centuries. From the internal courtyard is a lovely view of the beautiful facade, adorned with statues and various co-

loured marble decorations, begun in the early 15th cent. and finished in later times. The doorway is mainly the work of Benedetto Briosco (1483-1506) who followed the design of Giovanni Antonio Amadeo (c. 1447-1522). The simple and harmonious interior contains numerous works of art, including the Eternd by Perugino (1450-c. 1523), a St. Ambrose and Saints by Ambrogio da Fossano called Bergognone (c. 1455-1522), an Ecce Homo and Madonna and Child, also by Bergognone, frescoes by Daniele Crespi (c. 1600-1630), monument to Gian Galeazzo Visconti, founder of the Certosa, mainly carried out by Gian Cristoforo Romano (c. 1465-1512), 15th cent. windows, and monumental bronze candelabra. The doorway leading to the small courtyard is the work of Giovanni Antonio Amadeo. The large rectangular cloister is very interesting, with 122 arches, in the form that was common in the mid-15th cent. The Certosa Museum contains many valuable works including a Holy Conversation by Bartolomeo Montagna (c. 1450-1523).

** CERVETERI (Rome).

Attractive village on a tufa rise, with medieval quarter. The church of *Santa Maria* is a modern construction, added to a 12th cent. Romanesque church. It contains a panel of the Madonna and Child (1471) by Lorenzo da Viterbo, a Renaissance altar and panel depicting the Redeemer by an unknown 16th cent. artist. In the *Municipio* is a panel of a Saint by Perin del Vaga (1501-1547), and a 16th cent. Flemish triptych depicting the Adoration of the Magi. The *Necropoli di Cerveteri*, together with that of Tarquinia, is the most important of its kind. Exploration began in the mid-19th cent., and was intensified at the beginning of the present one. The 8th cent. B.C. tombs are open in the rock, the 7th cent. B.C. ones have stone covers and mounds, those from the 6th to the 2nd cent. B.C. are in the form of rooms with a vestibule, while those of the 4th-1st cent. B.C. are hypogea without mounds. Mention can be made here of the tomb of the Capitals, the tomb of the Funeral Beds, the tomb of the House with

Certaldo, Palazzo Pretorio.
Certosa di Pavia, facade.

Cerveteri, tomb of the alcove.

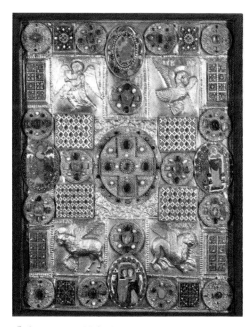

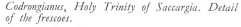

Codrongianus, Holy Trinity of Saccargia. Detail of the frescoes.

Città di Castello, Pinacoteca Comunale. Madonna enthroned, with angels and kneeling Dominican, detail.

Chiavenna, San Lorenzo. The Pax (prayer book cover).

Como, Museo Civico. Faustina and Liberata welcomed to the Convent, detail.

Como, Sant' Abbondio. Entry into Jerusalem and Journey towards Calvary.

Cremona, Cathedral. Jeremiah the Prophet.

Cremona, Museo Civico. Giuseppe Arcimboldi, Vegetable basket.

Cremona, Museo Civico. Benedetto Bembo, St. George, detail.

Thatched Roof, which is the most ancient of all; the tomb of the Dolii, the tomb of the Reliefs, also known as the Beautiful Tomb, the most interesting one in the whole necropolis, belonging to a Matuuna family, as the recently-deciphered Etruscan inscription reveals; the tomb of the Little House, made up of six communicating compartments, and the tomb of the Cornice; further off, outside the confines of the necropolis of Cerveteri, is the tomb of Marce Ursus, the tomb of the Greek Vases, the raised mound of the Colonel, the tumulus of Ophelia Maroi, from which Greek and Etruscan vases of the 6th cent. B.C. have been taken; the tomb of the Doric Columns, the tumulus of the Shields and Chairs, where there are small thrones and funeral beds, the tomb of the Painted Lions, and the Tumulus of the Painted Animals, with numerous compartments, the tumulus of the Ship in a room containing a picture of a ship, the tomb of the Sarcophaghi, with three alabaster sarcophaghi, the tomb of the Triclinium, the tomb of the Inscriptions or of the Tarquins, the tomb of the Alcove, etc. The *Necropoli del Sorbo* is a large ancient burial-ground, with individual tombs; in the Regolini-Galassi tomb (named after the scholars who explored it in 1837) there were a large number of fine oriental-style ornaments of the 6th cent. B.C. which have been transferred to the Gregorian Etruscan Museum. In the *Necropoli di Monte Abetone*, situated on tufa rocks, are the Campana tomb, and the Torlonia tumulus, with the tomb of the Chairs.

* **CERVIA** (Ravenna). Elegant seaside resort, also important for fishing. Little is left of the ancient Cervia, called Ficocle, as the area became unhealthy and the village was abandoned and demolished. The present-day town-centre was built to the design of Bellardino Berti (mentioned at the end of the 17th cent.). In the 18th cent. *Cattedrale dell'Assunta*, is a painting of the Madonna and Child by Barbara Longhi (1552-c.1638). *Milano Marittima* is a garden-town which has developed since 1950. The *Chiesetta della Madonna della Neve* or *delle Saline* is the only survival of Focicle.

* **CESENA** (Forlì). In the centre of the Romagna region, on the right bank of the Savio. The *Cattedrale*, dedicated to St. John the Baptist, was begun at the end of the 14th cent. and finished in the 15th. The large basilican interior has a nave and two aisles with marble statues representing Saints Leonard, Christopher and Eustace, by Lorenzo Bregno (recorded in 1523). The *Biblioteca Malatestiana*, on a basilican plan, has a nave and two aisles with eleven spans. It houses the Malatesta Novello codices, the codices of doctor Giovanni di Marco, and many other valuable texts. The church of *San Domenico* was rebuilt at the beginning of the 18th cent. to a design

by Francesco Zondini (recorded 1706-1745). It contains various works of art including a painting of the Madonna of the Rosary with St. Domenic and Petitioners, by Giuseppe Cesari called Cavalier d'Arpino (1568-1640), and St. Martin and the Beggar, a beautiful oval-shaped painting by Felice Torelli (1667-1748). The 12th cent. church of *Madonna del Monte* was rebuilt in the 18th cent. It has a spacious interior with a rich collection of votive offerings from the 15th cent. onwards, a painting of the Presentation of Christ in the Temple, by Francesco Raibolini called Francia (1450-1517), and an Annunciation by Bartolomeo Coda (recorded 1528-1562). The spectacular *Rocca Malatestiana* was rebuilt between 1466 and 1476.

* **CHERASCO** (Cuneo). The church of *San Martino* is Romanesque; and has an ancient bas-relief representing St. Martin on the facade. The church of *San Pietro* (13th cent.) has a bright Romanesque facade embellished with majolica cups and a fine marble frieze. The church of *Santa Maria del Popolo* was built in the 17th cent. The facade is high and intricate, and the interior is decorated with 18th cent. stuccowork. The *Museo Giambattista Adriani* contains an important collection of 12,000 coins.

* **CHIANCIANO** (Siena). In an attractive position, it lies within sight of Chianciano Terme, and Monte Cetona. It is probably Etruscan in origin. In the *Chiesetta della Misericordia* there is a fresco by Luca Signorelli (c. 1441-1523). The *Palazzo dell' Arcipretura* has a small collection of works from the Sienese and Tuscan schools.

* **CHIARAVALLE DELLA COLOMBA,** see Alseno.

* **CHIARAVALLE DI FIASTRA (ABBAZIA DI)** (Town of Tolentino, province of

Chiaravalle di Fiastra, Abbey.

89

Macerata). Situated in the valley of the Fiastra, it is an important Cistercian abbey which took the whole of the 12th cent. to complete. It was sacked in 1422 by the soldier of fortune Andrea Fortebracci, then well restored. The clear-lined facade has a fine Romanesque portal and the interior is impressive with Romanesque capitals. Behind the choir is a remarkable rose-window, in a quadrilobed circle, from which extend eight slender columns. The 14 or 15th cent. cloister and the Chapterhouse are worth visiting.

* CHIARAVALLE MILANESE, see Milan.

* CHIARI (Brescia). Small industrial town, with an ancient centre. The 15th cent. *Duomo*, dedicated to Saints Faustino and Giovita, was restructured in the 18th cent., and contains works of art including frescoes by Jacques Trécourt (1812-1882), a monument to Prevost Morelli by Gaetano Matteo Monti (1776-1847) and a Baptism of Christ carved by Abbondio Sangiorgio (1798-1879), as well as paintings by Cignaroli and Batoni. The 15th cent. church of *Santa Maria Maggiore* has a facade by Antonio Marchetti (1724-1791). The *Pinacoteca Repossi*, instituted in 1854, contains a large collection of engravings, statues and paintings, including St. James the Apostle, possibly by Caravaggio (1573-1610) and John the Baptist in a Cave, by Alessandro Magnasco (1667-1749).

* CHIAVARI (Genoa). On the right bank of the Entella, with an ancient and a modern part. The *Cattedrale* is dedicated to the Madonna dell'Orto and dates back to remote times. It was enlarged at the beginning of the 17th cent. and has an important pronaos (1841) by Luigi Poletti. The interior has many works in marble and gilded stucco, and a wooden composition representing the Temptations of St. Anthony, by Antonio Maria Maragliano (1664-1741). The *Biblioteca della Società Economica* contains fifty thousand volumes, eight

Chiavari, Fieschi Palace.

hundred manuscripts, and sixty incunabula. The 12th cent. church of *San Giovanni Battista*, completely restructured in later centuries, has a lovely modern marble facade, designed in 1935 by Gaetano Moretti. Worthwhile excursion to the *Basilica dei Fieschi*, built in the 13th cent. on the orders of Pope Innocent IV and his nephew Ottobono Fieschi; it is one of the most important and best-preserved monuments in eastern Liguria. A large tower rests on the cross-vault. Near the basilica is the *Palazzo dei Fieschi*, in Gothic-Pisan style.

* CHIAVENNA (Sondrio). On the banks of the Mera, dominated by high mountains. It is a tourist, commercial and industrial centre. The parish church of *San Lorenzo*, originally Romanesque in style, was rebuilt in 1538 after being destroyed by fire. It has an 18th cent. four-sided portico containing a painting of the Madonna and Child with Saints by Giovanni Pietro Ligari (1686-1752), and a Madonna and Child with St. Anthony by Giuseppe Nuvolone (1619-1703). In the Treasury are valuable works of art including a 12th cent. Pax or Evangelistary cover. The octagonal *Battistero* (8th cent.) has a Romanesque baptismal font dating from 1156. Worth seeing is the rock called *Paradiso* on which there was once a castle, destroyed in the 12th cent. by Frederick I Barbarossa.

** CHIERI (Turin). The *Cattedrale*, dedicated to Santa Maria della Scala, was built at the beginning of the 15th cent. The severe brick-work facade has a rich doorway. The interior contains eight round paintings depicting Doctors of the Church by Andrea Gastaldi (1826-1889), a fine 13th cent. baptistery, a marble icon, probably by Matteo Sanmicheli (recorded 1480-1534), 15-16th cent. Gothic-style wooden stalls, and a Treasury with rich reliquaries and frescoes by Gabriele Ferrero (1836-1906). Notice the chapel of the Madonna delle Grazie, erected by Bernardo Vittone in 1757-1759. The church of *San Domenico* was probably completed in 1307 but has been restructured several times. It has a large Gothic portal and, inside, paintings by Guglielmo Caccia called Moncalvo (c. 1568-1625). The Gothic church of *San Giorgio* stands at the highest point of the town. It contains a Madonna and Child, Massacre of the Innocents, and Resurrection, by Moncalvo, and a Head of St. George, in embossed silver, dating from the 13-14th cent. Notice also the church of *San Bernardino*, designed by Bernardo Antonio Vittone (c. 1704-1770) and the Baroque church of *Santa Margherita*, completed in 1671, with an impressive concave facade. Walk to the *Cappello del Cipresso*, possibly designed by Bernardo Antonio Vittone.

** CHIETI. Situated on the left bank of the Pescara, among olive-groves, with Roman and medieval remains. The ancient *Cattedrale di*

San Tommaso Apostolo, later St. Justin, was rebuilt in 840 by Bishop Teodorico I, and spoilt by restoration work carried out in the latter half of the last century. The campanile is tall and massive, with twin-columned, ogival mullions. It was begun in 1335 by Bartolomeo di Giacomo, and completed in 1498 by Antonio da Lodi. Inside, on the high altar, is an 18th cent. marble frontal representing Episodes from the Life of St. Justin, and, in the Treasury, a precious statue of the Saint. In four rooms of the *Palazzo Municipale* are precious pictures and antiques belonging to the African explorer Giovanni Chiarini (1849-1879). The *Villa Comunale* contains a bronze monument to the Fallen, by Pietro Canonica (1869-1962) and the bust of Giovanni Chiarini; it also houses the *Museo Archeologico*. The 1st cent. *Cisterna Romana* is one of the largest of its kind (60.20 m x 14.65 m). Worthy of attention in the *Museo di Arte Sacra* are a Barbarian cupital, of the 7th or 8th cent., a wooden statue of St. Benedict (12th cent.) and other wooden statues and busts of the 13-14th cent.

* **CHIGNOLO PO** (Pavia). Agricultural and industrial town, where one should pause to admire the *Castello Cusani Visconti*, now belonging to the Order of Malta; it is a Baroque transformation of a 15th cent. style, with high keep and turrets.

** **CHIOGGIA** (Venice). Picturesque little town on the southern tip of the Venetian Lagoon. The *Duomo*, which dates back to the 11th cent., was rebuilt in the 17th cent. to the design of Baldassare Longhena (1598-1682). It contains Venetian-school works of the 16-18th cent. In the Cathedral precinct is an important 14th cent. campanile. The *Chiesetta di San Martino* (1392) contains a polyptych of the school of Paolo Veneziano (recorded 1333-1362). The church of *San Domenico* was rebuilt in the 18th cent. It has a 14th cent. campanile and contains a painting of St. Paul by Vittore Carpaccio (c. 1455-c. 1526). *Forte di Brondolo* has a characteristic little church, dating back to the 10th cent.

* **CHIUSA** (Bolzano). Situated on the right bank of the Isarco, with 16th and 17th cent. houses. Annexed to the chapel of the *Ma-*

Chieti, Museo. Statuette of Hercules (from Venafro).

Chieti, Museo. The Warrior of Capestrano.

Chignolo Po, Castle, south facade.

91

donna di Loreto is a Treasury, formed in 1702, as a result of a donation by Queen Maria Anna of Spain. The most important paintings are a Madonna and Child, possibly by Bernardino Luini (c. 1490-1532), a San Giovannino, inspired by Leonardo da Vinci, an Immacolata by Luca Giordano (1632-1705), an Adoration of the Magi by the school of Albrecht Dürer (1471-1528), and Ascent to Calvary and Adoration of the Magi by the school of Peter Paul Rubens (1577-1640). The village is overlooked by the *Monastero di Sabiona*, built on the site of the Roman station of Sabiona. At the beginning of the 13th cent. there was a fortress here, which was converted into a Benedictine monastery in the years 1681-1685. The church of *Madonna*, designed by Giacomo Delai (active from 1648 to 1674) and Francesco Carloni (active in the 17th cent.) is octagonal in form. The dome is embellished with stuccoes and frescoes illustrating episodes from the Life of the Virgin by Stefano Kessler (1622-1700).

* **CHIUSI** (Siena). Once one of the most powerful of the twelve Etruscan Lucumons,

Chiusi, Museo Civico, Gualandi casket.

it is situated on a hill of olive trees. The 12th cent. *Duomo di San Secondiano* contains important paintings and frescoes. In the showcases in the Sacristy are 22 illuminated anthem books and objects of value. The *Museo Civico* houses an impressive collection of Etruscan objects, of great interest to scholars all over the world.

* **CHIVASSO** (Turin). On the left bank of the Po. The parish church of the *Assunta*, begun in the early 15th cent., has an ogival doorway decorated with terracottas representing the saints. Inside is a nave and two aisles divided by cruciform pillars. The 12th cent. octagonal tower in front of the church is all that remains of the castle of the Marquises of Montferrat.

* **CIANO D'ENZA** (Reggio Emilia). In ancient times called Cilianum, perhaps because it is perched on a ridge (*ciglio*) over the Enza. The 18th cent. *Parrocchiale* contains paintings of a Saint, a Warrior, and an Angel, attributed to Guido Reni (1575-1624). A road leads to the Panoramic *Castello di Rossena* (11th cent.).

** **CIMITILE** (Naples). Large agricultural centre near Nola, with early-Christian and medieval monuments. In a small square is the *Complesso di Basiliche* of exceptional scientific, early-Christian and medieval interest. It is dedicated to San Felice in Pincis, San Paolino, the Martyr Saints, and St. Caulonius. The basilica of St. Felice in Pincis, with valuable remains of mosaic decorations, is a four-sided portico in the centre of which there was once the tomb of St. Felice. The basilica of San Paolino has a nave and two aisles, and an apse with three choirs. The small basilica of the Martyr Saints is entered through a porch containing an inscription to Pope Leo III. It contains important frescoes and remains of a pagan hypogeum found during excavations.

** **CINGOLI** (Macerata). Situated on the slopes of Mount Cingulo or Circe, it is an attractive little town, completely built in stone,

Cingoli, Sant' Esuperanzio, interior.

with aristocratic mansions and picturesque streets. Owing to its position it is nicknamed the "Balcony of the Marches". The 13th cent. *Palazzo Municipale* is dominated by a Romanesque Clock-tower. It contains fragments of pre-Roman and Roman sculptures and inscriptions. It is the seat of the town archives, which include four hundred parchment scrolls from the 11th to 18th cent. The 17th cent. *Cattedrale* is a majestic building. Inside is a painting of San Gaetano da Thiene dying, by Pier Simone Fanelli (died 1703). The Canons' Sacristy is worth visiting; it contains a pentatych of the Madonna and Child with Saints, attributed to Antonio da Fabriano (active from 1450 to 1485). The *Balcone delle Marche* is one of the most wonderful vantage points in central Italy. The church of *San Domenico* contains a picture representing St. Domenic by Giovanni Andrea Lazzarini (1710-1801), a panel of the Madonna and Child enthroned and Saints, by Girolamo Nardini (active in the second decade of the 16th cent.) and, above all, a masterpiece of Lorenzo Lotto (1480-1556) depicting the Madonna and Child enthroned, Saints Esuperanzio, Catherine of Siena, Peter, Mary Magdalen, Thomas Aquinas, and Dominic, completed in the round by fifteen mysteries of the Rosary. The 13th cent. church of *Sant'Esuperanzio* is Romanesque-Gothic in form. It contains works of art including a fresco of the Madonna and Child, and Saints Esuperanzio and Bernardino by Antonio Solario (lived in the 15-16th cent.) or Pietro Paolo Agabiti (1470-1540), a polyptych representing the Madonna and Child with Saints, probably by Giovanni Antonio da Pesaro (recorded 1462-1511) and, in the priest's house, a Flagellation, late work of Sebastiano del Piombo (c. 1485-1547). In the sacristy of the church of *San Filippo* is a painting by Sebastiano Conca (c. 1680-1764).

* **CIRIÈ** (Turin). Situated at the beginning of the Valle di Lanzo. The 13-14th cent. *Duomo*, Romanesque-Gothic in style, was restored last century. The tripartite facade has a 15th cent. portal and is surmounted by a campanile decorated with mullioned openings. The interior is basilican, with a nave and two aisles; it contains a polyptych by Giuseppe Giovenone the Elder (1535) and a panel by Defendente Ferrari (active between 1511 and 1535). The church of *San Martino di Liramo* is Romanesque in origin (10-11th cent.) but was remodelled in the 18th cent. The original apses and campanile have been preserved; inside are 15th cent. frescoes.

* **CITTADELLA** (Padua). Agricultural and commercial centre, between the upper and lower plain of Venetia, it is surrounded by walls with four gateways corresponding to the cardinal points. The late 18th cent. *Parrocchiale*, neo-Classical in style, contains some important pictures, including a Supper at Emmaus by Jacopo da Ponte called Jacopo Bassano (c. 1510-1592), and Flagellation by Palma the Younger (1544-1628). Notice the well-preserved walls (*Antiche Mura*) with numerous rectangular towers.

* **CITTÀ DELLA PIEVE** (Perugia). Pleasant agricultural town overlooking the Chiani valley. The 12th cent. *Duomo dei Santi Gervasio e Protasio*, much restored in later centuries, is flanked by a Romanesque-Gothic companile. It contains a Madonna and Child, Two Angels, and Two Saints by Domenico Alfani (1480-1553), and a panel by Perugino (1445-1523) depicting the Madonna and Child with Saints Peter, Paul, Gervase, and Protasio. In the 13th cent. church of *San Francesco*, now a sanctuary of the Madonna of Fatima, is a painting of the Pentecost by Niccolò Circignani called Pomarancio (1580-1640). The *Oratorio di Santa Maria dei Bianchi* has a fresco of the Epiphany by Perugino. From Città della Pieve one can go to the *Santuario della Madonna di Mongiovino*. It has an octagonal dome, and was begun in 1513. Inside are frescoes depicting the Deposition from the Cross (1564) by Arrigo Fiammingo (c. 1530-1597), a fresco depicting the Resurrection (1569) by Niccolò Circignani called Pomarancio, fine portals and other valuable artistic works.

** **CITTÀ DI CASTELLO** (Perugia). Situated on the left bank of the Tiber, among fertile hills, with many medieval and Renaissance buildings. Illustrious artists worked here, such as Luca Signorelli (c. 1441-1523), Raphael (1483-1520), who produced here his famous Betrothal of the Virgin, now preserved in Milan, the Della Robbia (15th and early 16th cent.), the architect Antonio da Sangallo the Younger (1483-1546) and Giorgio Vasari (1511-1574). The 11th cent. *Duomo dei Santi Florido ed Amanzio*, has a valuable Gothic portal in a Baroque-inspired facade, and in the Treasury there is an altar-frontal in embossed and gilded silver, an admirable piece of goldsmith's work from the 12th cent., perhaps donated to the Cathedral by Pope Celestino II. In the *Pinacoteca* are rich artistic collections, including works by Antonio Vivarini (c. 1415-1476/84), Giovanni d'Alemagna (died 1450), Raphael,

Città di Castello, Palazzo Vitelli alla Cannoniera.

Luca Signorelli, and Domenico Ghirlandaio. The church of *Santa Maria Maggiore* is an important Renaissance construction. In the church of *San Francesco*, begun in Gothic style in 1237 and remodelled in the 18th cent. is the Cappella Vitelli, designed by Giorgio Vasari. Also worthy of attention are: the *Palazzo Comunale*, in rusticated stone, carried out between 1334 and 1352 by Angelo da Orvieto; the impressive Gothic church of *San Domenico*, containing 14th and 15th cent. frescoes; and the 16th cent. *Palazzo Vitelli alla Cannoniera*, possibly built to a design by Giorgio Vasari. Walks to the *Santuario della Madonna del Belvedere*, the *Terme di Fontecchio* and the *Eremo di Buonriposo*.

* CITTÀ SANT'ANGELO (Pescara). The 14th cent. *Collegiata di San Michele* is the town's most important monument. Its facade is almost hidden by an impressive bell-tower. The interior, mainly Baroque in style, contains the beautiful tomb of Amico di Buonamicizia, Bishop of Penne in the mid-15th cent. The church of *Santa Chiara* is interesting because it is built on an equilateral-triangle plan.

* CIVATE (Como). Situated on the southern edge of the Brianza area, and noted for the basilica of *San Pietro al Monte*, half-way up

Città Sant'Angelo, Collegiata.
Civate, Oratorio di San Benedetto.

Monte Cornizzolo. The basilica, dating from the mid-11th cent., originally had two facing apses; in a later period the present doorway was built in the eastern apse, whilst the altar and precious ciborium were moved to the centre of the aisleless nave. It has a trussed roof. Frescoes dating from the end of the 11th cent. are a valuable testimony of Romanesque art in Lombardy. The adjacent *Oratorio di San Benedetto*, built slightly after the basilica, to a cruciform plan, has three apses and an atrium covered by a cross-vault.

** CIVIDALE DEL FRIULI (Udine). Situated on the extreme edge of the Julian pre-Alps, with the Natisone flowing through it. The *Duomo*, dedicated to the *Assunta*, was rebuilt (1502) in Renaissance style by Pietro Lombardo (1435-1515). It has three pointed-arched doorways in the facade. The austere interior contains a gilded silver altarpiece depicting the Madonna and Child, Saints, Angels and the patriarch Pellegrino III, carried out at the turn of the 13th cent., a Last Supper by Jacopo Palma the Younger (1544-1628), an Annunciation, by Pomponio Amalteo (1505-1588), frescoes by Gaspare Diziani (1689-1767) and Giuseppe Diziani (lived in the 18th cent.), and the Equestrian Statue of Marcantonio di Manzano, a local nobleman (17th cent.). In the Treasury are objects of artistic and historical importance, such as reliquaries of Barbarian art, Bibles and 16th cent. tapestries. In the Christian Museum are high-medieval local sculptures, including the octagonal Baptistery of Callixtus, with Byzantine details, and the 8th cent. altar of Ratchis, donated by Duke Ratchis, decorated with relief-work exalting the Faith and condemning Arianism. The 8-9th cent. *Tempietto Longobardo* or *Oratorio di Santa Maria in Valle*, high-medieval in style, is the most famous and most characteristic monument in Cividale. It may have been built on the site of a temple to Vesta, but it could also correspond to a Longobard stronghold. It consists basically of a quadrilateral hall, with cross vault. In the apse are frescoes of Saints Peter and Paul, and a sarcophagus, said to

Civate, San Pietro al Monte. Celestial Jerusalem.

be of Piltrude, a legendary Queen of the Longobards, consisting of Longobard plutei; archaic wooden statues of the iconostasis, ancient stuccoes, and 15th cent. stalls have attracted scholars to this modest building, which is considered unique of its kind. The Palazzo Nordis houses the *Museo Archeologico Nazionale*, which has a rich collection of Lombard and patriarchal antiques including the sarcophagus of Duke Gisulfo, first Duke of Cividale Longobarda (early 7th cent.), the Veil of the Blessed Benvenuta Bojani (late 13th cent.), Longobard objects exacavated from the local area, pax of Duke Orso, and precious gold objects of the 8-9th cent. Notice also a triptych by Pellegrino da San Daniele (c. 1467-1547) and 17th cent. altarpieces by Andrea Vicentino, Jacopo Palma the Younger, and Giuseppe Diziani (lived in the 18th cent.). The church of *San Francesco* (latter half of the 13th cent.) contains damaged frescoes dating from the early 14th to the early 16th cent., some possibly by Vitale da Bologna (recorded 1330-1359). The 18th cent. church of *San Giovanni* or *Chiesa Esterna di Santa Maria in Valle* has a frescoed ceiling by Giuseppe Diziani and paintings by Pietro Antonio Novelli (1729-1804), Ercole Graziani (1688-1765) and Jacopo Palma the Younger. In the adjacent convent is a painting of the Risen Christ, probably by Paolo Caliari called Veronese (1528-1588). The 15th cent. Gothic church of *San Biagio*, contains a panel of St. Blaise and Two Angels by Pietro Miani (recorded 1486-1507), and Martyrdom of the Saint by Secante Secanti (1571-1637). The church of *Santi Silvestri e Valentino*, first built in the 13th cent., contains important Baroque altars and frescoes by Giulio Quaglia (1668-1751). Also worth seeing in Cividale are the 14th cent. *Palazzo Municipale;* the small church of *San Pietro ai*

Cividale del Friuli, Santa Maria in Valle. Row of Saints.
Cividale del Friuli, Duomo. Altar-frontal donated by Duke Ratchis.

Volti, 18th cent. reconstruction of a more ancient building; the daring Devil's Bridge (*Ponte del Diavolo*) which spans the river Natisone; the church of *Santa Maria dei Battuti* (1444), containing an important triptych by Pellegrino da San Daniele, and interesting remains of the *Celtic Hypogeum*.

* **CIVIDATE CAMUNO** (Brescia). Agricultural centre on the river Oglio. It corresponds to the Roman Civitas Camunnorum, but few traces of the ancient buildings have survived. The *Chiesa dell'Ospedale* has a Romanesque bell-tower and contains a painting of the Madonna and Saints Siro and Stephen by Domenico Carpinoni (1566-1658)' In the 18th cent. parish church of *Santa Maria Assunta* are frescoes by Pietro Scalvini (1718-1792) and a painting by Callisto Piazza (c. 1500-1561). The Romanesque church of *Santo Stefano* was restructured in the 17th cent. The bell-tower has an onion-shaped cusp.

** **CIVITA CASTELLANA** (Viterbo). Built on a tufa terrace, between the mouths of the Filetto and Maggiore. The 12th cent. *Duomo*, dedicated to St. Mary, is Romanesque. It has a tripartite facade in front of which is a large staircase with a portico on architrave columns, considered the masterpiece of the Roman

Civita Castellana, Duomo. Well with Sphinx.
Civita Castellana, Fortress.

marble-workers Jacopo di Lorenzo and Cosma, his son (active at the beginning of the 13th cent.). The interior has a Cosmatesque floor and contains a 14th cent. fresco of the Madonna and Child, a 15th cent. panel of the Madonna della Misericordia, a 7th cent. crypt, and ancient sacristy containing two magnificent marble plutei, one part of an inconostasis, with Cosmatesque decorations. The church of *San Pietro* has an 18th cent. interior and contains a panel of St. Bernardino of Siena, by Sano di Pietro (1406-1481), and a panel of the Adoration of the Child by Antoniazzo Romano (recorded 1461-1508). The Renaissance-style pentagonal *Rocca* was built on the site of 9th and 10th cent. fortresses for Pope Alexander VI (1492-1503). Excursion to *Falerii Novi*, a town built in the 3rd cent. B.C. by the Romans to gather together all the inhabitants of Falerii Veteres; one can see the remains of a wall over two kilometres long and sixteen feet high, and ruins of a theatre, a forum, and a swimming pool.

* **CIVITANOVA MARCHE** (Macerata). Well-known seaside resort at the mouth of the Chienti. The *Palazzo Comunale*, formerly the palace of Duke Sforza Cesarini, was built in the 13th cent. and remodelled in the 16th and 19th. It is a huge and impressive building. The church of *San Marone* was built in the 9th cent. and entirely rebuilt between 1890 and 1901 to a plan by Giuseppe Sacconi and Tito Azzolini. Nearby is *Civitanova Alta*, a walled town built in medieval times by fugitives from the coastal areas. Notice the 16th cent. *Palazzo Cesarini;* the *Collegiata* (rebuilt in the 18th cent.), with a painting representing the Birth of Mary by Pietro Andrea Briotti (lived in the 16-17th cent.); and the *Teatro Annibale Caro*, with a Renaissance doorway (second half of the 15th cent.).

Civitanova Alta, Marina Gate Tower.

** **CIVITAVECCHIA** (Rome). Important industrial centre spread out along the sea at the foot of the Tolfa mountains, it is the main port of Latium and the sailing point for Sardinia. The *Forte Michelangelo* is a solid Renaissance building. It was begun in 1508 by Donato Bramante (1444-1514), for Pope Julius II, continued by Antonio da Sangallo the Younger (1483-1546), and completed in 1557 by Michelangelo Buonarroti (1475-1564). Rectangular in shape, with four large cylindrical towers at each corner, and an octagonal keep, it has a vast, graceful courtyard inside. The *Museo Civico* has sections devoted to the early iron age, the Etruscan period (notice the Kylix by an artist signing himself as Hyschilos, of the 6th cent. B.C.), and Roman and medieval periods (notice the 15-16th cent. ceramics). The *Cattedrale* is dedicated to St. Francis and dates back to the second half of the 17th cent. It has a sober exterior, with a facade in two orders divided by half-columns, and a stately, aisleless interior. There are remains of a large Roman building *Edificio Romano*, presumably used as a military headquarters. Excursion to the *Terme Taurine*, with two buildings, one of the 1st cent. B.C. and the other of the first half of the 2nd cent., providing a most interesting group of Roman remains, completely excavated in the early 1950's. Excursion to the *Torre Bertolda* or *Sant'Agostino*, a popular seaside resort.

* **CIVITELLA DI ROMAGNA** (Forlì) Agricultural and arts and crafts centre, on the lower slopes of Monte Girone. In the *Santuario della Madonna della Suasia* (second half of the 16th cent.) is an important 15th cent. fresco of the Madonna and Child, and notable Baroccio-school paintings.

* **CLUSONE** (Bergamo). Commercial and industrial centre in the Valle Seriana, with important historical associations. The basilica of *Santa Maria Assunta* was rebuilt to a design by Giovanni Battista Quadrio (1659-1723). Inside are some valuable paintings, including an Assunta by Sebastiano Ricci (1659-1734) and a Martyrdom of St. Lawrence by Paolo Cavagna (1556-1627), as well as a Crucified Christ, in wood, by Andrea Fantoni (1659-1734). In the *Oratorio dei Disciplini* (1450) are some precious frescoes (1485) representing the Triumph of Death and Dance of Death, by an unknown Lombard artist. The *Palazzo Comunale* (Town Hall), rebuilt in the 15th cent., is linked to the remains of a medieval tower, with 17th cent. portal.

* **CODROIPO** (Pordenone). Situated in fertile countryside. The *Parrocchiale* was erected in the 18-19th cent. and contains a wooden Crucifix, probably by Alessandro Vittoria (1525-1608). A few km away, in the Passariano district, is the grand and famous *Villa Manin*, which belonged to Lodovico Manin (1720-1802), last Doge of Venice. Inside are tempera frescoes by Ludovico Dorigny (1654-1742).

** **CODRONGIANUS** (Sassari). The *Abbazia della Santissima Trinità di Saccargia* (Abbey of the Holy Trinity) is on the road from Sassari to Olbia. It was part of a Camaldolese abbey, which reclaimed the surrounding territory. It is an important Romanesque construction, in black basalt blocks and white limestone. The present-day building was erected in two stages, the first around 1116 A.D. and the second from 1180 to 1200. The interior is in the form of a Latin cross and has an aisleless nave. The apse contains a fascinating cycle of frescoes by an unknown painter from Latium, who lived in the 13th cent. The church of the Most Holy Trinity of Saccargia is within easy reach of the black *Nuraghe Nieddu*, situated on a slight rise.

* **COGNE** (Aosta). Situated among the pastures of Sant'Orso, most of its territory is included in the National Park of the Gran Paradiso. The surrounding area is characterized by chalets and rustic houses with pointed-arched doors and windows. The parish church of *Sant'Orso* has an aisleless nave, and contains five fine carved and gilded-wood altars of the 16th cent. In the *Castello*, built at the end of the 12th cent. by Bishop Valberto, the bishops of Aosta used to convene general assemblies and administer justice. Walks to the *Giardino Alpino Paradisia*, and to the *Miniera di Cogne*.

* **COLICO** (Como). On the northern tip of Lake Como. Close to the so-called Lake of Piona is the *Abbazia di Piona*, built by Cluniac monks in the second half of the 11th cent., in Renaissance style, and probably retouched in the following cent. The interior has an aisleless nave, semicircular apse and wooden ceiling, and is an elongated and irregular triangle in shape. The cloister dates back to the middle of the 13th cent.

Colico, Piona Abbey, cloister.

* **COLLECCHIO** (Parma). Agricultural and industrial town, on the right bank of the Taro. The 12th cent. parish church of *San Prospero* is Romanesque in style and has been restructured this century. It contains a 14th cent. bas-relief depicting Christ's Baptism.

** **COLLE DI VAL D'ELSA** (Siena). On the left bank of the Elsa, it is divided into two parts: Lower and Upper Colle. The facade of the church of *Sant'Agostino* dates back to the 13th cent. Inside is a Madonna and Child by Taddeo di Bartolo (c. 1362-1422), a Pietà and Saints by Ridolfo del Ghirlandaio (1483-1561), a Madonna and Child with Saints by Agnolo di Cosimo called Bronzino (1503-1572), and a marble tabernacle by Baccio da Montelupo (1469-1535). The *Duomo*, built at the beginning of the 17th cent. on the site of the ancient parish church of Santa Maria in Colle, contains a bronze Crucifix by Jean Boulogne (1524-1608) and a Nativity by Francesco Morandini called Poppi (1544-1584). The 12th cent. church of *Santa Maria in Canonica* is a notable construction in Pisan style. Not far away is the Romanesque church of *Santa Maria a Coneo* (1125); it has an interior in the form of a Latin cross, and an aisleless nave, and is all that remains of the ancient Abbey.

* **COLLEPARDO** (Frosinone). Scattered over a hillside overlooking a mountain stream. In the vicinity are the *Grotta Regina Margherita*, 150 m long, with a large number of stalagmites and stalactites; and the *Pozzo Santullo*, at the foot of Monte La Monna, and awesome chasm, formed by the collapse of the roof of an underground cave. The early 13th cent. church of *San Bartolomeo*, partly Baroque in its present state, contains pictures by Filippo Balbi (mentioned in 1855), the chapel of the Annunziata and the chapel of St. Bruno. Also in the neighbourhood is the *Certosa di Trisulti*, one of the most famous in Latium, composed of a group

Colle di Val d'Elsa (district), former Abbey of Santa Maria at Coneo.

of buildings surrounding a church; little remains of the Benedictine monastery, abandoned in 1204; the pharmacy, in the present-day Certosa contains pictorial decoration by Filippo Balbi, and a precious collection of 17th cent. terracottas from the Abruzzi region.

* **COLOGNO AL SERIO** (Bergamo). Industrial and agricultural centre, with medieval part still intact. The *Parrocchiale* was built in the second half of the 18th cent. to a design by Giovanni Battista Caniana (1671-1745). The facade is embellished with sculptures by Giovanni Antonio Sanz (1702-1787). The *Castello Visconteo*, with a moat, and 15th cent. facade, is in a perfect state of preservation. The *Palazzo Giovannelli* (18th cent.) has an arched and balconied loggia.

* **COMISO** (Ragusa). Set on a hillside, with mainly 18th cent. buildings, in an area rich in pre-historic remains. The *Chiesa Matrice* is dedicated to Santa Maria delle Stelle. It was built in the 15th cent. and rebuilt at the beginning of the 17th after a disastrous earthquake. The ceiling is enhanced with paintings by Antonio Alberti called Barbalonga (1600-1649). On the high altar is a Nativity of the Virgin, probably by Carlo Maratta (1625-1713). The 13th cent. church of *San Francesco* or *dell'Immacolata* was enlarged in the early 16th cent. by the Naselli family. It has an aisleless interior and open-trussed roof. The Naselli chapel presents a mixture of various styles such as Byzantine, Arab, Gothic and Renaissance, with theatrical effect. The church of the *Santissima Annunziata*, rebuilt in the second half of the 18th cent. to a design by Giovanni Battista Cascione, has a two-ordered facade and neo-Classical dome. The graceful interior, in the shape of a Latin cross, contains a 15th cent. polychrome-wood statue of St. Nicholas, a Crucifix, probably by the sculptor Umile da Petralia (1580-1639), a Death and Assumption of the Virgin by Narciso Cidonio (lived in the 16-17th cent.), and St. Gaetano, by Vito D'Anna (c. 1720-1769). The *Castello Feudale*, was built in the 13th cent. and modified in the 14th and 16th. Once the residence of the Naselli family, it boasts a sturdy square keep. and all in all is a most interesting building.

*** **COMO.** On the southern extremity of the west arm of Lake Lario (Como), in a hollow overlooked by the hill of Brunate. The *Broletto*, together with the adjacent *Torre del Comune*, was erected about 1215 and partly disfigured in later periods. It is faced with two-toned horizontal marble courses. The ground floor has a spacious portico with pointed arches, and the wall above is relieved with three large mullioned openings. The *Torre di Porta Vittoria* is one of the defensive constructions built in the 12th and 13th cent. together with the towers of San Vitale and Porta Nuova.

Como, San Fedele, portal relief.
Como, Sant'Abbondio, apse.

The *Duomo* consists of a longitudinal part dating back to the end of the 14th cent. (designed by Lorenzo degli Spazzi), and the 16th cent. cruciform eastern part (the apse being completed by Cristoforo Solari). The late-Gothic facade is divided by four pilaster-strips, decorated with niches containing small statues, and highlighted by an imitation porch, a rose-window and three portals decorated with sculptures by the Rodari family (15-16th cent.), who also carried out the side-entrances. The interior is divided into three by cruciform pillars with pointed arches, and has a cross vault. The point where the transepts cross the longitudinal part is marked by a tall slender dome, designed by Filippo Iuvara in 1731-44. Among the many works preserved in the Cathedral, special attention should be paid to: the tapestries produced by workshops in Ferrara, Florence, and Antwerp; a Holy Conversation and Adoration of the Shepherds by Bernardino Luini (1480/90-c. 1531); frescoes by Morazzone (1571-1626) in the Sacrestia dei Mansionari; a Deposition, relief-work by Tommaso Rodari (1498); and Marriage of the Virgin, by Gaudenzio Ferrari (c. 1475-1546). The church of *San Fedele* (probably erected at the turn of the 12th cent.) has a trefoil plan with a longitudinal part divided into a nave and two aisles. It is decorated on the outside by an accessible gallery and Romanesque sculptures. The church of *Sant'Abbondio*, consecrated in 1095, stands on the site of a 5th cent. basilica. Northern influence can be seen in the elongated apse and first bay which served as a narthex. The half-gable facade is decorated with small, round, hanging arches and a single doorway. Two bell-towers stand at either side before the choir section. The apse is decorated with mid-14th cent. frescoes. The church of *Sant'Agostino*, dating from the second half of the 14th cent., has a nave and two aisles, and a trussed roof. Externally the sides are enhanced with high single-lighted windows. Outside the ancient walls of the city is the basilica of *San Carpoforo*. It has a nave and two aisles, and was built in the 11-12th cent., probably on the site of a previous 4th cent. basilica. The *Museo Civico* preserves Roman and Romanesque works and fragments and, above all, archeological material from excavations in the Ca' Morta, Grandate, Breccia, and Rebbio areas. Adjacent to it is the *Museo del Risorgimento*. The neo-Classical *Tempio Voltiano*, built in 1927, contains antiques and objects connected with Alessandro Volta. Among the most noteworthy palaces are: *Palazzo Giovio* (17th cent. reconstruction of a previous 16th cent. palace); *Palazzo Natta* (one of the earliest examples of Lombard Mannerism); *Palazzo Rusconi* (Renaissance) and *Palazzo Odescalchi* (Baroque). In the Borgovico area are the *Villa Carminati* (late 18th cent.); *Villa "La Rotonda"*, built between 1790 and 1793 to a design by Leopold Pollack (1751-1806), consisting of a two-storey building around a central unit on a curvilinear plan; and *Villa Olmo*, built in 1782 by Simone Cantoni (1736-1818) and modified in 1882.

* **CONEGLIANO** (Treviso). Pretty little town situated partly on a hillside near the Monticano river. The foundation stone of the *Duomo* was laid in 1354, and the campanile was built in 1497. Inside are works of art including a painting by Giambattista Cima (1459-1518) of the Madonna and Child enthroned with Saints and Angels, and St. Francis receiving the stigmata with Saints, one of the finest paintings by Francesco Beccaruzzi (active in the first half of the 16th cent.); nearby is the important Sala dei Battuti (end of the 16th cent.). It has a wooden ceiling embellished with 16th cent. frescoes in twenty-seven panels, by various artists. The church of *San Rocco* (1630) contains an altarpiece depicting the Mystic Marriage of St. Catherine by Francesco Beccaruzzi, and the church of the *Madonna delle Grazie* has a Madonna and Child enthroned with Saints, also by Beccaruzzi. The church of *San Martino* (17-18th cent.) has a painting of the Last Supper by Sante Peranda (1566-1638). The *Museo Civico del Castello*, housed in the Torre della Campana, includes a lapidary collection, two frescoes by Giovanni Antonio de' Sacchis called Pordenone (c. 1484-1539) and two paintings by Jacopo Palma the Younger (1544-1628). In the neighbourhood, at *Castello di Roganzuolo*, is the church of Saints Peter and Paul, containing works of art including paintings by Pomponio Amalteo (1505-1588) and Titian (c. 1490-1576).

* **CONVERSANO** (Bari). Agricultural town and crossroads, on a high plateau of the Murge, with a panorama of the Adriatic coast from Bari to Monopoli; the medieval quarter is

Conversano, San Benedetto, campanile.

built on an oval-shaped plan; the modern part has straight roads. The Romanesque *Cattedrale* (11-12th cent.) was rebuilt in the 14th and has a well-preserved 14th cent. cusped facade, divided into three by pilaster-strips. The interior, in the form of a Latin cross, contains a 14th cent. wooden Cross, and a 15th cent. panel of the Resurrection, of the Central Italian school. The church of *San Benedetto* was built on the site of a monastery believed to have been founded by St. Mawr, disciple of St. Benedict, in the 9th cent. The Baroque campanile was perhaps designed by Paolo Domenico Finoglia (died 1632 or 1656); the interior is decorated in Baroque style and has, on the high altar, an important painting of St. Benedict and San Savino by Paolo Domenico Finoglia. The ancient crypt was part of the original church, which was destroyed by Saracens in 841. The church of *San Cosma* contains a rich collection of paintings and stuccoes, all by Finoglia. The massive *Castello* is of Norman origin but was restructured in later centuries. It stands on a trapezoidal plan and has a huge cylindrical tower (14th cent.), a large polygonal tower (15th cent.), three square towers (12th cent. and 13th cent.) and remains of pointed-arched and circular windows.

* **COPERTINO** (Lecce). Attractive little town in fertile countryside. The most important monument is the massive *Castello*, built in 1540 by Evangelista Menga for Alfonso Castriota, the feudal lord. The Angevin keep, strengthened by ramparts at the four corners, is in the centre of a trapezoidal bastion, the longest side measuring 117 metres. The rich doorway is in the form of a triumphal arch; the courtyard is trapezoid-shaped and has 14th cent. and Renaissance elements. The chapel of *San Marco* contains a Madonna by fra Angelo da Copertino (lived in the 16th cent.), and the tomb of Stefano Squarciafico (17th cent.). The *Collegiata*, dedicated to the Madonna delle Nevi, was first built in 1088 and rebuilt in 1235 and 1506, then modified at the beginning of the 18th cent. It has a Renaissance doorway and is overlooked by a sturdy Baroque campanile, designed between 1579 and 1603, probably by Evangelista Menga. The light and harmonious interior contains a monument to Tristano Chiaramonte (16th cent.), a Deposition from the Cross by Gianserio Strafella (lived in the 16th cent.), St. Peter weeping, by an unknown artist, and a Martyrdom of St. Sebastian by fra Angelo da Copertino.

* **COPPARO** (Ferrara). Large agricultural and industrial centre. The *Palazzo Comunale*, once the splendid mansion of the Este family, dates from the mid-16th cent. It contains frescoes by Benvenuto Tisi called Garofalo (1481-1559) and by Girolamo Sellari called Girolamo da Carpi (1501-1556); the building was restruc-

tured in 1875. The 12th cent. *Arcipretale di San Pietro* is Romanesque in layout but has been altered several times over the centuries. It contains paintings of the Madonna and Child with Saints, and Saints Peter and Paul, by Ippolito Scarsella (c. 1550-1620).

* **CORATO** (Bari). Situated in the heart of fertile countryside about 12 kilometres from Bisceglie, on the Adriatic coast. The well-preserved medieval centre is the hub of a network of modern roads. The 13th cent. *Chiesa Matrice* or *Santa Maria Maggiore* has been completely rebuilt over the centuries; all that remains of the original building is the architraved portal, with a lunette containing a bas-relief representing the Redeemer and the Madonna with St. John the Baptist; it has a remarkable 14th cent. campanile with mullioned openings. The *Chiesetta di San Domenico* is an important 13th cent. building in ogival style. In the medieval quarter are interesting remains of 16th cent. palaces, the most notable being the *Palazzo Gioia*.

* **CORCIANO** (Perugia). It has a beautiful castle surrounded by medieval walls and towers. The Town Hall (*Palazzo Comunale*) was one of the residences of the Della Corgna dukes. In the church of *Santa Maria* there is a standard depicting the Madonna of Mercy by Benedetto Bonfigli (c. 1420-1496), and an Annunciation and Nativity, considered to be one of the best mature works of Perugino (1445/50-1523). In the 14th cent. church of *San Francesco* is a panel by the school of Bartolomeo Caporali (c. 1420-1505). Notice the 16th cent. well in the square overlooked by the Town Hall.

* **COREGLIA ANTELMINELLI** (Lucca). The 13th cent. church of *San Michele* contains two statues of the Nino Pisano school (lived in the first half of the 14th cent.). The *Palazzo Rossi* contains a remarkable ethnographical collection.

* **CORFINIO** (L'Aquila). Walk to the *Basilica Valvense* or *San Pelino*, a very ancient building

Corfinio, Valvense Basilica.

sacked by the Saracens in 881, burnt down by the Hungarians in 937, and rebuilt in Romanesque style in the 11th and 12th cent. The present-day Baroque style is the result of considerable restoration work carried out after earthquakes. The facade is sombre, with a squat tower. The interior contains a superb parchment (1163) by Idolorico, frescoes and remains of frescoes of the 14th and 15th cent., and a painting of Christ Crucified by Teofilo Patini (1840-1906). The combination of the right side of the basilica and the church of St. Alexander has produced a graceful apse. The Museum contains local antiques.

* **CORI** (Latina). Picturesque, pyramid-shaped village, divided into upper (Cori a Monte) and lower (Cori a Valle) Cori. The *Collegiata*, also called Santa Maria della Pietà, was built on the remains of a temple to Fortune, in a period of transition from Renaissance to Baroque style. It has a sober facade relieved by three doorways, and contains a precious 12th cent. candelabra, for the Paschal candle, resting on a chimera. The church of *Sant'Oliva* is formed by two adjacent churches, one medieval, the other 15th cent. The latter contains frescoes depicting Episodes from the Old and New Testaments, carried out in 1553 by an unknown artist influenced by Michelangelo Buonarroti. In the medieval centre (*Nucleo Medievale*) is the characteristic Via del Porticato, leading to the Roman Ponte della Catena. There are remains of the Temple of Castor and Pollux, (*Tempio di Castore e Polluce*) dating from the first half of the 1st cent. B.C., and the important Doric-style Temple of Hercules (*Tempio di Ercole*) in travertine (also 1st cent. B.C.). Remains of Cyclopean walls (*Mura ciclopiche*).

* **CORREGGIO** (Reggio Emilia). Agricultural and industrial town, with wide streets flanked by porticoes. The 16th cent. basilica of *San Quirino* was designed by Jacopo Barozzi called Vignola (1507-1573). It contains a painting of St. Martin by Domenico Fetti (c. 1589-1624) and a fresco by Luigi Asioli (1817-1877) depicting the Apotheosis of St. Quirinus. The *Palazzo dei Principi*, built around 1500, has a fine doorway and houses the Civic Library and Museum, which boasts a Head of Christ by Andrea Mantegna (c. 1431-1506). Inside the 15th cent. church of *San Francesco* is a painting of St. Bernardino healing the Cripple, probably by Mattia Preti (1613-1699). In the neighbourhood is the ancient two-storeyed church of *San Paolo al Chienti*, with a facade flanked by two cylindrical towers. The construction dates back to the 11-12th cent.

** **CORRIDONIA** (Macerata). On the watershed that separates the valleys of the Chienti and the Cremone. The *Pinacoteca* contains some important pictures such as a Madonna and Child, Angels and five Saints, by Cristoforo

Roncalli called Pomarancio (c. 1552-1626), a triptych by Lorenzo di Alessandro (recorded 1465-1503), a Gothic-framed polyptych by Antonio Vivarini (c. 1420-ante 1484), a panel of the Madonna and Child by Carlo Crivelli (1430/35-1495/1500), a tempera depicting St. Francis, probably by Stefano di Giovanni called Sassetta (1392-1450), and paintings by Giovanni Francesco De Magistris (lived in the 16th cent.). The *Parrocchiale*, dedicated to Saints Peter, Paul, and Donat, was designed by Giuseppe Valadier (1762-1839).

* **CORTEMAGGIORE** (Piacenza). Village on the left bank of the Arda, in an exceptionally wealthy methane-producing area. The *Collegiata di Santa Maria delle Grazie* was begun in 1481 to a design by Gilberto Manzi (recorded at the end of the 15th cent.). It contains a remarkable fresco of Christ rising from the Tomb (1523) by an unknown painter. The *Chiesa dei Francescani* (1490) was designed by Gilberto Manzi, and contains a painting of the Deposition from the Cross, by Giovanni Antonio de' Sacchis, called Pordenone (c. 1484-1539). The chapel of St. Anne was frescoed in 1530 by the same painter.

* **CORTINA D'AMPEZZO** (Belluno). On the left bank of the Boite, in the centre of an undulating valley dominated by the most beautiful peaks of the Dolomites. The 13th cent. parish church of *Santi Filippo e Giacomo* has been altered several times over the centuries. It has an aisleless interior, with frescoes in the vault by Francesco Antonio Zeiller (1716-1792). On the high altar is a painting of the Madonna and Saints Philip and James by Giuseppe Zanchi (active in the first half of the 18th cent.). The campanile, designed by Ermanno Bergmann (1816-1886), is a characteristic landmark. The *Scuola d'Arte* contains works by contemporary Italian painters, including Massimo Campigli, Carlo Carrà, Giorgio De Chirico, Filippo De Pisis, Arturo Martini, Ottone Rosai, Gino Rossi and Pio Semeghini.

** **CORTONA** (Arezzo). In a panoramic position, it commands a sweeping view over

Corridonia, San Claudio al Chienti, view of the apses.

the Valdichiana and Lake Trasimeno. The *Duomo di Santa Maria* is admired especially for its facade (built over the previous Romanesque one dated about 1000 A.D.), the portal by Giuliano da Sangallo (1445-1516), and a Greco-Roman sarcophagus, depicting a struggle of Centaurs, Lapithae and Amazons with Bacchus. In the *Museo Diocesano* are preserved works by Beato Angelico (c. 1400-1455), Pietro Lorenzetti (1280-c. 1348), Sassetta (c. 1392-1450), Luca Signorelli (c. 1445-1523), and Giuseppe Maria Crespi called Spagnolo (1665-1747). The *Palazzo Pretorio* houses the Etruscan Academy, founded in 1727 as the Academy of the Occult by Onofrio Baldelli and Marco Venuti. It is also the home of a museum containing a rich Egyptian and Etruscan collection, with a bronze chandelier discovered in 1840 and considered the most interesting Etruscan work in bronze that has come down to us. The Palace also houses an art gallery with works by Luca Signorelli, Bernardino di Betto called Pinturicchio (1454-1513) and Pietro da Cortona (1596-1669), and a library including 676 paper and parchment codices, 1,160 parchments, 130 incunabula, and about 44,000 valuable books. The church of *Santa Margherita* contains the tomb of St. Margaret, a precious Gothic work (1362) by the local artists Angelo and Francesco di Pietro, and held to be one of the finest 14th cent tombs in existence. In the tiny church of *San Nicolò* are paintings by Luca Signorelli. The church of *San Domenico*, built at the turn of the 15th cent., is worth a visit, as are the 13th cent. Town Hall (*Palazzo Comunale*), the impressive *Palazzo Fierli* and *Petrella*, formerly Tommasoni, and the square-sided *Fortezza* called *Girifalco*. In the vicinity is the church of *Madonna del Calcinaio*, built to the design of Francesco di Giorgio Martini in 1485-1513. On a central plan, and surmounted by a high dome, it has a two-ordered exterior and a cheerful, simple interior. The windows are by Guglielmo Marcillat (c. 1470-1529). Above the altars are pictures by Tommaso Bernabei called Papacello (c. 1500-1559). The high altar preserves a venerated image of the Madonna.

** **COSENZA.** At the point where the Crati and Busento meet, it is formed by an ancient centre, on a hillside, and a modern part. The 15th cent. church of *San Domenico*, rebuilt in the 18th cent., has a fine door, carved in 1612. Inside is a Rosary Chapel, with Neapolitan-school marble reliefs by Giovanni da Nola called Mariliano (16th cent.), and remarkable 19th cent. paintings. In the Room of the Confraternity of the Holy Rosary is an important 17th cent. panel depicting the Eternal. The *Cattedrale*, built in Gothic-Cistercian style in the 12-13th cent., was modified in Baroque style in the second half of the 18th cent., and recently restored. It has a basilican interior, with frescoes representing the Assunta and Apostles, carried out in 1899 by Domenico Morelli and Paolo Vetri. The 15th cent. panel of the Madonna and Child, popularly known as the Madonna del Pilerio, a painting of the Immacolata by Luca Giordano (1632-1705), and the tomb of Isabella of Aragon, wife of Philippe III of France, who died here in 1271, are also worthy of attention. In the Treasury of the Bishop's Palace there is an admirable

Cortona, Madonna del Calcinaio.

Cosenza, Duomo. Detail of the monument to Isabella of Aragon.

gold reliquary Cross (possibly 12th cent.). The early-13th cent. church of *San Francesco d'Assisi* contains recognizable remains of Roman walls. Inside can be seen a late-Renaissance marble statue of the Madonna and Child, Gothic-influenced carved stalls (1505) and interesting 17th and 18th cent. paintings. The church is in the centre of a district characterized by stately mansions, unexpected steep flights of steps and picturesque little streets. The *Chiesa di Santa Maria di Costantinopoli* or dei *Riformati* was rebuilt in the 17th cent. It contains paintings including a self-portrait by the Flemish artist William Borremans (active from 1688 to 1720), and a beautiful polyptych altarpiece with an outstanding Madonna of Constantinople (a 17th cent. Neapolitan work). The *Museo Civico* contains material from the necropolis of Torre Mordillo, dating from the 9-7th cent. B.C.; weapons, oil lamps, small statues, fibulas, clay vases with geometric decorations, large painted tiles, and 16th and 17th cent, paintings and bas-reliefs. The church of *San Francesco di Paola*, rebuilt in the first half of the 18th cent. after a terrible earthquake, contains the imposing tomb of Ottavio Cesare Gaeta (end of the 16th cent.) and a large panel depicting the Madonna with Saints Paul and Luke the Evangelist, by Pietro Negroni called Zingarello (1503-1565).

* **COSSATO** (Vercelli). Spread along the banks of the Strona, with many factories and attractive villas. The parish church of the *Assunta* has a portico in the facade. The chancel contains a panel by Bernardino Lanino (c. 1512-1503) depicting the Assunta. One should walk to the chapel of *Sant'Anastasia*, where there is an interesting 16th cent. fresco.

** **CREMA** (Cremona). Important little agricultural and industrial town on the right bank of the Serio. The 13-14th cent. *Duomo*, dedicated to Santa Maria Assunta, is in Lombard-Gothic style. It contains numerous works of art, the most beautiful of which is a panel depicting Saints Sebastian, Roch and Christopher, considered the masterpiece of Vincenzo Civerchio (c. 1470-c. 1544). The expanse of the Renaissance-style *Palazzo del Comune* (1525) is broken up by the so-called Torrazzo tower, built at the same time. The *Palazzo Vimercati Sanseverino* was built at the turn of the 18th cent. The inner courtyards contain wrought-iron gates and railings by Alvisio Chaneval (active at the beginning of the 18th cent.). The fine Baroque church of the *Santissima Trinità*, was designed by Andrea Nono (lived in the 18th cent.). It contains paintings of the Deposition from the Cross by Pompeo Batoni (1708-1787), and an Adoration of the Child Jesus, by Callisto Piazza (c. 1500-1561). The church of *San Giacomo Maggiore*, rebuilt in the 18th cent., contains important paintings, including a St. Francis of Sales by Giovanni

Battista Lucini (active in the second half of the 18th cent.), a Madonna and Saints by Carlo Urbino (lived in the 16th cent.) and a Death of St. Andrew of Avellino, by Giambettino Cignaroli (1706-1770). The *Palazzo Terni de Gregori Bondenti* was built at the beginning of the 18th cent. to a design by Giuseppe Cozzi. The ex-monastery of St. Augustine houses the *Museo Civico*, which contains collections of archeological, historical and artistic material. Worthy of mention amongst the paintings are: Hostages of Crema by Gaetano Previati (1852-1920); a Redeemer and Saints by Giambettino Cignaroli, and Saints Roch and Jerome by Vincenzo Civerchio. Walk to the *Santuario di Santa Maria della Croce*, designed by Giovanni di Domenico Battagio (recorded 1465-1499). Inside are valuable frescoes and paintings by Antonio Campi (1524-1587) and Bernardino Campi (1522-1591).

*** **CREMONA**. Situated near the left bank of the Po, in fertile countryside. *Piazza del Comune* is the artistic centre of the town, overlooked by some fine buildings such as the 111-metre high Torre Campanaria called Torrazzo, dated 1267; and the Portico della Bertazzola, designed by Giovanni Battista Trotti called Malosso (1555-1619). The *Duomo*, begun in 1107, is one of the finest cathedrals in Northern Italy. The facade has two rows of small loggias, with a 16th cent. crown and 13th cent. porch. The relief work on the front represents agricultural labours, by the school of Antelami. Inside is a cycle of frescoes with Stories of Mary, by various Lombard-Venetian painters including B. Boccaccino, G. Romanino, and Pordenone. The two pulpits are works of Renaissance sculpture, with reliefs by Amadeo, and the tomb of Saints Peter and Marcellino in the crypt, by Benedetto Briosco. The Romanesque *Battistero* (1167) was designed by Teodosio Orlandino, and stands on an octagonal plan. The interior was partly spoilt by alterations in the 16th and 18th cent. The

Crema, Santa Maria della Croce.

103

Loggia dei Militi (1292), one of the most remarkable buildings in civil architecture in Lombardy, was called "dei Militi" because it was here that the captains of the communal armies gathered. The *Palazzo del Comune* or Palazzo dei Nobili or dei Ghibellini was rebuilt in the first half of the 13th cent., and largely transformed in 1575 by the architect Francesco Dattaro called Pizzafuoco. It contains works of art including pictures by Luigi Miradori called Genovesino (1600/10-1655/57), and Francesco Boccaccino (c. 1660-1750). In the Saletta dei Violini are three instruments by Antonio Stradivari (1648-1737). In the church of *San Girolamo* (latter half of the 14th cent.) is a Beheading of the Baptist, by Giacomo Guerrini (1718-1793) and a Madonna and St. Jerome by Francesco Monti (c. 1683-1768). The *Palazzo dell'Arte* houses the Natural Science and Stradivari Museums. *Palazzo Mina-Bolzesi*, designed by Carlo Sada (1809-1873). The 15th cent. church of *Santa Maria Maddalena* contains an Assunta and Saints Ursula and Anne by Vincenzo Campi (1536-1591), and a Madonna and Child with St. John of Damascus by Genovesino. The church of *San Michele*, founded originally in the 7th cent., and rebuilt in the 12th, contains a polyptych by Bernardino Campi depicting the Birth of the Redeemer, St. Leonard, and St. Bernardino. *Palazzo Fodri*, built at the turn of the 16th cent., is an elegant example of Renaissance architecture. The *Museo Civico* is housed in the Palazzo Affaitati; it includes an art gallery, an archeological and paleontographical section, the Cathedral Treasury, the Risorgimento museum, and a collection of coins. (In the art gallery are medieval and 15th cent. frescoes, Cremonese Mannerist

pictures, paintings by Alessandro Magnasco, works by local 19th cent. painters, etc.). The Gothic-style church of *San Luca* was modified in 1471. *Palazzo Raimondi* (1496) was designed by Bernardino De Lera (lived in the 15-16th cent.). *Palazzo del Popolo* or *dei Guelfi*, or *di Cittanova* (1256). The church of *Sant'Agata* (1077) was rebuilt at the end of the 15th cent. Inside is a double panel of St. Agatha, one of the finest examples of Northern Italian painting, Tomb of the Trecchi (turn of the 14th cent.), by Gian Cristoforo Romano (1470-1512), and an Assumption by Bernardino Campi. The church of *Sant'Agostino* is an imposing construction dating back to the first half of the 14th cent. Inside are frescoes by Bonifacio Bembo (recorded 1440-1478). The 16th cent. church of *San Pietro al Po* has a later facade. Inside are important pictures including a Madonna and Child, Saints and a Devotee by Gianfranco Bembo, called Vetraio (c. 1460-1526).

* **CRESCENTINO** (Vercelli). Destroyed by the river Po in the 9th cent., it was immediately rebuilt at the point where the Dora Baltea and the Po meet. The parish church of the *Assunta* has a nave and two aisles; above the fifth altar on the right-hand side is a Madonna of the Rosary by Guglielmo Caccia, called Moncalvo (1568-1625), and on the high altar a painting of the Assunta by Claude-François Beaumont (1694-1766).

* **CROTONE** (Catanzaro). Situated on a promontory jutting out into the Ionian Sea, it is one of the busiest towns in Calabria. The modest *Duomo* contains a 16th cent. font, and

Cremona, Duomo, interior.

a venerated Byzantine-type panel of the Madonna di Capocolonna. In the Treasury are two precious silver cross-staffs of the 18th cent. The Castle houses a notable *Museo Civico*, with collections of marbles, inscriptions, terracottas, vases, and Greek and Roman coins.

** **CUMA** (Town of Bacoli and Pozzuoli, province of Naples). Important archæological centre on the western tip of the Campi Flegrei. The Domitian-age *Arco Felice* is a monumental construction, forming a triumphal arch over the Via Domitiana where it cuts through Monte Grillo. Outside the city walls stood an amphitheatre, little of which is left apart from a Forum and a Capitoline Temple. The *Acropoli* contains the most interesting monuments: the Greek and Samnite-origin *Tempio di Apollo*, probably peripteral in form, suffered various alterations in the Augustan age and in the 6th and 7th cent. A.D., when it was transformed into a Christian basilica; the Greek-founded *Temple of Jupiter* suffered the same fate. The *Cripta Romana* is a long tunnel that cuts through the hill of Cuma, with straight and winding stretches. It is preceded by a vestibule decorated with four large recesses. The Cave of the Cumae Sibyl (*Antro della Sibilla Cumana*) also consists of a straight-walled tunnel ending in a rectangular room with vaulted ceiling and three recesses. The Necropoli covers a vast area, and the most ancient tombs date back to the 9-7th cent. B.C.

** **CUNEO.** On the road between Piedmont and Southern France, it stands on a wedge shaped piece of land, consisting of an ancient part and a rapidly expanding modern one. The former church of *San Francesco*, begun in 1227 in Romanesque-Gothic style, has a 15th cent. facade, divided into three by pilaster-strips and enhanced with a marble portal. The *Cattedrale*, built when the city was founded, is dedicated to Our Lady of the Woods. It was destroyed during sieges and rebuilt in 1662. The neo-Classical facade is by Antonio Bono. The *Museo Civico* contains collections of material connected with local art and history, together with documentary evidence of the sieges suffered by Cuneo. In the sixth room, which is devoted to pre-historic times, there is material taken from ancient tombs; in the seventh room, amphoras, bowls, bronzes, amulets and other items excavated in the surrounding area. The upper floor of the Museum houses the Civic Library, which contains five thousand books and forty-seven incunabula. The imposing *Municipio* was formerly a Jesuit monastery.

* **CUPRA MARITTIMA** (Ascoli Piceno). Divided into Lower Cupra, which is spread along the seashore, and Upper Cupra, the medieval part, which is clustered on the hill above. The *Collegiata* (1887) contains a triptych of the Adoration of the Madonna and Saints Sebastian and Basso, probably by Vittore Crivelli (c. 1440-1502). Upper Cupra is entirely surrounded with walls erected by Francesco Sforza (1401-1466). It boasts the ancient and characteristic little church of *Santa Maria in Castello;* the rectangular facade has a noteworthy Romanesque doorway and simple bell gable.

* **CUPRAMONTANA** (Ancona). Attractive little town in one of the most pleasant hilly areas of the Marches. The *Palazzo Comunale* was designed by Mattia Capponi (lived in the 18th cent.). It contains an important 17th cent. painting of the Martyrdom of St. Lawrence by an unknown artist, and a library with seventy-two incunabula. The ancient *Collegiata* was rebuilt first in the 13th cent., and again in the 18th. The facade has some fine statues, and inside is a painting of the Circumcision by Antonio Sarti (recorded 1613-1633), and a gilded wood altar-frontal by Andrea Scoccianti (1640-1730). Walk to the 16th cent. *Chiesa degli Zoccolanti* with altar designed by Fra Mattia della Robbia (1468-post 1534).

* **CUSANO MUTRI** (Benevento). A terraced village situated among hills, with medieval houses and streets. The church of *Santi Pietro e Paolo* was built in 944, and modified several times in the course of time. It has an insignificant exterior, but important basilican interior, with a fine high altar, behind which is a wooden Baroque construction, signed in 1661 by Domenico De Luca. The church of *San Giovanni* has an important inner portal, and contains a 14th cent. silver reliquary enclosing a thorn from Christ's crown. Ruins of the *Castello*, which was destroyed in 1780 during a peasants' revolt. Climb to Monte Mutria (1823 m).

* **CUTIGLIANO** (Pistoia). Pleasantly situated holiday resort. In the 14th cent. *Palazzo Pre-*

Cutigliano, Palazzo Pretorio, view from the loggia.

torio the so-called Captains of the Mountain held court, and their coats-of-arms can still be seen on the facade. The *Parrocchiale* and *Chiesa della Compagnia* contain some notable pictures.

* **DERUTA** (Perugia). Small town famous for its ceramics. The church of *San Francesco* was built in the second half of the 14th cent. It contains valuable works of art such as a detached fresco by Fiorenzo di Lorenzo (c. 1440-c. 1525) depicting the Eternal with Saints Roch and Romano and a view of Deruta, and a painting of the Madonna with Saints Francis and Bernardino by Domenico Alfani (recorded 1480-1553). The *Pinacoteca* in the Town Hall is worth a visit. It contains a panel of the Madonna with Saints Francis and Bernardino, Angels and Patron, by Niccolò di Liberatore, called Alunno (c. 1430-1502), interesting 17th and 18th cent. paintings, a 15th cent. monogram of St. Bernardino, on a wooden panel, chasubles, and Etruscan vases. Walk to the church of *Madonna di Bagno*, the interior of which is covered with hundreds of Majolica votive offerings of the 17th and 18th centuries.

* **DESENZANO DEL GARDA** (Brescia). Situated at the south-west tip of Lake Garda, on a morainic slope, it is built around a once-important port of the Venetian Republic. In the church of *Santa Maria Maddalena*, rebuilt in 1586 by Giulio Todeschini (1524-1603), are paintings by Gian Domenico Tiepolo (1727-1804), Zeno Donato called Zenon Veronese (1484-1554) and Palma the Younger (1544-1628). Ruins of a *Villa Romana* (middle of the 4th cent.) with polychrome mosaics.

Deruta, Museo Civico. Floor from the church of San Francesco, detail.

* **DOLIANOVA** (Cagliari). Large town formed by the merging of Sicci San Biagio and San Pantaleo. The Romanesque church of *San Pantaleo* is flanked by a campanile with two orders of single-lighted apertures. The late-5th cent. baptismal font in the apse is the only example of its kind on the island. The church contains an early-16th cent. Catalan-style altarpiece, and damaged 13th and 14th cent. Sardinian-school frescoes.

* **DOLO** (Venice). Large agricultural and industrial town on the banks of the Brenta canal. The parish church of *San Rocco*, dating from the second half of the 18th cent., has a soaring campanile; in a courtyard of the priest's house there is a well-curb carved by Bartolomeo Bon (lived in the 15th cent.). 18th cent. *Villa Andreuzzi-Bon*, Ionic in style; in the grounds is an attractive 16th cent. boathouse. 18th cent. *Villa Mocenigo-Spiga*. The *Villa Ferretti-Angeli* was designed by Vincenzo Scamozzi (1552-1616).

* **DOMODOSSOLA** (Novara). The most important centre in the Val d'Ossola on the Simplon road railway line. The *Collegiata dei Santi Gervaso e Protaso* was built at the end of the 18th cent. to a design by Matteo Zucchi; the facade is characterized by a small two-pillared doorway which was part of a 15th cent. building. The chancel contains a fresco by Lorenzo Peretti (1774-1851) representing the Martyrdom of Saints Gervase and Protaso; the second chapel on the right contains a painting by Tanzio da Varallo (c. 1575-1635) depicting St. Charles giving Communion to the Plague-stricken. *Palazzo Silva*, with cross-shaped windows, was built partly in 1519 and partly in 1640; inside are Roman tombs and objects, collections of local dress, pictures and prints. The *Palazzo di San Francesco* contains a museum of the war of independence, a natural history museum with a collection of reptiles, fish, insects, and local and exotic birds, mementoes of the construction of the Simplon tunnel and other interesting material. The Simplon Museum is in the *Collegio Mellerio Rosmini*. The little church of *Madonna della Neve*, built in the 15th cent. and rebuilt in the 17th, is well-known to pilgrims.

* **DOMUSNOVAS** (Cagliari). Founded in the middle ages, it lies where the San Giovanni stream flows into its valley. The *Grotta di San Giovanni* is a natural cleft, about 20 metres in height and width; it has two entrances with remains of cyclopean walls and traces of ancient chapels, one of which is dedicated to St. John, and gives its name to the grotto.

* **DRONERO** (Cuneo). Delightful, busy town set on a terrace, to the left of which flows the Maira stream. In Via Giolitti is the 15th cent. Romanesque-Gothic church of *Santi Andrea e*

Ponzio, with a vast Gothic facade flanked by spires, and a fine Gothic doorway. The interior has a nave and two aisles. Notice the Gothic holy-water stoup in the form of a chalice. The characteristic, octagonal *Loggia del Mercato* was built in the 15th cent.

* **EBOLI** (Salerno). Attractive little town with the medieval part spread over a hillside and modern area lying on the plain. The 13th cent. Romanesque church of *San Pietro alli Marmi* has no facade; the apse and campanile, Sicilian-Norman in profile, are all that remains of the original building. The basilican interior contains medieval frescoes depicting. St. Anthony and St. Francis, and wooden statues by Giacomo Colombo (recorded 1679-1705). The *Collegiata* (1782) is dedicated to Santa Maria della Pietà; it contains some interesting works of art, such as a wooden carving of the Pietà by Giacomo Colombo, and a panel depicting the Coronation of the Virgin, by an unknown artist working in the mid-15th cent. and referred to as the "Master of the Coronation of Eboli". In the 14th cent. church of *San Francesco* are 16th cent. frescoes, and a Crucifixion by Roberto Oderisi (active in the mid-14th cent.).

* **EDOLO** (Brescia). Picturesque village in the Upper Val Camonica, with access to the Valtellina, Trent and Upper Adige valleys. The church of *San Giovanni Battista* was rebuilt in the 15-16th cent. It has a tall, solitary bell-tower and contains frescoes illustrating the life of John the Baptist and Biblical scenes, held to be among the best works of Paolo Cailina the Younger (c. 1485-1545), although they have also been attributed to Callisto Piazza (1500-1561). *Casa Zuelli*, of the early 15th cent.

** **EMPOLI** (Florence). On the left bank of the Arno, at an important crossroads. The *Collegiata di Sant'Andrea* is thought to have originated in the 5th cent., and was certainly rebuilt in the 11th. The green and white marble facade has an interesting tympanum and square upper part. Inside is a fresco representing the Redeemer with the symbols of the Passion, by Raffaello Botticini (1477-1520). The Collegiata leads straight into the *Museo*, which is particularly rich in pictures, bas-reliefs and statues of high artistic value. The 14th cent. church of *Santo Stefano* is worth visiting. Inside, as well as important remains of frescoes and sinopias by Masolino da Panicale (1383?-c. 1440), there is a fresco by Masolino of the Madonna and Child with two Angels, and a painting of the Madonna handing the Rosary to St. Dominic (1634) by Francesco Furini (1604-1649).

** **ENNA.** On a horseshoe-shaped terrace in the centre of Sicily. The *Duomo*, the foundation stone of which was laid in 1307, is preceded by a broad flight of steps. It has a composite facade, with various interesting styles intermingled, and the interior, in the form of a Latin cross, contains some good works of art, especially altarpieces, by William Borremans (1670-1744), a Visitation, one of the most refined works of Filippo Paladino (c. 1544-1614), an altarpiece representing the Madonna delle Grazie and Saints Clare and Agnes, by Giuseppe Salerno called Zoppo di Gangi (recorded 1588-1630), and rare sacred vestments. In the cathedral treasury, gold jewellery and other valuable material, including silver candlesticks (1595) by Nibilio Gagini (recorded 1583-1607) and Pietro Rizzo (active in the 16-17th cent.); in the Alessi Museum, housed in the cathedral, there is a large collection of coins, ceramics, bronzes and prints of various periods, and some valuable pictures. The 14th

Empoli, Santo Stefano. Masolino da Panicale, a Saint, detail of the sinopia.

Enna, Duomo, facade.

107

cent. church of *San Francesco d'Assisi* contains a panel depicting the Epiphany, attributed to Simone de Wobreck (recorded 1557-1585), and a Nativity and Assumption of the Virgin by Francesco Ciotti (lived in the 17-18th cent.). In the church of *San Benedetto*, Deposition from the Cross, by Antonio Mercurio (active in the second half of the 18th cent.). The church of *Santa Chiara* built in the first half of the 18th cent. has a dynamic facade and important 18th cent. interior with floral-patterned majolica tiles as paving. The *Castello di Lombardia*, also known as the Cittadella, is one of the most interesting medieval castles in Sicily. The courtyard called of the Armati or San Nicola, the courtyard of the Maddalena, and the courtyard of San Martino are all worth visiting. The battlemented Pisan tower commands one of the finest views in Sicily. In the 17th cent. church of the *Anime Sante* there are frescoes by William Borremans. The 15th cent. church of *San Tommaso* contains an important marble group depicting the Annunciation, Evangelists and Pietà by Giuliano Mancino (active in the first half of the 16th cent.). The 13th cent. *Torre di Federico II di Svevia* is worth a visit.

* **EOLIE/AEOLIAN ISLANDS** (Messina). There are seven Aeolian and Lipari islands, the three largest of which (Vulcano, Lipari and Salina) are quite close together, while the other four, smaller ones are scattered over a wide expanse of sea (Alicudi, Filicudi, Panarea and Stromboli). The islands reveal archeological traces of every age from pre-historic to classical times. *Lipari*, the largest and most highly populated of the archipelago, has a Cathedral dedicated to St. Bartholomew, dating from the second half of the 11th cent.; the spacious Baroque interior contains frescoes illustrating stories from the Old Testament carried out in the 18th cent. The Archeological Museum, of prime scientific importance, is divided into sections relating to pre-historic and protohistoric Lipari, an epigraph department, a department concerning the lesser islands and one concerning the necropolises of Milazzo and Lipari. The excavations and archeological Park, with constructions of every period ranging from the bronze age (corresponding to the 16th cent. B.C. or thereabouts) right up to Roman times, are well worth a visit. *Panarea* on the Milazzo promontory: recent excavation work has unearthed an important bronze-age village of the 14th cent. B.C. near the village of San Pietro, and remains of a Hellenist-Roman settlement, dating from the 3rd cent. B.C. to the 2nd cent. A.D. *Stromboli* is the best-known island in the archipelago. Recent excavations have brought to light traces of an early-bronze-age settlement.

** **ERCOLANO/HERCULANEUM** (Town of Resina, province of Naples). On the slopes of Vesuvius, it is an extremely interesting archeo-

logical centre. Excavations were begun in the 18th cent., continued in the 19th, and systematically resumed in 1927. The north part of the ancient town, lying beneath present-day Resina, is still unexplored. The town is divided into neat, geometric sections, and is composed of plebeian dwellings and aristocratic villas with verandas and terraces facing the sea. The most interesting buildings include the *Casa dell'atrio a mosaico* with a geometric-design mosaic floor, the *Casa del tramezzo di legno*, with a wellpreserved front up to the second storey, and a wooden partition with three doors enclosing the triclinium; the *Casa sannitica*, the *Terme*, built in the Augustan age, with the layout typical of Roman baths, divided into male and female sections; the *Casa del mosaico di Nettuno e Anfitrite*; the *Casa del bicentenario*, the *Sacello degli Augustali*; the *Palestra*, and the suburban district with its own Baths. Most of the frescoes (which have provided scholars with valuable insight into ancient painting techniques) are preserved in the National Museum in Naples.

Ercolano (Herculaneum), Roman fresco, Robing Scene (now in the Museo Nazionale, Naples).
Ercolano (Herculaneum), Roman fresco, Actor (now in the Museo Nazionale, Naples).

** **ERICE** (Trapani). Set picturesquely on the summit of Mount Erice, with a commanding view and quaint medieval streets and houses. The early 14th cent. *Chiesa Matrice* is dedicated to the Assunta, and is flanked by a sturdy campanile, originally the watch tower. The church contains some works of art, such as the large marble altarpiece depicting the Madonna, Saints and scenes from the Passion, by Giuliano Mancino (active in the first half of the 16th cent.). The *Palazzo del Municipio* houses a library and museum, with archeological material including a small Praxiteles-style head of Aphrodite (4th cent. B.C.), a painting of Mary Magdalen by Andrea Carrera (lived in the 17th cent.), and a Crucifix by the sculptor Pietro Orlando (lived in the 18th cent.). The church of *San Giovanni Battista*, with 13th cent. portal, contains a statue of John the Baptist by Antonio Gagini (recorded 1541-1575) and another of St. John the Evangelist by Antonello Gagini (1478-1536). The *Castello di Venere* (Castle of Venus) was erected in the 12-13th cent. within the acropolis of the ancient city.

* **ESTE** (Padua). Attractive little town to the south of the Euganean Hills. The *Museo Nazionale Atestino*, housed in the Palazzo Mocenigo, is one of the most important in Italy for pre-Roman and Roman remains. The *Duomo*, dedicated to Santa Tecla, is an early-Christian basilica, rebuilt in the 11th cent. It contains some important works of art, including a magnificent painting by Giovan Battista Tiepolo (1696-1770), of Santa Tecla interceding with the Almighty on behalf of the plague-ridden city in 1630. The late-15th cent. basilica of *Santa Maria delle Grazie* was rebuilt at the

beginning of the 18th cent. It has some fine altars, sculptures and paintings. Notice also the 18th cent. *Palazzo del Municipio*, and the *Castello*, which was rebuilt in 1339 on the ruins of the previous, mid-11th cent. one: trapezoid-shaped in layout, it is the most characteristic monument in Este. The church of the *Beata Vergine delle Consolazioni*, known as the Zoccoli, was built in 1505, and contains a painting of the Madonna and Child by Giambattista Cima called Cima da Conegliano (c. 1459-1517). Also worth a visit are the church of the *Beata Vergine della Salute* (1639) and the Romanesque church of the *San Martino*, which contains two paintings by Antonio Zanchi (1631-1722).

** **FABRIANO** (Ancona). Situated in a large hollow on the eastern slope of the Umbrian-Marches Apennines, with an interesting medieval centre. The Bishop's Palace was built towards the middle of the 16th cent. It houses the *Pinacoteca Comunale* with many fine works of art by famous painters, mostly from Fabriano itself, such as Antonio da Fabriano (recorded 1450-1485), Simone de' Magistris (recorded 1534-1600), Neri di Bicci (1419-1491), Bicci di Lorenzo (1373-1452), Domiziano Domiziani (lived in the 16th cent.), Ambrogio Monaco (lived in the 17th cent.), Allegretto Nuzi (c. 1320-1373), and Biagio delle Lame (recorded 1511-1575). The *Duomo*, dating back to remote times and dedicated to San Venanzo, was rebuilt in 1617 by Muzio Oddi (1569-1639). The impressive facade is built in two orders of brickwork. Inside are works of art,

Fabriano, Ospedale del Buon Gesù. Wooden Madonna.

Erice, Castle of Venus.
Este, Duomo, Giambattista Tiepolo. S. Tecla frees Este from the plague, detail.

including paintings of St. Philip in Ecstasy by Giovanni Francesco Guerrini (1589-1655/59), and Purifying of the Souls, by Simone Cantarini (1612-1678); frescoes by Giovanni Battista Loreti (1686-1760) and Michelangelo Miliani (1780-1819). There are important 11-14th cent. parchments in the Chapter House. The *Palazzo del Podestà* was built in 1255 in Romanesque-Gothic style. 14th cent. *Palazzo Municipale*, restored by Antonio Antonini in 1690. The *Fontana Rotonda* in Piazza del Comune, the centre of the city, was built in 1285 by Jacopo di Grondolo. The church of *San Benedetto*, first built at the end of the 13th cent., contains works of art such as a painting of the Holy Innocents by Avanzino Nucci (c. 1552-1629) and paintings by Pasquale de' Rossi called Pasqualino (1641-1727) and Giacinto Brandi (1623-1691). The 14th cent. Gothic church of *Santa Lucia* has an unfinished facade. Inside is the chapel of St. Ursula, with a series of impressive frescoes, possibly by the Nuzi school. The church of *Santi Biagio e Romualdo*, built in the 13th cent. and rebuilt in Baroque style in the 18th, has an interesting dome frescoed by Giuseppe Malatesta (c. 1650-1719), and a painting depicting the Redeemer in glory with Saints, by Francesco Mancini (c. 1694-1758). A precious urn in the crypt contains the body of St. Romualdo, founder of the Camaldolite Order. The church of *Sant'Agostino*, first built at the beginning of the 13th cent., contains notable 14th cent. frescoes of the Fabriano-Rimini school. The church of *Sant'Onofrio* contains a beautiful Romanesque Crucifix of the German school, carried out in the second half of the 14th cent. In the 16th cent. church of *Santa Caterina* is a beautiful 17th cent. wooden tabernacle and a painting by Giuseppe Malatesta. The Ospedale del Buon Gesù, in late-Gothic-style brickwork, has a beautiful wooden sculpture of the Madonna and Child dating from the end of the 15th cent.

** **FAENZA** (Ravenna). Agricultural, commercial and industrial town on the Via Emilia, near the left bank of the river Lamone. The foundation-stone of the *Cattedrale*, dedicated to St. Peter, was laid on the 26th May 1474. It is the most famous example of Renaissance architecture in Romagna. The Tuscan style interior contains works of art including a Madonna and Child with Saints, one of the finest paintings by Innocenzo da Imola (1490/94-1547/50), the tomb of San Terenzio (second half of the 15th cent.), and the tomb of San Savino, masterpiece of Benedetto da Maiano (1442-1499). In the church of *Santa Maria Vecchia* or *Santa Maria Foris Portam*, rebuilt in the mid-17th cent., notice in particular the superb octagonal campanile (18th cent.), with single and double-lighted windows and belfry decorated with a double order of three-lighted apertures. The *Pinacoteca* and the *Museo Civico* contain important collections; in the art gallery, paintings by Marco Palmezzano (c. 1459-1539), Battista Dossi (recorded 1517-1553), Dosso Dossi (c. 1479-1542), Francesco Guardi (1712-1793). Antonio Rossellino (1427-c. 1479) and Augusto Rodin (1840-1917). Also worth a visit is the *Museo delle Ceramiche*, which has a collection of ceramics from every country and period. *Fontana Monumentale*, by Domenico Paganelli (1545-1624). The *Palazzo della Podestà* was built in the second half of the 12th cent. 13th cent. *Palazzo del Municipio*, in olden times known as the Palazzo del Popolo. The church of *San Francesco* was originally built in the 13th cent., and completely rebuilt in 1752. Inside is a painting of St. Francis by Pietro Fancelli (1764-1850). *Chiesa dei Santi Ippolito e Lorenzo*, built in 1773 to a design by Giuseppe Pistocchi (1744-1814).

* **FALCONARA MARITTIMA** (Ancona). Small town first built around Upper Falconara, with a magnificent view over the Esino valley,

Faenza, Pinacoteca. Giovanni da Rimini, Madonna and Child with Saints.

Falconara, Rocca Priora.

Ancona and the Adriatic. The parish church of *Santa Maria*, with a 14th cent. Gothic doorway, contains a few interesting works of art. Nearby is the *Rocca Priora*, an imposing fortress built by the people of Iesi in the 14th cent.

* **FANANO** (Modena). Holyday resort at the foot of Monte Cimone. The medieval *Chiesa Plebana*, dedicated to St. Silvester, was rebuilt at the beginning of the 17th cent. It contains a painting of the canonized Pope Silvester baptising Constantine, by Pellegrino da Fanano (active in the 17th cent.), a remarkable 18th cent. painting by an unknown artist depicting the Martyrdom of St. Cecilia, and a Holy Family by Domenico Cresti, called Passignano (c. 1558-1636). In the *Oratorio del Santissimo Sacramento* (1630) is a painting of Christ in the Garden of Gethsemane by an unknown late-16th cent. artist. The church of *San Giuseppe*, built at the beginning of the 17th cent., contains a Martyrdom of St. Catherine of Alexandria, probably by Giovanni Francesco Barbieri called Guercino (1591-1666).

** **FANO** (Pesaro). Situated at the mouth of the river Metauro, with numerous artistic monuments. The late-13th cent. Romanesque-Gothic *Palazzo della Ragione*, built in brickwork, has a five-arched portico. The *Corte Malatestiana* consists of two early-15th cent. buildings, and houses the Malatesta civic museum containing a vast collection of paintings of the Marches, Bolognese and Venetian schools, including St. Francis in Ecstasy, by Girolamo Donnini (1681-1743), St. Andrew, by Antonio Viviani (1560-1620), Saints Augustine and Monica, by Simone Cantarini (1612-1678), and Guardian Angel by Francesco Giovanni Barbieri, called Guercino (1591-1666). The museum also contains an important collection of coins. The *Palazzo Montevecchio*, designed by Andrea Vici (1744-1817) is one of the most important in the Marches. It has a fine doorway joined

Fano, Palazzo della Ragione.

to the large window on the first floor and small balcony on the second. The church of *Sant' Agostino* was built in the 13th cent. on the remains of a Roman building, and rebuilt in later periods. It contains reasonably interesting works of art, especially a chapel decorated with 14th and 15th cent. frescoes depicting scenes from the life of St. Lucy. The large 14th cent. church of *San Domenico* is built in Romanesque-Gothic style. The aisleless interior contains works of art including a fresco depicting the Madonna with Saints Dominic, Fortunato, Francis and Eusebio, by Giovanni Battista Ragazzini (lived in the 16th cent.), and paintings of the Birth of St. John the Baptist, by Federico Zuccari (c. 1540-1609), and St. Thomas Aquinas, by Iacopo Palma the Younger (1544-1628). The *Duomo* was begun before 1000 A.D. but on account of fires and earthquakes, it was rebuilt several times in the course of time. In the interior can be seen traces of the original Romanesque building, frescoes representing the Virgin in Glory, by Domenico Zampieri called Domenichino (1581-1641), a painting of the Madonna in Glory by Lodovico Carracci (1551-1619), and an Assumption by Sebastiano Ceccarini (1703-1783). Also worth seeing in Fano are: the 15th cent. *Logge di San Michele;* the Augustan arch (*Arco di Augusto*); the small church of *San Michele*, (second half of the 15th cent.), with a beautiful Renaissance doorway; the Augustan walls (*Mura Augustee*); the medieval church of *Santa Maria Nuova*, rebuilt in the 16th cent. and containing two remarkable panels by Pietro Vannucci called Perugino (1445/52-1523); the *Basilica di San Paterniano*, patron saint of the city, built in the 16th cent., probably by Iacopo Sansovino (1486-1570); the church of *San Pietro ad Vallum*, (beginning of the 17th cent.), with a Baroque interior; and the *Arche Malatestiane* (Malatesta tombs).

** **FARFA** (Town of Fara in Sabina, province of Rieti). Picturesque little town noted for its famous Abbey, made up of cottages with tiny shops which, at fair-time, were rented by the monks to pedlars. The village was restored by its last owner, Count Giovanni Volpi di Misurata (1877-1947). The *Abbazia di Farfa* was one of the richest and most powerful monastic centres in the Middle Ages, and its religious and cultural influence extended over a large part of central Italy. Built in 680 A.D., it became a veritable stronghold in Carolingian times, and reached the apex of its glory towards the end of the 9th cent., under Abbot Peter. The church of *Santa Maria di Farfa* was rebuilt at the end of the 15th cent. on the site of a Carolingian church. It has a facade divided by pilasters and a doorway in northern Gothic style, with a remarkable Umbrian-school fresco in the lunette, dating from the end of the 15th cent. The basilican type interior, Renaissance in style, has a nave and two aisles. It contains frescoes, some of which by Orazio Lomi called Gentileschi (c. 1563-1636/46), a large Last Judgement (1561) by Becker, a Flemish painter, traces of Cosmatesque mosaic paving, and a ciborium decorated with a Tuscan-school Gothic bas-relief of the 14th cent. The *Monastero* consists of buildings of various periods and styles; notice the small, so-called Longobard cloister, with Romanesque elements, the large cloister (17th cent.) leading to a vault containing a 3rd. cent. A.D. Roman sarcophagus, and the crypt, which was probably part of the original monastery.

* **FARRA DI SOLIGO** (Treviso). Agricultural town in a slightly hilly area. The badly-damaged church of *Santo Stefano* contains a painting by Paris Bordone (1500-1571) and a wooden crucifix by Andrea Brustolon (1662-1732). *Villa Savoini*, built at the beginning of the 16th cent., has a pretty facade decorated with attractive 16th cent. frescoes.

* **FASANO** (Brindisi). Situated at the foot of the *Murge dei Trulli*, only a few kilometres from the Adriatic, in the centre of fertile countryside. The *Chiesa Matrice*, built in 1600, is noted above all for its noble Renaissance facade, and has a beautiful rose-window. The *Chiesa del Purgatorio* contains numerous Baroque decorations. From Fasano one reaches Selva di Fasano, built on a spur of the upper Murge, with a beautiful panorama. Nearby is the most remarkable Karst-formation of the Murge, as well as the church of *Seppannibale*, and the *Cripta di San Procopio*, of ancient origin, as indicated by an 11th cent. inscription.

** **FELTRE** (Belluno). Built on the lower slopes of the so-called Goats' hill (delle Capre) in a particularly attractive area. The *Cattedrale*, dedicated to St. Peter, has been rebuilt several times, the last one being at the end of the 16th cent. It has a campanile dated 1392 and contains works of art including the tomb of Matteo Bellati by Tullio Lombardo (1455-1532), frescoes of various periods, including modern ones, and a Byzantine cross in boxwood dating from 542 A.D. The ancient church of *Ognissanti* contains a fresco of the Transfiguration and Saints Anthony and Lucy, considered the masterpiece of Lorenzo Luzzo (lived around 1476-1522). Notable the *Battistero* with 15th cent. apse and Renaissance doorway. The church of *Santa Maria degli Angeli* (1492) contains notable paintings, including one of the Madonna and Angels, possibly by Jacopo Bassano (c. 1517-1592). The Palazzo Villabruna houses the *Museo Civico*, with an archeological section and another one devoted to arts and crafts; there is also an art gallery with a fine collection of 16th, 17th and 18th cent. Venetian paintings. The Museum leads directly into the Historical Museum containing portraits, lithographs and autographs, especially

from the Renaissance period. The ex-Palazzo Cumano houses the *Galleria d'Arte Moderna*, which contains many paintings by Italian artists. There are interesting, mainly 16th cent. buildings on the *Via Mezzaterra*. The ex-*Palazzo Comunale*, one-time seat of the *Rettori Veneti*, was partly designed by Andrea Palladio (1508-1580). Notice the church of *San Rocco* (1599), with a harmonious interior consisting of a nave and two aisles. Excursion to the *Santuario dei Santi Vittore e Corona*, erected at the end of the 11th cent. and rebuilt in Romanesque-Byzantine style in the 12th. The interior contains 13th, 14th and 15th cent. frescoes.

* **FENIS** (Aosta). The trapezoidal *Castello* was built towards the middle of the 14th cent. and modified several times in later periods. The open gallery, which is entered from an interesting courtyard, contains frescoes by the school of Giacomo Jaquerio (recorded c. 1420-1453). The interior houses the Museum of Valdaostan Furniture.

** **FERENTILLO** (Terni). At the confluence of the Fosso Salto del Cieco and the Nera, in a gorge below two fortresses with towers jutting out over the steep slopes. The Nera divides the villages of Materella and Precetto. The 13th cent. church of *Santa Maria*, badly restored in later centuries, contains a Tabernacle of Holy Oil (1489), 16th cent. Umbrian-school frescoes, and, in the sacristy, a finely shaped cross by the painter Domenico di Giacomo da Leonessa (lived in the 15th cent.). The 15th cent. church of *Santo Stefano* is especially interesting for the baptismal font (1557) and the crypt. Near Ferentillo is the *Abbazia di San Pietro in Valle* on the lowest slopes of Monte Solenne. It was built around the tomb of two hermits by order of Faroaldo II, Duke of Spoleto. The *Chiesa* originates from the beginning of the 8th cent. The two side walls were decorated with frescoes, now in very poor condition, but which give an idea of Romanesque painting before the time of Pietro Cavallini (lived in the 13-14th cent.). It contains five remarkable Roman tombs, one of which is believed to hold the remains of Faroaldo II. Worth seeing is the harmonious 12th cent. cloister, in two orders, and the campanile, also 12th cent., with many 8th cent. fragments

Fenis, Castle.

112

Deruta. Plate with episodes from the Passion (now in the Museo Nazionale, Ravenna).

Fabriano, Pinacoteca Civica. Allegretto Nuzi, Madonna and Child, detail.

Domodossola, Parish Church. Tanzio da Varallo, St. Charles gives communion to the Plague-Victims, detail.

Faenza, Museo delle Ceramiche, Apothecary's jar.
Ferrara, Museo del Duomo. The month of October.

Ferrara, Museo del Duomo. Cosmè Tura, Virgin
of the Annunciation.

of marble reliefs from the ruins of the original church.

* FERENTINO (Frosinone). Situated on a hillside overlooking the Sacco valley The Romanesque, 11th cent. *Duomo*, dedicated to St. Ambrose the Martyr, has a plain facade with three doorways. The basilican interior has a wonderful Cosmatesque floor carried out in 1116 by a marble-worker called Paul, and contains a ciborium by Drudo da Trevio (lived in the 13th cent.), a Romanesque Bishop's chair, a spiral candelabra with Cosmatesque decorations, and, in the sacristy, a silver ciborium dating from the mid-17th cent. The rectangular *Acropoli*, a massive parallelepiped construction, dates from the Hernic period. Worthy of note are four large intercommunicating barrel-vaults above which there was probably once a terrace. The *Mercato Romano*, of the Republican age, is a large open area of stalls. *Porta Maggiore* or of *Casamari* is on the site of one of the original entrances to the Hernic town. *The Porta Sanguinaria*, a gateway in the polygonal walls of Ferentino, is partly Roman and partly medieval. The 14th cent. Cistercian-style church of *Santa Maria Maggiore* has a graceful facade with three doorways. The interior is made up of various well-blended architectural styles.

** FERMO (Ascoli Piceno). Situated between the valleys of the Tenna and Ete Vivo, it rises on a hill overlooked by the majestic

Ferentillo, Abbey of San Pietro in Valle. Sculpture on the cloister door.

Duomo. The building was erected in the 13th cent. and dedicated to the Assunta; it was rebuilt in the second half of the 18th cent. It has an asymmetrical facade and, inside, works of art such as statues of Hope and Faith, and medallions of Sixtus V and Pius III, by Gioacchino Varlè (1734-1806), paintings depicting the Purifying of the Souls, by Giovanni Battista Passeri (c. 1610-1679), and St. Ludovic of France, by Alessandro Ricci (lived in the 18th cent.). Notice the much admired remains of a 15th cent. mosaic pavement from an early Christian church, discovered in 1934; also worth a visit is the Chapel of the Blessed Sacrament, with paintings by Andrea Boscoli (c. 1550-1606) and Nicola Monti (1780-1864). In the basement can be seen remains of previous churches and a collection of archeological findings. The sacristy contains the famous chasuble of St. Thomas of Canterbury, a rare work beautifully embroidered in gold. The 13th cent. church of *Sant'Agostino* is Romanesque-Gothic in origin. It was restored in the first half of the 18th cent. and completely rebuilt in the present one. In the atrium there is a fresco representing the Madonna and Child with Saints, by an unknown 15th cent. artist, and a painting of Our Lady of Succour, by Giovanni Pagani (lived in the first half of the 16th cent.). The 18th cent. style interior contains remarkable works of art, including 14th and 15th cent. frescoes by unknown artists, a painting of the Nativity (1593) by Ercole Orfeo da Fano, an altarpiece depicting the Crown of Thorns, after the style of Tintoretto, and a Birth of the Virgin by Alessandro Vitali (1580-1640). *Piazza del Popolo* is the heart of Fermo, and is characterized by a series of porticoes (1569). The *Palazzo Comunale*, finis-

Fermo, Church of San Francesco, interior.

115

hed in 1525, houses an art gallery with a valuable collection of works, the most precious being a Nativity by Peter Paul Rubens (1577-1640). The *Oratorio di Santa Monica* (first half of the 15th cent.) contains notable works of art including a cycle of pictures illustrating Stories of John the Baptist and St. John, in international-Gothic style. The Romanesque-Gothic church of *San Domenico* (first half of the 13th cent.) has a bare facade with a fine doorway above which are cusps and a large round window dated 1455. The interior contains an altarpiece of the Last Supper by Nicola Monti (1780-1864) and magnificent Gothic wooden stalls carried out in 1448 by Giovanni da Montalparo. Also worth seeing at Fermo are: the *Biblioteca* containing one hundred thousand volumes, hundreds of incunabula, and thousands of fifteeners and correspondence of great historical importance; the *Loggiato di San Rocco* (first half of the 16th cent.); the gracious *Palazzo degli Studi*, designed by Girolamo Rainaldi (1570-1655); the *Museo Civico*, with a vast collection of archeological and medieval material; *Piazza del Girofalco*, which was once dominated by a 14th cent. fortress; *Palazzo Azzolino* (16th cent.;) the church of *Santa Maria del Carmine*, containing a panel of the Madonna and Child enthroned with four Saints, by Antonio Solario (lived in the 15-16th cent.); *Piscina Epuratoria Romana*, (first half of the 1st cent.); the church of *Santa Caterina*, rebuilt in the second half of the 15th

cent., containing a fresco representing St. Augustine with Saints Thomas of Canterbury and Ubaldo, Bishop of Gubbio, by Vincenzo Pagani (c. 1490-1568) and, finally, the church of *San Francesco*, begun in 1240, in Gothic style; the impressive interior contains the much-admired funeral monument of Lodovico Euffreducci, carried out in 1527, probably by Andrea Sansovino (1460-1529).

*** **FERRARA.** Agricultural, commercial and industrial town in a fertile valley on the right bank of the Po, with numerous historical associations. Building of the *Cattedrale* began in 1135 and continued for three and a half centuries; the facade, a blending of various styles, above all Romanesque and Gothic, has three beautiful Romanesque doorways. Inside are numerous works of art, including a Crucifixion altar by Carlo Pasetti (recorded 1639-1695), bronze statues of Saints Maurelius and George by Dominic of Paris (recorded 1450-1467), and a painting depicting the Universal Judgement by Sebastiano Filippi, called Bastianino (1532-1602). The *Museo del Duomo* contains magnificent temperas of St. George and the Annunciation by Cosmè Tura (c. 1430-1495) and a lovely statue of the Madonna of the Pomegranate with St. Maurelius, by Jacopo della Quercia (1367-1438). The *Castello Estense*, begun in 1385 to a design by Bartolino da Novara, was completed in the 16th cent. It consists of brick buildings, surrounded by a moat, with solid

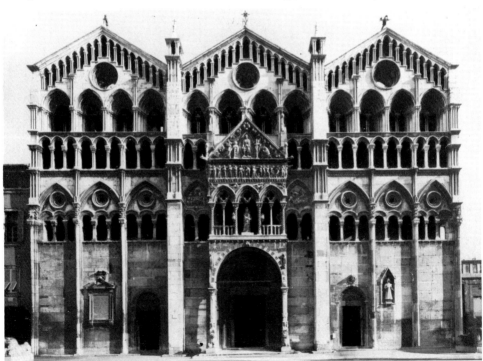

Ferrara, Cathedral, facade.

towers at the corners. The interior contains interesting rooms such as the large Games room (with frescoes, probably by Bastianino), the small Games room and the Aurora Hall, the chapel of Renée of France, small Loggia of the Orange-trees, and the Throne Room. The *Palazzo dei Diamanti*, so-called because its exterior is covered with twelve thousand small diamond-shaped pieces of marble. It was begun in the late 15th cent. and completed in the 16th. The interior houses the Town Art Gallery, which contains a large and valuable collection of pictures from the 15th cent. onwards; especially worthy of mention are paintings by Cosmè Tura, Vittore Carpaccio (c. 1465-1526) and Benevento Tisi, called Garofalo (1481-1559). The *Palazzo di Ludovico il Moro* is the unfinished masterpiece of Biagio Rossetti (1447-c. 1516); inside is the Spina archeological museum. The late-14th cent. *Palazzo di Schifanoia* or *Scandiana* was designed by Biagio Rossetti; in the Hall of the Months is one of the most interesting secular series of frescoes from the Renaissance period. In the Hall of the Enterprises can be seen Michelangelo's sketch of Moses (1475-1564). The 15th cent. *Casa Romei* is an example of a 15th cent. gentleman's residence. The mid-16th cent. *Palazzina di Marfisa* has ceilings decorated with grotesques, painted by Camillo Filippi (c. 1550-1574) and his sons Cesare and Sebastian. The *Palazzo Naselli-Crespi*, designed by Girolamo da Carpi (1501-1556) is an elegant example of Renaissance architecture. The Renaissance *Palazzo Roverella* was possibly built to a design by Biagio Rossetti. The *Basilica di Santa Maria in Vado* was begun in the 11th cent. and rebuilt by Biagio Rossetti; inside are important paintings by Carlo Bononi (1569-1632). The *Monastero di Sant'Antonio in Polesine* was founded in 1249 by Princess Beatrice II d'Este; it has a particularly attractive nuns' choir. The church of *San Giorgio* was a religious centre in remote times; it contains valuable works of art. The church of *San Benedetto* was built at the turn of the 16th cent.; notice in particular the two 16th cent. cloisters and the Lavabo room. *Via della Volta* is the most characteristic street of the ancient town, and numerous medieval buildings can be seen on both sides of it. *Corso Ercole I d'Este* is flanked by many noble dwellings. *Corso della Giovecca* is a wide and characteristic thoroughfare, overlooked by interesting medieval buildings. The *Certosa* (mid-15th cent.) contains the Municipal Chapel, where there is a bust of Leopoldo Cicognara by Antonio Canova (1757-1822). The *Casa di Ludovico Ariosto* (Ariosto's house) is a sombre building erected at the end of the 15th cent. or beginning of the 16th cent., and bought by the poet for his own residence.

* **FICULLE** (Terni). Pleasantly situated farming village, partly encircled by a medieval wall. The *Collegiata di Santa Vittoria* was built

Ferrara, Castle.
Ferrara, Palazzo dei Diamanti.
Ferrara, Palazzo Schifanoia. Francesco del Cossa, Pruning, detail of the Months.

at the beginning of the 17th cent. to a design by Ippolito Scalza. In the church of *Santa Maria Vecchia* are remains of 15th cent. frescoes and a wooden statue of the Assunta, of the same period. Walk to the *Castello della Sala*, erected by Angelo Monaldeschi della Vipera in 1350, and now owned by the Marquise Antinori of Florence; in the chapel are late-15th cent. frescoes by the Umbrian school.

* **FIDENZA** (Parma). Small agricultural and industrial town. The *Duomo*, dedicated to San Donnino, took the whole of the 13th cent. to build. The solemn facade is richly decorated and has a square tower at each side. The niches at the sides of the doorway contain Romanesque statues. The basilican interior contains a series of frescoes (late 13th cent.) depicting the Last Judgement, and other valuable works of art. The former church of *San Giorgio* (late 14th cent.) has a Gothic gable facade.

** **FIESOLE** (Florence). Situated in a particularly attractive position on a hill overlooking the valleys of the rivers Arno and Mugnone. The *Duomo*, dedicated to St. Romolo, was begun in 1024 by the order of Bishop James the Bavarian, enlarged in 1256, and modified during the second half of the last century. Inside are many works of art, including a statue of St. Romolo, Bishop of Fiesole, by Giovanni della Robbia (1469-post 1529), the Salutati chapel, tomb of Bishop Leonardo Sa-

Fidenza, Duomo. The prophet Ezekiel.

lutati (died in 1466), with a fine bust by Mino da Fiesole (c. 1430-1484), a triptych in a cusped frame depicting the Madonna enthroned and Child with Saints Alexander, Peter, Romolo and Donat, by Bicci di Lorenzo (1373-1452), and a marble altar divided into three sections by fluted columns, by Andrea Ferrucci (1465-1526). The 11th cent. *Palazzo Vescovile* contains the 14th cent. chapel of St. James, with a large fresco representing the Coronation of Mary with a host of Saints, by Rossello di Jacopo Franchi (c. 1377-1456); the garden is partly surrounded by Etruscan walls. The church of *Santa Maria Primerana*, once called the church of Santa Maria Intemerata, is an ancient oratory, with 16th cent. doorway. Inside are works of art including a self-portrait by the sculptor Francesco da Sangallo (1494-1576). The church of *Sant'Alessandro* was built on the site of an Etruscan, and later Roman, temple dedicated to Bacchus. It is almost impossible to know when it was constructed, although there is reason to believe that Theodoric, King of the Ostrogoths, had the pagan temple transformed into a Christian one at the beginning of the 6th cent. The interior consists of a nave and two aisles, divided by sixteen fine cipolin columns, oriental-style, with Ionic base and capitals, perhaps taken from the temple of Bacchus. It contains a few works of art: in the adjacent oratory of the Assunta is a panel representing the Assumption and Saints Michael and Peter, by Gerino da Pistoia (1480-post 1529). The chapel of St. Anthony, in the church of *San Francesco* (first

Fiesole, Badia Fiesolana, facade.

118

half of the 14th cent.), contains a remarkable stucco Crucifixion in Donatello style. The museum of the Franciscan Missions and magnificent remains of the fortress are worth a visit. The Roman Theatre (*Teatro Romano*) was built at the beginning of the Imperial era to hold three thousand spectators. The ruins of the *Terme* (also built at the beginning of the Imperial era, and enlarged under Hadrian) can be seen, consisting of high arches on pillars. A temple (*Tempio Romano*), discovered in 1792 and excavated during the following years, stands on the site of a primitive Etruscan temple. The three rooms of the *Museo* contain a large collection of archeological material excavated from the Fiesole area. The *Museo Bandini*, founded in 1795 by the renowned scholar-canon Angiolo Maria Bandini, contains many works of art by illustrious masters, including the painters Bicci di Lorenzo, Agnolo di Taddeo Gaddi (recorded 1369-1396), Neri di Bicci (1419-1491) and Francesco del Brina (c. 1540-1577), to mention but a few. The church of *San Domenico* was begun in 1406. Inside are works of art including a fresco representing the Glory of St. Domenic, by Matteo Bonechi (c. 1672-1752), and a panel, part of a triptych, depicting the Madonna and Child, with Angels and Saints Barnabas, Dominic, Thomas Aquinas and Peter the Martyr, by Beato Angelico (c. 1387-1455). The *Badia Fiesolana* is an austere and impressive abbey, until 1026 Fiesole cathedral, dedicated to St. Peter. During that year it was destroyed by the Camaldolese and rebuilt at the same time as the monastery. It is believed that the present Abbey was designed by Filippo Brunelleschi (1377-1446) who, however, died ten years before work began. The 15th cent. facade incorporated a 12th cent. Romanesque facade in white and green, and repeats architectural motifs from the Florence Baptistery and San Miniato. The interior contains works of art and, in the refectory, is a fresco depicting Christ attended by Angels, carried out in 1629 by Giovanni da San Giovanni (1592-1636).

* **FIGLINE VALDARNO** (Florence). On the left bank of the river Arno. The *Collegiata* (begun in the early 12th cent.) contains the Corpus Domini chapel; the walls are decorated

with a Sacrifice of Isaac and six Stories from the Old Testament by Tommaso Gherardini (1715-1797). Nearby are the *Resti di Castelvecchio*, ruins of an ancient town which stood here before Figline was founded. In the neighbourhood, at Gaville, is the parish church of *San Romualdo;* Romanesque in style, it has been recently restored.

* **FILOTTRANO** (Ancona). On a hill between the Rio Troscione and the Rio Fiumicello. The church of *San Francesco* has a slender unfinished facade in brick. The aisleless interior contains a panel representing the Raising of Lazarus, by Pompeo Morganti (lived in the 16th cent.), and in the sacristy there is a painting by Ercole Ramazzini (1571), and noteworthy confessionals and pews. The church of *San Michele* has valuable 16th and 17th sacred vestments. The 17th cent. church of *Assunta*, with a beautiful, harmonious brick facade, contains paintings by Ernesto da Utrecht (lived c. 1567-1626), and a Nativity after the style of Reni.

* **FINALE EMILIA** (Modena). On the left bank of the river Panaro. The town is dominated by a 15th cent. fortress, on a square plan with towers at the corners bearing the Este eagle. The collegiate church of *Santi Filippo e Giacomo*, originally 15th cent., contains remarkable paintings, including a St. Francis by Guercino (1591-1666), Nuptials of the Virgin by Sigismondo Caula (1637-post 1694), and Adoration of the Magi by Giuseppe Maria Crespi called Spagnolo (1665-1747).

* **FINALE LIGURE** (Savona). Built alongside a large beach between the mouth of the Pora and the Castelletto hill. The *Basilica di San Giovanni Battista* has a Baroque facade and contains many remarkable frescoes. The town is built on land watered by numerous streams (the Pora, Aquila, Sciusa and their tributaries)

Figline Valdarno (surroundings), Parish Church of San Romualdo a Gaville.

Finale Ligure, Church of San Giovanni Battista, facade.

and mostly made up of sandy miocene limestone, known as Finale stone. By studying this limestone one can obtain evidence of the slow evolution of the human species; the *Caverne del Finale* (Finale Caves) are, for this reason, of great paleontological interest. Walks to the White Sand and Fairy caves are recommended.

* FIORENZUOLA D'ARDA (Piacenza). Agricultural and industrial town. The *Collegiata di San Francesco* was erected in the early 14th cent. and rebuilt at the end of the 15th. It has a tripartite facade surmounted by pin-

nacles, and contains a series of frescoes by 16th cent. Lombard painters, a remarkable painting by Marco Benefial (1684-1764) depicting the Miracle of San Fiorenzo, and valuable sacred vestments and ornaments.

*** FIRENZE/FLORENCE. The city, divided by the river Arno, contains a collection of monuments of incomparable wealth. The Cathedral square is particularly beautiful for the many colours and slender lines of the buildings dominating it. The *Battistero* is an 11-12th cent. Romanesque building, with three bronze doors decorated with bas-reliefs by Andrea Pisano

Florence, Baptistery, interior.
Florence, Santa Maria Novella, facade.

Florence, S. Maria del Fiore, dome.

120

(c. 1290-c. 1349) and Lorenzo Ghiberti (1378-1455); the so-called Door of Paradise is especially famous. The interior contains Byzantine-style mosaics. The *Campanile di Giotto* was begun by Giotto (1267?-1337) and Andrea Pisano, and completed by Francesco Talenti (recorded 1325-1369). The *Duomo* or *Santa Maria del Fiore* was begun in 1269 by Arnolfo di Cambio (c. 1245-1302), continued by Francesco Talenti, and the cupola was finished by Filippo Brunelleschi (1377-1446); of particular interest along the northern side is the Porta della Mandorla; inside are works by Benedetto da Maiano (1441-1497), Andrea del Castagno (c. 1421-1457), Paolo Uccello (1397-1475), Ghiberti, Lucca della Robbia (c. 1400-1482) and Michelangelo Buonarroti (1475-1564). The *Museo dell'Opera del Duomo* contains, above all, 14th and 15th cent. Florentine sculpture. The church of *San Lorenzo* was built between 1442 and 1446 by Brunelleschi and by Antonio Manetti (1460), The Old Sacristy was decorated between 1435 and 1443 by Donatello (1386-1466). In the *Biblioteca Laurenziana* are the *Medici chapels* with the new sacristy designed by Michelangelo, and the famous Medici tombs (1520-1533). The *Palazzo Medici-Riccardi*, built by Michelozzo Michelozzi (1396-1472) is a

Florence, S. Maria del Fiore, apse section.

superb Renaissance building, housing the Medici Museum; in a chapel is a series of frescoes by Benozzo Gozzoli (1420-1497). The church of *Ognissanti*, founded in 1256 and almost completely rebuilt around 1627, contains a fresco of the Last Supper by Domenico Ghirlandaio (1449-1494). The church of *Orsanmichele*, built between 1337 and 1404, contains a series of valuable statues in Gothic niches carved in the pillars; famous tabernacle by Andrea di Cione called Orcagna (14th cent.). The *Piazza della Signoria* is dominated by the *Loggia dei Lanzi*, the *Fontana di Piazza* and the *Palazzo Vecchio*, built between 1299 and 1314, to a plan by Arnolfo di Cambio, and later enlarged by Bernardo Buontalenti (1536-1608) and Giorgio Vasari (1511-1574). The Palazzo degli Uffizi, designed by Vasari, houses the *Galleria degli Uffizi*, which is the richest art gallery in Italy. *Palazzo Pitti* was built round 1458 to the design of Brunelleschi, but remodelled and enlarged in later centuries. It houses the Modern Art Gallery, Silver Museum and Pitti or Palatine Gallery. The Boboli Gardens (*Giardino di Boboli*) are interesting; they were designed in 1550 by Tribolo (1550-1558) and others. The church of *Santo Spirito*, begun by Brunelleschi in 1444, was continued by Manetti and finished in 1487. In the church of *Santa Maria del Carmine* is the Brancacci chapel containing frescoes by Masaccio (1401-1428); the cycle, begun by Masolino and continued by Masaccio, was completed by Filippino Lippi. *Palazzo Strozzi* and *Palazzo Rucellai* are fine examples of Florentine architecture in the Renaissance; the Strozzi Palace was built in 1489 by Benedetto da Maiano and continued by Cronaca (1457-1508); the Rucellai Palace was built between 1446 and 1451 by Bernardo Rossellino (1409-1464) to the design of Leon Battista Alberti. The church of *Santa Trinità* was built during the second half of the 13th cent. and has a facade (1594) by Bernardo Buontalenti. The three-arched *Ponte di Santa Trinità* is the work of Bartolomeo Ammannati (1511-1592). *Santa Maria Novella* was built between 1244 and 1360, and the facade, designed by Alberti, dates from 1456-1470. Inside are numerous works of art, including a panel by Giotto, a statue by Nino Pisano and frescoes by Masaccio, Ghirlandaio and Filippino Lippi. Adjacent to the church are the Cloisters: the Chiostro Verde, the small Chiostrino dei Morti and the large Cappellone degli Spagnoli (Spanish chapel). St. Mark's monastery, rebuilt by Michelozzo Michelozzi between 1436 and 1443, houses the *Museo di San Marco*, which contains important documentation on the main works of Beato Angelico (1400-c. 1455). The *Galleria dell'Accademia* is famous for its collection of works by Michelangelo. The *Ospedale degli Innocenti* is by Brunelleschi (1426); it has a porticoed front surmounted by enamelled terracottas by Luca della Robbia (c. 1400-1482). The *Museo Archeologico* is especially interesting for

Florence, San Miniato al Monte, facade.
Florence, Bargello. Donatello, St. George.

Florence, Uffizi. Duccio da Boninsegna, Majesty, detail.

Florence, church of San Lorenzo. Donatello, Deposition from the Cross (detail of the first pulpit).

Florence, Bargello. Andrea del Verrocchio, David, detail.

Florence, Galleria dell'Accademia. Michelangelo, David, detail.

Florence, Loggia dei Lanzi. Benvenuto Cellini, Perseus, detail.

Florence, Church of Ognissanti. Domenico del Ghirlandaio, Last Supper, detail.

Foligno, Palazzo Trinci. Fresco in the room of the Planets, detail of Astrology.

Fontanellato, Fortress of San Vitale. Parmigianino, Stories of Diana and Actaeon, detail.

Forlì, Pinacoteca Civica. Antonio Canova, Hebe.

Fossa, Santa Maria ad Criptas. Last Supper, detail.

its Etruscan section. The *Museo Nazionale del Bargello* contains important 14-17th cent. sculptures and a valuable collection of arts and crafts, the most important being a group of sculptures by Michelangelo and Donatello. The church of *Santa Croce*, begun in 1295 to a design by Arnolfo di Cambio, is one of the most beautiful Franciscan churches there is; it has a plain interior with a nave and two aisles and contains a valuable collection of famous works of art (Giotto, Donatello, Benedetto da Maiano, Bernardo Rossellino, Maso di Banco). The *Cappella dei Pazzi* (built between 1430-1446), is one of Brunelleschi's finest works. The Romanesque church of *San Miniato al*

Monte (11-13th cent.) has a facade decorated with geometric designs. Also worthy of mention are: the *Chiesa della Badia*, begun at the end of the 10th cent. and enlarged during the 13th, containing sculptures by Mino da Fiesole (1429-1484); the 11th cent. church of the *Santi Apostoli;* the church of *Santa Maria Maddalena de' Pazzi* with a courtyard designed by Giuliano da Sangallo (1445-1516); and the *Palazzi Davanzati, Bardi, Capponi, Quarantesi and Lardarel.* In the neighbourhood of Florence are numerous villas, including the *Villa Capponi* called "the stone" ("la pietra"), one of the most attractive in the area; it was built in the 15th cent. and rebuilt in 1697 by Carlo Fon-

Florence, Santa Croce, interior.
Florence, Uffizi. Sandro Botticelli, Birth of Venus.

Florence, Museo dell'Opera del Duomo. Andrea Pisano, Giotto's Bell-tower panel.

tana (1634-1714) and contains an important collection of 14-17th cent. works of art. *Villa Salviati* was the manor house (14th cent.) first of the Del Palagio family and then of the Montegonzi. It is an austere-looking building with small towers at the corners. *Villa Medicea di Careggi*, situated in the centre of a thickly-wooded park, was first owned by the Lippi family and then by the Medici who bought it in 1417. It was later taken over by Cosimo the Elder who enlarged and embellished it with works by the sculptor Michelozzo Michelozzi (1396-1472); it has an attractive small, irregular-shaped courtyard designed by Michelozzo.

* **FIUGGI** (Frosinone). Composed of Fiuggi Fonte, the modern part, and Fiuggi town, which is mainly medieval. At Fiuggi Fonte are the *Fonte Bonifacio VIII* in the centre of a large park, and the *Fonte Anticolana*, also in a green setting. The church of *San Biagio* has two important paintings: Madonna enthroned, by Giuseppe Cesari called Cavalier d'Arpino (1568-1640), and St. Lawrence baptizing St. Blaise by Giovanni Battista Speranza (c. 1600-1640). The collegiate church of *San Pietro* has a painting of St. Francis in Ecstasy, a remarkable work by an unknown 17th cent. artist.

* **FIUMALBO** (Modena). At the confluence of the Rio Acquicciola and Rio delle Pozze. The parish church of *San Bartolomeo*, dating back to the beginning of the 13th cent., has a painting of St. Bartholomew, by Adeodato Malatesta (1806-1891), the so-called Fiumalba Cross (1494), vestments and reliquaries. The *Oratorio di San Rocco* (beginning of the 15th cent.) contains frescoes, some badly damaged, by Saccaccino Saccaccini (recorded 1503-1531).

*** **FLORENCE**, see Firenze.

** **FLORIDIA** (Syracuse). A few kilometres away is *Pantalica*, once the site of Hybla, which, from the 13-8th cent. B.C. was the capital of a people who had fled from the coastal towns on the arrival of the Sicules. It is an interesting archeological area which includes the necropolis of Filiporto, with nearly a thousand tombs; the north-west necropolis (12-11th cent. B.C.); the larger north necropolis, of the same period; the Cavetta necropolis (9-8th cent. B.C.) and the Anaktoron, the Prince's palace, which bears witness to the economic and political power attained by Hybla in the 12th and 11th cent. B.C.; it is a megalithic building, remains of which have been brought to light during recent excavations.

** **FOGGIA.** Main town of the Capitanata area, in the centre of the Tavoliere plain. The *Cattedrale*, dedicated to Santa Maria Icona Vetere, was built about 1170, according to the wishes of William II the Good, and rebuilt

in Baroque style after the earthquake in 1731. The interior, in the form of a Latin cross, contains a large painting by Francesco De Mura (1696-1784) of the Miracle of the Loaves, and the Chapel of the Icona Vetere or Madonna of the Seven Veils, built in 1672, and containing the miraculous image of the Madonna. The *Musei Civici* have an important archeological section, containing a collection of prehistoric material, above all stone weapons found in the Gargano area, terracottas, bronze and alabaster work; also worthy of note is the numismatic collection, with Arpane, Roman, medieval and Neapolitan coins; scientific section with thousands of Colcopter and Lapidoptera; historical section, Jordan section. The Museums also house a valuable art gallery containing 19th and 20th cent. paintings by Apulian artists, including Nicola Parisi (1827-1887) and Domenico Caldara (1814-1907). The *Chiesa del Calvario* or *delle Croci*, built at the end of the 17th and first half of the 18th cent., contains a remarkable fresco depicting the Ascent to Calvary by an unknown 18th cent. artist. The *Villa Comunale* has a rectangular-shaped park, designed in 1820 by Luigi Oberty, in which are stone images of famous sons of Foggia.

** **FOLIGNO** (Perugia). Flourishing commercial and industrial town, with Renaissance architecture, on the left bank of the river Topino. The *Duomo*, built in 1133 by a Master Atto, has a Romanesque facade with a rose-window surrounded by Evangelist symbols, and a magnificent Romanesque portal. The harmonious interior contains a fresco of the

Foggia, Chapel of the Seven Crosses.

Madonna with Angels (1500), carried out by Feliciano de' Muti; a canopy above the high altar, in imitation of the one by Gian Lorenzo Bernini (1598-1680) for St. Peter's in Rome, and the Chapel of the Blessed Sacrament designed by Antonio da Sangallo the Younger (1483-1546). The *Palazzo Trinci*, built at the turn of the 15th cent., houses the *Pinacoteca Civica*, which contains a rich collection of works of art; the Chapel, completely frescoed by Ottaviano Nelli (1375-1444/50); the Hall of the Liberal Arts and of the Planets; the Hall of the Giants, with fifteen large figures of Roman heroes painted by artists from the school of Nelli (beginning of the 15th cent.); and an archeological museum containing Roman sculptures and inscriptions. The Romanesque church of *Santa Maria Infraportas*, flanked by a sturdy Romanesque campanile, has a basilican interior and noteworthy Chapel of the Assunta. The church of *San Nicolò*, begun in the 14th cent., contains a large polyptych by Niccolò di Liberatore called Alunno (1430-1502). The *Chiesa della Nunziatella* (1494), with a Renaissance interior, has a valuable tabernacle stuccoed by Lattanzio di Niccolò Alunno (recorded 1480-1527). Walk to the church of *Santa Maria in Campis*.

* FOLLINA (Treviso). Fluorishing industrial centre, especially for textiles. The *Abbazia di Follina*, founded by the Cistercians in the 12th cent., and well repaired in the 20th, has a 14th cent. facade. The interior, partly Gothic and partly Romanesque, contains a fresco of the

Foligno, Duomo. Detail of the portal.

Madonna and Child with Saints and a worshipper (1507), probably carried out by pupils of Pordenone.

** FONDI (Latina). Situated at the foot of the Aurunci mountains. The church of *Santa Maria Assunta*, rebuilt at the end of the 15th cent., has a facade with three portals; the large interior, in the form of a Latin cross, contains a triptych of the Eternal between Saints James and John the Evangelist (1569) by Gabriele Feltrensis; a Pietà, probably by Giovanni da Gaeta (lived in the 16th cent.), a Nativity, also by Giovanni da Gaeta, and a Renaissance ciborium dated 1491. The *Duomo*, dedicated to St. Peter, was built on the remains of a pagan temple, and rebuilt in the first half of the 12th cent.; it has a travertine facade on which is a bas-relief representing Christ Blessing, four Apostles and two Angels. The basilican interior contains a triptych of the Madonna and Child, Onorato II and Saints Peter and Paul, by Antoniazzo Romano (c. 1435-c. 1517), a Cosmatesque pulpit, by the Roman marble worker Giovanni di Nicola (lived in the 13th cent.), and other artistic motifs. The church of *San Domenico* (1215), once called Santa Maria iuxta Amphitheatrum because it was built on the ruins of a Roman amphitheatre, is an interesting Gothic building; adjoining it is an attractive cloister which leads to a Chapter House with a Durazza-style portal. The *Palazzo del Principe* (second half of the 15th cent.) is enhanced by Angevin-Durazza-style and Gothic-Catalan architectural motifs. The *Castello* is an impressive, rectangular building (13-15th cent.). Beside it is the solitary, so-called Torrione. The church of *San Francesco* (late 14th cent.) has a Gothic porch, and a portal which already reveals Renaissance influence. Traces of the medieval walls (*Cinta Muraria*) can still be seen.

* FONTANELLATO (Parma). In the second half of the 14th cent. the town was fortified and took on its medieval appearance, which it still partly retains. The *Rocca* is one of the best preserved and most picturesque castles in Emilia. Built during the first half of the 15th cent., it has numerous rooms, the most interesting being that of Diana and Actaeon, with frescoes depicting Ovid's story of Actaeon surprising Diana bathing, and being changed into a stag. Also worth seeing is the so-called Room of Illusions where, thanks to a clever play of mirrors, one sees a reflection of the market-place and church square. The *Santuario della Madonna del Rosario* (17th cent.) has an impressive interior, with 19th cent. decorations. The *Monastero delle Domenicane* contains a small but interesting picture gallery with 16th, 17th and 18th cent. paintings.

***FORLÌ. Situated on the right bank of the river Montone, on the Via Emilia. It is rich

in history, monuments and works of art. The 12th cent. church of *San Mercuriale*, the most famous building in Forlì, has a facade with a marble portal; in the lunette is a beautiful 13th cent. relief of the Dream and Adoration of the Magi. Inside are numerous works of art, including many paintings by Marco Palmezzano (1459-1539), the tomb of Barbara Manfredi by Francesco di Simone Ferrucci (1437-1493), and that by Giacomo Bianchi (recorded 1514-1560) in the so-called Ferri chapel. The church is flanked by a square bell-tower, designed by Francesco Deddi (recorded 1178-1180). The 12th cent. *Duomo*, rebuilt in the 15th cent., is an imposing building containing works of art, the finest of which is a fresco representing the Annunciation by Carlo Cignani (1628-1719), who worked on it for 25 years. The *Rocca di Ravaldino* is a majestic, square, brick building, dating back to the 14th cent. The church of *Santa Maria dei Servi* (latter half of the 13th cent.) contains the Numai tomb by Tommaso Fiamberti (recorded 1498-1525), with bas-reliefs by Giovanni Ricci (lived c. 1440-1523); a 15th cent. choir and attractive 14th cent. chapel in the Chapter House. The *Pinacoteca Comunale* contains a rich collection of works of art, mostly from monasteries dissolved by Napoleon Bonaparte; it includes many works by Giovanni Francesco Barbieri, called Guercino (1591-1666), Guido Cagnacci (1601-1663), Marco Palmezzano, Melozzo da Forlì (1438-1494), Beato Angelico, and Antonio Canova (1757-1822). The same building houses the Romagna Ethnographic Museum and the important Archeological Museum. In the neighbourhood is the 15th cent. church of *Santa Maria delle Grazie di Fornò;* the unusual interior contains a Renaissance marble relief of the Trinity, attributed to either Antonio Rossellino (1427-1479) or Agostino di Duccio (1418-c. 1481). Also nearby is the 13th cent. parish church of *Santa Maria in Acquedotto*, in Romanesque style.

* **FORLIMPOPOLI** (Forlì). The ancient *Collegiata di San Rufillo* was rebuilt in the second

Forlì, Pinacoteca Civica. Guido Cagnacci, Glory of San Valeriano.

half of the 14th cent.; in the atrium are notable 16th cent. sculptures, and the interior contains fine paintings including a Madonna and Child with Saints, by Luca Longhi (1507-1580), and a Deposition, probably by Francesco Menzocchi (1502-1584). The massive *Rocca* (late 14th cent.) was rebuilt during the second half of the 15th cent. on a rectangular plan with cylindrical towers at the corners; it was the residence of various feudal lords.

* **FORMIA** (Latina). Attractive little town on the Bay of Gaeta, composed of two villages, the upper one called Castelnuovo (later known as Castellone), and the lower one Mola di Gaeta, on account of its mills. The 4th cent. *Teatro Romano* was the scene of the martyrdom of St. Erasmus the Bishop. *Villa Rubino* stands on the site of the villa of Marcus Tullius Cicero (106-43 B.C.). The *Peschiera Romana* is a group of large troughs used as fish-reserves, which must have belonged to a luxurious Roman villa. Nearby is the so-called *Tomb of Cicero*, 24 metres high; in the burial chamber is a cylindrical column formed of stone rings.

* **FORNOVO DI TARO** (Parma). Interesting village on the right bank of the river Taro, it is a cross-roads and railway junction between the Po valley and the Mediterranean coast. The 11th cent. *Parrocchiale*, dedicated to the Assunta, was probably built on the site of a Roman basilica. It has a gable facade and contains some works of art, such as Stories of St. Margaret, a marble relief by an unknown sculptor after the style of Benedetto Antelami (c. 1150-c. 1230).

** **FOSSA** (L'Aquila). The parish church of the *Assunta* dates back to the 15th cent. *Santa Maria delle Grotte* or *ad Cryptas* is a tiny church (latter half of the 13th cent.) in Cistercian-Gothic style. Inside, the walls are entirely covered with frescoes by 13th cent. masters. From the *Convento di Santo Spirito* (first half of the 13th cent.) one can go up to the *Castello d'Oro* and *Convento di Sant'Angelo* (also 13th cent.).

* **FOSSACESIA** (Chieti). In the neighbourhood is the church of *San Giovanni in Venere*, first built, together with the adjacent monastery, in the 8th cent. The church was enlarged in 1016 and remodelled in Cistercian style in the 12th cent. On the facade are some interesting Roman sculptures.

* **FOSSANO** (Cuneo). Noted as one of the most characteristic centres in Piedmont. The square, turreted *Castello dei Principi di Acaja* was built in 1314. Remarkable is the *Duomo*, erected in 1779. The church of the *Santissima Trinità* (first half of the 18th cent.) is a consummate piece of work by Francesco Gallo. It has a fine exterior and interior, with two

elevated chapels and valuable stuccoes and frescoes.

** **FOSSOMBRONE** (Pesaro). Situated on a hillside as regards the medieval part, and along the left bank of the river Metauro. The *Corte Alta*, originally built in the 13th cent., houses the Vernarecci Museum and an art gallery with important paintings, engravings and etchings by Harmenszoon van Rijn Rembrandt (1606-1669), Albrecht Dürer (1471-1528), Jacques Callot (1592-1635), and Giambattista Tiepolo (1696-1770). The *Cattedrale di San Maurizio*, once a Benedictine Abbey, was completely rebuilt in the 18th cent. by Cosimo Morelli (1732-1812). It has a tripartite facade and contains notable marble altars designed by Andrea Vici (1744-1817). Other places worth visiting in Fossombrone are: the 15th cent. *Palazzo Vescovile* (Bishop's Palace), in rusticated stonework, containing an important fresco of the Crucifixion by Timoteo Viti (1467-1525); the church of *San Filippo*, with a heavily Baroque interior (18th cent.), containing a Madonna di Loreto, probably by Guido Reni (1575-1642); the 13th cent. church of *Sant'Agostino*, with a high altar (1802) by Francesco Asconi da Sant'Ippolito; the 16th cent. *Palazzo Albani* or *Corte Rossa*, partly designed by Francesco di Giorgio Martini (1439-1502); the 18th cent. church of *San Francesco*, on the facade of which is a war-damaged bas-relief by Domenico Rosselli (1439-1498), and the *Cittadella*, with considerable remains of the Malatesta Fortress.

* **FRANCAVILLA FONTANA** (Brindisi). Graceful little town built to a regular plan, with straight roads, lying in the foothills of the south-eastern Murge. The *Palazzo Imperiale*, built in 1450, enlarged in 1536 and completed at the beginning of the 18th cent. by the Imperiali family, is a massive rectangular building, with projecting, towerlike arrises and

a wide 18th cent. doorway. Inside is the Council Chamber, containing important 16th, 17th and 18th cent. paintings. The *Duomo*, designed by Giuseppe Di Lauro between 1753 and 1759, has a modest Baroque facade offset by a superb, though unfinished bell-tower. The Greek-cross interior contains paintings by Domenico Carella (c. 1721-1813) and a silver reliquary bust of San Renato, by the 17th cent. Venetian school.

* **FRASCATI** (Rome). Situated in the Alban Hills, it is particularly interesting for the gorgeous villas built all around it. *Villa Torlonia*, with a park now belonging to the Town, has a spectacular fountain (Teatro delle Acque) by Carlo Maderno (1556-1629). The *Cattedrale* has a Baroque facade by Girolamo Fontana (1690-1714). The *Chiesa del Gesù* is attributed to Pietro da Cortona (1596-1669). The *Villa Aldobrandini* consists of a magnificent palace by Giacomo della Porta (1533-1602), Carlo Maderno and Giovanni Fontana (1540-1614), and a huge terraced park with spectacular "Teatro delle Acque" fountains. The *Villa*

Fossano, Castle.

Francavilla, Duomo, facade.
Frascati, Villa Aldobrandini.

Falconieri was erected in the mid-16th cent. but rebuilt later by Francesco Borromini (1599-1667). The palace of the *Villa Tuscolana* or *Ruffinella* was built by Luigi Vanvitelli (1700-1773).

* **FRASSINORO** (Modena). Pleasantly situated holiday resort. The *Parrocchiale* (parish church) dedicated to Santa Maria Assunta and San Claudio, stands on the remains of an 11th cent. Benedictine Abbey, and contains some interesting architectonic elements.

* **FRATTAMAGGIORE** (Naples). In the greater Naples areas. The *Chiesa Madre*, dedicated to Santa Maria degli Angeli and San Sossio, was built in the 12th cent. but altered during the Gothic period, and heavily overdecorated in Baroque style. In 1945 the elaborate additions were destroyed by fire, revealing the original structure of the building, which was then carefully restored. The facade has a notable Renaissance doorway.

* **FRATTA POLESINE** (Rovigo). Agricultural centre, medieval in origin, with a large number of villas, the loveliest and most renowned being *Villa Badoer* by Andrea Palladio (1508-1580), with two exedra porticoes and, in front, a wide flight of steps. The Palladian-style *Villa Bragadin-Mischiatti* has a Doric loggia. The 17th cent. *Casa Cornoldi* has an asymmetrical facade. The parish church of *Santi Pietro e Paolo* (mid-16th cent.) has a frescoed ceiling by Francesco Zugno (1709-1787), two wooden angels carved by Andrea Brustolon (1662-1732), and paintings of the Birth of Jesus and Adoration of the Magi, by Mattia Bortoloni (1696-1750).

Fratta Polesine, Villa Badoer.

* **FUCECCHIO** (Florence). On the lowest slope of Mount Albano. The 11th cent. collegiate church of *San Giovanni Battista* was extensively altered in the 18th cent. It contains an interesting Tuscan-school Madonna and Child (15th cent.). The church of *San Salvatore* stands on a low hill called Salamartano, on the site of the original Abbey of San Salvatore; inside are paintings by Giorgio Vasari (1511-1574).

** **GAETA** (Latina). In an attractive position, overlooking the Bay of Gaeta, it has some interesting architecture. The *Campanile del Duomo* is considered the city's most beautiful monument. It is built of rocks and monolithic columns taken from Roman buildings, whilst the three picturesque storeys were planned by the Roman marble worker Nicola di Angelo (recorded 1148-1174). The *Duomo*, dedicated to the patron saints of Gaeta, Erasmus and Martian, was first built in the 11th cent. and contains a much admired late-13th cent. marble candelabrum for the Paschal candle, with forty-eight bas-reliefs; a painting of the Martyrdom of St. Erasmus by Carlo Saraceni (1580-1620) and, on the high altar, the banner of Lepanto (1571). In the crypt is a Martyrdom of St. Erasmus by Giacinto Brandi (1623-1691). The Sagrestia dei Canonici contains a valuable panel by a follower of Raphael (1483-1520) depicting the Madonna and Child, St. Michael and six Angels. In the recently formed diocesan museum are valuable paintings, including a Madonna delle Itrie by Giovanni da Gaeta (lived in the 16th cent.), a Pietà by Massys Quentin (c. 1465-1530), a St. Catherine and Madonna and Child with St. Bernard by Andrea Vaccaro (1598-1670), and a Madonna and Child with Saints by Sebastiano Conca (c. 1680-1764). The church of the *Santissima Annunziata* (first built at the beginning of the 14th cent.) has a Baroque facade heightened in the 18th cent. The bright interior contains a polyptych by Giovanni Filippo Criscuolo (c. 1500-1584), a Nativity and Crucifixion by Luca Giordano (1632-1705), and a painting of the Madonna by Giacinto Brandi. Magnificent adjacent golden grotto or Chapel of the Immacolata, in Renaissance style. The 11th cent. sanctuary of the *Santissima Trinità* or of the *Montagna Spaccata* is connected with a monastery founded by the Benedictines, now a theological college, containing numerous paintings by Sebastiano Conca and other lesser painters of the 17th cent. The 10th cent. Romanesque church of *San Giovanni a Mare*, known locally as San Giuseppe, has a facade with a Gothic portal and a small bell gable. Inside are interesting but faded frescoes, probably 10th cent., and others of the 15th cent. The church of *Santa Lucia*, built in the 12th cent. and modified several times in later periods, contains 13th, 14th and 15th cent. frescoes, and a 13th cent. baptistery with Cosmatesque elements. The *Quartiere Medievale* includes the 13th cent. church of St. Catherine; the interior, tending towards Gothic, contains a Madonna del Buon Consiglio, by Luigi Stanziani (lived in the 19th cent.) and Madonna del Silenzio, by Luca Giordano, and the 15th cent. church of San Domenico, in late Gothic style with a large interior containing a painting of The Triumph of Faith by Mattia Preti (1613-1699) and a Madonna of the Rosary by Pompeo Landulfo (recorded 1588-1609). The *Castello*, first built in the 8th cent. and modified in 1227 by Frederick II, in 1289 by Charles II of Anjou, in 1436 by Alphonse I of Aragon, and in 1536 by Charles V, tells the story of the town's tormented past. The massive building is formed by the joining of the so-called Aragonese Castle with the Angevin Castle. In the mid-16th cent. church of the *Ulivi* is a painting of the Birth of the Virgin by Sebastiano Conca. In the church of *San Francesco*, at the top of a high flight of steps, is a statue of the Apostles by the brothers Giuseppe and Vincenzo d'Annibale (lived in the 19th cent.), and Assunta, painted by Girolamo Imparato (recorded 1573-1621). In the so-called *Torre d'Orlando* is the cylindrical tomb of Lucius Munarius Placus (22 B.C.). Also worth seeing is the circular mausoleum of Lucius Sempronius Atratinus (73-20 B.C.).

* **GALATINA** (Lecce). One of the most densely populated and busiest little towns on the Salentine peninsular. The 17th cent. parish church of *Santi Pietro e Paolo* has a rich Baroque facade. Inside is a painting of the Washing of the Feet, by Serafino Elmo (1696-c. 1770), and a 18th cent. marble statue of the Immacolata. The Franciscan church of *Santa Caterina di Alessandria*, built towards the end of the 14th cent., in accordance with the wishes of Raimondello Orsini, overlord of the territory, and completed under his son, Gian Antonio, has a tricuspid facade with an impressive main door (1397), flanked by columns based on lions with zoomorphic corbels. The interior contains frescoes by numerous artists, mostly from the Marches and Emilia, carried out in the early decades of the 15th cent. In the chancel is the tomb of Raimondello Orsini, and behind the high altar, a monument to Gian Antonio Orsini.

Galatina, Santa Caterina. Frescoes, detail.

* **GALATONE** (Lecce). Agricultural town situated in a fertile area, with Baroque buildings similar to those in the nearby town of Lecce. The most famous historical building in Galatone is the sanctuary of the *Crocifisso della Pietà*, built between 1696 and 1710, to a design by fra Nicola da Léquile. The facade is over-decorated and spoilt by too many statues. Inside, the dome is covered with frescoes and there is a massive high altar; the magnificently decorated ambo and organ (1699) are also interesting. The *Castello*, in front of the Sanctuary, and one-time residence of the Pignatelli-Belmonte family, is still in fairly good condition; it has characteristic 16th cent. windows and a square sloping-sided tower.

Galatone, Church of Crocifisso della Pietà.

* **GALEATA** (Forli). On the left bank of the Suasia. Originally Umbrian, called Mevaniola, it later became a Roman municipality. The church of *San Pietro* was rebuilt on foundations dating right back to the 4th cent. Inside are two 17th cent. Tuscan school altarpieces. The *Palazzo Potesterile*, rebuilt in 1636, has stone coats-of-arms on the facade. Walk to the *Abbazia di Sant'Ellero*: in the church (rebuilt in the 17th cent.) are remains of 11th cent. sculptures.

* **GALLIANO** (Town of Eupilio, province of Como). Situated in the Brianza area near Cantù, it has some interesting Romanesque buildings. The basilica of *San Vincenzo*, built before 1000 A.D., and restructured, especially in the apse section, in the time of Ariberto da Intimiano, contains a valuable collection of frescoes, mainly from the beginning of the 11th cent. In the apse are paintings depicting Christ in Majesty and Stories of St. Vincent. On the walls are Stories of St. Christopher, belonging to a later date than the frescoes in the apse, and older ones depicting Stories of

Adam and Eve, St. Margaret and Samson. The baptistery of *San Giovanni* was probably built around 1000 A.D. In the upper part of the four semi-circular exedrae is a women's gallery.

* **GALLICANO** (Lucca). At the confluence of the Turrite and Serchio. The parish church of *San Jacopo* contains a statue of the Madonna and Child with Saints in glazed terracotta from the workshop of Andrea della Robbia (1435-1528). Excursion to the *Eremo di Calomini* where there is a tiny church carved out of the rock at the foot of a steep precipice, much visited by pilgrims.

* **GALLIPOLI** (Lecce). Situated on a promontory and a small island jutting out for 3 km into the Ionian Sea. The *Cattedrale*, dedicated to St. Agatha, and built by Giovanni Bernardino Genuino (lived in the 17th cent.), has a splendid facade built in volcanic tufa. Inside, is a Madonna and St. Oronzo, the last painting by Giovanni Andrea Coppola (c. 1597-1659); there are many other paintings of his in the church; a Madonna delle Grazie or del Popolo, by Gian Domenico Catalano (lived in the 17-18th cent.), and a large painting by Nicola Malinconico (1673-1721) depicting Christ Driving the Moneychangers out of the Temple. The *Castello* (16th cent.) has a ravelin thrusting out into the harbour, and is protected by a large circular tower and square keep with towers at the corners. The *Fontana Ellenistica*, rebuilt in the middle of the 16th cent., is characterized by its caryatids and telamones supporting a Baroque gable. The *Museo Civico* contains ancient Messapian sarcophagi and vases, Greek vases, large proto-Italiot bowls decorated with red symbols, a small collection of coins, etc. The church of *San Francesco* (17-

Galliano, Baptistery.

18th cent.) contains wooden sculptures carved in an austere and simple style, by Vespasiano Genuino (second half of the 16th cent.), and a panel of St. Francis by Pordenone (c. 1484-1539). The church of *San Domenico* or *del Rosario*, built at the end of the 17th cent., contains a painting of the Crucifixion by Gian Domenico Catalano (lived in the 17-18th cent.), a Madonna of the Rosary by Giovanni Andrea Coppola, and four busts of Saints, probably the work of Antonio Vivarini (c. 1420-pre-1484).

** **GALLUZZO** (near Florence). Busy Florentine suburb, near the confluence of the Ema and Greve. The *Certosa del Galluzzo* or *di Firenze e di Val di Ema* was built according to the wishes of Niccolò Acciaiuoli. Work began in 1341 and the building was at various times enlarged and embellished during later centuries. The art gallery contains numerous works of art, although many were transferred elsewhere in Napoleonic times. Especially worthy of note are the five large frescoed lunettes by Jacopo Carrucci, called Pontormo (1494-c. 1556), inspired by prints by Dürer; Saints Francis and Jerome and, higher up, the Annunziata, part of a beautiful polyptych by either Masolino da Panicale (1383-c. 1447) or Beato Angelico (1387-1455), a panel of St. Peter Martyr and St. George, by Ridolfo del Ghirlandaio (1483-1561), and a cusped panel representing the Madonna and Child, by Jacopo del Casentino (1297-1358). The 16th cent. church of *San Lorenzo*, with a drystone facade, contains many works of art; particularly note worthy is the tomb of Cardinal Agnolo II Acciaiuoli, for many years believed to be the work of Donatello (1386-1466), but probably by Francesco da Sangallo (1494-1576). Also worth seeing are the 16th cent. middle cloister, the large

Gallipoli, Hellenistic Fountain.

132

cloister built at the turn of the 16th cent., the Chapter House, and the refectory containing an impressive 15th cent. drystone pulpit, probably the work of the sculptor and goldsmith, Giovanni Fancelli (recorded 1568-1586).

* **GANDINO** (Bergamo). Wool centre in the Valle Seriana. The basilica of *Santa Maria Assunta*, a masterpiece by Antonio Gandini (c. 1565-c. 1631), was restructured in the second half of the 17th cent. by Giovanni Maria Bettera. The interior contains a beautiful high dome, and a painting of the Birth of Jesus and Saints, by Johann Christophorus Storer (1611-1671). The *Museo della Basilica* contains a large collection of artistic works including 16th cent. Flemish tapestries and 15-18th cent. sacred vestments. In the 15th cent. church of *Santa Croce*, rebuilt in the Baroque period, is a wooden altar by Andrea Fantoni (1659-1734).

* **GARDA** (Verona). Popular holiday resort sheltered by the surrounding hills. An ancient Venetian necropolis shows it was once inhabited by tribes of lake-dwellers; later it became an important Roman and Longobard town. The 18th cent. *Parrocchiale*, dedicated to Santa Maria Maggiore, contains a painting of St. Blaise, by Jacopo Palma the Younger (1544-1628), and a painting by Francesco Paglia (1636-c. 1713). In the church of *Santo Stefano* is a painting of St. Stephen, by Paolo Farinati (c. 1524-1606). The *Punta di San Vigilio* is one of the most famous and attractive places on Lake Garda.

* **GARDONE RIVIERA** (Brescia). Situated at the entrance of Salò bay, it is formed by Gardone below, and by small holiday centres up in the hills, also popular in winter because of the exceptionally mild climate. Nearby is the *Vittoriale degli Italiani*, a flamboyant and over-elaborate group of buildings planned by Gian Carlo Maroni (1893-1952) for the poet Gabriele D'Annunzio (1863-1938), who later handed it over to the State.

* **GARGNANO** (Brescia). Situated at the narrowing point of Lake Garda, it is a popular holiday resort because of its very mild climate. The church of *San Francesco*, built in the second half of the 13th cent., has a damaged facade. It contains paintings by Andrea Celesti (1637-1712) and Andrea Bertanza (lived in the 17th cent.). Remarkable is the *Villa Feltrinelli*, erected in 1894.

* **GATTINARA** (Vercelli). The parish church of *San Pietro* (15th cent.) has a fine Lombard facade, remarkable for its tiny brickwork decorations. The neo-Classical apse contains five large and three small predella panels which were part of a polyptych by Bernardino Lanino (c. 1512-1583). Walks to the *Madonna della Consolazione* and to the *Santuario di Rado*.

* **GAVARDO** (Brescia). Wool centre with well-preserved historic quarter. The Gothic-inspired church of *San Rocco* contains a painting of the Madonna and Child with Saints by Antonio Gandini (c. 1565-1631). In the *Parrocchiale* are beautiful Baroque altars and a Pietà by Giulio Cesare Procaccini (1560-1625). The *Museo del Gruppo Grotte Gavardo* contains pre-historic and Roman objects excavated in the area.

* **GAVI** (Alessandria). At the confluence of the Neirone and Lemme, it is dominated by the massive *Castello* which was one of the most important fortresses of the Genoese Republic. The 13th cent. Romanesque-Gothic *Parrocchiale di San Giacomo* has a lovely main doorway, on the architrave of which is a beautiful carving of the Last Supper; there is also an attractive bell-tower. The sombre interior, with a nave and two aisles, has a panel representing the Madonna and Child with Saints James and John the Baptist, carried out in the late 14th or early 15th cent. by an unknown artist.

Gavi, Parish Church, campanile.

** **GELA** (Caltanissetta). Popular seaside resort on a hillside parallel to the beach. Built in 689 B.C., it was one of the most important Greek colonies in Sicily. In 1230 Frederick II of Swabia built a new town around the pre-existing one. The *Chiesa Matrice*, built in neo-Classical style in the second half of the 18th cent., contains a panel depicting the Death of the Virgin, by Deodato Guinaccia (recorded 1551-1581), and 18th cent. paintings. The *Museo Nazionale Archeologico* contains a valuable collection of material excavated in Gela itself and other areas in the province of Caltanissetta. Long stretches of walls (*Fortificazioni Greche*) remain, and are of great scientific interest. Remains of an ancient temple (*Tempio Dorico*) of the 5th cent. B.C. The 5th, 4th and 3rd cent. B.C. *Necropoli* of ancient Gela are inexhaustible sources of archeological material.

* **GEMONA DEL FRIULI** (Udine). Attractive little town near the Vegliato on the lowest slopes of the Glémina mountains. The *Duomo*, built towards the end of the 12th cent. and at the beginning of the 14th cent., by Giovanni Griglio, in Romanesque-Gothic style, has two characteristic statues at the sides of the main entrance. The Gothic interior contains a Roman sepulchral altar, the Dante bell cast in 1423, paintings by Giovanni Battista Grassi (lived in the 16th cent.), and a wooden altarpiece carved by Andrea Moranzone (recorded in the late 14th and early 15th cent.). The Deanery archives contain valuable illuminated manuscripts, including a 14th cent. antiphonary. The church of *Santa Maria delle Grazie* has a Renaissance portal and contains paintings of the Madonna and Child with Saints, by Cima da Conegliano (c. 1459-1518) and the Holy Family with St. Elizabeth, by Giovanni Francesco da Tolmezzo (recorded 1480-1510). The church of *San Giovanni*, possibly designed by Giovanni Griglio, has two portals in the facade,

one Romanesque and the other Gothic, and a huge head of St. Christopher with the Christ-Child. The interior has a ceiling made up of 40 coffered panels, painted by Pomponio Amalteo (1505-1588), and a Madonna and Saints, by Sebastiano Secante (1529-1558). In the *Palazzo del Comune* or *Loggia*, built at the beginning of the 16th cent., is a small art gallery.

* **GENAZZANO** (Rome). Situated on a lonely hillside in the foothills of the Prenestine mountains. From the huge Matteotti square, at the entrance to the town, can be seen the remains of a large nymphaeum (*Ninfeo*), a Bramante-style Renaissance construction. The sanctuary of the *Madonna del Buonconsiglio*, originally built in the 13th cent., modified during the first half of the 17th, and restored during the second half of the 19th, has a neo-Classical facade with a 15th cent. doorway. Inside, is a 15th cent. Gothic-Renaissance-style canopy supported by columns. The Gothic *Casa Apolloni* is one of the most beautiful buildings in Latium; it has a low-arched main doorway, three mullioned windows on the first floor, and three single apertures on the second. The church of *San Paolo*, modified in the 18th cent. and flanked by a remarkable Romanesque bell-tower, contains a baptismal font (1563), a medieval holy-water stoup supported by a small spiral column, and a Renaissance holy-water stoup. The medieval *Castello Colonna*, rebuilt in the 15th cent. by Ottone Colonna, who later became Pope Martin V, was modified in Baroque style and has a spectacular courtyard with a fountain and ancient water-tank.

*** **GENOVA/GENOA.** Built in the form of an amphitheatre rising from the sea to the lower slopes of the Apennine hills, it is one of the most important ports in the Mediterranean. The historical centre, with its narrow streets, is in striking contrast with the modern part, with its wide tree-lined avenues. The *Palazzo Municipale* was designed by Rocco Lurago (1501-1590); in the Mayor's office is the famous bronze tablet containing the text of a decree issued in Rome in 117 B.C., which was discovered at Isosecco in 1506 by a peasant, Ago-

Gemona del Friuli, Archivio Arcipretale, page from the Antiphonarium.

Genazzano, Nymphaeum.

stino Pedemonte. The *Palazzo Rosso*, so called because of its red facade, was designed by Pier Antonio Corradi (1613-1683). It contains an art gallery with valuable paintings, including some by Anthony van Dyck (1599-1641). The Palazzo Bianco (white palace), designed by Giovanni Orsolino and Domenico Ponzello (active in the second half of the 16th cent.) houses the Palazzo Bianco Art Gallery, with valuable works of art including Margaret of Brabant between two angels, a sculpture by Giovanni Pisano (1245-1314), Venus and Mars, by Peter Paul Rubens (1577-1640), and Flight into Egypt, by Bartolomeo Stefano Murillo (1617-1682). The 18th cent. *Palazzo Balbi* has an enormous staircase by Gregorio Petondi (1780). The 13th cent. *Chiesa del Carmine*, contains beautiful paintings in the square apse and in the side-chapels. The church of *San Filippo Neri* was finished in 1712. The interior, mainly 18th cent. in style, contains some notable works of art. In the Oratory of San Filippo Neri there are frescoes by Giacomo Antonio Boni (1688-1766). The church of the *Santissima Annunziata* (first built in the 13th cent.) has an interior rich in stucco work, gilding and frescoes, and contains numerous works of art. *Palazzo Durazzo Pallavicini*, now called Negrotto Cambiaso, is a fine example of Bartolomeo Bianco's work (1590-1657). The *Palazzo dell'Università* was also designed by Bartolomeo Bianco; nearby is the important University Library. The imposing *Palazzo Reale* was designed by Giovanni Angelo Falcone and Pier Francesco Cantone (lived in the 17th cent.). The church of *San Carlo*, was built from a model by Bartolomeo Bianco. The monument to Christopher Columbus (*Monumento a Cristoforo Colombo*) was designed by Michele Canzio (1787-1868). The *Chiesa del Gesù* or *dei Santi Ambrogio e Andrea*, built at the end of the 16th cent., contains marble stucco works and remarkable frescoes. The *Palazzo Ducale*, once the residence of the doges, was first built in 1291, and rebuilt in the 16th cent. by Andrea Vannone. *Torre del Popolo*, built in 1307. The *Palazzetto Criminale* (15th cent.) contains the archives pertaining to the State, the Genoese Republic, the Bank of St. George, and the Notaries. The *Cattedrale di San Lorenzo* has been involved in every important event in the history of Genoa for centuries. According to tradition it was built over a chapel on the site where St. Lawrence stayed, in 260 A.D. on his way from Spain to Rome. Completely rebuilt in the 11th cent. and altered in later periods, it is a blend of Romanesque-Gothic and Renaissance styles. The interior is rich in works of art. The Chapel of Senarega, Lercari, Cibo and St. John the Baptist are especially worth seeing; also the rich Treasury. The *Palazzo di San Giorgio* is formed by two buildings, the older one Gothic, the other 16th cent. The 12th cent. church of *San Giovanni di Prè*, restructured in Romanesque-Gothic style in the 14th cent. contains some remarkable paintings. The 16th cent. *Palazzo Doria Pamphily*, contains many works of art

Genoa, Palazzo Bianco Art Gallery. Giovanni Pisano, fragment from the tomb of Margaret of Brabant.

strips. *Casa di Andrea Doria*, built in the second half of the 15th cent. The *Palazzo Imperiale*, built to a design by Giovanni Battista Castello called Bergamasco (1509-1569), has a Doric doorway. The 10th cent. church of *Santa Maria delle Vigne*, (rebuilt in the 13th cent.) has a neo-Classical facade dated 1842. It contains several works of art, some by Domenico Piola (1627-1703). The church of *Santa Maria Maddalena*, first built in the 12th cent. was rebuilt in 1588 to a design by Andrea Vannone. It contains works of art including frescoes by Giovanni Battista Parodi (1674-1730). The church of *San Siro* (9th cent.) was Genoa's first cathedral; the interior has a nave and two aisles with high twin columns, and contains many valuable works of art. *Porta dei Vacca*, is a Gothic arch flanked by two towers which were part of the 12th cent. city wall. The church of *San Luca* (1138) contains decorations and frescoes by Domenico Piola and a Nativity considered to be the masterpiece of Giovanni Benedetto Castiglione, called Grechetto (1610-1665). *Loggia dei Mercanti* or *Borsa Merci*, designed by Galeazzo Alessi (1512-1572). The church of *San Pietro di Banchi* (dating from the 10th cent.), with an aisleless nave and dome, contains works by local artists. The 12th cent. *Torre degli Embriaci*. The Basilica of *Santa Maria di Castello*, rebuilt in the 12th cent. with material from the original building. It contains works of art including a statue of St. Dominic by Francesco Schiaffino (1689-1765) and a fresco of the Annunciation by Giusto d'Alemagna (mentioned in 1451). The church of *Santa Maria delle Grazie* has been the centre of a parish ever since 1183 it was rebuilt in the 17th cent. The *Oratorio di San Giacomo della Marina* contains painting by 17th cent. Genoese masters. The 13th cent. church of *Sant'Agostino* has a facade consisting of black and white strips. The 12th cent. church of *San Donato* is in Romanesque style. The church of *San Giorgio*, rebuilt in the 17th cent. contains paintings by Domenico Piola and Luca Cambiaso (1527-1588). The church of *Santi Cosma e Damiano* was first built in the 12th cent.; inside are remarkable paintings and frescos. The church of *Santa Caterina* or the *Santissima Annunziata di Portoria* (15-16th cent.) contains some fine paintings by Luca Cambiaso and Giovanni Battista Castello, called Bergamasco, Domenico Parodi (1668-1740), etc. The austere interior of the 16th cent. church of *Santa Maria Assunta di Carignano* contains works of art mainly by Genoese sculptors and painters. The 12th cent. *Chiostro di Sant'Andrea* is built to a rectangular plan and has slender twinfold columns. *Porta Soprana* or di *Sant'Andrea*, part of the city wall, dates from 1155. The church of *Santo Stefano* (12th cent.) has a black and white striped facade. *Santa Maria della Consolazione*, (second half of the 17th cent.) contains gilded stucco-work and fine paintings, mostly by local masters. The *Museo Civico di Storia*

and a wonderful Room of the Giants. The *Basilica di Gesù e Maria* or di *San Francesco di Paolo* was enlarged in the 17th cent. The characteristic feature and outstanding landmark of Genoa is the lighthouse known as the *Torre della Lanterna;* building began in the 14th and was continued during the following centuries. The church of *San Matteo* (1125) has a tripartite facade divided by black and white

Genoa, Palazzo dell'Università, the staircase.
Genoa, Palazzo Balbi. Valerio Castello, Decoration of the Gallery, detail.

Naturale, founded in 1873, contains some fine collections. The 14th cent. church of *San Francesco* contains 18th cent. frescoes. 16th cent. *Palazzo del Governo*, with an impressive marble doorway by Taddeo Carlone (1543-1613). The 19th cent. *Chiesa dell'Immacolata Concezione* contains sculptures and paintings by talented local artists. The church of *San Bartolomeo degli Armeni* was founded in 1308 by Byzantine monks who had fled from the massacres in Armenia. The 19th cent. *Castello D'Albertis* dominates the port and the city.

** GERACE (Reggio Calabria).

Built on a high impregnable mountain at the meeting point of the Merici and Novito streams. The *Cattedrale*, built during the first half of the 11th cent. and dedicated to the Assunta, is the largest church in the area. It is a huge majestic building with three semicircular apses. The basilican interior contains works of art such as a 16th cent. bas-relief of Doubting St. Thomas, the tombs of Giovanni Battista Carracciolo, Nicola Palizzi (14th cent.) and the Sacramental Chapel dating from the first half of the 15th cent. The *Castello* has been rebuilt several times and is now an attractive building with strong 15th cent. characteristics. Other places of interest in Gerace are the 13th cent. church of *San Francesco*, in Romanesque-Gothic style, the small Byzantine-inspired church of *San Giovannello*, which has been recently restored, and the *Chiesa dei Cappuccini* containing a beautiful painting of the Madonna and Child with St. Francis (second half of the 17th cent.).

* GIANO DELL'UMBRIA (Perugia).

Formed by the merging of two castles, with walls and postern gates, it is a summer and autumn resort with a delightful panorama. The 14th cent. church of *San Francesco* contains interesting 14th cent. frescoes. Remains of the ancient walls (*Resti di mura romane*). Sanctuary of the *Madonna del Fosco*.

Gerace, Cathedral, interior.

* GIOIA DEL COLLE (Bari).

Situated in a creek which separates the north-west and south-east Murge. The massive, dark *Castello*, which dominates the town, is one of the most impressive in Apulia. Built at the beginning of the 12th cent., it was modified and decorated in 1230 by Frederick II. Trapezoidal in form, it has two sturdy towers at either side of the facade, and walls strengthened by large red blocks of ashlar stone; the courtyard is an off-centre rectangle and it has a lively interior. The ex-monastery of St. Francis houses the *Museo Archeologico* with excavated material from the necropoles of Monte Sannace and Santo Mola.

* GIOVE (Terni).

Medieval town situated on a platform from which the Tiber can be seen, down to the left. The chapel of *San Rocco* contains a valuable 16th cent. fresco representing the Crucifixion, by the Foligno school. The 17th cent. *Palazzo Mattei*, never completed, has some fine decorations.

* GIOVINAZZO (Bari).

Busy town on the Adriatic coast between Molfetta and Bari, with notable ruins of medieval architecture. The 12th cent. *Cattedrale*, spoilt by alteration work carried out in later centuries, has a characteristic rose window on the facade, surrounded by animal figures. The apse is almost completely conserved in its original form; it has interlaced arches and single and mullioned apertures; the interior, consisting of a nave and two aisles, has a beautiful 13th cent. Byzantine-type panel representing the Madonna

Giovinazzo, Cathedral.

of Corsignano and the Risen Christ, and a gold-based panel, perhaps by Michele Giambono (recorded 1420-1462). The crypt is supported by ten pillars with Romanesque double-abacus capitals. In the medieval part of the town can be seen the *Torre Sagarriga* (13th cent.), the rusticated *Palazzo Donnanno* (14th cent.), the *Palazzi Paglia* and *Saraceno*, and the Casa Firlocco.

* GOITO (Mantua). Attractive little town near the river Mincio. The Baroque basilica of the *Madonna della Salute* (1729) contains a painting depicting the Handing over of the Keys by Giuseppe Bazzani (c. 1690-1769). The neo-Classical *Villa Moschini*, previously known as the Villa d'Arco, was designed by Giovanni Battista Marconi (recorded 1783-1789) and Giuseppe Crevola (active at the end of the 18th cent.).

** GORIZIA. On the border of Jugoslavia where the river Isonzo flows into the Friulian plain. The *Duomo*, built in 1684 and dedicated to Saints Ilaria and Taziano, was almost completely destroyed during the First World War. The interior has a nave and two aisles with black marble columns. It contains an Annunciation by Alessandro Varotari, called Padovanino (1588-1648), an altarpiece depicting the Madonna and Saints Hilary and Taziano, by Giuseppe Tominz (1790-1866), and stuccoes and gilded work by Francesco Grossi (lived in the present cent.). The Treasury contains works from the Basilica of Aquileia, an early 13th cent. embossed silver evangelistary, 14th and 15th cent. busts of saints, etc. The Baroque

Gorizia, Duomo. Reliquary bust.

church of *Sant'Ignazio*, built between 1654 and 1757, with a sumptuous facade, contains a large fresco of St. Ignatius in Glory, by Cristoforo Taucher (lived in the 18th cent.). The church of *Santo Spirito*, first built at the end of the 14th cent., contains a painting of the Assumption by Jacopo Palma the Younger (1544-1628). The massive *Castello*, enlarged in 1508 by the Venetians and partly destroyed during the First World War, contains paintings and furniture, mostly 16th and 17th cent. The *Museo Storico* contains a historical and numismatic Room, a De Baguer Room containing a collection of ancient armoury, and a room devoted to the works of Verdi. The modern, 20th cent. *Palazzo delle Poste e Telegrafi* was designed by Angelo Mazzoni and contains works by contemporary sculptors and painters including Mazzoni, Domenico Ponzi, Napoleone Martinuzzi and Guido Cadorin. Worth visiting are the nearby battlefields of *Carso and Medio Isonzo*, also the shrine of Oslavia, designed by Ghino Venturi, the *Zona Sacra del San Michele*, and the *Sacrario Militare di Redipuglia*, built to a plan by Giovanni Greppi and Giannino Castiglioni.

* GRADARA (Pesaro). Medieval village on a green hill, in a lovely setting, and surrounded by a wall. The most important piece of architecture and one which summarizes the history of Gradara, is the *Rocca*. It was begun in the first half of the 13th cent. on the site of a pre-existing fortress and completed by the Malatesta family; it has recently been entirely restored and furnished with period pieces.

** GRADO (Gorizia). On a small island between the sea and the lagoon, it is a popular seaside resort. The *Basilica di Sant'Eufemia*, once the cathedral, is composed of material excavated from Roman buildings. It was consecrated in 579 A.D. The sober double-sloped facade is preceded by a mid-15th cent. cusped bell-tower. The interior contains African-marble columns and has a 6th cent. mosaic floor; in the dome over the apse is a fresco in which can be distinghished the figures of Christ blessing the Virgin and Saints, with the symbols of the Evangelists. The Treasury was once well furnished but now only contains a few valuable objects, including two silver caskets for relics, the silver ark of Saints Ermagora and Fortunato (14th cent.) and two 11-12th cent. enamelled plates. The baptistery has a 6th cent. mosaic floor. The ancient *Basilica di Santa Maria delle Grazie* was modified in the 6th cent. and changed to Baroque style towards the middle of the 17th. It has a sober double-sloped facade, iconostases, and Byzantine capitals. The *Lapidario* contains Roman and early Christian objects. The *Basilica di Piazza Vittoria*, dating from the first half of the 5th cent., contains remains of mosaic pavements with inscriptions.

* **GRAGNANO** (Naples). Situated a few kilometres from Castellammare di Stabia on the Bay of Naples, with houses spread along both sides of the highway that runs into the Naples hinterland. The 16th cent. church of *Corpus Domini* contains 18th cent. stuccoes and has a frescoed ceiling (1753), a holy-water stoup (1571), a Transfiguration in Raphael style by Marco Pino (c. 1525-c. 1588) and numerous paintings by Giacinto Diana (1730-1803). Walk to the Castello, where there is the 12th cent. church of Santa Maria Assunta, with a pretty little Romanesque bell-tower.

* **GRAN SAN BERNARDO (COLLE DEL)/ GREAT ST. BERNARD PASS** (Aosta). 2473 metres above sea-level in a bare and wild valley, snow-covered for nine months of the year, it winds round the westernmost point of the Pennine Alps, between the Gran Combin range and the Mont Blanc Massif. Already inhabited in the bronze age. The Romans called it Mons Jovis and built two stages there and a small chapel, with an in-antis portico, dedicated to Jupiter Poeninus. The celebrated *Ospizio del Gran San Bernardo* is run by canons of the Augustinian order. It is here that the famous dogs are bred and trained to find and assist lost travellers and carry them to safety even during violent snowstorms. The museum contains a collection of coins, medals, small votive panels and Roman statuettes found in the area and thus proving the presence of the ancient Romans. Also, a rare collection of coleoptera and animals including three species of birds that pass the winter on the Great St. Bernard pass. The Baroque *Chiesa*, built in the second half of the 17th cent., contains the body of St. Faustina brought from the Roman catacombs, a fine carved-wood choir and relics of St. Bernard. The *Biblioteca* contains thirty thousand volumes, including numerous ancient records and a valuable 16th cent. illuminated missal.

* **GRAVEDONA** (Como). Facing the small Piona peninsular on Lake Como. The church of *Santa Maria del Tiglio* (St. Mary of the Limetree), built at the end of the 12th cent. reveals Burgundian influence and is characterized by its high campanile dominating the centre of the facade; the three semicircular apses are decorated with semi-columns and small arches. The simple and impressive interior has a timbered roof. The 11th cent. basilica of *San Vincenzo* was completely modified in the 17th and 18th cent.; it still contains an interesting crypt from the original building. The church of *Santa Maria delle Grazie* (second half of the 15th cent.) has a Renaissance facade with two carved marble portals; inside are 16th cent. Lombard frescoes. The *Palazzo Gallio*, designed by Pellegrino Tibaldi called Pellegrino Pellegrini (1527-1596) was built around 1586.

* **GRAVINA DI PUGLIA** (Bari). Unusual town with many Medieval and Renaissance remains. The *Duomo* was built during the last decade of the 12th cent. but extensively modified in the course of time. It is now a beautiful Renaissance building incorporating Romanesque and Gothic elements. The facade has a perfect rose-window with small pointed arches. The large sombre interior contains a few works of art. On the carved and gilded roof of the nave is a 16th cent. bas-relief of the Presentation of Mary at the Temple. The church *Grotta di San Michele*, known locally

Gravedona, Santa Maria del Tiglio, interior.
Gravina, San Sebastiano, cloister.

as St. Michael of the Grottoes, is carved out of the rock; the interior formed of a nave and four aisles, is divided by monolithic pillars. On the walls and pillars can be seen traces of frescoes. The Palazzo Pomarici Santomasi houses a *Museo* consisting of an archeological section with a Pre-historic Room, a Peucezia Room and an Apula Room, and an art gallery containing 16th, 17th and 18th cent. Neapolitan school paintings, some by Francesco Guarini da Solofra (1611-1654) and Saverio Persico (lived in the 18th cent.). The Renaissance church of *San Francesco*, with Baroque campanile, was built in 1766. It contains a panel of the Adoration of the Child by Sebastiano Pisano (lived during the 15th cent.). Walks to the *Grotta di San Vito Vecchio* containing remarkable 13th and 14th cent. frescoes and to the church of *San Sebastiano* where a remarkable Romanesque-Gothic cloister can be seen in the former monastery.

* **GREAT ST. BERNARD PASS,** see Gran San Bernardo.

* **GREVE** (Florence). Village on the left bank of the river Greve, grouped around an 11th cent. castle. The oratory of *San Francesco* contains a shrine with a Deposition and Saints, from the Giovanni Della Robbia workshop (1469-1529).

* **GROPINA** (Town of Loro Ciuffenna, province of Arezzo). The Romanesque parish church of *San Pietro* was probably built in the 12th cent.; a gallery runs round the outside of the apse, which is flanked by a massive 13th cent. bell-tower. The interior is formed of a nave and two aisles with monolithic columns and blends well with the attractive architectural style created by the varied capitals and the remarkable pulpit.

*** **GROSSETO.** Most important town in the Maremma area, it is divided into an ancient part enclosed within ramparts and a modern part which has grown up during the last fifty years. The church of *San Francesco* is bare externally. It contains a large panel of the Crucifixion, possibly late 13th cent., and 17th cent. frescoes by Francesco Nasini. The *Duomo di San Lorenzo* was built around the end of the 13th cent. by Comascan masters and rebuilt in 1294 by Sozzo di Rustichino of Siena. The red and white marble facade is decorated with symbols of the Evangelists and statues attributed to Sozzo di Rustichino. The interior is in the form of a nave and two aisles and has been modified several times. It contains an altar to the Madonna delle Grazie, much revered by the people of Grosseto, with a 15th cent. reredos by Antonio di Ghino of Siena and a valuable 16th cent. marble ciborium. The *Museo d'Arte Sacra* contains many works which were formerly in the Duomo, including a painting of the Virgin Mary and St. John, possibly by Simone Martini (1284-1344) and the Madonna of the Cherries, a masterpiece by Stefano di Giovanni, called Sassetta (1392-1450). The *Museo Archeologico*, the *Mura* and the nearby area known as *Bonifica Grossetana* are worth visiting.

Gropina, Parish Church, pulpit.

Grosseto, Museo d'Arte Sacra. Sassetta, Madonna of the Cherries.

* **GROTTAFERRATA** (Rome). The famous *Abbazia* is surrounded like a fortress by battlemented walls with large towers and moats; it was built at the end of the 15th cent. by Giuliano da Sangallo or Baccio Pontelli. The first courtyard leads to the Monastery where there is a museum containing remains of the old church, 15-18th cent. paintings, Byzantine objects and archeological remains from Etuscan and Roman times. The facade of the church of St. Mary, consecrated in 1025 but completely modified in the mid-18th cent., looks out onto the second courtyard. A colonnaded portico stands in front of the west entrance with a Byzantine marble doorway and mosaic lunette. To the left is a baptismal font (9-11th cent.). The 12th cent. Romanesque campanile is composed of five orders of three-mullioned windows. The basilica-style interior, with a nave and two aisles, has a Cosmatesque pavement and a coffered ceiling (16th cent.); the triumphal arch is decorated with 13th cent. mosaics depicting the Pentecost, while the upper part of the nave is covered with Byzantine-type frescoes. The chapel of St. Linus contains frescoes by Domenico Zampieri called Domenichino (1581-1614).

* **GROTTAGLIE** (Taranto). The *Chiesa Matrice*, built at the turn of the 12th cent., has an interesting facade, probably built in 1379 by Domenico da Martina, with a beautiful doorway in Romanesque-Apulian style. The interior is formed of an aisleless nave, and a high and beautiful Baroque dome. It contains altars to the patron saints of the town: Saints Ciro and Francesco de Geronimo; a painting of the Madonna of the Rosary, by Paolo De Matteis (1662-1728) and a 16th cent. high-relief in stone depicting the Annunciation. The *Castello* was built in the 14th cent. on the orders of the Bishops of Taranto. It has a square keep and a corner tower, both battlemented. Behind the castle are the so-called "Potteries".

* **GROTTAMMARE** (Ascoli Piceno). Situated at the mouth of the river Tesino, it is a well-known seaside resort. The 16th cent. church of *Sant'Agostino* has a fresco depicting the Madonna della Misericordia by Vincenzo Pagani (c. 1490-1568). The church of *Santa Lucia* was commissioned by Camilla Peretti in 1597, in memory of her brother Felice, Pope Sixtus V; it contains a few interesting works of art.

* **GUALDO TADINO** (Perugia). Small pleasantly situated town, with a healthy climate, noted for its artistic ceramics. The location of the town mentioned in the Eugubine Tables is unknown, but the Roman town of Tadinum was certainly on the Via Flaminia. The 13th cent. *Duomo di San Benedetto*, has a basilican interior decorated with bas-reliefs by the sculptor Guglielmo Ciani (1817-1890). The crypt contains an urn by Publio Morbiducci containing the body of the Patron Beato Angelo. The *Pinacoteca Comunale* contains notable works of art, especially by Matteo da Gualdo (1435-1507), as well as by Antonio da Fabriano (15th cent.), Niccolò di Liberatore called Alunno (1430-1503), and others.

* **GUALTIERI** (Reggio Emilia). Situated in the plain, near the river Po. The *Palazzo Bentivoglio* was begun in the late 16th cent. It contains the Room of the Giants, with decorations depicting episodes from the Liberation of Jerusalem, by Sisto Badalocchi (1585-1647), the Cardinal's room and the Cardinal's Chapel. The collegiate church of *Santa Maria della Neve* was first built in the 17th cent. The interior contains a Crucifixion by Camillo Ricci (active in the first half of the 17th cent.). The church of *Sant'Andrea* was first built in the 13th cent. and rebuilt at the beginning of the 18th.

Grottaglie, Chiesa Matrice. Angel of the Annunciation.

Gualtieri, Palazzo Bentivoglio.

* **GUARDIAGRELE** (Chieti). Near the massive range of the Abruzzi Apennines in the Maiella area, it is situated on a hill with an attractive panorama. The 12th cent. church of *Santa Maria Maggiore* has a facade with a beautiful pointed-arched doorway and fine decorations. The aisleless interior contains works of art including a beautifully carved walnut pulpit (1708). In the Treasury are seven illuminated chorals, tapestries and, most important of all, a famous silver cross by Nicola da Guardiagrele (active in the first half of the 15th cent.). The church of *San Francesco* (first half of the 14th cent.) has a Romanesque doorway beneath a triangular tympanum and contains paintings of the Assumption and the Apostles, inspired by the style of Raphael but probably by Simone De Magistris (c. 1543-c. 1600), a gilded statue of St. Anthony of Padua, interesting Baroque confessionals, an impressive Baroque organ and wooden choirstalls.

* **GUARDIA SANFRAMONDI** (Benevento). In a hilly area with a view over the Calore valley. An ancient stone utensil, found by chance, proved this area was inhabited in pre-historic times. The present village is believed to have been built around a tower constructed by the Sanframondi family, but it is probably much older than the tower. The church of *San Sebastiano*, with a 16th cent. doorway and 18th cent. interior, contains stuccoes by Domenico Antonio Vaccaro (c. 1680-c. 1750) and frescoes in the vault by Paolo De Matteis (1662-1728). The church of the *Annunziata* has an impressive gilded wooden ceiling (second half of the 18th cent.) and contains an Annunciation, probably by Paolo De Matteis. The ruins of the medieval *Castello* are worth seeing.

* **GUASTALLA** (Reggio Emilia). Small agricultural and industrial town on the right bank of the river Po. The *Cattedrale*, dedicated to St. Peter and designed by Francesco da Volterra (recorded in the second half of the 16th cent.) was consecrated in 1575 by St. Charles Borromeo. In Piazza Mazzini is a statue of Ferrante I Gonzaga by Leone Leoni (1509-1590). In the *Palazzo Vescovile* (Bishop's Palace) there is a painting by Pietro Faccini (1562-1602) of the Rest in Egypt. Walk to the *Basilica della Pieve*, built in 915 on the orders of Berengarius I, King of Italy. The basilican interior contains a painted terracotta Madonna and Child, probably by Guido Mazzoni (c. 1450-1518).

** **GUBBIO** (Perugia). One of the most characteristic towns in Umbria, truly medieval in appearance, with many important artistic monuments. The church of *San Francesco*, attributed by some experts to fra Bevignato da Perugia (recorded in the second half of the 13th cent.), has an unpretentious facade with a Gothic doorway. The interior has a huge nave and two aisles, and contains works of art by various masters such as Virgilio Nucci (1545-1621) and Ottaviano Nelli (1370-1450). The *Palazzo dei Consoli*, one of the most beautiful palaces in Italy, is a massive building with harmonious lines, believed to have been built between 1332 and 1337 by Angelo da Orvieto and Matteo Gattaponi. The lunette above the Gothic doorway contains an impressive fresco (1495) by Bernardino di Nanni dell'Eugenia, and the building is crowned with small pointed arches and rectangular merlons. It houses a Museum containing the celebrated Eugubine Tablets, discovered in 1444 either at Scheggia, or as some believe, in the Roman theatre, by Paolo di Gregorio who sold them to the Town in 1456. They consist of seven bronze plates, of varying sizes, inscribed in Etruscan and Latin with religious references which have enabled scholars to make some headway into an unexplored area of the three centuries preceding the birth of Christ. The large hall contains an 8th cent. pagan sarcophagus. The Palace also contains a large art gallery with many famous paintings such as the well-known Madonna of the Pomegranate, probably by Pier Francesco Fiorentino (recorded 1470-1500), a large panel with tabernacle by Timoteo Viti (1467-1525), and Matteo Balducci (lived in the 15-16th cent.). The 13th cent. Gothic *Duomo* has a spectacular interior, with numerous works of art

Gubbio, Palazzo dei Consoli. Barbarian sarcophagus.
Gubbio, Palazzo dei Consoli.

by illustrious masters such as Benedetto Nucci, a 16th cent. painter, the carver Girolamo Maffei (1557-1592) and Timoteo Viti. The *Palazzo Ducale*, called The Court, was begun in 1476 by Federico di Montefeltro. Inside is a superb rectangular courtyard. Many of the rooms have ancient brick floors with interesting quatrefoil graffiti. Unfortunately many of the original works of art have been lost and the beautiful Duke's Study, created by the best artists of the age, has been sold to the New York Metropolitan Museum. The church of *Sant'Agostino* (second half of the 13th cent.) is characterized by cylindrical buttresses and contains important works of art, including a fresco by Ottaviano Nelli (1375-1450) depicting the Last Judgement and paintings by Federico Brunori (1566-1649). It is worth visiting the well-preserved *Teatro Romano*, (1st cent.), the Gothic church of *San Pietro*, (13th cent.), *Santa Maria Nuova*, containing a beautiful fresco of the Madonna del Belvedere by Ottaviano Nelli and the *Palazzo del Bargello*. One should walk to the basilica of Sant'Ubaldo, which has a wonderful 16th cent. doorway.

* **GUIGLIA** (Modena). On a hillside with a fine view. In the neighbouring Monte Orsello area is the *Parrocchiale*, with a terracotta Madonna and Child by Antonio Begarelli (c. 1499-1565). Also in the neighbourhood, at Pieve Trebbio, is the Romanesque *Pieve di San Giovanni Battista* (9th cent.); it has a harmonious basilican interior consisting of a nave and two aisles.

** **HERCULANEUM,** see Ercolano.

* **IESI** (Ancona). Situated on a hill overlooking the left bank of the river Esino, with a walled medieval quarter. The *Duomo*, dedicated to San Settimo, was built in the 13-15th cent. It contains works of art including an enormous painting of the Martyrdom of St. Lawrence, by Gaetano Lapis (1706-1758); a Communion of the Apostles by Christopher Unterberger (1732-1798); John the Baptist preaching, by Filippo Bellini (1550/55-1604), and a 15th cent. baptismal font. To the left of the cathedral is the Baroque *Palazzo Balleani*, with a lovely balcony supported by caryatids, by Giovanni Toschini. The *Palazzo della Signoria* was designed by Francesco di Giorgio Martini (1439-1502), and houses a museum and an art gallery. The museum contains important works of art, including six headless Roman statues, Tuscan-school high-reliefs (14th cent.) Lombard-school bas-reliefs (16th cent.), coat-of-arms, putti and terracottas. In the art gallery are notable works of art including the magnificent panel (1531-32) of St. Lucy before Pascasio by Lorenzo Lotto (1480-1556), and others by Pietro Paolo Agabiti (1470-1540), Girolamo Marchesi da Cotignola (c. 1471-c. 1540), and Antonio Sarti (recorded

1613-1633). The City Walls (*Cinta delle Mura*), built over Roman ruins, are a fine example of 14th cent. defences. The church of *San Giovanni Battista* was rebuilt in the late 17th cent. It contains an important painting of the Madonna and Child with Saints, by Giovanni Peruzzini (1629-1694).

* **IGLESIAS** (Cagliari). Busy, picturesque little town, and mining centre of first-rate importance. The monument to *Quintino Sella* was carried out by Giuseppe Sartorio (1854-1922). The cathedral of *Santa Chiara* (13th cent.) has a Romanesque-Gothic facade and 13th cent. bell-tower with a bell cast in 1337 by Andrea Pisano. The church of *San Francesco*, with 15-16th cent. facade and interior, is important proof of the persistence of Gothic architecture in Sardinia. Inside, the Cappella Maggiore is worthy of note (1523). Important *Museo di Mineralogia*, containing eight thousand specimens.

* **ILLASI** (Verona). Agricultural centre around a hill on which are ruins of a fortress demolished by Ezzelino de Romano in 1439. The

Iesi, Palazzo Belleani. Balcony supported by Telamones.

Iglesias, San Francesco, interior.

143

Villa Carlotti, built in 1737 to a design by Alessandro Pompei (1705-1772), has a pronaos decorated with statues by Giuseppe Antonio Schiavi (1686-1758). The 19th cent. *Parrocchiale* contains a fresco of the Madonna and Child with Angels, by Stefano da Verona or da Zevi (c. 1374-c. 1438). The *Villa Sagramoso Perez Pompei*, completed during the first half of the 18th cent., is a large building characterized by barn-type roofs, with frescoes by Francesco Lorenzi (1706-1770) and Andrea Porta (1720-1805).

** **IMOLA** (Bologna). Important agricultural and commercial town on the left bank of the river Santerno. The 12th cent. *Palazzo Comunale*, once the residence of the feudal lord, has been restructured several times. Inside are four halls with valuable 18th cent. decorations. The Renaissance-style *Palazzo Sersanti* was built to a design by Giorgio Marchesi, called Giorgio Fiorentino (recorded 1471-1483). The ancient church of *Santa Maria in Regola* has a Baroque facade, flanked by an unevenly-rounded bell-tower (second half of the 12th cent.). Inside is a fine painting of the Madonna and Child with Saints by an 18th cent. Flemish painter, and other works of art. The church of *Sant'Agostino* dates from the end of the 13th cent.; the interior contains valuable paintings including Souls in Purgatory by Marcantonio Franceschini (1648-1729). The church of *Santa*

Maria dei Servi (first half of the 14th cent.) has a rich interior including paintings by Domenico Maria Viani (1668-1711). *Istituti Culturali del Comune*: in the art gallery are a few good paintings, including a Marriage of the Virgin by Gaspare Sacchi (recorded 1527-1536), a Marriage of St. Catherine by Sebastiano Filippi, called Bastianino (1532-1602), and Sacrifice of a Calf, by Lavinia Fontana (1552-1614). The *Cattedrale*, dedicated to San Cassiano, was built between 1187 and 1271 and rebuilt in 1781. It has a facade in two orders; the neo-Classical interior contains works of art such as a beautiful 15th cent. wooden Crucifix. The *Rocca* (1304) is now 15th cent. in style and contains a large collection of 15th, 16th and 17th cent. armoury. *Chiesa dell'Osservanza* (1473): inside is a tribune of Pope Julius II, dating from the early 16th cent., and a detached fresco of Our Lady of Peace, by Antonio Checci, called Guidaccio da Imola (recorded 1470-1473).

* **IMPERIA**. Mainly the result of the merging of the two communes of Oneglia and Porto Maurizio, it is divided by the Impero stream. The collegiate church of *San Giovanni Battista*, Baroque in style, was designed by Gaetano Amoretti (18th cent.); inside are marble, stucco and gilded works of art. The collegiate church of *San Maurizio*, mainly built during the last twenty years of the 18th cent., was designed

Imola, Sant'Agostino, interior.

144

by Gaetano Cantoni; the pronaos is supported by eight Doric columns, and it has a neo-classical facade, well-lit interior with a nave and two aisles, and impressive dome. The first side-chapel on the right contains the Baptism of Jesus, painted by Leonardo Massabó in 1867; and in the second chapel is a Death of St. Joseph, by the same artist. In the chancel are fine wooden stalls carried out in the 19th cent.; the organ has three thousand pipes. Worth visiting is the medieval *Città Vecchia*, with many doorways in black stone, and interesting houses which are well-preserved examples of medieval dwellings.

** **IMPRUNETA** (near Florence). Attractive little town situated in a green hilly area of great geological interest. Dating back to the Etruscans, it only became important in medieval times when, in the 11th cent., a Sanctuary was built there to enshrine a miracle-working image of the Madonna. The Basilica of *Santa Maria dell'Impruneta*, largely remodelled, first in the 14th and then in the 15th cent., is flanked by a slender 13th cent. crenellated bell-tower; inside are works of art including two outstanding side-chapels by Michelozzo Michelozzi (1396-1472); these two masterpieces were shattered by bombs during the Second World War, but were then carefully reconstructed, piece by piece, and can now be admired in their original beauty. The one on the right is called the chapel of the Cross, and has a lovely altarpiece by Luca della Robbia (1400-1482), while the one on the left is called the chapel of the Madonna, and also contains beautiful works by Luca della Robbia. The *Cripta*, part of the original 11th cent. parish church, has a semi-circular apse and columns with interesting capitals.

Impruneta, Basilica (formerly Parish Church of S. Maria), the crypt.

* **IRSINA** (Matera). Situated near the left bank of the river Bradano. The 13th cent. *Cattedrale*, dedicated to the *Assunta*, and rebuilt in the second half of the 18th cent., has an attractive rustic facade. Inside can be seen a baptismal font in red gravel (1761), 16th cent. polychrome marble statue of St. Euphemia; an Ecce homo (16th cent.) by an unknown Neapolitan artist, and other interesting paintings. The *Museo Ianora* is arranged in a 17th cent. house. It has a fine collection of paleolithic manufactures, Iron Age-type vases (8-7th cent. B.C.) and Italiot ones of the 4th-3rd cent. B.C. The church of *San Francesco* was rebuilt in the mid-16th cent. It contains an interesting holy-oil vessel and some fairly good 18th cent. paintings by the Neapolitan school; on the vault of the crypt are some remarkable frescoes (second half of the 14th cent.) by an unknown Neapolitan artist.

* **ISERNIA** (Campobasso). Busy and pleasant little town between the Carpino and Sordo rivers. The 14th cent. *Fontana Fraterna* is in a light and harmonious style, incorporating Roman marble work. The *Cattedrale di San Pietro*, rebuilt after an earthquake in 1805, contains frescoes by Amedeo Trivisonno (born in 1904), and a Byzantine panel. The *Antiquarium* contains remains of Grecian, Samnite and Roman sculptures; in the square of Santa Maria can be seen the doorway and Romanesque bell-tower (11th cent.) of the now-destroyed church of Santa Maria delle Monache.

* **ISSOGNE** (Aosta). Situated in a plain, at the mouth of the valley of the Boccoueil stream. The town is dominated by the *Castello di Issogne*, a heavy square-shaped building, partly Gothic and partly Renaissance in style. It was built in 1480, and sumptuously furnished, but later spoilt by alterations. In 1872 it was restored in such a way as to recreate the 15th cent. style; the courtyard is characterized by a beautiful octagonal-shaped fountain, with a pomegranate-tree in wrought iron, with water gushing out of the trunk. Worth visiting are the Dining-hall, the Kitchen, the Breakfast-room, the Bedrooms of Renato di Challant and Cardinal Madruzzo, the Chapel, the Writing room, the Room of the King of France or of the Lilies, and the Armoury. The lunettes in the portico are decorated with interesting frescoes.

** **IVREA** (Turin). Pleasantly situated in a Morainic amphitheatre, on either bank of the river Dora Baltea, it is the gateway to the Val d'Aosta. The *Duomo dell'Assunta*, was built in the 4th cent., probably on the site of a pagan temple, and restructured in the 11th cent. Of the original construction, only the tiburium, the two campaniles of the apse, and the crypt still stand. Inside is an altarpiece of the Madonna and Saints by Claude François

Beaumont (1584-1616); the Chapter Library contains rare illuminated liturgical codices, and in the Chapter Archives are records dating from the 13-18th cent. The *Castello* is an impressive square-shaped building with cylindrical towers at the corners, begun in 1358 by Amedeo VI of Savoy. The 15th cent. church of *San Bernardino* contains a cycle of twenty-one frescoes (1500) by Giovanni Martino Spanzotti. Walk to the remains of the oval-shaped *Anfiteatro Romano*, where excavations have brought to light part of the auditorium and foundations of the podium.

* **LACONI** (Nuoro). The most noted centre in Sarcidano, pleasantly situated at the foot of a limestone plateau. The lovely *Parco*, which is very big, surrounds the remains of the Aymerich castle. The 16th cent. *Parrocchiale*, originally in Gothic-Aragonese style, is flanked by an attractive campanile. Worth a visit is the small but interesting *Museo*, dedicated to St. Ignatius of Laconi, in honour of whom there is also a monument in the nearby square. Excursions can be made to the *Nuraghe Genna Corte* and the copper-mine (*Miniera di Fontana Raminosa*), which was certainly worked in remote times.

Ivrea, View of the city.

* **LAGONEGRO** (Potenza). Formed by an ancient town and a modern quarter. The *Parrocchiale*, dedicated to St. Nicholas, was rebuilt at the turn of the 19th cent.; inside is a picture of the Trinity by Salvatore Cascini (lived during that period). The church of *Sant'Anna* (second half of the 17th cent.) has a lovely facade; inside is a painting with a rich frame, by Francesco Gaetano (active in 1665). The facade of the *Chiesa del Rosario* is decorated with a faded fresco of the Last Judgement by Antonio Cascini (lived in the 18-19th cent.). The *Chiesa di San Nicola* (first built in Romanesque style during the 9-10th cent.) contains some fairly good works in wood. On the edge of the cliff, in the ancient part of Lagonegro, are remains of the *Palazzo Feudale*, the castle around which the town was built.

* **LAGOPÉSOLE** (Potenza). Situated in the Lucano Apennines, north of Potenza. Its name is derived from the nearby lake "Lacus Pensilis", which is the source of the Bradano. The few houses are overlooked by the *Castello di Lagopesole* standing on a hill, 809 m. above sea level. It was begun in 1242 by Frederick II, and is an impressive rectangular building of limestone blocks, which have turned reddish over the centuries on account of the iron content. It has two courtyards, a church incorporated in a tower, windows and doorways with interesting decorations. Two corbels contain images said to be at Frederick Barbarossa and his second wife Beatrice.

* **LAIGUEGLIA** (Savona). Quiet town situated at the extreme west of the bay between Cape Santa Croce and Cape Mele, with a large and sloping beach. It was noted in the 17th and 18th cent. for its coral fishing. The parish church of *San Matteo*, begun in 1715, has a Baroque interior with valuable works of art. The *Oratorio di Santa Maria Maddalena* (first half of the 17th cent.) has a beautiful altarpiece by Domenico Piola (1627-1703). Interesting walk to Cape Mele, along the Via Aurelia, with a view of the bay.

* **LANCIANO** (Chieti). Formed by the merging of an ancient quarter, consisting of medieval buildings, with a modern and industrial part. The *Cattedrale*, known locally as the Basilica di Santa Maria del Ponte because it is built over four arches of the Diocletian bridge, is nearly nine centuries old; it has been enlarged and altered several times. The interior, mainly 18th cent. in style, contains three frescoes in ellipses, by Giacinto Diana (1730-1803), a 15th cent. silver pastoral staff of the Sulmona school, and, in the Treasury, artistic votive offerings. The church of *Santa Maria Maggiore* was built in 1227 on the ruins of a temple to Apollo, in Cistercian style and has an impressive facade with a lovely doorway by Francesco Petrini (14th cent.).

The assymetrical interior, rather confused in style due to various works of reconstruction, contains works of art, including a perfect cross in engraved silver and enamel, by Nicola da Guardiagrele (recorded in the first half of the 15th cent.). The church of *Sant'Agostino* (1270) contains three precious reliquaries, one of which is by Nicola di Antonio di Pantaleone Pasquali (15th cent.). The 11th cent. *Porta di San Biagio*, is the only surviving gate of the original nine in the medieval walls.

** L'AQUILA.

Situated on a hillside on the left bank of the river Aterno, with a large number of Romanesque and Renaissance churches, and an imposing castle. The 13th cent. Romanesque church of *Santa Maria di Collemaggio*, with a fine central doorway, is an important historic and artistic monument; it contains the tomb of St. Peter Celestine, an impressive work in Renaissance-Lombard style by Girolamo da Vicenza (lived in the 15-16th cent.); also, notable works by Carlo Ruther (lived in the 17th cent.). The church of *San Bernardino* was built between 1454 and 1472 in honour of the great Franciscan Saint; the facade is by Nicola Filotesio called Cola dell'Amatrice (1489-1559). The interior is in the form of a Latin cross, ninety-six metres long, and has a magnificent carved wooden ceiling by Bernardo Mosca da Pescocostanzo; there is a terracotta by Andrea della Robbia (1435-1525); and the chapel of San Bernardino decorated with frescoes by Girolamo Cenatempo (lived in the 17-18th cent.), with the mausoleum of San Bernardino by the sculptor Silvestro dell'Aquila (recorded 1476-1505); also, the magnificent tomb of Maria Pereira, dell'Aquila's most successful work. The imposing *Castello* stands on the site of an Angevin fortress; built on a square

plan, with massive bastions at the corners, and encircled by a wide moat, it is a perfect example of a 16th cent. castle, especially in the underground section. It houses the *Museo Nazionale d'Abruzzo*, which consists of an archeological part, a medieval one, devoted above all to Abruzzi masters, and a modern one. The Romanesque church of *Santa Maria di Paganica* was built at the beginning of the 14th cent. but destroyed several times by earthquakes; the facade is enhanced by a harmonious doorway. The aisleless interior, in the shape of a Latin cross, contains works of art including an altarpiece representing the Saviour, by Alessandro Maganza (1556-1640). The church of *San Biagio di Amiterno* contains the Camponeschi monument by a "Gualtiero d'Alemania", possibly Walter of Munich (lived in the 14-15th cent.). The 13th cent. church of *Santa Giusta* has a plain and harmonious facade, and the church of *San Flaviano* (also 13th cent.), a fine Romanesque portal. The *Duomo* is dedicated to San Massimo, martyr of Aveia and patron saint of Aquila. It was erected towards the end of the 13th cent. but has been rebuilt several times owing to earthquakes. *Palazzo Benedetti* has a graceful Renaissance courtyard. The *Fontana delle Novantanove Cannelle* (beginning of the 15th cent.) is one of the town's most characteristic monuments.

* LARINO

(Campobasso). Attractive town, with Roman and medieval ruins. The 14th cent. *Duomo*, dedicated to the Assunta and San Pardo, is in Romanesque-Gothic style and has a beautiful doorway decorated with lions and griffins; inside are works of art, including a painting of the Immaculate Conception by Francesco Solimena (1657-1743), a valuable painting depicting St. Pardo, by an unknown

L'Aquila, Santa Maria di Collemaggio, portal.

L'Aquila, Palazzo Benedetti, courtyard.

artist, and wooden bas-reliefs, presumably 13th cent. In the dome of the church of *San Francesco* is a fresco depicting Paradise, by Paolo Gamba (1712-1782).

* LA SPEZIA. Industrial town, situated between the sea and green hills. In Roman times there was an important road, as can be seen from remains of baths, a bridge and a burial-ground. The *Duomo*, dedicated to Santa Maria Assunta, was completed in 1550. Inside, is a polychrome terracotta altarpiece by Andrea della Robbia (1435-1525), representing the Coronation of the Virgin. The *Museo Archeologico Lunense* contains a vast collection of material excavated near the town of Luni. The *Arsenale* housed a naval museum, which used to be the oldest and richest in Italy, but unfortunately its contents were transferred elsewhere after 1940, because of the war. One should walk to Porta Isolabella for a fine view over the town, the Arsenal and the bay, and to Biassa where there is the church of San Martino, containing valuable works of art.

** LASTRA A SIGNA (Florence). Large town at the confluence of the Vingone and the Arno. The original village used to be called Lastra a Gangalandi. It was encircled by a wall in 1380, on orders from Florence, and later completed by Filippo Brunelleschi (1367-1446). The *Spedale di Sant'Antonio*, with a seven-arched portico, was built for the Florentine Silk Guild, and is probably an early work of Filippo Brunelleschi. Walk to *Malmantile*, where there is a castle, the walls of which were rebuilt during the first half of the 15th cent.

* LATISANA (Udine). Agricultural centre on the left bank of the river Tagliamento. In the parish church of *San Giovanni Battista* is a painting of the Baptism of Jesus by Paolo Caliari, called Veronese (1528-1588), and a wooden Crucifix by Andrea Fosco (lived in the 16th cent.).

* LAURIA (Potenza). Neat and attractive village situated on uneven ground between Mt. Sirino and the Grande la Noce river. The *Parrocchiale* has a 15th cent. bell-tower; inside is the tomb of the reverend Domenico Lentini, with a picture by Fabio Cipolla (recorded only in 1454); a painting of St. Anthony by Salvatore Cascini (lived in the 18-19th cent.), and 15th cent. wooden statues of the Madonna and St. Nicholas. The church of *San Giacomo Maggiore* contains an important painting of the Madonna and Child with Saints by an unknown artist (possibly 16th cent.), wooden busts of the same period and later and beautifully carved wooden stalls (1554).

* LAVAGNA (Genoa). Spread out alongside a large beach, and sheltered by hills covered with olive-groves and pine-woods. Walk to the *Basilica dei Fieschi*, built in the mid-13th cent. by Pope Innocent IV and continued by Adrian V. It is one of the finest monuments in eastern Liguria; the upper parts of the doors in the lovely Gothic inspired facade, are composed of alternating light and dark bands. In front of the basilica are the remains of the Fieschi palace.

* LA VERNA (Town of Chiusi della Verna, province of Arezzo). Perched on the top of a limestone and miocene hill, characteristic in outline, it is surrounded by an old and beautiful wood. It is famous both for its natural beauty and Franciscan associations. The simple, mystic little *Chiesetta degli Angeli* was built in 1216 by St. Francis. Visits are recommended to the *Chiesa Maggiore*; the *Corridoio*, with frescoes depicting the life of St. Francis, and the *Cappella delle Stimmate*, built in 1263 by Count Simone da Battifolle. All these places have beautiful terracottas by Andrea della Robbia (1435-1525) and his followers.

*** LECCE. Important agricultural and commercial centre, on a limestone plateau, it is the historical and economic centre of the Salento peninsula. During the 17th and 18th cent. it was embellished with monuments and works of art, in Baroque style; the ancient part of the town abounds in exuberant examples of "Leccan Baroque", a style of architecture peculiar to Lecce and its neighbourhood. The *Basilica di Santa Croce* is the most impor-

Lecce, Chiesa del Rosario, facade.

Galliano, San Vincenzo. Martyrdom of St. Vincent.

Gualdo Tadino, Pinacoteca Comunale. Antonio da Fabriano, Triptych, detail.

Gubbio, Santa Maria Nova. Ottaviano Nelli, Madonna del Belvedere, detail.

Issogne, Castle. The Spice-dealer's, detail of the frescoes.

L'Aquila, Museo Nazionale d'Abruzzo. Maestro di San Giovanni da Capestrano. Stories of the Saint, detail.
Lodi, San Francesco. Antonio Fissiraga offering the Church to the Virgin.

L'Aquila, Museo Nazionale d'Abruzzo. Madonna at Prayer.
Lodi, Santa Maria Incoronata. Bergognone, Annunciation, detail.

tant example. It was begun in 1548 to a design by Gabriele Riccardi, who planned the general structure of the building; the porch is the work of Francesco Antonio Zimbalo (active in the 16-17th cent.); the upper part of the facade was carried out by Cesare Penna, (also active in the 16-17th cent.) and by Giuseppe Zimbalo called Zingarello (recorded 1620-1691); the mixtilinear pediment was also designed by Zingarello, but was carried out by Penna. The large and spectacular interior is remarkable for its sumptuous decoration; the wooden ceiling of the nave has carved and gilded panels (first half of the 17th cent.) and is embellished with a painting of the Trinity by Giovanni Grassi (lived in the 19th cent.); the altars are ponderous yet attractive, the one to San Francesco di Paola having a bas-relief depicting twelve stories concerning the Saint, by Francesco Antonio Zimbalo. Notice also a painting of St. Anthony by Oronzo Tiso (1729-1800), a 16th cent. fresco of the Madonna of Constantinople, and a beautiful altarpiece by the mannerist Gianserio Strafella (lived in the 16th cent.). The *Palazzo della Prefettura* was originally a Celestine Convent. After the Basilica di Santa Croce it is the building most typical of Leccan-Baroque architecture; its design is attributed to Zingarello, who almost certainly carried out the first plan. The magnificent facade is in two orders of rusticated stonework divided by pilasters. The four-sided portico, on columns, was begun by Gabriele Riccardi and finished by Giuseppe Zimbalo. The church of *Santi Nicolò e Cataldo* is an important example of Norman architecture; built in 1180 by Tancredi, Count of Lecce and penultimate Norman King, it has a Baroque facade which blends particularly well with the surviving Romanesque style. On the architrave of the doorway are six carvings of women's heads and, in the lunette, a 14th cent. faded fresco of the Madonna and Angels. The severe and impressive interior contains a statue of St. Nicholas by Gabriele Riccardi, paintings by Giovanni Battista Lama (lived in the 18th cent.), and grotesque and Raphael-style frescoes dating from the first half of the 17th cent. The *Palazzo del Seggio* or *Sedile* was built in 1592, during the mayoralty of Pietro Mocenigo. The ground floor is characterized by two spacious pointed arches, the upper parts decorated with panoplies. The square-shaped *Roman Amphitheatre*, partly hollowed out of tufa rock and partly built on sturdy arches, to hold 25,000 spectators, dates form the Trajan or Hadrian era. The church of *Santa Maria delle Grazie* was designed by Michele Coluzio (active in Lecce at the end of the 16th cent.) and contains paintings of the Presentation at the Temple, the Nativity, and the Assumption by Oronzo Tiso. The *Castello* was designed in 1539-1548 by Gian Iacopo dell'Acaja for Charles V. It is a large trapezoidal building, with strong lance-shaped bulwarks at the corners. The church of *Sant'Irene*, designed by Francesco Grimaldi (1543-1613) has a Roman-type facade; above the doorway is a statue of St. Irene (1717), one-time patron saint of the town, by Mauro Manieri. The interior contains rich

Lecce, Prefecture and Basilica of Santa Croce, facades.

altars by Francesco Antonio Zimbalo and important paintings by Oronzo Tiso. The *Duomo* is dedicated to the Assunta. It was erected in the 12th cent. and entirely rebuilt between 1659 and 1670 by Giuseppe Zimbalo. It has a modest main facade in two orders, with a triangular tympanum, and a sumptuous secondary facade. The interior, built in the form of a Latin cross, has wooden ceilings with important paintings; and magnificent altars in varying forms, with twisted columns laden with flowers, fruit and birds. The impressive, slender campanile was also designed by Giuseppe Zimbalo, and is formed of five floors tapering upwards, the top one being octagonal, with a four-pinnacled dome. The *Palazzo del Seminario*, designed by Giuseppe Cino between 1694 and 1709, has a smooth and rusticated facade divided by high parastas and crossed by two rows of windows; in the bright courtyard is a well, also by Giuseppe Cino. The *Chiesa del Carmine* (rebuilt between 1711 and 1717 by Giuseppe Cino) has a facade in three orders, with six statues in beautiful niches. The church of *San Matteo* is a typical example of Lecce-Baroque style, built between 1667 and 1700 by Achille Carducci; the lower part of the facade is convex, the upper part concave: the oval interior contains statues (1692) by Placido Buffelli representing the Apostles, on raised plinths, paintings of St. Oronzo and St. Anna by Serafino Elmo (1696-c. 1770), one of St. Agatha by Pasquale Grassi (lived in the 18-19th cent.), a 15th cent. fresco of Santa Maria della Luce, by an unknown painter, a wooden carving of St. Matthew (1691) by Gaetano Patalano, and an Our Lady of Sorrows, also in wood, by the 17th cent. Venetian school. The church of *Santa Chiara* was built at the end of the 17th cent. and first half of the 18th. Designed by Giuseppe Cino, it has a facade in two orders, with a rich portal. Inside are altars, possibly the work of Giuseppe Cino; a sketch of St. Agnes, by Francesco Solimena (1657-1747), and Death of St. Joseph, 18th cent. Neapolitan-school painting. The church of *Gesù* or *Buon Consiglio*, designed between 1575 and 1579 by the Jesuit Giovanni De Rosis, contains a painting of the Return of the Prodigal Son, by Antonio Verrio (c. 1639-1707), Doctors of the Church, by Oronzo Letizia (lived in the 17th cent.), and a high altar, with a concave profile, which is one of the most beautiful in the city and was probably made by Giuseppe Cino in 1696. The *Museo Provinciale Sigismondo Castromediano*, founded in 1868 by Duke Sigismondo Castromediano da Cavallino, contains a large collection of archeological remains, mostly ornaments, found in the area of Rudiae, and objects excavated from nearby areas. The church of *Sant'Angelo*, an imposing Baroque building erected in 1663, is believed to have been designed by Giuseppe Zimbalo; in the sacristy is a valuable 12th cent. Byzantine-style ciborium representing

Christ. Also worth seeing at Lecce are: the *Chiesa del Rosario* or *San Giovanni Battista*, (last work of Giuseppe Zimbalo); building was begun in 1691 and was completed in 1728; it has a bizarre and intricate facade; the *Teatro Romano*, the ruins of which were discovered in 1928; the *Arco di Trionfo*, built in 1548, in honour of Charles V, believed to have been designed by Gian Iacopo dell'Acaja, and the church of *San Francesco di Paola* or *Santa Maria degli Angeli* (1524) by Baldassare Peruzzi (1481-1536). Walk to the *Scavi di Rudiae*, Messapian centre and afterwards town hall in Roman times.

** **LEGHORN**, see Livorno.

* **LEGNAGO** (Verona). At the meeting-point of Venetia, Emilia and Lombardy. Pile-dwellings and other remains indicate that the area was inhabited in ancient times. After being a Longobard and Frankish centre, it was conquered by the Venetians, at the beginning of the 16th cent. They raised a fortress here, designed by Michele Sanmicheli (1484-1559), to act as a defensive stronghold against Mantua and Ferrara. The *Duomo*, rebuilt between 1773 and 1814, has a neo-Classical interior, and contains a 14-15th cent. polychrome statue of the Pietà. The *Museum* is housed in the Palazzo Fioroni, and is divided into various sections. There is a collection of weapons and fire-arms, barbarian farming implements, 15-16th cent. ceramics, 17th cent. furniture and historical relics from the Risorgimento.

* **LEGNANO** (Milan). The basilica of *San Magno* (1504), with 18th cent. campanile, has an interior in the form of a Greek cross, and

Legnano, San Magno.

contains a Madonna and Child, five Angel musicians and Saints, by Bernardino Luini (1480/90-c. 1531). Notice, also, the *Castello*, erected in the 13th cent. by Ottone Visconti, and the church of *Santa Maria delle Grazie* (1617).

* **LENDINARA** (Rovigo). Agricultural and industrial centre, on the left bank of the Adigetto canal. The *Duomo*, dedicated to St. Sophia, was rebuilt in the 18th cent. It has a lofty, soaring campanile (92m. high), designed by Francesco Antonio Baccari (1747-1835), and contains a Madonna and Child, and Souls in Purgatory, Saints Peter and Paul, by Antonio Zanchi (1631-1722), Pentecost, frescoes by Giorgio Anselmi (1723-1797), Domenico Maggiotto (1713-1794) and, in the sacristy, Madonna and Child with Angel musicians, painted by Domenico Mancini (recorded in 1511-12). In the *Santuario della Madonna del Pilastrello* (latter half of the 16th cent.), St. Anthony Abbot visiting St. Paul the Hermit, Jesus appearing to St. Anthony, by Tommaso Sciacca (1734-1795), and Baptism of Jesus, by Francesco Montemezzano (c. 1540-c. 1602); in the Chapel of the Bath, begun in the 16th cent., water flows which is reputed to have miraculous powers. The church of *San Biagio*, rebuilt in the early 19th cent., is entered through a 16th cent. portal. The interior, designed by Giacomo Baccari, contains notable pictures including Saints Nicholas, Anthony and others, by Andrea Vicentino (1539-1617), a Visitation by Sebastiano Filippi called Bastianino (1532-1602), Madonna of the Belt, by Antonio Zanchi, and Saints Peter, Diego and Pasquale by Gregorio Lazzarini (1655-1730).

* **LENNO** (Como). Attractive village facing Bellagio, the Grigna and Mount Legnone. The

Lenno, Baptistery.

parish church of *Santo Stefano*, built on the ruins of Roman baths, has a crypt consisting of a nave and two aisles, dating from the 11-12th cent., and a Luini-school picture of the Madonna and Child enthroned with Saints. Notice also an 11th cent. *Battistero*, octagonal in shape, a typical example of a Romanesque-Lombard building, neat and simple in construction.

* **LENTIAI** (Belluno). Agricultural village situated on undulating ground at the bottom of a valley. The parish church of *Santa Maria Assunta* was built at the end of the 15th cent., in Renaissance style. It contains works of art, including Stories of the Virgin and Deposition from the Cross, by Cesare Vecellio (1521-c. 1601); Baptism of Jesus, by Jacopo Palma the Younger (1544-1628), and a painting by Francesco Frigimelica (died in 1621). *Villa Pantz* is an interesting example of a 16th cent. gentleman's country house. 16th cent. *Villa Vergerio*, 19th cent. *Villa Crestini*.

* **LENTINI** (Syracuse). Built on hills divided by steep valleys, it is important for its citrus produce. Lentini was one of the first Greek colonies, formed in 729 B.C., at the same time as Catania. The *Chiesa Madre*, dedicated to Sant'Alfio, the first stone of which was laid in 1693, was rebuilt in the second half of the 18th cent. It has a harmonious 18th cent. facade in three orders. The interior contains the valuable 19th cent. silver ferculum of Sant'Alfio, and the 9th cent. Madonna Odigitria. In the *Museo Archeologico* are local remains dating from the 20th cent. B.C. onwards. The *Zona Archeologica di Leontinoi*, with an archeological park, contains fortifications of the Syracuse gate, a Hellenistic necropolis, and the walls around the southern crest of the San Mauro hill.

* **LEONESSA** (Rieti). Situated at the southern edge of the Ripa plain, dominated by Mount Tibia. The church of *San Francesco*, with a flat-topped facade and late-Gothic portal, is built in red stone; it contains a magnificent Crib, with polychrome terracotta figures in Abruzzi style, dating from the beginning of the 16th cent.; an Ascent to Calvary and Flagellation, paintings inspired by the style of Cola dell'Amatrice (1489-1559). The church of *Santa Maria del Popolo*, building of which began in the mid-15th cent., has a flat-topped facade, with a late-Gothic portal in red Aquila stone; the interior, altered in the 18th cent., contains a valuable 15th cent. processional Cross, in gilded silver. The church of *San Pietro*, previously called St. Augustine, standing away from the town centre, has a remarkable portal (1467) with carenated tympanum; the aisleless interior (renovated in the 18th cent., in Baroque style) contains 15th cent. votive frescoes in poor condition, and a large

16th cent. panel, probably by Jacopo Santori called Jacopo Siculo (died 1544). In the crypt is a terracotta Deposition by the Abruzzi artist De Nino (lived in the 16th cent.), and a wooden statue of St. Rocco by Silvestro dell'Aquila (lived in the 15th cent.).

* **LERICI** (La Spezia). Lovely little town, with houses arranged in a semi-circle, surrounded by green hills. The 13th cent. *Castello* was built by the Pisans; inside is the graceful chapel of St. Anastasia; the bastions and buttresses date from 1555. The church of *San Francesco*, rebuilt around 1730, contains important frescoes and 18th cent. paintings; in the adjacent oratory of San Bernardino is a painting of the Madonna between St. Bernardino of Siena and St. Francis by Domenico Fiasella, called Sarzana.

* **LEVANTO** (La Spezia). Seaside resort with a lovely sandy beach. Ruins of the *Mura* (14-16th cent.) and of the *Castello* are all that remains of the ancient municipality. The parish church of *Sant'Andrea*, built in 1200, but with an archway dating from the second half of the 15th cent., has a facade decorated with small arches, two mullioned windows with pointed arches, and a portal; the Gothic interior contains paintings by Carlo Braccesco (recorded 1478-1501). Also worth a visit is the *Chiesa dei Francescani* with adjacent monastery, built in the second half of the 15th cent., but rebuilt in 1615. Inside, is a painting of St. George slaying the dragon, by Pietro Francesco Sacchi (1485-1528), and the Miracle of St. Diego by Bernardo Strozzi (1581-1644); 13th cent. *Loggia del Comune*.

height called "Montagna". The *Chiesa del Carmine*, designed by Giovanni Biagio Amico (1684-1754), has a slender Baroque facade; the adjacent monastery has a cloister (1580) and 14th cent. Chapter House with a portal and two lovely mullioned windows. The church of *San Domenico* (beginning of the 17th cent.) contains paintings of St. Anthony Abbot and the Holy Trinity with Saints, by Filippo Paladino (c. 1544-1614). The *Chiesa Madre*, built at the beginning of the 16th cent. and modified during the 18th, contains a venerated 16th cent. wooden Crucifix. In the modern *Palazzo del Municipio* are mementoes of ancient Phintias, a statue of the Madonna and Child called "della Mazza" (1470), and a few valuable paintings.

** **LIVORNO/LEGHORN.** Tuscany's main port, situated between the hills and the sea, and clearly modern in style. It runs into the pretty villages of Ardenza and Antignano, which consist almost entirely of small villas and gardens. The *Duomo* is dedicated to St. Francis of Assisi, and was built at the beginning of the 17th cent. to a design by Alessandro Pieroni; the portico, with twin Doric columns, was designed either by Pieroni or by the English architect Inigo Jones (1605); the interior contains a marvellous ceiling and valuable paintings. The *Museo Civico* was founded in 1896, and consists of works of art belonging to the municipality and gifts from the citizens. It contains historical archives, with a wealthy collection of 13th cent. documents, paintings, drawings and etchings from past centuries; a hall dedicated to modern painters, mostly from Leghorn itself; an ar-

* **LICATA** (Agrigento). Commercial and industrial little town, with a good port, situated between the mouth of the river Salso and a

Levanto, Sant'Andrea, facade.

Leghorn, Monument to Ferdinand I. Pietro Tacca, detail of the Four Moors.

cheological collection; stone age weapons and tools; Etruscan and Roman objects. The church of *San Ferdinando*, also called Chiesa della Crocetta, is by Giovanni Battista Foggini (1652-1725); the aisleless interior contains lovely stucco decorations, marble work and statues. The *Monument to Ferdinand I*, called the monument of the Four Moors, was built in 1617 in memory of victories over the barbary pirates by the Knights of St. Stephen, the Grand Master of whom was Ferdinand I himself; the marble statue of the Grand-Duke is the work of Giovanni Bandini (1595), whilst the four bronze statues of enslaved barbars, popularly known as "the Moors", are by Pietro Tacca (1577-1640). Worth visiting are: the important *Palazzo De Larderel*, dating from the middle of the last century; church of the *Concezione* or of the *Madonna*, by Alessandro Pieroni (1599), containing the tomb of the Belgian sculptor Francesco Du Quesnoy (1594-1643); and the russet- coloured *Fortezza Vecchia*.

* LIZZANO IN BELVEDERE (Bologna).

Important holiday resort and good starting-point for excursions. The *Rotonda* is a characteristic pre-Romanesque building, built between the 8th and 10th cent. It is leaning, due to subsidence. The parish church of *San Mamante* was designed by Giuseppe Gualandi (1866-1945).

* LOCOROTONDO (Bari).

Characteristic village on a hilltop, in the heart of the Murgia dei Trulli area; it is built to a circular plan. The *Chiesa Madre di San Giorgio* is an important neo-Classical construction, built at the turn of the 19th cent.; inside are paintings by Federico Maldarelli (1826-1893), and wooden stalls which belonged to a previous church. The church of *La Greca* contains beautiful capitals and unusual half-columns supported by pillars.

* LOCRI (Reggio Calabria).

Popular seaside resort on the Ionic coast. The *Museo di Locri* houses a rich and important collection of archeological remains, mostly from the nearby necropolis, including a Nereid headless bust and mutilated statues, strigils, mirrors, vases, glass objects, helmets, discs and weapons. Trip to the *Rovine di Locri*, an extremely interesting archeological area.

** LODI (Milan).

Important agricultural and industrial centre, with historical connections, on the right bank of the river Adda. The *Duomo* was begun in 1160, and has a facade which has obviously been altered many times. The large, solemn interior contains important paintings including a polyptych by Callisto Piazza (c. 1500-1562) depicting the Massacre of the Innocents; and a polyptych of the Assunta by Martino Piazza (recorded 1514-1527); in the chancel are eleven works in marquetry by fra' Giovanni da Verona (c. 1457-1525). 18th cent. *Broletto*, with Baroque facade. The Renaissance-style *Santuario dell'Incoronata* (begun in 1488) contains important works of art, including four panels by Ambrogio da Fossano, called Bergognone (c. 1455-1522). The church of *San Cristoforo* was completely rebuilt to a design by Pellegrino Tibaldi called Pellegrino Pellegrini (1527-1596). The former monastery of St. Philip houses the *Museo Civico*, with a section containing 17-19th cent. ceramics, and an important art gallery, with works by Callisto Piazza, Cesare da Sesto (1477-1523), and other good artists. The church of *San Francesco*, built at the end of the 13th cent., in Gothic-Lombard style, contains extremely interesting 14th and 15th cent. frescoes by local and other Lombard painters. The *Ospedale Maggiore* (15-16th cent.) has an interesting courtyard (1473). The 14th cent. church of *Sant'Agnese* is in Gothic-Lombard style; inside is a polyptych by Albertino Piazza (c. 1475-1529). The church of *San Lorenzo* (12-13th cent.) contains a fresco of the Resurrection by Callisto Piazza, and a Pietà by Bernardino Campi (1552-1591). In the church of *San Bassiano*, which has a Gothic facade, is a valuable series of 14th cent. frescoes.

** LOMELLO (Pavia).

Ancient village giving its name to the area (Lomellina). The 5th cent. *Battistero di San Giovanni ad Fontes*, the upper part of which was rebuilt in the 8th cent. with

Lodi Vecchio, San Bassiano.
Lodi Vecchio, San Bassiano, interior.

a small tiburium, is surrounded by Roman tombs with tiled roofs. The church of *Santa Maria Maggiore* dates from the beginning of the 11th cent., the exterior is marked by pilasters and small hanging arches; the interior is lively but plain, as little of the original decoration remains. 12-13th cent. church of *San Michele*.

* **LONATO** (Brescia). Situated partly in the plain and partly on a hillside, overlooking Lake Garda. Pile-dwellings and household utensils prove this area was inhabited in the early Bronze Age, and Roman archeological remains have also been found in the area. The 18th cent. *Duomo*, dedicated to St. John the Baptist, contains paintings by Pietro Liberi (1614-1687), Paolo Farinati (c. 1524-1606), Giambettino Cignaroli (1706-1770) and Andrea Celesti (1637-1712).

* **LONEDO** (Town of Lugo di Vicenza, province of Vicenza). The *Villa Piovene Porto*

Lomello, Baptistery of San Giovanni ad fontes and Santa Maria Maggiore.
Lomello, Santa Maria Maggiore, interior.
Lonedo, Villa Godi Valmarana.

Godi, one of the early works of Andrea Palladio (1508-1580), was modified by Francesco Muttoni (active at the beginning of the 18th cent.) in 1700; in the park there is a 15th cent. chapel. Another work by Palladio is the *Villa Godi*, previously called Valmarana. It contains frescoes by Gualtiero Gualtieri (lived in the 16th cent.), Gian Battista Zelotti (1526-1578) and Battista del Moro (lived in the second half of the 16th cent.).

* **LONIGO** (Vicenza). Small agricultural and industrial town, on the lower slopes of the Berici mountains. The *Palazzo Comunale* (town hall), formerly Palazzo Pisani (second half of the 16th cent.) was inspired by the style of Michele Sanmicheli (1484-1559). The *Villa Giovanelli* once belonged to the Jesuits. It was rebuilt in 1877 to a design by Giuseppe Balzaretti (1801-1874); in the grounds of the villa is a Benedictine Abbey dedicated to Saints Fermo and Rustico, and rebuilt in the 19th cent. It contains paintings of the Martyrdom of Saints Fermo and Rustico by Francesco Montemezzano (lived c. 1540-1602), and the Marriage at Cana, St. Jerome and other Saints, by Alessandro Bonvicino, called Moretto da Brescia (c. 1498-1554). The *Rocca* was designed by Vincenzo Scamozzi (1552-1616). The parish church of *Santi Quirico e Giulietta*, rebuilt at the beginning of the 17th cent., contains paintings by Giambettino Cignaroli (1706-1770). In the neighbourhood is a 13th cent. Franciscan hermitage (*Eremitaggio Francescano di San Daniele*) and the sanctuary of the *Madonna dei Miracoli*, which contains a venerated image of the Madonna and small votive panels.

* **LOREO** (Rovigo). Agricultural and industrial village. The parish church of the *Assunta* was designed by Baldassare Longhena (1598-1682). It contains a few works of art, such as the high altar by Longhena, and Death of St. Joseph by Giovan Battista Piazzetta (1682-1754).

** **LORETO** (Ancona). Situated on an attractive hill on the right bank of the river Musone, with 16th cent. walls. The *Santuario della Santa Casa* was begun in 1468 and only completed towards the middle of the 18th cent.; it is one of the best-known monuments in Italy. The Renaissance facade was begun by Giovanni Boccalini (died 1580) and finished in 1587 by Giovanni Battista Ghioldi; the three bronze doors are embellished with magnificent bas-reliefs by Antonio di Bernardino Calcagni (1536-1593), Sebastiano Sebastiani da Camerino (died 1626), Tarquinio Iacometti da Recanati (lived in the 16-17th cent.), Antonio di Girolamo Lombardo (recorded 1608-1610), the brothers Pietro, Paolo and Giacomo Lombardo (active at the turn of the 17th cent.), Tiburzio Vergelli da Camerino (1555-1610), and Giovanni Battista Vitali (died 1640) who worked

Loreto, Santuario della Santa Casa. A. Lombardo, bronze panel with Expulsion from Paradise. Loreto, Piazza del Santuario.

there in 1596; the slender campanile is by Luigi Vanvitelli (1700-1773). The Sanctuary contains the so-called Santa Casa, with marble-faced walls designed by Donato Bramante (1444-1514), and many works of art including bronze works by Antonio Calcagni, Tiburzio Vergelli, Aurelio Lombardo (1501-1563), and Girolamo Lombardo (c. 1504-c. 1590), as well as valuable mosaics and paintings by the 20th cent. artist Giuseppe Pauri. The sacristy of St. Mark contains frescoes by Melozzo da Forlì (1438-c. 1494); in the sacristy of St. John are frescoes by Luca Signorelli, probably carried out towards the end of the 15th cent. Also of interest are the sacristy of St. Matthew and the Treasury. Although it lost most of its treasures to Napoleon I in 1797, it still has some notable works of art, such as paintings by Guido Reni (1575-1642), Alessandro Tiarini (1577-1668) and Francesco Mazzola, called Parmigianino (1503-1540), frescoes by Cristoforo Roncalli, called Pomarancio (c. 1552-1626), and precious majolicas, monstrances, diadems, mitres, chasubles, etc... The *Palazzo Apostolico* was begun by Donato Bramante and finished by such illustrious architects as Antonio da Sangallo the Younger (1483-1546), Raniero Nerucci (recorded 1530-1550) and Luigi Vanvitelli. It contains the historical archives of the "Santa Casa" with the famous accounts book (libro delle spese) of Lorenzo Lotto (1480-1556); the Papal appartment, with beautiful paintings by Lotto; the hall of mirrors, with paintings by Gaetano Gandolfi (1734-1802), Lotto, Girolamo Muziano (1528-1592), Carlo Maratta (1625-1713) and Felice Damiani (1530-1608); the Swiss hall, with valuable tapestries, and the Hall of the Tapestries.

* **LOVERE** (Bergamo). Situated on the shore of Lake Iseo, with historic buildings. The 15th cent. *Basilica di Santa Maria in Valvendra* has a spacious interior adorned with paintings by Ottavio Viviani (c. 1579-1641), Alessandro Bonvicino, called Moretto da Brescia (1498-1554) and other good artists. Palazzo Tadini houses the *Galleria dell'Accademia Tadini*, which contains valuable paintings including a Madonna and Child by Jacopo Bellini (1400-1471), a Madonna and Child by Lorenzo Veneziano (recorded 1356-1372), a Portrait of a Gentleman by Francesco Mazzola, called Parmigianino (1503-1540), and a Madonna and Child by Domenico Morone (c. 1442-1517). The church of *San Giorgio* was altered several times between the 17th and 19th cent.; inside is a painting of the Last Supper by Paolo Cavagna (1556-1627).

** **LUCCA.** Situated on the left bank of the river Serchio, at the beginning of the Garfagnana, in a vast and fertile plain. The city is still surrounded by its ancient, tree-lined walls, and its glorious links with the past are revealed in its churches, palaces and other monuments. The *Duomo di San Martino* was possibly founded in the 6th cent. by San Frediano; in the 8th cent. it was the seat of the bishopric; in 1060 it was rebuilt by Bishop Anselmo da Baggio, later Pope Alexander II. The Romanesque, assymetrical facade has a deep-set portico and three floors of loggettas; notice the wonderful marble statue of St. Martin on horseback and the Beggarman, a portent of Nicola Pisano's work (1225-1287); much admired portico and three doorways. The facade is flanked by a sturdy campanile, rising upwards with single-aperture and four-aperture windows; it is embellished with small hanging arches, and the summit is decorated with merlons in the form of a tower, the buttresses are adorned with Gothic niches. The interior is paved in polychrome marble. In the right aisle are altars with paintings, mostly late 16th cent.; while the right transept contains the tomb of Pietro da Noceto, by Matteo Civitali (1472). The left transept contains the chapel of Liberty, built by Charles IV (1369), in remembrance of the liberation of Lucca from the Pisans; the Sanctuary chapel, with a Madonna and Child enthroned between Saints Stephen and John the Baptist, considered one of the best works of Baccio della Porta called fra Bartolomeo (1475-1517), and, in the middle of the transept, the tomb of Ilaria del Carretto, masterpiece of Iacopo della Quercia (1367-1438). In the centre of the left aisle is the famous Tabernacle of the Holy Face, by Matteo Civitali (1482-1484); it contains an image of the Holy Face of Christ crucified, dating from the 11th or 12th cent. In the *Opera del Duomo* is a famous Treasury, containing, amongst many other objects, the

Lucca, Palazzo Pretorio.

158

gilt silver Crucifix, work of a Pisan goldsmith in the 15th cent., known as the Pisan Cross, a 15th cent. gilded silver pastoral staff, reliquiaries, Gothic closets and anthem books illuminated by many artists, including Bartolomeo della Gatta (1448-1502). The 12th cent. church of *San Michele* is a typical example of Pisan-Lucca architecture; the facade is very high, and on the cusp is an enormous statue of St. Michael the Archangel, killing the dragon. The Basilican-style interior, with a nave and two aisles, contains a Madonna and Child in enamelled terracotta, by Luca della Robbia (lived in the 15th cent.), and a panel depicting Saints Jerome, Sebastian, Roch and Helen, considered one of the finest works of Filippino Lippi (1457-1504). The church of *San Frediano*, built during the first half of the 12th cent., has a simple and beautiful facade with a large mosaic depicting the Ascension, in Italo-Byzantine style. Inside is a 12th cent. baptismal font by Roberto, formed by a bowl and a baldacchino decorated with simple reliefs; also works by Amico Aspertini (1474-1552), Matteo Civitali (1436-1501), Andrea della Robbia (1436-1525), and other famous artists. The church of *San Giovanni* consists of two buildings: the church of Santa Reparata e San Pantaleone, and the Baptistery dedicated to St. John. Built in the 12th cent., it was considerably altered in the course of time; it contains a Crucifix with a Madonna and Saints Francis and Catherine, by Francesco Vanni (1565-1609), a head of St. John in relief, after the Flemish style, and the funeral monument to Archbishop Giulio Arrigoni, by Augusto Passaglia (1838-1918). The *Pinacoteca Nazionale*,

housed in the *Palazzo della Provincia* (begun in 1578 by Bartolomeo Ammannati) has a rich collection of works of art by Ugolino Lorenzetti of Siena (lived in the 14th cent.), Sandro Botticelli (1444-1510), Cosimo Rosselli (1439-1507), fra Bartolomeo, Amico Aspertini, Andrea del Sarto (1486-1531), Jacopo Bassano (1510-1592), Harmenszoon Rembrandt (1606-1669), and Guido Reni (1575-1642). The *Museo Civico* contains Etruscan and Roman remains, and works by artists from the 9th cent. onwards; it also houses the War Museum, arranged in six rooms, with many relics from the Garibaldi era and the First World War. Also worth seeing in Lucca are: the ruins of the 14th cent. *Case dei Guinigi*; the *Oratorio di Santa Maria delle Rose* (built at the beginning of the 14th cent.); the 13th cent. church of *Santa Maria Forisportam*, also called church of *Santa Maria Bianca*; the Renaissance *Palazzo Pre-*

Lucca, San Giovanni, detail of the portal.

Lucca, Duomo, facade, detail.
Lucca, Palazzo Provinciale, courtyard.

159

torio, by Matteo Civitali, with a pillared portico and mullioned windows; the *Porta di San Gervasio* (ruins of the city wall built in 1260), and the *Casa di Monna Vanna* with the *Torre del Travaglio*, recently restored to its original 14th cent. aspect. Interesting walk round the tree-lined walls (*Giro delle Mura*); they were built in the 16th and 17th cent., and have eleven ramparts and a platform.

** LUCERA (Foggia).

Small agricultural and commercial town situated on a hill dominating the Tavoliere plain. The *Duomo*, dedicated to the Assunta, is an almost pure example of Angevin architecture; built between 1300 and 1317, it has a plain, cusped facade, with three narrow ogee-arched doorways surmounted by baldacchinoes; especially interesting are the area of the apse and the strong external buttresses. The vast and unadorned interior contains a fine pulpit (1560); a 16th cent. Madonna in Glory and Saints, of the Venetian school; and frescoes of the martyrdom of Apostles and Saints, by Belisario Corenzio (c. 1558-post 1640). The Gagliardi chapel contains valuable 16th cent. frescoes by an unknown artist; the tomb of Mozzagrugno (1605);, a wooden statue of Our Lady of Victory (second half of the 14th cent.) recording the victory of the Angevins over the Swabians; a Crucifixion and three Saints by Ippolito Borghese (lived in the 16-17th cent.); a panel of the Madonna between Saints Nicholas and John the Baptist, by Girolamo da Santacroce (recorded 1502-1537), and a late-16th cent. bas-relief of the Almighty, by the Neapolitan school. The church of *San Francesco* was built at the same time as the Cathedral. It has a cusped facade with a wide doorway surmounted by a baldacchino, a polygonal apse and strongly accentuated buttresses. Inside, are wooden statues by Giacomo Colombo (recorded 1679-1705), and important 14th, 15th and 16th cent. frescoes. The church of *San Bartolomeo* is incorporated in a large and insignificant 19th cent. building; inside is a painting of the Madonna and St. Gregory, by Ferdinando Sanfelice of Naples (1675-1748). The *Museo Civico Fiorelli* is housed in the De Nicastri palace; it contains a large collection of local antiques, including a beautiful bust of Proserpine; heads of Hercules and Apollo; headless statue of the Genius populi Lucerini; another headless statue of Venus, (copy of the original Praxiteles school one); capitals; bronze and glass objects. In the pre-historic section are objects from the Bronze Age, and the modern section contains interesting objects, too. The *Fortezza Angioina*, built in the second half of the 13th cent., was one of the most impregnable in Italy; it stands on a pentagonal plan, with the Tower of the Lioness, or of the Queen, and the Tower of the Lion which, even in its ruined condition, is an exceptionally interesting example of a military building. Walk to the Augustan-age *Anfiteatro Romano*.

** LUCIGNANO (Arezzo).

Situated between the Vertege hollow and the river Esse, with a panorama over the Valdichiana. The collegiate church of *San Michele* was built in 1594 by Orazio Porta; inside is a precious baptismal font (1672); also an impressive high altar by Andrea Pozzo (1642-1706) and, in the right aisle, St. Charles Borromeo showing the Cross to a woman, by the painter and engraver Giacinto Gemignani (1611-1681). The 13th cent. church of *San Francesco* has a Romanesque facade; inside are numerous remains of frescoes by Bartolo di Fredi (1330-1410). In the *Museo* are works by Luca di Tommé (1355-1389), Ugolino da Siena (1260-1339), Luca Signorelli (1441-1523), and various artists from Siena. Notice the *Cassero*, with its square tower.

Lucera, Castle.

* **LUCO DEI MARSI** (L'Aquila). It is believed that this village was founded to house slaves and clerks in the times of Imperial Rome; its name certainly derives from a sacred wood which surrounded the temple of the goddess Angitia called "lucus Angitiae". The *Parrocchiale* contains a valuable 16th cent. silver processional cross, and important works by goldsmiths from the Abruzzi area. The Romanesque church of *Santa Maria delle Grazie*, rebuilt in the 13th cent., stands on the site of the temple of Angitia; the interior, well-restored after the earthquake in 1915, contains interesting wooden statues, by an unknown Abruzzi artist.

* **LUGNANO IN TEVERINA** (Terni). Situated on a solitary hill, it consists of tall, large buildings, of ancient construction. The church of *Santa Maria Assunta* (second half of the 12th cent.) is one of the best examples of Romanesque churches in Umbria, even though the fine interior has been spoilt by later restoration work. In the apse is a triptych representing the Assunta and Saints Francis and Sebastian, by Nicolò di Liberatore, called Alunno (1430-1502). Also worthy of note are the walls (*Mura Medievali*), which were mostly built for Pope Pius II (1405-1464), and the *Convento di San Francesco* (1229).

* **LUGO** (Ravenna). Agricultural and industrial centre in the fertile plain between the Santerno and the Senio. The collegiate church of *San Francesco*, dating from the first half of the 13th cent., was rebuilt to a plan by Cosimo Morelli (1732-1812). It contains a few works of art, including a 16th cent. fresco of Our Lady of Succour, by an unknown artist, and St. Anthony reproaching Ezzelino da Romano, by Giacomo Zampa (1731-1808). In the church of *San Francesco di Paola* (end of the 19th cent.) are statues in coloured terracotta, Ferrara style, dating from the end of the 15th cent., and a Madonna and Child with Saints Matthew and Agatha, by Giovanni Battista Bertucci Juniore (c. 1540-1614). The Baroque-style church of

Lugnano in Teverina, Santa Maria Assunta.

the *Madonna delle Grazie* was built in 1667. Inside the *Chiesa della Croce Coperta* are 15th and 16th cent. frescoes of the Ferrara school. The *Rocca*, now the town hall, has a cylindrical, battlemented keep (14th cent.); inside is the Baracca Hall, which contains a collection of mementoes and objects belonging to the aviator Francesco Baracca (1888-1918). In front of the Rocca is the four-sided portico of the *Paviglione* (1783-1889).

* **LUINO** (Varese). At the mouth of the river Tresa. The 15th cent. church of the *Madonna del Carmine* contains some paintings from the 16th cent. Notice the *Oratorio di San Pietro*, rebuilt in the 17th cent., but still with its Romanesque bell-tower; inside is a fresco representing the Adoration of the Magi, possibly by Bernardino Luini (1480/90-1531). Also the church of *San Giuseppe* (18th cent.) and the *Prepositurale dei Santi Pietro e Paolo*, with four frescoes by Raffaele Casnedi (1822-1892) depicting the Evangelists.

* **LUNI** (Town of Ortonovo, province of La Spezia). On the plain east of the river Magra. Luni was a settlement in neolithic times, then a Roman colony from 177 B.C., flourishing on account of the exporting of Apuan marble from the nearby port. Excavations have unearthed the *Anfiteatro*, in the open countryside. It probably dates back to the 1st cent. and has twelve external marble stairways with double flights, and eight sectors.

* **MACERATA.** Built on an attractive hill, with an ancient quarter on a trapezoid plan, and modern quarters. The *Sferisterio*, an impressive building in neo-Classical style, was designed by Ireneo Aleandri (1795-1885). It is one of the most beautiful monuments of its type in central Italy, with a huge arena for the so-called "gioco del pallone al bracciale". The *Biblioteca Comunale Mozzi Borgetti* is considered one of the most important libraries in the Marches area, not only for the number of volumes, but above all for its valuable manuscripts and letters. The *Museo Civico* contains an interesting coin collection, and an archeological section consisting of objects (such as necklaces and various kinds of jewellery) found in the area around Macerata. The *Pinacoteca Comunale* has one section for ancient art, and

Lugo, porticoes of the Pavilion.

Macerata, Spheristerion.
Macerata, San Giovanni, part of the dome.

one for contemporary art. The former contains a Madonna and Child by Carlo Crivelli (1430/35-1495); a panel of the Madonna and Child, Angels and Saints, by Pietro da Montepulciano (active at the beginning of the 15th cent.); a painting representing Alexander III Farnese, by Antonio Moor (1519-c. 1575), and a large altarpiece depicting the Madonna della Cintola, by Andrea Boscoli (c. 1550-c. 1607). The church of *San Filippo* (turn of the 18th cent.) has a spectacular interior with a painting of the Birth of the Virgin by Francesco Boniforti (1594-1671), and one of San Filippo Neri, by Francesco Mancini (c. 1694-1758). In the church of *San Giovanni* (first half of the 17th cent.) is a Death of the Virgin by Giovanni Lanfranco (1582-1647). The *Duomo* was designed by Cosimo Morelli (1732-1812). It contains a painting representing the Madonna and Child with Saints Sebastian and Andrew, by Andrea Boscoli, and three paintings depicting the Last Supper, Supper at Emmaus, and Deposition from the Cross, by Filippo Bellini (1550/55-1604). The *Basilica della Madonna della Misericordia*, has a small and harmonious facade by Luigi Vanvitelli (1700-1773); inside are some fairly good works of art, including a Birth of the Virgin by Sebastiano Conca (c. 1680-1764). The *Loggia dei Mercanti* was built at the beginning of the 16th cent. and is a harmonious construction reminiscent of buildings in Tuscany. Walk to the church of *Santa Maria delle Vergini*, in late-Renaissance style, which contains a painting of the Flight into Egypt by Giuseppe Cesari, called Cavalier d'Arpino (1568-1640), and an Epiphany by Tintoretto (1518-1594).

* **MACOMER** (Nuoro). Important industrial and commercial town and centre of communications, built on a basaltic outcrop on the southernmost part of the Campeda plateau. Here stood the ancient Macopsissa; a castle was built in the Middle Ages (no ruins of which remain) and the new town was built around it. The 16th cent. parish church of *San Pantaleo*, in Gothic-Aragonese style, is flanked by a campanile built in 1573 by Michele Puig di Bolotana. Excursion to the *Nuraghe Santa Barbara*; the central tower, almost completely preserved, rises up from a large, megalithic base.

* **MADDALONI** (Caserta). Situated at the foot of Mt. San Michele. The Baroque church of *San Francesco d'Assisi* or *Sant'Antonio*, with a tall dome, contains some fairly good works of art, including a Madonna delle Grazie by an unknown 15th cent. Neapolitan painter. The church of the *Annunziata*, with a portico dated 1605, has a carved and painted ceiling (paintings by Giovanni Balducci – recorded 1560-1603), and tombs of the Carafa, Dukes of Maddaloni. Excursion to the *Ponti di Valle di Maddaloni* or *Ponti della Valle*, an enormous

construction by the architect Luigi Vanvitelli (1700-1773), through which passes the Caroline Aqueduct (named after King Charles of Bourbon), to feed the waterfalls in the park of the Royal Palace of Caserta.

* **MAGIONE** (Perugia). Village near Lake Trasimeno. The 15th cent. *Badia* or *Castello dei Cavalieri di Malta* is built on a square plan. In 1502 dispossessed nobles from Umbria and the Marches met there to join forces against Cesare Borgia, who wiped them all out at Senigallia. The church of the *Madonna delle Grazie* contains frescoes probably carried out in 1371 by Andrea di Giovanni da Orvieto.

* **MAGLIANO IN TOSCANA** (Grosseto). A village still living in a medieval atmosphere. Before the year 1,000 A.D. the Aldobrandeschi built a fortress there. It is surrounded by walls attributed to a 15th cent. military architect from Siena, called Bibbiena. Lovely 16th cent. *Porta Nuova*, in Sienese style, and the *Porta San Martino*, with remains of the Aldobrandeschi battlements. The church of *San Giovanni Battista*, initially in Romanesque style, with a Renaissance facade, contains a baptismal font, in travertine, dated 1492, and a Sienese fresco representing St. Sebastian. In the neighbourhood are the ruins of the church of *San Bruzio*, begun in the 11th cent. in Romanesque-Lombard style.

Magliano (surroundings), San Bruzio, archway.

* **MAGLIE** (Lecce). Commercial centre, with flourishing artisan industries. The 17th cent. church of the *Madonna delle Grazie* has a precious Baroque portal and a lovely Lecce-type altar. The 18th cent. *Parrocchiale*, with a characteristic convex facade, has a campanile which repeats the style of Lecce Cathedral. The Palazzo Capece, with a magnificent Baroque portal, looks on to the *Piazza del Municipio*. In the neighbourhood of Maglie are some menhirs (monolithic monuments).

* **MAIORI** (Salerno). Characteristic village, with houses arranged in the form of an amphitheatre, near the opening of the Tramonti valley. The church of *Santa Maria a Mare*, with a large cupola built of small majolica bricks, was built in the 12th cent. and modified several times in the course of time. It has a magnificent 16th cent. gilded lacunar ceiling, and, on the high altar, a 14th cent. polychrome wooden statue representing the Madonna and Child, which, according to legend, came from the sea. In the sacristy is an English alabaster frontal (15th cent.); also antiphonaries, valuable vestments, and a reliquary casket from the end of the 14th cent. The *Santuario di Santa Maria delle Grazie*, rebuilt after the floods in 1910, contains a remarkable 15th cent. painting representing the Visitation, and a 16th cent. marble font.

* **MALCESINE** (Verona). Attractive village surrounded by oliveyards, at the foot of Monte Baldo. The *Castello Scaligero* dominates the village. It was built in the 13th and 14th cent., and enlarged by the Venetians in the 17th; it has crenellated walls and a pentagonal tower. The 16th cent. *Palazzo dei Capitani*, the present-day town hall, contains the Meeting Hall, frescoed with 16th, 17th and 18th cent. coats of arms of the so-called Capitani del Lago, magistrates who were elected every three years by the Council of Veronese patricians.

* **MALLES VENOSTA** (Bolzano). Dominated by the Ortles group of mountains. The Gothic *Parrocchiale*, with picturesque bell-tower, contains works by M. Knoller (1725-1804): the Death of St. Joseph, St. Anne, and St. James. The 16th cent. church of *San Michele* contains frescoes of the same period. Remains of the *Castello Frölich*, with characteristic Romanesque cylindrical-shaped tower and Romanesque campanile. The 9th cent. church of *San Benedetto* has an aisleless interior, with remains of Romanesque-type frescoes.

* **MANDURIA** (Taranto). Agricultural centre situated on a shelf in the Taranto Murge. It stands on the site of one of the most important Messapian cities. The *Duomo*, dedicated to St. Gregory the Great, is Romanesque in origin, but was rebuilt in mainly Renaissance style. It has a facade with three portals, the middle

one of which was designed by Raimondo da Francavilla (lived in the 16th cent.). The campanile has single-lighted apertures, and dates back to the 13th cent. The interior consists of a nave and two aisles, and contains a large baptismal font with the figures of Christ and the Apostles (1534); a fine carved pulpit (1608); twelve statues of Saints in a Renaissance frame, by Placido Buffelli (1635-1693); paintings with stories of St. Gregory, by Pasquale Bianchi (lived in the 18th cent.), and Vincenzo Filotico (lived in the 17th cent.); and a Last Supper, probably by Francesco Solimena (1657-1747). The *Palazzo Imperiali* (1719) is enhanced by a spacious doorway and a corbelled balcony. The interior contains pictures by Vincenzo Filotico. The *Ghetto degli Ebrei*, facing the cathedral, is just as it was in the 15th and 16th cent. The 18th cent. ex-convento del Carmine houses the *Biblioteca Marco Gatti* which contains, among other things, maps of the Terra d'Otranto, hand drawn by Giuseppe Pacelli, local geographer (1764-1811), incunabula, fifteeners and local antiques. Also worth a visit in Manduria are the *Fonte Pliniano* (probably the lake Pliny mentions in his "Naturalis Historia)", a deep natural grotto going back to Roman times, from where the mineral-type water gushes out continuously, and the *Mura Megalitiche*, survivals of Messapanian Manduria, presumably erected between the 5th and 3rd cent. B.C.

** **MANFREDONIA** (Foggia). Between the Adriatic sea and the Gargano, at the mouth of the Capitanata, it is an agricultural and fishing centre, with a popular seaside resort

Manduria, Duomo, facade, detail.

along the lido di Siponto. The church of *San Domenico* has an original ogee-arched portal supported by two lions, dating back to the end of the 13th cent. It incorporates interesting remains of a previous chapel dedicated to Mary Magdalen, and contains important late-14th cent. frescoes of the Pietà, Tree of Jesse, Madonna and Child with St. Nicholas, and a valuable marble Madonna and Child of the early 16th cent. The *Cattedrale* was erected in 1680 by Pietro Francesco Orsini, later Pope Benedict XIII, after the Turks had destroyed the previous Gothic cathedral. It contains a Treasury with valuable sacred vestments, donated to the city by Pope Benedict, and a fine 17th cent., Neapolitan-school painting of the Deposition from the Cross. The *Castello*, built by King Manfredi but completed by later lords, was largely designed by Peter d'Angicourt (recorded 1269-1324). It has a square keep with one square tower and three cylindrical ones at the corners.

* **MANTA** (Cuneo). At the foot of the Saluzzo hills, it is situated among vineyards. It has medieval houses and an impressive 14th

cent. *Castello*. In the great hall are some well-preserved frescoes by Giacomo Jaquerio, including the lively "Fountain of Youth" and others with characters in scenes inspired by the medieval romance "Knight-errant" by Tommaso II da Saluzzo. There are some more 15th cent. frescoes in the ancient *Parrocchiale* and *Cappella di S. Maria del Monastero*.

*** **MANTOVA/MANTUA.** On the right bank of the Mincio, where it spreads out into a lake. It is a city rich in buildings and art treasures, especially of the 15th and 16th cent., when the Gonzaga family held one of the most brilliant courts in Europe here, and turned it into a Renaissance capital. The *Basilica di Sant' Andrea*, one of the most admired religious buildings of the Renaissance, was designed by Leon Battista Alberti (1404-1472). The interior is over a hundred metres long. It has an aisleless nave and contains a large number of artistic works: the mausoleum of Bishop Andreasi by Prospero Clementi (1516-1584), the Strozzi mausoleum (1529) above which is a Stoning of St. Stephen, attributed to A. Maria Viani, the tomb of Andrea Mantegna, who was buried

Manfredonia, Castle.

Mantua, Ducal Palace.
Mantua, Ducal Palace, Hall of Mirrors.

Lucca, San Frediano. Baptismal font by Roberto.
Malles, San Benedetto. Stories of David, detail.
Mantua, Ducal Palace. A. Mantegna, frescoes in the Bridal Chamber, detail.

Mantua, Ducal Palace. Pisanello, Two Ladies, detail of the fresco.

Mantua, Ducal Palace. Pisanello, Warriors, detail of the fresco.

Mantua, Ducal Palace. Frans Pourbus the younger, Eleonora dei Medici with her children, detail.

Mantua, Ducal Palace. Domenico Fetti, Feeding of the Five Thousand, detail.

Mantua, Ducal Palace. P. P. Rubens, The Gonzaga Family worshipping the Trinity, detail.

Mantua, Ducal Palace. P. P. Rubens, The Gonzaga Family worshipping the Trinity, detail.

Massa Marittima, Duomo. Goro di Gregorio, Tomb of S. Cerbone, detail.

Matelica, Museo Piersanti. Antonio da Fabriano, Madonna and Child.

Messina, Museo Nazionale. Caravaggio, Lazarus raised from the Dead, detail.

here in 1506, pictures from Mantegna's school, and a Madonna enthroned and Saints, altarpiece by Lorenzo Costa the Elder (c. 1450-1535). *Piazza delle Erbe* is overlooked by interesting buildings, partly dating back to the 15th cent. The *Rotonda di San Lorenzo* is a Romanesque church built by order of Contessa Matilde di Canossa. The *Torre dell'Orologio* (1473), was designed by Luca Fancelli (1430-c. 1495). The *Palazzo della Ragione* is a sturdy construction dating back to 1250, where the Rota and then the Senate met in the times of the Gonzagas. *Palazzo del Broletto*, with facade of 1227. *Piazza Sordello*, for centuries the heart of the political and artistic life of Mantua. The *Duomo*, dedicated to St. Peter, was rebuilt in the 16th cent.; it has a facade by Nicolò Baschiera (lived in the 18th cent.) and interior by Giulio Pippi called Giulio Romano. The *Palazzo Ducale* or *Reggia dei Gonzaga* is a group of buildings erected in various periods between the 13th and 18th cent. The splendid interior still gives an idea of the brilliance of the Gonzaga court in the Renaissance. Among its countless works of art are the magnificent painting by Peter Paul Rubens (1577-1640) of Dukes Guglielmo and Vincenzo Gonzaga, with their consorts Eleanor d'Austria and Eleanor de' Medici in Adoration of the Trinity,

Mantua, Palazzo del Te, view of the garden from the atrium.
Mantua, Sant'Andrea.

works by Foppa, Tintoretto, Van Dick, F. Pourbus the Younger, D. Fetti, G. Bazzani, and the frescoes of Andrea Mantegna (c. 1431-1506) and Pisanello (recorded 1395-1455). *Castello di San Giorgio*, with crenellated towers at the corners. *Teatro Scientifico*, in the Palazzo dell'Accademia Virgiliana, with facade by Giuseppe Piermarini (1734-1808). The 13th cent. church of *Santa Maria di Gradaro* is Romanesque-Gothic in style; in the chancel are 13th cent. Byzantine-inspired frescoes. The *Palazzo del Te*, one of the best preserved buildings of the 16th cent., was decorated by Giulio Pippi, called Giulio Romano (c. 1499-1546). *Chiesa di San Sebastiano*, designed by Leon Battista Alberti. *Casa di Andrea Mantegna*, probably designed by Mantegna himself. *Casa di Giulio Romano*, designed by Romano. The *Piazza Virgiliana* was re-ordered to suit neo-Classical taste in 1797. *Palazzo d'Arco* (1784); inside are seven enormous paintings illustrating stories of Alexander the Great by Giuseppe Bazzani (c. 1690-1769). The Gothic church of *San Francesco* dates back to the early 14th cent.; inside are some remarkable works of art.

* **MARIGLIANO** (Naples). Agricultural centre half-way between Naples and Avellino. The late-15th cent. *Collegiata*, dedicated to Santa Maria delle Grazie, is flanked by a sturdy campanile built over a great arch. It contains four pictures in the ceiling representing the Martyrdom of St. Sebastian, St. Francis Xavier, St. Roch and a Madonna delle Grazie, by Domenico Antonio Vaccaro (c. 1680-1750), and, in the chancel, the Miracles of Elia, by a follower of Luca Giordano (1632-1705). The 15th cent. church of *San Vito* has a coffered ceiling with a Deposition and Glory of San Vito, by Filippo Vitale (active 1613-1619). Also worthy of note is the *Palazzo Feudale*; the rooms are decorated with valuable paintings.

* **MAROSTICA** (Vicenza). Attractive little town on the slopes of the Asiago plateau, built to a checkerboard plan and surrounded by 14th cent. walls. The *Castello Inferiore*, formerly residence of the Venetian podestà, has an impressive tower and a lovely portico and loggia-style courtyard. Considerable remains of the *Castello Superiore* can be seen. The church of *Sant'Antonio* was rebuilt in the first half of the 18th cent.; it contains an altarpiece (1574) by Iacopo and Francesco Bassano the Younger depicting St. Paul preaching in Athens.

* **MARSALA** (Trapani). Situated on the promontory of Capo Boeo, it has an important ancient quarter and is a popular seaside resort. The 18th cent. *Duomo*, dedicated to St. Thomas

Mantua, Sant'Andrea, part of the dome.

of Canterbury, has an imposing facade. The interior has a nave and two aisles; it contains various sculptures by the school of Gagini, and eight wonderful 16th cent. Flemish tapestries. The 3rd cent. A.D. *Edificio Termale* is the most important ruin left from the Roman city; a tetrastyle atrium followed by a peristyle leads into the baths, where can be seen the remains of the tepidarium and the frigidarium; the pavements in the rooms are covered with polychrome mosaics, the most admired being the Mosaic of the Wild Beasts. Excursion to the Isola di San Pantaleo, nine kilometres north of Marsala, to the site of *Mozia*, first a Phoenician city and then a Carthaginian one. It was destroyed and forgotten and it is only recently that the name of Mozia has been identified with the Isola di San Pantaleo, the whole surface of which is completely covered with ancient ruins; remains of a large Punic-type building dating from the 6th cent. B.C. can be seen; in the Museum are findings from Lilibeo and Mozia.

* **MARTINA FRANCA** (Taranto). Interesting little town situated on the highest shelf of the southern Murge mountains. The collegiate church of *San Martino* is a massive 18th cent. building. The magnificent Baroque facade has a doorway surmounted by a marble group representing St. Martin and the beggar. In the interior, on the high altar, are polychrome marble pieces, dated 1733, the statues in silver of St. Martin and St. Comasia, carried out by De Blasio da Napoli between 1710 and 1716, and a painting of the Last Supper, by Domenico Carella (c. 1721-1813). The *Palazzo Ducale* was built in 1669 by Petracone V Caracciolo on the site where there was once a castle belonging to the Orsini family. The two-floor facade has a balcony running round it with Baroque iron balusters; inside are pictures of biblical or mythological themes, by Domenico Carella. From the terrace is a panorama of the entire countryside dotted with trulli. The 15th-cent. Gothic church of *Sant'Antonio*, once called

Santo Stefano, contains a huge painting of the Madonna delle Grazie by Leonardo Olivieri (1642-1745). The church of *San Domenico* (1760) has a magnificent Baroque facade; inside is a painting of the Madonna of the Rosary, by Domenico Carella.

* **MARTINENGO** (Bergamo). Agricultural and industrial centre, in a fertile plain. The church of the *Incoronata* (1476) has a slender campanile; inside are remarkable frescoes carried out at the turn of the 16th cent. by an unidentified artist. Medieval *Casa del Capitano*. Ruins of the convent of *Santa Chiara*; in one of the chapels is a large 15th cent. fresco by an unknown artist.

** **MARZABOTTO** (Bologna). On the left bank of the river Reno. *Zona archeologica*, on a plateau overlooking the exposed river-bed of the Reno, once the site of an Etruscan city, founded at the end of the 6th cent. B.C. and

Martina Franca, Colleggiate church of San Martino.

Marzabotto, Museum. Bronze statuette.

Maser, Villa Barbaro.
Maser, Villa Barbaro, The Great Hall. Paolo Veronese, Olympus, frescoes.

destroyed by the Gauls in the middle of the 4th cent. B.C. Archeological material excavated from the city and from the necropoles is collected in the Pompeo Aria Etruscan Museum, named after the first archeologist who became interested in that area. The museum contains pieces of exceptional interest, including a 5th cent. B.C. marble head of Kouros; a large part of the collection was destroyed during the Second World War.

** **MASER** (Treviso). In a hilly area, at the foot of Collalto. *Villa Barbaro*, now called Volpi, is one of the most beautiful villas in the area. It was built by Andrea Palladio (1508-1580) and contains frescoes by Paolo Caliari, called Veronese (1528-1588). In the neighbourhood is the *Barco della Regina*, a large building with a central loggia, the remains of a mansion built in 1490 for Queen Cornaro.

** **MASSA** (Massa Carrara). Situated between hills from which can be seen the serrated peaks of Mounts Cavallo and Tambura, with a mild climate. Massa Vecchia is built around the ancient Malaspina castle; Massa Nuova spreads out onto the plain. The *Duomo*, once dedicated to St. Francis, was built in the 15th cent. by Giacomo Malaspina; in the interior are funerary monuments to Lorenzo Cybo Malaspina and Eleonora Malaspina, by Pietro Aprili (lived in the 15-16th cent.), and, in the underground chapel, the tombs of the princes and dukes of Massa. The *Rocca*, formed by the merging of a medieval building and a Renaissance palace, is adorned with marble decorations round the windows and on the cornices.

* **MASSAFRA** (Taranto). Characteristic little town, at a short distance from Taranto, with an ancient quarter called Terra and a modern one called Borgo; the former has narrow, winding streets, the latter is built to a checkerboard plan. In the neighbourhood are the most important examples of a troglodyte city and Byzantine crypts in Apulia. The *Castello*, an imposing medieval construction, was al-

tered during the 16th cent. The *Duomo* is an impressive building with an Ionic pronaos (1853), designed by Achille Bruni, and finished in 1931; inside are remarkable 18th cent. paintings. The *Santuario della Madonna della Scala* (1731) contains a 12th or 13th cent. fresco representing the Madonna and Child between two kneeling deer; in the nearby *Crypta della Buona Nuova* is a 13th cent. fresco depicting the Madonna della Buona Nuova. The church-crypt of *San Marco* is the best preserved in Massafra, although it is not known exactly when it was built. One enters through a vestibule with a simple lunette. Inside there is a nave and two aisles. The walls were once covered with frescoes but they have almost all been obliterated by damp; the only fresco which is at all clear represents Saints Cosma and Damiano (13th cent.). The front section of the 14th cent. *Cripta di San Leonardo* is damaged; the crypt contains important frescoes representing Saints Andrew, Peter, Stephen and Nicholas of Bari. In the *Cappella-Cripta della Candelora* are frescoes (partly 13th cent.) the oldest and best-preserved of which represents the Presentation at the Temple. The church of *San Lorenzo* (1533) contains a few works of art, including a 16th cent. wooden statue of St. Lawrence.

** **MASSA MARITTIMA** (Grosseto). Situated on a hill, between the valleys of the rivers Pecora, Zanca and Noni, with many 13th and 14th cent. buildings. The town is made up of two parts: the Old Town, where the Romanesque style predominates, and the New Town, which is mostly composed of Gothic buildings. In front of the Romanesque-Gothic *Duomo*, dedicated to the Assunta and San Cerbone, is a wide flight of steps. The cathedral was designed in 1288 by a Comasque artist called Enrico – probably Enrico da Campione; the lower part of the facade has seven blind arches and, in the architrave, there is an interesting bas-relief depicting episodes

Massafra, Castle.

Massa Marittima, Duomo.

from the life of San Cerbone. Inside is a lovely travertine font with a rectangular basin, the work of Giroldo da Lugano (1267), also the tomb of San Cerbone (1324), a masterpiece by the Sienese artist Goro di Gregorio, the chapel of the reliquiaries, Gothic monument to Giuseppe Traversi (1779-1872), and important frescoes and paintings. Thirty coats-of-arms decorate the facade of the *Palazzo Pretorio del Podestà*, built at the beginning of the 13th cent.; it is a solemn building, first the seat of the podestà, then of the commissioners, then of the captains of justice, and, finally, of the King's vicars. The large Romanesque *Palazzo Comunale* contains a huge panel by Ambrogio Lorenzetti, carried out around 1330; it depicts symbolic figures of Faith, Hope and Charity, and is considered one of the most precious examples of Sienese painting. The Romanesque-Gothic church of *Sant'Agostino*, built at the beginning of the 14th cent., contains a painting of St. William the Hermit, by Antonio Nasini (1631-1716). Worthy of note are the *Casa dei Conti Biserno*, Romanesque in style, built in the 13th cent.; the *Torre di Biserno*; the *Fortezza dei Senesi*, probably by Agnolo di Ventura (recorded 1325-1349) and the *Museo di Mineralogia*.

* **MATELICA** (Macerata). Attractive little town at the meeting point of the Fosso di Braccano with the river Esino. The Palazzo Piersanti was built in the second half of the 15th cent. It houses the important *Museo Piersanti*, which contains many artistic works, including two vessels by Giovanni Francesco Barbieri called Guercino (1591-1666), a panel representing the Madonna and Child, by Antonio da Fabriano (active 1450-1485), and a large panel representing St. Anne and the Madonna and Child with Saints, by Lorenzo di Alessandro (lived in the 15th cent.). The church of *San Francesco*, first built in the 13th cent., contains a painting representing Purgatory by Ercole Ramazzani (c. 1530-1598), a Madonna and Child enthroned with Saints

Francis and Catherine of Alexandria, in its original frame, one of the best paintings of Marco Palmezzano (c. 1456-1539), a panel depicting three stories of St. Anthony, by Eusebio da San Giorgio (c. 1465-1540), and a Madonna and Child with Saints by Simone Cantarini (1612-1678). Notice the lovely *Piazza Valerio*, in the centre of which is a fine octagonal fountain, (1619), whilst on the righthand side is the harmonious *Loggia degli Ottoni* (1511). Looking out on to the square are the *Palazzo Ottoni*, part of which dates back to the 15th cent., and the 14th cent. *Palazzo Pretorio*, decorated with a crenellated tower. In the 14th cent. church of *Sant'Agostino* is a painting representing Noli me tangere, by Ercole Ramazzani.

** **MATERA.** In a picturesque position near the river Gravina, with characteristic churches (some carved out of the rock) and houses. The *Duomo* was built in the latter half of the 13th cent. in Romanesque-Apulian style. It has a tripartite facade and a bell-tower with three tiers of mullioned windows; the interior is partly Baroque and contains artistic works including a huge painting of the Assunta and Saints (1627), by an unknown artist, a choir carved in 1453 by Giovanni Tantino d'Ariano di Puglia, and sculptures by Altobello Persio (lived in the 16th cent.). The adjoining *Chiesetta di Santa Maria di Costantinopoli* has a fine Romanesque portal; the interior contains a painting of the Madonna and Child with St. Anne, attributed to Sebastian Maieski (a 17th cent. Polish artist), paintings by Giovanni Donato Oppido di Matera (lived in the 17th cent.), Domizio Persio di Matera (lived in the 16-17th cent.), and Francesco De Rosa, called Pacecco (died 1656); also, a silver and crystal urn containing the remains of San Giovanni da Matera, a hermit who lived in the Gargano in the 12th cent. The *Museo Domenico Ridola* is housed in the former convent of St. Clare, and contains a large collection of objects excavated in the area, of great paleontological interest. Other monuments worth seeing in Matera are: the church of *San Domenico*, ori-

Matelica, Loggia degli Ottoni.

Matera, the "Sassi", detail.

ginally Romanesque in style, containing the tomb of the Persio family (1649); the 18th cent. *Chiesetta di Mater Domini*, which used to belong to the Knights of Malta; the little church of *San Pietro Barisano* (12-13th cent.), partly carved out of the rock, and containing an important painting of Saints Peter and Paul by Giovanni Donato Oppido di Matera; the church of *Sant'Agostino* (second half of the 16th cent.), containing polychrome marble work and remarkable 18th cent. paintings; the little church of *Santa Maria de Idris*, almost entirely carved out of Mt. Errone, and the church of St. Francis of Assisi, which was founded long ago, and rebuilt in Baroque style in the second half of the 17th cent. It contains parts of a polyptych by Bartolomeo Vivarini (c. 1432-post 1499).

* MAZARA DEL VALLO (Trapani). Facing the sea, at the mouth of the Mazarò, embarkation centre for the Isola di Pantelleria. The *Cattedrale*, dedicated to the Saviour, was completely rebuilt towards the end of the 17th cent. It has a nave and two aisles on monolithic columns, and contains some artistic works, including a group of six marble statues representing the Transfiguration, by Antonio Gagini (recorded 1541-1575), and a medallion of Bishop Scavo, by the sculptor Ignazio Marabitti (1719-1797). The church of *Santa Caterina* was built at the beginning of the 14th cent. Inside are paintings and frescoes by Giuseppe Testa (lived in the 18-19th cent.). The church of *San Michele* (1637) contains paintings and frescoes by Tommaso Sciacca (1734-1795).

* MEDICINA (Bologna). Interesting little town with 17th and 18th cent. buildings. The parish church of *San Mamante* (first half of the 18th cent.), is flanked by a solitary bell-tower built between 1752 and 1777 and believed to be the masterpiece of Carlo Francesco Dotti (1670-1759); the interior contains a painting of the Madonna and Saints by Ercole Graziani the Younger (1688-1765), and one of Saints Ignatius, Lawrence, Anthony and Alò, by Ubaldo Gandolfi (1728-1781). The *Palazzo Comunale* was begun in the 16th cent. Until the 18th it was a notable philosophical, musical and artistic centre. The church of the *Assunta* or the *Santo Crocifisso* was designed by Alfonso Torreggiani (1682-1764).

* MELEGNANO (Milan). Agricultural and industrial centre divided by the river Lambro. The *Prepositurale* (provostry) *di San Giovanni Battista* is believed to go as far back as the 4th cent. In the 16th cent. Baptistery chapel is a painting of Christ's Baptism by Ambrogio da Fossano, called Bergognone (recorded 1481-1522). 16th cent. *Broletto*, with a portico and two arches. All that remains of the *Castello* are two heavy towers; inside, 16th cent. frescoes.

* MELFI (Potenza). Small town still partly surrounded by its ancient city wall, with buildings constructed out of lava taken from the secondary cone of Mount Vulture. The massive *Castello* was built by the Normans and altered in the 16th cent., but badly damaged in an earthquake in 1851. It is still an impressive sight in its lovely setting. The *Duomo*, de-

Melfi, Porta Venosina.

175

dicated to the Assunta, was first built in 1155 by William the Bad; it has a noteworthy fresco representing the Madonna and Child enthroned with two Angels, in mock-Byzantine style. The characteristic bell-tower was built in 1153 by Noslo di Remerio. The *Sarcofago di Rapolla*, so called because it was found in the Rapolla area in 1856, is a superb example of ancient art; it has fifteen niches, each containing a statuette representing a god or a hero.

** **MERANO** (Bolzano). Situated on the eastern foothills of the Giogaia di Tessa, in the fertile valley of the Adige. It is a popular holiday resort and spa. The Gothic *Duomo*, dedicated to St. Nicholas, was begun in 1367. It has an unusual facade with stepped crenellation and is flanked by a soaring Gothic campanile. Inside are Gothic, wooden and polychrome altars, paintings of the Assumption, Last Supper and Nativity, by Martino Knoller (1725-1804). The *Museo Civico* contains prehistoric, proto-historic and Roman items, minerals from the Upper Adige, ethnographical material from the Merano area, and paintings by Stefano Kessler (1622-1700), and 18-19th cent. artists from the Upper Adige. The 15th cent. *Castello Principesco* is an attractive building, where archdukes, kings and emperors have stayed; it is worth noting the Guards' room, with 16th cent. arms, the Hall of the Emperor, the Music Hall with 17th and 18th cent. instruments, the Games Room, etc. Walk along the lively *Via dei Portici* in the old city. In the neighbourhood of Merano are ruins of the *Castello San Zeno* (*Zenoburg*), the *Castel Tirol*

Merano (Maia Bassa), Santa Maria del Conforto, Crucifixion.

(*Schloss Tirol*), built at the beginning of the 12th cent. for the Counts of Venosta (from then onwards called the Counts of Tyrol) and the magnificent *Castello di Scena* (*Schloss Schenna*), dating from the mid-14th cent. At Maia Bassa is the Romanesque church of *Santa Maria del Conforto*, with an aisleless interior, where remarkable Romanesque frescoes have recently been discovered.

* **MERCATO SAN SEVERINO** (Salerno). Small commercial and industrial town in the Solofrana valley. The church of the *Minori Osservanti* has an 18th cent. interior containing the fine tomb of Thomas, Baron of Sanseverino and Constable of the Kingdom of Sicily, who died in 1358, the work of a talented unknown Neapolitan sculptor; above the altar is a painting of the Immaculate Conception by Giovanni Bernardo Lama (1506-post 1598). The *Palazzo Municipale* is one of the most important works by Carlo Vanvitelli (1739-1821). The remains of the *Castello* include large cylindrical towers and a good section of the walls. St. Thomas Aquinas stayed here, in 1273-74, just before he died.

* **MERCOGLIANO** (Avellino). Irpinian village on the slopes of Mount Partenio. Nearby is the Baroque *Palazzo Abbaziale di Loreto* (1735-1750) built to an octagonal plan by Domenico Antonio Vaccaro (1681-1750); in the Abbot's apartment are rich 16th cent. Flemish tapestries; the chapel contains an altarpiece by De Maio (18th cent.), and a beautiful choir; in the archives are Papal bulls, valuable codices and incunabula. The *Santuario di Montevergine* is in a lovely setting on the road to Avellino. It was begun in 1119 by Guglielmo da Vercelli (1085-1142) and consists of a fine group of buildings including the chapel of the *Scala Santa*, called the large tower, a newly-built Basilica (1952-1961), and the *Chiesa Vecchia*, which is linked to the new church by two archways. It has a nave and two aisles, and a chapel which has kept its original 14th cent. look. The chancel contains an Arabic-style abbot's chair. At the end of the right aisle are the interesting Gothic chapel of the Holy Sacrament, with a marble canopy, the tomb of Viscount B. de Lautrec and his son, revealing French influence, and the monument to Caterina Filangieri (15th cent.), decorated with four allegorical statues and bas-reliefs. In the *Monastero* can be seen the 18th cent. Chapter House, a museum containing Romanesque antiques, a 13th cent. Crucifix, and a Byzantine-inspired panel representing the Madonna.

* **MESAGNE** (Brindisi). Agricultural centre in the Brindisi area. It stands on the site of a Messapian city, of which the necropolis has been discovered. In Roman times it was probably a village under Brindisi. The *Chiesa Madre* was rebuilt (1653) in Baroque style to a design

by Francesco Capodieci (lived in the 16th cent.). The facade is decorated with statues; inside are 17th cent. paintings, the most important being a Nativity by Pietro Zullo (lived in the 17th cent.). The church of *Santa Maria in Betlemme* (1738), with interesting statues in the niches of the facade, is worth a visit. The present-day town hall (*Municipio*) is a simple building. It contains a collection of local antiques, including Messapian vases "a Trozzelle", arms and inscriptions found along the Appian Way. Important remains of the *Castello* which was built in 1062 for Robert Guiscard.

** MESSINA.

Gateway into Sicily from Calabria, situated on the lower slopes of the Peloritan mountains, overlooking the gulf of Messina. The town is completely new, having been rebuilt after the terrible earthquake on the 28th December 1908. In the cathedral square is the *Fontana di Orione*, by the Florentine artist G. A. Montorsoli. The *Duomo* is one of the most important buildings in Messina, and although it has been largely spoilt by alterations over the centuries it still preserves the beautiful lines of the original medieval structure; it was consecrated in 1197 and dedicated to St. Mary. The facade has a large main doorway with a high cusp which is the work of many artists and took a century to complete; the stonework and statues are mainly 16th cent. The vast, impressively sober interior contains a few artistic works, including the tomb of Archbishop Guidotto De Tabiatis, by the Sienese sculptor Goro di Gregorio (active at the beginning of the 15th cent.), the tomb of Archbishop Antonio La Lignamine, by Giovanni Battista Mazzola (recorded 1513-1550), and the tomb of Archbishop Bellorado, by the same sculptor. The Treasury contains a large and important collection of objects well arranged in glass show-cases, mostly 17th and 18th cent. The single bell-tower dominating the cathedral was designed by Francesco Valenti, at the beginning of this century; it has the biggest mechanical clock in the world, the work of the Strasbourg firm of Ungerer. The church of the *Annunziata dei Catalani* was built during the second half of the 12th cent., and reduced in size in the 13th, presumably after an earthquake. It has a noble 13th cent. facade and a harmonious interior. In front of the *Museo Nazionale*, founded in 1914, is a garden dotted with statues from churches and palaces destroyed by the earthquake, the most beautiful being a statue of Neptune (1557), from the Fountain of Neptune by Giovanni di fra Giovanni Angelo Montorsoli (1507-1563). The most valuable works in the Museum are: a 13th cent. Madonna and Child enthroned, with the artist's patron (called "la Ciambretta"), a triptych with folding panels of the Madonna and Child enthroned, Mary Magdalen and St.

Messina, Orion's Fountain and Duomo.

John, by the Dutch painter Jacob Cornelisz van Oostsanen (lived c. 1470-1533), St. John the Baptist and eight stories from his life, probably by the Belgian painter Henry de Bles, called Civetta (recorded 1515-1554), part of a panel depicting the Deposition from the Cross, by Colyn de Coter (active during the second half of the 15th cent.), a polyptych of St. Gregory, one of the masterpieces of Antonello da Messina (c. 1430-1479), a panel of the Madonna in Prayer, by Alessandro Allori, called Bronzino (1535-1607), Adoration of the Shepherds, a large painting carried out in 1604 by Michelangelo Merisi, called Caravaggio (1573-1610), the Raising of Lazarus, another dramatic masterpiece by Caravaggio, Virgin in Prayer, a beautiful marble bas-relief in Byzantine style, a marble statue of the Madonna and Child, by Goro di Gregorio (worked during the first half of the 14th cent.), a bronze Flemish lectern in the form of a pelican (14th cent.), a lovely marble statue of the Madonna and Child, by Francesco Laurana (recorded 1458-1500), marble ciborium of Jesus enthroned and Angels, by Antonello Gagini (1478-1536), fine wooden Crucifix by an unknown Sicilian artist, St. Anthony of Padua, by Antonello Gagini, and Scilla, by Giovanni Angelo Montorsoli.

* **MESTRE** (Venice). Rapidly expanding industrial town. The *Torre dell'Orologio* is the only remaining tower of the original eleven belonging to Mestre castle, a squat, massive building, dated 1108. The parish church of *San Lorenzo*, designed by Bernardo Maccaruzzi (lived in the 18th cent.), has a Romanesque campanile. *Provvederia*, with Romanesque portal and Renaissance windows. 18th cent. *Villa Combi*. 19th cent. *Villa Marini-Missana*, with a cloister decorated by Ippolito Caffi (1809-1866). *Villa Revedin*, rebuilt in 1736.

** **METAPONTO** (Town of Bernalda, province of Matera). Situated between the rivers Basento and Bradano, on the gulf of Taranto. *Ruins of Metaponto*, city of Magna Graecia. The Tavole Palatine are the ruins of a Doric temple dating from the 6th or 5th cent. B.C., dedicated to Athena or Hera. The ancient market place can be detected by means of a hump in the ground; ruins of the Doric temple to Apollo Lyceus. The *Antiquarium* contains archeological findings from the site of the ancient Greek colony.

Metaponto, Tavole Palatine.

*** **MILANO/MILAN.** Situated in the middle of the Po valley, between the pre-Alps and the river, the major industrial city in Italy. It is mainly modern in style, but rich in monuments which record its varied and difficult history. The rectangular *Piazza Duomo* took on its present-day aspect in the second half of the 19th cent. The *Duomo* is the most important Italian-Gothic monument in existence. It was begun in 1386 with the help of foreign masters (French and German) and masters from Como; work was continued on the apse in the 15th cent. and intensified in the 16th under the direction of Pellegrino Tibaldi called Pellegrino Pellegrini (1572-1586). The main spire was built in the 18th cent. and the facade finished in the 19th, while the spires and decorations have been completed this century. The facade has five 16th cent. doorways; it has been affected by the long-drawn-out building process, being Baroque-like in the lower part and Gothic above. The sides are very slender and the ensemble of the transept and polygonal apse is a very attractive sight. The interior is divided into a nave and four aisles by majestic columns, and contains valuable 15th cent. stained-glass windows; the chancel is by Tibaldi; in the crypt underneath is the body of St. Charles Borromeo. The ambulatory around the chancel provides one with a close view of the Gothic doorway to the medieval sacristy, the three windows in the apse, and the 16th cent. doorway to the northern sacristy. The neo-Classical *Palazzo Reale* is by Piermarini (1734-1808). All that

Milan, Sant'Ambrogio, atrium and facade.

Milan, Sant'Ambrogio, interior.
Milan, Campanile of San Gottardo in Corte seen from the Duomo.

Milan, Duomo, apse section.

remains of the original church of *San Gottardo* is its lovely bell-tower and apse. The *Museo del Duomo*, on the ground floor of the Royal Palace, contains sculptures of various periods, valuable stained-glass windows and a wooden model of the Duomo. The *Piazza della Scala* is reached through the *Galleria di Vittorio Emanuele II*, built in 1877 by G. Mengoni (1829-1877). The neo-Classical *Teatro alla Scala* was built by Piermarini in 1778. *Palazzo Marino*, in late-Renaissance style, was designed by G. Alessi (1500-1572); notice the inner courtyard. The *Museo Poldi Pezzoli* contains valuable objects such as enamelwork articles, jewellery, and a collection of arms and armour; the paintings are few in number but include some masterpieces: Portrait of a Woman, by Pollaiolo (1462-1498), View over the Lagoon, by F. Guardi (1712-1793), and works by the Venetian and Lombard schools. The *Brera* art gallery is housed in a 17th cent. palace; it contains a rich collection of Venetian and Lombard works from the 15-18th cent. The *Galleria d'Arte Moderna* is housed in the *Villa Comunale*, a pure neo-Classical building by L. Pollak (1751-1806); it contains a collection of mostly Lombard paintings and sculpture, of the neo-Classical and Romantic schools; the Grassi collection, on the second floor, consists of French masterpieces of the 19th and 20th cent., and Italian works of the same period. The *Museo Archeologico* contains a collection of Roman remains found in various areas, a collection of ceramics and vases, and evidence of pre-historic civilization. The *Casa dei Borromeo* contains interesting 15th cent. frescoes depicting various games. The *Ambrosiana* gallery, housed in a palace built in 1609, is made up of 16-18th cent. Lombard and Venetian works, and a rich collection of drawings. *Piazza Mercanti* contains the only group of medieval monuments left in Milan. Overlooking it are the 16th cent. *Palazzo dei Giureconsulti*, with its lovely windows, and the 13th cent. *Palazzo della Ragione*, with an open-arched ground floor (an upper storey was added in 1700). In a niche, at one side of the square, is a relief

Milan, Palazzo della Ragione. Oldrado da Tresseno.

Milan, Sant'Eustorgio, Portinari Chapel. Giovanni di Balduccio, detail of St. Peter the Martyr's tomb.

Milan, Musei Civici del Castello Sforzesco. Bonino da Campione, Monument to Bernabò Visconti, detail.

representing the podestà Oldrado da Treseno on horseback (13th cent.). The 14th cent. *Loggia degli Osii* is built in black and white marble. The 12th cent. *Palazzo Arcivescovile* has been rebuilt several times; the facade, as well as the fountain in the nearby square, is by Piermarini. The *Castello Sforzesco* was begun about 1450, and restored at the beginning of the 20th by L. Beltrami (1854-1933). It stands on a square plan and is surrounded by a moat with towers and battlements. The tower in the centre of the facade is a reproduction of the one built by A. Averlino called Filarete (1400-1469). Crossing a huge courtyard, called

the Soldiers' Square, one reaches the Ducal Court which leads to the castle museums. The ground floor of the *Musei Civici* consists of a collection of medieval and Renaissance sculpture, including the world-famous Pietà Rondanini, by Michelangelo (1475-1564); on the first floor is the art gallery, with a collection of paintings dating from the 15th to the 18th cent., mostly by Venetian and Lombard artists. The neo-Classical *Arena* was built in Napoleonic times. The *Arco della Pace*, by L. Cagnola (1762-1833) is one of the most famous monuments of the neo-Classical period. *Santa Maria delle Grazie*, one of the most important churches of the Renaissance period, was begun by P. A. Solari (1451-1493), still in Gothic style, and completed by Bramante (1444-1514), especially in the apse section. The interior is formed of a nave and two aisles, and contains a Story of the Passion, by G. Ferrari (1470-1546), and frescoes by Butinone (1445-1507); the beautiful cloister is the work of Bramante. Beside the church, in the refectory of the former

Milan, Sforza Castle.
Milan, San Satiro, baptistery of the Pietà.

Milan, Pinacoteca di Brera. Bramantino, Holy Family.
Milan, Santa Maria delle Grazie, interior.

Dominican monastery, is the fresco of the Last Supper by Leonardo, painted in 1495-1497. *Sant'Ambrogio* is a typical example of a Romanesque-Lombard church. It was begun in the 4th cent., but the apse dates from the 9th, and the rest of the church was completed between the 11th and 12th; the porticoed atrium is 12th cent. The gable facade is in the form of two open galleries, the upper part with five archways, and is flanked by two bell-towers dating from the 11th and 12th cent. It has three doorways; the interior has a nave and two aisles, with a cross vault; over the side aisles are women's galleries. The altar is covered with gold and silver leaf and is beautifully worked with precious stones; in the apse are Gothic-inspired wooden choirstalls, 4th cent. mosaics, a Madonna by Luini (1490-1523), and Christ and Angels by Bergognone (1481-1522). The interior of the *Monastero Maggiore* (early 16th cent.) is decorated throughout with frescoes by Luini and his school. The church of *San*

Satiro, by Bramante, is considered one of the most illustrious monuments of the early Renaissance; the interior has a nave and two aisles, and barrel-vault, in the centre of which is the dome. *San Lorenzo Maggiore* is a Roman and early-Christian basilica (4th cent.); the church square is surrounded by sixteen Roman columns. The church was rebuilt in the 16th cent. but the ancient plan was preserved. The interior is formed by a circular space with exedrae, women's galleries and a large dome and ambulatory. The *Cappella di Sant'Aquilino*, which has maintained its original structure, is octagonal, with niches; only a few fragments remain of the Early-Christian mosaic decorations. *Sant'Eustorgio* was erected in the 11th cent. and rebuilt in the 12th and 13th; behind the bell-tower, which stands on the right side, is the *Cappella Portinari*, a jewel of Renaissance art, attributed to Michelozzo (1396-1472), with a beautiful series of paintings by Vincenzo Foppa (1427-1515) and the Tomb of St. Peter the Martyr, by Giovanni di Balduccio and his

Milan, Santa Maria delle Grazie, detail of the apsidal tribune.

183

assistants. *Santa Maria presso San Celso*, erected between 1490 and 1565, has a fine facade by Alessi (1500-1572); inside are works by P. Bordone (1500-1571), G. Ferrari, and A. Bonvicino, called Moretto (1498-1554). *San Nazzaro Maggiore* was begun in the 4th cent. and rebuilt in the 11th. It is preceded by the funerary chapel of Trivulzio (1512), a magnificent work by B. Suardi, called Bramantino (1460-1576). *Ex-Ospedale Maggiore* (15th cent.); the right wing is the work of Filarete and is formed by an arched portico and a brick storey with mullioned windows. The courtyard was added in the 17th cent. by F. M. Richini (1583-1658).

Milan, Palazzo Marino, facade overlooking San Fedele.
Milan, Abbey of Chiaravalle, view of the cloister with bell-tower.

Milan, Abbey of Viboldone, facade.

Milan, Palazzo Borromeo. The "ball game", detail.
Milan, Sant'Eustorgio, Portinari Chapel. Vincenzo
Foppa, Miracle of St. Peter the Martyr, detail.

Milan, Museo Poldi Pezzoli. G. A. Boltraffio,
Madonna and Child, detail.

Milan, Duomo. Cerano, Miracle of Beatrice Cre-
spi, detail.

Modena, Duomo. Serafino Serafini, Coronation of
the Virgin, detail of the polyptych.
Modena, Duomo. Dosso Dossi, St. Sebastian,
detail of the altarpiece.

Monreale, Duomo. Barisano da Trani, S. Eustachio,
bronze door panel.
Monreale, Cloister.
Monreale, Duomo, view of the apses.

Santa Maria della Passione (14th cent.) has a facade added in the 18th cent. Inside are works by Luini, Bergognone, and G. Ferrari. *San Simpliciano* was founded in the 4th cent. but rebuilt in the Renaissance period. The *Abbazia di Chiaravalle*, founded in 1135 by the Cistercians, still has the characteristic church and campanile at the intersection. Inside, the nave is decorated with Flemish frescoes (17th cent.), while the 14th cent. frescoes in the tiburium are by a Tuscan master and Lombard assistants. The *Abbazia di Viboldone* was founded by the "Umiliati" in the 12th cent.; the Gothic church still contains important 14th cent. frescoes by pupils of Giotto, and works by Giusto de' Menabuoi.

** **MILAZZO** (Messina). On the isthmus of the Milazzo peninsula. The *Duomo Vecchio* (turn of the 17th cent.) is an important example of late-16th cent. Mannerist architecture. The *Duomo Nuovo*, a sober 20th cent. building, contains panels of a polyptych by Antonello De Saliba (recorded 1480-1535), a polyptych of St. Nicholas, stories of his life, and an Annunciation by Antonino Giuffrè (mentioned in 1493), and another Annunciation by the same artist. The church of *San Giacomo* (originally 15th cent.) contains a painting of the Martyrdom of St. Stephen by Leterio Palladino (1691-1743). The *Castello*, a large military type building completed under Frederick II of Swabia in the 13th cent., contains a graceful room with fireplace and arches. The castle walls afford a sweeping view over the city and Peloritani mountains as far as Etna. In the *Chiesa del Rosario*, frescoes by Domenico Giordano (died 1702).

* **MILENA** (Caltanissetta). Rural village, in rather barren surroundings. The *Vassallaggi* district contains an extensive archeological area, the importance of which has been brought to light by recent excavations. Vassallaggi became important in the first half of the 6th cent. B.C., with the introduction of Greek civilization among the Sicilian inhabitants. There are interesting remains of an ancient Sanctuary and terraced city, and a necropolis has also been discovered (5th cent. B.C.).

* **MINERVINO MURGE** (Bari). Farming centre situated on the edge of the Upper Murge (hence its name of the "balcony of Apulia"). The *Cattedrale*, dedicated to the Assunta, is of Norman origin and has a Renaissance facade. The 14th cent. *Castello Baronale*, now known as the *Palazzo di Città*, is worth noticing.

* **MINORI** (Salerno). In an attractive position along the Salerno coast. The *Basilica di Santa Trofimena* (11-12th cent.) is admired above all for its crypt under the chancel; there is an alabaster urn on the altar containing relics of Santa Trofimena, by Gennaro Ragozzino (lived

in the 18th cent.). The ground floor of the *Villa Romana* (1st cent.) was brought to light as recently as 1950-1954; many rooms can be distinguished including an enormous hall with stuccoes and frescoes.

* **MINTURNO** (Latina). Medieval centre in the foothills of the Aurunci mountains. The *Cattedrale*, dedicated to St. Peter, was begun in the middle of the 11th cent. and later altered and enlarged. It contains a candelabra for the Paschal candle, dated 1264, and a pulpit (1260). The 14th cent. church of the *Annunziata* contains frescoes of the Redeemer, Doctors of the Church, and Evangelists, belonging to the Neapolitan school, in which the transition from Gothic to Renaissance style can be noticed. The *Castello* is a sturdy building, with a round keep. The *Avanzi di Minturnae* are the ruins of the Ausonian city and later Roman colony, brought to light in excavations begun in 1817. Notice in particular the Theatre (1st cent.) in reticulated work, the Republican Forum, the Imperial Forum, with baths, and the temple to Marica, Italic goddess of fertility (6th cent. B.C.).

* **MIRABELLA ECLANO** (Avellino). In a hilly area between the rivers Calore and Ufita. The *Chiesa Matrice*, dedicated to Santa Maria Maggiore, was almost completely rebuilt at the end of the 19th cent. It has a ceiling painted by Giuseppe Tomaiuoli (recorded 1730-1749) and contains a carved and painted wooden crucifix (mid-12th cent.), which is an important example of Campanian-Romanesque art, with traces of southern French influence. In the Treasury are two Exultets from Quintodecimo. The church of the *Annunziata* contains paintings of the Mysteries and scenes from the Passion, with simple figures by local craftsmen, which are interesting examples of popular art in the 18th cent. *Scavi di Aeclanum*: remains of the ancient town, built on a triangular plateau. The public baths, market place, shops, houses and traces of walls, almost all in "opus reticulatum", have been identified. One should visit the *Necropoli Eneolotica della Madonna delle Grazie*, which goes back nearly three thousand years B.C. It is extremely important both for the quantity and quality of the grave goods excavated.

* **MIRANDOLA** (Modena). Small agricultural town with historical connections. The church of *San Francesco* was rebuilt in the 15th cent. and contains the interesting tombs of the Pico family. The 17th cent. *Chiesa del Gesù* contains a marble ciborium by Francesco Marchesini (active in the latter half of the 17th cent.), and a large altarpiece depicting the Circumcision, by Innocenzo Cristoforo Monti (recorded 1690-1713). The *Collegiata* was built in 1447 by the Pico family; it contains a Deposition by Sante Peranda (1566-1638).

*** **MODENA.** Situated in a fertile plain between the Secchia and Panaro rivers, on the Via Emilia. The *Duomo* is the town's most important monument; the first stone was laid on the 9th June 1099. The upper part of the facade (which is divided into three by columns) has a loggia; the central doorway, called the Porta Maggiore, has various reliefs by Wiligelmo (active at the beginning of the 12th cent.); the bell-tower is called La Ghirlandina and was built at the same time as the Duomo, by the apse. The Cathedral contains many artistic works, including a panel of the Madonna and Saints by Dosso Dossi (1479-1542), a polyptych by S. Serafini, the so-called "Pontile" resting on six decorated columns, and a group of five statues in polychrome terracotta called Madonna della Pappa, by Guido Mozzoni (c. 1450-1518). The *Aedes Muratoriana* houses the Muratori Museum which contains the works of the historian Ludovico Antonio Muratori (1672-1750), some of his personal belongings, mementoes, etc. The church of *Santa Maria Pomposa* was rebuilt on the orders of Ludovico Antonio Muratori; inside are paintings by Bernardino Cervi and Francesco Vellani (lived in the 17-18th cent.). The *Palazzo dei Musei* (1753) contains the valuable Este Gallery with works representing

Modena, Duomo, interior.
Modena, Duomo. Wiligelmo, Death of Cain, detail.

Modena, Galleria Estense. Cosmè Tura, St. Anthony of Padua.

artistic activity in the Po Valley area from the 14th to the 18th cent., and the equally valuable Este Museum. The *Museo Civico*, founded in 1872, contains a collection of prehistoric material from the Modena area, gradually added to over the years by gifts and donations of various collections, regarding the history and art of Modena, from the medieval period to modern times. The *Basilica Estense*, one of the richest in Italy, contains the precious 15th cent. Bible of Borso, with 1,200 illuminated pages by Taddeo Crivelli, Francesco De Russi and other artists who worked for the Este family. The *Galleria Campori* contains about one hundred valuable paintings. The *Palazzo Ducale* is one of the largest in Italy; building began in 1629 and was only finished in the 19th cent.; it has an impressively elegant facade and contains numerous works of art. The 13th cent. church of *Sant'Agostino* contains a detached fresco of the Madonna and Child, by Tommaso da Modena (1326-1379). *Chiesa di San Vincenzo*, pantheon of the Este family. The *Palazzo della Università* was built in 1774 to a design by Andrea Tarabusi (1701-1776). The church of *San Pietro*, rebuilt at the turn of the 16th cent., was designed by Pietro Barabani; inside are works of art including a painting of the Calling of St. Peter, by Girolamo Romani called Romanino (c. 1484-1566), and a panel depicting the Madonna with Saints Jerome and Sebastian, by Francesco Bianchi Ferrari (c. 1460-1510).

** **MODICA** (Ragusa). Important agricultural centre situated on a steep spur. In the church of *Santa Maria di Betlem*, built around 1400 and rebuilt after an earthquake in 1693, is a Sacramental Chapel, a notable example of late-Gothic architecture with signs of Arab, Norman and Catalan influence also; in the chapel is a stone sculpture of the Madonna and Child enthroned (16th cent.). On the high altar of the church is a huge altarpiece to the Assunta (1776) by Giovanni Battista Ragazzi. The *Chiesa Madre*, dedicated to St. George and designed by Rosario Gagliardi (recorded 1700-1770), is a prototype of other sacred buildings in this part of Sicily; it has an impressive facade of five orders of projecting columns. The interior contains a silver urn with relics of St. George, an altarpiece of nine panels narrating scenes from the life of St. George and evangelical scenes, probably by Girolamo Alibrandi (1470-c. 1524), and a painting of the Assunta (1610) by Filippo Paladino. In the church of *San Pietro* is a sculpture of St. Peter and the man sick of the palsy, by Benedetto Civiletti (1846-1892). The *Chiesa del Carmine*, with 15th cent. Gothic portal, contains an Annunciation by the sculptor Antonello Gagini (1478-1536), and a panel of St. Albert, probably by Angelo di Chirico (recorded 1513-1525). Excursion to the *Cava d'Ispica*, one of the most extensive caves in the limestone plateau of the Ibla mountains, with clear signs of human habitation from the aeneolithic to the classical age, such as necropoles, cave dwellings, 4-5th cent. catacombs and Byzantine oratories.

* **MODUGNO** (Bari). Busy agricultural centre a few kilometres from Bari. The village probably stands on the site of an ancient Apulian centre, as Peucitian material taken from tombs of the 4th, 3rd and 2nd cent. B.C. would seem to indicate. The church of the *Annunziata*, with late-Renaissance front section, has an elegant chancel; on the righthand side notice the bell-tower (17th cent.) in Romanesque style. Walk to the church of *San Pietro in Balsignano*, one of the most ancient Romanesque churches in Apulia, but unfortunately in a ruined state.

* **MOLA DI BARI** (Bari). On the Adriatic coast, with a medieval centre set on a promontory, and a modern one in the hinterland. The *Cattedrale*, dedicated to St. Nicholas, was rebuilt between 1545 and 1564 to a design by Francesco and Giovanni da Sebenico, and Giovanni da Corfù. In the facade is an ogival rose-window, belonging to the original church. The portal is flanked by columns supported by grotesque caryatids. The graceful interior has a nave and two aisles, and contains a monolithic baptismal font supported by a small pilaster decorated with four dancing putti, and a 15th cent. Byzantine-inspired panel of the Madonna and Child. The *Castello* was built in 1278 by Charles of Anjou, and rebuilt in the 16th cent. The corners are reinforced with sharply sloping ramparts and remains of square-sided towers. The church of the *Maddalena* contains some good 17-18th cent. painting of the Neapolitan school. The church of the *Ospedale* has fine marble altars (18th cent.), a Pietà in painted stone (also 18th cent.), and an important 16th cent. fresco.

** **MOLFETTA** (Bari). Mostly modern in style, but with a group of ancient buildings huddled on a headland stretching out into the Adriatic sea. The 17th cent. *Cattedrale*, dedicated to the Assunta, has a large Baroque facade. Inside, the aisleless nave is flanked by chapels, and the apse is a lovely example of Baroque architecture; it contains various artistic works such as the noteworthy painting of the Assunta by Corrado Giaquinto (1703-1765); Visitation, by Carlo Rosa (active in 1678); Our Lady of Sorrows, by Odoardo Fischetti (lived in the 19th cent.); a valuable 16th cent. Neapolitan-work monstrance, and a rare illuminated missal dating from the beginning of the 16th cent. The *Duomo Vecchio*, dedicated to St. Conrad, was begun in the second half of the 12th and only completed at the end of the 13th cent.; the interior,

fortunately still in good condition, contains four fine cruciform pillars and two chapels with small hemispherical domes; Byzantine, Romanesque-Lombard and Moslem styles are harmoniously merged. The church of *San Bernardino* was built in the 15th cent. and rebuilt in the 16th. It contains paintings of St. Jerome, by Francesco Fracanzano (1612-c. 1656); Madonna of the Needlework, by Francesco Cozza (1605-1682); Flight into Egypt, also by Cozza; and a Nativity by the Flemish painter Gaspare Hovic (lived in the 15-16th cent.). Walk to the church of the *Madonna dei Martiri*, built in 1162 near the Crusades Hospital; on the high altar is a rare Byzantine icon, stolen in 1188 from Constantinople, depicting the Madonna of the Martyrs.

* **MONASTIR** (Cagliari). Situated in a fertile area at the foot of rocky hills. The 16th cent. late-Gothic *Parrocchiale di San Pietro* has a remarkable portal and, inside, harmonious chapels. In the neighbourhood are the ruins of the *Monastero dei Camaldolesi* and the *Castello di Balardi* or *Baratuli*, probably 12th cent.

* **MONCALIERI** (Turin). Pleasant and busy little town, with houses partly scattered over one of the hills around Turin. The 15th cent. *Castello Reale* is an impressive building; it contains notable pictures of battles and portraits of the Savoy family. The church of *Santa Maria della Scala* was built in 1230, and rebuilt in Gothic style between 1330-36; it has a fine Gothic facade; the interior, consisting of four aisles, contains important works of art, including the statue of Princess Maria Clotilde at prayer, by Pietro Canonica (1869-1959), wooden rococo-style stalls and an impressive 15th cent. polychrome terracotta statue of the Pietà. In the neighbourhood of Testona, on the site

Molfetta, the Old Cathedral and wharf.

of the Roman village of the same name, excavations have brought to light many Roman remains and a barbarian fortress, possibly Longobard.

* **MONDOVÌ** (Cuneo). Attractive little town, formed by a lower part called Breo, and a higher part called Piazza. In Mondovi-Breo, the church of *San Filippo* is worth visiting; it was built in the first half of the 18th cent. by Francesco Gallo. It has an impressive and austere facade, and spacious interior in the form of a Greek cross. In Mondovi-Piazza is the *Chiesa della Missione*, dedicated to St. Francis Xavier, and designed by Giovenale Boetto in the latter half of the 17th cent. It is remarkable for its Baroque facade. The aisleless interior is decorated with a fine play of columns, and rich gilt work and frescoes on the vaults, carried out in 1679 by Andrea Pozzo. The *Cattedrale di San Donato*, begun in 1743, is considered one of the masterpieces of Francesco Gallo. The facade is in sandstone, rusticated in parts. The spectacular interior is richly decorated with gilt stuccoes, and in the sacristy there is a precious missal. On the *Belvedere* stands the ponderous Torre Civica (Civic Tower). Walk to the *Santuario di Vico Forte*, one of the most notable monuments in the region; it was begun in 1596 by Ascanio Vittozzi, a large oval dome was added by Francesco Gallo in the 18th cent. and the building was completed in the 19th. The main front is in mock-classical style, and the whole church is dominated by the dome, which is enclosed by buttresses, producing a dramatic effect. Inside are statues, frescoes, pictures and a monument to Margherita di Savoia-Gonzaga (1589-1655), daughter of Charles Emmanuel I, for whom the church was originally built.

* **MONFALCONE** (Gorizia). On the northern extremity of the gulf of Trieste, at the beginning of the Karst formation. It is an important industrial centre, especially for its shipbuilding, and has ten docks. In the surrounding area are *Avanzi di Terme Romane* (remains of Roman baths) which were well-known in ancient times and registered in the Tavola Peutingeriana. Also in the surrounding area, in the small village of *San Giovanni al Timavo*, is the church of *San Giovanni*, in authentic northern-Gothic style, incorporating remains of the 5th cent. Basilica. Inside are remains of the Basilica paving, and lapidary stones with inscriptions found in the area. A short way off are the Bocche del Timavo, an impressive phenomen of the river Timavo, with three bubbling springs produced by the Karst formation.

** **MONOPOLI** (Bari). Large centre on the Adriatic coast, with medieval quarter facing the sea, and modern districts. The *Cattedrale* was erected in the early 12th cent. and completed in the 18th. It is an important Baroque building, with high facade, on the left side of which stands a remarkable Baroque bell-tower. The interior is in the form of a Latin cross, with a nave and two aisles, and contains some valuable pictures including St. Michael by Jacopo Palma the Younger (1544-1628), St. James of Campostella by Paolo Domenico Finoglia (first half of the 17th cent.), a Last Supper, Sacrifice of Abraham, and Supper in Emmaus, by Francesco de Mura (1696-1784), a Madonna in Glory with Saints Roch and Sebastian, probably by Jacopo Palma the Younger, and a Circumcision, by Marco da Siena, called Marco Pino (1525-1588). In the apse is a Byzantine icon depicting the Madonna della Madia (1280). The Chapter-house contains an important Byzantine panel of the Madonna, and the Sacristy remains of 12th cent. sculptures taken from the original church; in the Bishop's Palace, Madonna and Saints, by Paolo Caliari, called Veronese (c. 1528-1588), Coronation of the Virgin, by Jacopo Palma the Younger, St. Jerome, possibly by Lazzaro Bastianini (c. 1430-1512), a Madonna and Saints, possibly by Polidoro da Lanciano (1515-1565), and important 17th cent. Neapolitan-school paintings. The church of *Santa Maria Amalfitana* was built in the early 12th cent. by traders from Amalfi who, for commercial reasons, were resident in Monopoli. The interior has a nave and two aisles, and contains elegant composite pillars with Romanesque capitals. The righthand aisle leads into a courtyard with three fine semi-circular apses, the central one (marked by slender semi-columns crowned by grotesque corbels) being the most impressive. In the council hall of the *Municipio* are pictures by Ignazio Perricci da Monopoli and other 17th cent. painters. A few kilometres from the town are the ruins of the ancient trade centre of Egnazia (*Rovine di Egnazia*) on the border between Messapia and Peucezia, later a Roman town hall. Also worthy of attention is the Porta Vecchia area is the Byzantine *Chiesa-Grotta*, built from a natural grotto; it has some interesting frescoes. In the *Chiesa del Purgatorio* is a fine painting of the Madonna of the Rosary by Paolo de Matteis (1662-1728). The church of *Sant'Angelo* contains a precious painting of the Madonna and Saints by Paolo Domenico Finoglia.

* **MONREALE** (Palermo). Situated on the slopes of Mount Caputo, overlooking the Oreto valley. The *Duomo*, a masterpiece of Norman architecture, was founded by William II in 1174 and almost completed by the end of the century. It was enlarged in the 16th and 19th centuries. The facade is flanked by two massive square towers and preceded by an 18th cent. portico, below which is a lovely portal with a pointed arch; the doors are the work of Bonanno Pisano (12th cent.) and consist of 42 panels depicting scenes from the Bible. The left flank of the cathedral has a 16th cent. portico with bronze doors made up of 28 panels, by Barisano da Trani (12th cent.). The basilican interior has a nave and two aisles with a deep-set chancel and three apses. The roof is open-trussed. The pillars support pointed, Arab-style arches, and the original mosaic floors still remain. The mosaics are very famous; they date from the 12th and 13th cent. and are the work of local artists assisted by Venetian

Monopoli, Cathedral, facade.

Monreale, the Cathedral bell-tower seen from the cloister.

the same time as the cathedral itself. It is one of Sicily's most famous and precious monuments, with its numerous twin pillars, decorated with mosaic inlays and arabesques. The *Seminario dei Chierici* (behind the town hall) was added to the residence of the Norman kings in the 18th cent.; the ancient mullioned windows have survived. In the neighbourhood of Monreale, at San Martino delle Scale, is the lovely *Abbazia Benedettina*, founded in the 6th cent. by St. Gregory the Great, but rebuilt at the beginning of the 14th by Angelo Senisio, and enlarged by Venanzio Marvuglia (1729-1814) towards the end of the 18th; inside, amongst other treasures, are 16-18th cent. sacred vestments, and a painting of St. Benedict by Pietro Novelli (1603-1647).

* **MONSELICE** (Padua). On the lower slopes of the Euganean hills, situated on the site of the Roman town of Mons Silicis. The Romanesque-Gothic *Duomo Vecchio* (1256), dedicated to St. Justina, has a 15th cent. porch; inside are a few works of art; the chancel contains remains of 16th cent. frescoes. The massive square *Torre Civica* (the first stone was laid in 1244), dominates the little town. The 13th cent. *Castello*, once called Ca' Marcello, now Cini, was the residence of Ezzelino da Romano, who had it built between 1249 and 1256; it was well restored between 1935-39 by Nino Barbantini and Aldo Scolari; inside is an armoury, 16th cent. apartment, Hall of Honour, and other interesting rooms. *Villa Duodo*, by Vincenzo Scamozzi (1552-1616); nearby is the Sanctuary of the Seven Churches, with six chapels, designed by Vincenzo Scamozzi; inside are paintings by Jacopo Palma the Younger (1544-1628).

* **MONTAGNANA** (Padua). Small, agricultural town and crossroads. The magnificent *Duomo*, rebuilt in the 15th cent., is dedicated to St. Mary; it contains many works of art, including a painting of the Transfiguration by Paolo Caliari, called Veronese (1528-1588), and a fresco depicting the Assumption of the Virgin, attributed to Giovanni Buonconsiglio called Marescalco (c. 1470-c. 1537). In the *Palazzo del Municipio*, designed by Michele Sanmicheli (1484-1559) are works of art including a painting of Moses receiving the Tablets, by Antonio Zanchi (1631-1722). *Villa Pisani*, now called Placco, was designed by Andrea Palladio (1508-1580). The 17th cent. church of *San Benedetto* contains a painting of the Madonna with Saints, by Jacopo Palma the Younger (1544-1628). The church of *San Francesco* was built in the 14th cent.; inside another painting by Jacopo Palma the Younger. The whole town is encircled by its walls (*Mura*) which are pierced by four gateways, the most beautiful being the Porta Legnago or Rocca degli Alberi (second half of the 14th cent.), designed by Francesco da Schicci.

ones. They depict stories from the Old and New Testament; notice in particular the stories from Genesis, in the nave, and Christ the Pantocrator in the central apse. Alongside the aisles are chapels with various tombs of great value. The square cloister (*Chiostro*) of the ancient Benedictine monastery is on the right side of the cathedral facade, and was built at

Monreale, Duomo, apses.
Monreale, Duomo, interior.

* **MONTALCINO** (Siena). Mainly agricultural centre, on a hill covered with olive-trees near the valleys of the Ombrone and Arno. The 13-14th cent. *Palazzo Comunale* has a high tower decorated with numerous coats of arms; it houses the museum which includes a terracotta altarpiece by the Della Robbia school, a Deposition by Bartolo di Fredi (1330-1410), a Madonna and Child from the school of Duccio da Boninsegna (1250-1319), and the same subject treated by Sano di Pietro (1406-1481). The church of *Sant'Egidio* (1325) has a trussed ceiling and contains a 15th cent. fresco of the Sienese school. The *Rocca* is perched on top of the hill, and is a beautiful example of 14th cent. military architecture. The *Museo Diocesano di Arte sacra*, housed in the Bishop's Seminary, contains valuable artistic works including a Madonna and Child by Bartolo di Fredi, various works by the Tuscan school, an important collection of wood-carvings, some of them polychrome. The Romanesque-Gothic church of *Sant'Agostino* has a gable facade; inside are 14th cent. frescoes by the Sienese school. The *Duomo* was rebuilt in neo-Classical style in the 19th cent. by Agostino Fantastici (1782-1845). In the neighbourhood is the pleasantly situated *Abbazia di Sant'Antimo*, built in the first half of the 12th cent. in Romanesque style. The open-sided porch has a rich portal decorated with bas-reliefs and sculptures, and on the left side of the abbey is a portal decorated with geometrical-type figures. The classically basilican interior has a nave and two aisles.

* **MONTALTO DI CASTRO** (Viterbo). Agricultural village which still preserves its medieval appearance. In the neighbourhood are the *Abbadia* (abbey) and the *Ponte*, an Etruscan-Roman bridge. The Abbey is a castle built on a trapezoidal plan, dominated by an imposing tower. It was begun in the 9th cent., destroyed by the Saracens, and rebuilt by the Cistercians in the 13th cent. It houses a collection of antiques, including remains from Etruscan tombs. The bridge is formed by a middle arch more than thirty metres high and two smaller arches. Beyond the Abbey is the *Necropoli di Vulci*, discovered in the 19th cent.; the military-religious monument called the *Coccumella*, in the form of an enormous mound, is still intact; the tombs consist of several chambers, and are built in the style of Etruscan houses.

* **MONTANARO** (Turin). The *Parrocchiale dell'Assunta* was designed by Antonio Bernardo Vittone (1704-1770); in the sacristy are precious cupboards made in 1769 by the joiner Pietro Antonio Actis da Rodallo. It is worth visiting the *Oratorio di Santa Marta*, also by Vittone; the *Castello* (rebuilt in 1353) and the 13th cent. church of *Santa Maria dell'Isola*, which has a characteristic bell-tower with rows of single,

double and triple-mullioned windows. In the *Camposanto* is the tomb of the poet and writer Giovanni Cena (1870-1917), by Leonardo Bistolfi (1859-1933).

* **MONTEBELLUNA** (Treviso). Agricultural, commercial and industrial centre, ancient in origin as remains of a Paleo-Venetian necropolis reveal. The *Prepositurale* or *Duomo Vecchio* (1613) has a lofty campanile set apart. Inside is a painting by Francesco Frigimelica (died 1621) of Saints Peter and Paul. The *Mercato Vecchio* stands on the site of the original town-centre.

* **MONTECASSINO** (Macerata). Walled village between the rivers Manocchia and Potenza. The *Palazzo Municipale* was designed by Antonio Lombardo (c. 1458-1516), and contains a picture representing Jacob's Dream by Ludovico Cardi, called Cigoli (1559-1613). The church of the *Assunta* was also designed by Antonio Lombardo. It contains a panel of the Coronation of the Virgin and four Saints, by Giacomo da Recanati (recorded 1443-1466) and the 14th cent. reliquary of the Holy Cross. In the 13th cent. *Oratorio di San Nicolò* are remarkable 15th cent. frescoes of the Umbrian-Marches school.

* **MONTECCHIO MAGGIORE** (Vicenza). Picturesque village at the foot of a hill. Above it, on the hilltop, stands the *Castello della Villa* or *di Romeo*, built by the Veronese in 1354, and demolished by the Venetians in 1514. On the same hill is the *Castello di Bellaguardia* or *di Giulietta*, also built in the mid-14th cent. by the Veronese, and later destroyed by the Venetians.

* **MONTECOSARO** (Macerata). In a hilly area between the Chienti and Tenna valleys.

Montecosaro, Santa Maria a Pie'di Chienti, interior.

It is a small village with remains of the 14th cent. walls. In the surrounding area is the 9th cent. Romanesque church of *Santa Maria a Pie' di Chienti* or *dell'Annunziata*, which has been altered many times. It has a two-storey basilican interior, with some remarkable works of art including frescoes of the Annunciation, St. Lucy and a Madonna and Child with Angels (second half of the 14th cent.) as well as some other, partly deteriorated votive frescoes.

* **MONTE D'ACCODDI** (Sassari). In the neighbourhood of Porto Torres. It is an impressive copper-age construction, consisting of a heap of stone and earth, with trapezoid base. It rests on drystone walls made of uneven blocks, and was originally a truncated pyramid in form. It is the only example, not only in Sardinia, but in the whole Western Mediterranean, of a megalithic altar, resembling the "ziggurat" of Mesopotamia. It reveals a building technique, using large blocks of stone, which would later be perfected in the Nuraghe. Fertility rites are presumed to have been celebrated on it; in the surrounding area can be seen remains of rectangular huts, probably parts of the sanctuary which culminated in this gigantic altar. Notice the huge sacrificial stone altar; a short way off is a sphere-shaped heap symbolizing the sun. A large amount of ceramic material has been excavated at Monte d'Accoddi, and is now arranged in the museum in Sassari.

** **MONTEFALCO** (Perugia). Called "the balcony of Umbria" because of the fine panorama which it affords, and famous for its church frescoes. The former church of *San Francesco* (1336-38) has a Renaissance portal and wooden door dated 1555. It has been converted into a museum, and contains an important collection that gives a clear idea of Umbrian painting; it includes works by Ottaviano Nelli (c. 1375-1445/50), Perugino (1445/50-1523), Francesco Melanzio (recorded 1487-1524), Pier Antonio Mezzastris, called Antonio da Foligno (1430-1506), Niccolò Alunno (c. 1438-1502), Antoniazzo Romano (recorded 1461-1508), Melozzo da Forlì (1438-1494), and Spagna (c. 1450-1528). The museum also contains some fine frescoes in the central apse, illustrating Stories of St. Francis, all by Benozzo Gozzoli (1420-1497). The Gothic church of *Sant'Agostino*, built in the second half of the 13th cent., has a sober facade, with many 14th, 15th and 16th cent. frescoes, including an early-15th cent. Madonna and Child by the Umbrian school, a Madonna della Misericordia (first half of the 15th cent.) and fragments of 15th cent. frescoes revealing the influence of the school of Ottaviano Nelli (1375-1450). In the church of *Santa Chiara* (13-14th cent.) is a high altar with beautiful gilt ciborium of the 17th cent. The adjacent chapel of the Holy Cross was completely frescoed in 1333 by Umbrian painters influenced by Giotto and the Sienese school, with varying results. In the 16th cent. church of *Santa Illuminata* are frescoes by Francesco Melanzio and Bernardino Mezzastris. The *Biblioteca Comunale* contains 500 law and educational works printed before 1500, seventy-six incunabula, and a 15th cent. fresco of the Gubbio school. In the neighbourhood is the church of *San Fortunato*, with frescoes by Benozzo Gozzoli and Tiberio d'Assisi (c. 1470-1524).

Monte d'Accoddi.

** **MONTEFIASCONE** (Viterbo). In a particularly attractive hilltop setting, with sweeping view over the lake of Bolsena. There was probably a Sanctuary dedicated to the Etruscan deity Volumna here. The town is in an easily defended position and goes back to the centuries of the Barbaric invasions. The 12th cent. church of *San Flaviano*, in pure Romanesque style, has an unfinished facade (1262) and spacious Gothic portal. The interior consists of two storeys, with a lower and an upper church, facing opposite ways. In the lower church is the so-called "tombstone" of the prelate Giovanni Fugger of Augusta, and on the walls much-admired frescoes, mainly 14th cent. The upper church is reached by thirty-nine steps and is less interesting than the first, but its being built immediately above the lower one has produced an extremely interesting result architecturally. The *Duomo*, dedicated to St. Margaret, was planned by Michele Sanmicheli (1484-1559) and completed by Carlo Fontana (1634-1714). It is an impressive building, mainly Renaissance in style. The facade is flanked by two campaniles and has a neo-Classical portal carried out in 1840-1843 by Paolo Garola. The octagonal interior, with radial chapels, contains a painting after the style of Giovanni Battista Salvi called Sassoferrato (1609-1685), of the Death of St. Joseph, and a huge Della Robbia altarpiece of the Madonna and Child with two Saints.

* **MONTEFIORE DELL'ASO** (Ascoli Piceno). On the right bank of the river Aso, with considerable remains of the ancient walls. The Romanesque *Collegiata di Santa Lucia*, rebuilt in 1850, has a polyptych by Carlo Crivelli (1430/35-c. 1495), which has unfortunately been badly damaged, paintings by Luigi Fontana (1827-1908), and a precious stylized Cross,

of the 16th cent. In the *Sala De Carolis* can be seen eighty-eight pictures by Adolfo De Carolis (1874-1928).

* **MONTEFORTE D'ALPONE** (Verona). Agricultural centre, on the lowest foothills of the Lessini mountains. The *Parrocchiale*, designed by Bartolomeo Giuliari (1783-1842), is

Montefiascone, Duomo, dome.

Montefiore dell'Aso, the Fortress.
Montefiore dell'Aso, Collegiate Church of Santa Lucia. Carlo Crivelli, Mary Magdalen (detail of a triptych).

flanked by a soaring late-19th cent. bell-tower, which stands out as an important landmark. Inside are pictures by Girolamo dai Libri (1474-1555) depicting Christ and the Samaritan Woman, and Visitation of St. Elizabeth, by Giovanni Caliari (1802-1850). *Palazzo Vescovile*, the bishop's palace, (mid-15th cent.) is linked to a small rectangular cloister, with a double loggia.

* **MONTEGIORGIO** (Ascoli Piceno). In a hilly area, not far from the left bank of the river Tenna, it is an agricultural centre, with narrow medieval streets. The collegiate church of *San Giovanni* contains frescoes by Luigi Fontana (1827-1908). In the Romanesque-Gothic church of *San Francesco*, with a fine portal designed in 1325 by Maestro Gallo, is the Cappella Farfense, containing an important series of late-Gothic frescoes. In the *Archivio Comunale*, precious 13th cent. parchments.

* **MONTEGROTTO TERME** (Padua). Health resort, already fashionable in Roman times, when it was known as Mons Aegrotorum (Mountain of the Sick). The church of *San Pietro*, rebuilt in the early 18th cent., has a ·neat interior, with several works of art. In the *Parco Archeologico*, remains of Roman baths and a theatre have been distinguished. The springs of the *Stabilimento delle Terme Neroniane* were restored in the second half of the 16th cent. by Bartolomeo Capodivacca. The enormous building called *Cataio* consists of walls and rectangular blocks with battlemented tops; it was commissioned in 1570-1572 by Pio Enea degli Obizi, and enlarged in later periods. It now includes 350 rooms, with picturesque inner courtyards and some outstanding halls decorated by such masters as Giovan Battista Zelotti (1526-1578).

* **MONTELEONE DI SPOLETO** (Perugia). Picturesque little village, built on the ruins of the ancient Brufa. The 15th cent. *Palazzo Bernabò* is a characteristic building. The *Torre dell'Orologio* is all that remains of a castle that has been almost completely destroyed over the centuries. The church of *San Francesco*, built in the 12th cent., modified in the 13th and 16th cent., and recently restored, is worth a visit. It has a graceful Gothic portal guarded by two lions resting on corbels. The pointed-arched cloister is decorated with a 12th cent. Umbrian-school fresco; the *Chiesa Sotterranea* was frescoed by Iacopo da Leonessa, who worked here in the 15th cent. Remains of a Bronze-age burial-ground have been discovered near the village, as well as a 6th cent. B.C. tomb containing precious ornaments and a war, or possibly ceremonial chariot, decorated with scenes from the life of Achilles. The chariot is now preserved in the Metropolitan Museum, New York.

* **MONTELEONE D'ORVIETO** (Terni). Picturesque village by the Chiani stream, among wooded hills. The *Collegiata* contains two panels: a Madonna and Child with Saints Peter and Paul, and a Pietà, from the school of Perugino. Notice the majestic high altar, Baroque in style, in the *Chiesa del Santissimo Crocifisso* (1637).

* **MONTELUPO FIORENTINO** (Florence). Village situated at the point where the Pesa stream flows into the river Arno, well known for its earthenware and artistic pottery. In the parish church of *San Giovanni Evangelista* is a Botticelli-inspired panel depicting Madonna and Child with four Saints. The *Ambrogiana*, an impressive turreted building, formerly a Medici villa, is worth a visit. It was built for Ferdinand I to a design by Bernardo Buontalenti (1536-1608).

* **MONTELUPONE** (Macerata). In the hilly area enclosed by the rivers Potenza to the north and Chienti to the south, with medieval roads and houses. The 14th cent. *Portico Medievale*, known as the Palazzo del Podestà, is overlooked by a Ghibelline tower, of the same century. The mid-13th cent. church of *San Francesco* has been subjected to much modification. It contains four Flemish-school statues representing Faith, Hope, Charity and the Church. In the *Collegiata* (first half of the 18th cent.) is a painting of the Madonna and Saints (1525) by Antonio da Faenza (1457-1535). Walk to the Romanesque *Abbazia di San Fermano* (10th cent.). There is a fine relief of the Crucifixion in the portal lunette, dating back to the time of the early construction. The basilican interior contains a polychrome terracotta by Ambrogio Della Robbia (1477-1527/28).

Montelupone, Palazzo del Podestà.

* **MONTE OLIVETO** (Town of Asciano, province of Siena). Situated in an isolated and attractive spot on a wooded hill. The *Abbazia di Monte Oliveto Maggiore* was founded in 1313, and can be reached after passing through a small square-towered fort begun in the late 14th and completed in the 16th cent.; on the door is a terracotta decoration from the school of the Della Robbia family. The church has a Gothic facade and elegant portal; the large rectangular cloister has a Renaissance well, and portico decorated with a cycle of frescoes with stories of St. Benedict, by Luca Signorelli (1441-1523) and Bazzi called Sodoma (1477-1549). In the passage to the church are two frescoes by Sodoma: Christ bearing the Cross and Flagellation. The aisleless interior is in the form of a Latin cross, and was altered by Antinori in 1772. Notice the precious wooden choir stalls by fra' Giovanni da Verona (1457-1525), and a large 13th cent. wooden Crucifix. The *Refettorio* is an impressive vaulted hall, with frescoes by Paolo Novelli, dated 1670. An inlaid door by fra' Giovanni da Verona leads into the *Biblioteca*, which is divided into three by columns with Corinthian capitals; it has some valuable 14th cent. chorals on show.

** **MONTEPULCIANO** (Siena). On the crest of a tufa hill, between Valdichiana and Val d'Orcia, it is a little town rich in Florentine-inspired Renaissance buildings. The *Duomo* was built between 1592 and 1630 to a design by Ippolito Scalza. It has a rather crude ex-

terior, but graceful interior. Behind the high altar is a fine triptych representing the Assumption (1401) by Taddeo di Bartolo. The church of *Sant'Agostino*, with a mainly Gothic facade, contains the Madonna della Cintola, by Federico Baroccio (1535-1612), and a Crucifixion with the Madonna and Mary Magdalen, by Lorenzo di Credi (1459-1537). The Gothic Palazzo Negri-Orselli (14th cent.) houses the important *Museo Civico*, with works by many eminent artists including Margaritone d'Arezzo (1216-1290), Andrea del Sarto (1486-1531),

Monte Oliveto, the Abbey.

Montepulciano, San Biagio.

Girolamo di Benevento (1470-1524), and Spinello Aretino (recorded 1373-1410). A visit should be made to the church of *Sant'Agnese*, with 14th cent. portal and present-century facade; *Palazzo Cervini*, begun by Cardinal Marcello Cervini, later Pope Marcellus II, to the design of Antonio da Sangallo the Elder (1455-1534), or Antonio Sangallo the Younger (1485-1546); the *Palazzo del Monte*, now called Palazzo Contucci, begun in 1519 by Antonio da Sangallo the Elder. In the immediate surroundings is the church of *San Biagio*, by Antonio da Sangallo the Elder; it is in the form of a Greek cross and is surmounted by a high dome.

* **MONTERIGGIONI** (Siena). Perched on a hill, 271m. high. It is a fortified village founded in the 13th cent. by Siena to prevent the Florentines from using the Via Cassia. It is still surrounded by its 570m. long walls, and fourteen square towers, which were once even higher than they are today, enough to make Dante compare them to giants (Inferno XXXI).

* **MONTERUBBIANO** (Ascoli Piceno). Village overlooking the Aso valley, fairly close to the left bank of the stream itself. The ancient *Collegiata di Santa Maria dei Letterati*, rebuilt in the 19th cent., contains a painting of the Assunta by Lattanzio Pagani (recorded 1535-1582), and wooden stalls (1778) by Alessio Donati da Offida. The *Palazzo Comunale* houses a Museum with excavated earthenware vessels and bronzes, Roman remains and pictures of the school of Pietro Alemanno (recorded 1475-1498).

* **MONTE SAN GIUSTO** (Macerata). Situated on a low hill, between the Chienti and the Ete Morto. In the *Palazzo Municipale*, formerly Palazzo Bonafede (first half of the 16th cent.) are three hundred drawings by 17th cent. masters, and in the church dedicated to *Santa Maria Telusiano* is a splendid Crucifixion by Lorenzo Lotto (c. 1480-1556).

* **MONTE SAN SAVINO** (Arezzo). Situated on a sunny hilltop dominating the Esse valley. Corso Sangallo is entered through the Ialta gateway, designed by Vasari. The church of *Santa Chiara* has an aisleless interior and contains a terracotta altar-frontal by A. Contucci, called Sansovino (1460-1529), a statue of Anthony by the Della Robbia school and an Adoration of the Sheperds by Giovanni Della Robbia (1469-1529). The *Loggia del Mercato*, by Antonio da Sangallo the Elder (1455-1534), is formed of a portico resting on four columns with Corinthian capitals. The *Palazzo Comunale*, also by Antonio da Sangallo the Elder, has an austere rusticated base and a single order of windows. The 14th cent. church of *Sant'Agostino* has 16th cent. additions; the

portal is by Sansovino. The church of *San Giovanni Battista* also has a portal by A. Sansovino. Excursion to the 13th cent. Sanctuary of *Santa Maria delle Vertighe*; it has a nave and two aisles, and trussed roof. The adjacent *Convento dei Francescani* contains various works of art including a fine 14th cent. wooden Crucifix of the Sienese school, and a picture by Michele Ghirlandaio (1503-1577).

** **MONTE SANT'ANGELO** (Foggia). The most important city on the Gargano promontory. It is perched on a spur, in an incomparable setting. The *Santuario di San Michele Arcangelo*, is one of the most ancient sanctuaries in the Christian world; its early construction dates back to the times of Lorenzo Maiorano, Bishop of Siponto, near the cave where the Archangel Michael is said to have appeared to him three times, between 490 and 493 A.D. It became the national sanctuary of the Longobards of Benevento, only to be sacked by the Greeks in 657 and several times by the Saracens in the second half of the 9th cent. and first part of the 10th cent. It flourished again during the Crusades, when the Gargano was a compulsory stopping-place on the route to Palestine. The facade (1865) has statues and capitals, almost entirely modern, but the bronze doors of the portal, consisting of twenty-four twin panels in silver and copper, were cast in 1076 in Constantinople by Pantaleone from Amalfi. Inside is the Archangel's Grotto with alabaster statue of St. Michael the Archangel, possibly by Andrea Contucci called Sansovino (1460-1529); the Baroque-style Chapel of the Holy Sacrament; St. Lucy's Chapel and altar of St. Francis of Assisi; 12th cent. bishop's throne and remains of a pulpit by Acceptus (11th cent.). The bell-tower, a real artistic treasure, was erected by the brothers Giordano and Maraldo da Monte Sant'Angelo, between 1273 and 1281, on the orders of Charles I of Anjou. Octagonal in plan, it has four storeys, and an internal spiral staircase. The *Tomba di Rotari* is a characteristic 12th cent. monument, the work of Pagano di Parma and Rodelgrimo di Monte Sant'Angelo, as is shown by an epigraph which, read wrongly, gave origin to its present

Monte Sant'Angelo, Castle.

name. It is presumed to have been an 11th cent. baptistery enlarged by Pagano and Rodelgrimo. The interior contains some valuable carved capitals depicting the sacrifice of Isaac, a Pilgrim at the Gargano, Announcement to the Shepherds, Avarice punished, allegorical bas-reliefs and remains of 14th cent. frescoes. The ancient church of *Santa Maria Maggiore* (rebuilt in the first half of the 12th cent.) has a facade with blind niches resting on slender pilaster-strips. The portal (1198), is surmounted by a canopy, and in the lunette there is a Madonna and Child with two Angels. Inside, holy-water stoup depicting the sun, and remains of Byzantine-inspired frescoes of the 12th and 13th centuries. The ruins of the *Castello* are most impressive: majestic, pentagonal Giants' Tower; the ruined interior contains some interesting remains; from the top, a sweeping view of Manfredonia and the great expanse of the Tavoliere is afforded.

* **MONTEVARCHI** (Arezzo). The 13th cent. *Collegiata* was rebuilt in 1700. It contains a small wooden shrine in the Sacristy, with figures attributed to Ridolfo del Ghirlandaio (1483-1561). 14th cent. *Oratorio di Gesù*. The *Convento di S. Ludovico* has a Renaissance cloister and houses the Valdarnese Academy, founded by Poggio Bracciolini; it has a particularly rich Library.

* **MONTEVERGINE** (Town of Mercogliano, province of Avellino). 1493 m. above sea level, in the Partenio chain of mountains, overlooking the hollow of Avellino. The *Santuario di Montevergine*, 1263 m. high, is close to the summit, and is one of the most striking monuments in Campania, both for its artistic importance and for the wonderful view it commands. It is the result of the merging of two churches. William of Vercelli (1085-1142) withdrew to Montevergine in 1119 to live in fasting and abstinence, and built a sanctuary dedicated to the Virgin; the Basilica was built in the 1150 to a design by Florestano Di Fausto. It contains works of art including a large panel

Monte Sant'Angelo, Tomba di Rotari. Internal capital.

of the Madonna di Montevergine known as "Mamma Schiavona" (second half of the 13th cent.), stained-glass windows illustrating the Coronation of the Virgin, and the splendid and impressive throne of the Madonna, with marble bas-reliefs and bronze statues. The crypt, with a nave and two aisles, contains the venerated body of St. William of Vercelli. The chancel leads into the Old Church, which has a nave and two aisles, and contains works of art such as the early-14th cent. monument to Caterina Valdemonte-Lionessa, 17th cent. high altar of the chancel, mosaic work with precious arabesques, carved-wood stalls (second half of the 16th cent.), Gothic Chapel of the Sacrament, with 13th cent. marble canopy decorated with mosaics, the monument to Baron Marcantonio Belli Simeoni (jurisprudent), which was repaired in the second half of the 17th cent., 15th cent. monument to Caterina Filangieri, and pictures and decorations by Vincenzo Volpe (1855-1929). The *Monastero* contains the vast 18th cent. Chapterhouse, now the Reception Hall, the walls of which are decorated with four medallions depicting St. Bernard, Ildefonso, Pier Damiani and Anselm, doctors of the Benedictine order, by Vincenzo Volpe, and a museum containing fairly interesting material including a Roman sarcophagus of the Imperial age, Romanesque antiques, a Byzantine-inspired painting of the Madonna of St. William, (last years of the 12th cent.), and small 16th cent. pictures by the Flemish school.

* **MONTICHIARI** (Brescia). Agricultural and industrial town. In the *Parrocchiale*, designed by Antonio Marchetti (1724-1791) are frescoes by Pietro Scalvini (1718-1792) and statues by Antonio Calegari (1698-c. 1777). The church of *San Pancrazio* (second half of the 12th cent.) has an unadorned facade and stern interior, noticeably influenced by Veronese art.

* **MONTIRONE** (Brescia). Agricultural centre in the Brescian plain. The Lombard-Venetian-style *Palazzo Lechi* was designed by Antonio Turbino (c. 1675-1756). Inside is a Portrait of Count Pietro Lechi, by Rosalba Carriera (1675-1757); an Assunta by Giovanni Battista Pittoni (1687-1767); another by Lattanzio Gambara (c. 1530-1574), and another by Domenico Zampieri, called Domenichino (1581-1641). Collection of weapons and firearms, and ancient ornaments. *Torre Emili* is all that remains of a 15th cent. castle which belonged to an anonymous family.

** **MONZA** (Milan). The *Arengario* or Town Hall (13th cent.) is supported by stone pillars. The upper part has two- and three-lighted windows and small hanging arches. A balcony (called "parlera") from where announcements were read juts out on one side. The *Duomo* or *Basilica di San Giovanni Battista* was foun-

ded by Theodolinda, queen of Lombardy; it was rebuilt in the 13th cent. and completed in the 14th. The majestic bell-tower was designed by Pellegrini (1675-1741). The central part of the facade is the work of Matteo da Campione (14th cent.), while the side parts were added later. The green and white marble facade is broken up by six pillars ending in niches and spires. The interior has a nave and two aisles, and 17th cent. decorations, a neo-Classical pulpit and various works by Matteo da Campione. The Chapel of Theodolinda contains the famous Iron Crown and is adorned with 15th cent. frescoes; the Stories of Theodolinda, by the Zavattari brothers, are interesting. The rich Cathedral Treasury is really remarkable, with precious late-Roman and high-medieval pieces (ivories and the Theodolinda collection in particular), as well as goldsmiths' items and wooden carvings of the Renaissance period. The neo-Classical *Villa Reale*, designed by Giuseppe Piermarini (1734-1808), houses the Civic Gallery, the History Museum and the Colonial Museum. The *Rotonda*, one of the individual buildings belonging to the Villa, stands alone in the large park; it is decorated by Andrea Appiani (1754-1817).

* **MORANO CALABRO** (Cosenza). In the upper basin of the Coscile, with picturesque houses dotted along the slopes of a cone-shaped hill. The church of *San Bernardino*, built about the mid-15th cent., is a rare example of Calabrian art of that period. The interior has a

Monza, Duomo. Iron Crown.
Monza, Villa Reale.

low, carinated 15th cent. ceiling, a 15th or 16th cent. wooden statue of San Bernardino, a huge polyptych by Bartolomeo Vivarini (recorded 1450-1499) and a wooden pulpit dated 1611. The *Collegiata della Maddalena*, a large Baroque building, contains a fine marble statue by Antonello Gagini (1478-1536) of the Madonna and Child, a late-16th cent. Gagini-school statue of the Madonna della Candelora, a painting of St. Francis Xavier, attributed to the Spanish artist, Francesco Palomino Lopez (lived in the 18th cent.), and an important painting of the Coronation of the Virgin, Saints Jerome and Nicholas of Bari, by Antonio Sarnelli (active 1742-1793). In the church of *San Pietro* are statues of St. Lucy and St. Catherine by Pietro Bernini (1562-1629), and a picture of the Madonna worshipped by Saints Blaise, Anne and Francis (1666), by Giovanni Battista Colimodio.

* **MORBEGNO** (Sondrio). At the head of the valley of the Bitto, which emerges from a gorge here. The *Arcipretale di San Giovanni Battista* (turn of the 18th cent.) contains frescoes and pictures by Giovanni Pietro Ligari (1686-1752); a Madonna and Child with San Filippo Neri, by Giovanni Battista Pittoni (1687-1767), and oval paintings by Giuseppe Antonio Petrini (1677-c. 1758). The 14th cent. church of *Sant'Antonio* has a Baroque facade and bell-tower, and contains frescoes, probably by Fermo Stella (recorded 1519-1562), and a Madonna by Cipriano Valorsa (recorded 1536-1597). In the adjacent ex-Dominican Monastery is a Pietà, probably by Cipriano Valorsa. The *Santuario dell'Assunta* or church of *San Lorenzo*, the foundation stone of which was laid in 1418, has a portal carved by Tommaso Rodari (recorded 1484-1526), and contains pictures by Cipriano Valorsa and Giovanni Pietro Ramegialli (lived in the 18th cent.), while the stained-glass windows are by Andrea Passeri (recorded 1487-1511).

* **MORTARA** (Pavia). Important agricultural and industrial centre in the so-called Lomellina

Mortara, San Lorenzo.

alluvial plain. The parish church of *San Lorenzo* or *Basilica Minore* was built between 1375 and 1380, to a design by Bartolino da Novara. It contains some important works of art including pictures by Gaudenzio Ferrari (c. 1470-1546), Giulio Cesare Procaccini (1560-1625), Panfilo Nuvolone (1581-c. 1651), Pier Francesco Mazzucchelli, called Morazzone (c. 1571-1626), and Luigi Miradori called Genovesino (recorded 1639-1654). The foundation stone of the church of *Santa Croce* was laid in 1080; the church contains some important pictures including a St. Michael by Guglielmo Caccia, called Moncalvo (c. 1565-1625). Mid-19th cent. *Municipio*: inside is a painting of Mary Stuart by Cherubino Cornienti (1816-1860) and some remarkable marble busts of Renaissance personalities. In the surrounding area is the *Abbazia di Sant' Albino*, which goes back originally to the 5th cent. A.D. In the Romanesque apse of the church are some remarkable early-15th cent. frescoes by Giovanni da Milano. The Romanesque bell-tower stands on the left side of the church.

* **MOTTA DI LIVENZA** (Treviso). Large agricultural and commercial centre, above the confluence of the Monticano and Livenza rivers. The *Santuario della Madonna dei Miracoli* was erected on the spot where the Madonna is said to have appeared, on 9th March 1510. The sanctuary has a fine curved facade divided into three parts. The interior contains some notable pictures including an Adoration of the Magi by Domenico Capriolo (1494-1528) and an Assumption by Jacopo Palma the Younger (1544-1628). The *Duomo* is dedicated to St. Nicholas; the foundation stone was laid at the beginning of the 16th cent. The cathedral has a fine, two-ordered facade and contains some notable pictures, including a Madonna and Child with Saints Nicholas, Roch and Sebastian, by Leandro Bassano (1557-1622), and a St. Louis and a Madonna with Saints by Pomponio Amalteo (1505-1588).

* **MOTTOLA** (Taranto). Large agricultural centre, in a panoramic setting on the Ionic side of the Murge. The 13th cent. *Cattedrale* is dedicated to the Assunta. It was enlarged at the beginning of the 16th cent., and has a facade reminiscent of the Venetian-Dalmatian style, with a central portal flanked by two medieval columns resting on lions. The interior, with a nave and two aisles, contains a painting of the Assumption by Nicola Malinconico (1673-1721). The surrounding district has interesting crypts and hypogean chapels.

* **MURO LUCANO** (Potenza). Situated on a mountainside, in an area containing remains of megalithic walls. The early-11th cent. *Cattedrale* was largely destroyed by an earthquake in 1694. It contains some frescoes by Giuseppe Avallone da Salerno (lived in the 19th cent.)

and a painting by Giuseppe Palmieri (1674-c. 1740). Interesting remains of the *Castello*, which collapsed in an earthquake at the end of the 17th cent.

*** **NAPOLI/NAPLES.** Beautiful city between the Campi Flegrei and Vesuvius, and busy industrial and commercial centre. The *Castel Nuovo*, commonly known as the "Maschio Angioino", was built in 1279-82 during the reign of Charles I of Anjou, by Pietro de Caulis (lived in the 13th cent.) but completely rebuilt in the times of Alfonso I of Aragon by Guillén Sagrera (died 1452/56). Between two of the three crenellated towers stands the *Arco di Trionfo*, a fine Renaissance archway in marble, erected in 1455-1468 to a design by Francesco Laurana (c. 1430-c. 1502). The *Palazzo Reale* (1600-1602) was built by Domenico Fontana (1543-1607) on the orders of the viceroy Ferrante di Castro. It has a facade with an arched portico and, inside, the Appartamento Storico with 17 rooms, including the Throne room and the Hercules suite. The *Palazzo Cuomo* is a Renaissance palace, built between 1464 and 1490, possibly to a design by Giuliano da Maiano (1432-1490). It houses the Museo Civico Filangieri. Among the many churches, special attention should be given to *S. Anna dei Lombardi*, also called Monteoliveto; it was begun in 1411 but modified in the 17th cent.

Naples, Triumphal Arch of Alfonso of Aragon.

by Gennaro Sacco (recorded from 1680), and is rich in Renaissance sculptures. Inside is a marble altarpiece by Benedetto da Maiano (1442-1497) depicting the Annunciation and two Saints, and many 16th cent. tombs. In the Oratorio del Santo Sepolcro is a terracotta group representing the Pietà by Guido Mazzoni (c. 1450-1518). Near the altar is a Crib scene and Saints by Antonio Rossellino (1427-c. 1479). The church of *Santa Chiara*, built between 1310 and 1328, is probably the work of Gagliardo Primario (died 1348) with Baroque decoration added in the 18th cent. Inside are the tombs of Maria di Valois, by Tino di Camaino (c. 1280-1337) and Robert I of Anjou. The adjacent Convent contains the Chiostro delle Clarisse. The *Duomo* or church of *San Gennaro* (late 13th cent. or early 14th) is built on the remains of an ancient, early-Christian basilica (5th cent.). Inside is the Cappella di San Gennaro, built between 1608 and 1637 to a design by Francesco Grimaldi (1543-c. 1630); a doorway leads into the church of *Santa Restituta*, 4th cent. Christian basilica, from which period the only survivals are the columns of the nave and two aisles, and some fragments of mosaics. Two churches go under the name of *Santa Maria Donnaregina*: a Baroque one designed by Giovanni Guarini (lived in the first half of the 17th cent.) and containing a 15th cent. wooden Crucifix and a large number of pictures including an Annunciation and

Immacolata by Carlo Mellin (c. 1597-1649); and the other one, built on the orders of Mary of Hungary in 1320. It contains the marble tomb of Queen Mary of Hungary, by Tino di Camaino and Gagliardo Primario, as well as some Giotto-school frescoes. From outside the church one can enter the Nuns' Choir, on the walls of which are important frescoes by Pietro Cavallini (recorded 1237-1308): a Last Judgment, and Stories of St. Catherine and St. Agnes. The church of *San Lorenzo Maggiore* medieval in origin but altered in the 18th cent., contains a 14th cent. wooden Crucifix, paintings by Mattia Preti (1613-1699) representing a Crucifixion and Franciscan Saints, and Madonna and Franciscan Saints, and the Tomb of Catherine of Austria, by Tino di Camaino. In the church of *San Giovanni a Carbonara*, erected in 1343, but rebuilt and modified in the early 15th cent. and first half of the 17th cent. respectively, are the Cappella Caracciolo di Vico and, by the high altar, the Monument to King Ladislaus, by Andrea Buonaiuti called Andrea da Firenze (active in the 14th cent.). The *Certosa di S. Martino* was begun in 1325 and completed in 1368 by Tino di Camaino and Francesco di Vito (active in the 14th cent.). It houses the *Museo Nazionale di San Martino*, which is sub-divided into three sections: historic, artistic and monumental. The villa *La Floridiana*, erected in 1817-19 by Antonio Niccolini (1772-1850) houses the *Museo Nazionale della Ceramica Duca di Martina*, which contains a precious collection of enamel, ivory, pottery and china from Italy and abroad. The *Museo Archeologico Nazionale* is considered one of the richest and most important in the world for the large number of sculptures and paintings which, together with mosaics, large and small bronzes and vases, afford an interesting illustration of the entire course of ancient Greek and Roman civilization. In the Royal Palace of Capodimonte are the *Museo e Galleria di Capodimonte*, containing numerous works of art including seven large tapestries with episodes from the Battle of Pavia; a Crucifixion by Masaccio (1401-1428); an Assunta by Masolino da Panicale (1383-1447); the Transfiguration by Giovanni Bellini (1430-1516); the *Collezione De Ciccio*, with over 1,300 pieces including majolicas, enamel-work, ivory, clocks, tapestries, sculptures, paintings, etc. The *Porta Capuana*, designed by Giuliano da Maiano in 1484, has a fine marble decoration on the external facade. There is only room here to mention a few examples of Naples great artistic wealth: the *Castello Sant'Elmo* or Belforte (1329); the *Castel dell'Ovo*; the church of *Santa Maria della Vittoria* (1628); the church of *Santa Maria del Parto* and the *Villa Comunale*.

* **NARDÒ** (Lecce). The largest centre in the province of Lecce, after Lecce itself. The *Cattedrale* was built at the end of the 11th cent. on the site of a previous Byzantine church,

Naples, Royal Palace. Story of Psyche, tapestry.

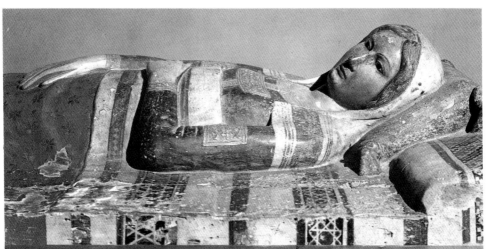

Montalcino, Museo d'Arte Sacra. Virgin of the
Annunciation.
Naples, Museo di S. Martino. Virgin of Nativity,
detail.

Naples, Museo di San Martino. Giuseppe Sanmartino, Crib figure.

203

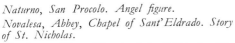

Naturno, San Procolo. Angel figure.
Novalesa, Abbey, Chapel of Sant'Eldrado. Story of St. Nicholas.
Novalesa, Abbey, Chapel of Sant'Eldrado. The Saint receiving the habit of the Benedictine order.

Novara, San Gaudenzio. Tanzio da Varallo, The Battle of Sennacherib, detail.
Orta, Isola di San Giulio, Basilica, pulpit.

and altered several times in later centuries (the latest restoration work being carried out in 1892-1900). It is artistically important especially for the interior, which consists of a nave and two aisles, marked by composite pillars, with three splendid altars carved in 1668 by Placido Buffelli. It contains other remarkable works of art including pictures by Ferdinando Sanfelice (1675-1748) and Francesco Solimena (1657-1747). Other important items include the so-called black Crucifix, in cedar-wood, possibly taken from a Byzantine coenobium, frescoes on the pillars and walls, of the 13th, 14th and 15th cent., and in the Treasury, silver statues of St. Gregory and the Immacolata, as well as an 18th cent. silver altar-frontal with an Assunta in relief-work. The church of *San Domenico* was erected in the 16th cent., and largely restored in the second half of the 18th. It is a splendid building, with facade richly decorated with columns and caryatids. The heart of the city is *Piazza Antonio Salandra*, surrounded by Baroque buildings and decorated in the centre with the spire of the Immacolata (18th cent.).

** **NARNI** (Terni). In a delightful setting overlooking the deep gorge of the river Nera and Terni plain. The *Duomo di San Giovenale* (369 A.D.) is dedicated to the first Bishop of Terni. It is a Romanesque building, containing the Sacellum of Saints Giovenale and Cassio, a fresco depicting the Deposition from the Cross, probably by Pier Antonio Mezzastris called Antonio da Foligno (1430-1506), the

tomb of Pietro Cesi, carried out in 1477 by Sebastiano di Francesco Pellegrini da Como, and a painting by Livio Agresti (recorded 1550-1580). The 15th cent. church of *Sant'Agostino* has an austere portal and, inside, a panel by Marcantonio Aquili or Marcantonio di Antoniazzo Romano (recorded 1511-1514). The *Palazzo del Podestà* is the result of the merging of three 13th cent. buildings, altered in the 16th cent. It houses an art gallery containing, above all, a large altarpiece carried out in 1486 by Ghirlandaio, a fragment of the Last Supper by Alessandro Torresani (c. 1530-c. 1590), and a valuable fresco of the Madonna and Child, by an unknown artist, for a long time wrongly attributed to Bartolomeo Torresani (c. 1500-1567). The Romanesque church of *San Domenico* has an important 12th cent. portal. The church of *San Francesco* was built in the 14th cent. on the spot where there was a splendid Gothic portal.

* **NARO** (Agrigento). Characteristic town on an isolated hill, with remains of 13th cent. crenellated walls. The church of *San Francesco* (first half of the 17th cent.) has a Baroque facade and contains frescoes by Domenico Provenzani, who worked on it in the second half of the 18th cent., and an altarpiece of the Immacolata by Vito D'Anna (c. 1720-1769). The convex-shaped facade of the *Santuario di San Calogero* (1599) is Baroque in style. Inside is a 16th cent. marble statue of the Flagellation. The *Chiesa Matrice della Santissima Annunziata* (first half of the 17th cent.) contains a Madonna

Nardò, San Domenico, facade.

Narni, Duomo, interior.
Narni, Duomo. Sacellum of S. Cassiano.

by the sculptor Vincenzo Gagini (1527-1595). In the church of *Sant'Agostino*, with vast 18th cent. facade, is a wooden statue of St. Francis of Paola, by Nicolò Bagnasco (lived in the 18-19th cent.), and pictures by Domenico Provenzani. The ruined *Matrice Vecchia* still preserves its fine, 14th cent. portal, and a few other remains.

* **NATURNO** (Bolzano). The Gothic *Parrocchiale di San Zeno* has two naves and contains remains of the early construction in the sacristy, with Romanesque frescoes, and on the outside a 16th cent. fresco depicting St. Christopher. In the neighbourhood are the *Castello Naturno* and the Romanesque church of *San Procolo*, possibly dating from the 8th cent. and rebuilt in the 11th, with 15th cent. frescoes.

* **NEMI** (Rome). Attractive town on Lake Nemi. The *Parrocchiale* contains, in the second chapel, a triptych from the school of Antoniazzo Romano (recorded 1461-1508), representing Christ Blessing between St. John the Baptist and St. John the Evangelist. The *Palazzo Ruspoli*, formerly *Baronale* preserves tempera pictures by Liborio Coccetti (lived in the 18-19th cent.) and, finally, the *Cappella della Crocifissione*.

** **NEPI** (Viterbo). Agricultural centre situated on a shelf between deep valleys and surrounded by massive walls. The *Duomo*, dedicated to the Assunta, is an ancient place of worship. Destroyed by the Longobards in 568 A.D., and rebuilt in the 9th cent., it was enlarged towards the end of the 12th cent., only to be burnt down by the French in 1789. All that is left of the Romanesque building is part of the structure, together with the three-arched

Naturno, San Procolo. Angel figure.

portico. The basilican interior, with a nave and four aisles, contains a pannelled triptych of Christ with Saints Romano and Tolomeo, by Giulio Pippi called Giulio Romano (c. 1499-1546), and tomb of St. Romano, in the style of Gian Lorenzo Bernini (1598-1680). The *Palazzo Comunale*, a solemn, aristocratic-looking building, was begun by Antonio da Sangallo the Younger (1483-1546). It has a rusticated portico, with a fountain, probably the work of Gian Lorenzo Bernini. The *Rocca* is a sturdy construction built in 1450 by Rodrigo Borgia, then modified by the Farnese family. Interesting remains of Etruscan walls (*Mura Etrusche*) are incorporated in the medieval walls. Two and a half kilometres away from Nepi is *Castel Sant'Elia*, where a large number of Etruscan hypogia have been found. The *Basilica di Sant'Elia*, an important Romanesque building, originally dates back to the beginning of the 6th cent. A.D. The Basilica, with a nave and two aisles, contains an ancient pulpit and, especially in the apse and transepts, a series of Byzantine-inspired frescoes carried out by two brothers, Giovanni and Stefano, and by their nephew Nicola, at the end of the 11th cent., or beginning of the 12th.

* **NERVI** (Genoa). Attractive little town surrounded by olive, orange and lemon groves; it is a fashionable seaside resort. Hundreds of works, providing a vast panorama of modern Ligurian painting, are arranged in eight halls and small rooms in the *Civica Galleria d'Arte Moderna*. The church of *San Siro* was erected in the 13th cent. and rebuilt in the 18th. It contains frescoes by Giuseppe Paganelli (recorded 1795-1822), Francesco Semini (1832-1883), Carlo Giuseppe Ratti (1737-1795), and statues by Francesco Schiaffino (1689-1765). The *Passeggiata Anita Garibaldi*, is a south-facing promenade, built on rocks eroded by the sea and interspersed with inlets of crystal-clear water. The *Parco Municipale*, with palms, pines and holm-oaks among its many varied plants, extends over an area of 80,000 square metres.

* **NETTUNO** (Rome). Almost a continuation of Anzio, with a medieval centre and modern quarters, it is a popular seaside resort, possibly Saracen in origin. The Anglo-American Anzio landings took place on its beaches. The *Forte*, erected between 1496 and 1503 on the orders of the Borgia Pope, Alexander VI, was designed by Antonio da Sangallo the Elder (1463-1534) and Baccio Pontelli (c. 1450-1492). It is a sturdy, square, brick construction standing on the coast. *Torre Astura* is an outstanding castle built on the seashore, historically associated with Corradino di Svevia (1252-1268).

* **NICASTRO** (Catanzaro). At the point where the Piazza stream flows into the plain of Santa Eufemia. Byzantine in origin, it flourished in

Norman times, and was rebuilt after a fearful earthquake in 1538. The church of *San Domenico* contains pictures by Francesco Colelli (lived in the 18th cent.). In the *Cattedrale* is a Last Supper, again by Colelli. The *Chiesa dei Cappuccini* contains an important painting of the Immacolata by Andrea Cefaly (1827-1907). In the *Tesoro del Vescovado* is a rare 17th cent. silver cross staff.

* **NICOSIA** (Enna). Picturesque town with houses dotted over the slopes of four rugged heights. The *Cattedrale* is dedicated to St. Nicholas, and dates back originally to the 14th cent. It has a massive campanile built against the facade. The Baroque interior contains some good works of art, including a Crucifix by the sculptor Giovanni Francesco Pintorno (1580-1639) and a painting of St. Bartholomew, probably by Giuseppe Ribera, called Spagnoletto (1588-1652). The church of *San Vincenzo* contains frescoes by William Borremans (1670-

Nicosia, the Cathedral and Campanile.

1744). The foundation stone of the church of *Santa Maria Maggiore* was laid in 1267. The facade has a spacious Baroque portal, and inside is a vast marble polyptych representing the Nativity of the Virgin, the Annunciation, Crib-scene, Death of the Virgin, and Saints, by Antonello Gagini (1478-1536). In the church of *San Biagio* are some fine 18th cent. stuccoes, and five paintings by Giuseppe Velasquez (1750-1827).

* **NOCERA SUPERIORE** (Salerno). Agricultural centre, divided into numerous districts, the most important being Santa Maria Maggiore, with the church of *Santa Maria Maggiore* or *Rotonda*, and 5th cent. baptistery, the dome of which was rebuilt after it had collapsed following an eruption of Vesuvius in 1944. The circular-plan interior contains a double round of monolithic columns, 14th and 15th cent. frescoes, large baptismal font for total immersion, with iconostases, and ancient architectonic fragments. Walk to the *Santuario di Santa Maria Mater Domini* (second half of the 12th cent.). On the facade are three large arches and, in the sober Baroque interior, Recovery of the miraculous panel and Apparition of Mary, by the painter Giacinto Diana (1730-1803), and a Byzantine-inspired panel of the Madonna and Child. In the Lady Chapel there is an important painting by Francesco Guarini (1611-1654) depicting the Madonna of the Rosary with Saints Pius V, Dominic, Thomas and Clare.

* **NOCERA UMBRA** (Perugia). Ancient-looking village, set panoramically on a lonely spur surrounded by mountains. The church of *San Francesco* was built at the end of the 14th cent., and houses an Art Gallery. On the walls are numerous frescoes by Matteo da Gualdo (c. 1435-1507) and an Annunciation, by Ercole di Giampaolo Ramazzani (lived in the 16th cent.). It is also worth noticing a polyptych (1483) by Niccolò di Liberatore, called Alunno (c. 1430-1502) and a panel of the Crucifixion by an Umbrian painter of the second half of the 13th cent. The *Duomo dell'Assunta*, was built in the 11th cent.; in the sacristy there is a valuable majolica floor. The *Torrione* is all that remains of the ancient Rocca.

Nocera Umbra.

* **NOLA** (Naples). An important agricultural and commercial centre on the south-eastern edge of the Campania plain, at the start of the sub-Apennine heights. The *Duomo*, dedicated to San Felice, was erected at the end of the 14th cent. and rebuilt at the turn of the 20th cent. to a design by Nicola Breglia (1831-1912). It is reached through a portico characterized by six Ionic columns. The interior is in the form of a Latin cross. It contains a painting of the fire that devastated the building in 1261, by Gaetano D'Agostino (1837-1914), and, on the ceiling, an Apotheosis of San Felice by Salvatore Postiglione (1861-1906). In the crypt (built on the remains of a temple to Jove) is a 13th cent. Byzantine-inspired relief of Christ and the Apostles, a marble Tabernacle and an altar-frontal of the early 16th cent. In the Baroque church of *Santa Chiara*, with majolica-tiled dome, are pictures by Ferdinando Sanfelice (1675-1748) and Giovanni Battista Caracciolo, called Battistello (c. 1570-1637). The aisleless *Ex Chiesa di Santa Chiara* contains traces of important 14th cent. frescoes. The ceiling of the former reception-room was painted by Angelo Mozzillo (active in the second half of the 18th and early 19th cent.). In the church of *Maria Santissima della Misericordia* or *San Biagio*, with Romanesque-Gothic campanile, is the tomb of Fabrizio Albertini, probably by Annibale Caccavello (c. 1515-1570). The *Palazzo Orsini* was built in 1461 by Orso Orsini. The facade has a Catalan-influenced portal. The church of the *Annunciata* or *San Felice* is Baroque-style in its present form; inside is a panel depicting the Annunciation, and Adoration of the Shepherds by Belisario Corenzio (c. 1560-post 1640). In the surrounding district, at Liveri, is the early 16th cent. Bramante-style *Santuario di Santa Maria a Parete*. It contains a panel of the Epiphany by Francesco Tolentino (active in the first half of the 16th cent.), Christ among the Shepherds by Jacopo Pastore (recorded in the first half of the 16th cent.) and frescoes by Belisario Corenzio.

* **NOLI** (Savona). Sheltered seaside resort between Punta del Vescovado and the Noli headland, surrounded by hills. The 11th cent. church of *San Paragorio* is Romanesque in style, with facade decorated with pilaster-strips and twin arches. Inside is a gigantic wooden Crucifix, known as the Holy Face, presumably carried out in the 12th cent., and inspired by eastern iconography. Noli boasts a large number of medieval palaces and towers, erected when the town was a free Commune.

Noli, San Paragorio.

** **NONANTOLA** (Modena). Agricultural and industrial centre, on the right bank of the river Panaro. An abbey was erected here in the middle of the 8th cent., and the medieval city grew up around it. The *Abbazia di Nonantola* was rebuilt in Romanesque style in the 12th, and altered in the 17th and 18th cent. The simple, majestic interior contains works of art including a polyptych by Michele di Matteo Lambertini (c. 1410-1470) of the Madonna and Child, Crucifixion and Saints. The 9th cent. parish church of *San Michele Arcangelo* was rebuilt several times in later centuries; in its present form it has a Baroque facade and basilican interior.

* **NORA** (Ruins of) (Town of Pula, province of Cagliari). First a Phoenician, then a Punic and finally a Roman centre. Nora still has remains of its ancient burial ground (*Necropoli*), with well-shaped trench and crematory tombs; the *Anfiteatro*, the Temple of the Goddess Tanit (*Tempio della dea Tanit*), the *Teatro*, of which the only traces of the portico are the stylobates; and beside it remains of a classical temple; the baths (*Grandi Terme*); and the *Terme a mare*, with a portico and pillars on both sides. Along the Via Sacra remains can be seen of the *Santuario delle divinità salutari*, a large group of buildings containing chapels and courtyards.

** **NORCIA** (Perugia). Surrounded by green mountains, in an area made fertile by the waters of the Sordo and Torbidone, and San Martino springs, it is a small town, but an important one for its history and monuments. The church of *San Benedetto* is very ancient, and tradition has it that it was erected on the site of the house of Euproprio Anicio and Abbondanza Reguardati, parents of the great St. Benedict. The church, in its present form, was almost entirely built in 1389, but the interior was completely restored in the 18th and 20th cent. The facade is characterized by a fine Gothic portal. Inside are some important works of art, including a 16th cent. fresco of the Madonna and Child, St. Barbara and St. Michael the Archangel, and a remarkable early 17th cent. painting of the Madonna and local Saints. The *Duomo*, dedicated to Santa Maria Argentea or of the People, dates back to the 16th cent., but had to be almost completely rebuilt after the disastrous earthquakes of 1703 and 1730. It is flanked by a sturdy campanile. The interior, with a nave and two aisles, contains some remarkably valuable works of art, including a vast 16th cent. panel representing the Madonna of the Rosary, apparently inspired by the style of Cola dell'Amatrice (recorded 1509-1547). The church of *Sant'Agostino*, erected in the 14th cent., has a graceful entrance-door, the lunette of which is decorated with a fresco by an unknown artist in 1388; it represents the Madonna and Child and Saints Augustine and Nicholas of Tolentino. The aisleless interior is richly frescoed; it contains an impressive organ, and carved choir stalls. The *Castellina* is a solid square fort, erected between 1554 and 1563 to a design by Jacopo Barozzi, called Vignola (1507-1573). The interior has been converted

Nonantola, Abbey Church. Lunette above the main entrance.

209

Norcia, Museo della Castellina. Deposition.

into a small Museum containing works by local artists on the whole. The *Edicola* or *Tempietto* is worthy of attention: built in 1354 to a design by Vanni Tuzi, in travertine, and only six metres high, it is a most graceful construction. Notice also the 14th cent. church of *San Giovanni*, with a two-aisled interior, and works of art including an Umbrian-school Madonna, by an unknown 15th cent. artist, and a 16th cent. wooden Crucifix. Norcia is the starting-point for interesting excursions: visits are especially recommended to the *Madonna della Neve*, a fine Renaissance church, containing some important works of art, to *Campi Vecchio*, a small village still with a medieval atmosphere, and to the *Abbazia di Sant'Entizio*, built before 1000 A.D., near the tombs of hermits who lived in the surrounding grottoes.

* **NORMA** (Latina). This village, still partly medieval, is on the way to the *Rovine di Norba*. Notice the ancient walls (*Mura*) dating back to the 4th cent. B.C. and the remains of the *Temple of Diana*, with corinthian capitals, columns and pillars in travertine (2nd cent. B.C.).

* **NOTARESCO** (Teramo). In the Vomano valley. *Santa Maria di Propezzano*: the only remains of the ancient monastery complex are the vast square-plan cloister, with a double order of arches, and the late-13th cent. church, with asymmetrical facade, flanked by a soaring campanile. In front of the church is a pointed-arched portico, and on one side is another, 14th cent. doorway known as the Porta Santa. The majestic basilican interior contains late 15th cent. frescoes. The church of *San Clemente al Vomano* dates back originally to the 9th cent.; the facade has an architraved portal with carved door-posts decorated with floral motifs. The basilican interior contains a rare 12th cent. ciborium, and a few works of art.

** **NOTO** (Syracuse). On a hillside, in the foothills of the Iblei mountains; its architecture is predominantly 18th cent. with unusual views and interesting panoramas. It was completely rebuilt in the 18th cent. after an earthquake had razed it to the ground in 1693. The city, in its present form, was designed by a scholar, Giovanni Battista Landolina, assisted by the architects Rosario Gagliardi (c. 1700-1770), Paolo Labisi (lived in the 17-18th cent.) and Antonio Mazza (lived in the 18th cent.). The *Duomo* is dedicated to St. Nicholas of Mira and St. Conrad. It was completed in 1776. There are three vast flights of steps in front and it is flanked on either side by a bell-tower. It contains fairly good works of art, some of them from the ancient town. The *Chiesa del Salvatore*, completed in 1801 to a design by Antonio Mazza, has a facade in which the transition from Baroque to neo-Classicism is well illustrated. The oval interior contains four paintings by Giuseppe Velasquez (1750-1827). The church of *San Domenico* was designed by Rosario Gagliardi. It has a flamboyant facade convex in the middle, and contains a painting of the Madonna of the Rosary probably by Vito D'Anna (c. 1720-1769). In the church of *Santa Chiara*, also designed by Rosario Gagliardi, are beautiful stuccoes and altars, Saints Benedict and Scolastica, by Salvatore Lo Forte (1807-1885), and a statue of the Madonna and Child, by Antonello Gagini (1478-1536). In the *Chiesa dell'Ecce Homo* is a painting of the Madonna and Child, probably by Antonio da Faenza (c. 1519-1609). The church of the *Santissimo Crocifisso*, completed in 1715, contains a Madonna and Child, popularly known as the Madonna of the Snow, one of the most successful works of the sculptor Francesco Laurana (recorded 1458-1500). The early-18th cent. *Monastero del Santissimo Salvatore* is a fanciful piece of architecture. *Palazzo Villadorata*, designed by Paolo Labisi, has a facade where the Classical-inspired elements mingle with Ionic and Baroque motifs. *Palazzo Astuto* is fundamentally Baroque in style. The *Museo Civico* is divided into an archeological section, arranged in seven rooms, comprising a large amount of pre-historic material taken from the surrounding countryside, and a modern section, in six rooms, containing antiques taken from ancient Noto, and an important collection of medals.

Noto, Duomo.

* **NOVAFELTRIA** (Pesaro). Attractive little town on the left bank of the Marecchia; the main centre in Montefeltro. The 14th cent. *Edicola di Santa Marina* is characterized by a small bell gable. The ancient parish church of *San Pietro in Culto* is documented as far back as 950 A.D. Notice the ruins of the walls of the early Romanesque construction. Excursion to *Talamello*; in the cemetery can be seen the interesting cell completely frescoed by Antonio di Guido Alberti da Ferrara (1390/1400-1449).

* **NOVALESA** (Turin). A resting-place for travellers on their way over the Mont Cenis pass before the Napoleonic road was opened. In the *Chiesa Parrocchiale* (parish church) are some paintings presented in 1813 by Napoleon to Abbot Gabet, prior of the Hospice of Mont Cenis. The *Abbazia della Novalesa* was founded in 716 by Abbone, governor of Susa, then handed over to the Benedictines, who transformed it into one of the most important cultural centres in Europe in the Middle Ages. It is an ensemble of buildings at the centre of which are the church and monastery, while four attractive chapels are scattered in the surrounding park. The interior of the Chapel of St. Eldrado is entirely covered with Romanesque frescoes.

Novalesa, Abbey. Story of St. Nicholas.

* **NOVA PONENTE** (Bolzano). Mountain village facing the Catinaccio and Latemar ranges. Visit the two-aisled Gothic church of *San Ulrico*, with wooden sculptures on the baptismal font and altars, by Giovanni da Judenburg (op. in the 15th cent.), and an altarpiece by Francesco Sebaldo Unterberger (1706-1776). The church of *Sant'Elena*, built in the 15-16th cent., has Bolzano-school pictures (1410) inside and outside. The 12th or 13th cent. church of *Sant'Agata*, was modified and restored in the 14th and 17th cent. It contains an altarpiece by Orazio Giovanelli (1580-c. 1636) depicting Saints Ulric and Wolfgang, and remains of 14th cent. frescoes.

** **NOVARA**. Almost on the border of Lombardy, it is a busy road junction and important industrial town. The *Basilica di San Gaudenzio* was built partly in the 16th and partly in the 17th cent., initially to a design by Pellegrino Tibaldi called Pellegrino Pellegrini (16th cent.); it has a deep-set apse, with three inter-communicating chapels divided by twin half-columns. The chancel is impressive, with a fine Baroque high altar. Notice works by Gaudenzio Ferrari, Morazzone, and Tanzio da Varallo (c. 1575-c. 1635). The *Duomo*, erected in honour of Santa Maria Assunta, was built in the last century to a design by Alessandro Antonelli. The facade is in the form of a tetrastyle Corinthian pronaos. The lower part of the campanile is Romanesque, dating from the 12th cent. The interior has a nave and two aisles, and contains a fine panel by Gaudenzio Ferrari (1470-1546) depicting the Marriage of St. Catherine and three Saints, caryatids, putti and mosaics in black and white. Visit the lower sacristy, decorated with important frescoes, and the Chapterhouse Library, which is one of the richest in the region. In front of the Cathedral stands the *Battistero*, possibly dating back to the 5th cent., and altered in later periods. Inside are frescoes by Pier Francesco Mazzucchelli called Morazzone (1571-1626). The *Museo Civico* contains an interesting archeological collection and many works by painters and sculptors, especially of the 15-18th cent. The *Galleria d'Arte Moderna* is housed on the first floor of the Palazzo del Podestà and two floors of the adjacent building.

Novara, San Gaudenzio.

* **NOVENTA VICENTINA** (Vicenza). Agricultural and industrial centre, at the junction of the provinces of Verona, Vicenza and Padua. In the mid-19th cent. *Duomo* is a painting of Saints Roch and Sebastian, by Giovan Battista Tiepolo (1696-1770). The 17th cent. *Villa Barbarigo*, with two superimposed loggias, contains paintings by Antonio Foler (c. 1529-1616) and Antonio Vassilacchi called Aliense (c. 1556-1629).

* **NOVI LIGURE** (Alessandria). On the southern edge of the plain of Alessandria, in the foothills of the Apennines; it is a road and railway junction. The *Chiesa della Maddalena*, erected at the end of the 17th cent., has a portal surmounted by a pretty Baroque statuette of Mary Magdalen. Two km. outside the town is the characteristic little church of *Madonna della Pieve*, built in the 12-13th centuries.

* **NUMANA** (Ancona). Pleasant village in the southern foothills of Mount Conero, divided into Upper and Lower Numana, on the sea-shore. The church of *Santa Maria di Portonovo*, erected in the first half of the 11th cent., is considered a real gem of Romanesque architecture. The *Santuario del Crocifisso*, built in the second half of the 16th cent., is believed to have been designed by Pellegrino Tibaldi called Pellegrino Pellegrini (1527-1596). It contains some remarkable works of art including a painting of Moses receiving the Ten Commandments and one of Moses parting the Waters, by Domenico Simonetti (born 1893). The ancient *Badia di San Pietro* was first a Benedectine, then a Camaldolese hermitage. It has an interesting Baroque portal, and is a graceful and characteristic building.

* **NUORO.** On an uneven plateau, at the foot of Mount Ortobene, facing the magnificent chain of the Sopramonte mountains. The 19th cent. *Duomo* contains a fine painting of the dead Christ, attributed to A. Tiarini. The *Museo Regionale del Costume* consists of about twenty large rooms, where the rural and village architecture of Sardinia is amply documented. Walk to the tiny church of *Nostra Signora della Solitudine*, built in 1625.

Nuoro, Duomo, interior.

* **ODERZO** (Treviso). Wine-producing and commercial centre. The *Duomo* dates back originally to the 10th cent. but was rebuilt in Gothic style in the 14th. It has a gable facade, and contains a fresco of John the Baptist and Santi Vescovi Opitergini by Jacopo Palma the Younger (1544-1628), and Resurrection, Transfiguration and Nativity, by Pomponio Amalteo (1505-1588). In the *Museo Civico* are Roman mosaics, medieval material and medallions.

* **OFFIDA** (Ascoli Piceno). On the ridge that separates the Tesino from the Tronto, with notable remains of 14-15th cent. city walls. The battlemented, 15th cent. *Palazzo Comunale* is one of the most elegant town halls in the Marches. Inside are some important pictures, including the Earthly and Underworld Kingdoms, by Simone De Magistris (1534-1600). The *Collegiata Nuova* was built in the 18th cent. to a design by Lazzaro Giosafatti (1694-1781). It contains some works of art, including a 16th cent. polychrome-wood statue of the Madonna and Child. Via Ciabattoni leads to the *Santuario di Sant'Agostino*, a majestic 14th cent. building, almost completely rebuilt in the 18th. It contains a painting of the Epiphany by Carlo Allegretti (lived in the 16th cent.). The church of *Santa Maria della Rocca* was rebuilt in 1330 in Romanesque style.

It has some works of art, especially frescoes and fresco fragments of the 14-15th cent. The crypt is also decorated with valuable, 14th cent. frescoes.

* **OLBIA** (Sassari). In a wide bay, surrounded by granite mountains, it is the main entrance to Sardinia from the mainland of Italy. *Olbia Marittima* is an important harbour and railway terminus for Cagliari. The church of *San Simplicio* was built in Romanesque style in the 11-12th cent. It is an austere building, with a basilican interior consisting of a nave and two aisles, and containing a collection of stone memorials. In the nearby *Necropoli* are hundreds of well-type tombs, where objects of the 4th-3rd cent. B.C. have been collected.

* **OLIENA** (Nuoro). In an attractive position, amid lush vegetation, in strong contrast with the barren rocky landscape of Sopramonte. The majestic *Parrocchiale* was built in the 17th cent., and contains a 17th cent., Spanish-inspired statue of St. Francis Xavier, and, in the sacristy, a valuable polyptych by an unknown, 16th cent. Sardinian artist. The 15th cent. Gothic church of *Santa Maria* is flanked by a fine bell-tower. Excursions to the *Grotta della Valle s'Abba Medica*, and *Punta Corrasi*, the highest peak of Sopramonte.

Offida, Town Hall.

* ORBETELLO (Grosseto). On a slender peninsula in the middle of the lagoon of Orbetello. The *Duomo* or *Collegiata dell'Assunta* was built in 1376 on the site of a previous church. It is noted for its portal which is surmounted by a rose-window surrounded by quadrilobes and a lower band of quadrilobes, each decorated with a stone head. One should visit the Etruscan-Roman *Antiquarium*, and the nearby village of Port'Ercole, the ancient Portus Herculis of Roman times. Heading south along the Via Aurelia one reaches *Cosa* (*Ansedonia*). It stands on a hill, 114 m high, and was a Roman colony from 273 B.C. The Etruscan walls still stand along a surface of 1500 m, with 14 square towers and two cylindrical ones. Down below, at sea level, are the *Tagliata Etrusca* and the *Bagno o Spacco della Regina*, two huge hydraulic constructions built by the Etruscans to prevent the harbour from silting up, which it now has.

* ORGOSOLO (Nuoro). Large village in an attractive position, with sweeping view as far as Nuoro. It lies among woods and game-reserves, and has a flourishing cattle-breeding industry. Orgosolo is not interesting for any building in particular, but its overall Sardinian atmosphere. The tiny church of *Sant'Anania*, built on the spot where Saint Anania and Saint Egidio were martyred, is worthy of attention.

* ORIA (Brindisi). On three hills dominating the so-called Tavoliere di Lecce plain. Hydra or Uria was one of the most important Messapian cities, as remains from tombs have proved. The most important building in the town is the *Castello*, built between 1227 and 1233 by Frederick II, and completed in the

14th cent. with the collaboration of the French architect Pierre d'Angicourt (recorded 1269-1324). It is an impressive and spectacular building, overlooked by the so-called Square tower, the torre del Cavaliere and the torre del Salto, slender cylindrical towers dating from the Angevin period. Inside is an enormous parade ground and Martini Carissimo collection, with a vast number of ancient coins and engraved stones, bronzes and Messapian vases, excavated in the area, as well as remains of Roman and medieval architecture. The *Cattedrale*, rebuilt in 1750, has a vast Baroque facade; the building is characterized by a tall polychrome-tiled dome.

** ORIAGO (Town of Mira, province of Venice). Large agricultural centre, crossed by the Brenta canal. The 16th cent. *Villa Gradenigo* is decorated inside by Benedetto Caliari (1538-1598). 18th cent. *Villa Mocenigo.* 16th cent. *Villa Moro.* 17th cent. *Villa Priuli.* Following the Brenta canal, one reaches *Villa Foscari* or *della Malcontenta*, by Andrea Palladio (1508-1580), in smooth rusticated work, with Ionic pronaos. The rooms inside contain important pictures and decorations.

* ORISTANO (Cagliari). On the gulf of Oristano; it is an agricultural and commercial centre. Oristano is believed to have been built on the site of the ancient Othoca. The large amount of archeological material used in the ecclesiastical buildings of the town probably comes from the ruins of Cornus and Tharros. The *Torre di San Cristoforo* or *Porta Manna* (1291) has a really impressive appearance. The *Antiquarium Arborense* houses an interesting art gallery and archeological collection, with neolithic, nuraghe, Punic and Roman remains. In

Oria, Castle.

Oristano (surroundings), Vitu Sotto, gateway.

the *Duomo*, only parts of the apse remain of the original 13th cent. building, which was rebuilt in the 18-19th cent. The 14th cent. polygonal bell-tower is still standing. Inside are the Chapter-hall, with illuminated chorals (13th cent.), a wooden statue of the Annunziata by Nino Pisano (early 14th cent.–1368), the Gothic Cappella del Rimedio, and, in the chancel, a painting by Sebastiano Conca (1679-1764), depicting the Madonna in Glory. In the church of *San Francesco* are preserved a 14th cent. wooden Crucifix, of the Spanish school, Bishop Saint (a marble statue by Nino Pisano) and, in the sacristy, St. Francis with Stigmata, by Pietro Cavaro (recorded from 1518 to 1537). Walks to the Romanesque church of *Santa Giusta*, built between 1135 and 1145; to the *Rovine di Tharros*, including, among other things, a Semite-style temple, two thermal buildings from Roman times, a 4th-3rd cent. B.C. Punic temple, a group of Punic-inspired houses and an Early-Christian baptistery, of the 5th cent.; and lastly, to the church of *San Giovanni in Sinis*, enlarged in 1000 A.D., but dating back to the 5th cent.

* **OROPA** (Town of Biella, province of Vercelli). In the Biella pre-Alps, it is famous for the *Santuario della Madonna d'Oropa* which was founded, according to tradition, by St. Eusebio in the 4th cent. It consists of a well-arranged ensemble of Baroque buildings, dating from the 17-18th cent. In the *Chiesa Vecchia* is the original chapel, containing a wooden Madonna decorated with gold and precious stones, as well as some 15th cent. frescoes. Behind the buildings stands the *Chiesa Nuova*, begun towards the end of the 19th cent. Twelve 7-8th cent. chapels are dotted over the hillside.

* **OROSEI** (Nuoro). At the mouth of the Cedrino stream, in an amphitheatre of heights dominated by the mass of Monte Tuttavista. Here stood the ancient Fanum Carisii, and in the Middle Ages the judges of Gallura built a castle, which was then passed over to the judges of Oristano and kings of Aragon. The *Chiesa Primaziale* has an attractive group of small domes, and is flanked by a remarkable bell-tower. Little remains of the *Castello Medievale*. Walk to the *Marina di Orosei*, at the mouth of the Cedrina.

* **ORTA SAN GIULIO** (Novara). In a pleasant position, with small Baroque palaces and quiet narrow streets. The *Palazzo Comunale* is a small but attractive-looking building. The 15th cent. parish church of *Santa Maria Assunta* has a porch supported by fine twin-columns. On the hill that rises on the peninsular of Orta San Giulio is the *Sacro Monte*, dedicated to St. Francis of Assisi, one of the most frequently visited sanctuaries in Piedmont. It consists of twenty chapels, containing 376 ter-

racotta statues representing Scenes from the life of St. Francis, carried out in the 18th cent. by Michele Prestinari, Dionigi Bussola and Carlo Beretta. On the islet of San Giulio is the ancient *Basilica di San Giulio*, rebuilt in the 11th cent., and altered again later. The medieval construction still preserves its lovely bell-tower; it contains a Romanesque ambo (11-12th cent.), 15th cent. frescoes, and some by Gaudenzio Ferrari (c. 1475-1546).

* **ORTE** (Viterbo). Situated on a tufa hill at a curve of the river Tiber. The Romanesque church of *San Silvestro* was built in the 12th cent. on the ruins of a Roman temple dedicated to Peace. The high, narrow facade has three single-lighted windows; on the left flank of the building are large Gothic arches. Inside is the Diocesan museum of sacred art, containing a mosaic fragment of the Madonna that, at the beginning of the 8th cent., was in St. Peter's in Rome; a Tuscan-school panel (1282) of St. Francis and stories of his life; 16th cent. Viterbo-school polyptych narrating stories of St. Egidio; a Viterbo-school panel (1501) depicting the Annunciation, and, finally, a large painting of the Madonna and Child with Saints, by Francesco da Castello (lived in the 16-17th cent.). The enormous *Cattedrale*, dedicated to the Assunta, was designed by Gregorio Castracchini (20th cent.). Inside is a panel of the Assunta by Taddeo di Bartolo (c. 1362-1422), and a large altarpiece of the Assunta and Martyrs, by Giuseppe Bottani (1717-1784).

* **ORTONA** (Chieti). The town is dominated by the Aragonese *Castello* (1452), which has

Orta, Isola di San Giulio, Basilica, detail of the pulpit.

been damaged by landslides and was bombed during the last war. The *Cattedrale di San Tommaso* was rebuilt in the first half of the 12th cent., and largely restructured in later periods. It is flanked by a sturdy bell-tower. Inside are two important antique bas-reliefs, representing Doubting St. Thomas, and St. Thomas's body being brought to shore. The *Porto*, built by the Frentani, was an important port in Roman times, and flourished again in the 16th cent. In the neighbourhood is the 8th cent. church of *San Giovanni in Venere*, one of the most important in the Abruzzi, built on the ruins of a temple to Venus the Peacemaker; notice the three elegant semicircular apses, with blind arches. Nearby are interesting ruins of a convent.

* **ORUNE** (Nuoro). Picturesque shepherds' village dominating the Rio Isalle valley. The neighbourhood is interesting because at Filitta or Fenosu there are many *domus de janas*, some simple, some complicated in construction, and a rare sacred nuraghe well, with remains of a sacellum of great architectonic interest.

*** **ORVIETO** (Terni). Standing high on a rock of volcanic tufa, in a panoramic setting, it is one of the prettiest towns in Italy. In ancient times it was a leading centre of Etruscan civilization, and the museums bear witness to the artistic genius of the Etruscans. The medieval streets lead up to the *Duomo*, which has been defined as "one of the seven wonders of the world"; it stands in a spacious, green square, affording incredibly beautiful views over the surrounding countryside. It is dedicated to the Assunta, and was begun at the end of the 13th cent. in Romanesque style, possibly to a design by Arnolfo di Cambio (c. 1245-1302) and directed by fra' Bevignate da Perugia; but from the beginning of the 14th cent., with Giovanni di Uguccione da Orvieto, the building took on a Gothic imprint. The cross vaults made it necessary to strengthen the walls, which was undertaken by Lorenzo Maitani (died 1330); he redesigned the apse, planned and began the erection of the facade. Many architects took part in the building process, throughout the 14th and 15th cent., modifying and adding to the initial plans. Again in the 16th and 17th

Ortona, Castle.

cent. work was carried out on the facade and some parts of the interior. The facade is in the form of a great triptych, and is strikingly beautiful, not only for its graceful lines, but also for the dazzling profusion of gold and mosaics. Notice in particular the reliefs by Maitani in the lower band (Biblical Scenes, Gospel Stories, Last Judgement), statues by Maitani and Andrea Pisano in the lunette of the central doorway, and the rose-window by Andrea di Cione called Orcagna (14th cent.). The basilican interior, with red limestone floor, contains many works of art including a fresco of the Madonna by Gentile da Fabriano (c. 1370-1427), a Crucifix by the school of Maitani, the wooden choir, with three orders of carved and inlaid choirstalls, carried out between 1331 and 1340 by Giovanni Ammannati and his assistants, and the Chapel of the Madonna of San Brizio, with a magnificent cycle of frescoes by Luca Signorelli (c. 1445-1523). The decoration of the Chapel was begun by Beato Angelico (c. 1387-1455) with the assistance of Benozzo Gozzoli (1420-1497), then interrupted and resumed several times, and finally entrusted to Signorelli in 1499, who completed it by 1504. In the Cappella del Corporale is the famous reliquary with the miraculous corporal and a "Madonna dei raccomandati" by Lippo Memmi (recorded 1317-1356). *Palazzo Soliano*, once called Palazzo dei Papi, is an impressive tufa building, with a fine flight of steps outside leading up to the State apartments, which include an immense salon. It was Pope Bonifice VIII who, on a visit to Orvieto in 1297, first ordered the building of this palace. It houses the *Museo dell'Opera del Duomo*, set up in the latter half of the last century, with a collection of artistic

Orvieto, Etruscan necropolis.

works, mostly from the Cathedral, and many of them by the great masters who worked on its construction and decoration. The *Palazzo Papale* is a fine 13th cent. building, now being restored to its original form. The *Pozzo della Rocca* or *di San Patrizio* was begun between December 1527 and May 1528 on the orders of Pope Clement VII, when he took refuge in Orvieto during the Sack of Rome. The well, dug in order to provide the besieged city with water, was designed by Antonio da Sangallo the Younger (1483-1546). In 1532 a pre-Etruscan tomb was discovered, at a depth of about 60 metres. The Romanesque-Gothic *Palazzo del Popolo* was begun in 1157 as a papal palace. It stands alone, between two

Orvieto, Duomo, facade.

217

squares, like several other palaces in Northern and Central Italy. The church of *Sant'Andrea* (actually dedicated to Saints Andrew and Bartholomew) is of ancient origin, as it was begun in the 6th cent. Later on, especially in the 11-12th cent., it was almost completely rebuilt. The basilican interior contains works of art by Ippolito Scalza (c. 1532-c. 1617), and followers of Luca Signorelli and Arnolfo di Cambio. Many other monuments are worth seeing in Orvieto, including the *Torre del Moro*, probably named after a relief-work Saracen's Head found there; the *Museo Claudio Faina*, with its rich collection of Greek vases; the tiny Romanesque church of *San Lorenzo in Arari*, and the church of *San Giovanni Evangelista*, with 16th cent. facade. From Orvieto there are walks to the *Necropoli Etrusca*, the *Convento della Trinità*, the *Tombe Etrusche di Settecamini*, and to the *Abbazia dei Santi Severo e Martirio*, founded in the high Middle Ages, rebuilt by the Benedictines in the 12th cent., and finally handed over to the French order of the Premonstratensians, who enlarged it. In the *Chiesa del Crocifisso* is an important 13th cent. fresco. The 12th cent. *Chiesa Antica* has a fine Cosmatesque floor, two Romanesque bas-reliefs, and a 12th cent. one-dimensional painting representing a Crucifixion, two Angels and four Saints.

* **OSIMO** (Ancona). Attractive little town, panoramically situated between the valleys of the Aspio and Musone. In the 4th cent. B.C. the area was invaded by the Gauls, from which

Osimo, San Marco. Arcangelo di Cola, Madonna enthroned.

period a vast necropolis remains. The *Duomo* is dedicated to San Leopardo, the first bishop of Osimo. It was erected in the 8th cent. on remains of a Capitol and Temple dedicated to Aesculapius and Hygeia. Modified in later centuries, it has a sober facade and contains some fairly interesting works of art. In the 12th cent. *Baptistery*, or church of *San Giovanni*, are a baptismal font by Pietro Paolo Iacometti (1580-1655), and Tarquinio Iacometti (lived in the 16-17th cent.), paintings by Antonio Sarti (recorded 1613-1633), Ercole Gennari (1597-1658), Giovanni Battista Gennari (1565-1615), Giulio Lazzarelli (1607-c. 1667), Pietro da Montepulciano (active in the early 15th cent.) and Simone De Magistris (1534-post 1600). The *Palazzo Municipale* is a fine building. It has a facade designed by Pompeo Floriani in 1675, and is flanked by a 13th cent. civic tower with Guelf crenellations. Inside are headless Roman statues, funerary cippi, and a polyptych, possibly carried out in 1464 by Antonio and Bartolomeo Vivarini. The brickwork *Collegio Campana* was designed by Andrea Vici (1744-1817): it contains a thousand fifteeners, and hundreds of parchments. The 13th cent. church of *San Giuseppe da Copertino* contains a few works of art, including 18th cent. paintings. The church of *San Marco* contains an interesting fresco by Arcangelo di Cola and a painting by Guercino.

* **OSPEDALETTO EUGANEO** (Padua). Its name derives from a hospital founded there in 1165. Walk to the *Santuario di Santa Maria del Tresto*. It was built in the second half of the 15th cent. and contains important pictures such as a 16th cent. Madonna and Child by an unknown artist.

* **OSPEDALETTO LODIGIANO** (Milan). Agricultural centre; it grew up around a 12th cent. hospital. The church of *Santi Pietro e Paolo* (1559) has a fine facade, and is flanked by a cusped bell-tower. Inside is a picture by Bernardino Luini (1480/90-c. 1531) depicting the Madonna and Child with Saints, and a 17th cent. wooden choir. Notice the annexed 16th cent. cloister.

* **OSTIA ANTICA** (Rome). South-west of Ostia Antica is the archeological area. The nearby *Castello* is a Renaissance work (1483-86) by Baccio Pontelli (1450-1495), consisting of sturdy bastions surrounded by a moat and surmounted by a tower. The Rocca museum is housed in the papal apartments. Via delle Tombe, so called because it is flanked by a large number of tombs dating from various periods, leads to the ruins of the Republican-age Porta Romana, and, on the left of the main road called Decumanus Maximus, can be seen an ancient statue of Minerva Vittoria (1st cent. A.D.). The *Terme di Nettuno* (baths of Neptune) are in the actual archeological area; they still have the Palestra and Tepidarium, with mosaics

Ostia, House of Diana.
Ostia, Horrea Epagathiana.

depicting Neptune and Amphitrite. The Augustan-age *Teatro* was completely rebuilt under Septimius Severus. In the centre of the *Piazzale delle Corporazioni* (with ruins of the fine double portico and mosaic paving) stands a temple to Ceres (*Tempio di Cerere*). The Forum contains the impressive *Capitolium*, dedicated to Jove, Juno and Minerva, and erected under Hadrian; the *Tempio di Roma ed Augusto* (1st cent. A.D. Corinthian prostyle, with a statue of Roma Victrix); the *Basilica*, a large rectangular hall with polychrome marble floor; the *Tempio Rotondo*, a roofless circular building (3rd cent. A.D.), most probably consecrated to the Emperor cult; the *Terme del Foro*, a spacious building of the 2nd cent. A.D., altered and enlarged in the 4th cent. On the right of the Via della Foce stands an area containing *three temples* of the Republican period, behind which a late-Imperial construction of the 4th cent. can be seen, called Domus of Eros and Psyche; the *Insula di Serapide*, and beside it the *Terme dei Sette Sapienti* (baths of the seven sages) with a round, domed hall. Continuing along Via della Foce one reaches the baths of Mithras (*Terme del Mitra*) and, at the far end on the left, a group of buildings belonging to the age of Hadrian, including: the *Terme della Trinacria*, with mosaics; the *Casa di Bacco e Arianna* (House of Bacchus and Ariadne), also with mosaics in some of the rooms, and the *Serapeum*, a temple dedicated to the Egyptian deity, Serapis. Returning to the Decumanus Maximus, one can see the so-called *Schola del Traiano*, an enormous building of the 2nd cent. A.D., possibly set up as the headquarters of the corporations; the *Tempio dei Fabri Navales;* a Christian *Basilica*, with Christian symbols on the architrave, and the *Terme delle sei colonne*. Standing next to the Baths is the *Insula degli Aurighi*, including a Temple to Mithras with a nave and two aisles. Among other places of interest is the house of *Fortuna Annonaria*, a late-Imperial aristocratic dwelling with mosaics, statues and pictures.

* **OSTIGLIA** (Mantua). Commercial and industrial centre, on the left bank of the river Po. The parish church of *Santa Maria Assunta*, designed by Pietro Saccardo (20th cent.), contains a St. Peter by Giandomenico Cignaroli (1722-1793). *Santuario della Madonna della Comuna*, designed by Giulio Romano (c. 1499-1546). Late 18th cent. *Palazzo Cavriani-Bonazzi*.

* **OSTUNI** (Brindisi). Situated on three hills at the edge of the Murge, a short distance away from the Adriatic coast, between Monopoli and Brindisi. The medieval village is clustered on one of the three hills. Messapian in origin, as inscriptions on vases excavated in the vast necropolis prove, it might correspond to the Roman Stulnium. The *Cattedrale*, erected in the 15th cent., has a splendid Gothic façade; in the lunette of the middle portal is an impor-

tant bas-relief representing the Madonna and Child. The interior, in the form of a Latin cross, was remodelled in 18th cent. style and has elegant Baroque chapels, and a Madonna and Child with Saints by Jacopo Palma the Younger (1544-1628). Notice the *Guglia di Sant'Oronzo*, 20.75 m high, by Giuseppe Greco (lived in the 18th cent.); the *Chiesetta dello Spirito Santo* (first half of the 17th cent.) with grand Renaissance portal; the Baroque *Palazzo Ducale Zevallos*, and remains of the *Castello*, built in the last years of the 12th cent., by Goffredo, Count of Lecce. Walk to Ceglie Messapico, where there is a fine 15-16th cent. *Castello*, with large cylindrical towers.

* **OTRANTO** (Lecce). In an inlet on the Costa Salentina, it stands on the west bank of the Otranto Canal, where it flows into the Adriatic sea. It is an isolated town, steeped in history. The *Cattedrale*, dedicated to the Annunziata, is the place where the Idruntini (inhabitants of Otranto) were massacred by the Turks in 1480. Built in the latter half of the 11th cent., and repaired in the latter half of the 15th cent., it recently underwent restoration work. The facade is decorated with a fine Baroque portal, (1764) and a magnificent rose-window with sixteen rays and exquisite Gothic tracery, dating from the last years of the 15th cent. The spacious, solemn interior contains 17-18th cent. frescoes, and the floor is covered with a vast mosaic by the priest Pantaleone, who worked on it between 1163 and 1166; notwithstanding the somewhat crude finish it is important for its dynamic design, against a white background. In the crypt (second half of the 11th cent.) are numerous columns and remains of Byzantine frescoes. The church of *San Pietro*, a simple Byzantine building of the 10th or 11th cent., contains frescoes of varying periods, some of them with Greek inscriptions. The *Castello* was built towards the end of the 15th cent. by Ferdinand of Aragon. It is a sturdy building on a square plan, with huge, cylindrical towers at each corner; the entrance-door still bears a large coat-of-arms of Charles V. The church of *San Francesco di Paola* or *Santa Maria dei Martiri* was erected to commemorate the massacre of 1480; it has Baroque altars

Otranto, Castle.

Orvieto, Duomo. Lorenzo Maitani, The Damned, detail.

Orvieto, Duomo. Reliquiary.

Padua, Church of the Eremitani. Andrea Mantegna, Stories of St. Christopher, detail.

Padua, Museo Civico. Guariento, Angels.

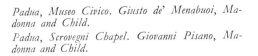

Padua, Museo Civico. Giusto de' Menabuoi, Madonna and Child.

Padua, Scrovegni Chapel. Giovanni Pisano, Madonna and Child.

Palermo, Museo Civico. Antonello da Messina, The Virgin of the Annunciation.

Palermo, Palatine Chapel. Mosaic depicting the Coronation of Roger.

and four stone tablets, with the names of the martyrs inscribed. In the direction of Capo d'Otranto are the ruins of the Romanesque-Gothic church of *San Nicola di Casole*, dating from 1100.

* **OTTANA** (Nuoro). Dairy-farming centre, in an area dotted with nuraghi and giants' tombs. The church of *San Nicola* (12th cent.) is an austere-looking Romanesque building. The aisleless interior contains a polyptych depicting Saints Francis and Nicholas of Mira, carried out in 1338-44 by a follower of Francesco Traini (1321-1363).

* **OZEGNA** (Turin). Agricultural centre, originally called Eugenia. Count Gottofredo di Biandrate, of the branch of San Giorgio, had the *Castello* built there in 1432. A cylindrical tower and three square ones, the courtyard, two superimposed loggias, and a huge fireplace still remain. The *Parrocchiale* was erected in 1831-42, to a design by Francesco Martelli.

* **OZIERI** (Sassari). In a panoramic setting, it is a main centre in the Logudoro area. The Gothic-Aragonese *Cattedrale* (16th cent.) was rebuilt in the 19th cent. in neo-Classical style. It contains a polyptych of the Madonna of Loreto by an unknown painter from Sassari, active in the first half of the 16th cent., and pictures by Giovanni Marghinotti (1798-1865). In the church of *Santa Lucia* is a late-14th cent. Spanish-made Crucifix. The mountains around the village contain a large number of caves, mostly inhabited in pre-historic times, including some of great archeological interest, such as the *Grotta di San Michele ai Cappuccini*, a natural cave used as a burial-place. It has a spacious mouth decorated with chalk-stone formations, and behind it lies another, smaller chamber. Excursions to *Sant'Antioco di Bisarcio*, a 12-13th cent. cathedral with a massive bell-tower.

*** **PADOVA/PADUA.** Large agricultural and industrial city, not far from the Euganean Hills. It stands at the intersection of the highways of Venetia with those leading to Trentino-Alto Adige, Venetia Giulia and Emilia. The most famous building in Padua is the basilica of *Sant'Antonio*, erected to hold the mortal remains of the Saint, who died at nearby Arcella in 1231. Romanesque-Gothic in form, and dominated by six domes and slender spires, it has an interior rich in bronzes, marbles, paintings, tribunes and monuments, produced by illustrious masters such as the artist Andrea Mantegna (1431-1506), and the architects and sculptors Iacopo Tatti, called Sansovino (1486-1570), Andrea Briosco called Riccio (1470-1532), Michele Sanmicheli (1484-1559), Donato de' Bardi, called Donatello (1386-1466), and Camillo Boito (1836-1914). In front of Sant'Antonio stands the famous *Monumento Equestre*

di Erasmo da Narni called *Gattamelata*, carried out in 1453 by Donatello. The basilica of *Santa Giustina* (5th cent. A.D.) was completely rebuilt in 1516-1521, to designs by Andrea Briosco modified by Alessandro Leopardi (1465-1523). It is a huge building, with a rough facade and spectacular interior. Of the many works of art contained inside, the most precious one is the Martyrdom of St. Justina, painted in 1575 by Paolo Caliari, called Veronese. The pride of Padua is the Romanesque oratory, *Cappella degli Scrovegni*, built at the beginning of the 14th cent. for a certain Enrico degli Scrovegni, who entrusted the decoration to

Padua, Monument to Gattamelata.
Padua, Basilica di Sant'Antonio.

Giotto di Bondone (1267?-1337). Giotto divided the walls into about forty squares, in each of which is a fresco representing an episode from the Story of the Redemption. Above the altar are a Madonna and two Angels, outstanding sculptures by Giovanni Pisano. The *Chiesa degli Eremitani* was built in the late 13th and early 14th cent. in Romanesque-Gothic style. It was seriously damaged by bombing on 11 March 1944. The Cappella degli Ovetari was also destroyed, together with the famous frescoes by Andrea Mantegna, Ansuino da Forlì (lived in the 15th cent.) and Bono da Ferrara (active 1450-1461). The *Palazzo della Ragione* was built in the 13-14th cent. as the seat of administration of civil and criminal justice. It is a grand rhombus shaped building overlooking Piazza delle Erbe, one of the busiest parts of the town. Inside is a huge salon, with richly frescoed walls. The 16-17th cent. *Palazzo del Bo*, is the seat of the most ancient university in Italy, after Bologna. The large *Caffè Pedrocchi* was built in 1830 by the Venetian architect Giuseppe Jappelli (1783-1852). *Prato della Valle* or *Piazza Vittorio Emanuele* covers a huge area; a square of incomparable beauty, it is surrounded by elegant palaces and mansions, and shaded by trees in the middle. In Roman times it was used as a circus. In the *Museo Civico* is an Art Gallery, with 14-17th cent. paintings and sculptures, a lapidary collection, and an archeological and Risorgimento Museum. The *Battistero del Duomo* is dedicated to Santa Maria Assunta. It dates back to the 9th cent., and contains a series of frescoes which form the masterpiece of Giusto de' Menabuoi (c.1320-c.1387). Notice, also, the Romanesque-Gothic church of *Santa Maria dei Servi* (second half of the 14th cent.); the 13th cent. *Palazzo Municipale*, formerly *del Podestà;* the *Loggia della Gran Guardia* or *del Consiglio*, a stately Lombardesque building, erected at the turn of the 16th cent.; the *Palazzo del Capitanio*, built between 1599 and 1605; the

Palazzo Papafava, formerly *Trento* (1763), designed by Giovan Battista Novello (1715-1799); the *Castello*, built around a defence tower called Torlonga, erected in 899 A.D.; *Santa Sofia*, the oldest church in Padua, founded in the 8th cent. on the site of a temple to Apollo, rebuilt in the 11th cent., and altered in later periods; the church of *Santa Maria*, formerly called *in Vanzo*, designed by Domenico Campolongo (lived in the 15th cent.); the church of *Santa Lucia* or *dell'Adorazione Perpetua*, rebuilt in 1740 to a design by Sante Benato (lived in the 18th cent.), with a painting of St. Luke by Giovan Battista Tiepolo (1696-1770); the *Scuola del Carmine* (1377) designed by Guglielmo del Sale; and remains of the *Bastione della Gatta*, a ponderous piece of Renaissance defence work. Walk to the *Santuario di Sant'Antonio dell'Arcella*, where St. Anthony died, on 13 June 1231.

* **PADULA** (Salerno). On the west side of the Vallo di Diano. The *Certosa di San Lorenzo* is a huge and impressive building. It was begun in 1306 and only finished in the early 19th cent. Among the various styles, Baroque dominates. The facade (1718) is decidedly Baroque, and decorated with statues in niches of Saints Bruno, Lawrence, Peter and Paul. The Church was partly built in the second half of the 14th cent. and contains two fine choirs: the Laymen's, carved in 1507 by Giovanni Gallo, and the Priests', with fine inlaid stalls, carved in the early 16th cent., and elaborated in later periods. The Hall of the Chapter-house contains 17th cent. frescoes representing Miracles of Christ. On the Library ceiling are paintings representing the Allegory of Aurora, the Last Judgement, and Allegory of Wisdom by Giovanni Olivieri (lived in the 18th cent.); the large rectangular Cloister covers an area of 15,000 sq. m. and has two orders of porticoes dating from the late 17th cent.; in the centre of the Procurators' Cloister is an important 17th cent. fountain; in the

Padua, Basilica di Sant'Antonio. Donatello, Miracle of St. Anthony.

224

Archeological Museum of Western Lucania is material excavated in the Vallo di Diano, such as cinerary urns of the early Iron age and grave goods.

** **PAESTUM** (Salerno). One of the most important archeological centres in Italy, on the south-eastern coast of the bay of Salerno, anciently known as Sinus Paestanus. The area was inhabited in very ancient times, as it is proved by remains of a neolithic-age necropolis excavated in the Gaudo district. In the 7th cent. B.C. it was a Greek colony, and in 273 B.C. subjugated by the Romans, who enriched it with some magnificent buildings. The ruins were discovered by chance around 1750, during construction work on a road which was ordered by the Bourbons, and is still in use. The *Basilica* is the most ancient temple, probably dating from the 6th cent. B.C. It is a vast peripteral enneastyle, surrounded by a portico which fortunately still has all its original Doric columns intact. In front of the Temple are the sacrificial altar, in fairly good condition, and well (bothros). The *Temple of Neptune*, the best-preserved temple in Paestum, was erected towards the middle of the 5th cent. B.C. It is a most impressive feat of architecture, and perfectly proportioned. In its votive cabinets, material has been found, thanks to which it has been possible to establish that it was consecrated to Hera Argiva, the goddess of motherhood and fertility. The *Forum* is a rectangular space 150 m by 57 on the site of the Greek Agorà. The *Tempio Italico*, erected in the 1st cent. B.C., presumably corresponds to the Capitolium, consecrated to Jove, Juno and Minerva. The *Temple of Ceres*, actually consecrated to Athena, as small clay statues and heads of the goddess, excavated in the area, prove, is a large Doric construction of the 4th cent. B.C. The *Via Sacra* can also be identified. Religious processions used to follow it, starting from the Gateway of Justice. The *Sacello Sotterraneo*, unearthed in 1954, has an interior decorated with white stuccowork. It

was here that five iron spears were found, wrapped in a woolen blanket, oil jars, bronze amphoras, and other material of great archeological importance. The ruined Sanctuary of Hera Argiva, discovered shortly before the outbreak of the Second World War, is very ancient indeed, as it certainly existed in the 7th cent. B.C. A great number of ex-voto have been found there, providing evidence of a violent battle which took place during the Italiot rebellion against the Lucani; it was despoiled by thieves in the 1st cent. B.C. and damaged in the eruption of Vesuvius in 79 A.D. Although its existence had been suspected by scholars for centuries, it was only proved between 1934 and 1940, by the archeologists Paola Zancani Montuoro and Umberto Zanotti Bianco. It is interesting to retrace the ancient walls (*Giro delle Mura*), which encircled the whole city (4,750 m in circumference). The enormous amount of archeological material found in the area, together with that found in the nearby necropoles, is well arranged in the *Paestum Museum*.

* **PAGANICA** (L'Aquila). In Roman times there were eighteen villas in this area; in the most important one, called the Paganico, possibly after a temple dedicated to Jupiter Paganicus, the survivors of a plague gathered together and formed the present Paganica, for a long time the feudal town of the Dukes of Costanza. The 17th cent. *Parrocchiale* is dedicated to the Assunta. It has a travertine facade and contains two wooden statues of the Madonna and Child, examples of 16th cent. Abruzzi art. Walk to the church of *San Giustino*, built in the 9th cent. and rebuilt in the 13th cent., with a basilican interior.

* **PALAZZO SAN GERVASIO** (Potenza). Interesting village of medieval origin. The *Pinacoteca d'Errico* contains three hundred paintings, including a lively Landscape by Salvatore Rosa (1615-1673), Wild Game, possibly by Andrea Belvedere (1642-1732), Guitar Player and Peasant, probably by Giuseppe Bonito (1707-1789), a Holy Family by Massimo Stanzione (1585-1656), a large Still Life by Abramo Breughel, called Napolitano (lived in the 17th cent.), another Landscape, possibly by Luca Giordano (1632-1705), and some fairly good 17th cent. paintings by the Flemish school.

* **PALAZZOLO ACREIDE** (Syracuse). Attractively situated in the Iblei mountains, between deep and picturesque valleys. The first stone of the church of *San Sebastiano* was laid in 1609; like other buildings of its kind in Sicily it stands at the top of a large flight of steps, and has a lively facade. The interior contains a painting of St. Rita, by Pietro Novelli (1603-1647). In the church of the *Immacolata*, with a convex Baroque facade, is a beautiful statue of the Madonna and Child, by

Paestum, Temple of Poseidon.

Francesco Laurana (recorded 1458-1500). Notice the 18th cent. *Palazzo Iudica, Palazzo Pizzo-Guglielmino*, with a fine portal, and church of *San Paolo*, with a Baroque facade in three orders, enlivened by statues and freizes. The *Antichità di Akrai*, on the high Acremonte plateau, surrounded by mountains, consist mainly of a simple Greek Theatre, two latomies (stone quarries) called Intagliata and Intagliatella, and the so-called Ferali Temples (a quarry cut in the rock and, above all, the famous Santoni crude but dynamic engravings, believed to date from the 3rd cent. B.C., and relating to the worship of the goddess Cybele, who is represented in various postures). There are numerous necropoles nearby, including the interesting one of Pantalica.

* **PALAZZOLO SULL'OGLIO** (Brescia). Situated on the banks of the river Oglio, with historic monuments and flourishing industries. The *Parrocchiale* was designed by Giorgio Massari (c. 1686-1766). It contains a polyptych of the Madonna and Saints by Vincenzo Civerchio (c. 1470-1544), a Last Supper by Pompeo Girolamo Batoni (1708-1787), and a painting by Giovanni Maria Morlaiter (1699-1781). In the church of *San Giovanni Evangelista* (rebuilt in the 18th cent.) is a painting by Andrea Celesti (1637-1712). The town is dominated by the cylindrical *Torre del Popolo*, a hundred metres high.

*** **PALERMO.** Capital of Sicily, situated on the northern coast. The Norman *Chiesa della Martorana* or Santa Maria dell'Ammiraglio dates from 1143, but was partially altered in the 16-17th cent. It has a four-storey bell-tower with mullions (belonging to the original building), communicating with the portico, on the front of which two mosaics can be seen: King Roger crowned by Christ and George of Antioch at the feet of the Virgin. The interior, originally of a square geometric shape, has Byzantine-style mosaics (1100) depicting various subjects (the Pantocrator, Archangels,

Prophets, Evangelists, Christ's Nativity, and Death of the Virgin). In place of the apse, which was destroyed in the 17th cent., there is a Baroque chapel with pictures by Antonino Grano (recorded 1683-1718) and, above a tabernacle, a picture by Vincenzo degli Azani (recorded 1519-1557), depicting the Annunciation. The church of *San Cataldo*, also Norman (c. 1160) but later restored to keep its original appearance, has three small semicircular domes, and a completely unadorned interior, with mosaic floor. The *Cattedrale* was started in the 12th cent., but is actually a mixture of styles owing to the various phases in its construction, as well as the many alterations it underwent in the 14-16th cent., and again in the late 18th and early 19th cent. The 14-15th cent. facade, with arches and a Gothic portal, is flanked by two towers and connected to the campanile. On the left is the Loggia dell'Incoronata (12th cent.), and the interior, modified to the plan of Ferdinando Fuga (1699-1781) in neo-Classical style, contains the imperial and royal tombs; a splendid silver urn (17th cent.) with the relics of Santa Rosalia; a 15th cent. wooden Crucifix; a carved-wood Gothic-Catalan choir; a 16th cent. holy-water stoup; a Bishop's throne and a Paschal candelabra (1100); statues of Apostles by Antonello Gagini (1478-1536); a Madonna and Child by Francesco Laurana (c. 1430-c. 1502), and a rich treasury; in the 12th cent. crypt are various sarcophagi. The sacristy leads into a chapel containing a Madonna by Antonello Gagini. The Bishops' Palace houses the *Museo Diocesano*, containing, above all, statues and pictures taken from destroyed and deconsecrated churches. The oriental-looking church of *San Giovanni degli Eremiti* consists of five, red balloon-shaped domes dating from the Norman period (1132). It has an aisleless interior; in the garden

Palermo, Museo Archeologico. Metope from Temple E of Selinunto.

Palazzolo Acreide, reliefs in the necropoles of Akrai.

is a 13th cent. cloister and the remains of an Arabic cistern. The 15th cent. church of *Santa Maria della Catena* includes Gothic, Catalan, and Renaissance elements. It has a three-arched portico below which are three doorways decorated with bas-reliefs by Antonello Gagini; the interior has a nave and two aisles, and contains 15th and 16th cent. statues, mainly by the Gagini school. The church of *San Francesco d'Assisi* was built during the second half of the 13th cent., but frequently altered in the course of time. The facade, restored by Giuseppe Patricolo (1834-1905) at the end of the last century, has a Gothic main doorway and two smaller ones in Renaissance style. Inside are Gothic and Renaissance chapels containing various kinds of marble sculptures by the Gagini school, and in the fourth chapel on the left there is an arch by Francesco Laurana and Pietro de Bontade (died before 1495); 16th cent. wooden stalls, and eight allegorical statues by Giacomo Serpotta (1652-1732). The *Chiesa del Gesù* or church of the Casa Professa, in Sicilian-Baroque style, with 17th cent. dome, was built between the second half of the 16th and second half of the 17th cent.; inside are stuccoes by Giacomo Serpotta, marble groups with Biblical characters, by Gioacchino Vitaliano (active in the second half of the 17th cent.) and, amongst other works of art, a marble sculpture of the Madonna and Child, by the Gagini school. The interior of the

oratory of the *Rosario di San Domenico* is skilfully decorated with stuccoes by Giacomo Serpotta; it contains a Madonna of the Rosary with St. Dominic and the Patron Saints of Palermo, by Sir Anthony van Dyck (1599-1641), and the Mysteries, by Pietro Novelli (1603-1647), Giacomo Lo Verde (active in the first half of the 17th cent.), Mattia Stomer (c. 1600-post 1650). The oratory of *Santa Zita* is reached through the church of St. Zita (second half of the 14th cent.). It has sculptures by Antonello Gagini and contains the 18th cent. Rosary Chapel, also stuccoes by Giacomo Serpotta; near the altar is a Madonna of the Rosary by Carlo Maratta (1625-1713). The oratory of *San Lorenzo* with stuccoes by Giacomo Serpotta, contains a Nativity of Jesus by Caravaggio (1573-1610). The *Palazzo Abatellis*, built in a mixture of Gothic-Catalan and Renaissance styles, was begun by Matteo Carnelivani (active in the second half of the 15th cent.) and completed by others in the course of five years. The front is flanked by two battlemented towers with triple-mullioned openings and a portal. The *Palazzo dei Normanni*, a 9th cent. Arab-style construction, was later enlarged by the Normans, in 1100, from which period the Tower of Santa Ninfa still survives, with the Treasure room, on the right of the 16-18th cent. facade. The 17th cent. courtyard gives access to the Norman *Cappella Palatina* (1132) with mosaic floor and artistic wooden

Palermo, Duomo.

ceiling, of the first half of the 12th cent. It contains the royal throne with mosaics, a mosaic pulpit and Paschal candelabrum (1100). The entire sanctuary is decorated with incredibly lovely Byzantine-style mosaics (12th cent.) with scenes from the Old and New Testaments, episodes from the lives of St. Paul and St. Peter, Christ the Pantocrator surrounded by Archangels, Prophets and Evangelists. Among the royal apartments the Hall of King Roger, with its mosaic decorations, is especially important. The *Palazzo Chiaromonte* was built for the Chiaromonte family in the 14th cent. The Great Hall has an artistic wooden ceiling painted with Biblical and Chivalrous scenes, by Simone da Corleone (recorded 1377-1380) and Darenu da Palermo, also recorded from 1377 to 1380. The *Orto Botanico*, founded in 1789, is of considerable importance, including, in its 25 acres, plants from all over the world. As regards the buildings, the central one, the Ginnasio, is by Leone Dufourny (1754-1818) and the side ones, that is the Calidarium and the Tepidarium, are both by Venanzio Marvuglia (1729-1814). The *Museo Archeologico*, housed in the former monastery of the Filippini, contains very important archeological material, such as sculptures from the Selinuntine temples unearthed during excavations in Selinuntis, and an Etruscan collection from Chiusi, with remains from the 7th – 1st cent. B.C. The *Galleria Nazionale della Sicilia*, housed in the above-mentioned Palazzo Abbatellis, contains some masterpieces, such as a fresco depicting the Triumph of Death, of the first half of the 15th cent., the Bust of Eleonora of Aragon, by Francesco Laurana; an Annunziata, and three Saints by Antonello da Messina (c. 1430-1479). Notice, finally, the late-16th cent. church of *Santa Caterina*, with a statue of St. Catherine, by Antonello Gagini; the early-17th cent. church of *San Giuseppe dei Teatini*, with some frescoes including a Crucifixion by fra' Umile da Petralia (1580-1639); the late-16th cent. *Chiesa dell'Olivella*, or di *Sant'Ignazio*, with a Baroque facade, containing paintings by Sebastiano Conca (1679-1764), on the right of which is the neo-Classical oratory of St. Philip Neri; the 16th cent. *Chiesa de La Gancia* or St. Mary of the Angels, with Gothic portals and, inside, sculptures by Antonello Gagini; the *Palazzo Zisa*, a rectangular, Arab-style building, begun during the reign of William I, and later completed by his son; and the *Cuba*, a building similar to the Zisa pavilion in the Norman park, which William II commissioned in 1180. The sanctuary of *Santa Rosalia*, on the slopes of Mount Pellegrino, consists of a grotto-chapel and a convent.

** **PALESTRINA** (Rome). Situated on the southern slope of Mount Ginestro, in the Prenestini chain, with a medieval centre. The *Tempio della Fortuna Primigenia* was one of the

Palermo, *San Cataldo.*
Palermo, *San Giovanni degli Eremitani.*

most important sanctuaries in ancient times, and was large enough to cover an area equal in size to the entire modern town. It was abandoned in the 4th cent., and Civitas Praenestina formed on its ruins. The Upper Sanctuary is a wide courtyard, divided into four by columns of which some traces are left. It gives access to the rectangular absidal hall, while at the opposite end is the Cave of Destiny, hollowed out of the rock, with fine mosaic paving, of the 1st cent. B.C. In the Upper Sanctuary are the Terrazza degli Emicicli, the Terrazza dei Fornici, and the Terrazza della Cortina. In the Barberini Palace, rebuilt towards the middle of the 17th cent., is the *Museo Archeologico Prenestino*, where a large collection of rare material, excavated in the Praenestis area, is arranged. Room I contains elements from the Temple of Fortune; Room II, busts and cippi from the necropolis,

of the 4th and 3rd cent. B.C.; Room III, a tall, mutilated statue of Fortune (2nd cent. B.C.); Rooms IV, V and VI, altars, statues and other material from the 2nd cent. B.C. to the 1st cent. A.D.; Room VII, terracottas from the 6th to the 2nd cent. B.C.; Rooms VIII and IX, bronze mirrors, boxes and toilet items, grave goods; in Room X, mosaic floors and a model of the Temple of Fortuna Primigenia; lastly, in Rooms XI and XII, the famous mosaic depicting the Nile in Flood (1st cent. B.C.). The *Duomo* was rebuilt in the 12th cent. It still retains parts of the original construction and its remarkable belltower.

* **PALLANZA** (Town of Verbania, province of Novara). World-famous health-resort, pleasantly situated on the northern shore of the Borromeo bay, facing Stresa. On the first floor

Palestrina, Temple of Fortune Primigenia, terrace of the hemicycles.

of the 18th cent. *Palazzo Dugnani* is the history, art and natural science Museum. There are many pleasant walks and excursions to be made in the surrounding area; a visit to the Isola Madre, with its famous *Botanical Garden*, is especially worthwhile. In the neighbourhood is the church known as the *Madonna di Campagna*, erected in 1519 on the site of a Romanesque building, which still preserves a small single-lighted and mullioned bell-tower. The octagonal tiburium, crossed by an elegant gallery, is the most interesting architectural element.

* **PALMANOVA** (Udine). In the lower Friuli area. In 1593 Venice, having been obliged to give up Gradisca after the war of the Cambrai League, built a fortified polygonal-plan city here, in the shape of a star, corresponding to present-day Palmanova, a much-admired feat of military engineering. The polygon has nine points, each with a rampart. The ramparts were called Grimani, Savorgann, Foscarini, Villachiara, Contarini, Gazzoni, Monte, Donato and Barbaro. The *Duomo* is a simple building, begun in 1615 to designs by Baldassarre Longhena (1598-1692), and Vincenzo Scamozzi (1553-1616). The interior contains a St. Barnabas and other Saints by Alessandro Varotari, called Padovanino (1588-1648). *Porta Udine, Ci-*

vidale, and *Aquileia* are military constructions, apparently designed by Vincenzo Scamozzi.

* **PALMI** (Reggio Calabria). On a terrace jutting out towards the sea. The church of the *Immacolata* contains bas-reliefs and statues of the Gagini school (16th cent.). The Town Hall houses a small *Museum*, consisting of archeological, ethnographical, and folklore sections. Trip to the *Monte Sant'Elia*, which commands a fine view over the entire southwestern portion of Calabria; on the summit is a sacred shrine, Byzantine in origin.

* **PALO DEL COLLE** (Bari). One of the leading agricultural centres in the province of Bari, it is the result of the union of a medieval centre, called Terra di Palo, and a newer part, called Borgo, lying in the plain. It boasts a 12th cent. *Cattedrale* dedicated to Santa Maria della Porta, Romanesque in style, and damaged in the second half of the 16th cent. It is one of the most interesting buildings in the region; the facade, divided into three by pilaster-strips, is decorated with a beautiful rose-window with archivolt supported by corbels on caryatids. The slender, elegant campanile is Romanesque, and the interior contains interesting imitation matronei (women's galleries) and an attractive crypt supported by columns.

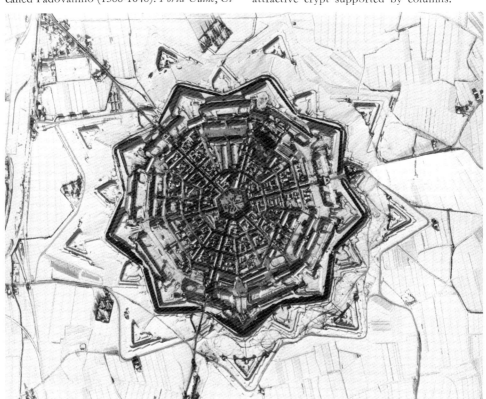

Palmanova, aerial view of the city.

Parma, Duomo. Two Saints in a section of the high altar.

Parma, Galleria Nazionale. Correggio, The Madonna of St. Jerome, detail.

Parma, Galleria Nazionale. Parmigianino, Portrait of a Young Woman.

Parma, Palazzo del Giardino. Carlo Cicognani, Bacchus and Ariadne.

Perugia, Galleria Nazionale dell'Umbria. Arnolfo di Cambio, Young Woman at the Well, detail. Perugia, San Bernardino.

Perugia, Galleria Nazionale dell'Umbria. Giovanni Boccati, Madonna of the Pergola, detail. Pesaro, Museo Civico. The Betrothed at Table, ceramic group.

* **PAOLA** (Cosenza). On the extreme edge of the coastal chain of Calabria. The church of *San Giacomo* was begun in the second half of the 15th cent. but rebuilt in later periods. It contains a panel of the Madonna delle Grazie, probably by Domenico Beccafumi (c. 1486-1551). The sanctuary of *San Francesco* is a group of buildings varying in style from the 15th cent. onwards, situated in a gorge of the Isca. The Monastery, with 15-16th cent. cloister, the so-called "area of miracles" (zona dei prodigi) and the Devil's Bridge, over the Isca, are all worth visiting.

*** **PARMA.** On the Via Emilia, where the Baganza and Parma streams meet. The *Palazzo del Municipio*, begun in 1627 to a design by Giovanni Battista Magnani (1571-1653), is a two-storeyed brick building. The buildings around the *Piazza del Duomo* form an exceptionally harmonious group. The *Duomo*, dedicated to the Assunta, and already in existence towards the middle of the 11th cent., is Romanesque in style. It has a majestic facade crossed by three orders of loggias, and is flanked by a late-13th cent. Gothic bell-tower. Inside are many works of art, including a Deposition in relief work by the sculptor Benedetto Antelami (recorded 1178-1230), and Assumption of the Virgin, a masterpiece by Antonio Allegri, called Correggio (1489-1534). The *Battistero* is a most significant monument denoting the transition from Romanesque to Gothic. Begun in 1196, it was completed in 1260. It is built on an octagonal plan, in red Verona marble and enriched with plastic decoration inspired by moral and religious facts and doctrines, almost all by Benedetto Antelami. The 10th cent. church of *San Giovanni Evangelista*, rebuilt at the turn of the 16th cent., has a sumptuous Baroque facade in its present state. The interior is rich in works of art, especially the famous frescoes in the dome, which were carried out between 1520 and 1523 by Correggio. The *Storica Farmacia di San Giovanni Evangelista* was founded by the Benedictines in the 9th or 10th cent. It has three Halls called del Fuoco, dei Mortai, and delle Sirene, adorned with 16th cent. frescoes and ornaments of the same period. The *Palazzo della Pilotta* is so called after the game of the "pelota" which used to be played in one of the courtyards. It is a grandiose building, begun in 1583 to a design by Giovanni Boscoli (1524-1589), but left unfinished. It houses the Museo Nazionale d'Antichità, the Biblioteca Palatina, with the Museo Bodoniano, and the Galleria Nazionale, which is remarkable for the quantity and quality of the works exhibited, including paintings by Giovan Battista Cima da Conegliano (c. 1459-1518), Sebastiano del Piombo (c. 1485-1547), Correggio, Hans Holbein the Younger (c. 1497-1543), and Francesco Mazzola, called Parmigianino (1503-1540). The *Teatro Farnese* was built in 1618, to a design by Giovanni Battista Aleotti, called Argenta (1546-1636), who took his inspiration from the Palladian Teatro Olimpico in

Parma, Duomo and Baptistery.

233

Vicenza. *Camera del Correggio* or *di San Paolo*: Correggio, invited to decorate it in 1518, gave the first great demonstration of his art here, producing one of his most valued masterpieces. The *Museo Civico Glauco Lombardi* contains collections of pictures, sculptures, drawings, jewels, and many articles from the 18th and 19th cent. The church of the *Madonna della Steccata* was designed by Bernardino and Giovanni Francesco Zaccagni, who built it in Bramante style, between 1521 and 1539. Inside are many works of art, including frescoes by Francesco Mazzola, called Parmigianino. The church of the *Santissima Annunziata* was begun in 1566, after a design by Giovanni Battista Fornovo (1521-1575). Inside, behind the high altar, is a Madonna and Child enthroned with Saints, by Francesco Zaganelli, called Cotignola (c. 1470-1531). The *Palazzo dell'Università* is a grandiose 16th cent. building, designed by Galeazzo Alessi (1512-1572), and Jacopo Barozzi, called Vignola (1507-1573). The *Pinacoteca Giuseppe Stuard*, has the most important private collection in the city. The *Museo d'Arte Cinese*, one of the most interesting of its kind in Europe, contains material from the 9th cent. B.C. to the 13th cent. A.D. The *Cittadella*, a majestic pentagonal building, was begun in 1591 by Alessandro Farnese. The *Palazzo del Giardino* contains some interesting works of art. The church of *Santo Sepolcro*, rebuilt in 1257 and altered in 1460, contains works of art including pictures by Alessandro Bernabei (1580-1630), and Pier Antonio Bernabei (1565-c. 1630). The church of *Sant'Antonio Abate*, designed by Ferdinando Bibiena (1657-1743) contains pictures by Giambettino Cignaroli (1706-1770) and Giuseppe Peroni (1710-1776).

* PASSIGNANO SUL TRASIMENO (Perugia). Small centre situated on the northern shore of Lake Trasimeno, with remains of medieval walls. The late-15th cent. church of *San Bernardino* contains a 17th cent. wooden statue of the Assunta and a Madonna on a small panel (second half of the 16th cent.). On the Isola Maggiore stands the church of *San Michele Arcangelo*, with 15th and 16th cent. frescoes, and a panel of the Crucifixion by Bartolomeo Caporali (c. 1420-1505). Excursion to Castel Rigone, where the ruins of the 13th cent. *Castello* can be admired. There is also the Renaissance church of the *Madonna dei Miracoli* (1494), with a portal by Domenico Bertini (recorded 1486-1518); inside is a 16th cent. statue of St. Anthony Abbot and a Madonna of the Rosary by Bernardo di Girolamo Rosselli (recorded 1532-1569).

* PATERNÒ (Catania). Overlooked by a great rock on which stand a church and the Norman Castle. The church of the *Abbadia della Santissima Annunziata*, contains a painting of St. Benedict by Giacinto Platania (1647-1720). The *Castello* was built in 1073 for Roger the Norman, but altered in the 14th cent. It has an enormous solid exterior and well-preserved interior, with vast armoury. From the top there is a fine view of Etna and the plain of Catania. The church of *Santa Maria della Valle di Giosafat* or *della Gancia*, dating back originally to the second half of the 11th cent., is entered through a fine 14th cent. Gothic portal.

Parma, Galleria Nazionale. Simone Lamberti, St. Peter the Martyr, detail of the polyptych.

Paternò, Castle.

* **PATTI** (Messina). One of the most attractive little towns on the northern coast of Sicily, situated on a hill overlooking a lovely beach. *Scavi di Tindari:* Tyndaris was one of the last Greek colonies in Sicily, founded in 396 B.C. by Diogenes I. The *Teatro Greco*, of the 3rd or 2nd cent. B.C., but altered in Roman times, has a diameter of 63 metres. All that is left is the auditorium facing the sea, divided into eleven wedge-shaped sections with twenty-eight steps. The *Basilica*, erected in late-Imperial times, consisted of three storeys, of which only the bottom one is still in a fairly good condition. The 3rd cent. B.C. *Edificio termale*, has a vast porticoed courtyard and two simple rooms, possibly changing-rooms, with lovely mosaic floors. The *Museo* contains documents concerning Tyndaris, two winged Nikai, possibly acroteria of a 4th or 3rd cent. B.C. temple, a gigantic Head of Augustus, ceramics, terracottas, cinerary urns, and Hellenistic and Roman items. The 3rd cent. B.C. *Mura di Tyndaris* completely encircled the hill on which the ancient city stood. The most important stretch, in an excellent state of preservation, was unearthed during recent excavations, and is quite awe-inspiring in its magnitude.

* **PATÙ** (Lecce). Situated at the foot of the Serra del Vareto in an area rich in olive groves. The remains of the 16th cent. *Castello* – four large towers and the walls – give proof of the defences set up by the inhabitants against enemy attacks from the sea. In front of the 12th cent. church of *San Giovanni* stands the megalithic construction known as the *Centopietre*. This interesting monument has a controversial origin: some consider it Messapian, others Medieval; the rectangular-shaped little church has a double-sloped roof, and the interior, consisting of two dissimilar aisles, contains traces of Byzantine frescoes.

*** **PAVIA.** On the left bank of the river Ticino, an agricultural, commercial and industrial city, strongly associated with the period when it was the capital of the Longobards, and rich in Romanesque churches. The *Duomo*, built on the remains of two Romanesque cathedrals, was begun in 1488, and work continued throughout the 16th cent., with the collaboration of famous architects, including Leonardo da Vinci himself (1452-1519). It is an imposing monument, built on a central plan, and contains works of art of various periods. The 12th cent. Romanesque church of *San Teodoro* contains artistic works, including frescoes depicting Stories of St. Agnes by an unknown artist, active at the beginning of the 16th cent. The basilica of *San Michele*, originally Longobard, but rebuilt in Romanesque style in the 12th cent., has a gabled facade and contains numerous works of art; a Crucifix worked in embossed silver-leaf, possibly dating from the second half of the 10th cent., is especially worthy of attention. The *Università* is an impressive building. The main part dates back to the 14-15th cent. but it has been restructured several times in the course of time. The *Castello Visconteo* was built between 1360 and 1365 by Galeazzo II Visconti, and completed by his son, Giangaleazzo. It stands on a square plan with large towers at the corners and wall surfaces enlivened by Gothic mullions and crenellations. A portico and richly-decorated loggia open on to the vast courtyard. Inside are housed the Civic Museums: the Archeological Museum, Sculpture Museum, Risorgimento Museum, and the rich *Pinacoteca*. Among the many beautiful and precious paintings, notice particularly the Bottigella altarpiece by Vincenzo Foppa (c. 1427-c. 1516), Christ followed by the Carthusians, by Ambrogio da Fossano, called Bergognone (recorded 1481-1522), Madonna and Child by

Pavia, Visconti Castle.

Giovanni Bellini called Giambellino (c. 1430-1516); Portrait of a Man by Antonello da Messina (c. 1430-1479). The 12th cent. Longobard-style basilica of *San Pietro in Ciel d'Oro* has a gabled facade; above the high altar is the famous Tomb of St. Augustine, carried out in various periods by Lombard masters, partly influenced by the style of Giovanni di Balduccio da Pisa. The 11th cent. *Chiesa del Santo Sepolcro*, commonly known as the church of San Lanfranco, contains the famous Tomb of San Lanfranco by Giovanni Antonio Amadeo.

* **PECETTO TORINESE** (near Turin). An attractive village situated on a low hill. The parish church of *Santa Maria della Neve*, with brick facade, was designed by Bernardo Antonio Vittone (1705-1770). It is flanked by a medieval tower, believed to have been erected in 1106; inside there is an important painting by Vittorio Amedeo Rapous (c. 1728-c. 1800). The church of the *Confraternità dei Flagellati* was built between 1625 and 1736, by the architects Luigi Molinari d'Andorno and Ludovico Parrucchetti (lived in the 17-18th cent.). Inside are vestments and statues taken from the Hermitage (an impressive group of buildings erected at the beginning of the 17th cent. on the orders of Carlo Emanuele I, and destroyed by the French in 1797), a gilded-wood tabernacle on the high altar, designed by Francesco Tanadei (1770-1828), and carried out by Antonio Bosco (18th cent. engraver), a polychrome-wood statue of the Madonna and Child by

Pavia, San Michele, facade.

Stefano Maria Clemente (1719-1794), a painting of the Crucifixion by the school of Jacopo Robusti, called Tintoretto (1518-1594), and other works of art. The Romanesque church of *San Sebastiano* contains a fresco depicting the Nativity, by Jacobino Longo (died c. 1542), a Madonna and Child with Saints, by Gregorio Cartorio (lived in the 17th cent.), a Madonna of the Rosary Saints Cassiano, Dominic and Worshippers, by Cristoforo Alberti (lived in the 16-17th cent.). *Villa la Moglia*, situated on an attractive hillside, is a typical example of an 18th cent. Piedmontese villa; it was erected in 1760 to a design by Count Nicolis di Robilant. Inside is the remarkable Sala degli Angeli.

* **PEGLI** (Genoa). Industrial town and popular seaside resort. The *Villa Durazzo Pallavicini*, designed and carried out between 1837 and 1846 by Michele Canzio, has a famous park spread over an area of 120,000 sq m, with many specimens of tropical vegetation, statues, summer-houses and fountains. The *Museo Civico di Archeologia Ligure* contains a large amount of archeological material. *Villa Doria* (16th cent.) is said to have been erected for the illustrious Admiral Andrea Doria (1466-1560) to whom it most certainly belonged. The *Civico Museo Navale* provides valuable insight into the history of the Ligurian and Italian Navies and, to a lesser extent, to the history of European marine activity in general. Of particular interest, in the so-called Hall of the Maps, are the globe and map of the heavens, produced towards the end of the 17th cent. by Vincenzo Coronelli. On the walls are well-known pictures by Genoese and Flemish artists, all concerning the sea.

* **PENNE** (Pescara). Situated on two hills, between the valleys of the rivers Fino and Tavo. The whole town, including the streets, is built in brick, and has a large number of medieval remains. The ancient *Cattedrale*, dedicated to Santa Maria degli Angeli or San Massimo the martyr, was begun before 1000 A.D., but greatly altered in later periods. Inside can be seen an attractive baptismal font with bronze bas-relief, dated 1665, and the silver statue of San Massimo, by a certain San Martino da Napoli. Walk to the church of *Santa Maria in Colleromano*, which was built in the first half of the 14th cent. and was once a powerful abbey. The basilican interior contains some important pictures.

* **PERETOLA** (near Florence). The church of *Santa Maria*, originally Romanesque but altered in the 15th cent., contains a marble stoup by Francesco di Simone Ferrucci (1437-1493), a fresco depicting Saints James, Anthony Abbot and Giles, probably by Giusto d'Andrea Manzini (1440-1496), and a tabernacle by Luca Della Robbia (1400-1482). From Peretola one can

reach *Campi Bisenzio*, on the banks of the Bisenzio. The castle dates back to the times of Charlemagne. The parish church of *Santo Stefano*, built in 936 but enlarged in later centuries, contains fine holy-water stoups, a 16th cent. wooden Crucifix, and other works of art.

* **PERGOLA** (Pesaro). At the confluence of the Cinisco and Cesano, with medieval streets and houses. The *Duomo*, erected towards the middle of the 13th cent., contains some fairly valuable works of art, including the 15th cent. Gothic reliquiary of San Secondo. The 13th cent. Gothic church of *San Francesco*, with asymmetrical exterior, contains some works of art, the most important being a painting of the Flight into Egypt, probably by Claudio Ridolfi (c. 1570-1644).

* **PERTOSA** (Salerno). Situated on a slight elevation, on the site of a Roman settlement. In the limestone expanse of Monte Alburno is the *Grotta di Pertosa* or *dell'Angelo* or *San Michele* (as it is dedicated to St. Michael), one of the finest caves in southern Italy. Stakes and neolithic objects discovered there in 1897 prove that this vast cave was inhabited from the bronze age onwards; it was known and used by the Greeks and Romans, and in the 11th cent. A.D. it was transformed into a Christian sanctuary. One should visit the hall and chamber where the spring gushes out, the main cavity, the bats' chamber, the chamber of wonders, and the hall of the Madonna, with a statue of the Virgin surrounded by candle-like stalagmites and stalactites, the throne room, the great hall, the room of the sponges and of the virgins, all with clearly formed concretions.

*** **PERUGIA**. Important artistic, industrial and commercial centre, situated on a rugged hill, overlooking the Tiber valley, with exceptionally beautiful views. From the 3rd to the 2nd cent. B.C., it was surrounded by stout walls, with fine gateways; and vast burial grounds were created around it. The *Fontana Maggiore* or di Piazza, is one of the most elegant fountains in Italy. It was designed by Giovanni Pisano (c. 1248-post 1314) and Nicola Pisano (c. 1220-1278/84), who decorated it with valuable sculptures. Altered and damaged in later centuries (in 1348 it was almost completely rebuilt after being destroyed by an earthquake), it was repaired and restored to its former beauty in 1948-49. Notice the fine bas-reliefs on the lower basin and delicate statuettes on the upper one. The Gothic *Cattedrale di San Lorenzo*, begun in 1445 and completed in 1490, has an unfinished facade, with Baroque portal, carried out by Pietro Carattoli (1703-post 1760). On the left of one entrance is the bronze statue of Pope Julius III, by Vincenzo Danti (1530-1576). The portal on the left side is by Galeazzo Alessi (1512-1572).

The interior, 68 m long, contains many works of art, including a picture of the Madonna delle Grazie, probably by Giannicola di Paolo (c. 1460-c. 1544); the Chapel of San Bernardino, with a Deposition, by Baroccio (1535-1612); the Chapel of the Crucifixion; the Altar of the Gonfalone, with standard depicting Mary imploring Jesus to put an end to the Plague, by Berto di Giovanni (recorded 1497-1529); the Chapel of Sant'Anello, where the legendary wedding ring of Christ's mother is preserved; a wooden choir with decorative motifs by Giuliano da Maiano (1432-1490) and Domenico del Tasso (1440-1508); a Bishop's throne designed by Rocco di Tommaso da Vicenza (recorded 1494-1526) and carried out by Ciancio di Pierfrancesco (recorded 1501-1527); inlaid cabinets by Mariotto di Paolo Sensi, called Terzuolo (recorded 1492-1497), and some fragments of a Pietà Altarpiece. The *Palazzo Comunale* or dei Priori, known in the middle ages as the People's New Palace, is a powerful construction begun in 1293 to a design by Giacomo di Servadio (recorded at the end of the 13th cent.) and Giovanello di Benvenuto (also recorded at the end of the 13th cent.). The most characteristic side of the building is the one facing the square, as it is the oldest. On the first floor is the Notaries' Hall, one time People's Hall, with frescoes by the school of Pietro Cavallini (lived in the 13-14th cent.), depicting legends alternated with Biblical episodes. The *Galleria Nazionale dell'Umbria* is arranged on the third floor of the palace; it contains the richest collection of Umbrian painting in existence in Italy, and shows the development of the school

Perugia, Hypogea of the Volumni. Relief of Aule Velimnas on cinerary urn.

over the centuries. Among the hundreds of works on display in the 24 rooms, the most important ones from an artistic point of view include: Madonna and Angels by Duccio di Buoninsegna (recorded 1278-1319); Madonna and Child, Angels and Saints, by Beato Angelico (1387-1455); Madonna and Child with Saints, by Pietro della Francesca (1415/20-1492); Pietà and Adoration of the Magi by Pietro Vannucci, called Perugino (1445/50-1523); Flagellation, a bronze moulding by Francesco di Giorgio Martini (1439-1502); the niche of St. Bernardino of Siena, together with Standard, by Benedetto Bonfigli (c. 1420-1496) and the Priors' Chapel, frescoed by Bonfigli. The *Sala del Collegio della Mercanzia* was donated by the Commune to the Merchants in 1390, and decorated in the first half of the 15th cent. in late-Gothic style. Notice the small carved figures in bas-relief, depicting Fortitude, Justice, Prudence and Temperance. The *Collegio del Cambio*, seat of the money-changers, was built between 1452 and 1457 by Bartolomeo da Mattiolo (recorded 1447-1473) and by Lodovico di Antonibo (active 1452-1474). The Audience Hall in the Exchange contains some

famous frescoes by Perugino and a few of his disciples, including the Self-portrait, Fortitude, Prophets and Sibyls, and God the Father. There is also a long carved bench by Domenico del Tasso (1440-1508) and a terracotta Justice, possibly by Benedetto da Maiano (1442-1479). The *Palazzo del Capitano del Popolo* is an elegant Renaissance building designed by Gasparino di Antonio (recorded 1467-1486) and Leone di Matteo (recorded 1473-1481). It has a graceful doorway, with two Griffins. The church of *San Severo*, built in 1007, supposedly on the site of a pagan temple dedicated to the Sun, was restored in the 18th cent. and preserves a fresco by Raphael (1483-1520). The church of *San Bernardino* was built between 1457 and 1461 by Agostino di Duccio (1418-c. 1481); the sober interior, divided into three bays, contains some remarkable works of art. The church of *Sant'Angelo*, an important Early-Christian building, was erected at the beginning of the 6th cent. Inside are Roman Corinthian columns and frescoes. The church of *Santa Maria di Monteluce* or *della Madonna di Monteluce*, was erected in the 13th cent. and rebuilt after a fire in the first half of the 14th.

Perugia, Fontana Maggiore.

The interior contains a marble tabernacle by Francesco di Simone Ferrucci, and the walls were decorated in 1607 by Giovanni Maria Visconti (recorded 1565-1610). The *Arco etrusco*, or Augustan Arch, is a sturdy construction of the 2nd or 1st cent. B.C., flanked by two large trapezoidal towers. The Etruscan-age *Porta Marzia* probably dates back to the 2nd or 1st cent. B.C. The *Via Bagliona* branches off within the precincts of the *Rocca Paolina*, built in the first half of the 16th cent. for Pope Paul III, who commissioned Antonio da Sangallo the Younger (1483-1546) to design it. The basilica of *San Domenico*, begun in Gothic style in 1305, has an impressive unadorned facade, flanked by a massive bell-tower by Gasparino di Antonio (recorded 1467-1486). Inside is the funerary monument of Benedict XI, carried out by followers of Arnolfo di Cambio (c. 1245-1302) or Lorenzo Maitani (?-1330), and the altar, with an architectural decoration depicting the Madonna and Angels, Annunciation, and Saints, by Agostino di Duccio (1418-c. 1481). The *Museo Archeologico Nazionale dell'Umbria* has pre-historic and Etrusco-Roman sections, and one of the most important and best-arranged State Archives in Italy. The basilica of *San Pietro*, built towards the end of the 10th cent. and preceded by a 17th cent. porticoed courtyard, has an octagonal bell-tower (second half of the 15th cent.) with Gothic mullions, designed by Bernardo

Perugia, Palazzo dei Priori.
Perugia, Sant'Angelo, part of the interior.

239

Rossellino (1409-1464) and carried out by Giovanni di Betto (lived in the 15th cent.) and Puccio di Paolo (active in the second half of the 15th cent.). Inside are a Pietà and four small pictures by Perugino, depicting Saints Constance, Peter the Abbot, Sant'Ercolano and San Placido; eleven paintings by Antonio Vassilacchi called Aliense (1556-1629); carved and inlaid wooden stalls by Bernardino di Luca Antonibi (recorded 1516-1526) and Stefano Zambelli (active in the first half of the 16th cent.); four pieces of marquetry by Damiano Zambelli (1490-1549); a varnished terracotta washbasin by Benedetto Buglioni (1461-1521), and a marble tabernacle, possibly by Mino da Fiesole (1429-1484). The *Porta San Pietro* or Porta Romana, consists of two gateways, the inner one dating from the 14th cent., and the outer one Renaissance, with two unfinished niches, by Agostino di Duccio (1418-c. 1481). In the neighbourhood of Perugia is the *Ipogeo dei Volumni*, an exceptionally fine example of an Etruscan noble's tomb, discovered by chance in 1840. The interior has figured scenes depicting-mythological subjects, and seven stucco-covered funerary urns, one in marble and six in travertine.

** **PESARO.** Crossed by the river Foglia, it has a medieval centre, modern districts and bathing resort. It is famous for its works of art and also for its majolica industry. The most important building is the *Palazzo Ducale* or *del Governo*, built for Alessandro Sforza in the second half of the 15th cent., with a graceful exterior and solemn interior. Special attention should be paid to the so-called courtyard of honour, and especially to the spacious Metaurus Hall. The 13th cent. Gothic church of *San Domenico*, no longer used as a place of worship, attracts visitors especially for its magnificent pink and white doorway, designed and erected in 1395 following the canons of the Dalle Masegne. The *Musei Civici* contain a rich picture gallery, the pride of which is the so-called altarpiece of Pesaro, a masterpiece by Giovanni Bellini (c. 1430-1516), and the Ceramics Museum. The *Cattedrale* was built at the turn of the 14th cent. on the remains of a Roman basilica. It has a well-defined Gothic portal and, inside, some fairly good works of art including a wonderful ivory ciborium (6th cent.). *Rocca Costanza*, a sturdy 15th cent. military construction, was ordered by Costanzo Sforza, and carried out by Luciano Laurana (c. 1420-1479). The Gothic portal (carried out between 1356 and 1378) of the church of *San Francesco* is worth noticing, as is another Gothic portal, built in 1413 in Istria stone, for the church of *Sant'Agostino*. *San Giovanni Battista*, on the Via Passeri, one of the most attractive and least damaged churches in old Pesaro, was designed by Girolamo Genga (c. 1476-1551) and completed by his son, Bartolomeo Genga (1516-1559). The facade is enriched with an elegant Serlian triple-lighted window. Inside is an important wooden Crucifix, carved in 1636 by Innocenzo da Pe-

Pesaro, Ducal Palace.

tralia. The *Ex Chiesa della Maddalena*, by Luigi Vanvitelli (1700-1773), has a fine concave facade and elegant interior, in the form of a Greek cross. The Palazzo Almerici houses the *Museo* and the *Biblioteca Oliveriani*, with important displays of archeological remains, statues and fragments of statues especially of Roman origin, a famous bilingual inscription, in Etruscan and Latin, of exceptional glossological importance, a hundred thousand volumes (partly 16th cent.), 260 incunabula, parchments and the "Map of Pesaro", a famous nautical chart probably traced in 1505. The *Conservatorio Rossini* contains a bronze monument to Rossini by Carlo Marocchetti (1805-1867), a music library, a 19th cent. auditorium, and a Rossini "shrine" containing mementoes of the composer. In the surrounding area, at *Sassocorvaro*, is the 15th cent. Rocca, a masterpiece of military architecture, designed to reproduce the form of a ship, by Francesco di Giorgio Martini (1439-1502).

* **PESCARA.** Produced by the merging of the municipalities of Castellammare Adriatico and Pescara, on either side of the river Pescara. It is an active, lively town, the main commercial and industrial centre in the Abruzzi. The modern *Palazzo del Governo* is an impressive-looking building. Inside is the famous picture, La Figlia di Iorio, by Francesco Paolo Michetti (1851-1929). The *Tempio Nazionale della Conciliazione* was designed by Cesare Bazzani (1873-1939) and is dedicated to the canonized popes. Inside is a St. Francis, probably by Guercino (1591-1666) or his school, and a bronze reproduction of a Crucifix by Donatello (1386-1466).

* **PESCIA** (Pistoia). A small industrial and agricultural town divided into two by the Pe-

scia stream. The *Duomo* was rebuilt in the 17th cent. but has traces of the original Romanesque construction including the bell-tower (1306). It contains several works of art including the Mausoleum of Baldassarre Turini, by Raffaello da Montelupo (1505-1566). The late-13th cent. church of *San Francesco* has a facade rebuilt in the early 16th and modified in the first half of the 17th cent. It contains paintings by Bonaventura Berlinghieri (recorded 1235-1274) depicting St. Francis and six Stories of his life, and, in the Cardini Chapel by Andrea Cavalcanti (1412-1462), a 15th cent. wooden Crucifix, and Founders of the Chapel with Patron Saints, by Neri di Bicci (1419-c. 1491). The small church of *Sant'Antonio* (second half of the 14th cent.) contains frescoes by Bicci di Lorenzo (c. 1368-1452) depicting Stories of St. Anthony Abbot, and a 13th cent. group of wooden sculptures depicting the Deposition. The *Palazzo Comunale*, together with other buildings of various periods, faces the attrac-

Pesaro, Sant'Agostino. Choir, inlay.

Pescia, Town Hall.

241

tive Piazza Mazzini. One can walk to Uzzano, where there is the small church of *Santi Iacopo e Martino*, modified in the 14th cent., and restored at the beginning of the present one. Inside are two loggettas with 15th cent. frescoes including a Marriage of the Virgin, by Alessandro Gemignani, and a 14th cent. Crucifix.

* **PESCHIERA DEL GARDA** (Verona). Situated on the south-eastern tip of Lake Garda, where the river Mincio flows out of the lake. It was first a prehistoric settlement, then a Roman centre called Arilica, and important in medieval times. The Venetians fortified it in the mid-16th cent., and three military constructions were built in the Napoleonic period. Notice the *Porta Brescia* and the 18th cent. church of *San Martino*. One should walk to the 16th cent. sanctuary of the *Madonna del Frassino*, rebuilt at the beginning of the present cent., inside which are paintings by Paolo Farinati (1524-1606) and frescoes by Bernardino Muttoni the Younger (active in the second half of the 17th cent.).

* **PESCOCOSTANZO** (L'Aquila). Attractive village on the slopes of Mount Calvario, with 15-16th cent. houses. The most remarkable monument is the *Collegiata*, dedicated to Santa Maria del Colle: built in the 14th cent., it was destroyed by earthquakes, rebuilt in the second half of the 15th cent., and enlarged in the 16th. The interior contains a magnificent wooden ceiling, with designs by Carlo Sabatini (17th cent. engraver) and paintings by Giovan Angelo Bucci (lived in the 17th cent.),

a Baroque baptismal font, a large gilded and carved organ, and a wrought-iron gate in front of the Sacramental Chapel. The Piazza Umberto I is overlooked by the Town Hall and the facade of a monastery, designed in 1624 by Cosimo Fanzago.

* **PETRALIA SOPRANA** (Palermo). The highest municipality in the province of Palermo, on an elevated mountain-spur. The facade-less church of *Santi Pietro e Paolo*, with a basilican interior, contains some precious gold ornaments and rare materials. In the 18th cent. church of *Santa Maria di Loreto* is a marble altarpiece (late 15th cent.), probably by Domenico Gagini (1420/25-1492). Petralia Soprana commands a sweeping view of the Madonie, as far as Etna.

* **PETRALIA SOTTANA** (Palermo). Situated in the mountainous area of the Madonie, it is a popular summer resort. The *Chiesa Matrice*, dedicated to the Assunta, and rebuilt in the 17th cent., has a 16th cent. Gothic-Catalan portal. The majestic facade is equalled by a fine interior, with interesting works of art such as a 16th cent. marble ancon, a 17th cent. statue of the Madonna and Child, and a triptych painted towards the middle of the 15th cent. by an unknown artist in Marches-Sicilian style. The entrance-door to the church of *Santa Maria della Fontana* or *della Vittoria* is also Gothic-Catalan. In the Baroque church of *San Francesco* are some fairly good paintings, especially a Stigmata of St. Francis by Giuseppe Salerno (called Zoppo di Gangi) recorded 1588-1630.

Pescocostanzo, Palazzo del Convento.

** **PIACENZA.** Situated on the Via Emilia, on the right bank of the river Po, it is largely medieval in appearance. The *Palazzo del Comune*, known as the "Gothic" Town Hall, is a masterpiece of 13th cent. civic architecture in Lombardy. Building began in 1280, to designs by four local architects, Pietro da Cagnano, Negro de' Negri, Gherardo Campanaro and Pietro da Borghetto. The facade is divided into two orders, the upper one relieved by three large rounded windows; the sides repeat the same characteristics as the front. Inside is a look-out tower, known as the Lanterna. The equestrian statues of the Farnese (*Statue equestri dei Farnese*), in front of the Town Hall, are by Francesco Mochi (1580-1654). The basilica of *San Francesco* (second half of the 13th cent.) has a Lombard facade, but is mainly

Gothic in style, with central doorway. The Gothic interior contains a huge painting by Benedetto Marini (c. 1590-1627) depicting the Miracle of the Bread and Fishes, and 15th cent. frescoes. The *Duomo* was begun in 1122. It is a magnificent Lombard construction, with a solemn gable facade enhanced by two fine doorways. Behind the facade stands the bell-tower, completed in 1333. Inside the asymmetrical-plan building are works of art such as the Death of the Madonna, a huge painting by Camillo Procaccini (c. 1551-1629), and Prophets, by Pier Francesco Mazzucchelli, called Morazzone (c. 1571-1626) and Giovanni Francesco Barbieri, called Guercino (1591-1666). Behind the high altar is a large, Venetian-inspired Gothic altarpiece; the niches contain a Redeemer, Madonna and Saints, dated 1479, by a certain Tuscanus. The basilica of *San Savino*, dating back to 903, but radically altered in the course of time, has a basilican interior, and contains works of art such as a black marble altar, with bronze decoration, by Giuseppe Filiberti (recorded 1733-1775), and a 12th cent. Romanesque Crucifix in wood. The basilica of *Sant'Antonio*, which served as a cathedral from the 4th to the 9th cent., was rebuilt at the start of the 11th. Preceding the original facade is the so-called "Paradise" atrium, designed by Pietro Vago (recorded 1341-1350). In the *Galleria d'Arte Moderna Ricci-Oddi* are exhibited seven hundred works, including Madame Noblet and Ecce Puer, by Medardo Rosso (1858-1928). The Renaissance church of the *Madonna di Campagna* was built between 1522 and 1528 to a design by Alessio Tramello (1455-1535). Inside are many works of art including a fresco depicting St. Augustine, by Giovanni Antonio de' Sacchis, called Pordenone (c. 1484-1539), and pictures by Daniele Crespi (c. 1590-1630), Alessandro Tiarini (1577-1668), and Giovanni Francesco Barbieri, called Guercino (1591-1666). The frescoes in the dome are especially beautiful, most of them by Pordenone. The church of *San Sisto* was built at the turn of the 16th cent., to a design by Alessio Tramello. The interior contains works of art including a panel by Sebastiano Novelli (mentioned in 1540), and an inlaid choir by Bartolomeo Spinelli da Busseto (active in 1514) and Giampietro Panbianchi da Colorno (recorded from 1514). The *Palazzo Farnese* was begun in 1558 to a design by Francesco Paciotto (1521-1591) and continued under the direction of Jacopo Barozzi, called Vignola (1507-1573). It houses the Civic Museum, with sections devoted to archeology, painting, sculpture, and handicrafts. The *Collegio Alberoni* has an art gallery containing pictures, tapestries, and sacred vestments. Among the most important works on show are an Ecce Homo by Antonello da Messina (c. 1430-1479), a Madonna enthroned, by Jean Provost (1462-1529), and a Holy Family by the school of Raphael (1483-1520).

Piacenza, Piazza Cavalli. Francesco Mochi, Monument to Ranuccio Farnese.

Piacenza, Duomo, interior.

* **PIADENA** (Cremona). Agricultural and industrial centre as well as an important crossroads. The area was inhabited in ancient times, as is proved by pre-historic remains of the Neolithic and Bronze ages. The 17th cent. Town Hall houses the *Museo Civico*, with prehistoric, Gallic and Roman collections. It has an interesting mosaic depicting the Minotaur in the Labyrinth. In the *Parrocchiale* (rebuilt in Baroque style towards the middle of the 18th cent.) are paintings by Gabriele Zocchi (lived in the 16-17th cent.), Sigismondo Benini (c. 1670-1720), and Gian Angelo Borroni (1684-1772).

* **PIANELLA** (Pescara). Small agricultural centre between the Tavo and Pescara valleys. A short distance away is the 12th cent. Romanesque church of *Sant'Angelo* or the church of Santa Maria Maggiore. It has a portal with interesting door-posts and bas-reliefs, and the interior contains 13th cent. frescoes and a 12th cent. pulpit. Excursion to Moscufo, where stands the 13th cent. church of *Santa Maria del Lago*, containing traces of 13th and 14th cent. frescoes, and a travertine pulpit by Nicodemo da Guardiagrele (active in the second half of the 12th cent.).

** **PIAZZA ARMERINA** (Enna). Spread over three heights, it is in an agricultural area rich in sulphur mines and quarries. The *Duomo*, dedicated to the Assunta, was originally begun in 1604 to a design by Orazio Torriani (recorded 1613-1655). It is a severe-looking, impressive building, in the Mannerist style of the late 16th cent. The aisleless interior, in the form of a Latin cross, contains a panel of the Crucifixion painted on both sides (1485), a splendid work by an unknown artist indicated as the "Master of the Cross of Piazza Armerina"; a Martyrdom of St. Agatha by Jacopo Ligozzi (c. 1547-1626), an Assunta by Filippo Paladino (c. 1544-1614), a Byzantine-style Madonna, inside an embossed-silver frame, carried out in 1625 by Giuseppe Capra, and a well-furnished treasury. The church of *San Giovanni Evangelista* is frescoed throughout by William Borremans (1670-1744) and his pupils. In the late-Renaissance church of *San Pietro* (early 17th cent.) can be seen a typical 18th cent. frame in carved wood on the high altar, and a fine Nativity by an unknown artist working in the 17th cent. In the church of *Sant'Andrea* (end of the 11th cent.) is an attractive cycle of frescoes of the 12th, 13th, and 15th cent. Piazza Armerina is well-known in the archeological world because of the *Zona Archeologica* in the Casale district. The Villa Romana of Casale, brought to light by recent excavations, was at the centre of a rural village, presumably formed at the turn of the 4th cent. A.D., and enlarged in later centuries. The Villa contains a magnificent group of mosaics. The Thermae

have been identified, with octagonal frigidarium and apse-shaped tepidarium, and calidarium. In the quadriportico of the vast peristyle, with Corinthian columns, can be seen a tessellated pavement of medallions, with images of animal heads. The mosaic floor of the so-called ambulatory of the Great Hunt depicts two personified Lands, one of which (obviously Arabia) is represented by the mythical Phoenix. In the great hall are two apse-shaped recesses, with mosaic floors relating myths and episodes from Roman life. Finally there is the Triclinium, a vast square hall, with three apses boasting magnificent mosaic compositions of Hercules killing the giants with his arrows, the labours of Hercules, the metamorphosis of Daphne, and other mythological episodes.

* **PIAZZOLA SUL BRENTA** (Padua). Rapidly expanding agricultural and industrial centre. The *Villa Camerini* is an impressive construction, in the middle of the village. Built in 1546 on the remains of a castle, it was heavily decorated later in Baroque style. The audience hall and the statue-filled music hall (known as the Guitar on account of its shape) are worthy of note.

* **PICERNO** (Potenza). Picturesque village overlooking the Picerno valley. In the *Chiesa dei Cappuccini* is an important picture by the Flemish artist Wenceslas Coberger (1561-1634). The *Chiesa Parrocchiale* contains a notable 16th cent. altarpiece. The Chapel of the *Annunziata* is an interesting building, with a pointed-arched doorway and stone relief-work below the archivolt.

* **PIEDIMONTE D'ALIFE** (Caserta). At the edge of the limestone mass of the Matese, crossed by the river Torano. Stone weapons, terracottas and remains of megalithic walls show that the area was inhabited in neolithic times. The church of *San Tommaso d'Aquino* or *San Domenico* (begun in the early 15th cent.) has a sober ogival doorway and is flanked by a cusped octagonal bell-tower. It contains a panel by Belisario Corenzio (c. 1558-post 1640),

Piazza Armerina, Mosaics in the Villa Romana del Casale.

a picture of the Nativity of the Virgin, probably by Fabrizio Santafede (c. 1560-1628), and early 17th cent. frescoes by Giuseppe Cesari, called Cavaliere d'Arpino (1568-1640) and Bernardino Cesari (mentioned in 1614). The mid-17th cent. sanctuary of the *Santissima Annunziata* contains precious stuccoes and carved-wood altars, together with a panel of the Annunciation by Giovanni Balducci (recorded 1560-1603), the Marriage at Cana, a vast picture crowded with sixty figures, by Nicola Maria Rossi (c. 1699-1755), a statue of the Immacolata, carved in 1762 by Gennaro D'Amore, and carved-wood stalls (1748) by Aniello Giordano. The church of *San Salvatore*, designed by Cosimo Fanzago (1594-1678), has a Baroque interior, and is decorated with marble-work and stuccoes. In the church of *San Biagio*, built at the beginning of the 15th cent., are frescoes with Stories from the Old and New Testaments, and Episodes from the Life of St. Blaise (15th cent.). The *Museo Alifano* contains a large amount of archeological, artistic, and historical material connected with the area.

** **PIENZA** (Siena). A particularly interesting little town and real pearl of the Renaissance, named after Pope Pius II (1405-1464). It flourished in the 14th cent. thanks to the Piccolomini, one of the leading families of the time. The entire rectangular plan of the town, built around an axis, is by Bernardo Rossellino (1409-1464). The axis includes Piazza Pio II, with a well also by Rossellino, and the main buildings. The *Cattedrale*, dedicated to the Assunta, has a Renaissance facade in travertine and, on the left, an octagonal bell-tower. The interior, with a nave and two aisles, contains some remarkable works of art including a wooden Gothic choir (second half of the 15th cent.), and an Assumption of the Virgin with Saints Catherine, Callixtus, Agatha, and Pius I, by Lorenzo di Pietro, called Vecchietta (c. 1412-1480). The crypt contains a baptismal font by Bernardo Rossellino. The *Museo della Cattedrale* houses an art gallery with interesting works, including a Madonna and Child with four Saints by Vecchietta; Madonna della Misericordia, by Bartolo di Fredi (c. 1330-1410); Flemish tapestries and collections of chalices, ciboriums, pyxes, monstrances and medals; incense-holders and copes of inestimable value; a 15th cent. silver pax, and the cope of Pius II. The *Palazzo Piccolomini* is held to be Bernardo Rossellino's masterpiece, and was inspired by the Rucellai palace in Florence. It is built on a square plan and has a fine hanging garden. The interior contains Pius II's bedroom, and many mementoes of that great pontiff. A visit should be made to

Pienza, Piazza Pio II.

Palazzo Ammannati, now called Palazzo Newton, built in the 15th cent. by Giacomo Ammannati, Cardinal of Pavia and favourite companion of Pius II. In Via del Corso, surrounded by 15th cent. buildings, stands the 13th cent. church of *San Francesco*. The interior contains a vast 14-15th cent. fresco decoration, depicting the Annunciation, Deposition, Stigmata of St. Francis, Prayer in the Garden, and Saints, possibly by Cristoforo di Bindoccio (recorded 1361-1406). In the ex-monastery is a 16th cent. cloister. One should walk to the Romanesque *Pieve di Corsignano*. The church of the ancient Corsignano was built in the 11-12th century, it has a cylindrical bell-tower. Inside is a beautiful 14th cent. wooden Crucifix, of the Sienese school.

* **PIETRA LIGURE** (Savona). Overlooked by Monte Trabocchetto, it is a fashionable bathing resort. The parish church of *San Nicola di Bari* was built in the 18th cent. The high

Pienza, Cathedral.
Pienza, Palazzo Piccolomini, facade.

vault over the aisleless nave is frescoed with a Glory of St. Nicholas.

* **PIETRASANTA** (Lucca). At the foot of green hills of olive groves and vineyards, beyond which are the Apuan Alps. The 14th cent. Romanesque-Gothic *Duomo di San Martino*, has a tripartite marble facade, with three doorways. The interior, with a nave and two aisles, contains a Madonna of the Rosary by Matteo Rosselli (1649) and a Nativity by Pietro Dandini (1677). The choir is much admired, with its twenty-four marble choirstalls. In the nearby baptistery is a goblet-shaped baptismal font, by Donato Benti (1509). The church of *Sant'Agostino*, founded in the 14th cent., has a facade with three large blind arches and, inside, the altar of the Annunziata, or Nativity altar, by Donato Benti.

* **PIEVE DI CADORE** (Belluno). Small mountain town, in a panoramic setting, backed by the Marmarole range. The early-19th cent. *Parrocchiale*, designed by Domenico Schiavi, has a facade decorated with a fresco depicting the Nativity of the Virgin by Goffredo Sommavilla (lived in the 19th cent.), and an altarpiece of the Madonna and Child, Saints Titian and Andrew, and the artist himself as a donor, by Tiziano Vecellio (1490-1576). Titian's birthplace, *Casa Natale di Tiziano*, with its own Museum, is rich in mementoes of the great painter. In the *Palazzo della Magnifica Comunità Cadorina*, rebuilt in 1525, ·is an ancient Venetian archeological museum.

* **PIEVE DI SANTO STEFANO** (Arezzo). A small commercial town on the right bank of the Tiber. The collegiate church of *Santo Stefano* has an interior in the form of a Latin cross, and houses some remarkable works of art including a 15th cent. terracotta, statue of St. Sebastian, in Della Robbia style, and a 14th cent. wooden Crucifix. The facade of the

Pietra Ligure, Parish Church.

Palazzo Pretorio deserves attention, with its ninety magnificent coats-of-arms by Della Robbia.

* **PINEROLO** (Turin). Commercial and industrial centre, consisting of an ancient part spread over the Hill of San Maurizio, and a modern part on the plain. The *Duomo*, dedicated to San Donato, is about a thousand years old, but the original parts are interspersed with later additions so that the final appearance of the building is fundamentally Gothic. *Via Principi d'Acaja*, a narrow little street, flanked with quaint houses, some of them with projecting upper storeys, winds through the oldest and most picturesque part of the city. The 11th cent. church of *San Maurizio* is flanked by a majestic Romanesque bell-tower with three orders of double and triple-lighted openings. The interior, with a nave and four aisles, contains the tombs of eight princes of Acaja and Savoy.

* **PINZOLO** (Trento). Holiday resort in the Val Rendena. The parish church of *San Lorenzo* (rebuilt in the second half of the 18th cent.) contains some frescoes by Bartolomeo Zeni (lived in the 18th cent.). One should walk to the 16th cent. church of *San Vigilio*, with a fresco on one side depicting the Dance of Death, by Simone Baschenis (recorded 1519-1547).

* **PIOMBINO** (Leghorn). Situated on the tip of the small Mount Massoncello peninsula. It is an industrial town with iron and steel works, once the Roman port of Falesia. In the neighbourhood was founded the famous Benedictine Abbey of San Giustiniano di Falesia, at the beginning of the 11th cent. The *Porta S. Antonio* is joined to a large sturdy tower, dated 1213. The 14th cent. parish church of *Santi Antimo e Lorenzo*, restored before the Second World War, contains the 14th cent. tomb of Iacopo d'Appiano, by the Pisan school, and a marble baptismal font, with a Gothic-style base, carried out by Andrea Guardi in 1470. The 13th cent. *Palazzo Comunale* has been remodelled several times. The *Torre dell'Orologio* was built in 1598 to a square plan, and has two storeys.

** **PIOMBINO DESE** (Padua). The beautiful *Villa Cornaro* by Andrea Palladio (1508-1580), recently well restored, contains frescoes by Mattia Bortoloni (1696-1750), and sculptures by Camillo Mariani (1567-1611).

*** **PISA.** Situated in the plain, ten kilometres from the Tyrrhenian Sea, and crossed by the river Arno. Borgo Stretto is an ancient Pisan street flanked by lovely buildings with colonnaded doorways dating from 1000-1600, and the church of *San Michele in Borgo*, built in 990 probably on the site of a pagan temple didi-

Pisa, Duomo and Leaning Tower.

cated to Mars; the 14th cent. facade by Fra Guglielmo Agnelli (c. 1238-c. 1312), is a blend of Romanesque and Gothic architecture. The interior, with a nave and two aisles, contains a 13th cent. fresco of St. Michael, by an unknown artist; a painting of St. Lawrence and other Saints by Baccio Domi (active in the second half of the 16th cent.); a triptych by Taddeo di Bartolo (c. 1362-1422) depicting the Madonna, Angels and four Saints, and a late-14th cent. Crucifix by the Pisan school. The buildings surrounding the Piazza dei Cavalieri are partly the work of Giorgio Vasari (1511-1574); to the right of the Square is the church of *Santo Stefano dei Cavalieri*, with a 17th cent. marble facade. It was designed by Vasari in the second half of the 16th cent., and the campanile is also by him. Inside it has a wooden ceiling and several holy-water stoups designed by Vasari, a bust of San Lussorio Niccolò by Donatello (1386-1466), a silver Crucifix designed by Pietro Tenerani (1789-1869), Stories of St. Stephen, possibly by Vasari, and paintings by Iacopo di Chimenti (1551-1640), Iacopo Ligozzi (1547-1626), Cristoforo

Allori (1577-1621), and a Stoning of St. Stephen by Vasari. The *Duomo*, in Romanesque-Pisan style, was begun by the architect Buscheto (active in the second half of the 11th cent. and first decade of the 12th), and continued and finished by Rainaldo (active in the 12th cent.). The facade, also the work of Rainaldo, has colonnaded arches in the lower part and four orders of small loggias in the upper part. The three bronze doors are decorated with Stories of Mary and the Redeemer, by the school of Jean Boulogne (1529-1608). To the left of the apse is the bronze door called Porta di San Ranieri; it is decorated with Stories from the Life of the Redeemer by Bonanno Pisano (recorded 1451-1470). The interior, in the form of a nave and four aisles, contains works of notable artistic importance including a pulpit by Giovanni Pisano (c. 1248-post 1314), the tomb of Arrigo VII, by Tino di Camaino (c. 1280-1337), paintings of Saints Agnes, Margaret, Catherine, Peter and John the Baptist by Andrea del Sarto (1486-1530), and a 13th cent. mosaic representing the Redeemer between Mary and St. John the Evangelist by

Pisa, Duomo, transept, interior.

Pisa, Museum. Nino Pisano, Madonna and Child.
Pisa, Duomo. Giovanni Pisano, Annunciation,
detail of the San Ranieri door.

Pisa, Duomo. Giovanni Pisano, Pulpit.
Pisa, Museum. Andrea Pisano, Virgin of the An-
nunciation.

Pistoia, Ospedale del Ceppo. Santi Viviani, Feeding the Hungry.
Pomposa, Abbey Refectory. Last Supper.

Cimabue (recorded 1272-1302). The church of *Santa Caterina* (13-14th cent.) contains a painting of the Apotheosis of St. Thomas by Francesco Traini (recorded 1321-1363), a statue of an Angel and the Annunziata by Nino Pisano (c. 1300-1368), and the Tomb of Archbishop Simone Saltarelli, also by Pisano and his assistants. The church of *San Francesco*, begun during the first ten years of the 13th cent., was continued during the period 1265-1270 by Giovanni di Simone (recorded from 1275), and finished during the first half of the 13th cent. The upper part of the facade dates from 1603. Inside can be seen a fresco of the Madonna and Saints by Tommaso Pisano (recorded from 1363), frescoes depicting the Monastic Virtues by Taddeo Gaddi (c. 1290-1366) and, in the sacristy, frescoes depicting Stories of the Virgin Mary, by Taddeo di Bartolo (c. 1362-1422). From the cloister one enters the Chapter-house of St. Bonaventura, which contains frescoes by Niccolò di Pietro Gerini (recorded 1368-1415), representing the Crucifixion and Stories of the Passion, Resurrection and Pentecost, Christ Blessing, Evangelists and Prophets. The church of *Santa Maria della Spina*, in Romanesque-Gothic style, was originally an oratory dedicated to Santa Maria di Pontenovo; later (1323) it was enlarged and took on its present form. The exterior is decorated with sculptures by the school of Giovanni Pisano and the interior with statues by Nino Pisano and his school depicting the Madonna and Child between St. Peter and St. John. The 9th cent. church of *San Paolo a Ripa d'Arno* was rebuilt between 1000 A.D. and 1100 A.D.; the facade dates from the beginning of the 12th cent.; inside can be seen the Burgundio Tomb, Roman sarcophagus. Behind the church is the Romanesque chapel of *Sant'Agata* (1100) in brickwork. The *Palazzo dei Cavalieri*, also called della Carovana, is actually the ancient Palazzo degli Anziani, restored by Vasari; it has a three-storeyed facade and a 19th cent. external staircase decorated with graffiti. The *Campanile*, or Leaning Tower, begun in the second half of the 12th cent., possibly by Bonanno Pisano, was continued from the third floor by Giovanni di Simone (recorded from 1275), and eventually finished in the second half of the 14th cent., apparently by Tommaso di Andrea da Pontedera (active in the second half of the 14th cent.). The Romanesque *Battistero*, built to a circular plan, was begun by Diotisalvi (recorded 1150-1153) during the second half of the 12th cent., continued by Nicola and Giovanni Pisano in the 13th cent., and finished by Cellino di Nese (recorded 1338-1359) and others, towards the end of the 14th cent. It has four doorways, the most beautiful of which is the main one. The interior contains a pulpit by Nicola Pisano, with five reliefs representing the Nativity, Epiphany, Presentation in the Temple, Crucifixion, and Last Judgement; statues of the

Madonna and Child, Evangelists and Prophets, by Giovanni and Nicola Pisano and their school, and an octagonal baptismal font, by Guido Bigianelli (recorded 1230-1250). The *Camposanto* is built to a rectangular plan, with a marble wall and blind arches, the work of Giovanni di Simone; above the door on the right is a tabernacle in Gothic style, and underneath a lovely Madonna and Saints, by the school of Giovanni Pisano. In the *Museo Nazionale di San Matteo* are valuable Pisan sculptures and paintings by the Tuscan school dating from 1100 to 1400, including a Madonna and Child by Nino Pisano; the Virgin of the Annunciation, by Andrea Pisano; a

dancing figure; a Saint with reliquary and two other Saints, by Giovanni Pisano; St. Lawrence, by Jacopo della Quercia (c. 1371-1438); bust of the Redeemer, by Verrocchio (1435-1488); polyptych of the Madonna and Saints, by Simone Martini (1284?-1344); St. Paul, by Masaccio (1401-1428); and the Redeemer by Beato Angelico (c. 1400-1455). It is also worth noticing *La Gherardesca* or *Palazzo dell'Orologio*, built to a design by Vasari; the church of *San Sisto* (second half of the 11th cent.); the church of *Sant'Anna*, containing a valuable wooden Crucifix dating from 1000-1100 A.D., by the French or Catalan school; the church of *San Ranierino*, with a painting of the Crucifixion, Madonna and four Saints by Aurelio Lomi (1556-1622); the 11-13th cent. church of *San Matteo;* the Gothic church of *San Martino* (1332), containing a relief, possibly by Andrea Pisano (c. 1290-c. 1349); and the 14th cent. *Palazzo Gambacorti*, in Gothic style. Excursions to *San Piero a Grado*, a Romanesque basilica dating from 1000 A.D.; the interior has a nave and two aisles, and contains frescoes dating from the second half of the 13th cent.

* **PISOGNE** (Brescia). On Lake Iseo, at the entrance to the Val Camonica. The 15th cent. church of the *Madonna della Neve* contains a wonderful series of frescoes representing scenes from the Passion of Christ by Girolamo Romani, called Romanino (c. 1484-1566). 14th

Pisa, Palazzo dei Cavalieri.

cent. *Torre del Vescovo*. The late-18th cent. *Parrocchiale* contains frescoes and paintings by Sante Cattaneo (1739-1819), Ponziano Loverini (1845-1929), Gaetano Cresseri (1870-1933), Antonio Guadagnini (1817-1900), and Alessandro Sala (1771-1841).

* PISTICCI (Matera). An important agricultural centre between the rivers Basento and Cavone. It is of Greek origin, and archeological material has been found in the necropolis. The *Chiesa Madre* or church of *Santi Pietro e Paolo* was built during the first half of the 16th cent. on the ruins of a church dating from 1100, of which the bell-tower still remains. The interior, in the form of a nave and two aisles, contains 18th cent. paintings, including a Deposition and Marriage at Cana. The former-church of the *Riformati* contains works by Giovanni Tommaso Guarino (1611-1654), including the Porziuncola. The *Castello* is in ruins. One should walk to the *Abbazia di Santa Maria del Casale*, built towards the end of the 11th cent.; it has a lovely doorway and rose window.

*** PISTOIA. Built at the northernmost part of the Ombrone plain, it has many buildings from the period of the Communes, and Romanesque-Pisan churches. The church of *San Giovanni Fuorcivitas* is so called because in ancient times it actually was outside the city wall. It was built at the beginning of the 8th cent., but rebuilt between the 12th and 14th. The architrave of the doorway is decorated with a bas-relief depicting Jesus at Supper

Pistoia, San Giovanni Fuorcivitas, detail.

with the Apostles, believed to have been carried out in 1162 by Gruamonte (active in the second half of the 12th cent.). Inside can be seen a lovely pulpit by Fra Guglielmo Agnelli da Pisa (c.1238-c.1312), a beautiful Visitation in glazed terracotta, attributed to either Andrea della Robbia (1435-1525) or Luca della Robbia (1400-1482), and a holy-water stoup with decorations representing the three theological virtues, by Giovanni Pisano. The *Duomo* was already founded in the 5th cent. It has a Romanesque facade with three orders of loggias, and in a lunette above the central doorway is a Madonna and Child between two Angels, by Andrea della Robbia. The extensively-altered interior contains, amongst other works of art, a silver altar-frontal of St. James, begun in 1287 and completed in 1456, including the much-admired Nine Stories from the Life of St. James, by Leonardo di Giovanni (recorded 1361-1371); the monumental tomb of Cino da Pistoia; the Chapter-house Museum, housing the Treasury, the famous "sagrestia di belli arredi" (sacristy of the beautiful vestments and vessels) mentioned by Dante; a bronze candelabra, by Naso di Bartolomeo (1406-1456); a monument to Cardinal Niccolò Forteguerri; a sculptured stele in high-relief with bust of Bishop Donato de' Medici, attributed to either Antonio Rossellino (1427-c. 1479) or Verrocchio (1435-1488); a baptismal font, designed by Benedetto da Maiano (1442-1497) and carried out by Andrea Ferrucci (1465-1526); and a Madonna and Child enthroned between Saints John the Baptist and Zeno, by Verrocchio and one of his followers, Lorenzo di Credi (1456/60-1537); in the sacristy is a panel of the Crucifixion with Six Stories painted on a gold-leaf base. The octagonal *Battistero*, begun in the first half of the 14th cent. by Cellino di Nese (recorded 1338-1359), is faced with white and green marble; on the architrave are valuable bas-reliefs representing Stories in the Life of St. John the Baptist. The *Palazzo del Comune* was built by the Guelphs at the end of the 13th cent., while Giano della Bella was Podestà. It was later modified and enlarged at various times, and contains a strange statue in black marble, believed to be by Filippo Tedici, about which there are several legends. Inside, the Hall of the Pages and the Ghibelline Hall are especially worth seeing. The *Museo Civico* is also worth a visit. It houses an important collection of works of art, including a 14th cent. panel of the Deposition by the Pistoian school; a Holy Family by Andrea del Brescianino (recorded 1506-1525); a Portrait of Tommaso Puccini by Giovanni Battista Foggini (1652-1725); and a Resurrection in terracotta, by Benedetto Buglioni (1461-1521). *Ospedale del Ceppo*, founded towards the end of the 13th cent. is worth a visit, as are: the church of *San Bartolomeo in Pantano*, containing a lovely pulpit by Guido da Como (recorded 1230-1250); the church of the *Madonna dell'Umiltà*, designed by Ventura Vitoni (1442-1532); the imposing church of *San Francesco*, built at the turn of the 14th cent., and containing 14th cent. frescoes by the school of Giotto (1266-1336); the church of *Sant'Andrea*, built in 1166 by Gruamonte and his brother Adeodato, containing a wooden Crucifix and a hexagonal pulpit, carried out between 1298 and 1301 by Giovanni Pisano and considered one of his masterpieces; and the church of *San Domenico*, built at the end of the 13th cent., containing a fresco of the Madonna and Child by Baccio della Porta, called Fra Bartolomeo (1475-1517), and busts attributed to Gian Lorenzo Bernini (1598-1680).

* **PITIGLIANO** (Grosseto). Attractive little town in a characteristic position built on the gullies in the Meleta, Lente, and Prochio ravines, with houses perched on the edge of the cliffs. The *Duomo*, dedicated to St. Mark, is flanked by a high bell-tower; inside are paintings by Pietro Aldi (1852-1888). The crenellated *Palazzo Orsini*, begun during the last few years of the 14th cent., was sacked in 1547 during a local revolt. One should walk to the *Villa Orsini*, where there are the ruins of an enormous statue, commonly known as Orlando, flanked by another statue representing a woman, carved out of the rock. Excursion to *Sovana*, a picturesque medieval village situated between the ravines of the Folonia and Calesina gorges.

* **PIZZIGHETTONE** (Cremona). Agricultural and industrial town divided by the river Adda; built in a star shape, it still retains traces of the 16th cent. city wall. In the 12th cent. the Cremonese built a castle there, of which only the main tower remains. The parish church of *San Bassano* (rebuilt in the 12th cent.) contains a large fresco representing the Crucifixion by Bernardino Campi (1552-1591); and important reliefs of the Annunciation, Epiphany, and Nativity, by an unknown 14th cent. sculptor. The *Museo* contains Gallic and Roman archeological remains and 16th cent. marbles.

* **PIZZO** (Catanzaro). Situated on a steep cliff facing the sea. The collegiate church of *San Giorgio*, with a Baroque facade dating from the first half of the 17th cent., is decorated with marble bas-reliefs by Bartolomeo Berrettaro (recorded 1500-1517), and contains a painting depicting Our Lady of Succour (1832) by Michele Foggia, another of the Martyrdom of St. George, painted by Emanuele Paparo (1779-1828), and John the Baptist, attributed to Pietro Bernini (1562-1629).

* **POGGIBONSI** (Siena). Situated at the confluence of the Staggia and the Elsa. The *Palazzo Comunale* is flanked by a crenellated me-

dieval tower. The collegiate church of the *Assunta*, built during the last century, contains a panel representing the Resurrection, possibly by Vincenzo Tamagni (1492-1529), and a Holy Family, after the style of Andrea del Sarto (1486-1531). The 14th cent. church of *Santi Lorenzo ed Agostino* contains a panel representing St. Nicholas of Tolentino, by Neri di Bicci (1419-1491), and a wooden Crucifix, probably the work of Giovanni di Agostino (recorded 1310-1345). One should walk to the 14th cent. church of *San Lucchese;* the Gothic-French interior contains a few valuable paintings, including a Noli me tangere, possibly by Raffaellino del Garbo (1466-1525) and the *Pieve* (parish church) dedicated to Santa Maria Assunta, at Staggia; inside can be seen a painting of the Communion of St. Mary Egiziaca, by Pollaiolo (1431-1498) and some badly damaged 14th cent. frescoes.

** **POGGIO A CAIANO** (near Florence). *Villa Medicea*, the most beautiful villa in the Florence area, was a stronghold of the Cancellieri family of Pistoia until it became the residence of the Strozzi family; about 1480

Poggibonsi, Town Hall.
Poggio a Caiano, Villa Medicea.

253

it was bought by Lorenzo the Magnificent, who had it rebuilt to the design of Giuliano da Sangallo (1445-1516), after which it was further embellished by his son Giovanni, the future Pope Leo X. Below the main entrance, which stands in the middle of a vast expanse of gardens, are four Roman sarcophagi. The interior is rich and harmonious; the drawing room of Bianca Cappello and the Salon being especially worth noticing. They contain many works of art, the most important being a huge composition with Vertumnus and Pomona, a masterpiece by Jacopo Carrucci, called Pontormo (1494-1556). The terrace commands a beautiful view over Florence, Prato, Pistoia and the surrounding hills.

* **POLICORO** (Matera). Agricultural centre situated in the plain between the rivers Agri and Sinni. In the direction of Tursi are the *Scavi archeologici dell'antica Heraclea* (the central part of the ancient city, built in 400 B.C. to a rectangular plan, has been brought to light); the *Sanctuary of Demeter* (600 B.C.) and two bronze *Tavole di Heraclea*. In the *Museo Nazionale della Siritide* are archeological remains which provide evidence of the various stages in the civilization of the entire area dominated by Heraclea and Siris. Excursion to the cathedral of *Santa Maria d'Anglona*, dating back to 1000 A.D. but later modified several times. From inside one can enter the Bishop's Palace, which contains a Byzantine fresco representing the Martyrdom of a Saint (1000-1100 A.D.).

* **POLIGNANO A MARE** (Bari). On the Adriatic coast, between Monopoli and Bari. The medieval quarter lies on the edge of a steep cliff, which is pierced by a large number of attractive grottoes. The *Chiesa Matrice*, dedicated to the Assunta and originally Romanesque in style, was consecrated at the end of the 13th cent., and modified several times in later centuries. The facade has a late-Renaissance doorway and is dominated by a sturdy bell-tower. The interior, in the form of a nave and two aisles, has been modified several times, and is now predominantly 16th cent. It contains a beautiful five-panelled polyptych (1472), by the Murano artist Bartolomeo Vivarini. A large stone crib by Stefano da Putignano di Apulia (lived in the 15-16th cent.) is also worth noticing. The church of *Sant'Antonio* contains a painting of the Madonna and Child with Saints by Alessandro Varotari, called Padovanino (1588-1648), and another very large painting, depicting the Virgin Mary and Franciscan Saints, by the Flemish artist Gaspare Hovic (lived in the 15-16th cent.). A visit to the *Grotta Palazzese* is worthwhile. It is the most interesting of all the grottoes which, as mentioned above, open out in the cliff underneath the medieval centre. The *Grotta dei Colombi*, *Grotta della Colonna*, *Grotta Ardito*, *Grotta Pietropaolo*, *Grotta Stalattitica*, and *Grotta della Foca* are alsto characteristic grottoes. Walk to the church of *San Vito*, built over the sacellum containing the body of San Vito, a Sicilian youth martyred in Diocletian times (303 A.D.).

* **POLLA** (Salerno). Picturesque village at the northern end of the Vallo di Diano. The church of *Sant'Antonio da Padova*, built in the 16-17th cent., has an interesting porch. Inside is a ceiling covered with numerous paintings depicting Stories from the Old and New Testament by Michele Regolia (recorded 1632-1686), a wooden Crucifix by Fra Umile da Petralia (1580-1639), and other works of art. The vast and complicated *Grotta di Polla* is an awe-inspiring sight; remains of Quaternary fauna and bronze-age objects have been discovered there.

* **POMIGLIANO D'ARCO** (Naples). Large agricultural and industrial centre near the slopes of Mount Somma. The parish church of *San Felice* has been rebuilt several times but still retains its original bell-tower. The Baroque *Chiesa del Carmine* contains the noteworthy tomb of Teresa Strambone. In the cemetery is the *Cappella Gentilizia degli Imbriani* where the famous Neapolitan writer, Paolo Emilio Imbriani (1808-1877) is buried.

*** **POMPEII** (Naples). Very important archeological centre to the south-east of Vesuvius; the site of the ancient city of Pompeii which was destroyed during a volcanic eruption in 79 A.D. The archeological area is reached through the so-called *Porta Marina*, which originally had two passageways and, in a niche, a statue of Minerva. To the right is the *An-*

Polignano a Mare, Chiesa Matrice.

tiquarium, with four rooms containing archeological remains from Pompeii, arranged according to the periods of Pompeiian civilization. The first room contains archeological remains from the pre-Samnite period (9-5th cent. B.C.), including numerous pieces of terracotta excavated from the Temple of Apollo and the Temple of Hercules. The second room, dedicated to the Samnite period (425-90 B.C.), contains a Sphinx in Italic-Campanian style, a bust of a satyr, busts of a husband and wife, portrait of a woman, and a head of Zeus. The third and fourth rooms, devoted to the Roman era, contain a bronze bowl discovered in the House of Menander bronze vases, surgical instruments, and plastercasts of some of the victims of the eruption, as well as a wheel, a tree, and a cupboard. Between the second and third room is the Room of Livia and of Iconography, where a statue of Livia, found in the Villa of Mysteries, a herma portrait of C. Cornelius Rufus, one

Pompeii, Amphitheatre.
Pompeii, House of the Vetii, peristyle.

255

of Vesonius Primus, and a portrait of Marcellus can be admired. Beyond the site of the *Tempio di Venere Pompeiana*, (very few traces of which remain), stands the *Tempio di Apollo* surrounded by a wall and a colonnaded portico, modified during the reign of Nero. There are two bronze statues, (one of Apollo and the other of Diana) in front of the portico, and an altar before the steps. The *Foro*, where all the everyday activities took place, is built to a rectangular plan, with a portico having columns on three sides only and a square with the main buildings. The *Tempio di Giove*, reached by a double stairway, and dedicated to Jupiter, Juno and Minerva, was built about the first half of the 2nd cent. B.C., and enlarged by the Romans; it was flanked by two triumphal arches, only one of which remains. To the right is the *Macellum* (the meat market, dating from the Imperial era). The *Edificio di Eumachia*, dedicated to the Concordia Augusta and to the Pietà, has a fine doorway and preceding vestibule; it was the headquarters of the fullones (cloth-fullers). The *Basilica*, built to a rectangular plan and divided into a nave and two aisles by 28 columns, was used as a law court. The *Terme del Foro* (c. 80 B.C.) still retain, in the men's section, the tepidarium and the calidarium. The *Teatro Grande*, built in 400 B.C., and later enlarged, had three orders of terraces divided into five sectors and three doorways leading onto the stage. The *Teatro Piccolo* (c. 80-75 B.C.) had two orders of terraces, divided into five sectors. Behind the *Tempio di Giove Meilichios*, where a bust of Minerva and two terracotta statues of Jupiter and Juno were found, is the *Temple of Isis*, built in 100 B.C., standing on a platform, with a pronaos. The *Casa del Menandro*, dating from the Imperial era, so called because a portrait of Menander was found there, has in the atrium an exedra with three paintings representing epic scenes from the Trojan War, such as the Trojan Horse and the Death of Laocoon; the west side and the calidarium are decorated with mosaics and frescoes. The luxurious *Casa di Loreius Tiburtinus* has an attractive garden and rectangular atrium; the best rooms were situated along the loggia; of these the triclinium is worth noticing; it is famous for its decorations depicting episodes from the Labours of Hercules and the Iliad. The *Anfiteatro* (c. 80 B.C.) is built to an oval plan; three entrances lead into the arena (without trace of underground passages), and to the tripartite auditorium. The *Terme Stabiane* were built in Samnite times and modified in the Imperial era; all the buildings are grouped around the courtyard of the palaestra. Surrounded on three sides by a columned portico, it houses public and private baths, and halls equipped for games. In the men's section can be seen two changing-rooms, the frigidarium, tepidarium, and calidarium. In the women's section the frigidarium is missing. The roof

and walls are stuccoed. The *Casa dei Vettii*, owned by the wealthy merchants Aulus Vettius Conviva and Aulus Vettius Restitutus, has a painting depicting Priapus against the evil eye in the entrance; to the left are two richly decorated rooms, and to the right is the servants' entrance; in the peristyle is a fine triclinium, decorated with mythological scenes. At the entrance to the *Casa degli Amorini Dorati* are two passages with paintings depicting Leda and the Swan, Narcissus at the Spring, Winged Mercury, and Paris and Helen at Sparta; the porticoed peristyle is embellished with hermae and bas-reliefs. The *Casa di Fauno*, dating from the Samnite era (100 B.C.), blends Italic and Greek styles, with the Greek style predominating; crossing the vestibule one enters the first peristyle, which has a colonnaded portico. The noble *Villa di Diomede* has a peristyle entered by a small staircase beside which is a bathroom with a portico and swimming pool. The *Villa dei Misteri*, built in the first half of the first cent. B.C., but modified in later periods, has a remarkable room called the Hall of the Great Frescoes, the most important artistically being the fresco depicting the Initiation of a Bride to the Dionysian Mysteries, made up of various scenes. It is also worth noticing the *Via dei Sepolcri*, so called because three tombs can be seen there: of the builder Gaius Vestarius Priscus, of Arellia Tertulla, and Septimia; the *Caserma dei Gladiatori*, a large square used as barracks for gladiators in Nero's times; the *Necropoli di Via Nuceria*, dotted with tombs; the *Casa delle Nozze d'argento* (house of the Silver Wedding) built in the Samnite era and modified in Imperial times; the *Casa del Centenario*, with porticoed peristyle; the *Tempio della Fortuna Augusta*, built in 3 B.C. and dedicated to the Imperial cult; a 500 B.C. *Tempio Dorico*, of which only a few traces can be seen; and the *Palestra Sannitica*.

* POMPOSA (Ferrara). Agricultural centre at the junction of the roads leading to Ferrara, on the western side of the Giralda valley. The land has been completely reclaimed in recent years. The *Abbazia di Pomposa*, a Benedictine monastery, is linked to the history of Italian medieval culture; it was probably built in the 7th cent., and at the end of the 10th cent. passed under the jurisdiction of the Archbishops of Ravenna. The impressive building, one of the most important in Romanesque style, is dominated by a campanile built in 1036. The *Chiesa Abbaziale* or basilica of *Santa Maria* dates back to the 8-9th cent. in its present form. The interior, formed of a nave and two aisles, with a raised chancel, contains works of art including frescoes by Vitale da Bologna (1309?-pre-1361). To the right of the basilica is the *Monastero* containing early-14th cent. frescoes by an unknown pupil of Giotto (1266-1336), valuable paintings and a Renaissance ciborium. The 12th cent. *Palazzo della*

Ragione, where the abbot dispensed justice, is built in Venetian style, with a portico in the lower storey and a loggia; inside can be seen remains of interesting frescoes.

* **PONTASSIEVE** (Florence). Important agricultural and industrial centre at the confluence of the rivers Sieve and Arno. Excursions to *Montefiesole*, *Poggio di Bardellone* and *San Martino*

Pomposa, Abbey.
Pontassieve, Parish Church of Remole, bell-tower.

a Quona, where a beautiful 14th cent. Madonna and Child can be admired. Nearby, at Remole, is the parish church of *San Giovanni;* the interior is divided by pillars and there is a slender and characteristic campanile.

* **PONTEDERA** (Pisa). Situated at the confluence of the Era and the Arno. The *Castello*, built at the beginning of the 13th cent., was for a long period contested by the Pisans and the Florentines; in 1554 the walls were pulled down by order of Pietro Strozzi, to punish the town for having given shelter to the French and the Sienese. The *Palazzo Pretorio*, dating from the beginning of the 17th cent., has a doorway decorated with valuable podestà coats-of-arms in stone, and is flanked by a clock tower. In the church of *Santi Iacopo e Filippo* is a 14th cent. wooden statue of St. Lucy, by the Pisan school.

* **PONTERANICA** (Bergamo). In the Valle Brembana, on the left side of the narrow Morla valley. The parish church of *Santi Vincenzo e Alessandro*, with a 15th cent. facade and a round-arched doorway, contains a polyptych in six sections by Lorenzo Lotto (1480-1550), depicting the Risen Christ between the Angel and the Virgin Mary, Saints Peter, John the Baptist, and Paul.

* **PONTIDA** (Bergamo). Small agricultural town on the slopes of Mount Canto, surrounded by vineyards and chestnut woods. The *Abbazia di Pontida* was founded in the 11th cent. The basilica, dedicated to *San Giacomo* and built between the 14th and 19th cent., contains a few works of art including 14th cent. frescoes and 17th cent. paintings. The monastery, rebuilt after 1485, has an Upper Cloister, possibly to a design by Pietro Isabello (c. 1480-1550), and a Lower Cloister (1490).

* **PONTREMOLI** (Massa Carrara). Main centre of the Lunigiana area, surrounded by hills covered with chestnut woods. The *Torre dell'Orologio* or *del Campanone* is in the centre of the defence wall built in 1322 by the Luccan soldier-of-fortune Castruccio Castracani degli Antelminelli, to prevent clashes between the Guelphs and the Ghibellines. The church of *San Francesco* (completed at the beginning of the 16th cent.) contains interesting tombstones, a bas-relief depicting the Madonna and Child, attributed to Agostino di Duccio (1418-c. 1481), and a Crucifixion by Giulio Cesare Procaccini (1560-1620).

* **PONT SAINT MARTIN** (Aosta). At the beginning of the Lys valley and the Val d'Aosta. A fine, well-preserved Roman bridge (*Ponte Romano*) of the 1st cent. A.D. spans the Lys stream. The *Castellaccio* is all that remains of a fortification built in the 11th cent. on the

orders of Edoardo di Bard. The *Cappella di San Rocco* contains some interesting medieval frescoes.

* **POPOLI** (Pescara). Attractive little town by the so-called Tremonti or Popoli gorges. The 15th cent. church of *San Francesco* has a Romanesque doorway surmounted by a quadrilobed rose-window. Inside there is an important 15th cent. fresco representing the Pietà, by an unknown artist. The *Taverna Ducale* is a rare and lovely example of medieval architecture in the Abruzzi. It was probably built in the mid-14th cent. for Giovanni Cantelmo, feudal lord of Popoli, who needed it as a storehouse and market for the farm produce due to him from the peasants. To the right of it is the University or New Tavern, built in 1574 by Duke Ottavio Cantelmo.

* **POPPI** (Arezzo). Elegant little town; nearly all the streets are porticoed. The church of *San Fedele* contains a painting of the Madonna and Child with four Saints (1527) by Antonio Solosmeo, a Martyrdom of St. Lawrence by Pietro Sorri; a Martyrdom of St. John the Evangelist by Francesco Morandini, called Poppi (1544-1584), and a 13th cent. panel of the Crucifixion. The 13th cent. *Palazzo Pretorio*, once the residence of the Counts Guidi, has a facade divided by a protruding tower, and a harmonious courtyard. In the large hall on the top floor is a 16th cent. Della Robbia-style terracotta representing the Assumption with Saints Jerome and Thomas; the chapel on the second floor contains a frescoed polyptych and paintings by Taddeo Gaddi (c. 1300-1366). The *Torre dei Diavoli*, residence of the Guidi family before the castle was built, is now the magistrate's court.

* **POPULONIA** (Leghorn). It is worth visiting the *Rocca*, with a large cylindrical tower, and the *Mura Etrusche*, formed of horizontal blocks of stone smaller than those found in other towns. From Populonia one goes down to Porto Baratti, where the *Necropoli Arcaica* of Populonia was discovered in 1908.

** **PORDENONE**. One of the most important industrial centres in Friuli, on the right bank of the river Noncello. The *Duomo*, dedicated to St. Mark, was built in the second half of the 15th cent. in late-Gothic style. In the facade there is an Italian-Renaissance doorway by Giovanni Antonio Pilacorte (recorded 1484-1531). Overlooking the Duomo is a beautiful Romanesque campanile with Gothic elements, built in the 13-14th cent. The cathedral contains an Our Lady of Mercy, painted by Giovanni Antonio Sacchiense called Pordenone (1484-1539), Saints Erasmus and Roch and the Madonna and Child, also by Pordenone, frescoes by Giovanni Maria Calderari (c. 1500-1570), an altarpiece representing St. Francis between Saints John the Baptist and Daniel by Marcello Fogolino (c. 1480-1548), and the Flight into Egypt, by Pomponio Amalteo (1505-1588). In the sacristy there is one of Pordenone's early works, depicting the Resurrection. The Treasury contains reliquaries from the 13th to the 16th cent. The *Pinacoteca Civica*, housed in the Gothic Town Hall, contains more paintings by Por-

Pont-Saint-Martin, Roman bridge.
Poppi, Castle of the Conti Guidi.

Pordenone, Town Hall.

denone, as well as by Michelangelo Grigoletti (1808-1870), Alessandro Varotari, called Padovanino (1588-1648) and other 16th cent. Venetian masters. Part of the cloister of the *Ex-Chiesa di San Francesco* is frescoed by Pordenone. In the church of *San Giorgio* (made of Istrian stone) are Saints Lucy, Paul and Sebastian, by Michelangelo Grigoletti, and a painting of St. George by Gaspare Narvesa (active in the second half of the 16th cent.). The *Castello* is one of the most remarkable of its kind in the area, in spite of being badly restored in recent times.

* **PORRETTA TERME** (Bologna). Important spa, on the left bank of the river Reno. In the parish church of *Santa Maria Maddalena* (1690) are important paintings, including the Marriage of St. Catherine, Christ and the Centurion, by an unknown 17th cent. painter, a Madonna and Saints Francis and Bernardino by Alessandro Tiarini (1577-1668), and a Noli me Tangere by Denijs Calvaert (1540-1619). Walk to the sanctuary of the *Madonna del Ponte*, restructured in Doric style, to a design by Saverio Bianchi (active in the second half of the 19th cent.). Inside are paintings by Alessandro Guardassoni (1819-1888).

* **PORTOFERRAIO** (Main town of the Isle of Elba, province of Leghorn). Attractive little town with important iron and steel works, situated on a promontory, with a lovely panorama. In 1548 Cosimo I de' Medici founded a town on this site which he called Cosmopolis, but which later became known as Portoferraio. In the early days three forts were built here: the stately Fort Falcone, the star-shaped Stella Fort, and the Linguella Fort thrusting out into the sea. The *Pinacoteca Foresiana* contains a collection of books, paintings, sculptures, prints, and other objects of artistic interest. One should walk to the *Villa San Martino* or *Villa Napoleone*, a store-house converted by Napoleon into a summer residence, during his esile.

* **PORTOGRUARO** (Venice). Busy town, mostly agricultural, but also with modern industries. The 17th cent. *Duomo*, dedicated to St. Andrew, contains altarpieces by Giovanni Martini (recorded 1497-1535), Gregorio Lazzarini (1665-1730) and Pomponio Amalteo (1505-1588). The 14th cent. *Palazzo Comunale* is an interesting example of Gothic architecture. In the *Museo Concordiese* is a collection of material from Julia Concordia. In the neighbourhood is *Concordia Sagittaria* with a *Cattedrale*, Gothic-Renaissance in style, but considerably altered by the restoration work; inside are two important holy-water stoups, one in the form of a Roman capital, dating from the 2nd cent. Near the church is a small 12th cent. Romanesque *Battistero*: the interior has three apses and contains 14th cent. frescoes.

Excavations begun in the area after the Second World War have unearthed a 4-5th cent. Early-Christian burial ground.

* **PORTO SAN GIORGIO** (Ascoli Piceno). One of the most popular seaside resorts in central Italy. The square, battlemented *Rocca*, built in 1276 on the orders of Lorenzo Tiepolo, later Doge of Venice, has turrets and a large keep. The neo-Classical *Chiesa del Suffragio*, (beginning of the 17th cent.) contains an important painting of Souls in Purgatory by Francesco Trevisani (1656-1746). *Torre di Palme* is a small village nearby, perched on a commanding hilltop. Here can be seen the characteristic *Chiesetta di San Giovanni*, built about 1000 A.D.; the 12th cent. parish church of *Sant'Agostino* containing a large polyptych representing the Madonna and Child with Saints, by Vittorio Crivelli (c. 1440-1502); and the 12th cent. church of *Santa Maria a Mare* with a panel depicting the Madonna and Saints by Vincenzo Pagani (c. 1490-1568).

* **PORTO TORRES** (Sassari). Situated on the innermost part of the Bay of Asinara. The church of *San Gavino*, once the ancient cathedral of Torres, is the oldest Romanesque church in Sardinia. It was built in the second half of the 11th cent. in Pisan style, and has a basilican interior with a nave and two aisles. It contains a 7-8th cent. Byzantine inscription commemorating the victory of the Sardinians over the Longobards who had attacked Torres, and an antecrypt with sarcophagi, the most important being a 3rd cent. Roman one, with the nine muses.

* **PORTOVENERE** (La Spezia). Overlooking the narrow stretch of water between the mainland and the island of Palmaria, with a lovely view. The 13th cent. church of *San Pietro*, in Genoese-Gothic style, was restored in the 1930's; the interior has an inlaid marble floor. The 12th cent. parish church of *San Lorenzo*, several times altered and restored, has a spacious interior containing a 15th cent. polyptych representing Saints Martin, Augustine and Nicholas of Tolentino; in the sacristy is a treasury

Portovenere, San Pietro and the small Castle.

containing three 10-11th cent. Syriac ivory caskets. The *Castello*, built by the Genoese in 1113, was called Castrum Superior; the top affords a wonderful view of Portovenere. Worthwhile excursion to the Isola Palmaria 105 m from the mainland, where there is the Grotta dei Colombi, containing mesolithic and stone-age remains.

* **POSITANO** (Salerno). Ancient village on the Amalfi coast and well-known holiday resort. The houses are built on terraces on the slopes of the Comune and Sant'Angelo a Tre Pizzi mountains. The village is surrounded by lush vegetation. The parish church of *Santa Maria Assunta*, with a large majolica dome, contains a painting of the Circumcision by Fabrizio Santafede (c. 1560-1628) and, on the high altar, a Byzantine-style panel of the Madonna and Child, by an unknown 13th cent. artist. On the campanile is a 13th cent. bas-relief depicting a sea monster, a fish and a fox. Ruins of a *Villa Romana*. In the nearby cave known as the *Porta*, higher-paleolithic material and mesolithic hunting implements have been found.

* **POSSAGNO** (Treviso). Small agricultural town in a hilly area. The *Tempio di Canova*, begun in 1819 to a design by Canova, is a round building after the style of the Pantheon. It is entered through a double pronaos with eight Doric columns; inside are remarkable paintings including a St. Francis of Paula by Luca Giordano (1632-1705), Jesus in the Garden of Gethsemane by Jacopo Palma the Younger (1544-1628), and a Deposition from the Cross and Trinity, by Antonio Canova; also, Canova's tomb, which he carved himself. The *Birthplace of Antonio Canova* houses a gallery of plaster casts, including nearly all the casts and original models by the famous sculptor.

* **POTENZA**. Situated high up in the hills with a lovely view over the Basento valley. The *Museo Provinciale Lucano* contains prehistoric and proto-historic remains excavated in the area, Greco-Roman remains, material from medieval times, ceramics, and a numi-

Possagno, Gipsoteca Canoviana. Antonio Canova, Love and Psyche.

smatic collection. The *Cattedrale*, dedicated to San Gerardo and first built at the end of the 12th cent., contains a few fairly good works of art, and an 18th cent. ciborium made of inlaid marble. The church of *San Francesco*, built in 1274 around an oratory founded by followers of the great saint, has an important Durazza-style portal and a fine 15th cent. carved-wood door; inside are a Renaissance tomb of Donato de Grasis (1534), and beautiful 13th and 17th cent. paintings.

* **POTENZA PICENA** (Macerata). Walled city on a hillside. The most important monuments are: the church of *San Francesco* (restored in the 18th cent.); the *Palazzo del Podestà* (14th cent.); the *Palazzo Municipale*, containing a terracotta by Ambrogio Della Robbia (1477-1527/28), numerous Papal Bulls from 1351 to 1700, and letters from Venetian Doges; the church of *Sant'Agostino* which contains a Crucifixion by Cristoforo Roncalli, called Pomarancio (c. 1552-1626); the church of *San Giacomo*, containing a triptych by Paolo Bontulli (recorded 1507-1531); and the *Istituto dell'Addolorata*, with ancient looms that produce wonderful damasks. In the modern parish church of *Porto Potenza Picena* there is a remarkable painting representing the Madonna, St. Anne and St. Joachim, by Pomarancio.

** **POZZUOLI** (Naples). In a splendid setting, built on a promontory of tufa rock jutting out into the Bay of Pozzuoli. The *Serapeo* or *Tempio di Serapide* was actually the market-place of the Roman town built during the Flavian era; it has been well preserved and is one of the most interesting buildings in the Phlegraean area. The adjacent *Antiquarium Flegreo* contains sculptures and marble works excavated from the area. The *Anfiteatro Flavio*, built during the second half of the 1st cent. A.D., is the third largest amphitheatre in Italy, after the

Potenza, Museum. Corinthian helmet from Vaglio.

Colosseum and the one at Santa Maria Capua Vetere; it is 149 m long and 116 m wide, and could hold forty thousand spectators. The vast subterranean part, still well preserved, gives an idea of how spectacles of fights with wild animals were organized. The *Duomo*, first built in the 11th cent., and rebuilt during the first half of the 17th cent., contains paintings by Artemisia Gentileschi (1597-c. 1652), Giovanni Lanfranco (1582-1647), and Francesco and Cesare Fracanzano (lived in the 17th cent.). The *Rovine di Liternum* (in ancient times the mouth of the river Clanis was called Liternus) are of exceptional scientific interest. During excavations carried out from 1932 to 1947, the forum, temple, basilica and theatre of the ancient city were brought to light.

* **PRAGLIA** (Padua). The *Abbazia* stands in one of the most attractive spots in the Euganean hills. It was founded in 1080 by the Benedictine monk Isalberto de' Tadi and completely rebuilt in the 15-16th cent. The church of the *Assunta*, rebuilt between 1490 and 1548 to a design by Tullio Lombardo (c. 1455-1532), has a Romanesque bell-tower; the Renaissance interior, in the form of a Latin cross, with a dome, contains many frescoes by Luca Longhi (1507-1580), Dario Varotari (1534-1596), Giovan Battista Zelotti (1526-1578), Jacopo Palma the Younger (1544-1628), and Padovanino (1588-1648). In the sacristy there is an interesting painted-wood Crucifix of the 14th cent. The adjacent *Monastero* has many interesting rooms, in varying styles, such as the Conference Hall, Reception Hall, Hall of the Stuccoes, the picturesque Hancing Cloister, large Refectory containing nine enormous canvases by Giovan Battista Zelotti (1526-1578) and a fresco of the Crucifixion by Bartolomeo Montagna (c. 1450-1523), Communal Refectory, double east Cloister, Old Library (with paintings by Giovan Battista Zelotti), New Library, and Chapter-house with a large fresco of the Deposition by Girolamo Tessari (1480-1550).

* **PRALBOINO** (Brescia). The stately *Parrocchiale*, built towards the end of the 18th

Pozzuoli, Amphitheatre.

cent., contains important paintings including a Visitation of Mary by Callisto Piazza (c. 1500-1562), a Madonna with Donors by Girolamo Romani, called Romanino (c. 1484-1566), and two paintings depicting the Madonna and Saints, by Alessandro Bonvicino, called Moretto da Brescia (1498-1554). Imposing 18th cent. *Palazzo Gambara.*

* **PRATA D'ANSIDONIA** (L'Aquila). The Baroque parish church of *San Nicola* was built on the ruins of a 13th cent. church. It contains the finest ambo in the Abruzzi, carried out in 1240 and transferred here in 1796 from the nearby church of *San Paolo di Peltuino*, which stands on the remains of the Roman town of Peltuinum and was rebuilt at the beginning of the 13th cent.

** **PRATO** (Florence). On the right bank of the Bisenzio, at the foot of the Calvana moun-

Prato, Duomo.
Prato, Duomo. Filippo Lippi, Salomè dancing before Herod.

261

tains. The *Duomo* was built in the 10th cent. and called the parish church of Santo Stefano di Borgo al Cornio. In 1211 the facade was decorated with pilaster-strips and Lucca-style arches by Guidetto da Como. The fine Holy Girdle pulpit is the work of Donatello (1386-1466) and Michelozzo Michelozzi (1396-1472); the marvellous Dancing Cupids, composed of seven panels divided by small twin columns, is by Donatello. The church has a rich collection of works of art including frescoes by Fra' Filippo Lippi (1406-1469), who lived for many years in Prato, and the large bronze Crucifix by Pietro Tacca (1577-1640). The late-14th cent. *Cappella del Sacro Cingolo* contains frescoes painted in 1367 by Agnolo Gaddi depicting the Legend of the Holy Girdle. The beautiful gate of the chapel of the Holy Girdle was carried out by Mario di Bartolomeo, Antonio di Sebola and Pasquino di Matteo da Montepulciano between 1438 and 1467. In the *Galleria Comunale* are works representing Tuscan art from the beginnings to the 15th cent. The exterior of the church of *Santa Maria delle Carceri*, built between 1484 and 1495 by Giuliano da Sangallo, is faced in polychrome marble; the spacious interior is considered one of the masterpieces of Renaissance architecture. Various other monuments worth seeing at Prato are the *Castello dell'Imperatore*, unique of its kind in northern Italy; *Palazzo Pretorio;* and the church of *San Domenico*.

* **PRATOVECCHIO** (Arezzo). Large village, dominated by the Romena castle, on the left bank of the river Arno. Walk to *Santa Maria a Poppiena*, first a Benedictine then a Camaldolese abbey; inside is an Annunciation and Saints John the Baptist and Mary Magdalen, by Giovanni del Ponte (1385-post 1437).

* **PREDAPPIO** (Forlì). Agricultural and industrial town, modern in appearance. The 11th cent. church of *San Cassiano in Appennino*, restructured in 1934, has a tripartite facade surmounted by small arches. One should walk to the 18th cent. *Santuario della Madonna*, containing valuable stuccoes and paintings, and to the *Rocca delle Caminate*, built before the 11th cent., possibly on the site of a Roman fort.

* **PRIVERNO** (Latina). Situated on a hill, overlooking the Amaseno valley. The 13th cent. *Duomo*, dedicated to Maria Assunta, is Cistercian-Gothic in style. It contains a Madonna and Child, part of a 15th cent. polyptych, and relics of St. Thomas Aquinas. The ancient church of *San Giovanni Evangelista*, which is falling into ruins, contains many frescoes dating from various periods, the most attractive being one representing Stories in the Life of St. Catherine of Alexandria, carried out in the 14-15th cent. The *Palazzo Comunale* (13-14th cent.) with two and three-mullioned windows on the first floor, and two-mullioned windows on the second floor, is worth noticing. Walk to the *Rovine di Privernum*, discovered at the end of the 19th cent., with ruins of the Palace of Tiberius. From Priverno the *Abbazia di Fossanova* can easily be reached; Cistercian-Gothic in style, it was founded by the Benedictines in the 9th cent. The church was begun by the Cistercians in 1187 and has a plain and impressive facade. The interior, with a nave and two aisles, contains some beautiful chapels and a deep-set choir, in which there are a few works of art. In the monastery, it is worth noticing the mystic cloister (Romanesque on three sides and Gothic on the fourth) the refectory, the Chapter-house, and the guest rooms.

* **PUTIGNANO** (Bari). Attractive and busy little town in the Murge mountains. The *Chiesa Madre di San Pietro* was built in the 12th cent., rebuilt in the 15th and again in the 17th. It has a beautiful rose-window in the facade, and is flanked by a massive bell-tower built in 1615. The interior, now Baroque, contains three paintings representing the Miracle of the Loaves, Manna from Heaven, and Crossing of the Red Sea, probably by Luca Giordano (1632-1705). One should walk to the *Grotte di Putignano*, discovered by chance in 1931.

* **QUARTU SANT'ELENA** (Cagliari). The church of the *Cappuccini* (13th cent.) was later altered. The harmonious square apse and small hanging arches are all that remain of the original building. The *Parrocchiale* contains a valuable 17-18th cent. statue of St. Helen, and a large altarpiece depicting Plato amongst Saints and Prophets, probably by Antioco Mainas, follower of Pietro Cavaro (recorded 1518-1537). In Piazza Azuni, the Roman column or capital, with a 15th cent. Gothic Cross, is worth seeing.

* **QUINZANO D'OGLIO** (Brescia). Large agricultural and industrial centre crossed by the Roggia Saverona. The neo-Classical *Parrocchiale* contains two paintings, one depicting the Miracles of St. Anthony, attributed to Cesare Pronti, called Baciocchi (1616-1708), and the other of the Risen Christ and Saints, probably by Floriano Ferramola (c. 1480-1528). The church of *Santa Maria Assunta*, built at the end of the 12th cent., and restructured in the 17th, still has its original Romanesque-style apse. Late 16th cent. church of *San Rocco*.

* **RACCONIGI** (Cuneo). The former Royal Palace (*Castello Reale*) is a huge construction, in which the most diverse styles are combined (begun in 1681, it was completed in 1834). The interior, renovated by Charles Albert, is sumptuous, and enriched with artistic treasures of inestimable value. Behind it is an immense park, refreshed by streams and little lakes.

** **RAGUSA.** Situated on a mountain-spur that extends in the direction of the valley of the river Irminio, between two steep valleys called the Cava di San Leonardo and the Cava di Santa Domenica. There is a predominantly modern part called Ragusa Superiore, and an older quarter called Ragusa Ibla. The latter is supposed to have risen on the site of the Sikelian Hybla Heraia. The *Cattedrale*, dedicated to St. John the Baptist, is an imposing building erected in the first half of the 18th cent. The facade has Corinthian columns. The interior is divided into a nave and two aisles by Corinthian columns, and richly decorated with stucco work and marble, as well as marble high-reliefs, including the Sacrifice of Melchisedec and the Last Supper by Giuseppe Prinzi (1833-1893). The *Basilica di San Giorgio* was designed by Rosario Gagliardi (c. 1700-c. 1770). It has an exuberant Baroque facade, a high neo-Classical dome, and paintings of the Immacolata and St. Nicholas by Vito d'Anna (c. 1720-1769). The *Museo Archeologico* has many findings from the 6th cent. B.C. onwards, discovered in the area around Ragusa. The church of *Santa Maria delle Scale* still retains something of the original construction that was destroyed by an earthquake in 1693, while the interior bears traces of the Catalan-Gothic and Renaissance styles of the 15th and 16th centuries. The church of *San Giuseppe* (1590) has a Baroque facade, and contains a painting of the Holy Family by Matteo Battaglia (lived in the 18th cent.) and another of St. Benedict by Sebastiano Lo Monaco (lived in the 18th cent.). In the church of the *Cappuccini Vecchi* are paintings of the Assumption with Apostles and Angels, St. Agatha in prison, and the Martyrdom of St. Agnes, by Pietro Novelli (1603-1647). In the *Palazzo Donnafugata* is an art gallery: among other things, it contains a Madonna and Child, probably by Antonello da Messina (c. 1430-1479), paintings by Dario Querici (born 1831), and ceramic works by Giacomo Bongiovanni (1772-1859).

* **RANDAZZO** (Catania). Situated on the right of the river Alcantara, with houses built of lavic stone. Though only 15 km from the summit of Etna, it has never been touched

Racconigi, Castle.

by lavaflows. The *Basilica di Santa Maria* was built for the first time in the first half of the 13th cent. and reflects the influence of the Norman-Swabian style. It is flanked by a slender, cusped bell-tower, and contains some fairly interesting works of art, such as the panel depicting the Death, Assumption, and Coronation of the Virgin by Giovanni Caniglia (lived in the 16th cent.), a Holy Family and an Assumption by Giuseppe Velasquez (1750-1827), a Madonna and Child enthroned by Giuseppe Sciuti (1834-1911), and a particularly rich treasury. The originally 14th cent. church of *San Nicolò* was rebuilt in 1583. It has an interior in the form of a Latin cross, a high dome with marble reliefs by Antonello Gagini (1478-1536) and Giacomo Gagini (1517-1598), and a painting of the Passion of Christ as the fountain of Grace by Onofrio Gabriello (1610-1706). The church of *San Martino* was badly damaged by bombing in the Second World War. It has a bare 17th cent. facade, and a harmonious 14th cent. bell-tower, with two orders of coupled single-lighted windows. It contains a statue of the Madonna delle Grazie by Vincenzo Gagini (1527-1595), a polyptych depicting the Madonna and Child with Saints Magdalen and Martha, the Deposition, and the Annunciation, probably by Antonello de Saliba (1466-c. 1535), and a rich treasury.

* **RAPALLO** (Genoa). A little town situated in the innermost part of the gulf of Tigullio. The very ancient *Collegiata dei Santi Gervaso e Protaso* has a neo-Classical facade (1857), and a leaning bell-tower. The interior is divided into a nave and two aisles, and contains a marble group representing the Madonna di Montallegro by Enrico Quattrini (1926). The *Lungomare Vittorio Veneto* is planted with flowers and trees, and there are monuments to Garibaldi and Columbus. Excursion to the 16th cent. sanctuary of the *Madonna di Montallegro*, and to the ruins of the *Monastero di Valle Christi*, erected in 1204 in the French Gothic style.

Rapallo, Church of Valle Christi.

263

* **RAPOLLA** (Potenza). Near the river Mèlfia. The little Norman church of *Santa Lucia* has two small domes; it is rather spectacular, especially inside. On the right of the *Cattedrale*, rebuilt in the first half of the 13th cent. and completed in 1253 by Melchiorre da Montalbano (sculptor active in 1253-1279), is the fine *Campanile*, the work of Master Sarolo da Muro Lucano (mentioned in 1209), who also did the two large bas-reliefs depicting the Annunciation and Original Sin.

** **RAVELLO** (Salerno). A peaceful, isolated little town, situated on the ridge that separates the valley of the Dragone from that of the Reginna; the pearl of the coast of Amalfi, it commands a view of incomparable beauty. The *Duomo* is preceded by a steep flight of steps. Dedicated to San Pantaleone, it was built in the second half of the 11th cent. and altered in the second half of the 18th. The sober facade has a central doorway in marble, the precious bronze doors of which were cast in 1179 and divided up into fifty-four square panels, with Saints, scenes of the Passion, and two grotesque masks. The fine 13th cent. belltower rises on the right side of the church, which contains works of art, the most important being the pulpit by Nicolò di Bartolomeo (active in the second half of the 13th cent.), and an ambo of 1130, with mosaics representing Jonah being swallowed and vomited by the whale. The Chapel of San Pantaleone, the patron saint of the town, was rebuilt in 1782. The *Palazzo Rufolo*, situated on a terrace overlooking the gulf, is the result of the fusion of various constructions built in the Sicilian-

Arab style. It was erected in the second half of the 13th cent. by the aristocratic Rufolo family. The courtyard is in the form of a small cloister with high walls, and with two storeys of loggias formed by small Sicilian-Arab columns. The garden surrounding the palace is full of exotic plants. The church of *San Giovanni del Toro* was built in the middle of the 11th cent. The facade has three doorways, the central one with an ancient entablature. The bell-tower on the left of the church is also in the Sicilian-Arab style. In the nave is a superb pulpit, commissioned by the Bovio family, and carried out by Alfano da Termoli (lived in the 12-13th cent.), with mosaics representing Jonah and the whale. The crypt has three apses, and is decorated with 14th cent. frescoes of Christ, the Saints, and the symbols of the Evangelists. The church of *Santa Maria a Gradillo*, built in the late 12th cent., has three doorways, the central one with an ancient architrave; the interior is divided into a nave and two aisles, while the columns supporting the pointed arches have tall piers. The *Villa Cimbrone* consists of a building dominated by two towers, and a courtyard put together out of antique remains, in the centre of which is a precious pluteal. From the garden, which abounds in plants of every kind, one reaches the Belvedere on the extreme edge of the spur of rock on which Ravello is built, which commands a view of stunning beauty, from Atrani to the Gulf of Salerno, as far as Paestum.

*** **RAVENNA.** Situated in the north-western plain of Romagna, the city once occupied a

Ravenna, Sant'Apollinare in Classe, interior.

site on the Adriatic coast. One of the most famous centres of art in Italy, it preserves the art produced in two eras, that of the late Roman age and that of the Byzantine. The *Basilica di San Vitale*, the city's greatest example of Byzantine art, was erected about 525 A.D. by G. Argentario. It has an octagonal plan, the dome resting on high arches; the chancel and apse are decorated with mosaics of the 6th cent. The *Tomba di Galla Placidia* was erected in the 5th cent. in the form of a Latin cross, the exterior being decorated with arcadings and pilasters, the interior with superb mosaics carried out before 450. The *Museo Nazionale dell'Antichità* is housed in a Benedictine monastery, and has Roman, Early Christian, and Byzantine remains. The church of *San Giovanni Battista*, erected in the 5th cent., was rebuilt in 1600. The *Battistero degli Ariani* is an octagonal construction built at the end of the 5th cent. The cupola is decorated with a mosaic of the 5th cent. The *Duomo*, built in the 5th cent., was completely rebuilt in the 18th to a design by G. F. Buonamici (1692-1759): the facade is of the Baroque kind, and the two columns that support the arch of the portico are all that remains of the original basilica; the interior is in the form of a Latin cross, with a nave and two aisles, and contains a 6th cent. ambo and two beautiful 5th cent. sarcophagi. Beside the cathedral is the *Battistero degli Ortodossi*, an octagonal construction built in the 5th cent., with arcadings in its upper part; inside, two orders of arches support the dome, which is decorated with superb mosaics carried out at the same time as the construction of the baptistery. The Museum

of the Bishop's Palace (*Museo dell'Arcivescovado*) contains objects belonging to the cathedral: besides fragments of mosaics, there is the famous Throne of Maximian, the work of artists from Alexandria (6th cent.), decorated with beautiful ivory reliefs. Adjoining the *Accademia di Belle Arti* is an important art gallery; it has works by Romagnole, Venetian and Tuscan painters, from the 14th to the 17th cent., as well as the extremely beautiful statue of Guidarello Guidarelli by Tullio Lombardo (1455-1532). Inside Dante's tomb (*Sepolcro di Dante*), erected in 1780, is a bas-relief of the poet by Pietro Lombardo (1435-1515). *San Francesco*, erected in the 5th cent. and rebuilt in the 10th, was destroyed in the last war, and has been recently rebuilt. It has a brick facade and a beautiful Romanesque bell-tower. The interior is of the basilican type, with a nave and two aisles. The crypt, decorated with Byzantine and Romanesque capitals, has four central columns, and another series of inner columns. *Sant'Agata Maggiore* was begun in the 5th cent. and restored in 1400. The facade is preceded by a beautiful porch, while the basilican interior has a nave and two aisles. The *Basilica di Santa Maria in Porto* was built in the 16th cent., but had to be rebuilt after being damaged during the war; the facade is neo-Classical. The *Loggia del Giardino*, an elegant Renaissance construction, consists of a portico with five arches and a loggia; from the portico one passes to the Renaissance cloister. *Sant'Apollinare Nuovo*, an Arian church built in the 6th cent. by Theodoric, passed over to the practice of Catholic rites in the 9th. The facade has a 16th cent.

Ravenna, San Vitale, exterior.

portico (put together with antique materials). The basilican interior is divided into a nave and two aisles by columns with precious Byzantine capitals, and is decorated with magnificent 6th cent. mosaics, partly classical (the Life of Christ, Saints, and Prophets), and partly in the Byzantine style (the sequence of Martyrs and Virgins). The church of *San Giovanni Evangelista* goes back to the 5th cent., but was restored after damage suffered in the last war. In the neighbourhood is the *Mausoleum of Theodoric*, erected in the 6th cent. The construction has two storeys, the lower, ten-sided one having a deep recess in each side, while the upper is covered over by a cupola composed of a single block of Istrian limestone. *Sant'Apollinare in Classe*, the only remaining evidence of the ancient port of Ravenna, was built in the 6th cent. On its left side is a 10th cent. cylindrical bell-tower, with mullioned windows divided into one or more lights by small columns. The basilican interior is divided into a nave and two aisles by marble columns with acanthus-leaf capitals, and contains sarcophagi of the 5th cent., as well as Byzantine-like mosaics representing the Transfiguration, the Emperor Constantine IV, and portraits of Bishops.

Ravenna, Sant'Apollinare Nuovo, interior.
Ravenna, Baptistery of the Orthodox.

Ravenna, Tomb of Galla Placidia, interior.

Ravenna, Sant'Apollinare Nuovo. Mosaic with the Three Kings.
Ravenna, San Vitale. The Empress Theodora with her court.

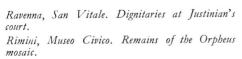

Ravenna, San Vitale. Dignitaries at Justinian's court.
Rimini, Museo Civico. Remains of the Orpheus mosaic.

Rimini, Tempio Malatestiano. Agostino di Duccio, Cherubs playing.

** **RECANATI** (Macerata). Spread out over
a hill between the valleys of the Musone and
the Potenza, it occupies one of the most
pleasant areas in the Marches, and commands
a fine view. The *Palazzo Comunale* houses an
art gallery with wonderful paintings by Lorenzo Lotto (c. 1480-1556) and, above all, a
polyptych carried out in 1508, and considered
the masterpiece of this great painter's early
period; it also houses the Museo Beniamino
Gigli (1890-1957), which has many souvenirs
of the famous tenor. The *Cattedrale*, dedicated
to St. Flavian, was rebuilt in the last years
of the 14th cent., and later underwent further
alterations. It has a fine lacunar ceiling, on
which Andrea Costa the wood-carver, and the
Venetian painter Antonio Rizzo worked in
1920. The tombs of Bishop Angelo Cino, who
built the church, and died in 1412, and Gregory XII (1325-1417) are also interesting.
The *Museo diocesano* contains archaeological
findings and works of art, including an interesting lion (once the base of a pillar), a bronze
bust by Antonio di Bernardino Calcagni (1536-
1593), a Holy Family, probably by Andrea
Mantegna (1431-1506), a polyptych representing
the Madonna and Child with Angels, St. Benedict and St. Sebastian by Ludovico Urbani
(active 1460-1493), and a panel depicting the
Glory of Mary by Cristoforo Gherardi (1508-
1556). The most admirable feature of the
church of *San Domenico*, which was rebuilt in
the 14th cent., is the fine marble portal, believed to have been designed by Giuliano da

Maiano in 1481; inside is a superb fresco of
St. Vincent Ferrer by Lorenzo Lotto. The
14th cent. church of *Sant'Agostino* has a portal
made out of Istrian stone, the work of Giuliano da Maiano, and a grandiose interior, with
paintings by Filippo Bellini (1550/55-1604). The
Palazzo Leopardi is an 18th cent. building; the
Sala Leopardi contains manuscripts by the
poet Giacomo Leopardi (1798-1837), while the
library, with its twenty-five thousand volumes,
was put together by Monaldo Leopardi, Giacomo's father. Walk to the Romanesque church
of *Santa Maria di Castelnuovo;* it has a fine
doorway, and in the lunette a wonderful bas-
relief representing the Madonna and Child
enthroned with the Archangels Gabriel and
Michael, by Nicola d'Ancona (mentioned 1253).
At *Porto Recanati* is a 15th cent. castle, with a
strong corbelled tower, built to defend the
coastal villages against the continual raids of
pirates.

** **REGGIO CALABRIA.** Well situated on
the eastern side of the strait of Messina, it is
a popular bathing resort. Completely destroyed
by the earthquake of 28 December 1908, it
has been rebuilt on a larger and more orderly
scale. The *Museo Nazionale di Reggio Calabria*
contains, among other things, a collection of
coins, another of Attic-style vases, figured terracottas, pinakes from Locri, Greek statues in
marble, and a wonderful glass cup of the 3rd
cent. B.C. In the medieval section of the museum is important architectural and decorative
material from Reggio, Arab-like stuccoes, and
coats-of-arms. In the archaeological section are
statues from the Hellenistic and Roman ages,
an imposing acroterial group from the Doric
temple of Casa Marafloti at Locri, objects from
the early Iron Age, small votive statues, bronzes, amber and glass-paste necklaces, pre-historic material, a stone baptismal font, possibly of the 11th cent., and a fine 15th cent.
wooden door. The *Museo Comunale* contains
a non-European ethnographic section, as well
as furnishings, terracotta figures, acroteria,
and other antique objects from Rhegion (the
ancient Reggio), Greek inscriptions, Byzantine seals, and fragments of mosaics. The art
gallery contains paintings of the 17th, 18th,
and 19th centuries, especially of the Neapolitan school, most of which come from buildings that were destroyed in the 1908 earthquake. In the *Duomo* is a marble pulpit with
a bas-relief by Francesco Ierace (1854-1937),
while the large Chapel of the Blessed Sacrament is decorated with polychrome marble
inlays of the 17th and 18th centuries. In the
church of the *Ottimati* are important remains
of a Cosmatesque floor of the Norman period.
In Via Torrione, part of a Hellenistic odeon.

** **REGGIO EMILIA.** An important historical, commercial, and industrial town situated in the plain, along the Via Emilia. The

*Recanati, Pinacoteca Civica. Lorenzo Lotto, Annun-
ciation.*

269

Reggio Emilia, Municipal Theatre.
Reggio Emilia, San Girolamo, Rotunda of Saints Simeon and Thaddaeus, interior.

Duomo, built for the first time in the 9th cent., was remodelled in the 13th and 14th, and further altered in later times. It has three doorways, the statues of Adam and Eve above the central one being the work of Prospero Sogari, called Prospero Spani (1516-1584). The interior is in the form of a Latin cross, with a nave and two aisles, and there are numerous works of art, including the tomb of Valerio Malaguzzi by Bartolomeo Spani (1468-1539), the tomb of Bishop Ugo Rangone, again by Prospero Spani, and a painting of the Assumption with Saints Peter and Jerome by Giovanni Francesco Barbieri, called Guercino (1591-1666). The *Basilica di San Prospero* was founded in the 10th cent. and rebuilt in the 16th. It is flanked by an octagonal bell-tower, and contains many works of art, the most admired being the frescoes by Camillo Procaccini (c. 1551-1629). The Sanctuary of the *Madonna della Ghiara* was begun in 1597 to a design by Alessandro Balbi (recorded 1590-1610). It contains many works of art, including frescoes, especially from the 17th cent., and marble and statues which reflect the beginning of the Baroque age. The church of *San Girolamo* was built by Gaspare Vigarani (1586-1663) in 1646. The *Museo Civico* include the Spallanzani Museum of natural history, a collection of Roman, Romanesque, Renaissance, and modern stone inscriptions, the Chierici Museum of Palaeontology, the Museum of the Risorgimento, and the Fontanesi Art Gallery: particularly admired are the Madonna and Child by Alessandro Tiarini (1577-1668), the Deposition by Jacopo Palma the Younger (1554-1628), and the Massacre of the Innocents by Domenico Pellizzi (1818-1874). The *Civica Galleria Parmeggiani* was created by Luigi and Anna Parmeggiani, who donated it to the town in 1933. It has important works by Italian and foreign painters, especially Spanish primitives, and a very large collection of arts and crafts. Walk to the *Villa Mauriziano*, where the poet Ludovico Ariosto (1474-1533) loved to stay.

* **REVERE** (Mantua). An agricultural and commercial town, situated parallel to the river Po. In the 18th cent. parish church (*Parrocchiale dell'Annunciazione*), with its characteristically curved facade, are paintings by Giuseppe Bazzani (c. 1690-1769). The *Palazzo Ducale* is a grandiose 15th cent. construction.

*** **RIETI.** Capital of the province of Sabina, situated on the edge of a fertile plain near the river Velino, beneath Monte Terminillo. It was once the capital of the Sabines, who called it Reate. The *Museo Civico* is housed in the 13th cent. Palazzo Comunale, a construction that was altered in later times. It contains archaeological material from the early Iron and Etruscan ages, a pentaptych of the Madonna and Child with Saints, carried out in 1370 by

Luca di Tommé (recorded 1330-1389), a triptych depicting the Resurrection (1511) by Marcantonio d'Antoniazzo (lived in the 15-16th cent.), other works by the same painter and his disciples, a Crucifixion with Franciscan Saints by Zannino di Pietro (lived in the 15th cent.), St. Gregory by Giovanni Battista Benaschi (1636-1688), St. Andrew the Apostle by Ascanio Manenti (1568-1663), St. Leonard visiting a prisoner by Antonio Gherardi (1644-1702), St. Cecilia and King David by Lattanzio Niccoli (recorded 1627-1660), a plaster cast of Hebe by Antonio Canova (1757-1822), an Old Woman spinning, Landscapes with shepherds and animals, and an Old Beggar, all attributed to Filippo Pietro Roos (c. 1655-1706), Still Life paintings by Giovan Paolo Spadino (lived in the 17-18th cent.), a Young Boy drinking by Antonio Amorosi (c. 1660-post 1736), a Young Boy writing by Amorosi, a Madonna, probably by Guido Reni (1575-1642), as well as court costumes, illuminated manuscripts, and drawings. The foundation stone of the *Duomo*, dedicated to the Assunta, was laid at the turn of the 12th cent. The church is preceded by an imposing Romanesque campanile with two storeys of coupled mullioned windows, and a portico built in the middle of the 15th cent. The Baroque interior is in the form of a Latin cross, and contains a panel of the Madonna and Child with Saints Vincent and Nicholas of Bari by Bartolomeo Torresani (c. 1500-1567), a painting of a Guardian Angel by Andrea Sacchi (1599-1661), and paintings of the Sacrifice of Noah and the Last Supper by Giovanni Francesco Romanelli (1610-1662). In the Chapel of the Relics or Coro d'Inverno (Winter Choir) is a Martyrdom of St. Barbara by Giovanni Andrea Lazzarini (1710-1801). In the main sacristy are precious 16th cent. reliquaries. One of the chapels in the aisle on the left is the result of work carried out by Gian Lorenzo Bernini (1598-1680), Carlo Fontana (1634-1714), and Sebastiano Cipriani (recorded 1696-1733). Other works worthy of notice include a much-admired statue of St. Barbara, designed by Gian Lorenzo Bernini and carried out by Giovanni Antonio Mari (recorded 1653-1661, the last date being the year of his death), a bas-relief of the Immaculate Conception by Lorenzo Ottoni (1648-1736), statues by the same sculptor, and a fresco of the Madonna and Child with two Saints by Antoniazzo Romano (c. 1435-1517). In the baptistery, a precious 16th cent. baptismal font. The Bishop's Palace (*Palazzo Vescovile*) was first built in 1283, by a certain Master Andrea; it faces Piazza Vittori, and has a fine loggia supported by two arches, built in 1288. Inside, one should notice the so-called "vaults of the Bishop's Palace", a large two-aisled portico, with pillars supporting Gothic arches; the Bishop's Arch was built by Pope Boniface VIII. The medieval walls (*Mura Medievali*), parts of which go back to the 13th cent., have survived intact. The 13th cent. Gothic church of *Santo Agostino* has a 14th cent. doorway, and its interior is in the form of a Latin cross. It contains a painting of the Madonna and Child with Saints by Giovanni Giacomo Pandolfi (recorded 1595-1630), and a cycle of 18th cent. paintings illustrating scenes from the life of St. Augustine. The Romanesque church of *San Pietro* dates from the middle of the 12th cent. It has a sober, gabled facade with a 13th cent. Romanesque doorway. By the side of the church is the late-Renaissance *Palazzo Vecchierelli*, parts of which foreshadow the Baroque; it has a spectacular courtyard. Other interesting buildings in Rieti include the *Palazzo del Governo*, formerly Vicentini, which was restored in the last years of the 16th cent. and has a loggia in the style of Vignola, the *Teatro Flavio Vespasiano*, the *Palazzo della Cassa di Risparmio*, formerly Crispolti, with a doorway carried out in 1818 by Giuseppe Gubleyras, the little church of *San Giuseppe*, which contains a painting of the Death of St. Joseph by Vincenzo Manenti (1600-1674), and the church of *San Francesco*, founded in 1245. The latter has a Romanesque doorway, while the interior is in the form of a Latin cross, with an aisleless nave. It contains a fresco of the Deposition, St. Agatha, and the Ascension by Lorenzo Torresani (c. 1500-1564), a St. Francis by Vincenzo Manenti and other frescoes and paintings, especially from the 13th, 14th and 15th centuries. In neighbourhood of Rieti are the famous Franciscan Sanctuaries, (*Santuari Francescani*) which should be visited: the Convento la Foresta or Santa Maria della Foresta, the Convento di Fonte Colombo, the Convento di Grecciò, and the Convento di San Giacomo, which grew up in the first half of the 13th cent., with a beautiful cloister, from where one climbs up to the Romitorio, St. Francis' favourite refuge.

* **RIFREDI** (neighbourhood of Florence). On the banks of the Terzolle. The Romanesque church of *Santo Stefano in Pane*, or *alle Panche*, formerly *Santo Stefano in Arcore*, was built in the 10-11th cent. and rebuilt in the 13th. The facade has a 16th cent. portico, with columns supporting its roof. In the lunette above the central doorway is a Pietà of the 15th cent. The interior is divided into a nave and two aisles, and contains a St. Francis by Jacopo Vignali (1592-1664), a 15th cent. della Robbia polychrome terracottas representing the Marriage of the Virgin, a small panel depicting the Madonna and Child from the Florentine school of the second half of the 15th cent., and in the nave a trap-door that leads down to the crypt. Walking down Via delle Panche, one comes to the 14th cent. villa of *La Quiete*, formerly Palagio di Quarto, which contains works by Jean Boulogne (1524-1608), by the painter Ridolfo del Ghirlandaio (1483-1561), from the school of Botticelli, and a beautiful

13th cent. panel depicting the Crucifixion. The imposing Baroque *Villa Corsini*, formerly the "Palagetto" (little palace) of the Strozzi family, has a vast facade and a 16th cent. garden. The *Villa Medicea della Petraia* was designed by Bernardo Buontalenti (1536-1608): the interior is sumptuous, with frescoes celebrating the deeds of the Medici family by Baldassare Franceschini, called Volterrano (1611-1689), furnishings and tapestry, mainly from the 17th cent. Particularly noteworthy is the upper terrace of the garden with the fountain by Niccolò Pericoli, called Tribolo (1500-1558). The *Villa Medicea di Castello*, built before the 14th cent. and called "Il Vivaio" (the nursery), was the favourite residence of the Medici, who enlarged it, commissioning Jacopo Carrucci, called Pontormo (1494-c.1556), to decorate it with paintings which, unfortunately, no longer exist. Ransacked and burnt after the decline of the Medici, it was restored by Giorgio Vasari (1511-1574), and Cosimo I enriched it with outstanding works of art, including the famous ones of the Birth of Venus and Spring by Botticelli (c. 1445-1510). Damaged in the Second World War, it was later restored.

** **RIMINI** (Forlì). Situated on the Adriatic coast, on the right bank of the river Marecchia, at the point where the ancient Roman roads, the Via Flaminia and Via Emilia meet. The *Tempio Malatestiano*, dedicated to St. Francis, is a magnificent Renaissance construction, though it was originally built in the second half of the 13th cent. Towards the middle of the 15th cent. work was begun on its outer facing and interior with the help of Leon Battista Alberti (1404-1472), who designed the magnificent facade. The interior consists of an aisleless nave, and contains the tomb of Sigismondo Malatesta, the work of Bernardo Ciuffagni (1381-1457) and Francesco di Simone Ferrucci (1437-1493), that of Isotta degli Atti,

Rimini, Augustan Arch.

272

Sigismondo's third wife, probably by Matteo de' Pasti (recorded 1441-1472), bas-reliefs representing the liberal Arts and Sciences by Agostino di Duccio (1418-post 1481), and the Chapel of the Ancestors and Descendants, also by Agostino di Duccio. The *Arco d'Augusto* is the most ancient Roman arch to have survived, and one of the most admired; it was erected in 27 B.C. in honour of Julius Caesar Octavius Augustus. The *Ponte di Tiberio* over the river Marecchia is built of Istrian stone, and has five arches. The Romanesque-Gothic church of *Sant'Agostino*, or San Giovanni Evangelista, dates from 1247: inside, it has the form of a rectangle, and contains some fine 14th cent. frescoes, brought to light during work carried out after the disastrous earthquake of 1916. The church of *San Giuliano* is mentioned as early as 816 A.D.: it contains a dramatic painting of the Martyrdom of St. Julian by Paolo Caliari, called Veronese (1528-1588), and a polyptych of St. Julian and scenes from his life by Bitino da Faenza (recorded 1398-1427). The *Museo e Pinacoteca Comunale* contains a Pietà by Giovanni Bellini (c. 1430-1516), St. Vincent Ferrer with Saints Sebastian and Roch, a masterpiece by Domenico Bigordi, called Ghirlandaio (1449-1494), and the Calling of St. Matthew by Guido Cagnacci (1601-1663). Walk to the church of *San Giovanni Battista*, rebuilt in the 17-18th cent. It contains one of Guido Cagnacci's most admired paintings, a Madonna with Saints. Walk to the Sanctuary of the *Madonna delle Grazie*, built in

the second half of the 14th cent., with a facade dating from 1578; it contains a painting of the Nativity by Giovanni Laurentini, called Arrigoni (c. 1550-1633). The *Palazzo dell'Arengario* is a Romanesque-Gothic building begun in the early 13th cent. After undergoing various alterations over the centuries, it was restored to its original form in 1900. It has two storeys, the lower one, which has six rows of arches, resting on massive pillars. The upper floor is decorated with mullioned windows, and the palace is surmounted by battlements. Next to it is the *Palazzo del Podestà*, which dates from the first half of the 14th cent. The *Roman Amphitheatre*, of which very little remains, was built in the time of Augustus or Tiberius. Discovered in the last century, it is the only one to have survived in Emilia. It consisted of four concentric circles, with an arena almost as big as that of the Colosseum.

* **RIONERO IN VULTURE** (Potenza). Situated on two hills, near the volcano of Vulture. The *Chiesa dei Morti* has a 16th cent. painting of the Madonna and Child with St. John, and precious wood carvings. In the ancient little church of *Sant'Antonio Abate* are some fair 18th cent. paintings, and a fine tabernacle of the Madonna del Carmine. Excursion to the *Abbey of San Michele di Monticchio*, or *del Vulture*, situated in a solitary, romantic spot; the abbey grew up out of the grottoes occupied by Basilian hermits before 1000 A.D. Inside, is the very ancient Chapel of St. Michael.

Rimini, Tempio Malatestiano.

* **RIPATRANSONE** (Ascoli Piceno). Situated on the hills that separate the valleys of the Menocchia and the Tesino, it commands a fine view. A recently discovered necropolis has shown that the area was already inhabited in pre-historic times. The *Cattedrale* is dedicated to Saints Gregory and Margaret, and was begun in 1597 to a design by Gaspare Guerra. It has an elegant interior, with paintings of the Madonna and Child with Saints Gregory and Magdalen by Giulio Lazzarelli (1607-c.1667) and St. Charles by Alessandro Turchi, called Orbetto (1578-1649), as well as a pulpit and a magistrate's bench by Desiderio Bonfini (a 17th cent. wood-carver). The *Palazzo Municipale* is an imposing building that was rebuilt in the second half of the 17th cent. It houses the town library, archives, notarial archives, museum, and an art gallery with important works of art, including a fresco of St. Gregory's Mass by Giacomo da Campli (lived in the second half of the 15th cent.), panels of polyptyches by Vittore Crivelli (c. 1440-1502) and Pietro Alemanno (recorded 1475-1498), and terracottas by Fra Mattia della Robbia (recorded 1468-1534) and Giovanni Francesco Gagliardelli (lived in the 16th cent.). Other interesting monuments are the *Porta di Monte Antico*, once the entrance to the town, the *Palazzo del Podestà*, erected in the early 14th cent., the church of *San Domenico*, which contains fifteen small panels representing the Mysteries of the Rosary by Ascanio Condivi (c. 1525-1574), and the small church of *San Pastore*, with its elegant little portico by Lucio Bonomi (lived in the 17-18th cent.).

* **RIVA** (Trent). A pleasant resort situated at the northernmost tip of Lake Garda, beneath the steep Monte Rocchetta. In the *Chiesa dell'Inviolata*, which was begun in 1603 to a design drawn up by an anonymous Portuguese architect, are frescoes by Pietro Ricchi, called Lucchese (1606-1675), and Teofilo Turri (lived in the 17th cent.). The 12th cent. *Rocca* is the town's most unusual construction. It was first enlarged by the Scaliger family, and later by the Venetians, but badly neglected by the Austrians, who used it as a barracks in the last century. It houses a civic museum, which contains many Egyptian objects, pagan altars, Roman funerary cippi, remains of proto-historic and Roman tombs, Roman and medieval furnishings, objects and documents concerning the history of Riva, ancient coins, as well as ornithological and mineralogical collections. The parish church of the *Assunta* was built in the early 18th cent., and contains an Assumption by Giuseppe Craffonara (1790-1837), a Madonna of the Rosary with two Saints by Giambettino Cignaroli (1706-1770), and paintings by Giuseppe Alberti (1640-1716).

* **RIVERA** (Agrigento). Built to a reticular plan in a pleasant hillside position within sight of the sea. Excursion to *Eraclea Minoa*, which was founded by the inhabitants of Selinunte, who called it Minoa; the first name, Eraclea, was added by Spartan colonists who arrived at the end of the 6th cent. Part of the wall with two towers has survived. An amphitheatre once stood on top of the hill, but very little of it has survived. A Greek necropolis has been discovered. In 1951 a theatre was discovered in a new archaeological area, and the urban nucleus was brought to light. The *Antiquarium* contains material excavated in the surrounding areas.

* **RIVOLI** (Turin). A small town situated on the slope of a morainic amphitheatre. The highest part is grouped around the 18th cent. *Castello*, which has some medieval remains. In the same district is the church of *Sant'Antonio di Ranverso*, one of the most important examples of medieval architecture in Piedmont, which reflects the influence of the French Gothic style. Built in the late 12th cent., but altered on numerous occasions (the facade dates from the 14-15th cent.), it contains an important cycle of frescoes by Giacomo Jaquerio of the 15th cent., and a large pentaptych by Defendente Ferrari (active 1511-1535).

* **ROBBIO** (Pavia). An agricultural and industrial town. It may have been the Roman Retovium. The 13th cent. church of *San Pietro* was restored in the 15th cent., and has a doorway with a pointed arch. The church of *San Michele* has remains of an ornamental doorway with a pointed arch, and contains fragments of 15th cent. frescoes. The 14th cent. *Castello* has recently been remodelled.

* **ROCCA DI PAPA** (Rome). Pleasantly situated to the north of Monte Cavo, it has a medieval and a modern part. The church of the *Assunta* (1664-1754) was rebuilt as a result of an earthquake in 1800, with a neo-Classical facade by L. Bracci. It contains paintings of the 19th cent., a panel depicting the Redeemer enthroned, carried out in 1523 and attributed to Pietro Buonaccorsi, called Perin del Vaga (1501-1547), and M. Venusti (1512-1579), a fine Renaissance tabernacle, and a Madonna and Child of the 14th cent. Sienese school. Excursion to the 16th cent. *Madonna del Tufo*, with a fresco painted on tufa rock by A. Romano (1435-1508).

* **ROCCALBEGNA** (Grosseto). A picturesque town built at the foot of two rocky mountains, near the confluence of the Marlancione. The ground is very unstable as a result of the clay soil beneath the rock. The 13th cent. church of *Santi Pietro e Paolo* is Romanesque, and the lowered architrave demonstrates the instability of the ground; the interior is in ruins, and the roof has been demolished. The works of art that were once in the church are now in

the priest's house: Madonna and Child by A. Lorenzetti (active in the first half of the 14th cent.), and a Deposition by Ventura Salimbeni (1557-1613). The *Oratorio del Crocifisso* (1388) has a bell gable, and contains a Crucifixion by Luca di Tommè (1355-1389).

* ROCCAMONFINA (Caserta). Situated on the eastern side of the crater of the volcano of Roccamonfina, in an unusual and picturesque position. The *Collegiata di Santa Maria Maggiore*, rebuilt in the second decade of the 18th cent., has a facade with a 17th cent. porch, and is flanked by a tapered 18th cent. belltower. The high altar has marble inlays, and there are fine 18th cent. metal gates af the entrance to the two side chapels. Walk to the 15th cent. sanctuary of *Maria Santissima dei Lattani*, which is what attracts tourists and scholars to Roccamonfina. In front of the church still grows the chestnut-tree planted by St. Bernardino of Siena, who, together with S. Giacomo della Marca, founded the sanctuary. In the inner courtyard, on the left, is the well-restored hermitage of San Bernardino, and the little 15th cent. fountain of the Madonna. The wooden doors of the portal are divided up into twenty squares, an interesting work that dates from the early 16th cent. The interior consists of an aisleless nave, with 15th cent. frescoes, an anonymous 15th cent. panel of the Crucifixion with Saints, and a painting of the Pardon of Assisi, attributed to Salvatore Rosa (1615-1673). In the Chapel of the Vergine dei Lattani is a polychrome basalt image of the Madonna and Child, made before 1000 A.D.

*** ROMA/ROME. The capital of Italy is built on the banks of the Tiber amongst beautiful hills, not far from the sea.
Ancient Rome: the *Forum Romanum* was the commercial, religious, and political centre of Roman life, and included the *Curia*, where the Senate met, the present brick building being a reconstruction that goes back to the time

Roccalbegna, Church of Santi Pietro e Paolo. Ambrogio Lorenzetti, Saint Peter, detail.
Rome, Castel Sant'Angelo and Bridge.

275

of Diocletian, the *Temple of Saturn*, where the State Treasury was kept, a building begun in 497 B.C. and continually altered up to the 3rd cent B.C., the *Temple of the Dioscuri*, dedicated in 484 to Castor and Pollux, the *Casa delle Vestali* (House of the Vestal Virgins), the *Arch of Titus*, erected in 81 A.D., which consists of a single archway with fluted half-columns, the vault being decorated with beautiful friezes, the *Temple of Antoninus and Faustina*, the *Arch of Septimius Severus*, erected in 203 with three archways and richly decorated with reliefs, and *Santa Maria Antiqua*, erected in the 6th cent. and preceded by an atrium with fragments of frescoes; the interior is divided into a nave and two aisles, and there are numerous frescoes from the 6th and 7th centuries. On the Palatine Hill: *House of Livia*, a typical example of a Roman dwelling; the *Palace of the Flavians*, built in the 1st cent. A.D.; *Domus Augustana*, the emperor's private habitation; *Stadium*, built by Domitian, and surrounded by two tiers of

Rome, Tomb of Cecilia Metella.
Rome, Roman Forum.

arcades; *Thermae of Severius*. The *Fori Imperiali* were built by the emperors when the ancient Forum proved inadequate; they consist of: the *Forum Julium;* the *Forum of Augustus;* the *Pantheon*, built in 27 B.C., but rebuilt in the time of Hadrian. Its brick structure is in the form of a cylinder, preceded by a pronaos with Corinthian columns, and decorated with a triangular pediment; the *Ara Pacis Augustae*, erected in 13-9 B.C. (rebuilt in 1938), consists of an altar surrounded by a marble wall decorated with fine reliefs; the *Colosseum*, begun by Vespasian in 72 A.D. and continued by Titus in 80, is an elliptical structure with three storeys of arcades, and a fourth decorated with pilasters and corbels. The front seats all around the arena formed a podium, part of which was reserved for the emperor and his retinue; of the *Trajan Markets and Fora*, an architectural complex built by Apollodorus of Damascus (111-114 A.D.), only the *Basilica Ulpia* and the celebrated *Trajan's Column*, with its spiral band of magnificent relief-sculpture, have survived; the *Column of Marcus Aurelius*, erected between 176 and 193, is composed of blocks of marble beautifully decorated with a spiral band of reliefs representing military events; the *Thermae of Caracalla*, the most imposing of Roman baths, was also equipped with libraries and many other rooms; the *Basilica of Maxentius*, begun in 306 and completed by Constantine, was divided into a nave and two aisles by four massive pillars, and the three barrel-vaults in the right aisle still survive; the *Arch of Constantine* was erected in 315, and has three richly decorated archways. Along the *Via Appia Antica* we find the *Tomb of Cecilia Metella*, erected in the last decades of the Republic in the form of a cylinder, and decorated

Rome, Arch of Titus.
Rome, Ara Pacis.
Rome, Trajan Markets.

277

with an elegant frieze, as well as the *Catacombs of San Callisto* of the 2nd cent., with the tomb of St. Cecilia and frescoes of the 7-8th cent. One enters the catacombs, which include four storeys of galleries, through the 4th cent. church of *San Sebastiano*.

Medieval Rome: Santa Maria d'Aracoeli, built in the 4th or 5th cent., was later remodelled

Rome, Pantheon, interior.
Rome, statue of Marcus Aurelius.

in the Romanesque-Gothic style. The 4th cent. church of *Sant'Agnese* was rebuilt in the 7th; it is divided into a nave and two aisles, with matronei (women's galleries), and has a precious 7th cent. mosaic in the apse. *Santa Costanza* is a 4th cent. circular building (it was first built as a mausoleum); the nave is decorated with mosaics carried out in the same period as the foundation of the church. The church of *Santi Giovanni e Paolo* was erected in the 4th cent., though the apse, portico, and campanile were added later in the Romanesque period. The church of *Santi Quattro Coronati*

is of Early-Christian origin, but was rebuilt in the 12th cent. The 4th cent. *San Clemente* was destroyed by the Normans, and rebuilt in the 12th cent. One enters the church by passing through a colonnaded courtyard. The interior is divided into a nave and two aisles, and has a Cosmatesque-type floor; there is a 12th cent. mosaic in the apse, and frescoes by Masolino da Panicale (1383-1477) in the Chapel of St. Catherine. One may also see the remains of the lower church, with frescoes from the 6th to the 12th cent. The 5th cent. *San Pietro in Vincoli* has a basilican interior, with a nave

Rome, Santa Maria in Cosmedin, interior.
Rome, Basilica of Maxentius.

Rome, Santa Sabina, interior.

and two aisles, and contains the Tomb of Julius II by Michelangelo (1475-1564), with the famous statue of Moses. *Santa Maria Maggiore*, founded in 431, still retains its early Christian structure, though the apse was rebuilt in 1200, and the church altered in 1600. The interior is divided into a nave and two aisles, with a 16th cent. timber ceiling and precious 5th cent. mosaics. *Santa Prassede* was begun in the 5th cent., and rebuilt in 1822. The interior is divided into a nave and two aisles by trabeated columns, and contains precious 9th cent. mosaics. *San Lorenzo fuori le mura* was founded by Constantine, but has been altered many times; it has a 13th cent. portico, while the interior is divided into a nave and two aisles by ancient columns, with a matroneum (women's gallery). One passes through the 13th cent. Romanesque cloister in order to reach the catacombs of St. Ciriacus. *Santa Sabina* is a typical early basilica erected in the 5th cent. *San Paolo fuori le mura*, a patriarchal basilica erected in the 4th cent. and completed in the 5th by Galla Placidia, was destroyed by fire in 1823, and later rebuilt; the interior is divided into a nave and four aisles, and is faced in marble. It contains mosaics from the 5th cent. and others by Cavallini (active in the 13th cent.), as well as a Gothic candlestick by Arnolfo di Cambio (1240-1302). The cloister dates from the 13th cent. *Santa Cecilia in Trastevere*, founded in the 4-5th cent., was rebuilt in the 9th and altered in 1700. In its present form, *Santa Maria in Trastevere* dates from the 12th cent.; it contains 12th cent. mosaics and works by Cavallini. *Santa Maria in Cosmedin* was built in the 6th cent., but remodelled in the 12th, the same century in which the bell-tower was

added; it contains various Cosmatesque works (floor, ambones, candlestick).

Renaissance Rome: Palazzo della Cancelleria, erected in the second half of the 15th cent., perhaps by A. Bregno (1418-1513), with the collaboration of Bramante (1441-1514). *Palazzo Venezia* (now the seat of a Museum of Arts and Crafts), erected in 1455 to a design attributed to Alberti (1404-1472); the colonnade in the courtyard is the work of Giuliano da Maiano (1432-1490). *Santa Maria del Popolo*, built in the second half of the 15th cent., perhaps by B. Pontelli, contains frescoes by Pinturicchio, as well as a Conversion of St. Paul and a Crucifixion of St. Peter by Caravaggio; the Chigi Chapel was designed by Raphael. *Santa Maria della Pace*, attributed to B. Pontelli (1450-1492), has a Baroque rear facade, while its aisleless nave is decorated with Sybils by Raphael (1483-1520); the cloister, by Bramante, is in the form of two superimposed loggias. *Santa Maria sopra Minerva*, erected upon an ancient temple, was rebuilt in the Gothic style, but has a beautiful Renaissance facade. In the courtyard of the church of *San Pietro in Montorio* is Bramante's Tempietto, a harmonius circular building with a dome. *Santo Agostino*, with its two-storeyed Renaissance facade, has an interior divided into a nave and two aisles, restored by Vanvitelli (1700-1773). The church of the *Trinità dei Monti* was built in the 16th cent., and the facade is flanked on both sides by a campanile; situated at the top of the fantastically steep steps, it dominates Piazza di Spagna. *St. Peter's*: the present church was begun in 1506 by Julius II, but it rises upon a much earlier Christian basilica. Though Rossellino (1409-1464) was commissioned to

Rome, Santa Maria Maggiore, interior.

Rome, Capitol.

Rome, The consul in his chariot and four circus guards, inlay from the Basilica of Giunio Basso.
Rome, San Lorenzo fuori le mura. Mosaic on the great arch.

Rome, San Pietro in Vaticano, Treasury. Justin's Cross.

Rome, Santi Cosma e Damiano. Mosaic in the apse, detail.

Rome, Santa Maria Antiqua. St. Andrew.

Rome, San Clemente, subterranean church. Madonna Regina.

carry it out, the design drawn up by Bramante was the one eventually adopted. Various artists collaborated in its construction, such as Raphael, B. Peruzzi (1481-1536), A. Sangallo the Younger, and finally, in 1546, Michelangelo. On Michelangelo's death, the work was continued by I. Barozzi, called Vignola (1507-1573), and others. The ground plan was changed from that of a Greek cross to a Latin one, one of the sides of the church being extended by C. Maderno (1556-1629), who also designed the facade. The imposing nave and two aisles of the interior are decorated with numerous paintings and statues. The *Farnesina* is one of the most harmonious examples of Renaissance architecture: built by B. Peruzzi (1481-1536), it is decorated with precious frescoes by Raphael, Sebastiano del Piombo (1485-1547), and Sodoma (1477-1549). The *Palazzo Farnese* was begun by A. Sangallo the Younger, and continued by Michelangelo; it has a Bramantesque courtyard. The *Piccola Farnesina* (which houses the Museo Barraco of classical sculpture) was built in 1523. The *Palazzo Massimo alle Colonne*, the masterpiece of B. Peruzzi (1481-1536) and A. Sangallo the Younger (1483-1546), has a convex rusticated front. The *Piazza del Campidoglio* was designed by Michelangelo (1475-1563) in 1536. *Santa Maria degli Angeli* was built by Michelangelo in 1566, and later altered by Vanvitelli.

Baroque Rome: the *Chiesa del Gesù* was begun by Vignola in 1568, and completed by G. Della Porta (1540-1602), who also designed the facade. Many architects, such as Fontana, Maderno, Pozzo and others, worked on the *Palazzo del Quirinale*, which was begun in 1574; the doorway of the facade is by Bernini. *Santo Andrea della Valle*, with its huge dome, was begun at the end of the 16th cent. and completed in 1625 by Maderno; its facade was designed by G. Rainaldi (1570-1655). *Sant'Ignazio*, built in 1626-1630 by O. Grassi (1583-1654), has an interior richly decorated with marble and frescoes. The *Palazzo di Montecitorio*, begun by Bernini, was completed by Fontana (1634-1714) with a majestic facade. The *Oratorio dei Filippini*, a splendid example of the Baroque style, near the Chiesa Nuova, is the work of Borromini. *Piazza Navona* has an elliptical shape, and is dominated by Bernini's *Fontana dei Fiumi* (Fountain of Rivers); on one side of the square is the Baroque church of *Sant'Agnese* by Borromini. *San Giovanni in Laterano* was founded in the 4th cent. and rebuilt by Borromini. The facade is by A. Galilei (1691-1736). The interior is divided into a nave and four aisles, with a Cosmatesque floor and a precious Renaissance timber ceiling. *Piazza San Pietro*, Bernini's masterpiece, acts as a vestibule to the Basilica of St. Peter's; it consists of two hemicycles, each comprising

Rome, Villa Farnesina.

Rome, St. Peter's.
Rome, Palazzo Venezia.

Rome, St. Peter's Square.
Rome, Sant'Ivo alla Sapienza.

three passages, surmounted by numerous statues. The church of *Sant'Ivo alla Sapienza* is a very stylish work of Borromini, carried out in 1660. *Piazza di Spagna*, with the majestic staircase of the Trinità dei Monti designed by A. Specchi (1668-1729) and F. de Sanctis (1693-1740); the fountain in the centre is by Bernini. On one side of the square is Bernini's *Palazzo di Propaganda Fide*. The *Fontana di Trevi* is the work of Niccolò Salvi (1697-1751). *Santi Apostoli* was rebuilt in 1702 by C. Fontana, but goes back to the 5th cent., and has a 15th cent. portico; the interior is interesting, and is divided into a nave and two aisles. *Santa Croce in Gerusalemme* was founded in the 4th cent., though its facade dates from the 18th; it has a very imposing Baroque interior, with a Cosmatesque floor.

Neo-Classical Rome: Piazza del Popolo owes its present design to G. Valadier (1762-1839); the *Parco del Pincio* was laid out in the last century, together with the Casina Valadier; *Vittoriano* dates from the 19-20th cent.; *Teatro dell'Opera; EUR. Musei;* the *Museo Capitolino* is housed in a palace designed by Michelangelo, and has a collection of classical sculpture. The *Museo dei Conservatori* is housed in the palace of the same name designed by Michelangelo, and contains Greek and Roman sculpture. In the same building is the *Pinacoteca Capitolina*, with paintings from the various schools of the 14-17th cent., and the *Museo Nuovo*, with a collection of Greek art. The *Galleria Doria-Pamphili* contains Italian and foreign masterpieces of the 15-17th cent. The *Museo di Roma* is housed in the 18th cent. Palazzo Braschi, and contains material illustrating the life of Rome. The *Museo di Castel Sant'Angelo* is to be found in the castle of the same name, built by Hadrian in 135-139 A.D. as his mausoleum, but greatly altered later, especially in the Renaissance (the bastions were constructed by Sangallo). There is a collection of weapons, and it is worth visiting the Hall of Justice, the prisons, and the Pope's Apartment (with valuable paintings). The *Vatican Museums and Art Galleries* are housed in the Vatican Palace, a grandiose architectural complex begun in the 13th cent., in the construction of which all the most famous architects of Rome collaborated, from Bramante to Sangallo, from Fontana to Bernini. The art gallery contains works from the primitives up to the 18th cent., Raphael's tapestries being particularly famous;

Rome, Trinità dei Monti.

Rome, Santa Maria Nova. Madonna.

Rome, The Borgia apartment in the Vatican. Pinturicchio, Temptation of Saints Anthony and Paul, detail.

Rome, The Borgia apartment in the Vatican. Pinturicchio, Visitation, detail.

Rome, Galleria Borghese. Gian Lorenzo Bernini, David.

Rome, Trevi Fountain. Pietro Bracci, The Ocean.

Rome, Galleria Borghese. Gian Lorenzo Bernini, The rape of Proserpine.

Rome, Santa Maria della Vittoria. Gian Lorenzo Bernini, St. Theresa in ecstasy.

the *Museo Pio-Clementino* has a collection of Greek and Roman sculpture, with the famous statue of the Laocoon (1st cent. B.C.); the *Etruscan Museum;* the *Egyptian Museum;* the *Borgia Apartment,* decorated by Pinturicchio and his followers; the *Sistine Chapel,* with frescoes by Michelangelo depicting scenes from Genesis, and the Last Judgement; *Raphael's Stanze and Loggie.* The *Galleria Nazionale d'Arte Antica* is housed in the splendid Baroque Palazzo Barberini, erected by Maderno and Borromini and completed by Bernini, and contains paintings from the 13-16th cent. The *Galleria Borghese,* situated in the beautiful park of the Villa Borghese, has a collection of antique sculpture and many works by Canova (including the famous Venus) and Bernini (Apollo and Daphne, David, the Rape of Proserpine) on the ground floor; on the first floor are Roman and Venetian paintings of the Renaissance. The *Galleria d'Arte Moderna* has a very rich collection of modern paintings and sculpture, including foreign works, from 1800 to the present day. The *Museo di Villa Giulia,* housed in the villa built by Vignola for Pope Julius III, is an archaeological museum. The *Museo Nazionale Romano* has a rich collection of archaeological material, as well as Greek and Hellenistic sculpture; on the upper floor are stuccoes and paintings from the Augustan age and in the Pompeyan style, as well as others from the Farnesina.

* **ROMANO DI LOMBARDIA** (Bergamo).

A modern, commercial and industrial town, with an older centre. The parish church (*Parrocchiale di Santa Maria Assunta*) was remodelled in the 16th cent., and contains a Last Supper by Giovanni Battista Moroni (c. 1526-1578), an Immaculate Conception by Jacopo Palma the Younger (1544-1628), and an altar-frontal representing the Crucifixion, inlaid by Giovanni Battista Caniana (1671-1754). The *Palazzo del Podestà* is a Venetian construction of the 16-17th cent. The remains of the 11-12th cent. *Castello Visconteo* include corner towers.

* **RONCIGLIONE** (Viterbo). Situated on a

southern ramification of the Ciminian mountains, the town has a medieval urban centre, and a more modern part that developed in the 17-18th cent. The *Duomo* was designed by Carlo Rainaldi (1611-1691) in the Baroque style, with a two-storeyed facade. The grandiose interior is divided into a nave and two aisles, and contains marble altars, an altarpiece depicting the Assumption by Francesco Trevisani (1656-1746), and an altarpiece representing the Madonna of the Rosary by Giuseppe Ghezzi (1634-1721). The church of *Santa Maria della Pace* was first built in 1575, and its facade is decorated with pilasters: it contains parts of a triptych by Antoniazzo Romano (c. 1435-1517) depicting Saints Catherine and Peter, a 15th cent. fresco of the Madonna of Peace by a painter of the Viterbo school, and, in the sacristy, a precious panel representing the Madonna of the Rosary and the fifteen Mysteries, which dates from the end of the 16th cent. The ruined 12-13th cent. church of *Sant'Andrea* has a stylish campanile, erected in 1430 by Galasto da Como, incorporated in its facade. The church of *Santa Maria della Provvidenza* is of medieval origin, but was repaired towards the middle of the 18th cent., and again in 1954, after part of it had collapsed into the ravine below; it has a small portico, and a small, slender, Romanesque-looking campanile which dates from the 12-13th cent. Its interior is bare, though there are frescoes of the 15th cent. The facade of *Santa Maria degli Angeli,* called *del Collegio,* is decorated with pilasters and coupled columns, but the church is most admired for the pure Baroque lines of the interior. It is worth visiting the nearby *Lake Vico,* the lacus Ciminus of antiquity, situated in the Ciminian mountains.

* **ROSANO** (neighbourhood of Florence). A

little village on the banks of the river Arno, gathered around a *Benedictine Monastery* that was built in 780, rebuilt in the 12th cent., and repaired in the 16th and 18th centuries;

Romano di Lombardia, Visconti Castle.

it is one of the most ancient and famous monasteries in Tuscany. A 12th cent. bell-tower rises above the courtyard. The church of the Santissima Annunziata contains works of art, including an exquisite triptych depicting the Annunciation, Saints Eugene and Benedict, John the Baptist and Nicholas, by Giovanni del Ponte (1385-1437), a cusped panel depicting the Annunciation, perhaps by Jacopo di Cione, called Jacopo Orcagna (recorded 1365-1398), a panel depicting the Crucifixion and scenes of the Passion by an artist of the 13th cent. Tuscan school, and a fine baptismal font.

* **ROSCIANO** (Pescara). Situated in a beautiful position, with a splendid medieval *Castello*. Excursion to the Cistercian church of *Santa Maria Arabona* (1208), the first of its kind to be built in the Abruzzi. The front part of the edifice is missing, but the exterior is still imposing, while the apse has the typical Cistercian form. The interior is divided into a nave and two aisles, with a cross-vaulted ceiling.

* **ROSCIOLO** (L'Aquila). Starting-point for interesting excursions, and especially for the ascent of Monte Velino. The 15th cent. church of *Santa Maria delle Grazie*, on which two masters called Giovanni and Martino worked, as an inscription on the facade recalls, is flanked by a bell-tower supported by two large arches, based on large cylindrical pillars. The parts of the church discovered during the restoration work carried out in 1935, especially those inside, are interesting; some of them are frescoed. Walk to the 11th cent. Romanesque church of *Santa Maria in Valle Porclaneta*, which contains an important 12th cent. ambo, and an iconostasis, with four small columns and Corinthian capitals, also of the 12th cent.

* **ROSETO DEGLI ABRUZZI** (Teramo). Excursion to *Santa Maria di Propezzano*, a Romanesque-Gothic church of the 13th cent. It has a facade with two Gothic doorways. The only part of the originally Romanesque church of *San Clemente al Vomano* that has survived, is the doorway; inside, there is a beautiful ciborium.

* **ROSSANO** (Cosenza). Situated on a hill covered with olive-groves, it has many traces of its Byzantine past. Recent discoveries seem to prove the town's Roman origin. The *Cattedrale*, dedicated to the Assunta, has a basilican interior, with sumptuous carved gilt timber ceilings. Both the latter and the church itself are very ancient, but were well restored at the beginning of this century. The Madonna Achiropita (painted miraculously) is an ancient and revered Byzantine fresco. In the sacristy is a 15th cent. panel of the Madonna della Pietà in a Byzantine style. In the Bishop's Palace is the 6th cent. *Codex Rossanensis*, or *Purpureus*, the oldest and most precious of Greek miniatured evangelaria (books containing passages from the Gospels). The church of *San Marco*, built on a rock, is an interesting 11th cent. Byzantine building: it has three semicircular apses on the outside, and contains a Byzantine fresco of the Madonna, which dates from the same period as the church. The little churches of *Santa Maria del Piliere* and *San Nicola al Vallone*, both of Byzantine origin, are also interesting.

* **ROVERETO** (Trent). An important cultural and industrial town, situated in a pleasant hollow, where the Leno runs into the Adige. The *Palazzo del Municipio*, formerly occupied by the Pretura, was enlarged in the 15th cent., and contains the coats-of-arms of the Castelbarco family, the ancient lords of the city, of the Venetian podestà, and of the Hapsburgs. The *Castle* was built in the 14th cent. by Guglielmo di Castelbarco, and extended in the 15th by the Venetians. It houses the *Museo Storico della Guerra* (Historical War Museum), which has a collection of material illustrating both World Wars. In the big Malipiero tower is the Campana dei Caduti (Bell of the Fallen), cast in 1925 with bronze supplied by all the countries involved in the First World War. The church of *San Marco* was begun in 1462: it has a modern facade, and contains frescoes by Luigi Cavenaghi (1844-1918), statues by Domenico Molin (1691-1761) and Antonio Giuseppe Sartori (1712-1792), as well as paintings by Domenico Ricci, called Brusasorci (c. 1516-1567) and Gaspare Antonio Baroni di Cavalcabò (1682-1759). The *Museo Civico* has a natural science section, and an archaeological col-

Rosciolo, Santa Maria in Valle Porclaneta, pulpit.

lection from the 5th cent. B.C. onwards. The interior of the church of *Santa Maria del Carmine* is decorated by the contemporary painter, Giorgio Wenter Marini.

* ROVEZZANO (neighbourhood of Florence). The church of *Sant'Andrea a Rovezzano* is a very ancient construction, but has been remodelled many times. It is flanked by a fine Romanesque campanile, and contains works of art, which include a small statue of the Madonna and Child by Piero di Bartolo Gargalli (15th cent.), a terracotta of the Madonna and Child gathering a lily, from the workshop of Luca della Robbia, and a Madonna and Child with two Angels by an artist of the Florentine school (second half of the 13th cent.). The smallish Baroque bell gable near the ancient little church of *San Jacopo al Girone* is a characteristic landmark.

** ROVIGO. A rapidly expanding agricultural and industrial town, it is the capital of the province of Polesine. The *Palazzo dell'Accademia dei Concordi* was designed by Sante Baseggio (1794-1861), and houses an art gallery with many works of art, including a Madonna and Child by Giovanni Bellini, called Giambellino (c. 1430-1516), Christ carrying the Cross by the same painter, Venus and the looking-glass by Jean Gossaert (c. 1472-1533), the Death of Cleopatra, Lot and his daughters, the Finding of Moses by Sebastiano Mazzoni (c. 1611-1678), Ulysses and Calypso by Luca Giordano (1632-1705), St. Francis of Paola by Giovan Battista Piazzetta (1682-1754), a Portrait of Antonio Riccoboni by Giovan Battista Tiepolo (1696-1770), and a Portrait of a Woman by Rosalba Carriera (1675-1757). The 10th cent. *Duomo* dedicated to St. Stephen the Pope, was rebuilt in 1696 to a design by Girolamo Frigimelica (1653-1732). Its works of art include a Resurrection with Saints Bellino and Stephen the Pope, by one of the school of Jacopo Palma the Younger (1544-1628). The church of the Beata Vergine del Soccorso, called the Rotonda, was designed by Francesco Zamberlan (1529-1606). The Gothic church of *San Francesco* was built in the 14-15th cent. The *Porta San Bartolo* was built in 1482-1486, after Rovigo had been handed over to the Venetians. The *Palazzo del Municipio*, formerly the Loggia dei Notai, dates from the 16th cent.

* RUBIERA (Reggio Emilia). Situated on the left bank of the river Secchia. It was here that the inhabitants of Reggio built a massive castle to defend the Via Emilia and the passage over the Secchia at the beginning of the 13th cent. The 18th cent. parish church of *Santi Donnino e Biagio* contains works by the goldsmith Francesco Spani (died in 1530). In the same district is the *Pieve dei Santi Faustino e Giovita*, which contains a 13th cent. fresco; in the sacristy is a painting of Saints Faustinus

and Giovita by one of the school of Benvenuto Tisi, called Garofalo (1481-1559).

* RUTIGLIANO (Bari). Situated between Bari and Monopoli, not far from the Adriatic coast. It occupies the site of an ancient Apulian town. The church of *Santa Maria della Colonna* was built at the very beginning of the 12th cent. by the Norman Count Hugo, but has undergone many alterations since. The architrave of the doorway is decorated with a fine piece of sculpture representing Christ and the Apostles and, higher up, the Annunciation. The interior has a nave and two aisles, and contains a polyptych of the Madonna and Saints, carried out in 1450 by Antonio Vivarini.

** RUVO DI PUGLIA (Bari). Situated in fertile country with the Adriatic coast as a

Ruvo di Puglia, Cathedral.
Ruvo di Puglia, Cathedral. Telamon.

boundary on one side, near the ports of Bisceglie, Molfetta, and Bari. The Romanesque *Cattedrale* was built with dark stone in the 12-13th cent. Its facade is enlivened by a magnificent rose-window (1237) divided into twelve sections, niches with statues, relieving arches on half columns, human and animal heads, and leaf patterns. It has a wonderful central portal, the archivolt of which rests on two gryphons supported by small columns with lions for bases; the latter, in their turn, are supported by crouching caryatids. The detached bell-tower, a very ancient construction, was once used for defence. The cathedral's works of art include frescoes, the memorial plaques of bishops from the 15th and 16th centuries, a Romanesque-style ciborium designed by Ettore Bernich (1845-1914), and a painting by Marco Pino, (c. 1525-1588). In the Palazzo Jatta is the *Museo Jatta*, which has more than one thousand seven hundred vases found in the immediate neighbourhood; they illustrate the entire development of local ceramic ware from the 4th cent. B.C. to the first centuries of the Christian era. In the first room the finest objects are the large

askoi of the kind produced at Canusium (modern Canosa); in the second room are red-figure vases, as well as Attic, proto-Italiot and Apulian vases, mainly of the 5th and 4th centuries B.C.; in the third room is a superb 5th cent. Attic krater, with the figure of Dionysus surrounded by Sileni and personifications; in the fourth room is an Attic krater of the end of the 5th cent. B.C., with a representation of the death of Talos, the bronze monster who guarded the shores of Crete; the fifth room contains helmets, leggings, spears and bronze objects found in the necropolis of Ruvo.

* **SABBIONETA** (Mantua). A picturesque little town, with traces of the Gonzaga family. The construction of the *Palazzo del Giardino* was begun in 1568: the modesty of its exterior conceals an interesting interior, some of the rooms being finely decorated with frescoes. Above all, one should visit the so-called Galleria degli Antichi (Gallery of the Ancients) where there are frescoes by Pietro Martire Pesenti (recorded 1563-1594), and Giovanni and Cherubino Alberti (active in the second half

Sabbioneta, Church of the Incoronata, interior.

of the 16th cent.). The *Teatro all'Antica* or *Olimpico* was designed by Vincenzo Scamozzi (1552-1616), who considered it his masterpiece. The *Palazzo Ducale* dates from the 16th cent.: it houses the Galleria degli Antenati (Ancestors' Gallery) and contains fragments of decorations by Bernardino Campi (1522-1591), Alberto Cavalli (active in the first half of the 16th cent.), Pietro Martire Pesenti, and Fornaretto Mantovano (lived in the 16th cent.). The church of the *Incoronata* contains the tomb of Vespasiano Gonzaga, the work of Giovanni Battista della Porta (c. 1542-1597). The parish church of *Santa Maria Assunta* was designed by Pietro Martire Pesenti.

* **SACILE** (Pordenone). An agricultural and industrial town on the Livenza. The *Duomo* was built in the 15th cent. on the remains of a 14th cent. structure: it has a fine facade with a slender campanile; the Madonna and Saints is by Francesco Bassano the Elder (c. 1470-1540). The Madonna della Salute in the little church of *San Gregorio* is by Pietro Liberi (1614-1687). The *Palazzo Flagini* now *Bilia*, built in the 15-16th cent., is worth visiting.

Sabbioneta, Church of the Incoronata, exterior.
Sabbioneta, Olympic Theatre, interior.

* SACRA DI SAN MICHELE (Town of Chiusa San Michele, province of Turin). An abbey built on Monte Pirchiriano. The Abbey church was built in the 10th cent. and dedicated to St. Michael. The impressive interior is a mixture of 13th cent. Gothic and Romanesque styles. It contains a triptych by Defendente Ferrari (active 1510-1531) and some tombs of the House of Savoy. The crypt consists of three chapels dating from the 15th, 18th and 20th centuries. Nearby are the ruins of the Sepolcro dei Monaci (Monks' Tomb), which has an octagonal plan and dates from 1000 A.D.

* SALA CONSILINA (Salerno). A picturesque town situated on the eastern side of the Vallo di Diano, with houses perched on the slope of a jagged mountain. The *Palazzo di Alberico Grammatico*, built in 1722, has unusual Baroque decorations. The church of *San Pietro* is very ancient, but was rebuilt in the Baroque style in the second half of the 18th cent. In the area of *Pietra Chiatta* there is a large Villanovan urnfield dating from the 9-8th cent. B.C., with cremation burials.

* SALEMI (Trapani). Well-situated, it is the meeting-point for the roads from Trapani, Palermo and Agrigento. Pre-historic in origin, it flourished under the Romans. Its inhabitants became converts to Christianity in the 4th cent., as it is proved by the remains of a basilica with superimposed mosaic floors carried out in an unmistakable African style. The *Castello*, built by Frederick II of Swabia in the 13th cent., has a trapezoid plan, and three of its original four towers still stand. The *Duomo*, the foundation stone of which was laid in 1619, contains a baptismal font by Domenico Gagini (c. 1420-1492), a statue of St. Julian, probably by Francesco Laurana (recorded 1458-1500), a Madonna of the Angels by Mariano Smiriglio (1561-1636), and a silver processional cross, by Giovanni Cioni (mentioned in 1386). In the Baroque *Chiesa del Collegio*, designed by the Jesuit Vincenzo Cascio (active in the 17-18th cent.), is a painting of St. Francis Borgia by Giuseppe Felice (1661-1734). In the *Chiesa del Crocifisso* is a wooden crucifix by Fra Umile da Petralia (1580-1639).

** SALERNO. A charming town, delightfully situated in the northern extremity of the bay of Salerno. Like many other towns of central-southern Italy, it has a medieval quarter consisting of narrow, irregular streets, built on a hillside dominated by the ruins of a castle, and a modern quarter, with broad, straight streets, built lower down near the sea. Nothing is known for certain about the town's origins, though a necropolis of the 6-5th cent. B.C. shows that the area was already inhabited at that time. In the Middle Ages it was renowned throughout Europe for its medical school.

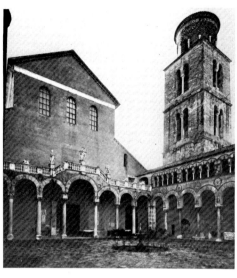

The *Duomo* is dedicated to St. Matthew, and is the town's most important monument. Built towards the end of the 11th cent., it was rebuilt later in the first half of the 18th. Close by the "atrium facade" is a two-aisled hall, which is supposed to be that of the ancient medical school. In the atrium, which is surrounded by ancient columns supporting arches of an Islamic kind, there is a granite bath dating from antiquity. Under the arcades are Roman and medieval sarcophagi, and on the Baroque balustrade of the front are statues of St. Matthew, S. Bonosio and S. Grammazio, works carried out in 1733 by Matteo Bottiglieri. The bronze parts of the main door were cast in Constantinople in 1099, and are made up of fifty-four square sections. The much altered and restored interior contains a great number of works of art, including two magnificent 12th cent. ambones, an iconostasis made in 1175 and decorated with beautiful mosaics, and paintings by Angelo Solimena (c. 1630-1716), Francesco Solimena (1657-1747), and Gabriele Chiarella (active in the mid-18th cent.). There are also frescoes from the 14th cent. onwards, tombs and monuments. The Baroque crypt contains early-17th cent. polychrome marble, and frescoes by Belisario Corenzio (c. 1560-1640). There are more works of art in the Cathedral museum, such as the famous 12th cent. altar-frontal, an Ecce Homo by Giovanni Bernardo Lama (1506-post 1598), an Adoration of the Magi by Luca Giordano (1632-1705), a parchment manuscript of an Exultet decorated with 13th cent. miniatures, the so-called jewelled cross of Robert Guiscard (11th cent.), various Roman furnishings and a collection of papal medals from 1417 to the present day. Built in the first half of the 12th cent., the Romanesque bell-tower is a particularly fine structure, with its three storeys of

Salerno, Duomo and Campanile.

Rossano Calabro, Cathedral Treasury. Miniature from the Codex Purpureus.
Saluzzo, Casa Cavassa. Maestro di Celle Macra, Our Lady of Mercy.

San Gimignano, Collegiata. Jacopo della Quercia,
Virgin of the Annunciation.

San Gimignano, Collegiata. Jacopo della Quercia,
Angel of the Annunciation.

arched, mullioned openings and its cylindrical crown. The 13th cent. *Episcopio* (bishop's palace) has been successfully restored in recent years, and is one of the town's most interesting buildings. Its 13th cent. interior is a large, two-aisled hall, with pointed arches supported by six sturdy antique columns taken from the Italic Temple at Paestum. The Baroque church of *San Giorgio* has an interior richly decorated with gilt stucco work and frescoes, and contains paintings by Andrea da Salerno (c. 1490-1530), Angelo Solimena, and Francesco Solimena. The *Museo Provinciale* has a collection of antique objects and works of art, which illustrates the historical and cultural development of the area from pre-historic to modern times. In the art gallery is a triptych by the so-called "Master of the Coronation of Eboli" (lived in the 15th cent.), and a polyptych by Andrea da Salerno, depicting the Madonna delle Grazie, St. Anthony, St. Augustine, and St. Michael the Archangel. There are some rare works in the *Biblioteca Provinciale*, such as the "Raccolta Salernitana", which illustrates the history of the medical school of Salerno. Also worthy of notice is the little church of *Sant'Andrea*, rebuilt in the 18th cent., the *Chiesa del Crocifisso*, built in the 10-11th cent., where there is a late-12th cent. Crucifix on parchment attached to a wood panel, and the *Via dei Mercanti*, the most characteristic street in the old part of the city. The 8th cent. *Acquedotto Medievale*, remains of which have survived, was repaired by the Normans in the 11th cent. for the Monastery of St. Benedict.

* **SALÒ** (Brescia). A little town in a bay on the south-western shore of Lake Garda, with a mild climate, so a much frequented resort. The *Duomo*, dedicated to the Virgin Annunciate, was begun in 1453 by Filippo Dalle Vacche. The Renaissance portal is the work of Antonio Tamagnino, called Antonio della Porta (recorded 1491-1520), and Gasparo da Cairano (lived in the 15-16th cent.). The imposing interior has ten side chapels, and important paintings, such as the St. Jerome by Zeno Donato, called Zenon Veronese (c. 1484-1554), a Deposition and a Christ in Limbo by the same artist, a polyptych of the Madonna and Saints by Paolo Veneziano (recorded 1333-1362), a Madonna and Child with Saints Bonaventure and Sebastian by Girolamo Romani, called Romanino (c. 1484-1559), St. Charles and the Plague-stricken by Alessandro Maganza (c. 1556-1640), a Madonna with Saints by Ercole Graziani (1688-1765), and landscapes by Giovanni Battista Trotti, called Malosso (1555-1619). There are other notable paintings in the chancel by Jacopo Palma the Younger (1544-1628), Aliense, and Zenon Veronese. The *Palazzo del Comune* is a reconstruction of the one destroyed by an earthquake in 1901: it contains the Triumph of the Cross by Andrea Bertanza (lived in the 17th cent.), and has a

collection of documents from the Napoleonic period to the Second World War. In the *Palazzo degli Uffizi Finanziari* are the remains of Roman inscriptions found in the surrounding district.

* **SALSOMAGGIORE TERME** (Parma). A health resort, with saline waters, situated in the foothills of the Parmesan Apennines. The little town is a point of departure for walks to *Tabiano Bagni* (the castle of Tabiano was built in the 11th cent. by the Pallavicino family), *Bargone* (the 12th cent. castle belonged to the Pallavicino family), *Scipione* (the 12th cent. castle has a cylindrical tower), *San Giovanni in Contignaco* (in the church of the same name is a very good fresco of St. Lucy, painted in 1517), and to *Vigoleno* (the 12th cent. castle was built by the Scotti family).

* **SALUZZO** (Cuneo). Built on the easternmost spur of the Monviso Alps, it is typical of many of the Piedmontese towns that lie at the foot of the great mountain chain, and has an unmistakably medieval atmosphere. The 15th cent. *Cattedrale* is dedicated to the Virgin Annunciate, and is one of the most imposing in the whole of Piedmont. The cusped brick portal and the Baroque door are remarkable. The large interior is divided into a nave and two aisles by sixteen polystyle pillars, and contains a great number of very valuable paintings and frescoes, including an anonymous 15th cent. triptych of the Madonna with Saints Cosmas and Damian. The Chapel of the Blessed Sacrament contains parts of another beautiful anonymous polyptych of c. 15th cent., depicting S. Chiaffredo presenting the Marquis Ludovic II of Saluzzo, St. Constance presenting the Marquess Margaret of Foix, and Saints George and Sebastian, as well as a wooden crucifix of the first half of the 15th cent. *Casa Cavassa* is a charming 15th cent. building rebuilt in the Renaissance style in the early 16th cent. It has a simple facade, and the finely made marble portal bears the signature of Matteo Sanmicheli (recorded 1480-1534), who completed it in the third decade of the 16th cent. In the entrance-

Saluzzo, Cathedral, interior.

hall is a fresco of the Blessed Sacrament, which recalls the struggle against the heretics. In the Hall of Justice, the Hall of Alliance, the so-called Margaret of Foix Hall, the Hall of the Emperors, and in other rooms of the palace are paintings, tapestries, ancient weapons and other precious objects. The church of *San Giovanni*, begun in the early 14th cent., but not completed until 1504, has a large facade decorated with an enormous 19th cent. fresco of St. Christopher. The apse, called the Chapel of the Holy Sepulchre, contains fine Gothic choir-stalls. The chapter house, which one reaches by passing through the cloister, contains the tomb of Galeazzo Cavassa, by Sanmicheli. The *Castello*, built in the second half of the 13th cent. and reconstructed in 1826, is another notable construction.

* SAN BARTOLOMEO IN GALDO (Benevento).

In a very hilly region, with a view over the valley of the Fortore. The facade of the church of *San Bartolomeo* has two important late-Gothic cusped portals, taken from the Abbey of Santa Maria at Mazzocca. The church of the *Annunziata* has a portal identical to the above-mentioned, in the lunette of which is a bas-relief of the Annunciation dating from 1398.

* SAN BENEDETTO PO (Mantua).

Agricultural and industrial town near the river Po. The basilica of *San Benedetto* is all that remains of the Abbey of Polirone, one of the most important Benedictine foundations from 1000 A.D. onwards. In its present form, the church is that designed by Giulio Pippi, called Giulio

Romano (c. 1499-1546). The Gothic interior is divided into a nave and two aisles, and contains fine paintings, including a Christ Blessing by Paris Bordone (1500-1571), and St. Benedict's Last Communion by Giambettino Cignaroli (1706-1770). On the left of the church is the Romanesque cloister of St. Benedict.

* SAN BENIGNO CANAVESE (Turin).

An agricultural village, with remains of the

San Benedetto Po, Basilica of San Benedetto.

Cluniac *Abbazia di Fruttuaria*, founded in 998 A.D. by Guglielmo di Volpiano. The remains of the abbey are now part of the Salesian Institute founded by St. John Bosco. The parish church (*Chiesa Parrocchiale*) is consecrated to the Assumption, and was built by Quarini to a design of Vittone's in the second half of the 18th cent. The adjoining Romanesque campanile was once part of the ancient abbey.

* SAN CANDIDO (Bolzano).

A much-frequented holiday resort. Once the site of a small Roman fort, a Benedictine monastery was built here in the 8th cent., thus giving rise to the name of San Candido; a cluster of houses grew up around the monastery. The

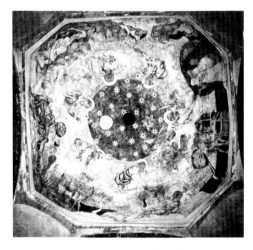

San Benigno Canavese, the Abbey bell-tower.
San Candido, Collegiata. Tiburium frescoes.

Collegiata dei Santi Candido e Corbiniano was originally an 8th cent. Benedictine abbey, but is now an essentially 13th cent. Romanesque structure, in which local art is dominated by Lombard influence. In the interior, which one enters through a doorway surmounted by a pointed arch, is an early 13th cent. wood carving of Christ on the Cross between the Madonna and St. John, a polychrome wood statue of S. Corbiniano done in the 13th cent. Romanesque style, and other works of art. Note the twinfold *Chiesa*, built in 1635, which imitates the plan of the Oratory of the Holy Sepulchre in Jerusalem, and that of the Sanctuary of Altotting in Bavaria.

* SAN CASCIANO IN VAL DI PESA

(Florence). Town situated between the valleys of the Greve and Pesa. The *Chiesa della Misericordia*, or of *Santa Maria del Prato*, was built in the first half of the 14th cent. The interior contains a pulpit with bas-reliefs by Giovanni di Balduccio (recorded 1317-1349) depicting the Annunciation, St. Dominic and St. Peter Martyr, a Crucifixion on wood, perhaps by Simone Martini (1280/85-1344), and a Madonna and Child enthroned with Saints Francis, Peter, and donor by Ugolino di Neri (active in the first half of the 14th cent.). The church of *Santa Maria del Gesù* or *del Suffragio* has a Madonna and Child painted on wood, a work of the 14th cent. Florentine school. The church of *San Francesco*, built towards the end of the 15th cent., together with the adjoining Convent of the Cross, has an early- 15th cent. wooden crucifix, and an Eternal with Angels by Giovanni Battista Bertucci (1465/70-1516). Walk to the *Pieve di Santa Cecilia*, built in 1000 A.D., to which the portico and campanile were added in the 16th cent.

* SAN COLOMBANO AL LAMBRO (Milan). Agricultural town at the foot of the hill

San Colombano al Lambro, partial view of the Castle.

of San Colombano. The 14th cent. *Parrocchiale* (parish church) has a neo-Classical pronaos, and frescoes by Bernardino Campi (c. 1552-1591). Only a crenellated tower of the *Castello* remains.

* SAN DANIELE DEL FRIULI (Udine).

The town stands on the morainic amphitheatre of the Tagliamento. The *Duomo*, dedicated to St. Michael, has a richly decorated 18th cent. facade. The campanile was designed by Giovanni da Udine (1487-1564). The interior contains a Trinity by Giovanni Antonio de' Sacchis, called Pordenone (1484-1539), and a Marriage of Mary and a Circumcision by Pomponio Amalteo (1505-1588). The Library has some rare works, including an 11th cent. Bible. In the church of *Sant'Antonio Abate* there is a series of Gothic frescoes (St. Sebastian, Descent of Christ to Limbo, Crucifixion, Christ washing the feet of the Apostles, and Doctors of the Church), which are the finest works of Pellegrino da San Daniele (c. 1467-1547).

* SAN DEMETRIO CORONE (Cosenza).

Situated in uneven countryside formed by narrow valleys and rivers that run down into the Ionian Sea. The church of *Sant'Adriano* is now part of a modern building, but has very ancient origins. Its interior is considered one of the most interesting in the region, and though mainly Norman, has traces of various styles. The most notable objects are the holy-water stoup, carved out of an early Byzantine capital, two shapeless lions, which came from the porch of the facade that was demolished towards the middle of the last century, and the floor, part of which is in "opus sectile".

* SAN DONNINO (near Florence). An an-

cient village. The church of *Sant'Andrea a Brozzi* was built in the 11th cent. and remodelled in the 15th, while its portico and columns date from the 17th cent. It contains a triptych depicting the Annunciation with Saints Eustachius and Anthony Abbot by the Portuguese painter Alvaro Pirez (lived in the 15th cent.), a Madonna enthroned with four Saints, a painting on wood, probably by Francesco Botticini (1446-1497), and frescoes by Domenico Bigordi, called Ghirlandaio (1449-1494). The *Torre dei Tornaquinci* is a massive medieval brick construction. The 11th cent. church of *San Donnino* has some fine paintings, including a polyptych that is probably the work of Giovanni del Biondo (recorded 1356-1392).

* SAN GALGANO (ABBAZIA DI) (Town

of Chiusdino, province of Siena). In the heart of the countryside. It was built in 1224-80 by Cistercian monks. The partly unfinished facade is faced in travertine and brickwork. The interior is in the form of a Latin cross, 69 m long. The lofty nave has slender little columns resting on corbels, and is made even more striking by the absence of the roof, which collapsed in the 18th cent; the floor is overgrown with grass. The Abbey was originally a great cultural and administrative centre, but it began to decline in the 14th cent. It is one of the few examples of ruins which have become even more attractive by being left untouched. Beside it stand the remains of the Monastery, with fine arches on slender columns.

* **SAN GEMINI** (Terni). A small town, half medieval and half modern, well-known as a spa. The facade of the 15th cent. church of *San Francesco* has a fine Gothic portal, while the interior has seven interesting pointed arches of some size, and a polygonal apse. It is worth noticing the 14th cent. facade of the *Duomo*, the interior of which is neo-Classical. One should also walk to *Carsulae*, a place of very ancient origins in an area of archaeological interest.

** **SAN GIMIGNANO** (Siena). Situated on a hill overlooking the Val d'Elsa, it is famous because its 13th and 14th cent. streets, palaces, and towers have come down to us intact. It is justly considered one of the most attractive little towns in Italy. Founded by the Etruscans, as the discovery of a burial-ground proves, it became a populous town before 1000 A.D. The *Collegiata*, or Cathedral of *Santa Maria Assunta*, was consecrated by Pope Eugenius III in 1148. The interior abounds in precious works of art, but the following are particularly admirable: the frescoes depicting scenes from the New Testament by the Sienese painter Barna, who, according to Vasari, died in 1381, after falling from a platform while painting the Crucifixion. These frescoes were completed by his nephew and pupil, Giovanni d'Asciano, who lived in the 14th cent.; the Chapel of Santa Fina, a local saint, is a masterpiece of Florentine Renaissance architecture, carried out by Giuliano da Maiano in 1468. The altar of the chapel has a beautiful reredos, and a marble canopy carried out by Benedetto da Maiano in 1475. In the same chapel are important frescoes by Domenico Bigordi, called Domenico Ghirlandaio (1449-1494). Another series of frescoes in the left aisle, depicting scenes

San Gimignano, Cathedral square.

San Gimignano, Collegiata. Barna da Siena, Annunciation.

San Gimignano, Collegiata. Barna da Siena, Christ Captured.

San Gimignano, Collegiata. Barna da Siena. The Way to Calvary, detail.

San Gimignano, Sant'Agostino. Benozzo Gozzoli, St. Augustine reader of rhetoric in Rome.

San Gimignano, Collegiata. Domenico del Ghirlandaio, Exequies of S. Fina, detail.

San Gimignano, Collegiata. Barna da Siena, Crucifixion, detail.
San Ginesio, Collegiata crypt. Lorenzo Salimbeni, Martyrdom of St. Stephen, detail.

built by the Florentines in the middle of the 14th cent., the *Fonti*, a fugue of round and pointed arches built between the 12th and 14th centuries, and the Romanesque church of *San Lorenzo in Ponte*, which dates from the middle of the 13th cent. The latter contains frescoes by Francesco di Ser Cenni (recorded 1597-1630).

* **SAN GINESIO** (Macerata). A pleasant, busy little town situated between the river Chienti and the Fiastra. It has a fine view of the Sibylline mountains, and for this reason is also called the "Balcony of the Sibyllines". The facade of the Romanesque *Collegiata* has a fine brick decoration (1421), and by the side of it rises a strong-looking campanile with a bulbous cusp. The church contains a few works of art, including a fresco of the Madonna and Child with two Saints by Stefano Folchetti (active 1492-1513), three paintings representing the Fall beneath the Cross, the Last Supper, and the Crucifixion by Simone De' Magistris (lived c. 1534-1600), and a wood panel depicting the Madonna of Mercy by Pietro Alemanno (recorded 1475-1498). The 13th cent. *Ospedale dei Pellegrini* (Pilgrims' Hospital) is a simple, stylish building; its portico has alternate round and octagonal columns, while the loggia is a 15th cent. addition. The small 14th cent. church of San Sebastiano is now the *Museo Comunale*, and contains Picene objects, Gallic bronzes, Roman remains, a Madonna and Child with Saints by Vincenzo Pagani (c. 1490-1568), a Pietà by Simone De' Magistris, and wood panels by Stefano Folchetti. Adjacent is the *Oratorio di San Biagio* with frescoes by the Salimbeni brothers, Jacopo and Lorenzo (lived in the 14-15th cent.). The church of *San Francesco* has a 13th cent. Romanesque doorway, some notable frescoes, and an Assumption by Andrea Boscoli (c. 1550-1606).

from the Old Testament, is the work of Bartolo di Fredi. The *Palazzo del Popolo* or *Palazzo Nuovo del Podestà*, now the Palazzo Comunale, was begun towards the end of the 13th cent. and is characterized by the so-called Torre Grossa, which was begun in 1298, and added to by each successive podestà. In the Council Chamber is a huge fresco (Maestà) by Lippo Memmi, dated 1317. The adjoining *Museo Civico* has a wonderful collection of works of art, including frescoes, paintings, cloths, chests, lace, and carpets. It is surmounted by a tower with three bells, the largest dates from 1328, the middle one from 1341, and the smallest from 1245. From the top of the tower one can see the whole range of encircling mountains, from the Apuan Alps to the Apennines above Modena and Pistoia, to Monte Falterona, Pratomagno, the upper Chianti region, and as far as Montagnola Senese. The sober exterior of the Romanesque-Gothic church of *Sant'Agostino*, built towards the end of the 13th cent., forms a contrast with the interior, with its many works of art; these include a marble altar carried out in 1494 by Benedetto da Maiano, and a cycle of frescoes based on the life of St. Augustine, which bear the signature of Benozzo Gozzoli, who painted them with the help of his pupils in 1464-65. Other monuments of considerable interest include the superb *Porta San Giovanni* (1262), the 14th cent. *Palazzo Pratellesi*, which houses the town library, with its forty thousand volumes and precious codexes, the triangular *Piazza della Cisterna*, the *Palazzo Antico del Podestà* surmounted by the Torre della Rognosa, the *Museo d'Arte Sacra*, the ruined *Rocca*

San Gimignano, Collegiata. Taddeo di Bartolo, Hell, detail.

San Ginesio, Collegiata.

* **SAN GIOVANNI IN PERSICETO** (Bologna). Small agricultural town just a few kilometres from Sant'Agata Bolognese. In the *Palazzo Municipale* is a painting of St. John the Baptist by Francesco Raibolini, called Francia (c. 1450-1517). In the *Collegiata di San Giovanni* is a painting of St. Anthony of Padua and the Child Jesus by Giovanni Francesco Barbieri, called Guercino (1591-1666). The so-called *Palazzaccio* is also interesting.

* **SAN GIOVANNI ROTONDO** (Foggia). Small agricultural town, which grew up in the 11th cent. in an area with a plentiful supply of spring-water. In 1220 fifteen towers were built around the town, and their remains may be seen incorporated in some of the houses. Archaeological research has established that the site was already inhabited in pre-historic times. The little church of *San Giovanni* or *della Rotonda* is a very old building, and legend has it that it rose upon the ruins of a temple dedicated to Janus. The church of *Sant'Onofrio* is a notable 14th cent. structure with a beautiful doorway surmounted by a pointed arch. The ancient chapel of the *Madonna di Loreto* was built by pilgrims from the Marches on their way to Monte Sant'Angelo, but it is not known when. In the 17th cent. church of *Sant'Orsola* is an interesting 16th cent. Deposition of the Venetian school. The Capuchin monastery of *Santa Maria delle Grazie* was built in the 16th cent., and was the home of Padre Pio da Pietralcina. Overlooking the town is the *Casa di Sollievo della Sofferenza*, the large modern hospital Padre Pio was able to build, thanks to the donations of the faithful.

* **SAN GIOVANNI VALDARNO** (Arezzo). On the left bank of the river Arno. The 15th cent. basilica of *Santa Maria delle Grazie* has a portico with a glazed terracotta by Giovanni della Robbia (1469-1529), and contains 15th cent. frescoes. Next to the basilica is the small *Pinacoteca Parrocchiale*, where, amongst other things, there is an Annunciation attributed to Jacopo del Sellaio (1442-1493), and a Madonna and Child by the "Maestro del Cassone Adimari", formerly attributed to Masaccio. The *Palazzo Pretorio* is a medieval building.

San Giovanni Valdarno, Palazzo Pretorio.

* SAN GODENZO (Florence). A holiday resort, built on a mountainous spur among olive-groves and chestnut-trees. The town grew up around the Benedictine abbey (*Badia Benedettina*) founded in 1029. Inside the abbey church is a 14th cent. Florentine pentyptych of the Madonna with Saints, a wooden statue of St. Sebastian by Bartolomeo d'Agnolo Baglioni, called Baccio d'Agnolo (1462-1543), and a mosaic of the Coronation of the Virgin designed by Giuseppe Cassioli (1865-1942). The crypt contains the mummified remains of St. Gaudentius, a 6th cent. Benedictine.

* SAN LEO (Pesaro). Commands a fine view, being built on a rocky shelf facing the valley of the river Marecchia. The medieval *Forte di San Leo* is an unusual construction, and was described by the Venetian writer Pietro Bembo as "the largest and most beautiful instrument

of war in the region". Carrying out the assignment given him by Federico II of Montefeltro, Francesco di Giorgio Martini (1439-1502) enlarged the fortification, and gave it its present form. It houses a small art gallery. The *Duomo*, built entirely of sandstone in the 12th and 13th centuries, seems to have been constructed upon the remains of a temple dedicated to Jupiter Feretrius. It has a beautiful tripartite facade, and some fair works of art. The *Pieve*, or *Basilica*, is a sturdy 9th cent. pre-Romanesque structure, with a basilican interior, in which there is a fine 9th cent. ciborium.

* SAN LORENZO IN CAMPO (Pesaro). According to tradition, the name of this little town derives from a Benedictine abbey, of which the very ancient church of *San Lorenzo* is all that remains. The church is supposed to have been built for the first time as far back as the 5th cent. Its present exterior bears the traces of numerous alterations effected over the centuries. An attempt has been made to restore the interior to its original form. It contains some fairly interesting works of art, including a painting of the Madonna and Child with Saints, as well as Scenes of the Passion by Ercole Ramazzani (c. 1530-1598).

* SANLURI (Cagliari). A town of medieval origin on the edge of the plain of Campidano. The recently restored 14th cent. *Castello di Eleonora d'Arborea* belonged to the Giudici

San Leo, view of the Fort and town.
San Lorenzo in Campo, San Lorenzo, interior.

family of Cagliari, and was strategically important in the Middle Ages. The castle interior contains medieval and Napoleonic remains, as well as autographs of Gabriele D'Annunzio. Walk to Sardara, where there is the 13th cent. Romanesque-Gothic church of *San Gregorio*, and a monumental nuraghe shaped like a well, which dates from 900 B.C.

* SAN MARCELLO PISTOIESE (Pistoia). A favourite resort in the summer months, situated in a pleasant dale. The church of *San Marcello* is of Romanesque origin, but was completely rebuilt at the beginning of the 17th cent. It contains the Invention of the Cross by Agostino Ciampelli (c. 1577-1642), and frescoes by Giuseppe Gricci (lived in the 18th cent.). The town is a starting point for interesting excursions.

* SAN MARINO (Town of). A small, independent State wedged between Emilia-Romagna and the Marches, built on the crest of Monte Titano, about fifteen kilometres from Rimini. Work was begun on the church of *San Francesco* in 1361 by Menetto da San Marino (active in 1361) and continued by Battista da Como (active in the 14th cent.), but many alterations have been made since. The 14th cent. facade is covered by a 16th cent. portico, and an upper structure added in the last century. The interior was altered in the 18th cent. It contains a 13th cent. wooden crucifix, fragments of frescoes depicting the Adoration of the Magi and the Stigmata of St. Francis, by the 14th cent. school of Rimini, a Presentation in the Temple by an artist of the school of Baroccio (1528/35-1612), and St. Francis receiving the Stigmata by Guercino (1591-1666). The *Basilica di San Marino*, with its neo-Classical facade and 14th cent. campanile, rises on the foundations of the ancient parish church, and was built in 1826-1836 to a design by Antonio Serra (1783-1847). It contains a Noli me Tangere by Elisabetta Sirani (1638-1665), and a St. Agatha appearing to the Republic by Oreste Monacelli (lived in the 18-19th cent.). The *Rocca* or *Guaita* stands on the top of a sheer cliff, and was almost certainly built in 1000 A.D. It was later rebuilt in the 15th and 16th centuries, and restored in the 16th and first half of the 17th. Its inner and outer walls have large corner towers. The walls of the Fratta date from the 14th cent. and the Cesta tower from the 13th, but they have undergone many alterations, and were restored to their original form in the first twenty years of this century. The Montale tower also dates from the 13th cent., and was restored in the 18th and 19th. In the rooms of the *Museo e Pinacoteca Governativi*, which are housed in the *Palazzo Valloni*, whose two wings were built in different periods (1477 and the 17th cent.), are numerous works of art, including a St. Philip Neri by Guercino, a

St. Jerome by Jacopo Palma the Younger (1544-1628), the Driving of the Merchants from the Temple, probably by Tintoretto (1518-1594), and the Burning of Sodom and Gomorrha, attributed to Domenico Zampieri, called Domenichino (1581-1641). *The Palazzo del Governo* or Palazzo Pubblico was designed by Francesco Azzurri (1831-1901), and its facade bears the coats-of-arms of the castles scattered in the surrounding area. The interior is notable for its Conference Hall, Audience Room, and the Camera di Scrutinio, where there is a painting of San Marino, attributed to Giovanni Lanfranco (1582-1647). Walk to the *Chiesa dei Cappuccini*, or San Quirino, a Capuchin church built in the first half of the 16th cent. It has a facade with a five-arched portico, and contains a Deposition, perhaps the work of Taddeo Zuccari (1529-1566).

* SAN MICHELE EXTRA (Verona). On the outskirts of Verona. It grew up around a Benedictine monastery in the 8th cent. Church of the *Madonna di Campagna*, or *della Pace*, with a circular ground-plan, perhaps designed by Michele Sanmicheli (1484-1559). It contains some noteworthy paintings, such as the Deposition by Felice Ricci, called Brusasorci (1546-1605), the Scourging at the Pillar by the same painter, a Nativity by Paolo Farinati (1524-1606), and a 14th cent. fresco of the Madonna and Child enthroned with Saints Bartholomew and Anthony Abbot, for the protection of which the church was built. Church of *San Michele*, rebuilt by Adriano Cristofali (1717-1788).

* SAN MINIATO (Pisa). Already a village in Roman times, in the early Middle Ages it was fortified with a castle, either by Desiderius, the last king of the Longobards, who died in 774 A.D., or by the Emperor Otto I. The church of *San Jacopo de Foris Portam*, known as the church of San Domenico, was rebuilt in 1330, and its chapels contain important paintings and frescoes signed by Agnolo Gaddi (c. 1333-1396), Francesco Morandini, called Poppi (1544-1597), and other famous artists. The *Duomo dell'Assunta e di San Genesio* was built in the 12th cent., but modified later, and is flanked by a massive bell-tower. It contains a crucifix by the sculptor Baccio Sinibaldi, called Baccio da Montelupo (1479-1535), and frescoes by Annibale Gatti (1828-1909). The church of *San Francesco*, rebuilt in 1276 upon an earlier structure, completely altered in the 15th cent., has a nave which opens out into two aisles. It is also worth visiting the *Santuario del Crocifisso*, built between 1705 and 1718, the *Chiesa della Trinità* (1566), which contains a fresco of the school of Giotto and a large panel depicting the Madonna with Angels and Saints of the school of Ghirlandaio, and the characteristic *Chiesa della Compagnia della Crocetta*.

* **SAN PIER D'ARENA** (Genoa). Industrial suburb on the left bank of the Polcevera. The 13th cent. church of *Santa Maria della Cella* has a neo-Classical facade and an elliptical dome. Its sumptuous interior is decorated with paintings by Nicolò Barabino (1832-1891), Giovanni Andrea Ansaldo (1584-1638), Domenico Fiasella, called Sarzana (1589-1669), Luca Cambiaso (1527-1585), and Giovanni Battista Carlone (1592-1677). On 9 June 1944, a bombardment destroyed the adjacent cloister, uncovering the wholly unsuspected remains of the church of San Pietro dell'Arena, around which the early settlement had grown up. The *Palazzo Scassi*, called "della Bellezza", was designed by Galeazzo Alessi (1512-1572), and its construction supervised by Domenico Ponzello (lived in the 16th cent.). It is an imposing building, and contains works by the painters Giovanni Andrea Carlone, called Genovese (1590-1630), and Bernardo Castello (1557-1629). Walk to the *Belvedere*, to the sanctuary of Our Lady of Belvedere. This was first built in the 13th cent. It contains a fine anonymous painting of the Madonna and Child, which may date back to the early 14th cent.

* **SAN PIETRO IN LAMA** (Lecce). Agricultural town surrounded by fertile land, and remembered for its parish church (*Chiesa Parrocchiale*), an important example of local Baroque, built between 1636 and 1715.

* **SAN POLO D'ENZA** (Reggio Emilia). On the right bank of the river Enza, and starting point for excursions to the ruins of the castle of Canossa. In the church of *San Pietro*, a fresco of the Adoration of the Magi by Nicolò dell'Abate (c. 1509-1571). Nine kilometres from the town is the *Castello di Canossa*, built on whitish sandstone towards 940 A.D. (the name of Canossa, formerly Canusia, derives from the Latin "canus", meaning white). It was here that the most dramatic episode in the Investiture Contest between Pope and Emperor took place. In 1255 the militia of Reggio destroyed the castle, which was later rebuilt and destroyed many times. What little remains is the result of reconstruction-work.

* **SAN QUIRICO D'ORCIA** (Siena). Called San Quirico in Osenna in ancient times, it was an important town in the Middle Ages. Nowadays it is visited mainly because of the *Collegiata*, or *Pieve di Osenna*. This has an imposing Romanesque doorway, and contains a triptych by Sano di Pietro (1406-1491), and beautiful choir-stalls with inlays by Antonio Barili (1453-1516). In the adjoining *Chiesa della Misericordia* is a painting of the Madonna and Child with Saints Sebastian and Leonard in the manner of Giovanni Antonio Bazzi, called Sodoma (1477-1549). The austere 17th cent. *Palazzo Chigi*, and the park called *Orti Leonini* are worth noticing.

* **SANREMO** (Imperia). The town is divided into two parts: a modern one on the flat land and near the coast, with luxury hotels and sumptuous villas, and an older one, called

San Quirico d'Orcia, Collegiata, main entrance. San Remo, Russian Church.

Pigna, on the slopes of a hill between the mountain-streams of San Francesco and San Romolo. Though of earlier origins, the *Collegiata di San Siro* was completely rebuilt in the Lombard Gothic style of the 14th cent. Its doorway is surmounted by a pointed arch and a rose-window, but the facade was altered in the Baroque period. It contains an anonymous panel of the middle of the 16th cent. depicting Saints Peter, Paul, Sirus, John the Baptist and Romulus. The *Corso dell'Imperatrice* runs along the sea-front, and is planted with palm-trees; it commemorates the visit to Sanremo of the Empress of Russia, Maria Alexandrovna. Nearby is the Russian church (*Chiesa Russa*), and the *Casinò Municipale* built by Eugene Ferret in 1904-06.

* SAN SALVATORE TELESINO (Benevento).

On a hill near the right bank of the Calore, a tributary of the river Volturno. It takes its name from the abbey that existed in the 10th cent. The parish church (*Parrocchiale*) contains a Transfiguration carried out in the manner of Luca Giordano (1632-1705). There are some interesting ruins of the Samnite town of Telesia, mentioned for the first time in 217 B.C. These *Rovine di Telesia*, scattered along the sides of the road, make it possible to distinguish the remains of a wall in "opus reticulatum", a circus, an amphitheatre, a "macellum", and thermal baths.

* SANSEPOLCRO (Arezzo).

A large commercial town at the lower end of the Tiber valley. The *Duomo*, dedicated to St. John the Evangelist, is an ancient abbey founded by the Camaldolese in 1012. Romanesque, but considerably altered on various occasions, it has an austere facade. It contains many works of art, including an Ascension, perhaps the work of Pietro Vannucci, called Perugino (c. 1445-1523), and an Assumption with Apostles by Jacopo Palma the Younger (1544-1628). The most important work in the *Pinacoteca Comunale*, housed in the Palazzo Comunale, is a wonderful fresco depicting the Resurrection by Piero della Francesca (c. 1420-1492). The art gallery has other important paintings by Piero. One should also visit the church of *San Francesco*, and the *Chiesa dei Servi*, built between 1294 and 1371.

* SAN SEVERINO MARCHE (Macerata).

On the right bank of the Potenza, divided into a lower part, called the Borgo, and an upper, more ancient part, called the Castello. The *Palazzo Municipale*, built in the second half of the 18th cent., houses an important art gallery, which is dominated by the frescoes by Jacopo Salimbeni (died after 1427), Lorenzo Salimbeni (1374-c. 1420), and their pupils. The 13th cent. *Duomo Nuovo* (*New Cathedral*) has a 15th cent. facade, embellished by a Gothic doorway set in a stylishly decorated frame,

and a basilican interior with many works of art, the most important of which is undoubtedly the so-called Madonna della Pace, the masterpiece of Bernardino di Betto, called Pinturicchio (c. 1454-1513). The very ancient church of *San Lorenzo in Doliolo* may even go back as far as the 8th cent., though it has been greatly altered since. Its most important works of art are the Adoration of the Child Jesus with donor and the Madonna and Child by Lorenzo di Alessandro (lived in the second half of the 15th cent.), and the painting of Saints Lawrence and Philomena by Cristoforo Roncalli, called Pomarancio (c. 1552-1626). The *Duomo Antico* (Old Cathedral), dedicated to San Severino, was built in the late 10th and early 11th cent. It has a fine 14th cent. Gothic facade, and contains frescoes by the Salimbeni brothers, as well as the magnificent choir-stalls begun by Domenico di Antonello Indivini (c. 1445-1502) and completed by his pupils. The spectacular *Piazza del Popolo* was set out in the 14th cent., and is one of the best-proportioned in the Marches.

* SAN SEVERO (Foggia).

West of the Gargano promontory, it is a major communications centre. Of remote origins, it did not develop until the Middle Ages, when it became

San Severino Marche, San Lorenzo in Doliolo, bell-tower.

the property of the Benedictine monastery of Torremaggiore. The *Cattedrale*, dedicated to Santa Maria Assunta, was built in the 11th cent., but has been disfigured by Baroque alterations; it has a spectacular, aisleless nave. The right side of the 12th cent. church of *San Severino* was originally an early Romanesque facade. The doorway is surmounted by an arch decorated with acanthus leaves and supported by lion-shaped sphinxes. The lower part of the massive bell-tower is Romanesque, and has mullioned openings. The church of *San Lorenzo*, or *delle Benedettine*, was built in 1712, and has an elegant Baroque facade. In the *Camposanto* is the tomb of Raffaele Fraccacreta, the work of Amleto Cataldi (1882-1930).

* **SANTA CESAREA TERME** (Lecce). A solitary, picturesque town on the cliffs overlooking the Strait of Otranto. Excursion to the *Grotta Romanelli*, discovered in 1879, which contains Aeolian rock deposits of considerable scientific interest. Leaving the town, and passing Porto Migiano, one reaches the *Grotta Zinzalusa*, which contains the Corridoio delle Meraviglie (Corridor of wonders), with its abundant limestone deposits, the *Duomo*, a deep, irregular cathedral-like cavity, and other awe-inspiring caves.

* **SANTA FIORA** (Grosseto). A colourful town which has retained a distinctly medieval atmosphere. The houses are all built out of trachytic rock, so that they have become almost black with the passage of time. The *Pieve*, dedicated to Saints Flora and Lucilla, has a partly Romanesque and partly Renaissance facade. Its interior has a nave and two aisles, and contains terracottas by the della Robbia school. It is worth visiting the *Borgo*, where there is the church of Sant'Agostino, and the Peschiera, out of which the water of the river Flora gushes.

* **SANT'AGATA DEI GOTI** (Benevento). Attractive town, finely situated on a terrace between two tributaries of the river Isclero, near Monte Maineto. The *Duomo*, dedicated to the Assumption, was built in the second half of the 10th cent., but rebuilt and restored in later periods. It has a facade with a large vestibule, the 16th cent. Holy Oil Tabernacle, a St. Anne with the Virgin and Child by Giovanni Battista Antonino (a 17th cent. sculptor), ancient mosaic pavements, and a 14th cent. crypt, with twelve delicate columns and frescoes. The church of *San Menna* was built in the early 12th cent. It contains the remains of a mosaic pavement with geometrical patterns, and partly damaged frescoes from the 14th and 15th centuries. The *Chiesa dell'Annunziata*, originally a Gothic structure, has a fine late-Renaissance marble portal. It contains a painting of the Annunciation by Giuseppe Cosenza (born in 1847), and an Annunciation on wood by an anonymous 14th cent. painter. The 13th cent. church of *San Francesco* was completely rebuilt in the 18th cent. It contains the important tomb of Ludovico Artus, lord of the town in the 14th cent., and fragments of a triptych by Angelillo Arcuccio (recorded 1464-1492). Roman remains (*Avanzi Romani*), such as burial cippi, inscriptions and pillars are scattered throughout the little town.

* **SANTA MARIA MONTE** (Pisa). A large town, and formerly one of the most important citadels in the Valdarno. In the *Collegiata di San Giovanni Evangelista* is a marble baptismal font by Domenico Rosselli da Rovezzano (15th cent.), and a precious 13th cent. pulpit. Worth noticing is the *Palazzetto Pretorio*, which incorporates parts of the castle of Castruccio Castracani degli Antelminelli (1281-1328) and other medieval remains.

** **SANTA MARIA CAPUA VETERE** (Caserta). One of the busiest towns in the Terra di Lavoro (Land of work), not far from the Volturno. Though very ancient (it stands on the ruins of Capua, a primitive Oscan town, developed into a city by the Etruscans in the second half of the 6th cent. B.C.), it is built according to modern criteria, with broad, straight streets. The *Duomo*, or *Collegiata di Santa Maria*, is extremely ancient, since it was built in 497 A.D. by San Simmaco, the bishop of the town, upon the catacombs and grotto of San Prisco. It has been enlarged and restored many times over the centuries. The interior has fifty-one antique columns with mainly Corinthian capitals, a high Renaissance ciborium, the Chapel of Death, with a Deposition by Francesco De Mura (1696-1784), the Chapel of Consolation, and the Chapel of Our Lady of Succour. The *Amphitheatre Campano* is one of the most impressive examples of its kind to survive. Originally it was as big as the Colosseum in Rome. It is not known exactly when it was built, but it was certainly restored in 119 A.D. under the Emperor Hadrian. Nearby is the *Antiquarium*, where there are remains of decorations and inscriptions dating from the 2nd and 1st centuries B.C., votive and architectural terracottas, Oscan inscriptions of the 6-2nd cent. B.C., small squares of mosaic, etc. The *Mithraeum* is one of the best-preserved temples dedicated to the worship of the Persian god, Mithras. Built in the 2nd or 3rd cent. A.D., it consists of a rectangular, underground room, the ceiling of which is painted with stars characterized by six green and reddish points. On the bottom wall is a 2nd cent. fresco of Mithras killing a bull. Other frescoes represent the seven successive degrees of initiation. The Arch of Hadrian (*Arco di Adriano*) or of *Capua*, which once rose above the Via Appia, and the remains of an ancient crypto-porticus (*Avanzi d'un Antico Criptoportico*) are of considerable interest.

* **SANTA MARIA DI LEUCA** (Town of Castrignano del Capo, province of Lecce). Situated on the southern extremity of the Salentino peninsula, which is composed of white limestone cliffs. The sanctuary of *Santa Maria di Leuca*, or *De Finibus Terrae*, rebuilt in the 18th cent., stands on the site where the temple dedicated to Minerva (mentioned by Strabo) once stood. It contains the Altar of Minerva and a Madonna and Child by Andrea Cunaci da Mesagne (painter who lived in the 16-17th cent.).

** **SANTA MARIA DI RONZANO** (Town of Castel Castagna, province of Teramo). The church of *Santa Maria di Ronzano*, built in 1171, is one of the most outstanding Romanesque constructions in the Abruzzi, mainly because of its frescoes. It has a lively, elegant facade, and contains important frescoes (1171) depicting scenes from the Old and New Testament, besides the Blessed in the company of the Patriarchs, a Saint enthroned with two angels, a Christ Blessing with two Saints, an Annunciation, Angels, Prophets, and episodes from the Gospels. Two of the altars were formerly used in pagan rites. Nearby is the Romanesque church of *San Giovanni al Mavone* or *ad Insulam*, built in the 12th and 13th centuries, its facade characterized by a circular window set between two mullioned windows. Inside, there are 15th cent. frescoes and a crypt with nine bays.

* **SANTA MARINELLA** (Rome). Popular seaside resort, stretching along the coast as far as Capo Linaro, on the site of the ancient Punicum, an Etruscan-Roman settlement. In the park (*Giardino del Municipio*) is a tomb put together with findings of the 4th and 3rd centuries B.C. taken from a burial-ground discovered in the Zona Castellina. *Roman Stele* dating from the very first years of the 3rd cent. Roman bridge (*Ponte Romano*) made of large square rocks fitted together without mortar, reconstructed at the beginning of this century. The 15th cent. *Castello Odescalchi* stands on the site of an earlier 11th cent. fortress. The *Repubblica dei Ragazzi* (Boys' Town) is a re-educational institute, founded by John Patrick Carrol-Abbnj, and consists of an agricultural village, an industrial village, and a seaside village, the latter centred around the square, medieval Torre Marangone.

* **SANT'ANATOLIA DI NARCO** (Perugia). Situated on a rocky prominence beside the river Nera. A castle was built here in 1198, and the town grew up around it. The area is of archaeological interest, and many findings are now kept in the Etruscan Museum in Florence. In the Oratory of *Santa Maria delle Grazie*, built in 1570, is a fine Madonna and Child with St. John the Evangelist and another Saint by an unknown painter of the 15th cent., and frescoes by Pier Matteo Gigli

(recorded 1561-1596). If one takes the road to Ruscio, it is worth stopping a moment in the little village of *Caso*, where there is a fresco of the Coronation of the Virgin by Pierino Cesarei (c. 1530-1602) in the apse of the parish church (*Chiesa Parrocchiale*).

* **SANT'ANGELO DEI LOMBARDI** (Avellino). On a hill where the river Ofanto rises. The *Cattedrale*, built in the 11th cent. and rebuilt in the 16th, has a late-Renaissance doorway; it contains the 17th cent. Ceceri tomb. One reaches the *Casa Ceceri* through an interesting outer Renaissance doorway (1537), and an inner one with small columns. Walk to the *Abbazia di San Guglielmo al Goleto*, an abbey founded between 1132 and 1138 by St. William of Vercelli. While the large church is to a great extent ruined and of little interest, the small church, consisting of an upper and a lower part, is a remarkable artistic monument, the upper half being a rare example of architectural grace, probably designed and built in 1250 by Melchiorre di Montalbano. The massive campanile (1152), ancient remains having been incorporated in its construction, and the tower (1212) are also interesting.

* **SANT'ANGELO IN FORMIS,** see Capua.

* **SANT'ANGELO IN VADO** (Pesaro). Busy, attractive town, situated at the point where the Morsina flows into the Metauro. The church of *Santa Maria dei Servi*, a bare structure built in 1331, has two Renaissance doorways. Its 15th cent. interior is embellished

Sant'Angelo in Vado, San Filippo. Statue of the Virgin.

with sumptuous Baroque altars and works of art, such as S. Pellegrino Laziosi healed by the Cross, by Francesco Mancini (1679-1758), a panel of the Madonna and Child with Saints by Raffaello del Colle, called Raffaellino (born in the second half of the 15th cent., died in 1556), and a bronze relief of the Madonna by Lorenzo Ghiberti (1378-1455). The *Duomo* was built in the 12th cent. and rebuilt in the 17th. It has a basilican interior with a nave and two aisles, and contains a panel of the Madonna del Pianto in the chapel of the same name, a Venetian-Marchigian work carried out in the first years of the 16th cent. In the apse is a painting of the Triumph of St. Michael by Francesco Mancini.

* SANT'ANGELO LODIGIANO (Milan).

Agricultural and industrial centre on the banks of the Lambro. The *Castello* is a picturesque building, with its turrets and battlements. It was enlarged in the 14th cent. In its seventeen rooms is housed the Gian Giacomo Morando Bolognini Museum, with various objects from the 15th and 16th centuries, a well-stocked armoury, and a rich library.

* **SANT'ANTIMO,** Abbey of, see Montalcino.

* SANT'ANTIOCO DI BISARCIO (Sas-

sari). The town grew up around the church of *Sant'Antioco di Bisarcio*, one of the most important Romanesque buildings in Sardinia. It was once the cathedral of the diocese of Bisarcio, which was abolished in 1503, and has been built gradually over the centuries, though the oldest part certainly goes back to the 11th cent.; it has a sturdy bell-tower. The lower, projecting part of the facade consists of three finely proportioned arches, while the outer walls are decorated with arcadings. The interior follows a basilican plan, with a nave and two aisles, formed by massive columns of red trachyte surmounted by graceful capitals.

* SANT'ANTONIO DI RANVERSO, see

Rivoli.

* SANT'ARCANGELO DI ROMAGNA

(Forlì). Agricultural and industrial centre situated on a pleasant knoll called Montegiove. The neo-Classical *Palazzo Comunale* was designed by Luigi Poletti (1792-1869), and con-

tains a polyptych of the Madonna and Child with Saints by Jacobello di Bonomo (active in the second half of the 14th cent.). The *Collegiata* was designed by Gian Francesco Buonamici (1692-1759), and contains a few works of art, including paintings of Christ as a Young Man and Saints Joseph, Eligius, and Ignatius by Guido Cagnacci (1601-1663). The *Rocca* was built in the 13th cent. by the Malatesta family. Its rooms are in good order, and decorated with 17th cent. furniture. Beneath the old town centre are about ten artificial grottoes, which were presumably cells hewn out of the rock by Basilian monks in the 6th and 7th centuries. Walk to the *Pieve di San Michele*, and 11th cent. Romanesque church, built on the foundations of an earlier one.

* SANTA SCOLASTICA, Monastery of, see

Subiaco.

* SANTA SEVERA (Town of Santa Mari-

nella, province of Rome). Little seaside village, with good beach, and important for its *Castello*, a large castle facing the Tyrrhenian Sea. It was built about 1000 A.D. within a triple-walled circle on the site of the ancient Pyrgi, one of the ports of the Etruscan city of Caere. Within its boundaries is the *Chiesa dell'Assunta* (1595), and parts of the polygonal walls of a Roman fortification, which are of considerable scientific interest; there are also remains of Etruscan walls. In the area of the *Scavi di Pyrgi* have been found the foundations of the temple of Leucothea with pronaos.

* SANTA SEVERINA (Catanzaro). Situated

in hilly country, close to the right bank of the

Sant'Angelo Lodigiano, Castle.

Sant'Arcangelo di Romagna, Collegiata.

river Neto. It grew up in the Middle Ages on the ruins of the Greco-Roman town of Siberene. The *Cattedrale*, dedicated to Sant'Anastasia, was built in the second half of the 13th cent., but has undergone numerous alterations since. It has a fine central doorway with a pointed arch. Inside, there is a 17th cent. marble pulpit, the 16th cent. tombstone of a knight, polychrome marble, and, in the sacristy, croziers, chalices and monstrances of the 17-18-19th cent. The adjoining baptistery is a well-preserved Byzantine structure of the 8th or 9th cent. and contains a primitive baptismal font. The *Castello* is believed to have been built by Robert Guiscard.

* **SANT'ELPIDIO A MARE** (Ascoli Piceno). Stituated on a hill between a mountain-stream called the Ete Morto and the river Tenna. The most important monuments are: the 16th cent. *Chiesa della Misericordia*, whose barrel-vaulted roof is frescoed with scenes from the life of the Virgin by Cristoforo Roncalli, called Pomarancio (c. 1552-1626), and which also contains paintings by Andrea Lilli (1555-1610) and Andrea Boscoli (c. 1550-1606); the mock Romanesque *Collegiata*, which has remains of an earlier 14th cent. Gothic construction on its left side; and the *Palazzo Comunale*, on which Pellegrino Pellegrini (1527-1596) is believed to have worked, and which contains works by Vittore Crivelli (c. 1440-1502).

* **SANTE LUSSURGIU** (Cagliari). Small town near the eastern slopes of Monte Ferru. A few kilometres away, in the village of San Leonardo de Siete Fuéntes is the small Romanesque-Gothic church of *San Leonardo*, built in the second half of the 13th cent. Excursion to Bonarcado, where we find the 12th cent. church of *Santa Maria*, built in Romanesque style, but altered in the 13th and 18th centuries, with a triple-arched facade, and the Sanctuary of the *Madonna di Bonaccattu*, with its Byzantinelike features and 13th cent. alterations.

* **SAN VINCENZO AL VOLTURNO (ABBAZIA DI)** (Town of Cerro al Volturno, province of Isernia). The abbey was built by three noblemen from Benevento, the brothers Tatone and Tasone, and their cousin, Paldone, in an area where a chapel dedicated to St. Vincent existed at the beginning of the 8th cent. It was almost totally destroyed by an earthquake in 848, and two years after its rapid reconstruction, it was sacked by the Saracens. The church still bears traces of the 13th cent. (remains of the smaller apses) and 14th (the chancel with four columns). The

Santa Severina, Castle.
Sant'Elpidio a Mare, Collegiata. Roman sarcophagus, detail.

Sansepolcro, Pinacoteca Comunale. Piero della Francesca, St. Julian, detail.

Sarnano, Santa Maria di Piazza. Gerolamo di
Giovanni, Annunciation, detail.

San Severino Marche, Pinacoteca Civica. Lorenzo
Salimbeni, Mystic Marriage of St. Catherine, detail.

Saronno, Sanctuary. Bernardino Luini, Adoration
of the Magi, detail.

Sassari, Duomo. Saint Veronica, processional
banner.

area is rich in remains from various periods, especially in fragments of Roman architecture. Not far from the abbey is the crypt of St. Lawrence, (*Cripta di San Lorenzo*) originally called San Lorenzo in Insula, built by a certain Abbot Epifanio in the ninth century. It contains frescoes of Saints, Angels, the Life of Jesus, and the Martyrdoms of Saints Lawrence and Stephen by the Benedictine school of the same period. Little, however, is left of the church.

* **SAN VITO** (near Turin). Charming little village, with sweeping, attractive views. The church of *Santi Vito, Modesto e Crescenzio* was built prior to the 11th cent., and in spite of numerous alterations, especially those of 1605, still has interesting Romanesque features; in particular, the lower part of the bell-tower.

* **SAN VITO AL TAGLIAMENTO** (Pordenone). Agricultural and industrial town on the right bank of the Tagliamento. The *Duomo*, dedicated to S. Vito, S. Modesto and S. Crescenzio, was completely rebuilt in 1745, but still retains its original Romanesque campanile. It contains important paintings, such as that of Saints Sebastian, Roch, and Apollonius by Pomponio Amalteo (1505-1588), a Resurrection by the same painter, a Deposition by Alessandro Varotari, called Padovanino (1588-1648), and a polyptych by Andrea Bellunello (c. 1430-1494). In the church of *San Lorenzo Salvaroli*, called "I Frari", is the tomb of Pomponio Amalteo, and a fresco of St. Vincent Ferrer by Andrea Bellunello. *Casa Natale di Paolo Sarpi* (Birthplace of Paolo Sarpi), Servite friar, historian, politician and orator (1552-1623).

* **SAN VITO DEI NORMANNI** (Brindisi). Large agricultural town on the road to Brindisi. The Baroque *Parrocchiale*, called Santa Maria della Vittoria was built to commemorate the naval battle of Lepanto (1571). Interesting 15th cent. feudal *Castello*, considerably altered in later centuries. In the neighbourhood is the rectangular *Grotta di San Biagio*, dug in a deep, narrow little valley, with a small apse decorated with frescoes bearing Greek inscriptions, probably from the second half of the 12th cent., and the *Grotta di San Giovanni*, which has frescoes with Latin inscriptions.

* **SAN VITO DI CADORE** (Belluno). Popular tourist resort surrounded by some of the most beautiful mountains in the Dolomites. In the *Parrocchiale* (1764) is an altarpiece depicting the Madonna and Child enthroned with Saints by Francesco Vecellio (c. 1475-1560). In the small, early-16th cent. church of *Madonna della Difesa* is a triptych, probably by Francesco Vecellio.

* **SAN VITTORE DELLE CHIUSE** (Town of Genga, province of Ancona). The church of *San Vittore delle Chiuse* is one of the most outstanding Romanesque buildings in the Marches. It is thought to have been built in the 11th cent. Against the facade is a truncated campanile and a cylindrical tower. There are two small apses in both the left and right walls of the church, and three large ones in the bottom. The structure is surmounted by a tiburium decorated with arcadings all around it. One reaches the *Grotta dei Frasassi* after passing through the gorge of Frasassi, which is more than two kilometres long. Inside is a small octagonal church, built in accordance with the wishes of Leo XII, and designed by Giuseppe Valadier (1762-1839).

* **SANZENO** (Trent). Charming town in the Val di Non. Archaeological findings have proved that the area was already inhabited in the 4th cent. B.C. The parish church of *Santi Sisinio, Martino e Alessandro*, who were martyred here in 397 A.D., was built in the second half of the 15th cent. It has a grandiose facade dating from the middle of the 16th cent., and contains a painting of the Three Martyrs by Giovanni Battista Lampi the Elder (1751-1830). In the Chapel of the Holy Martyrs are Gothic reliefs in wood depicting the tortures inflicted on the saints. In the neighbourhood is the Sanctuary of *San Romedio*, built on a steep rock, consisting of the Chapel of St. George, called Clesiana, which dates from the second half of the 15th cent. and contains a few interesting frescoes, the Chapel of St. Michael or of the Most Holy Sacrament, the Chapel of Our Lady of Sorrows, the main Chapel (1536), the Chapel of St. Vigilius, and the mystical Chapel of S. Romedio, built parhaps in the 7th cent.

* **SARNANO** (Macerata). On the right bank of the Tennacola, with an old town centre on a steep slope. In the church of *Santa Maria di Piazza*, which incorporates 13th cent. Romanesque-Gothic remains, is a fresco of the Eternal with Angels by Lorenzo di Alessandro (lived in the 15-16th cent.), panels by Niccolò Alunno (c. 1430-1502), and a wooden standard

San Vittore delle Chiuse, exterior of the church.

315

by Girolamo di Giovanni (active 1449-1473). The *Palazzo Municipale* houses an art gallery, which contains a picture of the Last Supper painted in 1607 by Giuseppe De Magistris, a Crucifixion by Stefano Folchetti (active 1492-1513), and a Madonna by Carlo Maratta (1625-1713). In the same building is the town library, with 14th and 15th cent. treatises on law and theology, as well as sixty incunabola. The *Fonte di San Giacomo* is important for the production of mineral water.

* **SARONNO** (Varese). Industrial town northeast of Milan. The facade of the Sanctuary of the *Madonna dei Miracoli*, a monument begun in the late 15th cent. by Giovanni Antonio Amadeo (c. 1447-1522) and continued later by Vincenzo Seregni (1509-1594), has a late 16th and early-17th cent. facade, and was designed by Pellegrino Tibaldi (1527-1596). The interior consists of a nave and two aisles, and contains a fresco entitled Concert of Angels by Gaudenzio Ferrari (c. 1475-1556), a Dispute in the Temple, the Marriage of Mary and the Adoration of the Magi by Bernardino Luini (1480/90-c. 1531), and a Deposition in marble by Pompeo Marchesi (1789-1858). *San Francesco*, built in the 15th cent. on the foundations of an earlier church dedicated to St. Peter, has a Baroque facade, and an interior with a nave and two aisles.

Saronno, Sanctuary.

* **SARSINA** (Forlì). Agricultural and industrial locality. Once a Roman town of Umbrian origin. The *Cattedrale*, of Romanesque origin, was rebuilt towards 1000 A.D., and has been considerably altered since. It has a nave and two aisles, and contains some interesting paintings, the most important being the Mass of

St. Gregory, the work of an anonymous 17th cent. painter from the Romagna. The *Museo Archeologico Sarsinate* is important for knowledge of life in the area under the Romans. It contains the tomb of Aeflonius Rufus, the base of Cetrania Severina, the funeral monument of Verginius Paetus, and an abundance of other material.

* **SARZANA** (La Spezia). At the junction of the road to the Cisa Pass (the Roman Via Emilia Scauri) and the Via Aurelia, some traces of which have survived. The *Cattedrale di Santa Maria Assunta*, begun in the early 13th cent. but not completed until the end of the 15th, is partly Romanesque-Gothic and partly Renaissance. In the second chapel on the right are statues representing Faith and Charity by Domenico Guidi (1625-1701). The chapel on the right side of the transept has an altar called after the Presentation in the Temple, with an imposing marble altarpiece by Leonardo and Francesco Riccomanni (the first lived in the 15th cent., the second in the 16th). In the Cappella del Crocefisso is a crucifix painted on wood by Master Guglielmo in 1138; an object of veneration, it is an archetype of all similar crucifixes to be found throughout Tuscany and Umbria. The 12th cent. Romanesque church of *Sant'Andrea* has been almost completely altered in the course of time. It has a barrel-vault, and to the left of the entrance is the 14th cent. tombstone of a magistrate. Walk to the *Fortezza di Sarzanello*, built in 1322 on the site of the ancient Castrum Sarzanae by Castruccio Castracani, a condottiere from Lucca. The fortress was the residence of all the lords of the town.

** **SASSARI**. Situated on a slightly sloping limestone plateau, on the edge of the plain that runs down to the sea near Porto Torres. It is divided into an older part, with narrow, winding streets, and a more modern one, in

Sarsina, Museum. Mosaic depicting the triumph of Dionysius.

316

a stage of rapid expansion. The district of Sassari is rich in archaeological remains from pre-historic times, especially from the early Copper Age. The *Museo Nazionale Giovanni Antonio Sanna* was presented to the nation by the Sanna Castoldi family. It contains an art gallery with works by Sardinian painters from both Italian and foreign schools of the 14-20th cent. The archaeological section has findings that range from the Copper and early Bronze Ages to that of Imperial Rome, while the Gavino Clemente ethnographic section contains thousands of objects illustrating the whole of Sardinian folklore, in which one can see the reflection of a history and culture, from their remote beginnings, thousands of years before Christ, up to the present century. The *Duomo* is an unusual building in which various styles are combined. It was built in the 13th cent. as a simple parish church, and rebuilt between 1480 and 1505, when the episcopal see was transferred from Porto Torres to Sassari. Much work has been done to restore the interior to its original state, but with results that invite criticism. One should notice the baptismal font in the Piedmontese Baroque style, the Last Supper by Giovanni Marghinotti (1798-1865), the tomb of Placido Benedetto of Savoy, Duke of Moriana, the brother of Charles Emmanuel IV, the Madonna of Humility in the chapter house by Charles van Loo, a painter from Nice, and the processional banner by a 16th cent. Catalan painter. *Fonte Rosello* is a graceful quadrilateral construction erected in the early 18th cent. The church of

Sassari, Duomo, portico vault.

Santa Maria di Betlem was built in the second half of the 13th cent. and rebuilt in the second half of the 15th. Inside is an interesting 14th cent. wooden Gothic statue of the Madonna and Child. In the cloister is an ancient 14th cent. fountain with bronze heads of monsters, popularly known as Brigliadore. In the *Biblioteca dell'Università* are more than a hundred thousand volumes, Latin and Spanish manuscripts, and a Sardinian parchment codex of the 12-13th cent. Excursions to the following places: the church of *San Michele di Plaianu*, built in two different periods, the first in the second half of the 11th cent.; the *Santissima Trinità di Saccargia*, built in the Pisan Romanesque style of 1100, which, together with the campanile, is all that remains of the once adjoining Camaldolese abbey. It contains admirable frescoes by a 13th cent. painter from Latium; the church of *San Michele di Salvenero*, built in 1100 in the Pisan Romanesque style, with a 15th cent. statue of St. Michael; Ploghe, where the *Parrocchiale* contains paintings by Michele Cavaro (?-1584) and Filippino Lippi (1457-1504); Monte d'Accaddi, where there are the fine remains of a megalithic altar of the Neolithic Age, and nearby, those of a sanctuary-village.

* SASSOFERRATO (Ancona). The town consists of the Borgo, or lower part, and the Castello, the upper. The church of *Santa Maria del Piano* has a fine, early-17th cent. facade, and contains some excellent works of art, including paintings by Giovanni Francesco Guerrieri (1589-1655/59), and a panel of the Madonna and Child with Saints Catherine and John the Baptist by Pietro Paolo Agabiti (1470-1540). In the 14th cent. *Palazzo dei Priori*, much altered in later centuries, is the Civic Museum, with collections of findings from Sentinum, paintings, including two by Pietro Paolo Agabiti, Flemish caskets, and silver crosses etc. Walk to the early 12th cent. Lombard Romanesque church of *Santa Croce*, which contains a polyptych depicting the Madonna and Child, the Crucifixion, and Saints by Giovanni Antonio da Pesaro (recorded 1462-1511), a panel by Pietro Paolo Agabiti, and frescoes of the 14th cent. Fabrianese school. Walk to the ruins of Sentinum (*Ruderi di Sentinum*). In the same district is the abbey of *Santa Maria di Sitria*, founded in the early 11th cent. by St. Romuald; it has an important Romanesque-Gothic altar. One should visit the small cell, called "St. Romuald's Prison", where the saint was shut in for almost a year by the other monks.

** SASSOVIVO (ABBAZIA DI) (Town of Foligno, province of Perugia). Founded about 1000 A.D., it was a flourishing centre of studies in the 14th cent., but declined in the 15th. In a room called *Il Paradiso* are fragments of 15th cent. monochrome frescoes. There is a beautiful Romanesque cloister (*Chiostro*) built in 1229 by Master Pietro De Maria, with one hundred and twenty-eight slender, spiral, double columns supporting fully-rounded arches. A hundred metres away is a 14th cent. portico, beneath which is an 11th cent. crypt, called *Cappella del Beato Alano*. This was once part of the Benedictine abbey of Santa Maria del Vecchio, or della Valle, the first construction to be erected at Sassovivo.

* **SASSUOLO** (Modena). Small, but important industrial town on the right bank of the Secchia. The *Palazzo degli Estensi*, built in 1634 upon a 15th cent. fortification, has a number of large statues, and some interesting rooms, such as the Hall of Fortune, the Room of Love, the Room of the Este Virtues, and the Gallery, frescoed by Jean Boulanger (1566-1660). The parish church of *San Giorgio* has Baroque altars, and a painting of the Madonna and Child with Saints by Jean Boulanger. In the church of *San Francesco* is a painting of St. Francis in Ecstasy by Michele Desubleo, called Michele Fiammingo (c. 1601-1676).

* **SAVIGLIANO** (Cuneo). A communications centre in the middle of the plain of Cuneo, between the Maira and the Mellea. The *Chiesa Abbaziale di San Pietro dei Cassinesi* has a fine facade, Renaissance doorway, and Baroque bell-tower. The church interior is decorated in a heavy Baroque style, but contains an admirable polyptych of the Madonna and Child with Angels, an Annunciation and Pietà, and

Sassuolo, Ducal Palace, grand staircase.

Saints, carried out in 1510 by Gandolfino di Asti. The *Collegiata di Sant'Andrea* was built at the beginning of the 15th cent., but badly damaged by 18th cent. alterations; it has a fine bell-tower. The *Palazzo Cravetta*, built towards the end of the 16th cent., has an interesting courtyard.

* **SAVIGNANO SUL RUBICONE** (Forlì). Agricultural, commercial town on the right bank of the Rubicon. The *Palazzo Comunale* dates from the end of the 18th cent. The *Biblioteche Comunale ed Accademica* are well stocked, especially with 18th cent. works. The *Collegiata di Santa Lucia* was designed by Girolamo Theodoli (1677-1766). It is decorated in the style of the early 18th cent. and contains some important paintings, including a St. Anthony by Giovanni Andrea Lazzarini (1710-1801), a St. Francis of Paola, probably by Nicola Lapiccola (1730-1790), the Martyrdom of St. Lucy by Sebastiano Ceccarini (1703-1783), and a huge canvas by Ubaldo Gandolfi (1728-1781). Walk to *San Mauro Pascoli*, an agricultural and industrial town, to visit the birth place of the poet Giovanni Pascoli (1855-1912).

* **SAVONA**. An important harbour situated at the mouth of the Letimbro, beneath the hill of the Capuchins. The old quarters have sumptuous palaces, while the modern part is characterized by regular streets running at right angles to each other. The *Duomo* was built in the 16-17th cent., and the marble facade bears the signature of Guglielmo Calderini (1886). It contains a marble crucifix by Angelo Giovanni Molinari (1499), a magnificent baptistery with friezes prior to 1000 A.D., a hexagonal pulpit, also by Angelo Giovanni Molinari, and a triptych by Ludovico Brea. In the chancel are carved-wood choirstalls, a Baroque high altar surmounted by a ciborium, and on the walls two huge frescoes by Francesco Coghetti (1802-1875), representing Sixtus IV blessing the Crusaders, and Julius II laying

Savigliano, Palazzo Cravetta.

the foundation stone of the basilica of St. Peter's. The 18th cent. church of *Sant'Andrea* contains a 16th cent. panel of Our Lady of Good Counsel. The *Cappella Sistina* was built by Sixtus IV in memory of his parents, but was later rebuilt in the Rococo style of the 18th cent. It contains an admirable statue of Pope Sixtus presenting his parents to the Virgin, carried out by Michele and Giovanni De Aria about 1490. The *Palazzo Pozzobonello* was begun in the 13th cent. It houses the Civic Art Gallery, which has many interesting works of art, and the Museum, which contained collections of pre-historic, historic, ethnographic, botanical and zoological interest, unfortunately almost completely destroyed in the bombardments of the Second World War. The *Fortezza Priamar* was built by the Genoese in 1542, and has survived in a considerably altered state. The *Teatro Chiabrera*, designed by Carlo Falconieri (1853), has a facade with two orders of Doric and Ionic columns. In the oratory of *Santa Maria di Castello* is a grandiose polyptych, partly the work of Vincenzo Foppa (c. 1430-c. 1515) and Lodovico Brea (recorded 1475-1522).

* **SCALA** (Salerno). Town near Ravello, dating from the first centuries A.D. The construction of the *Duomo di San Lorenzo* goes back to the 12th cent. The church contains works of art, such as a pulpit supported by four columns with mosaic decorations, a 13th

Savona, Pinacoteca. Donato de' Bardi, Calvary.

cent. mitre decorated with enamels, and paintings by Andrea da Salerno (c. 1490-1530) and the Fleming Pietro Todos (lived in the 16th cent.). One should also visit the vast, well-lighted crypt. Walk to *Minuto*, to the Chiesa dell'Annunziata, whose crypt has 11th and 12th cent. frescoes, mainly of scenes from the Old and New Testament.

* **SCANDIANO** (Reggio Emilia). Picturesque town, where the Tresinaro flows into the plain. It grew up around a castle erected in 1262. The parish church of *Santa Maria* has a 15th cent. bell-tower, besides containing an important 17th cent. polychrome wooden statue of the Madonna of the Rosary, the tombs of the Boiardo family, and the tomb of L. Spallanzani. The clock-tower (*Torre dell'Orologio*) is 16th cent. The church of the *Convento dei Cappuccini* contains a Deposition and a St. Lawrence of Brindisi, the works of Giuseppe Solieri, called Fra Stefano da Carpi (1710-1796).

** **SCANDICCI** (Florence). Nearby is Borgo a Settimo, with the *Badia di San Salvatore*. Mentioned as early as the 10th cent., it was completely surrounded by walls and towers in 1371. In 1236 Pope Gregory IX handed over the abbey to the Cistercians of San Galgano, who restored it and kept it until 1782. Badly damaged in the Second World War, it has been well restored, and the bell-tower, which had been destroyed by bombs, has been completely rebuilt. The 13th cent. Romanesque facade is divided into three part by pilasters. The church contains works of art, including a marble tabernacle, probably the work of Giuliano da Maiano (1432-1490). One should notice the Chapel of San Quintino, completely decorated with frescoes by Giovanni Mannozzi, called Giovanni da San Giovanni (1592-1636), and the 15th cent. main cloister leading to the vast lay-brothers Room and the Chapter house, with its columns half buried in the ground.

* **SCANNO** (L'Aquila). In a deep, narrow valley, into which flow the Tasso and one of its tributaries. The *Chiesa Madre*, dedicated to Santa Maria della Valle, was built in the 16th cent. The rectangular facade has three doorways, the most interesting being the middle, Romanesque one. In the basilican interior are fine holy-water stoups by Nicodemo Mancini (lived in the 18th cent.) and Loreto di Ciccio (of the same century), and four confessionals and a pulpit carved in 1744-1745 by Venanzio and Rosario Bencivegna.

* **SCARPERIA** (Florence). In the valley of the Mugello, still partly surrounded by walls. The oratory of the *Madonna dei Terremoti* contains a fresco of the Madonna and Child in the manner of Filippo Lippi (1406-1469). In the oratory of the *Madonna di Piazza* is a fine 15th cent. marble tabernacle, and a Madonna and

Child by Iacopo del Casentino (1297-1358). In the square is the *Palazzo Pretorio*, built in 1306, with frescoes of the 14-15th cent. in the hall and in the rooms on the first floor. In front of the palace is the *Chiesa Prepositurale*, with remains of a small 15th cent. cloister; it contains a marble tondo by Benedetto da Maiano. Walk to *Giogo di Scarperia*, and excursions to the *Badia di Moscheta* and the *Pieve Romanica* at S. Agata.

* **SCHEGGINO** (Perugia). An old town, at the junction of the Narco Valley and the river Nera, with medieval walls built high up on the rocks. The church of *San Nicolò*, built in the 13th cent. and rebuilt in the 16th, has a nave and two aisles, with frescoes depicting the Coronation of the Virgin, Saints John the Baptist and Nicholas, and the Nativity, signed by Giovanni di Pietro, called Spagna (c. 1450-1528); unfortunately, they are badly damaged. Near the town are the limpid *Fonti di Valcasana*, which spring up in a very pleasant spot among trees.

* **SCHIO** (Vicenza). Charming little town, at the mouth of the Val Leogra. There are remains of a Roman fort. The *Duomo*, dedicated to St. Peter, is a large construction, the rebuilding of which was begun in 1740 by Giovanni Miazzi (1699-1797) and completed by Antonio Caregaro Negrini (1821-1892). It contains an altarpiece representing the Pleading of Saints Joseph and Theresa, and frescoes by Valentino Puppin (1830-1886). In the sacristy is a painting

Scarperia, Pieve di Fagna, Baptismal font, detail.

of the Madonna with St. Catherine and St. John the Baptist by Jacopo Palma the Elder (c. 1480-1528). The interior of the Gothic church of *San Francesco*, founded in 1436, is decorated with frescoes by Francesco Verla (recorded 1490-1520). In the apse are wooden choirstalls made by Bernardino de Ronchius in 1509.

* **SCIACCA** (Agrigento). In a hilly area, which slopes down steeply towards the sea, and dominated on its eastern side by Monte San Calogero. A Selinuntian colony, until conquered by the Romans, it really began to develop under Arab rule. It was fortified in 1336 by Federick II of Aragon. The *Duomo*, dedicated to St. Mary Magdalen, was first built in the 12th cent., and is one of the most interesting monuments in the area. The Baroque facade has been left unfinished. The vault was decorated with frescoes by Tommaso Rossi in 1829, and the church contains the 16th cent. tomb of Bartolomeo Tagliavia, a statue of the Madonna della Catena by Giuliano Mancino (active in the first half of the 16th cent.), and a marble tabernacle by Antonino Gagini (recorded 1541-1575). The church of *Santa Margherita*, erected in 1342, has a Gothic-Renaissance portal in one side, one of the best works of Francesco Laurana (recorded 1458-1500): in the lunette an image of St. Margaret and Angels; in the cusp, the Eternal with Angels, and on the sides, Saints Calogero and Mary Magdalen. The interior consists of an aisleless nave, and is completely decorated with polychrome stucco work by Orazio Ferraro, (recorded 1594-1622), and frescoes by Ferraro, Giovanni Portalone (active in the first half of the 17th cent.), Michele Blasco (1628-1685), and Gaspare Testone (lived in the 18th cent.). The *Steripinto* is a bizarre 15th cent. palace built in a Sicilian-Catalan style, with a graceful Renaissance doorway. As far as it is known, the Selinuntian Baths (*Terme Selinuntine*) were the first to be used for therapeutic purposes, and were already frequented by the ancient Greeks. The originally Norman church of *Santa Maria delle Giummare*, or *di Valverde*, was completely rebuilt in the 16th cent. The battlemented facade has an 18th cent. doorway, and is framed by two towers with mullioned windows surmounted by pointed arches. Inside, the decorative stucco is by A. Ferraiolo (lived in the 18th cent.), while the vault was frescoed by a local painter, Mariano Rossi (1731-1807). Excursion to *Monte San Calogero*, the Greek Kronion, on the summit of which is the sanctuary of San Calogero, with a notable statue of the saint by Giacomo Gagini (1517-1598).

* **SCICLI** (Ragusa). Destroyed by an earthquake in 1693, it was rebuilt in its present Baroque form. The 18th cent. *Chiesa Matrice*, or *del Collegio*, dedicated to St. Ignatius, has a flamboyant facade with a large doorway. It

contains a notable painting of the Madonna delle Milizie by Francesco Pascucci (recorded 1787-1793). The 18th cent. church of *San Bartolomeo* has a neo-Classical facade, and contains a huge altarpiece depicting the Martyrdom of St. Bartholomew by Francesco Pascucci, and a Deposition by Mattia Preti (1613-1699). The harmonious facade of the *Chiesa del Carmine* is clearly inspired by the style of Rosario Gagliardi (c. 1700-c. 1770). In the church of *Santa Maria la Nova* is a Nativity of Mary by Sebastiano Conca (c. 1680-1764).

* **SEDINI** (Sassari). Pleasantly situated, with houses running down into a steep gorge, in such a way that they appear to be built on top of each other. The church of *Sant'Andrea*, erected in 1517, has a fine Aragonese-Gothic facade. The interior consists of a nave, with graceful arches above the entrances to the side chapels, and a reproduction of Raphael's Transfiguration in the apse, the work of Andrea Lusso (recorded 1593-1610). Very important is the *Domus de Janas*, hewn out of a great mass of limestone, with a number of small burial chambers. Excursion to the ruins of *San Nicola di Silanis*, surrounded by prickly pears, once a Benedictine abbey.

** **SEGESTA** (Town of Calatafimi, province of Trapani). An extremely important archaeo-logical area. The Doric Temple (*Tempio*) stands solitary and majestic in the desolate countryside. It is a peripteros-hexastylos, and its entablature and two pediments are still intact. It is supposed to have been built in the 5th cent. B.C., though nothing certain is known about its origins. The Theatre (*Teatro*) is a large semicircle, with steps hewn out of the bare rock. In 1928 the remains of what were probably religious constructions of the 10-9th cent. B.C. were discovered beneath the stage and auditorium.

* **SEGNI** (Rome). Situated on the northern side of the Lepini mountains; the Volscian town of Signum was surrounded by two kilometres of walls in the 6-5th cent. B.C., and their perimeter can still be traced. The originally Romanesque *Cattedrale*, rebuilt in the first half of the 17th cent., is over-decorated. It contains a fresco of the Coronation of Mary with the Evangelists by Fra Antonio Courtois (lived in the 17th cent.), Scenes from the Life of St. Bruno frescoed by Lazzaro Baldi (c. 1624-1703), a painting of the Madonna and Child with Saints Dominic and Catherine of Siena by Pietro da Cortona (1596-1669), and a Glorification of the Cross by Giacomo Courtois, called Borgognone (1621-1675). In the rectangular *Acropoli*, with its polygonal blocks of stone, were three rooms dedicated to the

Segesta, Temple.

Capitoline triad; the middle one is now the foundation of the 13th cent. church of St. Peter. One should also notice the Saracen Gate (*Porta Saracena*), whose name probably commemorates a Saracen attack, the *Cisterna*, a circular swimming-pool of the 6th cent. B.C., and the medieval quarter (*Quartiere Medievale*).

** **SELINUNTE** (Town of Castelvetrano, province of Trapani). An indispensable point of reference for any visitor to Sicily, because of the extent of its archaeological area, which offers one of the most complete pictures of a 5th cent. Greek city. It was built about 650 B.C., and was a Greek colony of considerable importance for some time. The most flourishing period in its history coincided with the 5th cent. It was destroyed by the Carthaginians in 409 B.C., while most of its buildings, which had retained their antique grandeur, collapsed as the result of an earthquake at some unknown date during the Byzantine period. For centuries its wonderful marble was carried away and used in the construction of country villas. This pillage was partly stopped by an order issued by King Ferdinand III in 1779. The systematic exploration of its ruins began in the 18th cent., partly thanks to English archaeologists, such as William Harris, and research has continued at a greater pace up to the present day, with the aid of increasingly refined techniques. There are three *Templi Orientali*: the one dedicated to Apollo (temple G), the tutelary god of the Selinuntians, is one of the most colossal examples of Greek architecture. It was built between 550 and 480

B.C., and in the centre of its numerous remains is a column, the size of which gives one an idea of how huge the original structure must have been; the second (temple F), a peripteros-hexastylos built in the 6th cent. B.C., is the one that has suffered most from plunder; the third (temple E), consecrated to Hera, is another peripteros-hexastylos, with thirty-eight columns. Built in the 5th cent. B.C., it is a perfect example of the Doric style. The *Acropoli* is a vast terrace with an irregular perimeter, and was once crowded with monuments, though only five towers and four doorways have been discovered so far. The *Torre di Polluce*, which gave its name in Arab times to a village recorded in ancient documents as Terra di Pulci (land of fleas), was erected in the 16th cent. as a bulwark against pirates, and the ruins of an old tower, or lighthouse, were used in its construction. The remains of other temples may be found in the area of the Acropolis. The *Santuario della Malophoros*, called also the sanctuary of Gaggera, after the name of the district, was a place of worship outside the city. It was discovered in 1874 by Francesco Saverio Cavallari, one of the most active and gifted scholars who have explored the Selinunte of Grecian times. It is a quadrilateral measuring 50 x 60 metres, which is reached through a 5th century propyleaum. Inside one sees a rather narrow space and an imposing sacrificial altar. Farther on are numerous and important remains of a temple dedicated to the goddess Malophoros, who was probably the equivalent of the Greek Demeter.

Selinunte, Temple C.

322

* **SEMINARA** (Reggio Calabria). Situated in hilly countryside, with a view of Monte Santo Elia. Founded in the 5th cent., it was completely rebuilt after the earthquake in 1908. It had an important fortress in the Middle Ages. In the church of *San Marco*, rebuilt after 1908, like all the other buildings in the town, are some fairly interesting works of art by the sculptor Antonello Gagini (1478-1536) and other artists. In the building that houses the prefecture and the town hall are five important 16th cent. bas-reliefs representing battle scenes. In the Sanctuary of the *Madonna dei Poveri* is a 12-13th cent. Madonna and Child in cedar wood, a marble statue of Mary Magdalen by Rinaldo Bonanno (recorded 1577-1591), and embossed silver reliquaries of the 17-18th cent.

* **SENIGALLIA** (Ancona). Small town near the mouth of the Misa. The old centre is surrounded by walls built by the Rovere family and the Popes, while the modern part of the town runs down to the beaches. The *Rocca*, probably designed by Luciano Laurana (1420/25-1479) is a notable example of Renaissance military architecture. The *Chiesa della Croce*, first built in 1576, contains some fair works of art, such as the Burial of Christ in the Sepulchre by Federico Baroccio (c. 1528-1612), and other paintings by Giovanni Anastasi (c. 1654-1704). The *Duomo*, built in the late 18th cent., contains some interesting works of art, including a painting of Sant'Andrea Avellino dying, probably by Domenico Corvi (1721-1803), Saints Francis and Dominic by Emilio

Savonanzi (1580-1660), and the Baptism of Christ by Andrea Lilli (1555-1610). The *Palazzetto Baviera* is a modest Renaissance construction. It was rebuilt in the 15th cent. by Giacomo Baviera, with a small courtyard, and contains some fairly interesting works of art. Walk to the church of *Santa Maria delle Grazie*, designed in 1491 by Baccio Pontelli (c. 1450-1492), or by Girolamo Genga (1445/52-1523).

* **SENORBI** (Cagliari). The most important town in the Trexenta district. The construction of the parish church of *Santo Antioco* was begun in the 16th cent. in the late-Gothic style. It contains a crucifix and wooden statues by Giuseppe Antonio Lonis (lived in the 18-19th cent.). The little church of *Santa Mariedda*, built in the 13-14th cent., is a remarkable Romanesque country chapel, with blind arcades and a charming bell gable.

* **SERAVEZZA** (Lucca). Important for its marble industry, it lies at the confluence of the Serra and the Vezza. In the *Cattedrale dei Santi Lorenzo e Barbara*, rebuilt in the first years of the 16th cent., is a fine altar-frontal on the high altar depicting St. Lawrence, the work of Jacopo Benti (recorded 1644-1659), and a baptismal font by Stagio Stagi (c. 1496-1563). On the facade of the 15th cent. *Oratorio della Santissima Annunziata*, or *Chiesa della Misericordia*, is a bas-relief of the Madonna and Child by Donato Benti (1470-c. 1536), and inside is a painting of the Three Marys at the Sepulchre by Pietro da Cortona (1596-1669). The *Pa-*

Senigallia, the Fort.

lazzo Mediceo, the summer residence of the Grand Dukes of Tuscany, was designed and built in 1555 by Bartolomeo Ammannati (1511-1592) for Duke Cosimo I.

* **SERMONETA** (Latina). With a view overlooking the Pontine plain. The *Cattedrale*, consecrated to the Assunta, and built in the 13th cent. on the ruins of a temple dedicated to Cybele, is a much altered Romanesque-Gothic construction. In the lunette above the entrance is a fresco of the Virgin and Child with two Saints by Pietro Coleberti (active in the first half of the 15th cent.). Inside is a fine 16th cent. holy-water stoup, frescoes depicting episodes in the life of Mary, and a panel of the Madonna of the Angels by Benozzo Gozzoli (1420-1497). The well-preserved *Castello Caetani* was built in the first half of the 13th cent. by the Annibaldi family, and later enlarged by the Caetani family, who had the so-called "Camere Pinte" (painted rooms) frescoed with symbolic and mythological figures by an anonymous disciple of Pinturicchio. From Sermoneta one can reach the *Abbazia di Valvisciolo*, consecrated to Saints Peter and Paul, and surrounded by eucalyptus trees. It was founded by Greek monks in the 8th cent., and rebuilt in the 13th by the Knights of the Holy Temple. Inside the Cistercian-Gothic church are frescoes by Nicolò Circignani, called Pomarancio (c. 1517-1596), a 17th cent. painting of the Madonna, and an 18th cent. one of St. Lawrence baptising a convert.

* **SERRA SAN BRUNO** (Catanzaro). This town grew up between the 11th and 12th centuries near the famous Charterhouse of S. Stefano del Bosco, founded by the Carthusian Brunone of Cologne, perhaps in 1090. The *Chiesa Matrice*, dedicated to St. Blaise, was built at the end of the 18th cent. with a Baroque facade. It contains marble statues, taken from the above-mentioned monastery, bas-reliefs which recall the Flemish school, signed "David Müller tudesco 1611", a Baroque pulpit by the Scaramuzzino family of wood-carvers (active in the 18-19th cent.), and a Flemish-style painting of the Martyrdom of St. Stephen from the 16th cent. The *Chiesa dell'Addolorata* has a small Baroque facade, and was designed by one of the Scaramuzzino family. The interior is in the form of a Latin cross, and contains a valuable painting of the Death of St. Anne by an artist of the neo-Classical Roman school, a splendid ciborium made out of the great ciborium designed by Cosimo Fanzago (1593-1678) for the Charterhouse and destroyed by the earthquake of 1783, and a painting of the Apparition of the Madonna to St. Bruno by Paolo De Matteis (1662-1728). Walk to the *Certosa di San Bruno*: on the vast inner lawn are the ruins of the ancient Charterhouse of S. Stefano del Bosco. This building had fallen into almost complete

ruin before its reconstruction in the late 16th cent., possibly to a design drawn up by Andrea Palladio (1508-1580); it collapsed later during the 1783 earthquake. The ruins, which were propped up at the beginning of this century, include parts of the facade and cloister. One passes from the old monastery to the new, built in 1900, which contains some works of art, including a 16th cent. silver bust of St. Bruno. The place is ideal for walks amongst forests of tall firs, one of which is called St. Mary's Wood.

* **SERRAVALLE SCRIVIA** (Alessandria). Centre of a road and rail network, it was probably founded by the inhabitants of Tortona on the ruins of the Roman Libarna. Archaeologically important on account of excavations *Libarna* (*Scavi di Libarna*), it is situated on the alluvial terrace of the river Scrivia.

* **SERRI** (Nuoro). An area exceptionally rich in archaeological remains. Excursion to the *Giara di Serri* or *sa Giara*, a plateau with slabs of basalt rock, called "giare". There are some notable remains of a religious centre dating from the age of the Nuraghi. Particularly worthy of attention is the "recinto delle riunioni" (meetings' enclosure), an elliptical space occupied by circular huts.

* **SESSA AURUNCA** (Caserta). On the trachytic slopes of the volcano of Roccamontina. Corresponds to Suessa, the most important

Serra San Bruno, Church of the Assunta.

324

city of the Aurunci, as is proved by the recently discovered burial hoards of the 8-7th cent. The town's most important monument is the *Duomo*, dedicated to St. Peter, and rebuilt in the early 11th cent. with material taken from Roman buildings. The facade has an austere 13th cent. portico. On the archivolt of the central archway are important bas-reliefs of scenes from the life of St. Peter. The portal of the Bishop's Palace has an architrave in Roman marble decorated with panthers and masks. The interior has a basilican plan, and is divided into a nave and two aisles by monolithic columns. It has an interesting mosaic floor, and notable works of art, including a superb pulpit decorated with essentially geometrical patterns in mosaic, begun by a marble-cutter called Pellegrino in the first half of the 13th cent., and an Easter candlestick decorated with mosaics by the same craftsman. In the centre of the 12th cent. nave is the Baroque Chapel of the Blessed Sacrament, with a painting of the Communion of the Apostles by Luca Giordano (1632-1705). The crypt is supported by small antique columns. The *Chiesa dell'Annunziata*, the facade of which is framed by two bell-towers, is a successful example of Baroque architecture; it contains a precious panel of St. Agatha by an unknown painter. There are many remains of the Roman Theatre (*Teatro Romano*), encompassed on three sides by a cryptoporticus. In the church of *San Giovanni* are notable works of art, including an early 15th cent. Crucifixion painted on wood, and paintings after the style · of Francesco Solimena (1657-1747). The 18th cent. interior of the church of *San Germano* is a magnificent sight. In Piazza Umberto I is the important *Fontana dell'Ercole*, with a marble statue of Hercules slaying the Nemean lion, a sign that the worship of this divinity was practised by the ancient inhabitants of Suessa. Walk to the Auruncan bridge (*Ponte degli Aurunci*), with its twenty-one round arches, which commands a magnificent view over the Travata.

* **SESTO AL REGHENA** (Pordenone). About ten kilometres from San Vito al Tagliamento. The *Abbazia di Santa Maria in Sylvis*, founded in the first half of the 8th cent., with a Byzantine-Romanesque basilica of the 12-13th cent., is rich in frescoes dating from different periods. In the abbey crypt is the precious 8th cent. urn of S. Anastasia.

* **SESTO FIORENTINO** (Florence). The markedly Romanesque *Pieve di San Martino* was built in the 9th cent. It contains a precious tabernacle (1388), a painted crucifix, probably the work of Agnolo di Taddeo Gaddi (recorded 1369-1396), and a painting of the four Patron Saints of Sesto by Santi di Tito (1536-1603). Interesting excursion to *Monte Morello* for its fine views.

For the *Pieve di Sant'Andrea a Cercina*, see Cercina.

* **SESTRI LEVANTE** (Genoa). Situated on the Golfo Tigullio, it stretches over the alluvial plain of the Gromolo, and is an important summer and winter seaside resort. The parish church of *Santa Maria di Nazareth*, built at the beginning of the 17th cent., has a Madonna del Carmine with Saints Lawrence and John the Baptist by Lazzaro Tavarone (1556-1641), a Death of St. Joseph by Orazio De Ferrari (1606-1657), and a Pentecost by Domenico Fiasella, called Sarzana. The *Pinacoteca Rizzi* has an important collection of pictures, including a Head of St. Francis of Paola by Giovanni Battista Tiepolo (1696-1770), a sketch by Gian Domenico Tiepolo (1727-1804), a Roman Charity by Michelangelo Merisi, called Caravaggio (1570-1610), a small panel of the Adoration in the Garden by Raphael (1483-1520), a cartoon of Adam and Eve by Michelangelo, which the artist used when painting the frescoes of the Sistine Chapel, and a Portrait of Vincenzo Gonzaga II by Peter Paul Rubens (1577-1640).

* **SESTRI PONENTE** (Genoa). Industrial town, a few kilometres from Genoa. The *Chiesa dell'Assunta*, built in 1620, has a facade with a bronze relief of the Assunta, and statues of Saints Joseph and John the Baptist by the contemporary sculptor, Luigi Venzano. The church contains a painting of the Virgin Assumed into Heaven by Giulio Benso (1601-1668), Jesus in the boat awoken by St. Peter, by Domenico Fiasella, called Sarzana (1589-1669), and a Baptism of Christ by Domenico Piola (1627-1703).

Sesto Fiorentino, Parish church of Sant'Andrea at Cercina, interior.

* **SESTU** (Cagliari). The 16th cent. parish church of *San Giorgio* is in late-Gothic style, and has a campanile in the form of a tower. The interior consists of an aisleless nave, and has a harmonious apse and chapels. Walk to the church of *San Gemiliano*, which, in spite of the unfortunate alterations carried out after the 16th cent., is a notable example of Sardinian Romanesque art. It was built by Arab workmen for the Victorine monks.

* **SETTIGNANO** (neighbourhood of Florence). Pleasant town on a green hill scattered with villas, within a few kilometres of Florence. In the 15th cent. *Parrocchiale dell'Assunta* is a pulpit designed by Bernardo Buonaiuti (1536-1608) and carried out by Gherardo Silvani (1579-1675). Not far from Settignano is the villa called *I Tatti*, surrounded by a vast Italian garden. It was bought in 1905 by the American art critic Bernard Berenson (1865-1959), who repaired it, and filled it with precious books and works of art. On the death of Berenson "I Tatti" became the seat of the Harvard Centre for the History of the Italian Renaissance. The *Berenson Collection*, which is set out in the various rooms of the villa, has many important works of art, including a Madonna and Child of the 14th cent. Florentine school, Saints Lucy and Catherine, probably by Simone Martini (1284?-1344), a Madonna and Child by Pietro Lorenzetti (1280-c. 1348), St. Michael enthroned by Michele Giambono (?-1462), a Madonna and Child by Domenico Veneziano (?-1461), St. Francis with John the Baptist and Ranieri Rasini by Sassetta (c. 1392-1450), Portraits of Camillo and Vitellozzo Vitelli by Luca Signorelli (c. 1445-1523), St. Sebastian by Cima da Conegliano (c. 1459-1517), and a Madonna della Siepe and Madonna and Child by Vincenzo Foppa (c. 1427-c. 1515).

* **SEZZE** (Latina). Overlooking the Pontine plain. The construction of the *Duomo* was begun in the Romanesque period and completed in 1347. It was considerably altered in the 16th and 17th centuries, so that it is now a very ungainly structure. Long stretches of the *Cinta Muraria Difensiva* (defensive walls), which are claimed to have been built before 382 B.C., have survived, together with prominent bastions. Worth visiting is the *Teatro Sacro Italico*, a natural amphitheatre set in the Pontine plain.

*** **SIENA.** Considered to be one of Italy's most fascinating cities, it is situated between the valleys of the Orbia and Elsa, and extends over three hills, a fact that gives it great physical variety. It may be said that every stone in Siena has a history. Consequently, one can only provide a list of the main monuments the visitor should see. The *Loggia della Mercanzia* or *dei Mercanti* or *di San Paolo*, with its transitional Gothic-to-Renaissance style, was built between 1417 and 1428 to a design by Sano di Matteo. The pillars form niches, with the statues of St. Paul by Lorenzo di Pietro, called Vecchietta (1412-1480), St. Victor by Antonio Federighi (1420-1490), St. Ansanus by Federighi, St. Peter by Vecchietta, and St. Savinus by Federighi, placed in that order. Beneath the portico are two marble benches, the finest being that by Federighi, with heads of Cicero, Cato, Scipio Maior, Curius Dentatus, Furius and Scipio Africanus. The decoration of the vaults, carried out by Lorenzo Rustici (1521-1572), is also admirable. *Piazza del Campo*, or just the Campo, is one of the most beautiful in Europe. Formerly Campus Fori, it spreads out like the valve of a scallop-shell, at the very point where the three hills of the city meet. It is surrounded on all sides by 14th cent. palaces. It has been the heart of the city for centuries; in the centre of the square is the imposing Fonte Gaia. The original reliefs by Jacopo della Quercia are now kept in the Loggia in the *Palazzo Pubblico*, which is the most imposing Gothic construction in Tuscany. Built between 1297 and 1310, and enlarged in later times, it was the seat of the Signoria and of the Podestà. Rising above it is the famous Torre del Mangia, a slender, graceful structure built by the Perugian brothers, Minuccio and Francesco di Rinaldo, between 1338 and 1348. The palace contains art treasures signed by many of the greatest painters and sculptors of the 14th and 15th centuries. Particular attention should be paid to the immense fresco of the Maestà by Simone Martini (1284-1344)

Settignano, Berenson Collection. Luca Signorelli, Vitellozzo Vitelli.

Siena, Duomo. Pulpit by Nicola Pisano.
Siena, Battistero. Lorenzo Ghiberti, Christ's Baptism.

Siena, Duomo. Nicola Pisano, Visitation, panel from the pulpit.

Siena, Museo dell'Opera del Duomo. Giovanni Pisano, Prophet's head.

Siena, Sant'Agostino. Simone Martini, Miracle of the Blessed Agostino Novello, detail.

Siena, Sant'Agostino. Simone Martini, Miracle of the Blessed Agostino Novello, detail.

in the Map Room, and to the cycle of frescoes carried out in 1338 by Ambrogio Lorenzetti in the Hall of Peace. The construction of the *Duomo dell'Assunta* probably began towards the middle of the 12th cent. The white marble facade, enlivened with red and green marble, was begun by Giovanni Pisano (recorded 1245-1314). The rich interior has many works of art, such as the famous 15-16th cent. terracotta busts of Popes, the Cappella del Voto, or Chigi Chapel, commissioned by Fabio Chigi of Siena, later Pope Alexander VII, and designed in 1661 by Benedetto Giovannelli. The pulpit is by Nicola Pisano (1220-1287). The

Siena, Museo dell'Opera del Duomo. Duccio da Buoninsegna, Peter's Betrayal, detail.

Piccolòmini Library contains frescoes by Pinturicchio and precious illuminated manuscripts. The floor of the cathedral is covered with beautiful marble inlays, on which numerous artists worked from 1369 to 1547. The *Battistero*, or *San Giovanni* (1316-1325), is the cathedral crypt. It has a Gothic facade (1382), which is attributed to Mino di Neri del Pellicciaio. It contains a precious baptismal font, carved in 1417 by Jacopo della Quercia, with bas-reliefs by Jacopo, Donatello and Ghiberti. In the *Museo dell'Opera del Duomo* are various art collections, but perhaps its real jewel is the Maestà by Duccio di Buoninsegna (1255-1318). The Palazzo Buonsignori houses the *Pinacoteca*, in which almost the whole Sienese school is represented, except Simone Martini. The church of *Sant'Agostino*, built in 1258, has many works of art, including a Crucifixion by Pietro Vannucci, called Perugino (1445-1523), an Epiphany by Giovanni Antonio Bazzi, called Sodoma (1477-1549), a Blessed Agostino Novello inspired by an Angel and four Miracles of the Saint by Simone Martini, and a Maestà by Ambrogio Lorenzetti. The 13th cent. church of *Santa Maria dei Servi*, formerly of the Immaculate Conception, has an interior in the form of a Latin cross, with a nave and two aisles. It also has many fine works of art, such as the Madonna and Child, called "del

Siena, Duomo, interior.

Siena, Museo dell'Opera del Duomo. Duccio da
Buoninsegna, The Marriage at Cana, detail.

Siena, Museo dell'Opera del Duomo. Duccio da
Buoninsegna, The Miraculous Catch, detail.

Siena, Pinacoteca Nazionale. Giovanni di Paolo,
Universal Judgment, detail.

Siena, Pinacoteca Nazionale. Giovanni di Paolo,
Presentation of Christ at the Temple, detail.

Siena, Pinacoteca Nazionale. Domenico di Bartolo,
Our Lady of Humility.

Siena, Pinacoteca Nazionale. Francesco di Giorgio
Martini, Coronation of the Virgin, detail.

Bordone", carried out in 1261 by the Florentine Coppo di Marcovaldo, a fresco of the Massacre of the Innocents by Pietro Lorenzetti (1280-c. 1348), and the Madonna del Popolo by Lippo Memmi (recorded 1317-1347). The *Palazzo Piccolòmini*, an imposing stone edifice in the style of the Florentine Quattrocento, was probably designed by Bernardo Rossellino (1409-1464), while its construction was begun in 1469 by Pietro Paolo Porrina da Casole. It now houses the important State Archives and the collection of "tavolette" (covers of registers) from the Biccherna (revenue office). The church of *San Francesco* was begun in the Gothic style in 1326. It has a brick facade, with a rose-window surrounded by the symbols of the Evangelists. The interior is in the form of an Egyptian cross, with a vast aisleless nave,

Siena, Town Hall, rear view.

and contains frescoes by Martino di Bartolomeo (recorded 1389-1434); in the transept are detached frescoes by Pietro and Ambrogio Lorenzetti. The 14th cent. *Palazzo Salimbeni* is now the seat of the famous Monte dei Paschi Bank. The *Palazzo Tolomei* already existed in 1205, and is the oldest of the city's private palaces; it is an austere, aristocratic building, constructed wholly out of stone. The *Fonte Branda*, which is mentioned in documents as early as 1081, was enlarged in the late 12th cent. and remodelled in the middle of the 13th. The *Santuario e Casa di Santa Caterina* was converted into an oratory in 1464. Inside the austere, massive church of *San Domenico*, begun in 1226, is the Chapel of St. Catherine, with frescoes by Sodoma, Francesco Vanni (1565-1609), and other famous artists. The church of *Fontegiusta* has a Renaissance facade, and a superb marble door by Urbano da Cortona (lived in the 15th cent.). Nor can one overlook the *Cappella di Piazza, Palazzo Sansedoni, Palazzo Saracini, Palazzo del Capitano di Giustizia, Palazzo del Magnifico, Spedale di Santa Maria della Scala*, the church of *Santa Maria del Carmine*, the church of *Santo Spirito* and the *Logge del Papa*.

* **SIGILLO** (Perugia). Founded by the Longobards and developed by the inhabitants of Perugia, at the foot of the bare, rugged Monte

Siena, Pinacoteca Nazionale. Francesco di Giorgio Martini, Annunciation.

Cucco. The church of *Sant'Agostino* contains a beautiful panel of the Annunciation, painted by Ippolito Borghese (local painter of the 16-17th cent.) in 1617. The church of *Sant'Anna*, in the cemetery, has a fine facade, carried out in the early 16th cent., with votive frescoes by Matteo da Gualdo (c. 1435-1507). Excursion to the *Grotta di Monte Cucco*, one of the most remarkable Karst formations in central Italy.

* **SILANUS** (Nuoro). Nearby is the *Nuraghe Madrone*, also called the Orolis. Important on account of the beauty of its structure and fluent architectural lines, it is believed to have had four lobes. The site commands a magnificent view of the valley of the river Tirso.

* **SINALUNGA** (Siena). On a hill, overlooking the Valdichiana. In the *Collegiata di San Martino* is a Madonna and Child with four Saints by Sodoma (1477-1549). In the 17th cent. church of the *Madonna delle Nevi* is a Madonna and Child by Benvenuto di Giovanni (1436-c. 1518), and other notable paintings. Walk to the church of *San Bernardino* or *dei Cappuccini*, near which is a well-proportioned, octagonal chapel, with interesting panels by the painter and miniaturist, Guidoccio Cozzarelli (recorded 1450-1506), Sano di Pietro (1406-1481), and Benvenuto di Giovanni.

** **SIPONTO** (Town of Manfredonia, province of Foggia). Situated on the Gargano promontory. Nearby are two beautiful chur-

Sinalunga, San Bernardino. Benvenuto di Giovanni, Annunciation, detail.

334

boldly articulated facade was designed by Andrea Palma (1664-1730). The basilican interior contains many works of art, including a panel with gilt background depicting S. Zosimo, probably the work of Antonello da Messina (c. 1430-1479), two marble medallions depicting St. Lucy and St. Eutichius, probably by Ignazio Marabitti (1719-1797), frescoes by Agostino Scilla (1629-1700), a ciborium in the form of a small temple by Luigi Vanvitelli (1700-1773), thirteen panels of a polyptych depicting Christ, Apostles and Evangelists, perhaps by Marco Costanzo (recorded 1468-1500), a Madonna della Neve by Antonello Gagini (1478-1536), and other statues by Antonello and Domenico Gagini. In the *Museo Archeologico Nazionale*, indispensable for the study of the pre- and proto-history of Sicily, are pre-Hellenic collections, and a topographical section on Greek Sicily (small terracotta statues from a

ches: the church of *Santa Maria* was built in the Romanesque style in the very first years of the 11th cent. on the remains of an earlier temple. Its facade has a beautiful Apulian-style portal, over which is an eagle, part of an ambo carved by Acceptus (11th cent.). It is interesting to note the depressed arch of the dome, and its lantern with eight small arches, as well as the Romanesque holy-water stoup with its stone lion base. In the crypt is an important painted sculpture of the Madonna and Child from the early Middle Ages. Excavations carried out in the left side of the church have brought to light the remains of an early Christian basilica, probably built upon a temple dedicated to Diana. The *Chiesa Abbaziale di San Leonardo di Siponto*, or *di Lama Volara*, was built at the very end of the 11th or beginning of the 12th cent. On its left side is a superb doorway, possibly dating from the first half of the 12th cent., with figured capitals. The church terminates in three finely designed apses, and has two octagonal domes, one of which is decorated with 14th cent. arcadings. The nave is covered by a barrel-vault and domes, the aisles by semi-barrel-vaults. It contains an important painted wood crucifix of the first half of the 13th cent.

*** SIRACUSA/SYRACUSE.

Spread over the island of Ortigia and the neighbouring coast, behind which the countryside is covered with rich, prevalently Mediterranean vegetation, it enjoys a wonderful climate. It is a modern-looking city, though notable medieval and Baroque monuments are to be found in the centre. The *Duomo*, dedicated to Santa Maria del Piliero, or delle Colonne, was built in the 7th cent. over the temple of Athena. The huge

Siponto, San Leonardo, doorway.

Syracuse, Museo Archeologico. Venus Anadyomene, called Landolina.

sanctuary dedicated to Demeter and Kore, a votive deposit from the temple of Ares, archaic wooden statuines of the 7th cent. B.C., terracotta busts of Demeter and Kore, a bronze mask of Gorgon from the 4th cent. B.C., grave goods from the tomb of a warrior of the 4th cent. B.C., polychrome terracotta relief with winged Gorgon, a monstrous Gorgon, an acroterium in the form of a horseman, archaic limestone head). In Room IX is the much admired statue of Venus Anadyomene, discovered in the city in 1804, and that of Heracles from the school of Lysippus (c. 300 B.C.). On the ground floor of the *Museo Nazionale di Palazzo Bellomo* is a collection of statues, with works by Domenico Gagini (c. 1420-1492), Francesco Laurana (recorded 1458-1500), Giovanni Battista Mazzola (recorded 1513-1550) and others. On the first floor is the art gallery, with works by Lorenzo Veneziano (recorded 1356-1379), Giovanni Francesco da Rimini (recorded 1450-1561), Marco Costanzo, Antonello da Palermo (recorded 1497-1528), Alessandro Padovano (recorded 1507-1529), Andrea da Salerno (c. 1484-1530), Giovanni Maria da Treviso (recorded 1506-1513), Simon de Wobreck (recorded 1557-1585), Wilhelm Borremans (1670-1744), and, above all, by Antonello da Messina, author of the finest painting in the whole collection, an Annunciation, dated 1474. In Largo XXV Luglio are the important ruins of the *Temple of Apollo*, or *Artemis*, which date from the late 7th or early 6th cent. B.C. The most ancient of its kind among the great Greek temples of Sicily,

it was found in 1862, and revealed in its entirety between 1938 and 1943. Particularly famous is the Fountain of Arethusa (*Fonte Aretusa*). The *Castello Maniace* is named after Giorgio Maniace, the Byzantine general who conquered the city in 1038. Built on a spur barring the eastern approach to the Porto Grande, it has been the centre of important military events. Though badly damaged in November 1704 by the explosion of an ammunition depot, as well as being struck by lightning, it still retains its 13th cent. exterior, including a fine Gothic doorway, and cylindrical towers at its corners. The church of *Santa Lucia* was first built in the 6th cent. on the spot where, according to tradition, the Syracusan virgin was martyred. In the apse is a painting of the Burial of St. Lucy, one of the masterpieces of Michelangelo Merisi, called Caravaggio (1573-1610). In the octagonal cappella del Sepolcro, designed by the architect Giovanni Vermexio (recorded 1621-1657), is a niche where the remains of the saint were kept before they were transferred to the church of St. Jeremiah in Venice in 1204; one should visit the catacombs of St. Lucy. The *Chiesa del Collegio* was built in the second half of the 17th cent. It has an imposing facade, high altar, and rich marble works by Giovanni Battista Marino (recorded 1728-1765), as well as a statue of St. Ignatius by Ignazio Marabitti. Ruins of the so-called *Ginnasio Romano*, probably from the second half of the 1st cent. The *Parco Monumentale della Neapolis* encompasses nearly all the classical monuments built

Syracuse, Greek Theatre.

Siena, Pinacoteca Nazionale. Pinturicchio, Holy Family with S. Giovannino, detail.

Siena, Palazzo Pubblico. Il Sodoma, Holy Family with S. Leonardo, detail.

Syracuse, Museo Archeologico. Painted vases.

Syracuse, Museo Archeologico. Corinthian oenochoe and ciborium.

Syracuse, Museo Archeologico. Painted pottery vases.

Sorrento, Museo Correale. Pluteus with hippogryphs, detail.

Sulmona, Museo Civico. Giovanni da Sulmona, Tabernacle, detail.

Spoleto, Duomo. Alberto Sozio, painted Cross.

Sulmona, Museo Civico. Giovanni da Sulmona. Tabernacle panel, detail.

by the Greeks and Romans in Syracuse. The 5th cent. Greek Theatre (*Teatro Greco*) is the most important example of ancient theatre architecture and Classical scenic technique that has survived. The Latomia del Paradiso is a quarry 45 m deep, wherein is the famous Ear of Dionysius, a grotto hewn in the rock, 65 m long, the name of which is based on the legend that it was built by Dionysius so that he could hear from above everything his political prisoners said, or even whispered. The Latomia di Santa Venera has been converted into a pleasant garden, and has four little niches in the corners, once dedicated to the worship of heroes. The Roman Amphitheatre is an imposing construction erected under the Empire, and dating from the 3rd-4th cent. The Grotta dei Corsari has an irregular vault, supported by pillars that taper downwards like large stalactites. The Altar of Hiero II is huge, and was used to celebrate the city's public sacrifices. The *Catacombe di San Giovanni* form a large, subterranean necropolis, almost wholly unexplored; on the walls are interesting, but unfortunately faint traces of frescoes. The Castle of Euryelus (*Castello Eurialo*) is one of the best-preserved examples of a Greek fortification. Built by Dionysius I in six years, between 402 and 397 B.C., it was vital in the defence against the Carthaginians. It was conquered by the Romans in 212 B.C.

* **SIRMIONE** (Verona). In a magnificent position, near the tip of the promontory of Sirmione, which projects into Lake Garda. The *Rocca Scaligera* is a spectacular building erected in the middle of the 13th cent. It seems to have been built by Mastino II Della Scala, and has three entrances and a massive keep: the wet dock once served to harbour the Scaligers' fleet. The 15th cent. church of *Santa Maria Maggiore* has an aisleless nave, with frescoes of the 15-16th centuries, and paintings by Luigi Voltolini (1814-1864). The portico of the facade has a column, the first on the left, which was used as a milestone in the time of the Emperor Flavius Claudius Julianus, called the Apostate. The *Grotte di Catullo* are the remains of a large Roman villa of the 1st cent.

* **SOAVE** (Verona). An ancient town, still surrounded by walls. The 18th cent. *Parrocchiale* has a painting of Saints Bovo, Francis, and Anthony Abbot by Paolo Farinati (1524-1606), a Madonna and Child enthroned with Saints Roch and Jerome by Francesco Morone (1471-1529), and three 15th cent. bas-reliefs. The 8th cent. *Abbazia di San Pietro Apostolo* was rebuilt in the first half of the 12th cent., and has undergone alterations at various periods. Part of the facade is in nenfro marble, while the Romanesque interior contains late 14th cent. frescoes illustrating episodes in the life of St. Benedict, a St. Michael, the Coronation of Mary with other Saints by an unknown

15th cent. painter, and a stone altarpiece, probably by Bartolomeo Giolfino (c. 1401-1486). The *Castello* was built in the early Middle Ages, and later fortified by the Scaligers and the Venetians. It has an irregular plan, with two courtyards separated by walls; worth visiting are the Corpo di Guardia (Guards' Room) the Stanza della Caminata, the bedroom, with its 14th and 15th cent. frescoes, and the dining-room, with period furniture. The *Palazzo di Giustizia* (1375) has battlements and a portico. The *Palazzo Cavalli* is built in the Venetian Gothic style of the early 15th cent. The badly damaged frescoes of the facade are attributed to Falconetto (1468-1540). The town walls (*Cinta Muraria*), begun by Cansignorio, and completed in 1369, have survived intact.

* **SOLETO** (Lecce). In the heart of the Salentino peninsula. Its most famous monument is the *Campanile*, popularly known as the Guglia di Raimondello, which stands against the parish church of Santa Maria Assunta. It was built by Raimondello Orsini, lord of Soleto, in the last years of the 14th cent. Romanesque and Gothic elements combine to make it a harmonious whole. The small, stylish 14th cent. church of *Santo Stefano*, or *Santa Sofia*, has a Gothic facade, dated 1347, with traces of Romanesque. The architraved doorway is decorated with a little rose-window and small arches. The interior is decorated with frescoes of Biblical scenes from two quite different periods (13th and 14th centuries). Particularly outstanding is the Last Judgement, carried out in accordance with the canons of Byzantine iconography.

* **SOLOFRA** (Avellino). Surrounded by high mountains, the town has both traces of the past, and modern factories. The 16th cent. *Collegiata di San Michele* has an imposing 17th cent. Baroque facade, and three portals with wooden doors. The spectacular interior is in the form of a Latin cross, and has decorations of the 17th cent., including twenty paintings of Archangels by Giovanni Tommaso Guarino (died in 1637), twenty-one paintings of scenes from the New Testament by Francesco Guarini (1611-1654), a remarkable Renaissance tomb (1520), and Music-making Angels by Giovanni Bernardo (1506-c. 1598). The late-16th cent. *Palazzo Ducale*, formerly the Palazzo degli Orsini, and later the Palazzo dei Grimaldi, is a massive block, with a large doorway and square courtyard. Inside are tempera paintings of the palaces of the Orsini family, and one of the Fair of Gravina di Puglia, the most important feud of the Orsini. In the church of *San Domenico* is a Madonna of the Rosary and portraits of members of the Orsini family by Francesco Guarini, as well as the Vision of St. Cyril of Alexandria by Angelo (c. 1630-1716) and Francesco Solimena (1657-1747). In the church of *San Giuliano* is a panel depicting St. Julian

and the Madonna di Monte Vergine by Felice Guarino (lived in the 16-17th cent.).

* **SOMMA LOMBARDO** (Varese). Small industrial town near the Alps. The 13th cent. church of *San Vito* has a 17th cent. bell-tower, and a triptych of the Madonna and Child with Saints Vitus and Modestus by Giovanni Ambrogio Bevilacqua (recorded 1481-1502). The Visconti castle (*Castello Visconteo*) was built in 1100, but later altered, and finally rebuilt in the 15th cent. Walk to Arsago Seprio, to the 11th cent. *Battistero*, and the *Basilica di San Vittore*, built in the 9th cent., with a nave and two aisles. The bell-tower is of the same period.

* **SONCINO** (Cremona). Agricultural and industrial town, situated within the ring of defensive walls built by the Sforzas. The *Rocca*, built by Galeazzo Maria Sforza in 1473 to a design by Bartolomeo Gadio (1414-1484), was restored by Luca Beltrami (1854-1933). In the church of *San Giacomo*, rebuilt in the 17th cent., is a 15th cent. group of polychrome terracotta statues representing the Deposition. The 15th cent. *Casa degli Azzanelli* is a much-admired example of secular architecture, with terracottas, probably by Rinaldo de Stauris (recorded 1461-1490). The church of *Santa Maria delle Grazie* was built in the late 15th and early 16th cent. It contains beautiful frescoes from the first half of the 16th cent., including a Last Judgement. In the apse is the Stampa tomb and funeral monument.

* **SONDRIO**. Situated in a beautiful position, where the Mallero flows into the Adda. In the *Collegiata dei Santi Gervasio e Protasio*, designed by Giovanni Pietro Ligari (1686-1752), are paintings by the same artist, an Annunciation by Giovanni Gavazzeni (1841-1907), and two large canvases by Giacomo Pallavicini (c. 1660-1729). The *Museo Valtellinese di Storia e Arte* is housed in the Palazzo Quadrio, and contains collections illustrating the history and art of the Valtelline. Walk to the Sanctuary of the *Madonna della Sassella*, set amongst luxuriant vineyards. Inside is a Nativity by Gaudenzio Ferrari (c. 1470-1546), and frescoes by Andrea De Passeri (recorded 1487-1511).

Soncino, the Fort.

* **SORA** (Frosinone). The most important little town in the valley of the Liri, dominated by the bare Monte San Casto. The *Duomo*, dedicated to St. Mary, dates from the 12th cent., but has been altered twice since. The facade has a 13th cent. Romanesque doorway, while the basilican interior is mainly Gothic. The church of *San Bartolomeo* has a neo-Classical facade, and a painting of the Madonna and Child by Sebastiano Conca (c. 1680-1764).

* **SORAGNA** (Parma). Agricultural town on the left of the Stirone. The *Rocca* is a grandiose, square construction, but has been altered radically since the late 16th cent. There are some interesting rooms inside, such as the Room of Fountains, the Yellow, or Campi Room (on the walls four vast frescoes by Giulio Campi, c. 1500-1572), the billiard-room, the Sala degli Stucchi, the Poets' Gallery, and the Nuns' Gallery. The parish church of *San Giacomo*, or *Santuario della Sacra Famiglia*, was built in 1769. The *Chiesa del Carmine*, or *di San Rocco*, was built in 1754, and its high altar is crowded with statues.

* **SORESINA** (Cremona). Agricultural town about thirty kilometres from Cremona. The parish church of *San Siro* was rebuilt towards the end of the 16th cent. Its separate campanile dates from the 19th cent., and the facade from the first half of the 20th. It contains a Last Supper and a Miracle of St. Bernard by Genovesino (1600/10-1655/57), the Distribution of the Loaves by Francesco Boccaccino (1660-1750), and a Madonna with Saints by Malosso (1555-1619). In the church of *Santa Croce* is

Sondrio, Pinacoteca. Gian Pietro Ligari, Self-portrait.

a painting of an Apostle by Andrea Mainardi (c. 1550-1613), and a Baptism of Christ by Malosso. In the *Chiesa della Madonnina*, or Santa Maria del Cingano, is the Miracle of the Mule, another work by Genovesino.

* **SORIANO NEL CIMINO** (Viterbo). Built on a spur of Monte Cimino. The *Palazzo Chigi*, formerly Albani, is one of the finest works of Jacopo Barozzi, called Vignola (1507-1573). The Paracqua Fountain, called the "queen of the waters", is a bizarre 16th cent. Mannerist invention. The *Castello Orsini* is one of the most refined and best-preserved in the region. In 1278 it was enlarged by Pope Nicholas III. It is dominated by a massive tower and surrounded by battlements. The 18th cent. *Collegiata* has a large brick facade framed by two bell-towers, and its vast neo-Classical interior contains a notable Renaissance font. The *Casina degli Specchi*, built by the Albani family, deserves to be mentioned on account of an 18th cent. room with painted mirrors, and a vestibule containing precious Flemish maiolica.

* **SORRENTO** (Naples). Situated on a terrace of tufa rock, which rises steeply from the sea. The *Duomo* was rebuilt in the 15th cent. The *Basilica di Sant'Antonino* was constructed out of an oratory erected near the Saint's Sepulchre, which already existed in the early 14th cent. The *Museo Correale di Terranova* is housed in the 18th cent. palace of the same name. It is especially interesting for its collection of art and craft objects from the 17th and 18th centuries.

* **SPELLO** (Perugia). An ancient-looking town on the southern slope of Monte Subasio, with interesting Roman remains and notable Renaissance works of art. The church of *Santa Maria Maggiore* was completed in 1285, and is flanked by a sturdy Romanesque campanile. Inside, the Baglioni Chapel, also called the Cappella Bella, is covered with frescoes by Bernardino di Betto, called Pinturicchio (c. 1454-1513). The church has a tabernacle on the high altar by Rocco di Tommaso da Vicenza (recorded 1494-1526), while the Chapel of the Blessed Sacrament has a tabernacle by Gian Domenico da Carrara (recorded 1545-1573). It is advisable to visit the adjoining Museum, which has some notable works of art, including a diptych representing the Crucifixion and the Coronation of the Virgin signed by Cola Petruccioli (active in the second half of the 14th cent.). The interior of the 13th cent. church of *Sant'Andrea* is in the form of a Latin cross, and contains a fresco believed to be the work of Michelangelo Carducci (recorded 1555-1571), as well as a huge panel by Pinturicchio. The *Porta Venere* is an imposing Augustan construction, and takes its name from a temple dedicated to Venus which is supposed to have existed nearby. The church

of *San Lorenzo* was built in the early 12th cent. on the site of the former church of St. Ercolanus, erected in 560. It has a nave and two aisles, and contains a superb Holy Oil tabernacle, while the inlays of the baptismal font are the work of Cruciano Egidiucci (lived in the 16-17th cent.). The *Belvedere* commands fine views of the plain of Topino and the range of hills between Montefalco and Assisi. Walks to the 12th cent. Romanesque church of *San Claudio*, built on the remains of a Roman edifice, to the Roman Amphitheatre (*Anfiteatro Romano*), believed to have been built in the 1st cent., and to the Augustan *Porta Urbica*.

* **SPERLONGA** (Latina). The ancient part of the town is concentrated on a spur of rock that rises sheer above the sea. The *Museo Archeologico Nazionale di Sperlonga* contains material collected from the Grotto of Tiberius. Particularly important are the statues of Menelaus with the body of Patroclus, presumably a work from Rhodes, of Scylla, of a Male Figure fighting with a large serpent, and of Attis about to be carried off by Jove's eagle. The *Grotta di Tiberio* is a deep, awe-inspiring cave, explored for the first time in 1957, with the result that about seven thousand statues, of fragments of statues, have been found and arranged in the Archaeological Museum.

* **SPILIMBERGO** (Pordenone). Agricultural town on the right bank of the Tagliamento. The Gothic *Duomo* has a Romanesque portal on the left side, called the Porta Moresca, the work of Zenone da Campione (lived in the 14th cent.). In the Chapel of the Rosary are works by the sculptor Giovanni Antonio Pilacorte (recorded 1484-1531), and by Porde-

Spello, Santa Maria Maggiore. Pinturicchio, Adoration of the Child, detail.

with vine-branches, as well as a Renaissance doorway with five arches, the work of Ambrogio da Milano (lived in the 15-16th cent.) and Pippo di Antonio Fiorentino (recorded in the late 15th cent.). The campanile was built with the remains of Roman buildings, the belfry being designed by Cola da Caprarola (recorded 1494-1518). The church contains many works of art, including a Bust of Urban VIII by Gian Lorenzo Bernini (1598-1680), a fresco depicting the Pietà by Pinturicchio (c. 1454-1513), the Eroli Chapel or Cappella dell'Assunta, the Chapel of the Blessed Sacrament, and the magnificent frescoes in the apse by Fra Filippo Lippi (c. 1406-1469). In the Chapter Archives are documents, manuscripts, and an autograph letter from St. Francis of Assisi to Fra Leone. The imposing Augustan bridge, *Ponte Romano* or *Sanguinario*, is built out of

none (1484-1539), who is the author of the Fall of Simon Magus and the Conversion of St. Paul. In the central apse are important frescoes by anonymous painters of the 14th and 15th centuries, a fresco of the Assumption by Pordenone, and paintings by Pellegrino da San Daniele (c. 1467-1547). There are some notable miniatures in the Archives. The *Castello*, which was first constructed in the first half of the 8th cent., now appears as a group of Gothic and Renaissance buildings called the Palazzo Dipinto (painted palace), because of the frescoes on its facade, the Palazzo Spilimbergo-Ciriano, which contains paintings by Giovanni da Udine (1487-1564), the Palazzo Troilo, and the Palazzo Tadea. The churches of *San Giovanni Battista*, built in the middle of the 14th cent., and *San Giuseppe* or *San Pantaleone*, which dates from the 14th cent. and contains choirstalls by Marco di Giampietro Cozzi (active in the second half of the 15th cent.), are also interesting. The little doors of the organ were painted by Pordenone.

*** **SPOLETO** (Perugia). Situated on a prominent hill dominated by a fortress, Spoleto is one of the most interesting towns in Italy, and the destination of a great many tourists. Its streets are somewhat severe, but made beautiful by the many palaces and other medieval and Renaissance monuments that line them. The *Duomo*, dedicated to the Assunta, was built in Romanesque style in the late 12th cent. on the site of the earlier cathedral destroyed by Barbarossa in 1155, though its interior was rebuilt in the 17th cent. It is a fine building, and one of the most beautiful in Umbria. The facade, divided horizontally into three zones, has a Romanesque portal with magnificent jambs and an architrave decorated

Spilimbergo, Parish Archives. Illuminated page from Ms. 3, detail.

Spoleto, SS. Giovanni e Paolo. Martyrdom of St. Thomas Becket, detail.

Spoleto, San Pietro, facade.

blocks of travertine. The 11th cent. church of *San Gregorio Magno* has been damaged more than once by fire and floods. It has a 16th cent. portico, and nearby is the 14th cent. Chapel of the Innocents, now the baptistery, with important frescoes. The sturdy campanile was erected in the 11-12th cent. with the remains of Roman buildings. The church contains valuable frescoes of the 12-15th cent., a fine tabernacle, probably by Benedetto da Rovezzano (1474-post 1552), a Renaissance tabernacle for the Holy Oil, and a fresco of the Madonna and Child with Angels and Eve by an anonymous Umbrian master of the 15th cent. Remains of the 2nd cent. Roman Amphitheatre (*Anfiteatro Romano*), converted into a fortress by Totila. Walls (*Mura*), with tower and postern. *Teatro Romano* built in the early years of the Empire. The 13th cent. church of *San Domenico*, formerly San Salvatore, contains an important 15th cent. fresco of the Triumph of St. Thomas Aquinas, the Montevecchio Chapel, with a silver reliquary made in 1726 by Ludovico Barchi containing a nail of the Holy Cross, Christ arrested in the Garden by Cesare Nebbia (c. 1536-c. 1614), and a huge canvas of the Madonna and Child with four Saints by Giovanni Lanfranco (1582-1647). The 12th cent. church of *Santi Giovanni e Paolo* is a sober building, containing votive frescoes of the 12-14th cent., including a Martyrdom of St. Thomas of Canterbury, probably by Alberto Sozio (lived in the 12th cent.), the fragment of a Banquet of Herod, and scenes from the lives of Saints John and Paul, by the same painter. *Arco di Druso, Tempio Romano* and *Cripta Cristiana*, the arch built by the Senate of Spoleto in honour of Drusus the Younger (the son of Tiberius) and Germanicus, the temple dedicated to an unknown divinity, and the crypt dedicated to Saints Isaac and Martial, two Syriac monks who sought refuge from persecution at Spoleto. The crypt has a rectangular plan, and is rich in frescoes, including a Beheading of John the Baptist, a Christ, and a Last Supper, the works of anonymous 11-12th cent. painters. The 13th cent. town hall houses the *Pinacoteca Comunale*, which contains, among other things, works by Bernardino Campilli (lived in the 15-16th cent.), Antonello de Saliba (c. 1466-c. 1535), Niccolò di Liberatore, called Alunno (c. 1430-1502), Giovanni di Pietro, called Spagna (c. 1450-1528), Giacomo di Giovanni (recorded 1515-1522), and Giovanni Francesco Barbieri, called Guercino (1591-1666). *Casa Romana* of the 1st cent., where the atrium, impluvium, the cubicola, triclinium and tablinum are clearly identifiable. The church of *Sant'Eufemia*, possibly of the 12th cent., contains important works of art, including a 13th cent. marble altar-frontal, and a precious triptych by an Umbrian painter of the second half of the 15th cent. The *Museo Civico* is on the first floor of an imposing 14th cent. palace, and is particularly rich in works

of art, some of which illustrate Spoleto's great cultural past. The *Ponte delle Torri* spans the ravine that separates the castle hill from Monteluco, and has ten arches. In its present form it dates from the second half of the 14th cent., and was probably designed by Matteo di Giovannello, called Gattaponi (died after 1376). There are various other buildings worth visiting at Spoleto, such as the church of *San Pietro*, built in the early 5th cent. on the site of a necropolis, and continually altered from the 13th cent. onwards, which contains a relic of St. Peter's chains. Another is the *Basilica di San Salvatore*, or *del Crocifisso*, built in the late 4th and early 5th cent., but altered in many different periods; it contains interesting frescoes. There is also the *Galleria Comunale d'Arte Moderna*, the park (*Giardini Pubblici*), with an enchanting view of the valley of the Tessino, and the Franciscan sanctuary of *Monteluco*.

* **SQUILLACE** (Catanzaro). Built on a granite rock, near the Ionian Sea. The *Duomo*, dedicated to the Trinity, was completely rebuilt in the late 18th cent. after being destroyed by an earthquake. It has a basilican interior, and its paintings were carried out at the beginning of this century by Carmelo Zimatore. In the sacristy is the stylish marble front of a ciborium, with Angels at prayer, a product of the 16th cent. Neapolitan school. In the roof of the Bishop's Palace is an Adoration of the Magi by Francesco Basile (active c. 1700). The *Castello*, erected in the 9th or 10th cent., now almost completely ruined, has an interesting cylindrical tower, and another polygonal one. From the top, one can see the whole bay.

* **STAFFARDA (ABBAZIA DI)** (Town of Revello, province of Cuneo). The *Abbazia di Staffarda* is a group of buildings dating from

Staffarda, Abbey, interior.

the first half of the 12th cent. The Romanesque facade of the Abbey church was altered in the late 15th cent. Inside, there are some 15-16th cent. wooden statues of the German school representing the Crucifixion, Mary and St. John, and a 14th cent. French Gothic wooden pulpit. Little remains of the once vast 13-14th cent. cloister; beyond the garden is the Gothic Chapterhouse. The *Abbazia di Santa Maria* was built in the 11th cent. but completely altered in the 18th. The bell-tower is 15th cent.; the crypt has a nave and two aisles.

* **STIA** (Arezzo). At the foot of Monte Falterona, where the Staggia flows into the Arno. In the oratory of the *Madonna del Ponte* is a glazed della Robbia terracotta dated 1531, representing a Madonna and Child with Saints Roch and Sebastian. The *Parrocchiale* has a Romanesque interior, and contains a panel of the Madonna and Child with two Angels by the "Maestro di Varlungo" (13-14th cent.), a panel of a polyptych of the Florentine school, dated 1408 representing the Assumption, and a wonderful Madonna and Child by Andrea della Robbia (1435-1525). Walk to the Renaissance church of *Santa Maria delle Grazie*, once a farmhouse belonging to the Hospital

of Santa Maria Nuova in Florence.

* **STILO** (Reggio Calabria). Commanding a fine view, with medieval streets and houses, not far from the Ionian Sea. The most important monument is the famous *Cattolica*, a small Byzantine temple, similar to those frequently found in Georgia, Armenia, and Anatolia. Of very ancient origin, it is a square structure with five small domes, four in the corners, and one in the centre. The columns of the interior have inverted capitals and were

Stia, Parish Church, a capital.

taken from antique constructions. Interesting traces of Byzantine frescoes can be seen. In the church of *San Francesco* is the Madonna del Borgo, an important panel of the 16th cent. Sicilian school.

* **STRA** (Venice). Agricultural and industrial town, where the Brenta divides into two branches. The *Villa Pisani*, the most imposing of the villas on the Brenta, was built for the Venetian family of the Pisani to a design by Girolamo Frigimelica (1653-1732), and completely remodelled by Francesco Maria Preti (1701-1774). The facade consists of a central structure with caryatids supporting the loggia, above which rise Corinthian half-columns, upon which rest the cornice and pediment. The latter are decorated with statues, while two wings have Ionic pillars. Passing through the solemn, harmonious entrance-hall one reaches the "piano nobile". The numerous rooms contain frescoes and paintings by Francesco Zuccarelli (1702-1788), Bartolomeo Nazzari (1699-1758), and Alessandro Longhi (1733-1813), as well as valuable period furniture, precious objects, and historical relics. The ballroom is large and well-lighted; on the ceiling is a Glory of the Pisani House, and a fresco of Venice escorting the Pisani family to its Apotheosis, one of Giovan Battista Tiepolo's masterpieces, carried out in 1761-62. In the park is a maze, 19th cent. buildings, and a little palace for the stables. The *Villa Lazara Pisani* is a large, 18th cent. construction, called La Barbariga, since it was the residence of the Venetian Barbarigo family. It contains precious stuccoes and 18th cent. furnishings. The Clock-Tower dates from the early 18th cent.

* **STRESA** (Novara). Delightful walk around the town, which is situated on the Borromeo Gulf of Lake Maggiore. The 19th cent. *Villa Pallavicini* has a vast park with age-old trees and a lovely garden of rhododendrons. Ex-

Stilo, the Cattolica.

cursion to the *Isola Bella*, whose beauty is enhanced by the natural environment. Here is the imposing Palazzo Borromeo, where one should visit the Ball-room, the Sala dell'Alcova, the Throne-room, and the Sala della Quadreria, which is a rich art gallery, with works mainly by Lombard painters of the 16-17th cent. It also contains paintings by Anthony Van Dyck (1599-1641), Antonio Tempesta (1555-1630), Giovanni Battista Tiepolo (1696-1770), and Francesco Zuccarelli (1702-1788). In the chapel are statues by Amadeo and Bambaia. Another interesting excursion is to the *Isola dei Pescatori*.

** **STUPINIGI** (neighbourhood of Turin). This is the site of the *Palazzina di Caccia*, an

imposing Baroque architectural complex, designed by Filippo Juvarra (1676-1736) for Victor Amadeus II. Well-known architects such as Giuseppe Ignazio Bertola (c. 1647-1719) and Ludovico Bo (active 1764-1774) collaborated in the completion of the building. It is one of the best examples of Piedmontese Rococò. The decoratios and furniture are typical of an 18th cent. royal residence. Inside, the *Museo d'Arte e d'Ammobiliamento* includes the Portrait Gallery, the Library, the New Apartment, the main Salon, and the King's Apartment. These rooms contain notable works of art, such as paintings, busts, and furnishings.

** **SUBIACO** (Rome). Charming little medieval town among wooded mountains in the

Stupinigi, Palazzina di Caccia.
Stupinigi, Palazzina di Caccia, central hall.

upper valley of the river Aniene. The church of *San Francesco*, erected in 1327, has a single nave of Franciscan austerity, and contains a triptych of the Madonna and Child with Saints Francis and Anthony of Padua by Antoniazzo Romano (c. 1435-1517), and frescoes of figures dressed in the costumes of Subiaco, probably by Giovanni Antonio Bazzi, called Sodoma (1477-1549). The church of *Sant'Andrea*, the work of Pietro Camporese the Elder (1726-1781), has a large facade, flanked by two small campaniles. It contains the Dream of St. Joseph by Pietro Cavallini (recorded 1291-1321), the Miraculous Draught of Fishes by Sebastiano Conca (c. 1680-1764), and a Madonna and Child by Carlo Dolci (1616-1686). The church of *Santa Maria della Valle* is a neo-Classical construction, and has a sober, two storeyed facade. It contains a polychrome-wood statue of the Madonna of Perpetual Succour in a Byzantine style, and a painting of the Resurrection of the son of the widow of Naim by Vincenzo Manenti (1600-1674). The *Rocca Abbaziale* (Abbey fortress) was erected in the 11th cent. by a certain Abbot Giovanni to protect the monks and intimidate the inhabitants of Subiaco, who had grown tired of their abuses. In the apartment of the Colonnas is a fresco by Federico and Taddeo Zuccari (lived in the 16th cent.). In the apartment of Pius VI are frescoes of the towns and churches that belonged to the Abbey of Subiaco, as well as the Room of Pius VI, with the Pope's own writing-desk. Walk to the *Monastero di Santa Scolastica*, a large group of buildings gathered round three cloisters and a church. The first 16th cent. cloister was badly damaged by bombing in the Second World War, and later partially reconstructed. The second cloister, whose construction was begun in 1052, has a large 16th cent. Gothic arch and leads to the Monastery Library, which contains thirty-five thousand volumes, some of great value, and fifteen thousand documents. The third cloister was built by the Cosmati masters from the end of the 12th cent. onwards. The church, consecrated by Pope Benedict VII in 980, was remodelled in the Cistercian-Gothic style in the second half of the 13th cent., and altered again in the 18th. The Romanesque campanile, with its five storeys of mullioned apertures, was erected in 1052-53. In the sacristy is a Madonna and Child with St. Anselm, probably by Carlo Maratta (1625-1713). The *Sacro Speco*, or *Monastero di San Benedetto*, grew up in the early 13th cent. around the cave in which St. Benedict passed the first three years of his monastic life. It is a characteristic group of buildings, consisting of two modest churches built one on top of the other, and a series of chapels and grottoes connected by stairs. The so-called Upper Church, a mystical mid-14th cent. edifice, has numerous frescoes of the 14th cent. Sienese school, including St. Benedict's Last Conversation with St. Scho-

lastica, the Saviour, St. Benedict watching St. Scholastica being transformed into a dove with two Angels, by Ottaviano di Martino Nelli (c. 1370-1450), a St. Agnes by the same painter, and a beautiful 13th cent. altar-frontal. In the Lower Church is the Cappelletta called after S. Romano, the Sacro Speco, and the Chapel of St. Gregory the Great, also called the Cappella degli Angeli, with Byzantine-like frescoes from the early 13th cent., including one of St. Francis, carried out when the saint visited Subiaco in 1223. Frescoes by the same artists who worked in the Upper Church decorate the passages that lead to the surrounding chapels.

* **SULMONA** (L'Aquila). At the confluence of the Vella with the Gizio in the fertile hollow of the Peligna valley, washed by the waters of five rivers (the Gizio, the Vella, the Sa-

Sulmona, Duomo. Bas-relief in the crypt.

gittario, the Aterno and the Pescara) and surrounded by high mountains on all sides. The *Cattedrale*, built on a temple dedicated to Apollo and Vesta, is a very ancient edifice. It was almost completely destroyed by fire in 1228, and rebuilt ten years later. The facade has a doorway with a pointed arch, and two columns supported by lions. In the lunette is a faded fresco of the Deposition, perhaps by Leonardo da Teramo (lived in the first half of the 15th cent.). The church has a basilican interior and an interesting crypt, with notable works of art, including a wooden statue of St. Teresa by Giacomo Colombo (lived in the 16th cent.). There are other important works and objects in the Treasury. The *Annunziata*, built in 1320 by the Confraternita della Penitenza, is the most important monument in the town; the right side of the Palace of the Annunziata constitutes the left side of the church of the same name. It combines Romanesque, Gothic, Renaissance, and Baroque characteristics with surprising results. One should visit the Civic Museum and the Treasury, in which, among other things, is a local 14th cent. processional cross, a box-shaped reliquary of the first half of the 15th cent., and an enamelled jewel of the 16th. The church of *San Francesco della Scarpa*, perhaps built in 1290 by Charles II of Anjou, is dedicated to St. Mary Magdalen. It contains a large Baroque organ carved by Domenico Antonio Fedeli in 1754, and a painting of St. Anthony of Padua, carried out in 1766 by Eugenio Porretta. The church of *Santa Maria della Tomba* or *di Loreto* was built on the spot where a temple dedicated to Jupiter once stood, and is mentioned as early as the first half of the 13th cent. It contains works of art, including a terracotta of the Madonna and the Child Jesus standing on her knees, in the manner of Giovanni Francesco Gagliardelli (recorded 1524-26). In ancient times, Sulmona had twelve gateways, the most imposing of which, the *Porta Napoli*, has survived intact; it was probably erected in the 14th cent., and has an unusual shape. Walks to the *Badia Morronese* or *di Santo Spirito* and to *Sant'Onofrio*, which was the hermitage of Pietro Angeleri, later Pope Celestine V.

* **SUPERGA** (Turin). A few kilometres from Turin, on the northern side of the Torinese hills. The *Basilica di Superga*, dedicated to the Nativity of Mary, is an imposing circular building built in 1717-1731 to a design by Filippo Juvarra (1676-1736), and is one of the most important 18th cent. monuments in Piedmont. The facade has a deep, Corinthian, tetrastyle pronaos. The interior is vast and spectacular, with many works of art, including a St. Maurice by Sebastiano Ricci (1659-1734), a marble high-relief of the Nativity of Mary by Agostino Cornacchini (1685-post 1740), and a Blessed Margaret of Savoy and St. Charles by Claude Francis Beaumont (1694-1766). Behind the ba-

silica is a large building erected for the Congregation of secular Priests to a design by Filippo Juvarra. It contains important works of art, such as the marble statue of St. Michael driving Lucifer from Heaven by Carlo Finelli (1785-1853), and statues of Faith, Charity, Peace and Genius, and the Arts by Ignazio Collino (1724-1793) and Filippo Collino (1737-1800). There is also a bas-relief representing the Pietà by Agostino Cornacchini (1685-post 1740).

* **SUSA** (Turin). In a strategic position on the banks of the Doria Riparia, and surrounded by high mountains. The *Cattedrale*, dedicated to St. Justus, was built in the 11th cent., and has undergone many alterations. It has a high facade with a simple doorway, flanked on the right by an 11th cent. Romanesque campanile, considered one of the finest in Piedmont. The interior is asymmetrical, and houses the Chapel of Relics. The baptistery probably dates from the 9th or 10th cent. *Porta Savoia*, one of the gateways in the old town walls, was built to protect the town from barbarian invaders. One passes through Porta Savoia before entering the *Parco di Augusto*, the most attractive part of Susa.

** **SUTRI** (Viterbo). Situated on a narrow ridge of tufa, at the confluence of the Promonte and the Rotari. The *Duomo*, dedicated to the Assunta, is in the Romanesque style, but was greatly altered in the 18-19th cent. It is flanked by a fine campanile (1207). The deep, predominantly 18th cent. interior has a beautiful Byzantine-like panel of Christ Blessing, which dates from the first half of the 13th cent., and the Renaissance altar of St. Pius V, who was Bishop of Sutri for six years. The *Anfiteatro*, an amphitheatre completely hewn out of the tufa rock, is one of the characteristic monuments of the region. It is not

Susa, Cathedral bell-tower.

known when it was built, but the majority believe it to be an Etruscan work, used for cultural purposes. The *Sacello della Madonna del Parto* is a subterranean Etruscan tomb, originally Mithran, but later converted to Christian worship. There are frescoes of various periods in the vestibule, nave and aisles. A few kilometres away is *Bassano Romano*, a medieval-looking village, where we find the *Palazzo Anguillara*, an ancient manor converted in the 16th cent. into the residential villa of the Giustiniani family, a massive square structure. It is well worth seeing the Salone dei Cesari, with busts of twelve Caesars, the dining-room completely covered with paintings of mythological scenes by Francesco Albani (1578-1660), and a small room with frescoes depicting the legends of Diana by Domenico Zampieri, called Domenichino (1581-1641).

*** **SYRACUSE,** see Siracusa.

* **TAGGIA** (Imperia). Surrounded by wooded hills. The parish church of *Santi Giacomo e Filippo* is a late 17th cent. reconstruction. It contains a statue of the Madonna of the Sacred Heart, popularly known as the Madonna di Taggia, the work of Salvatore Revelli (1816-1859). The church of *San Domenico* was built in 1460 by masters from Como. It contains a polyptych of the Annunciation, a Madonna of the Rosary by Lodovico Brea (c. 1450-1523), a Baroque altar with marble statues and, in the sacristy, a Pietà by Lodovico Brea. One should visit the church's 15th cent. cloister. Walk to the Sanctuary of *Lampedusa*, with its sober facade flanked by two small picturesque campaniles.

* **TAGLIACOZZO** (L'Aquila). Small town situated on a steep slope, with interesting medieval monuments. In the church of *San Francesco*, built in the 14th cent., is a valuable 16th cent. polychrome wood crucifix, and the urn of Blessed Thomas of Celano. The *Palazzo Ducale*, built by the Orsini family in the 14th cent. and completed in the 15th, is a massive, solemn building, with an important Renaissance portal. It contains excellent frescoes and other works of art.

*** **TAORMINA** (Messina). Situated on Monte Tauro, over-hanging the sea, and surrounded by a wealth of vegetation, with archaeological and other remains. The *Greek Theatre*, built perhaps in the 3rd cent. B.C. and enlarged in the 2nd, has a diameter of 109 m. The auditorium is hewn out of the rock and once had nine tiers. Much of the stage has survived, and the acoustics are still good. The theatre commands one of the most extraordinary views in the whole Mediterranean, especially at dawn and sunset. The Roman *Odeon* or *Teatrino*, built during the Empire, was partially revealed in 1893. The Roman *Naumachia*, after its restoration in 1943, may now be seen in all its original grandeur, its front measuring 122 m. The *Edificio Termale*, is another Roman monument that dates from the Empire. In the *Antiquarium* are the collected remains of the buildings of Taormina, including a Hellenistic torso of Apollo, administrative tablets of the civic magistrature, and votive epigraphs. The *Palazzo Corvaia*, erected at the beginning of the 15th cent., was the seat of the Sicilian Parliament in 1410. Its battlemented facade has mullioned windows with round arches, and

Taormina, the Duomo, square and fountain.

inside is the Parliament Hall. The *Palazzo Ciampoli* is in the Catalan-Gothic style, and dates from the beginning of the 15th cent. The *Palazzo dei Duchi di Santo Stefano*, an aristocratic structure in the Sicilian style, was built between the 14-15th cent. The 13th cent. *Duomo*, dedicated to St. Nicholas, has a Renaissance doorway (1636), and contains a panel of the Visitation and Saints Joseph and Zacharias by Antonino Giuffrè (recorded in 1493), a polyptych by Antonello De Saliba (c. 1466-1535), and a statue of St. Agatha by Martino Montanini (recorded 1557-1562). The *Badia Vecchia* or *Badiazza* is a stylish 14th cent. building. Excursion to *Cape Schisò*, once the site of Naxos, the first Greek colony in Sicily (735 B.C.). Recent excavations have succeeded in identifying the town's walls, built in the 6th cent. B.C. It commands a superb view of Etna, Taormina, and Capo Sant'Alessio.

** **TARANTO.** Situated on the Ionic coast, at the innermost point of the vast Gulf of Taranto. It consists of a modern part (Città Moderna) on the mainland, and an older one (Città Vecchia) on a little island, between the so-called Mar Grande and the Mar Piccolo. It was one of the most flourishing cities of Magna Graecia, and reached the zenith of its political and commercial power in the first half of the 4th cent. B.C. Visiting the *Museo Nazionale* is like opening a window on the art and civilisation of Magna Graecia. The main part of its collection is made up of the archaeological remains found in Taranto: the first, second, and third rooms on the first floor are dedicated to sculpture, in marble and local stone, and mosaics; the fourth room contains statues in sandstone, antefixes and other pictorial and architectural elements found in the Tarantine burial places, or in the "naiskoi" (niches) above the burial chambers; the fifth room contains the grave goods and vases found in the Tarantine necropolis, aryballi, and amphoras decorated with animal patterns; the sixth room also contains grave goods; the seventh is reserved mainly for black-figured Attic ware, the eighth, Attic ceramic ware; the ninth, objects from the Tarantine necropolis; the tenth many ceramic objects of the kind produced at Egnazia; the eleventh, called the room of gold, contains gold and silver jewellery from Taranto and other towns in Apulia, dating from the 6th cent. B.C. onwards. On the same floor are various corridors; the twelfth has numerous terracottas figured with scenes both sacred and profane; the thirteenth continues the exhibition of sacred terracottas; the fourteenth has more terracottas of the same kind, while the fifteenth is reserved for Hellenistic figured terracottas, nearly all taken from tombs, with a greater number of female figures, such as Aphrodite, Nike, and the Muses. On the second floor is the pre-historic section, with a collection of objects from the whole of Apulia, as well as from some neighbouring regions. The most important collections are the following: Terranera di Venosa, which has some of the first known artifacts of the palaeolithic age; Gargano, rich in artifacts that are partly unclassifiable from the chronological point of view; Taranto, which has many objects from the Bronze Age, long-handled pails with bands, and Mycenaean vases; Torre Castelluccia, rich in material from the transitional period between the Bronze and Iron Ages, and from the early Iron Age, including bronzes, and amber and glass-paste necklaces found in houses and in the cinerary tombs; Leporano, rich in material, nearly all vases from the Bronze to the early Iron Age; Monte Timari, with many cinerary urns, fibulae, brooches, rings, rasors, etc. The museum also has a topographical section, the Apulian part of which is arranged to illustrate the ancient topographical sub-divisions of the region: Messapia, with local vases, called "trozzelle", Corinthian or Attic vases from Greece, and red-figured Apulian vases; Peucezia, where many important archaeological sites of the province are represented; Daunia, with long-handled, plates and basins, local vases, and votive offerings; Lucania, with many red-figured Apulian vases; and Calabria, represented by the Candida di Locri Epizefiri Collection, with finely made "pinakes" (terracotta plaques). The *Duomo*, dedicated to S. Cataldo, was built in the second half of the 11th cent. on the ruins of an earlier church, and has been much altered since. It has a Baroque facade, carried out in 1713. Inside, is a baptismal font surmounted by a baldacchino dating from 1571, and the tomb of Archbishop Tommaso Caracciolo (1663). The Chapel of S. Cataldo, also called the Cappellone, was rebuilt in 1657, with frescoes by Paolo De Matteis (1662-1728), statues by Giuseppe Pagano (lived in the 18-19th cent.), and a silver statue of S. Cataldo by Vincenzo Catello (lived in the 19th cent.). The 11th cent. church of *San Domenico Maggiore* was rebuilt in the early 14th cent. Its facade rises above a steep, Baroque, double flight of steps, and is characterized by a large doorway surmounted by a pointed arch and baldacchino and by a rose-window encompassed by an archivolt supported by two hanging columns. The interior is in the form of a Latin cross; on the left is a lavish Baroque altar, while the wooden ceiling was painted in 1717 by Carlo Martinelli. The *Palazzo degli Uffizi*, one of the city's most massive buildings, was designed in 1896 by Giovanni Galeone and houses an important geophysical meteorological observatory. The *Istituto Sperimentale Talassografico* in Via Roma is also important and has an interesting collection of marine fauna, with a well-stocked library on the subject. The *Villa Peripato* has a magnificent, large garden from where one can see the Mar Piccolo, divided into two bays by the peninsula of Punta Penna.

*** TARQUINIA (Viterbo). On a hill overlooking the Tyrrhenian, on the left side of the river Marta. The Gothic-Renaissance *Palazzo Vitelleschi* was built in 1436-1439 by Cardinal Giovanni Vitelleschi. The facade, the upper part of which is rusticated, represents a particularly successful fusion of the Gothic and Renaissance styles. It is now the *Museo Nazionale Tarquinese*. This museum is the richest, or contains one of the richest collections of Etruscan antiquity, of which only the most important items can be mentioned here: on the ground floor, sarcophagi of the Alvethna family in tufa from the 4th to the 1st cent. B.C. and the Laris Palenas or Magistrate's sarcophagus, with a figure of the defunct on the lid, holding a scroll with a long Etruscan inscription. Sarcophagus of the so-called Magnate, with scenes of hunting and crouching sphinxes, and the sarcophagus of the so-called Obesus, with a splendid male figure on the lid; on the first floor, in a glass case, the rhyton of Karinos, a precious example of 6th cent. B.C. Greek ceramic ware, and the famous terracotta high-relief of the Winged Horses, regarded as one of the masterpieces of Etruscan sculpture, which already reflects Greek influence. On the second floor, besides fragments of sculpture and architectural elements up to the 16th cent., are the following works of art: a panel of St. Anthony with Saints Sebastian and Roch by Costantino di Jacopo Zelli (lived in the 16th cent.), Portrait of Count Nicola Soderini by Pompeo Batoni (1708-1787), Portrait of Pius VII by Vincenzo Camuccini (1771-1844), and a wooden ceiling with a cycle of precious frescoes by an unknown artist of the 16th cent. In the Salone d'Armi is the Tomb of Triclinium, probably dating from the first half of the 5th cent. B.C., and the most beautiful of all Tarquinia's tombs for its colours and designs, together with the Tomb of the Olympics, with scenes of discus-throwing, running, and charioteering, which dates from the second half of the 6th cent. B.C. The *Duomo*, dedicated to St. Margaret, was rebuilt towards the second half of the 17th cent. The facade is modern however, the work of Piero Magnani, and dated 1933. It contains frescoes depicting the Marriage of Mary, the Birth of Mary, the Coronation of the Virgin, and Saints and Sybil, carried out by Antonio da Viterbo, called Pastura (recorded 1478-1509). The 12th cent. Romanesque church of *Santa Maria di Castello* has a rectangular facade surmounted by a small bell gable. It has a vast basilican interior, and contains a Cosmatesque pulpit by Giovanni di Guittone (lived in the 12-13th cent.), and a baptismal font with eight sides, made out of marble taken from an ancient tomb. The 13th cent. church of *San Giovanni Battista* or *San Giovanin Gerosolomitano*, formerly of the Knights of Malta, has a facade with three doorways; it contains a 15th cent. fresco of the Deposition, and a Renaissance tabernacle

for the Holy Oil. In the church of *Santa Lucia* is a Deposition and a St. Benedict handing the Rules to St. Scholastica by Pietro Gagliardi (1809-1890). The *Palazzo Comunale* is an imposing Romanesque construction, with a large external staircase. Inside is a fine anonymous fresco dated 1429, depicting legendary and true episodes in the history of Tarquinia and Corneto. The church of *San Pancrazio* is a successful example of 13th cent. Romanesque-Gothic. On its right side is a low campanile, with two storeys of Romanesque mullioned windows and a cusp. The 13th cent. Romanesque-Gothic church of *San Francesco* nestles beneath a 16th cent. bell-tower, while its bare, mystical interior is decorated with some fair Baroque stucco work. The church of the *Annunziata*, built between the end of the 12th and beginning of the 13th cent., has a small Romanesque facade, the doorway of which bears some traces of the Norman-Sicilian style. The remains of the *Palazzo dei Priori*, together with the small ancient houses around it, form a typical medieval centre. The *Necropolis*, also called Monterozzi because of its underground stone tumuli, is 1½ km. long and ranges in time from about the 7th cent. B.C. to the Roman period. Discovered by chance in the 15th cent., it was not really explored and studied until the last years of the 18th. These tombs are of exceptional importance because of their numerous Etruscan paintings: in the Tomb of the Chase and Fishing (6th cent.) are floral decorations, dancers and musicians among trees, two horsemen preceded by a servant urging on two dogs, a hare in flight, hunters with slings, boats with fishermen, bathers, etc.; in the Tomb of the Jugglers (6-5th cent.), panther and lion, young girl with a candlestick on her head, to whom a young boy is throwing a ring, an old man leaning on a stick; in the Tomb of the Hunter (4th cent.), horsemen, bulls, lions, stags, and dogs; in the Tomb of the Warrior (4th cent.), a warrior with a blue cloak; in the Cardarelli Tomb (6th cent.), a lion killing a gazzelle, a dancer, and a citharist; in the Bartoccini Tomb (6th cent.), banqueting scene, and green-blue sea-horses; in the Tomb of the Charons (3rd cent.), booted figures gripping swords and hammers; in the Tomb of the Saplings (4th cent.), a gorgoneion with its tongue cut out; in the Tomb of the Lioness (6th cent.), feline figures with swollen breasts; in the Tomb of the Baron, or the Horses (6th cent.), young horsemen, and groups of people conversing; in the Tomb of the Young Girl (5th cent.), a tender figure of a young girl; in the Tomb of the Festoons (2nd cent.), shields decorated with festoons of leaves and ribbons; in the Tomb of the Leopards (5th cent.), leopards and panthers; in the Tomb of Typhon (2nd cent.), which belonged to a certain Pumpu family, are three large steps hewn in the rock, on which sarcophagi and friezes decorated

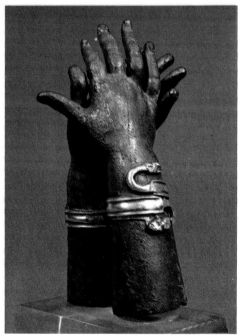

Tagliacozzo, Ducal Palace. Nativity.
Taranto, Museo Nazionale. Bronze forearms of a woman, 3-2nd cent. B.C.

Taranto, Museo Nazionale. Gold ear-ring, 3rd cent. B.C.

Tarquinia, Tomb of the Triclinium. A flute-player.
Tarquinia, Tomb of the Triclinium. Dancers.

with Greek frets, rosettes, and dolphins were once placed. Other tombs include the Tomb of the Death-bed (5th cent.), the Tomb of the Bacchantes (6th cent.), the Tomb of the Boar-hunt, or Guerciola Tomb (5th cent.), the Tomba della Marcareccia (3rd cent.), the Tomb of the Dead Man (6th cent.), the Tomb of the Shields, or Four Rooms (end of 4th or beginning of 3rd cent.), the Tomb of the Cardinal (2nd cent.), the Tomb of the Augurs (6th cent.), the Tomb of Pulcinella (6th cent.), the Tomb of the Bulls (6th cent.), the Tomb of the Red Lions (6th cent.), the Tomb of the Sea, or Two Rooms (6th cent.), the Tomb of the Dying Man (6th cent.), the Tomb of the Old Man (6th cent.), the Tomb of Polyphemus, or the Ogre (4-3rd cent.), the Tomb of the Painted Vases (6th cent.), and the tumuli della Doganaccia (7th cent.). Visit to the ruins of *Tarquinia Antica*, excavated and explored mainly in the period 1934-1938.

* **TAVARNELLE VAL DI PESA** (Florence). Very ancient town on the road between the old Florentia and Rome. Inside the 16th cent. Franciscan parish church (*Parrocchiale*) is a 14th cent. Crucifixion painted on canvas and fixed to a wood panel, the interesting remains of an early 15th cent. fresco and an Annunciation carried out in 1471 by Neri di Bicci. Walks to the Romanesque church of *San Pietro in Bossolo*, and to Morrocco, to the 15th cent. *Pieve di Santa Maria*, which contains three panels by Neri di Bicci (1419-1491).

* **TAVERNA** (Catanzaro). Pleasant, isolated little town. The church of *San Domenico*, rebuilt in the Baroque style in the second half of the 17th cent., contains a vast cycle of works by Mattia Preti (1613-1699) and an early 17th cent. marble Pietà by Giovanni Battista Ortega. In the church of *San Nicola* is a superb painting of the Madonna of Purity by Mattia Preti. The parish church of *Santa Barbara* was rebuilt in 1930, and contains numerous paintings by Preti, as well as an Immaculate Conception by the Neapolitan painter Girolamo Imparato (recorded 1573-1621).

* **TEANO** (Caserta). At the foot of the volcano of Roccamonfina, in the middle of luxuriant countryside. The 12th cent. *Duomo*, dedicated to St. Clement, was re-designed in 1630 by Andrea Vaccaro. It has a sober portico, an arcade on the right, and a large campanile, in the lower part of which are antique marble sections. The church has a basilican interior, and contains a 13th cent. pulpit with spiral columns, a painting of the Flight into Egypt and St. Martin by Francesco De Mura (1696-1784), a Crucifixion painted on wood by Roberto Oderisi (active in the second half of the 14th cent.) and a carved Roman sarcophagus. Important remains of the *Roman Theatre* have survived in a place called Le Grotte.

Nearby are parts of walls in opus reticulatum, while in the locality called Loreto are traces of a pre-Roman sanctuary and four Hellenistic temples. In the 18th cent. Baroque church of *Santa Caterina* are white and rose-coloured stuccoes.

* **TEGGIANO** (Salerno). Situated on a solitary hill, on the western extremity of the Vallo di Diano. The *Cattedrale*, dedicated to Santa Maria Maggiore, dates from the second half of the 13th cent. The portal is a vigorous piece of sculpture by Melchiorre di Montalbano (active in the second half of the 13th cent.), and on the right is another notable Renaissance doorway. Inside there are some good works of art, such as the pulpit with the symbols of the Evangelists carried out by Melchiorre di Montalbano in 1271, tombs from the 14th and 15th centuries, and wooden statues of Angels from the 16th. In the church of *Sant'Andrea*, which dates from the Angevin period, is a Madonna and Child with Saints and two 14th cent. triptyches. In the church of the *Annunziata*, of the same period, is a 15th cent. panel of the Annunciation and, on the high altar, a polyptych of the second half of the 16th cent. depicting the Annunciation, the Martyrdom of St. Catherine of Alexandria and Saints. The church of *Sant'Angelo* was erected on the ruins of an ancient theatre; it contains 11th cent. marble reliefs of the symbols of the Evangelists. The former Angevin church of *San Pietro*, which may have been built on the ruins of a temple dedicated to Euscalapius, now houses the civic museum, and contains Roman ornaments and marble works, medieval and Renaissance coats-of-arms and tombs and 18th cent. wood carvings. The Gothic *Chiesa della Pietà* has a portal dated 1475 and a 15th cent. cloister, embellished with interesting remains of decorations.

* **TEGLIO** (Sondrio). Situated on a mountainridge, beneath the slopes of Monte Combolo. In the parish church of *Sant'Eufemia*, rebuilt at the end of the 15th cent., are ancient frescoes and a processional cross by Giovanni Pietro

Teglio, Palazzo Besta, courtyard.

Lierni (active in the first half of the 16th cent.). On the facade of the *Oratorio della Confraternita dei Bianchi* is depicted the Dance of Death and some other damaged 16th cent. frescoes. The *Palazzo Besta* was remodelled in the Renaissance style at the beginning of the 16th cent. It has a harmonious facade, interesting frescoes and paintings, and rare furnishings. It is a good example of a 16th cent. gentleman's residence in the Valtelline.

* **TEOLO** (Padua). A resort situated in a fertile hollow scattered with villas and the starting-point for walks in the Euganean hills. The church of *Santa Giustina* was first built at the beginning of the 13th cent. It contains frescoes by Giacomo Manzoni (1840-1912) and a painting of the Assumption and the Baptism of St. Justina by Domenico Campagnola (lived in the 16th cent.). Excursion to the sanctuary of the *Madonna del Monte*.

** **TERAMO**. Situated at the confluence of the Tordino and the Vezzola. Much of the town is modern, but there are many traces of the Middle Ages in its buildings and churches. The *Cattedrale*, destroyed and rebuilt more than once, was well repaired in 1935. Much of the facade, which is asymmetrical in relation to the dome, goes back to the 12th cent., and is graced with a harmonious main doorway, the work of Diodato Romano (1294-1332). In the vast, austere interior are some notable works of art, the most important being a famous silver altar-frontal, considered the masterpiece of Nicola da Guardiagrele, jeweller and sculptor (c. 1395-c. 1426). The church of *San Francesco* or *Sant'Antonio*, built at the beginning of the 13th cent., enlarged in the 14th, and rebuilt in the 16th, has a superb Romanesque portal. The church of the *Madonna delle Grazie* was built in the 12th cent. but completely reconstructed in 1900. It contains a wooden group of the Madonna and Child, probably by Silvestro dell'Aquila (recorded 1476-1505), and frescoes by Cesare Mariani (1826-1901). In the 14th cent. church of *Sant'Agostino* is a superb polyptych by the Venetian painter, Iacobello del Fiore (died in 1439), and a fresco of the Madonna and Child by the Austrian painter, Pietro Alemanno (active in the second half of the 15th cent.). One should also visit the ruins of the *Roman Theatre*, and the *Art Gallery* in the museum (*Museo Civico*), which contains pre-Roman objects, marble capitals, Roman terracotta decorations, and some notable paintings. Walk to the *Osservatorio Astronomico Vincenzo Cerulli di Collurania*, founded in 1890 by the eminent astronomer, Vincenzo Cerulli.

* **TERLANO** (Bolzano). Wine centre and holiday resort. The facade of the Gothic parish church of *Santa Maria Assunta* still has a 14th cent. sculptural group and a 15th cent. fresco; it is flanked by a mullioned Gothic bell-tower. Inside, the church has a Giottesque cycle of frescoes (1400), and a beautiful baptismal font.

** **TERMINI IMERESE** (Palermo). On the slopes of a promontory, dominated by Monte San Calogero; a health and bathing resort. The *Duomo*, dedicated to St. Nicholas of Bari, was rebuilt in the 17th cent. It contains a statue of the Madonna della Mazza, or of Succour, by Giorgio da Milano (active 1487-1496), a marble oval of the Madonna del Ponte by Ignazio Marabitti (1719-1797), marble high-reliefs again by Marabitti and Federico Siragusa (lived in the 18-19th cent.), and a superb Gothic-style cross painted on both sides by Pietro Ruzzolone (recorded 1484-1526). The *Museo Civico* has sections on prehistory, archaeology, epigraphy, numismatics, geology, mineralogy, natural history and the fine arts. The last-mentioned contains, among other things, the Holy Mass by Vito d'Anna (c. 1720-1769), a Deposition by Giacomo Graffeo (active 1476-1516), a St. Sebastian, probably by Guido Reni (1575-1642), and Flemish tapestries. The church of the *Madonna della Consolazione* has an ancient apse, which was once the facade, while the front is preceded by a Baroque staircase; its stucco work is by Serpotta. Also worth visiting are the ruins of the *Roman Amphitheatre*, the *Principe Umberto Belvedere*, on the site of a Roman forum, and *Piazza Bagni*, where the termal waters gush out. Visit to the *Ruins of Imera*, the most western of the Greek colonies, on the northern coast of Sicily. The most notable ruin is the Doric Temple, a peripteros-hexastylos of the 5th cent. B.C. It was discovered in 1823, and revealed in its present form in 1929-1935.

* **TERMOLI** (Campobasso). The most important town on the Adriatic coast between Vasto and the Gargano, and the only port in Molise. The *Cattedrale di San Basso* is considered the most outstanding building in the region of Molise, and was probably built in the 6th cent. on the ruins of a Roman temple. It has been rebuilt since, after being sacked and destroyed by fire. The facade is built entirely of stone, and bears clear Apulian Romanesque traces of Norman inspiration. The interior has been completely altered; it contains a beautiful chancel and a modern crypt, where one can see part of the church as it was in the 6-7th cent.

** **TERNI**. At the confluence of the Serra and the river Nera and surrounded by green hills. It is important both for its works of art and its industries. The circular church of *San Salvatore* was probably built on the site of an earlier pagan temple dedicated to the sun and contains important frescoes. The originally Romanesque *Duomo* was rebuilt in 1653 and the facade is decorated with statues by Corrado

Vigni (born in 1888). The interior is in the form of a Latin cross, and has a nave and two aisles; it contains an anonymous 17th cent. painting of Christ in the Garden, and a picture of the Immaculate Conception, probably of the Flemish school. Notable also are the carved walnut choir-stalls, carried out in 1559 by Domenico Corsi. Buried in the crypt is St. Anastasius, a former bishop of Terni. The church of *Sant'Alò* may have been built in the 11th cent., but was badly damaged by bombing in the Second World War. It was restored in its original Romanesque form in 1955. The walls are decorated with frescoes by artists of the 13-16th cent. The *Roman Amphitheatre* was built in 32 A.D. by Faustus Titius Liberalis and many ruins have survived. The church of *San Pietro*, built in the 14th cent., has a facade with a doorway surmounted by a pointed arch and, in the tympanum, is a valuable 15th cent. relief of Christ Blessing. It contains a few works of art, nearly all anonymous. The huge 14th cent. cloister, partially rebuilt in the 16th cent., is both typical and harmonious. In the *Musei Civici*, which include an art gallery and an archaeological museum, are some interesting works, such as the panel in tempera of the Marriage of St. Catherine, with Saints Lucy, Francis and Bartholomew, the work of Benozzo Gozzoli (1420-1497), a Madonna of Mercy with three Saints by Pietro di Giovanni Ambrosi (1409-1449), a wooden crucifix by Giovanni d'Enrico d'Alemagna (lived in the second half of the 15th cent.), and a vast triptych in tempera depicting the Madonna enthroned with Saints, dated 1485, possibly the work of the Master of the Gardner Annunciation, and considered one of the finest works of the period in Umbria. In the archaeological museum are altars, sarcophagi, bas-reliefs, dedicatory inscriptions, and architectural fragments; the pre-historic section once contained objects found during the excavation of a large Iron Age necropolis, but unfortunately they were nearly all destroyed during the bombing. The 13th cent. Gothic church of *San Francesco* may have been designed by Fra Filippo da Campello. The facade has Gothic traces, while inside the church is the Paradisi Chapel, built by the nephews of Giovanni Paradisi of Terni, Paolo and Angelo, Captains of the people in Florence in 1333-1335. Terni lies in the centre of a picturesque region of great natural variety, and is a starting-point for many walks and excursions. Walks to the *Chiesa del Camposanto* or *Chiesa di Santa Maria del Monumento*, to the *Chiesa delle Grazie*, and to *San Valentino*. Excursion to the *Cascata delle Marmore*, one of the most attractive natural beauties in Italy.

* **TERRACINA** (Latina). On the southern edge of the Pontine plain, at the foot of the Lepini mountains. The *Duomo*, dedicated to San Cesareo, is the most important building in the city, and part of it was once an Augustan temple. Eighteen steps lead up to the facade, which has a portico with six ancient columns on medieval bases and an admirable Sicilian-Norman mosaic frieze of the 12th cent. The 13th cent. Romanesque-Gothic campanile is one of the finest towers in Latium. The church contains a spiral Easter candlestick (1241), a Cosmatesque ambo from the middle of the 13th cent., and a superb mosaic floor. In the *Museo Archeologico* is material found in the surrounding districts, ranging from the 4th to the 1st cent. B.C. The *Palazzo Venditti* dates from the first half of the 14th cent. Numerous remains of the *Capitoline Temple* of the 1st cent. B.C. These came to light as a result of bombing during the Second World War. Excursion to the ruins of the *Temple* of *Anxur* of the 1st cent. B.C.

Terracina, Temple of Jupiter Anxur.

* THARROS (RUINS OF) (Town of Cabras, province of Cagliari). Situated on a height near the sea. It was founded by the Phoenicians after the 10th cent. B.C., and conquered by the Romans in the 3rd. A network of roads (from north to south, and east to west) separates the *insulae* (blocks of houses). The houses are built like the Punic ones (from two to six rooms with a central courtyard). The walls are either of the traditional Punic frame kind, or of the isodomon variety. The brightly painted plaster of the walls has been greatly damaged, and only fragments of it remain. The houses probably had two storeys. *Castellum Aquae*, a square construction preceded by a clarification bed, has an interior consisting of a nave and two aisles, and was probably used as a meeting-place by Christians. The *Tempio Punico Monolitico*, built in a Greek-Egyptian style in the 4-3rd cent., consists of a base with a semi-circular side and Doric pillars; on top of the ramp-like platform was a chapel or tabernacle. The *Tempio Semitico* is a square space, with traces of a tabernacle in the centre and two at the sides. *Thermae; Early Christian Baptistery*, in the form of a square, with an apse on one side; Small Temple (*Tempietto*), consisting of a cell, with altar and nearby the remains of a building that once contained the Treasury; *Acropolis; Torre di San Giovanni*, built at the end of the 16th cent. by Phillip II; *Remains of a Necropolis*, where the most common type of tomb is called a *dromos* (room approached by means of a ramp-like corridor, or stairway). Climbing the little hill that dominates the ruins of the town, one reaches the *tophet*, or holy place, where rites were celebrated to propitiate the gods.

* THIENE (Vicenza). Commercial and industrial town, almost at the entrance to the valley of the Astico. The *Duomo*, rebuilt in the first half of the 17th cent. and enlarged in the 20th, has a lacunar ceiling by Ottone Calderari (1730-1803), and paintings by Sebastiano Ricci (1659-1734), Alessandro Maganza (c. 1556-1640), Giulio Carpioni (1611-1674), and Giovan Battista Pittoni (1687-1767). The Gothic-Renaissance *Palazzo Porto Colleoni*, called the Castello di Santa Maria, was built in the 15th cent. on the site of a medieval castle. It contains frescoes by Giovanni Antonio Fasolo (c. 1530-1572) and Giovan Battista Zelotti (1526-1578). In the *Palazzo Fabris* are 18th cent. furnishings and tapestries. The *Palazzo Cornaggia-Colleoni* is 16th cent., and the *Palazzo Miola* 17th cent.

* THIESI (Sassari). A big town situated on a limestone plateau. The parish church of *Santa Vittoria*, built in the Aragonese Gothic style in the last years of the 15th cent., is dominated by a huge polygonal bell-tower, and embellished with a portal decorated with lilies. Walks to the *Ipogei Eneolitici*, and to the grotto of *Monte Maiore*, where the vast caves have interesting concretions and attractive stalactites and stalagmites.

** TIVOLI (Rome). Pleasant, lively town, through which flows the river Aniene. *Hadrian's Villa* is one of the most grandiose archaeological complexes of Roman antiquity. The foundations of the *Duomo*, renovated in the middle of the 17th cent., are mixed up with the remains of a Roman basilica. The church is preceded by a fine portico and flanked by a 12th cent. Romanesque bell-tower. It contains a big 13th cent. wooden group of the Deposition, and a much admired triptych of the Saviour between the Virgin and St. John of the 11-12th cent. In the Romanesque church of *San Silvestro* is an apse with important frescoes of the 12th and 13th centuries. The 13th cent. church of *Santa Maria Maggiore* has a facade with a Gothic doorway and rose-window. The *Temple of Vesta*, probably dedicated to Hercules, is a circular, classical construction with Corinthian columns erected in the last period of the Roman Republic. Nearby is the rectangular *Temple of the Sybil*, or of *Tiburnus*, built in the same period, with Ionic columns. The *Villa Gregoriana* has a vast park into which the famous waterfalls, fed by the river Aniene cascade from a height of 160 m. The interior of the *Villa d'Este* is decorated with 16th cent. frescoes. One should notice the Fontana del Bicchierone (of the large glass) by Gian Lorenzo Bernini (1598-1680), the Avenue of the Hundred Fountains, the Fontana dell'Ovato and the Fountain of the Dragons by Pirro Ligorio (c. 1510-1583). The *Rocca Pia* is a solid structure built in the 15th cent. by Pope Pius II on the remains of a Roman amphitheatre. In the church of *San Giovanni Evangelista* is an important cycle of frescoes, probably by Antoniazzo Romano (c. 1435-1517).

Tivoli, Villa d'Este. Pirro Ligorio, Organ Fountain.

** **TODI** (Perugia). On a hill by the confluence of the Naia and the Tiber, rich in medieval monuments, with Etruscan and Roman remains. The austere, crenellated *Palazzo dei Priori* was begun at the end of the 13th cent. and completed in the first half of the 14th. One should notice the bronze Eagle of Todi, cast in 1339 by Giovanni di Giliacco, and the trapezoidal tower erected in the second half of the 14th cent. The solemn, graceful *Palazzo del Popolo* was built in the 13th cent. and has a marble statue of the Todi Eagle. The *Palazzo del Capitano*, built at the end of the 13th cent., has a spacious colonnade and houses an art gallery with notable works of art, including four Saints on two panels, the remains of a triptych by Bicci di Lorenzo (1373-1452), a huge oil-painting of the Trinity, the central part of which is attributed to Giovanni di Pietro, called Spagna (c. 1450-1528), a Deposition by Felice Damiani (c. 1530-1608), a bronze crucifix, probably by Jean Boulogne (c. 1524-1608), and wardrobes with maiolica, chalices, and processional crosses. In the same building is the Etruscan Roman Museum, with bucchero vases, and male and female statuines. The *Duomo*, dedicated to the Santissima Annunziata, is believed to have been built on the site of a Roman monument. Its construction was begun in the first years of the 12th cent., then continued and completed later. The facade is Gothic, with three doorways and a beautiful rose-window of the first half of the 16th cent. The basilican interior has four aisles and contains many works of art, including a fresco of the Last Judgement by Ferraù da Faenza (1562-1645) and the fragment of a fresco of the Trinity by Spagna. The construction of the church of *San Fortunato* was begun at the end of the 13th cent., but not completed until the second half of the 15th. Its facade, with three dorways, was designed by Giovanni di Santuccio da Fiorenzuola di Spoleto (lived in the first half of

the 15th cent.): the portal (1420-1436), with its numerous bands of small spiral columns, vine-tendrils and little figures, is superb in its richness and grandeur. The luminous interior is vast and harmonious, with a nave and two aisles of identical height, and there are some notable works of art, including a fresco of the Madonna and Child with two Angels by Masolino da Panicale (1383-c. 1447), fragments of frescoes by Nicola Vannucci (recorded 1373-1400), a painting of the Coronation of Mary with four Saints by Andrea Polinari (recorded 1612-1643), fragments of 14th cent. frescoes of the school of Giotto and the tomb of Fra Jacopone da Todi. The Renaissance church of *Santa Maria della Consolazione* was begun at the end of 1508 by Cola di Matteuccio da Caprarola (recorded 1494-1518), who was succeeded by Ambrogio da Milano (lived

Tivoli, Hadrian's Villa, canopus.

Todi, Santa Maria della Consolazione.

in 15-16th cent.) and Francesco de Vita (re-corded 1521-1524). Its plain, well-proportioned interior has pendentives decorated with figures of the Evangelists by Gian Battista Gardona da Ligornetto (lived in the second half of the 16th cent.) and Francesco Casella (recorded 1570-1598), as well as Baroque altars and columns of mixed black marble. The four large *Roman Niches* in Piazza Mercato Vecchio, with a Doric entablature, are probably the remains of a large structure.

** **TOLENTINO** (Macerata). On the left bank of the river Chienti, surrounded by hills on all sides. The *Basilica di San Nicolò da Tolentino* is one of the most famous buildings in the region. It was built for the first time in the 13th cent., but was greatly restored in the 16th. The stylishly articulated facade has a beautiful late-Gothic doorway, on which Nanni di Bartolo called "il Rosso" worked; he was active in the first half of the 15th cent. Inside is the Cappellone di San Nicola of the first half of the 14th cent. Its walls are decorated with magnificent frescoes by famous masters, including an anonymous pupil of Pietro da Rimini (lived in the first half of the 14th cent.), Giovanni Baronzio (mentioned towards the middle of the 14th cent.), an unknown follower of Giuliano da Rimini (active more or less in the same period), and an anonymous disciple of Agostino di Duccio (15th cent.). Adjacent to the basilica is the *Museo delle Ceramiche*, with collections of Etruscan, Roman, Chinese, and Japanese pottery, and the *Museo Civico*, with objects from the early and late

Tolentino, Basilica di San Nicola, doorway.

Iron Age. The *Duomo*, dedicated to San Catervo, the town's patron saint, was first built in the 8-9th cent., rebuilt in the 13th, and amply restored in the first half of the 19th. It contains works of art, such as a Baroque holy-water stoup, as small as it is precious, carved panels by Giovanni Oravia (active in 1425), and frescoes by Francesco da Tolentino (lived in the 16th cent.). The 13th cent. church of *San Francesco* was originally built in a Romanesque-Gothic style, but was almost completely rebuilt according to Baroque principles in the 18th cent. It contains works of art, including a much admired Crucifixion of the Marchigian school carried out in 1361, and a painting of St. Vincent Ferrer of the school of Guercino. There is also an Eternal enthroned by an artist of the Riminese school (c. 1330). Other buildings worthy of mention are the *Palazzo Benadducci*, with two Renaissance doorways, fire-places and a 15th cent. portico in the courtyard and the *Palazzo Bezzi*.

* **TOLMEZZO** (Udine). The main commercial and industrial centre of Carnia. In the *Museo Carnico delle Arti e delle Tradizioni Popolari* are rooms specially arranged with interesting collections of objects to illustrate local customs and tradition (lace, embroidery, wrought iron, chests, little bronzes, carnival masks, decorated tools, etc.). On the walls are painting by Nicola Grassi (c. 1682-1750) and frescoes by Francesco Chiarottini (1748-1796). The *Duomo*, dedicated to St. Martin, was rebuilt towards the middle of the 18th cent. It contains an altar-piece depicting the Madonna with Saints Martin and Charles Borromeo by Francesco Fontebasso (1709-1769), and paintings of Apostles by Nicola Grassi. In the church of *Santa Caterina*, rebuilt at the end of the 18th cent., is a painting of the Madonna with Saints Lucy, Catherine and Apollonia by Pomponio Amalteo (1505-1588). Walk to the ruins of the *Torre Picotta*, erected in 1477 as a defence against Turkish invaders.

*** **TORINO/TURIN.** Situated on the banks of the Po beneath a spectacular circle of mountains, the city still retains the air of a capital (formerly of the kingdom of Sardinia) above all in the regular, geometrical lay-out of its streets and houses, for the centre is surrounded by squares and streets rather like a chess-board. *Palazzo Madama* stands in Piazza Castello, which was designed in the 16th cent. by Ascanio Vittozzi (1539-1615). It rises upon a castle which had incorporated an earlier Roman gateway. It was enlarged in the 15th cent., and in the 17th became the residence of the royal family. In 1721 the beautiful facade was carried out by Filippo Juvarra (1676-1736). It now houses the *Museo Civico d'Arte Antica*, which, besides other objects, also has an art gallery with a beautiful portrait by Antonello da Messina (1430-1479) and various miniatures. The church of *San Lorenzo* was designed in 1667 by Guarino Guarini (1624-1683); *Teatro Regio;* the Royal armoury (*Armeria Reale*), a remarkable collection of weapons and armour; the *Palazzo Reale*, built in 1660, the royal residence of the House of Savoy, with magnificently furnished rooms, in particular, the Scala delle Forbici (Scissors Staircase) by Filippo Juvarra. The *Duomo* is built in a very simple Renaissance style, and flanked by a massive bell-tower; inside is the Chapel of the Sacra Sindone (Holy Shroud), designed by Guarini. The *Porta Palatina* is a two-arched gateway of the Augustan period, flanked by two sixteen-sided towers. The church of *San Filippo Neri* was begun in the 17th cent. and continued by Juvarra; it has a classical pronaos. The *Palazzo dell'Accademia delle Scienze* is a Baroque building, and houses the Egyptian Museum, the Museum of Antiquities, and the Picture Gallery. The Egyptian museum (*Museo Egizio*) is one of the richest of its kind in Europe: besides various objects such as mummies, papyri, tools, it has a very fine collection of statues. The Museum of Antiquities (*Museo d'Antichità*) contains archaeological material ranging from pre-historic to Roman times. The *Galleria Sabauda* is a very important picture

Turin, Castello del Valentino.
Turin, Palazzo Madama, grand staircase.

Turin, Palazzo Reale, Scala delle forbici.

gallery, containing works by Piedmontese painters of the 15th and 16th centuries, Italian painters of the 17th and 18th, and a group of Dutch and Flemish paintings. *Palazzo Carignano* is the work of Guarini. The *Santuario della Consolata*, a hexagonal structure erected by Guarini in 1703, has a richly decorated interior. The *Galleria d'Arte Moderna* contains works by Piedmontese, Venetian, and Lombard painters of the 19th cent.: on the second floor, the collection ranges from the Futurists to the present day, with works not only by Italian, but European artists as well. The *Parco Valentino* is a magnificent park laid out in 1830, the Castello del Valentino being a structure erected in 1630 in the style of the 16th cent. French castles. The church of *Corpus Domini* was designed by Vittozzi and the Baroque interior is decorated with red and black marble. The *Galleria dell'Accademia Albertina* consists mainly of a collection of 17th cent. paintings. The *Mole Antonelliana* was built by Alessandro Antonelli (1798-1888). Excursions to the *Basilica di Superga*, built by Filippo Juvarra on classical lines to a central plan. The *Villa Reale di Stupinigi* is a pure Rococo construction of Juvarra. The *Villa della Regina* is an imposing Baroque construction built by Ascanio Vittozzi, but radically altered in later times. The facade by Masazza di Valdondona (1710-1785) was damaged by bombing in the Second World

Turin, San Lorenzo, dome.
Turin, Palazzo Reale, great hall.

361

War, but has since been restored. It was the residence of Lodovica Cristina of Savoy and assumed its present name from the time when it was inhabited for a brief period by Queen Anne of Orleans, the wife of Victor Amadeus III. The Baroque interior contains frescoes by Giovanni Battista Crosato (1697-1756) and Corrado Giaquinto (1703-1765).

* **TORNO** (Como). Situated in a pleasant spot. The church of *Santa Tecla*, built in 1480, has a beautiful facade decorated with a marble portal and a rose-window. It contains a Passion of Christ by B. Benzi (active in the 15-16th cent.), and a panel dated 1400. The church of *San Giovanni* has a richly ornamental Renaissance doorway; inside, Renaissance frescoes and 17th cent. paintings. Excursion to the 16th cent. *Villa Pliniana*.

* **TORRALBA** (Sassari). The Nuraghe Santu Antine, or Santinu, or Sa Domu de Su Rei, which means "the royal palace". This, together with the Su Nuraxi at Barumini, is the best-preserved nuraghe in Sardinia, and one of the most outstanding examples of megalithic, towered architecture in the western Mediterranean. It dominates the plain of Cabu Abbas, which is scattered with nuraghi. The exterior is squat, the interior well finished and it reveals a surprisingly advanced building technique. It is thought that the central tower was erected in the 11-10th cent. B.C. The little Romanesque church of *Nostra Signora di Cabu Abbas* is a simple, suggestive construction of the 12-13th cent.

* **TORRECHIARA** (Town of Langhirano, province of Parma). Village at the foot of the famous *Castello di Torrechiara*, a grandiose rectangular castle, with three defensive walls and towers at its corners, built between 1448 and 1460 by Pier Maria Rossi. Inside, on the right of the entrance, is a Madonna with Saints Roch and Sebastian, an interesting fresco of the second half of the 15th cent., probably by Francesco Tacconi (recorded 1458-1500). On the vault of the Chapel of St. Nicodemus are 18th cent. frescoes. The Camera d'Oro (Room of Gold) was decorated by Benedetto Bembo (recorded 1461-1475). The towers command a fine view of the surrounding plain and the valley of the river Parma. Walk to the *Badia di Torrechiara*, built on the banks of the river

Torrechiara, Castle.

Parma in 1471; in the church, rebuilt in the 18th cent., is a valuable anonymous 14th cent. fresco of the Madonna and Child.

* **TORRE DE' PASSERI** (Pescara). Nearby is the *Abbazia di San Clemente a Casauria*, the most attractive church in the area, which reflects the change from the Romanesque to the Cistercian style. There was once a Roman village nearby, with a temple which may have been called the "casa aurea". This would explain the origin of the name, Casauria. The monastery, together with the church of the Most Holy Trinity, was built in 871 by Emperor Ludovic II, in fulfillment of a vow made after his liberation from imprisonment in the duchy of Benevento. The facade is superb, and particularly notable is the bronze door dated 1191. Inside is an ancient, solemn pulpit, carved by a certain Fra Giacomo, and the crypt, with two rings of apses, on the outside of which are the remains of the 9th cent. construction. In the Museo Casauriense are archaeological findings from the Roman age, architectural fragments from monasteries, and objects in stone.

* **TORREGLIA** (Padua). A pleasant agricultural village. Starting-point for excursion to the 16th cent. *Villa dei Vescovi*, now Alcese, behind which is the church of St. Martin. The latter contains an altarpiece depicting St. Martin with beggar and other Saints, Christ and two Cherubims, and a Benedictine monk at prayer, the work of Girolamo da Santacroce (recorded 1502-1537). Excursion to the Hermitage of Rua (*Eremo di Rua*), built in 1339 and rebuilt in 1537 by the Camaldolites, whose church contains notable paintings, such as a Crucifixion by Jacopo Palma the Younger (1544-1628).

* **TORRI DEL BENACO** (Verona). In a wonderful position, with a view of Lake Garda. The *Castello Scaligero* dates from the 14th cent. and has towers with battlements. The church of the *Santissima Trinità* contains 15th cent. frescoes.

Torre de' Passeri. Abbey of San Clemente a Casauria, lunette above main entrance.

* **TORTONA** (Alessandria). An agricultural and industrial town of historical and cultural importance, situated on a ridge of the Ligurian Apennines, on the site of the ancient Ligurian town of Dertona. The heart of the town is *Piazza Duomo*. The *Cattedrale*, dedicated to the Assunta and St. Lawrence, is an austere, imposing edifice, whose construction was begun in 1574 by Pius V, and its facade looks on to the square. Inside is a large Baroque high altar, the tomb of Cardinal Carlo Perosi and that of his brother, the musician Lorenzo Perosi, and a Treasury with precious reliquaries. The 15th cent. *Palazzo Guidobono* was restored in 1939. It houses the Tortona Institute of Education, Antiquity and Art, as well as the *Museo Civico*, which includes a Roman section with findings from the Roman colony of Julia Dertona, a modern section, with medieval and modern works of art, and an abundance of historical material. Walk to the Sanctuary of the *Madonna della Guardia*, erected in 1931.

* **TOSCOLANO MADERNO** (Brescia). Situated in a small delta, among olive-groves. The church of *Santi Pietro e Paolo* was founded in 1584. It has a Baroque doorway, and contains valuable 16th cent. wooden statues, paintings by Andrea Celesti (1637-1712), and stained-glass windows by Luigi Balmet (lived in the 19-20th cent.). At Maderno is the 12th cent. Romanesque church of *Sant'Andrea*, its graceful facade presenting a row of half-columns. The interior has been restored to its original form, and contains a panel of the Madonna and Child by Paolo Veneziano (recorded 1333-1362).

** **TRANI** (Bari). A charming, neatly planned town on the Apulian coast, with a small, well-protected harbour. The *Cattedrale*, dedicated to San Nicola Pellegrino, is the finest Romanesque building in the region and rises on a site once occupied by a 7th cent. church dedicated to St. Mary. Its construction was begun in the last years of the 11th cent. and completed in the 13th. Its vast, rose-coloured stone facade is enlivened by a circular window framed by figures of animals, windows with tracery, and elegant decorations. The beautiful bronze door was carried out between 1175 and 1179 by Barisano da Trani. Attached to the facade is a slender bell-tower, one of the most beautiful in Apulia. The bare, predominantly Romanesque interior has a number of works of art. In the crypt of St. Nicholas are many columns of Parian marble, with curious capitals. The 12th cent. Romanesque *Chiesa di Ognissanti* is surrounded by old houses typical of the region and is preceded by a double portico. Inside, there are columns supporting round arches with a double extrados, a Madonna and Child of the 16th cent. Venetian-Cretan school, and a painting of the Madonna with Saints of the same century. The small, originally Romanesque church of *San Giacomo*

has a portal, the archivolt of which is decorated with leaf patterns. Parts of the early building came to light as a result of a fire in August 1902. The church of *Sant'Andrea* is a small 11th cent. Byzantine basilica. The interior is in the form of a Greek cross drawn within a rectangle, and it has three fine semi-circular apses. The church of *San Francesco* was built in the 12th cent. and completely altered at the end of the 19th. It has a bare facade, surmounted by a pediment decorated with arcadings. It has three beautiful domes, the middle one resting on an octagonal drum decorated with arcadings and a serrated cornice. The *Castello* was built in 1233 by Fredrick II, and enlarged in later times; the keep and the three corner towers are quite remarkable. The *Palazzo Caccetta* is a harmonious, late-Gothic building of the middle of the 15th cent. Walk to the abbey of *Santa Maria di Colonna*, built by the Benedictines in the first years of the 12th cent.

* **TRAPANI.** The city consists of an old part situated on a sickle-shaped promontory, and a new part spread out on the slopes of Monte Erice. The *Santuario dell'Annunziata* is its most important monument. Built in the first half of the 14th cent., and decorated in later times, it has a sober facade with a lovely rose-window. Inside, the 14th cent. Fishermen's Chapel is decorated with 16th cent. frescoes depicting scenes from Genesis; the 16th cent. Seamen's Chapel is in the Renaissance style, while the Chapel of the Virgin Mary contains the famous statue of the Madonna of Trapani by Nino Pisano (active in the early 14th cent.). The *Museo Nazionale Pepoli* is housed in the Car-

Trani, Cathedral.

melite convent of the Annunziata, and contains collections of archaeological findings, statues, and paintings. The most outstanding paintings include a Pietà by Roberto di Oderisio, dated 1380, a polyptych of the Virgin crowning St. Catherine with Saints by the Master of the polyptych of Trapani, carried out at the beginning of the 14th cent., a Madonna and Child enthroned with Angels holding up curtains by an unknown Palermitan painter of the middle of the 15th cent., a triptych by Antonio Massaro, called Pastura (second half of the 14th cent.), a St. Francis receiving the Stigmata by Tiziano Vecellio (1490-1576) and a Madonna by Massimo Stanzione (1585-1656). The 17th cent. church of the Jesuit College (*Collegio dei Gesuiti*) has a richly decorated Baroque facade, designed by Natale Masucci in 1636; on the high altar is a marble bas-relief of the Immacolata by Ignazio Marabitti (1719-1797). The *Cattedrale*, dedicated to St. Lawrence, has a Baroque facade dated 1740, and inside is a Crucifixion by Anthony van Dyck (1599-1641). The church of *Santa Maria del Gesù* dates from the first half of the 16th cent. and has a precious glazed polychrome terracotta of the Madonna degli Angeli by Andrea della Robbia (1435-1528). Other outstanding buildings include the 14th cent. church of *Sant'Agostino*, formerly of the Templars, the *Palazzo della Giudecca*, a bizarre 16th cent. construction in a Catalan style and the *Palazzo*, a massive, medieval structure, which has been enlarged on various occasions. Trapani is the port of embarcation for the *Isole Egadi* (Aegadian Islands). In Levanzo, one of the islands, extremely interesting pre-historic graffiti have been found in the Grotta del Genovese. One can also see how tunny-fish are captured and killed in the archipelago.

* **TREIA** (Macerata). A pleasant town commanding fine views, with medieval walls, houses, and streets. The 12th cent. *Duomo* was rebuilt in the 18th cent. It has a brick facade, surmounted by a 12th cent. cusped bell-tower. It contains a few works of art, such as an Assumption by the painter Vincenzo Pagani (c. 1490-1568), and the tomb of Cardinal Nicola Grimaldi, with small statues of Apostles by Andrea Bregno (1418-1503). The *Palazzo Municipale*, built in the 16-17th cent., faces the stylish Piazza della Repubblica; the facade is decorated with the coats-of-arms of noble families, and with an important travertine high-relief of the Madonna of Loreto. In the *Biblioteca dell'Accademia dei Sollevati*, which is housed in the palace of the Accademia Georgica, is a panel depicting the Madonna by Lorenzo di Alessandro (lived in the 15-16th cent.), as a well as incunabula, parchment manuscripts, Papal Bulls, etc.

* **TREMITI (ISLANDS)** (Foggia). There are three islands: San Nicola, San Domino and

Capraia, but only the first two are inhabited. The Island of *San Nicola* is the most interesting in the archipelago, for it has ruins as well and it is here one can see the characteristic houses of the fishermen. The *Chiesa Abbaziale di Santa Maria a Mare* was built by the Benedictines in the early 11th cent., and then altered in the 14th and 15th centuries. The facade has an important Renaissance doorway, the work of Andrea Alessi from Durazzo (c. 1425-1505) and Nicolò di Giovanni Cocari from Florence (lived in the 15th cent.). Inside is an 18th cent. painted wooden ceiling, the floor has fragments of mosaics, and besides a Gothic polyptych on wood, there is a panel depicting the Crucifixion, probably from the 12th cent. The big tower called the "Cavalier di San Nicola", because it bestrides the ridge of the island, is an imposing structure.

** **TRENTO/TRENT.** Situated on the left bank of the river Adige and on its tributary the Fersina and encircled by mountains. It stands at the cross-roads of the thoroughfares that run from Lake Garda, Verona, and Bassano towards the Brenner Pass and the Dolomites. The *Duomo*, dedicated to San Vigilio, is the most important monument in Trent, both for its art and history and reflects various styles, ranging from the beginning of the 13th cent. to the end of the 19th. The facade has an outstanding Gothic rose-window, and a deeply moulded portal. From the left corner

Trent, Castello del Buon Consiglio. Frescoes of the Months: October.

Tivoli, Duomo. Deposition.
Turin, Museo Civico. Macrino d'Alba. Madonna and Child with Saints, detail.

Turin, Galleria Sabauda. Gaudenzio Ferrari, Crucifixion.
Turin, Galleria Sabauda. Martino Spanzotti, Madonna between Saints Ubaldo and Sebastian.
Turin, Museo Civico. Martino Spanzotti, Holy Conversation.

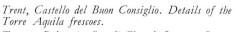

Trent, Castello del Buon Consiglio. Details of the Torre Aquila frescoes.

Trescore Balneario, Suardi Chapel. Lorenzo Lotto, Stories of Santa Barbara.

Treviso, Museo Diocesano. Fresco fragment.

Trescore Balneario, Suardi Chapel. Lorenzo Lotto, Stories of Santa Barbara.

Trieste, Church of San Giusto. St. Justin (detail), painted on silk.

of the church rises a large campanile, completed in 1531. The interior is in the form of a Latin cross and has a nave and two aisles. It includes the Cappella del Crocifisso, where the historical crucifix, before which the decrees of the Council of Trent were emanated, is kept; it is the work of Sixtus Frey of Nurimberg (recorded 1500-1515). There is also a panel depicting the Crucifixion by Giacomo da Vicenza (recorded 1502-1519), a painting of the Madonna and Child with Saints by Marcello Fogolino (active 1510-1548), important 15th cent. frescoes, and numerous tombs of bishops and other important personages of Trent. In the Cathedral Museum are precious objects and seven superb Flemish arrasses by Pietr Van Aelsi (recorded 1497-1537). The red marble *Basilica di Santa Maria Maggiore* dates from the first half of the 16th cent., and has an imposing doorway. It was here that the preliminary sessions of the Council of Trent took place. It contains paintings by Giovanni Maria Falconetto (lived in the 15-16th cent.), Giambettino Cignaroli (1706-1770), Giovanni Battista Moroni (1520-1578) and Michele da Salisburgo (mentioned 1467). The *Palazzo Tabarelli*, designed by Alessio Longhi (recorded 1522-1550), has a beautiful rusticated facade decorated with friezes. The Romanesque church of *San Lorenzo*, which dates from the second half of the 12th cent., rises beside a Baroque campanile. The *Castello del Buonconsiglio* is a large construction built in different periods and formerly inhabited by the Bishop Princes. It is the result of the fusion of the Castelvecchio, the Magno Palazzo, and the Giunta Albertiana. Notice the beautiful Cortile dei Leoni (Lions' Courtyard), the Audience Room, decorated with frescoes by Girolamo Romani, called Romanino (1484-1559), the Room of the Black Fireplace, the two halls of the Giunta Albertiana, where the painter Giuseppe Alberti (1640-1716) worked, the Torre dell'Aquila (Eagle's Tower), which contains important frescoes depicting the twelve months of the year, carried out in 1407, the Camera degli Scarlatti, the Sala delle Stampe (Print Room), the Sala dei Lampi, with paintings by Giovanni Battista Lampi the Elder (1751-1830), the Venetian Loggia, and the modern art gallery. One should also visit the Fossa dei Martiri, where Italian patriots were kept as prisoners, and the Museum of the Risorgimento in the Castelvecchio. In the Baroque church of the *Santissima Annunziata*, designed by Antonio Brusinelli (recorded 1690-1730), is an Annunciation by Michelangelo Grigoletti (1801-1870). In the 16th cent. *Palazzo del Municipio* are frescoes by Domenico Ricci, called Brusasorci (c. 1516-1567). The facade of the 16th cent. *Palazzo Geremia* is decorated with frescoes, probably by Marcello Fogolino. The *Palazzo Galasso* was built at the beginning of the 17th cent. for the banker Georg Fugger. The 13th cent. *Torre Vanga* is a typically military construction built to defend a bridge over the river Adige. In the neighbourhood of the city, the *Mausoleo di Cesare Battisti*, and the *Cascata di Pont' Alto*.

** TRESCORE BALNEARIO (Bergamo).

Industrial town and health resort. In the 15th cent. church of *Santa Barbara*, rebuilt in the 19th cent., are magnificent frescoes by Lorenzo Lotto (1480-c. 1556). In the neo-Classical parish church of *San Pietro* are frescoes by Ponziano Loverini (1845-1929), as well as paintings by Sebastiano Ricci (1659-1734) and Antonio Balestra (1666-1740). The *Villa Terzi* is a group of buildings designed by Filippo Alessandri (1713-1773).

* TREVI (Perugia).

In one of the most pleasant parts of Umbria, with far-ranging views of the surrounding countryside. The church of *Sant'Emiliano* is a Romanesque construction of the 12th cent. which has been greatly altered in later ages. In the tympanum of the 15th cent. portal is an important high-relief of St. Emilian and the two Lions. Inside, one can admire the superb altar of the Blessed Sacrament, which is a combination of three niches,

Trevi, panorama.

the work of Rocco di Tommaso da Vicenza (recorded 1494-1526) and an interesting wooden statue of St. Emilian, carved by an anonymous German artist in 1551. The 13th cent. Gothic church of *San Francesco* consists of a single nave and contains some notable paintings and frescoes, unfortunately somewhat damaged. The *Pinacoteca* (art gallery) has a notable collection of works of art, especially paintings, arranged in two rooms. Walk to the Renaissance church of the *Madonna delle Lacrime*, built to a design by Antonio Marchisi (1451-1522). Its fine doorway was carved by Giovanni di Gian Pietro da Venezia (recorded 1492-1511). It contains many frescoes and paintings, as well as the tomb of Cardinal Erminio Valenti, Bishop of Faenza, carried out in 1618.

* **TREVIGLIO** (Bergamo). An industrial town and important railway junction, at the point where the roads for Bergamo, Lodi, and Crema

Treviglio, Collegiate Church of San Martino. Details of polyptych by B. Butinone and B. Zenale.

join up with the main national thoroughfare of the upper Po valley. The *Collegiata ai San Martino* was founded in 1008 and rebuilt in the Lombard Gothic style at the turn of the 16th century. It is flanked by a grandiose Romanesque campanile with Gothic elements. It contains a much admired polyptych of the Madonna with Saints by Bernardino Butinone (c. 1445-1507) and Bernardino Zenale (c. 1436-1526). In the chancel are paintings by Paolo Cavagna (1556-1627). Beyond the choir is an Assumption by Camillo Procaccini (c. 1551-1629). The Sanctuary of the *Beata Vergine delle Lacrime* was built in the 16-17th cent., with an octagonal dome. It contains a painting of the Conversion of St. Paul by Bernardino Galliari (1707-1794). In the church of *San Rocco* is an important 16th cent. polychrome terracotta Pietà.

* **TREVIGNANO ROMANO** (Rome). Picturesque village on the shore of Lake Bracciano. The 16th cent. church of the *Assunta* consists of aisleless nave and contains a large fresco of the Assumption and Coronation of Mary, carried out in 1517 by an anonymous artist influenced by Raffaello Sanzio (1483-1520), a 16th cent. fresco of the Madonna and Child enthroned with Saints Anthony of Padua and Jerome and praying child, and a 15th cent. triptych of the Saviour, Angel, the Virgin and Saints John the Evangelist and Peter, signed by Nicolò di Pietro Paolo and his son, Pietro. In the church of *Santa Caterina*, built within a Roman edifice, of which some remains have survived, is a 17th cent. polychrome statue of St. Anthony Abbot, and the tomb of Abbot Tommaso Silvestri (1744-1789).

** **TREVISO.** Charming town, intersected by canals and foot-paths. The Romanesque *Palazzo dei Trecento* (so called because it was here that the town's Greater Council, composed of three hundred citizens, used to meet) is Treviso's most characteristic building. The *Battistero* or *San Giovanni del Battesimo* is an important Romanesque construction of the 11-12th cent. The *Duomo*, consecrated to St. Peter and built in the 11-12th cent., has seven hemispherical domes. It contains many works of art, including an altarpiece of the Adoration of the Shepherds by Paris Bordone (1500-1571), a painting of the Madonna and Child enthroned with Saints Roch and Sebastian, called the Madonna of the Flower, by Girolamo da Treviso (lived in the second half of the 15th cent.), and a panel depicting the Annunciation by Tiziano Vecellio (1490-1576). In the chancel, designed by Pietro Lombardo (c. 1435-1515) and his sons, Tullio and Antonio, is the tomb of Biship Giovanni Zanetto, again the work of Pietro Lombardo. The *Museo della Casa Trevigiana* is housed in a Gothic edifice of the first half of the 15th cent. It has collections of wrought iron, banners, funerary sculpture, and terracottas. The *Museo Civico* contains the town's most important artistic and archaeological collections: paintings by Giovanni Bellini (c. 1430-1516), Giambattista Cima da Conegliano (c. 1459-1518), Lorenzo Lotto (c. 1480-1556), Tiziano Vecellio, Pietro Longhi (1702-1785), Alessandro Longhi (1733-1813); Rosalba Carriera (1675-1757), and sculptures by Antonio Canova (1757-1812). The Romanesque-Gothic church of *San Nicolò* was built in the 13-14th cent. with three polygonal apses. The large interior contains works of art such as the frescoes of Saints Agnes, Romuald and John the Baptist by Tommaso da Modena (c. 1325-1379). In the chancel is the tomb of Senator Agostino Ovigo, the sculptured part being the work of Antonio Rizzo (1465-1499), and the paintings by Lorenzo Lotto. The *Seminario Vescovile* is a group of buildings built between the 13th and 16th centuries and known above all for the frescoes by Tommaso da Modena which decorate the Dominican Chapter Room. The *Cappella dei Rettori* is a 17th cent. rectangular chapel, with a richly decorated apse. The church of *Santa Lucia* is 14th cent. In the Chapel of the Crucifixion is a fresco of the Madonna delle Carceri by Tommaso da Modena. The 12th cent. church of *San Vito* was rebuilt in 1568; it contains an altarpiece depicting the Madonna with Saints by Marco Vecellio (1545-1611). The Romanesque *Loggia dei Cavalieri*, once a meeting-place for the nobility, was built in the 10-13th cent. *Santa Caterina dei Servi di Maria* dates from the 14th cent. It has some notable paintings, a few by Tommaso da Modena. The church of *Santo Agostino* was built to a design by Fra Francesco Vecelli (lived in the 18th cent.); it contains some precious paintings, including two by Karl Loth (1632-1698). The 13th cent. Romanesque-Gothic church of *San Francesco* has a bare facade, and contains a fresco of the Madonna with Saints by Tommaso da Modena. The *Porta San Tommaso* was designed by Guglielmo Bergamasco, or d'Alzano (died in 1550). *Santa Maria Maggiore*, called the Madonna Grande, dates from the 9th cent.

* **TREZZO SULL'ADDA** (Milan). On the right bank of the Adda. The parish church of

Trezzo sull'Adda, Castle ruins.

Santi Gervaso e Protaso has been restored in the present century, but still retains the polygonal apse of the original 14th cent. structure. It contains frescoes by Bernardino Campi (c. 1552-1591) and other 15th cent. frescoes. The *Castello di Trezzo*, of which only the grandiose ruins now stand, was one of the most important in Lombardy, closely connected with the history of the Longobards and later restored by the Viscontis. A large, square tower, the Tower of Barbarossa, and the prisons have survived.

* **TRICARICO** (Matera). In spite of its medieval aspect, the town already existed in the Byzantine era. The *Cattedrale* has a Baroque interior and contains the tomb of Bishop Diomede Carafa, carried out in 1639. The church of *Santa Chiara* was built in the first half of the 14th cent. and contains some fair paintings, including an Immaculate Conception attributed to Pietro Antonio Ferri (lived in the 17th cent.) and a 16th cent. painting of the Porziuncola. The church of *Sant'Antonio da Padova* was built at the end of the 15th cent. and has an interesting Durazzo-style portal; inside, Baroque stucco work.

** **TRIESTE.** A modern city situated in a beautiful position in the bay of Trieste, and a very important industrial and commercial centre. The recently discovered *Roman Theatre* of the 1st cent. A.D. shows that the city was a rich Roman colony. *San Giusto* is an amalgamation of two earlier Romanesque basilicas. The facade is decorated with a Gothic rose-window, and flanked by a 15th cent. campanile. The interior is divided into a nave and four aisles, the nave having a wooden ceiling. There are 14th cent. frescoes, a mosaic of the same period depicting Christ with Saints Giustus and Servolus and a panel by B. Carpaccio (active in the 15th cent.). The *Castello* was erected in the 15th cent. and completed in the 17th: one should visit the Venetian Room, the patrol's rounds, the parade-ground and the Chapel, which contains a triptych from the school of Carpaccio. *San Michele* is Gothic. The *Museo di Storia dell'Arte* includes a collection of Greek and Egyptian antiquities and a small art gallery with works by Marco Ricci (1676-1729), Magnasco (1667?-1749), P. Veneziano (1321-1358) and drawings by Giambattista Tiepolo (1696-1770). The church of *Sant'Antonio* is neo-Classical. Excursion to the *Castello di Miramare*, erected on a promontory with a beautiful park, which contains an historical museum; in the park is an Ancient Art Gallery, with works mainly by Venetian painters of the 16-18th cent.

** **TROIA** (Foggia). An agricultural town situated on top of a hill, with a fine view of the Tavoliere. The *Cattedrale*, dedicated to the Assunta, is one of the most important mo-

numents in Apulia. Its construction was begun in 1093 and continued in the Romanesque style for the next three centuries. The facade is the most wonderful part of the church, its lower part decorated with free-standing arcades, and its portal embellished with Oriental-looking bas-reliefs and closed by a superb bronze door, cast in 1119 by Oderisio da Benevento. On the right side is another bronze door, which Oderisio carried out in 1127. On the left side is a fine doorway, with a bas-relief in the lunette. The semi-circular apse, with its upper row of small arches, is both grandiose and harmonious. The church contains a few works of art: in the sacristy is a Treasury, with silver statues of the 17th cent., silver candlesticks of the 15th and 18th centuries, finely chiselled chalices, rare pyxes, richly embroidered copes, chasubles, precious Exultets (Easter hymnals), and Papal Bulls. The church of *San Basilio* is an important Romanesque building, mentioned for the first time in a document dated 1078; it has a bare exterior, while the interior, divided into a nave and two aisles, is simple and refined. In the Bishop's Palace (*Palazzo Vescovile*), which dates from the second half of the 18th cent., is a painted statue of the Madonna and Child by Giovanni da Casalbore (lived in the 13th cent.).

* TROPEA (Catanzaro). Situated on the terraced coast overlooking the sea, it commands a fine view. The 11th cent. *Cattedrale* contains some fair works of art, including the two Baroque tombs of the Galluppi family, an important black wooden crucifix of the 15th or 16th cent. and the portraits of the Bishops of Tropea from 499 A.D. onwards. In the Treasury of the Bishop's Palace (*Palazzo Vescovile*) is a precious 15th cent. silver crozier, called Count Ruggero's. In the church of *San Pietro ad Ripas*, probably built in the second half of the 13th cent., is a statue of the Immacolata, perhaps the work of Giuseppe Albino, called Sozzo (1550-1611). Also worth visiting is the *Chiesa della Sanità* or *dei Cappuccini*, which contains a painting of the Madonna della Sanità by Giovanni Angelo d'Amato (lived in the 16th cent.) and the church of *Santa Chiara*, where there is a beautiful painted marble statue of St. Francis of Assisi, which dates from the 16th cent.

Troia, Duomo. Lunette above side door.

* TURSI (Matera). Situated in a hilly district near the river Agri. The church of the *Rabatana* takes its name from the Arab "rabhadi", which means village; it was rebuilt in the 18th cent. It has a fine 15th cent. portal, and a 14th cent. triptych on wood, called the Madonna of the Icon. The church of *San Filippo* was built in the second half of the 17th cent. It contains a beautiful Neapolitan painting of the same period, depicting St. Philip, frescoes illustrating episodes in the life of St. Philip by Domenico Simone Oliva (lived in the 18-19th cent.), and three altars with artistic inlays. In the same district is the former 13th cent. cathedral of *Santa Maria d'Anglona*, which was the seat of the episcopal see before the latter was moved to Tursi. It is worth noticing the portal with its serrated decorations, the frescoes of episodes in the lives of saints, one of which is an 11th cent. Byzantine representation of the Martyrdom of a female Saint, and a characteristic apse with a window flanked by two little columns. The upper part of the square campanile has fine mullioned windows with small coupled columns.

** TUSCANIA (Viterbo). A medieval-looking, agricultural town, situated on a hill of tufa, south of the Volsini mountains. The church of *San Pietro*, which was first built in the 8th cent., and whose present Lombard Romanesque form is the result of alterations carried out over the centuries, is regarded as one of the most interesting buildings of the Italian Middle Ages. The facade was well restored at the end of the 19th cent. It has a portal surmounted by a small blind loggia and a rose-window with the symbols of the Evangelists. The sides of the church are decorated with small blind arcades supported by slender columns. The bare, austere interior has a ciborium supported by columns (1093), an ambo with fragments of decorations from the 7-8th cent., a fresco depicting episodes in the life of St. Peter, carried out in the first half of the 12th cent., and a fresco of Christ between Angels and Apostles, a work of the Roman school with traces of Byzantine influence. In the crypt are numerous columns taken from Roman buildings. Nearby, in the Bishop's Palace, is a Civic Museum, with many terracotta sarcophagi dating from the 2nd and 1st centuries B.C. The church of *Santa Maria Maggiore* is another magnificent example of Romanesque architecture, with traces of Gothic influence. Its first construction goes back to the 8th cent., but it has been almost completely rebuilt since then. It is preceded by a massive, squat, Romanesque bell-tower. The facade is the same as that of the church of St. Peter and is decorated with Umbrian motifs. Of the three doorways, the most beautiful is the middle one in white marble. It is deeply moulded and the jambs

Tuscania, Santa Maria Maggiore. Main doorway, Sacrifice of Isaac.
Tuscania, Santa Maria Maggiore, interior.

interesting 15th cent. statues in niches, a huge polyptych depicting the Madonna and Child enthroned with Saints Louis of France, Paul, Peter, Francis and donor by Andrea di Bartolo (mentioned in 1428), a panel of Saint Bernardino and two Angels by Sano di Pietro (1406-1481) and a much admired 16th cent. painting of St. James Major in the sacristy. The church of *Santa Maria del Riposo* was built at the end of the 15th cent. Its facade is supported by three powerful buttresses and it has a richly decorated portal (1522). It contains a 14th cent. nenfro marble holy-water stoup, paintings by Giulio Pierino d'Amelia and Antonio da Viterbo, called Pastura (recorded 1478-1509), and a Presentation of Mary in the Temple by Girolamo Sicciolante, called Sermoneta (1521-1580). In the characteristic *Via degli Archi* there are ancient medieval houses and, above all, a 14th cent. house with an outside staircase in Viterbo style, with a Romanesque-Gothic mullioned window.

** **UDINE.** The most important city in Friuli, gathered around a little hill, on the top of which rises a 16th cent. castle. The *Castello* is the symbol of the city. It was built between 1517 and 1595 to a design by Giovanni Fontana (active in the first half of the 16th cent.), with whom Giovanni da Udine (1487-1564) is supposed to have collaborated. The facade faces Piazza della Libertà, the most important square in Udine. The castle houses the Civic Museum, the Ancient Art Gallery, the Modern Art Gallery, and the Museum of the Risorgimento. In the Civic Museum are architectural remains from the times when the city was governed by the Bishops and the Venetians, and a fresco of the Madonna dell'Uva by Giovanni Antonio Pordenone (1484-1539). In the Ancient Art Gallery one should notice, above all, the terracotta crucifix by Antonio Canova (1757-1822), the painting of the Madonna at prayer by Giovanni Battista Salvi, called Sassoferrato (1609-1685), the Ecstasy of St. Francis by Michelangelo Merisi, called Caravaggio (1573-1610), the Blood of Christ by Vittore Carpaccio (c. 1465-1526), the Consilium in Arena, the Guardian Angel, St. Francis of Sales, and Fortitude and Wisdom by Giovanni Battista Tiepolo (1696-1770). In the Modern Art Gallery there are many works of art of the 19th and 20th centuries, as well as ancient and modern sections dedicated to prints and drawings. In the Museum of the Risorgimento are objects and documents concerning the Risorgimento dating from the first years of the 19th cent. There are also collections of stamps and jewellery, including artistically wrought precious stones from the Roman period, and medals produced by Friulan medallists. At the top of the castle is an observatory, from where one can see the Carnic and Julian Alps. *Santa Maria di Castello* was built for the first time in the 13th cent. It has a Renaissance facade, and a

are decorated with bas-reliefs (the figures of Saints Peter and Paul are clearly recognisable), while the lunette has a bas-relief of the Madonna and Child enthroned, flanked by the mystical Lamb and the Sacrifice of Abraham. The interior is particularly harmonious and is divided into a nave and two aisles by columns and pillars with Roman capitals. It contains an octagonal baptismal font, a pulpit built of several marble fragments from the 8th, 9th, and 12th centuries, a Gothic ciborium, a huge anonymous 13th cent. fresco of the Last Judgement, and a Byzantine-style fresco of Apostles in the apse, dating from the end of the 13th cent. The 14th cent. church of *Santa Maria della Rosa* is a building in which the Romanesque prevails over the Gothic style; it has a brown, asymmetrical facade. The interior is also asymmetrical and contains a carved wooden altarpiece depicting Saints and scenes from the Gospels by Giulio Pierino d'Amelia (recorded 1543-1581), as well as a painting of the Madonna Liberatrice, placed in a Renaissance niche. This title is explained by the tradition that the Madonna raised the terrible storm which forced Charles VIII's mercenaries to interrupt the sack of the town in 1495. The *Duomo* was rebuilt in the 18th cent., but has retained its simple, two-storeyed, 16th cent. facade. The basilican interior contains the Chapel of Saints Justus and Julianus, with

Tuscania, San Pietro, facade.

massive 16th cent. campanile designed by Gaspare Negro (recorded 1525-1588). It contains an important series of paintings, the work of anonymous artists towards the middle of the 13th cent. The *Duomo*, dedicated to the Annunziata, was begun in 1225, but continually altered in later times. It has a brick facade, with a notable, deeply moulded central doorway, while the campanile was erected between 1441 and 1450 by Bartolomeo della Cisterna and Cristoforo da Milano. The interior is in the form of a Latin cross, and there are paintings by Giovanni Battista Tiepolo, Pomponio Amalteo (1505-1588), Francesco Fontebasso (1709-1769), Ludovico Dorigny (1654-1742), Francesco Floriani and Giovanni Battista Grassi (active in the second half of the 16th cent.) and Pellegrino da San Daniele (c. 1467-1547). To the left of the apse are frescoes depicting the funeral of St. Nicholas by Vitale da Bologna (recorded 1330-1359). In the *Oratorio della Purità* (1757) is an Assumption by Giovanni Battista Tiepolo, and a cycle of monochrome frescoes by Gian Domenico Tiepolo (1727-1804). In the Bishop's Palace (*Palazzo Arcivescovile*), the core of which dates from the 16th cent., while the wings were added in the 18th, are important paintings by Giovanni Battista Tiepolo and Giovanni da Udine, the painter who worked on the so-called Room of Giovanni da Udine. Also worth noting is the architectural complex formed by *Piazza della Libertà* and the typically Venetian Gothic *Palazzo della Loggia del Lionello* or *Palazzo del Comune*, designed by Nicolò Lionello (1400-1462). The *Loggia di San Giovanni* is a beautiful Renaissance structure, surmounted by a clocktower. The *Casa della Contadinanza* contains an armoury with pre-historic, Oriental, African, Mexican, Longobard, and Italian objects, which

continues up to the 17th cent. The church of the *Madonna del Carmine* was built in the first half of the 16th cent. The *Basilica Santuario della Madonna delle Grazie* was first built in the 15th cent. and altered in the early 19th; it contains a revered 14th cent. Madonna and Child. The *Palazzo degli Antonini*, now occupied by the Banca d'Italia, was designed by Andrea Palladio (1508-1580). The *Palazzo del Monte di Pietà*, now occupied by the Cassa di Risparmio, was built in the early 16th cent. The church of *San Giacomo* was built in the second half of the 14th cent., and contains a painting of Purgatory by Michelangelo Grigoletti (1801-1870). *San Francesco* is a 13th cent. Romanesque church, while the *Cappella Manin* is a Baroque masterpiece, probably built to a design by Domenico Rossi (1687-1742).

* **UMBERTIDE** (Perugia). On the left bank of the river Tiber, at its confluence with the river Reggia. The church of *Santa Maria della Roggia* is an imposing, octagonal building. It was built to a design by Bino Sozi (recorded 1573-1603), who was succeeded by Francesco Laparelli (1521-1570), an architect from Cortona. The church of *Santa Croce* was erected in 1651, and contains a Baroque high altar, with a panel representing the Deposition by Luca Signorelli (c. 1445-1523). Walk to the *Castello di Civitella Ranieri*, the best-preserved in the area. Nearby is the abbey of *San Salvatore di Monte Corona*, a 12th cent. Romanesque construction, badly altered in the Baroque period. The church is interesting because fragments of early-14th cent. frescoes, together with remains of the original chancel, have recently been discovered; notice the 8th cent. ciborium decorated with reliefs. Eight kilometres away is *Monte Corona*, a hermitage

Udine, Palazzo della Provincia.

founded in a forest of fir-trees by St. Romuald; its belvedere commands one of the most beautiful views in Umbria.

* URBANIA (Pesaro). On the banks of the Metauro, with an interesting 15th cent. quarter. The pre-Romanesque *Cattedrale di San Cristoforo* was remodelled in the Renaissance, and almost wholly rebuilt in 1759 by Giuseppe Tosi. It contains some notable works of art, including a painting of the Madonna with Saints Roch and Sebastian by Domenico Peruzzini, the Nativity of San Giovannino by Giorgio Picchi (c. 1550-c. 1599), a wonderful panel of the Madonna nursing the Child Jesus by an anonymous painter of the 15th cent. Venetian-Marchigian school, inscriptions from the 3rd, 4th, and 5th centuries, silver-ware from the 16-18th, and reliquaries. The church of *San Francesco*, wholly rebuilt in the second half of the 18th cent., has a late-Baroque interior, with works of art by Domenico Peruzzini, Giorgio Picchi, and the Venetian Claudio Ridolfi (c. 1570-1644). The *Oratorio del Corpus Domini*, which was first built in the 14th cent., has some notable works of art signed by Giorgio Picchi, Raffaello del Colle, called Raffaellino (born towards the end of the 15th cent. and died in 1556) and Giovanni Francesco Guerrieri (1589-1655/59). The *Palazzo Ducale*, a massive structure built in the late 14th cent., houses a public library which was founded long ago, before being despoiled by Pope Alexander VII in 1667, a museum with collections of maps, parchments, engravings, and book-bindings, and an art gallery with works by Giovanni Francesco Guerrieri, Giustino de' Salvolini, called Episcopio (recorded 1545-1609), Domenico Peruzzini, Federico Barocci (c. 1528-1612), Lucio Dolci (recorded 1536-1589), and Francesco Mancini (c. 1694-1758).

*** URBINO (Pesaro). An enchanting little town on a hill, with wonderful views all around. It abounds in monuments and works of art, especially from the Renaissance. The *Duomo*, begun by Francesco di Giorgio Martini (1439-1502) and completed by Muzio Oddi (1569-1639), is as majestic outside as it is inside, and is crowned by a large dome. It contains many works of art signed by painters such as Federico Fiori, called Baroccio (c. 1528-1612), Lodovico Viviani (died in 1649), Carlo Cignani (1628-1719), Carlo Maratta (1625-1713), Cristoforo Unterberger (1732-1798), Claudio Ridolfi (c. 1570-1644), and Jacopo Palma the Younger (1544-1628). One should visit the recently reorganised Diocesan Museum, which has many works of art. The *Palazzo Ducale*, one of the jewels of Renaissance architecture, was begun towards the middle of the 15th cent. to a design by Luciano Laurana (1420/25-1479), and completed by famous architects such as Francesco di Giorgio Martini (1439-1502) and Girolamo Genga (c. 1476-1551). It is both graceful and imposing, and its beauty is fully revealed in the so-called "facade of the two little towers", which bears the unmistakable imprint of Luciano Laurana's genius. The palace houses the *Galleria Nazionale delle Marche*, one of the most important art galleries in Europe, which contains priceless works of art signed by such painters as Marino Angeli (lived in the 15th cent.), Giovanni Baronzio (recorded 1345-1362), Giovanni Bellini (c. 1429-1516), Simone Cantarini (1612-1678), Carlo Crivelli (1430/35-1495), Carlo da Camerino (active in the second half of the 14th cent.), Gentile da Fabriano (c. 1370-1427), Francesco da Rimini (lived in the first half of the 14th cent.), Lorenzo di Alessandro da Sanseverino (lived in the 15th cent.), Andrea di Cione, called Verrocchio (1435-1488), Piero della Francesca (1415/20-1492), Andrea di Bartolo di

Urbino, Ducal Palace.

374

Fredi (recorded 1389-1428), Justus of Ghent (recorded 1460-1475), Sandro di Mariano Filipepi, called Botticelli (1445-1510), Nicola Filotesio, called Cola dell'Amatrice (recorded 1509-1547), Giovanni Mansueti (recorded 1485-1527), Luca Signorelli (c. 1445-1523), Raffaello Sanzio (1483-1520), Tiziano Vecellio (1490-1576), Timoteo Viti (1467-1525), Alvise Vivarini (c. 1446-1506), Paolo Uccello (1397-1475), by sculptors such as Ambrogio Barocci (recorded 1470-1516), Francesco di Simone Ferrucci (1437-1493), Francesco di Giorgio Martini, Baccio Pontelli (c. 1450-1492), as well as by tapestry-weavers such as Francis van den Hecke (recorded 1629-1640). The Gothic church of *San Domenico*, built in the first half of the 14th cent., has a stone portal, a masterpiece by Maso di Bartolomeo (1406-c. 1456); it contains works of art. The *Oratorio di San Giovanni Battista*, built in the second half of the 14th cent., is in the centre of a quarter characterized by picturesque, narrow streets, and contains the famous frescoes carried out in 1416 by the Salimbeni brothers, Jacopo and Lorenzo. In the Baroque *Oratorio di San Giuseppe* is a stucco crib by Federico Brandani (c. 1520-1575). The church of *San Giorgio* contains a painting of the Martyrdom of St. George by Claudio Ridolfi, and paintings by Girolamo di Bartolomeo Cialdieri (1593-1680). The 15th cent. *Casa di Raffaello* (Raphael's House) was the great painter's birthplace; it is well preserved inside, and contains beautiful works by Raphael, as well as works by Orlando Merlini (recorded 1475-1510), Giovanni Santi (active 1484-1494), Federico Zuccari (1540-1609), and Simone Cantarini (1612-1678).

Urbino, Ducal Palace, courtyard.

* **URBISAGLIA** (Macerata). On the left bank of the Fiastra. The *Theatre* is the most important archaeological monument in the Marches and was built in the 1st cent. by Caius Salvius Liberalis, as is testified by an inscription discovered in the 18th cent. It was very big, the front measuring over 100 m. Portraits and statues have also been found. The *Amphitheatre of Urbs Salvia*, of which important remains have been discovered in recent years, dates from the 2nd cent.

* **URGNANO** (Bergamo). An industrial and agricultural town. The parish church (*Parrocchiale*), rebuilt in the 18-19th cent., has a cylindrical bell-tower by Luigi Cagnola (1762-1833), and contains a Birth of Jesus by Francesco Bassano the Younger (1540-1592), a Deposition by Andrea Celesti (1637-1712), and Christ deposed from the Cross by Jacopo Robusti, called Tintoretto (1518-1594). The *Castello* is a notable building, and its construction was begun in 1354. At Basella is the 15th cent. sanctuary of the *Madonna della Basella*.

* **URZULEI** (Nuoro). A characteristic, isolated town. The *Oratorio* contains a 17th cent. painting. Excursion to the mountaintop called *Is Gruttas*, where one can visit various grottoes, one of which has seven separate caves. Votive objects from the age of the Nuraghi have been found in one of the grottoes.

* **USSEL** (Aosta). A little village situated on a height, shaded by chestnut-trees. The *Castello di Ussel* was built to a rectangular plan in 1350, and combines the style of the castle-fortress with that of the castle-residence.

* **USSITA** (Macerata). Summer holiday resort. The 14th cent. *Chiesa di Pieve* was restored by Cardinal Pietro Gasparri. It has some 15th cent. frescoes and a beautiful ciborium. Excursion to the Bramantesque *Santuario di Macereto*, built by Giovanni Battista da Lugano (active in the 16th cent.). It contains a 15th cent. polychrome-wood statue of the Madonna.

* **USTICA** (Palermo). The inhabited centre is on the volcanic island of Ustica, which has both fertile areas and others composed of lava and volcanic material. The first inhabitants were Phoenicians or Carthaginians, and were later superseded by the Romans. From the 8th to the 10th cent. it was in the hands of the Saracens. It then fell under Norman rule, before finally passing to the Bourbons. The *Fortezza* (Fortress) has a square tower. The *Torre di Santa Maria* is a little fort built to defend the creek of the same name. There is also the *Cappella di San Francesco* and the *Madonna della Croce*, a little chapel on the top of a height, commanding a view of all the surrounding countryside.

* **UTA** (Cagliari). A big agricultural town. The late-Gothic parish church (*Parrocchiale*) has a beautiful doorway. The church of *Santa Maria* (1135-1145) is the most beautiful of those built by the Victorine monks. The rusticated façade has a rectangular doorway with Arab-like decorative elements. The sides and apse of the church are decorated with arcadings and pilasters.

* **UZZANO** (Florence). A beautiful, pleasantly situated town. A large *Villa* stands on the ruins of a medieval castle. The church of *San Martino* contains a triptych by Bicci di Lorenzo (1373-1452). In the church of *Villa*

Urgnano, Castle. Marble statue on the balustrade over the courtyard.

Uzzano, Palazzo del Podestà.

Udine, Archbishop's Palace. Giambattista Tiepolo, detail of Sarah and the Angel.

Udine, Archbishop's Palace. Giambattista Tiepolo,
Rachel hiding the Idols, detail.
Urbino, Galleria Nazionale. Piero della Francesca,
Our Lady of Senigallia.

Urbino, Galleria Nazionale. Carlo da Camerino,
Annunciation, detail.

Casale is a panel of the 13th cent. Florentine school. Nearby is the *Castello di Verrazzano*, built before 1000 A.D. The chapel contains a 16th cent. panel of the Florentine school. *San Donato a Citille*, a little church rebuilt after the last war, has a polyptych by the so-called Master of the Madonna of Straus.

* **VADO LIGURE** (Savona). Situated near that part of the sea which goes by the same name. The *Museo Civico* has collections of sculptures, grave goods, inscriptions, and four hundred coins of the 2nd cent. The *Casa di Arturo Martini* contains works, sketches, casts, and designs by this famous sculptor from Treviso (1885-1947).

* **VALDAGNO** (Vicenza). A very important little commercial and industrial town on the right bank of the Agno. The 18th cent. parish church of *San Clemente* was designed by Giovanni Miazzi (1699-1797), and contains a polychrome stone polyptych of St. Anne with Mary, the Child Jesus and four Saints by Girolamo da Vicenza (mentioned in the early 16th cent.), as well as altarpieces by Gerolamo Ciesa (active in the second half of the 18th cent.) and Antonio de' Pieri (lived in the 17-18th cent.). Worth noticing too, is the *Villa Gaianigo*, built at the beginning of the 19th cent., and the *Villa Valle*, now Marzotto, built at the beginning of the 18th.

* **VALDOBBIADENE** (Treviso). The parish church (*Chiesa Arcipretale*) goes back to the 14th cent., and contains paintings by Jacopo Palma the Younger (1544-1628), Paris Bordone (1500-1571), and Claudio Ridolfi (1570-1644). In the church of *San Gregorio* (1482) is a Madonna of the Rosary by Domenico Ricci, called Brusasorci (c. 1516-1567), and a painting of St. Venantius Fortunatus by Rosa Bortolan (1817-1892).

* **VALLE DI CADORE** (Belluno). Pleasant holiday resort, and quite important industrial town. The church of *San Martino* was completely rebuilt at the beginning of the 18th cent., and contains an altarpiece depicting the Madonna and Child with Saints and Angels by Francesco da Milano (active in the first half of the 16th cent.), and a painting of the Death of St. Joseph by Antonio Lazzarini (1672-1732).

* **VALLO DI NERA** (Perugia). On a hill, with picturesque streets, and the ruins of medieval walls. The 13th cent. Gothic church of *Santa Maria*, or *San Francesco*, has a fine portal with a pointed arch, and contains frescoes carried out in 1383 by Cola di Pietro da Camerino and Francesco di Antonio. In the neighbourhood of the town is an interesting shrine (*Edicola della Madonna delle Forche*), with votive frescoes of the 15th cent.

* **VAPRIO D'ADDA** (Milan). Situated upon a terrace overlooking the Adda. The *Palazzo Melzi d'Eril* was erected in the second half of the 15th cent. on the ruins of a medieval castle, and enlarged in the 17th. Inside, there is a fresco called the Madonnone, which some consider to be the work of Leonardo da Vinci (1452-1518), as well as 18th cent. stucco work. On the left side of the small 11-12th cent. Romanesque church of *San Colombano* is a statue of St. Columbanus imparting his blessing.

* **VARALLO SESIA** (Vercelli). The most important town in the Val Sesia. It lies in a hollow, surrounded by wooded mountains, at the foot of the famous sanctuary of the Sacro Monte, and at the confluence of the Mastallone. The 13th cent. *Collegiata di San Gaudenzio* stands on a solitary rock, and has a fine arcade running all round it. The vast interior has numerous 18th cent. polychrome marble altars, and in the apse is a polyptych of the Marriage of St. Catherine by Gaudenzio Ferrari. The church of the *Madonna delle Grazie*, or *dei Frari*, was built in the 15-16th cent., and contains an admirable cycle of frescoes carried out in 1513 by Gaudenzio Ferrari, representing the life of Christ in twenty-one separate sections. The *Palazzo dei Musei* houses a permanent handicraft exhibition, the Calderini Museum, and an art gallery, which has a collection of mainly local artists from the 15-19th cent. The *Sacro Monte*, which one can

Varallo Sesia, Sacro Monte. Tanzio da Varallo and Giovanni d'Enrico, Christ before Herod, detail.

Varallo Sesia, Sacro Monte. Tanzio da Varallo and Giovanni d'Enrico, Christ before Pilate.
Varallo Sesia, Sacro Monte. Morazzone, Ecce Homo Chapel, detail.

reach either on foot, by car, or by cable car, is one of the most famous sanctuaries in Italy. It is a huge monumental construction, and was founded towards the end of the 15th cent. by the Friar Minor, Bernardino Caimi of Milan. The architects mainly responsible for the building were Pellegrino Tibaldi (1527-1596) and Galeazzo Alessi (1512-1572), while the decoration is mainly the work of Gaudenzio Ferrari (1470-1546), Nicholas Wespin, called Nicola Tabacchetti (1577-post 1616), and Giovanni d'Enrico (c. 1560-1644). The pictorial decoration is mainly by Gaudenzio Ferrari, Pier Francesco Mazzucchelli, called Morazzone (1571-1626) and Antonio D'Errico, called Tanzio da Varallo (c. 1575-c. 1635). The sanctuary consists of the church dedicated to the Assumption, surrounded by forty-five chapels, called the New Jerusalem and consecrated to the Life of Christ, decorated with numerous statues and frescoes, most of which signed by the artists already mentioned, who also collaborated in the construction of the Sacro Monte. One should visit the *Cappella della Madonna of Loreto*, one of the most important works of art in the Valsesia: the Chapel is a fine Renaissance structure, rich in 16th cent. frescoes by various artists, many of which are attributed to Antonio Zanetti, called Bugnato. The most important are the Creation, the Fall, the Expulsion from Paradise, the Adoration of the Child Jesus, all by Gaudenzio Ferrari, the Assumption with Apostles and Angel offering St. Thomas a sash, by Andrea Solario (1460-post 1527), the Annunciation and the Death of the Virgin.

* **VARAZZE** (Savona). Situated in a creek between Punta della Mola and Punta dell'Aspe-

Varallo Sesia, Sacro Monte. Giovanni d'Enrico, Virgin of the Annunciation.

Varazze, Sant'Ambrogio, Campanile.

ra, with a beautiful beach. The *Collegiata di Sant'Ambrogio* has a Romanesque-Gothic campanile, and a modern facade (1916). The Baroque interior contains a Madonna with Saints by an artist of the school of Luca Cambiaso (1527-1585), and a polyptych representing St. Ambrose and Saints, carried out by Giovanni Barbagelata in 1500.

* **VASTO** (Chieti). The *Cattedrale di San Giuseppe*, formerly of St. Augustine, and earlier still, of St. Margaret, was built in the last years of the 13th cent., destroyed by the Turks towards the middle of the 16th and rebuilt in 1568. The 13th cent. facade has a beautiful portal with a pointed arch and a big rose-window, the work of Ruggero de Fragenis (lived in the 13th cent.). The church of *Santa Maria Maggiore*, built in the 11th cent., almost destroyed by the Turks in 1566, and by a fire in 1645, was rebuilt and enlarged in 1785. The basilican interior contains the Cappella della Spina, where a relic of the Holy Thorn, and a painting called "of the Thorn", possibly by Titian (1477-1576), are kept. The church of *San Pietro* was built in the 13th cent. on the remains of a temple dedicated to Ceres, and almost completely rebuilt in 1754. The facade has a fine portal with a pointed arch, probably the work of Ruggero de Fragenis. It contains a painting called Ecce Agnus Dei by Filippo Palizzi (1818-1899). One should visit the museum (*Museo Civico*), which has an interesting collection of archaeological findings and works of art, including two Oscan bronze inscriptions, architectural fragments, seals, terracottas, gold, silver, bronze, iron and amber objects from the excavation sites of Histanium and Buca, a collection of coins, as well as the paintings of Filippo Palizzi and other local artists.

** **VEIO** (**RUINS OF**) (Rome). An Etruscan city, and later a Roman colony. Excavation began in this century and has brought to light a great amount of material. From the village of Isola Farnese, with its beautiful medieval castle, one reaches the ruins of Veio. Parts of the *piscina* and *platea* of the *Temple* of Apollo have survived. The *Ponte Sodo* is a tunnel, which the Etruscans dug for the purpose of channelling water. The *Campana Tomb* is very interesting, for it bears witness to a period of transition from flat-roof to vaulted constructions; the interior is decorated with archaic frescoes.

* **VELLEIA** (Piacenza). A Roman town situated in the Apennines near Piacenza; one of the most important archaeological sites in Emilia. *Archaeological excavation*, begun in the second half of the 18th cent., has brought to light an extremely important group of monuments. Particularly interesting is the rectangular, paved forum surrounded by columns, the basilica, where important inscriptions have been found, and the twelve statues of members of the Julian-Claudian imperial family. Velleia is interesting, not so much for its monuments, as for its inscriptions, especially the so-called *tavola alimentare* (agricultural law) of Trajan, which is essential for an understanding of agricultural property between the 1st and 2nd centuries.

* **VELLETRI** (Rome). The town's houses are grouped together on a volcanic spur of Monte Artemisio. The 4th cent. *Cattedrale* has been rebuilt in later ages. It has a Renaissance portal, the work of Traiano da Palestrina (active in the early 16th cent.) and contains a panel of the Madonna and Child by Antoniazzo Romano (c. 1435-1517). The *Museo Capitolino* contains a panel of the Madonna and Child with Angels by Gentile da Fabriano (c. 1370-1427), two paintings of the Madonna and Child by Antoniazzo Romano, and an 11th cent. crucifix-reliquary. The colonnaded *Palazzo Comunale* is the work of Giacomo Della Porta (1540-1602).

* **VENAFRO** (Isernia). Dominated by Monte Santa Croce. Particularly interesting is the predominantly Baroque *Chiesa del Purgatorio*,

Velleia, view of the Forum and Temple.

Varallo Sesia, Pinacoteca. Tanzio da Varallo, David, detail.

Venice, Istituto Ellenico. The Virgin, Prophets,
Apostles and Saints, detail.
Venice, St. Mark's Treasury. The Virgin's Grotto
and votive crown of Leo VI.

Venice, St. Mark's Treasury. St. Michael.

the austere, battlemented *Palazzo Caracciolo*, the medieval *Cattedrale* (spoilt by restoration), the church of the *Annunziata*, with its Baroque interior and notable 18th cent. frescoes, and the *Museo Civico*, with its statues and Roman remains.

*** VENEZIA/VENICE.

The city rises on a group of small islands between the lagoon and the sea. This position, together with its innumerable monuments, makes it one of the most unusual cities in the world. The rectangular *Piazza San Marco* is enclosed on all sides by palaces and arcades: the *Procuratie Vecchie* were begun by B. Bon (active in the first half of the 16th cent.); the *Procuratie Nuove* were begun by V. Scamozzi (1552-1616) and completed by B. Longhena (1598-1682) in the 17th cent.; the *Ala Napoleonica* was added in 1810; the *Torre dell'Orologio* is the work of M. Coducci (1440-1504). At the bottom of the square rises the *Basilica of St. Mark*, a masterpiece of Byzantine-Romanesque art. It is surmounted by five domes, while the facade is divided into two storeys covered with mosaics, most of which have been restored. The five doorways of the facade are decorated with extremely beautiful Byzantine-style reliefs. The interior, preceded by an atrium decorated with 13th cent. mosaics, is in the form of a Greek cross, with a nave and two aisles; there are also *matronei* (women's galleries). The mosaics are the work of Venetian-Byzantine artists of the 12-14th cent., but have been greatly restored

since. The raised presbytery is separated from the rest of the church by a rood screen with statues by the Dalle Masegne brothers (active in the 14th cent.), and on the altar is a most beautiful altarpiece of the 10-14th cent. The baptistery is a fine work by Sansovino (1486-1570), whereas the campanile was completely rebuilt in 1912. The *Loggetta* near the campanile is also the work of Sansovino. The *Museo Correr* is housed in the Ala Napoleonica, and besides its collection of objects illustrating the life of the city, has a very important art gallery, with works mainly by Venetian artists. On the right of *Piazzetta San Marco* is the *Libreria Vecchia*, Sansovino's masterpiece, which houses the *Biblioteca Marciana* (with paintings by Titian, Tintoretto, and Veronese) and the *Museo Archeologico*, with its Greek and Roman sculpture; on the left is the *Doge's Palace*. The latter, built between 1309 and 1442, is a typical example of Venetian Gothic architecture, with empty wall surfaces predominating over full, and elegantly faced with polychrome marble. Above the ground-floor arcade runs a loggia with interlaced arches. Two balconies of the 14th and 16th centuries interrupt the sequence of numerous ogee-arched windows. Passing through the Gothic Porta della Carta, one enters the fine courtyard, two of its sides being in the Gothic style, and one in the Renaissance. The Scala dei Giganti (Giants' Staircase), decorated with statues by Sansovino, faces the Baroque facade of the Orologio and the Foscari arch.

Venice, St. Mark's, interior.

The Scala d'Oro (Golden Staircase) leads up to the piano nobile, to lavishly decorated rooms with paintings and frescoes of considerable value, including works by Tintoretto, Veronese, Francesco Bassano, and Titian. On the quay rises the *Palazzo della Zecca*, the work of Sansovino and towards the Riva degli Schiavoni is the Bridge of Sighs (*Ponte dei Sospiri*). The *Grand Canal* (Canal Grande), which runs right through the city, dividing it into two, is flanked on both sides by extremely beautiful palaces, especially Gothic ones of the 14th and 15th centuries, of which only the most representative can be mentioned here. On the left: the *Palazzo Dario*, a Renaissance palace designed by Pietro Lombardo (1435-1515), decorated with beautiful four-lighted windows and faced with marble; the *Palazzo Contarini degli Scrigni*, partly designed by Scamozzi (1552-1616); the Gothic *Palazzo Loredan;* the Baroque *Palazzo Rezzonico*, designed by Longhena (1598-1682); the Gothic *Palazzi Giustinian;* the *Ca' Foscari*, a 15th cent. Gothic construction with two loggias, each with eight arches; the classical-looking *Palazzo Balbi*, designed by Alessandro Vittoria (1524-1608); the

Gothic *Palazzi Pisani;* the beautiful Lombard-style *Palazzo Grimani;* the Renaissance *Palazzo dei Dieci Savi*, built by A. Abbondi, called Scarpagnino (active in the first half of the 16th cent.); the *Ponte Rialto*, built in 1592, and consisting of a single arch surmounted by other arches; the Renaissance *Palazzo dei Camerlenghi;* the *Fabbriche Vecchie di Rialto* by Scarpagnino; the *Fabbriche Nuove di Rialto* by Sansovino; the *Palazzo Corner della Regina*, a classical structure by D. Rossi (1678-1742); the *Palazzo Pesaro*, a Baroque work by Longhena; the *Palazzo Belloni Battagià* by Longhena; the *Deposito del Megio*, a 15th cent. battlemented construction, once used as a granary; the Venetian-Byzantine *Fondaco dei Turchi*, completely rebuilt in the 19th cent. On the right: the Gothic *Palazzo Giustinian;* the Gothic *Palazzo Contarin-Fasan;* the *Palazzo Corner*, a work by Sansovino, with a three-ordered facade; the *Palazzo Giustinian Lolin*, built in the 17th cent. by Longhena; the *Palazzo Grassi*, in the Baroque style; the Renaissance *Palazzo Contarin delle Figure;* the *Palazzo Mocenigo*, which consists of four buildings of the 16-18th cent.; the *Palazzo Corner-Spinelli*, a masterpiece by M.

Venice, St. Mark's, the Crafts, detail.   *Venice, St. Mark's, the Month of February.*

Venice, Galleria dell'Accademia. Gentile Bellini, Procession of the Relic of the Cross in St. Mark's Square, detail.
Venice, Galleria dell'Accademia. Gentile Bellini, Miracle of the Cross in St. Lawrence's Canal.

Venice, Galleria dell' Accademia. Vittore Carpaccio, Arrival of the English Ambassadors, detail of the Legend of St. Ursula cycle.

Venice, Doge's Palace.
Venice, Ca' d'Oro.

Venice, Doge's Palace, courtyard.
Venice, Doge's Palace. Vittore Carpaccio, The Lion of St. Mark.

Coducci (1440-1504); the *Palazzo Grimani*, a masterpiece by Sanmicheli (1484-1559); the *Palazzo Farsetti*, a typical Venetian-Byzantine construction of the period 1100-1200; the Renaissance *Palazzo Manin* by I. Sansovino; the *Fondaco dei Tedeschi* by Scarpagnino; the *Ca' del Mosto*, a Venetian-Byzantine construction; the *Ca' d'Oro*, a masterpiece of the 15th cent. by B. Bon and M. Raverti (active in the first half of the 15th cent.), faced with marble of different colours, with two loggias characterized by interlacing arches; the *Palazzo Vendramin Calergi*, designed by M. Coducci and completed by the Lombardo in a beautiful Renaissance style; the *Palazzo Correr Contarini*, a construction of the 17th cent. Moreover, there are another two bridges of recent construction over the Grand Canal, the Ponte dell'Accademia and the Ponte degli Scalzi. The church of *San Moisè*, an example of the Venetian Baroque style, is near the church of *Santa Maria di Zobenigo*, another lavish, flamboyant Baroque construction, containing works by Tintoretto and Rubens (1577-1640). The church of *Santo Stefano*, built in the 14-15th cent., has a very beautiful decorated Gothic portal; it contains paintings by Bartolomeo Vivarini (1432-1499), Tintoretto, and others. Near this church, in the Campo Pisani, is the *Palazzo Pisani*, built in the 16-18th cent. Crossing the Ponte dell'Accademia, one comes to the *Galleria dell'Accademia*, which is housed in a 15th cent. convent, and which contains the largest collection of Venetian art from the period 1400-1700. The *Museo del Settecento*, wich is housed in the Palazzo Rezzonico, besides its collection of objects and documents illustrating the history of Venice, contains works by Venetian painters such as Alessandro Longhi (1733-1812), Canaletto (1697-1768), F. Guardi (1712-1793), and frescoes by

Venice, Campo SS. Giovanni e Paolo. Monument to Colleoni.

D. Tiepolo (1720/27-1804). In the *Scuola dei Carmini* are works by G. B. Tiepolo (1696-1770); the Gothic *Chiesa dei Carmini* has a Renaissance facade. The 16th cent. church of *San Sebastiano* is famous tor its paintings by Veronese, which include scenes from the life of Queen Esther and the Martyrdom of St. Sebastian. The church of *San Trovaso* dates from the 16th cent. The 18th cent. *church of the Jesuits* has works by Piazzetta (1683-1754) and Tiepolo. The church of *Santa Maria della Salute* is an extremely beautiful example of Baroque architecture by Longhena. It has an octagonal ground-plan, an imposing stair-case, and a very large dome; it contains works by Titian and Tintoretto. The *Mercerie* connect Piazza San Marco with the Rialto. Along one of these streets is the church of *San Salvatore*, which contains the tomb of Sansovino and Titian's Annunciation. The church of *Santa Maria Mater Domini*, which rises in the very characteristic *campo* (square) of the same name, is attributed to Sansovino. The 12th cent. church of *San Giacomo dell'Orio* is divided into a nave and two

Venice, Santa Maria della Salute.

Venice, Galleria dell'Accademia. Giorgione, The Tempest, detail.

Venice, Doge's Palace. Paolo Veronese, The Triumph of Venice, detail.

Venice, Doge's Palace. Giambattista Tiepolo, Neptune offering Gifts to Venice, detail.

Venice, Doge's Palace. Paolo Veronese, Juno offering Gifts to Venice, detail.

aisles, and has a beautiful hull-shaped wooden ceiling; in the sacristy is an altarpiece and paintings by Veronese, and in the old sacristy are paintings by Palma the Younger (1544-1628). The *School of San Giovanni Evangelista* was designed by P. Lombardo; it contains a Gothic church, and a school with a most beautiful staircase by M. Coducci. The church of *Santa Maria Gloriosa dei Frari* was erected by the Franciscans in the monumental Gothic style of the 14-15th cent. It has a very beautiful, lively apse, and is decorated with richly ornamented doorways. The interior is divided into a nave and two aisles, and there are a great number of paintings, statues, and tombs of Doges. The *School of San Rocco* has a facade by Scarpagnino and its rooms are decorated with very important works by Tintoretto, depicting scenes from the Old and New Testament. The church of *San Rocco*, rebuilt in the 18th cent., contains works by Tintoretto. The church of *Santa Maria Formosa*, which stands in the characteristic little square of the same name surrounded by interesting buildings, is the work of Coducci; it contains a triptych by B. Vivarini and a polyptych by Palma the Elder (1480-1528). In the *Pinacoteca Querini Stampalia* is a collection of Venetian art from the 14-18th cent. In the *Campo di San Zanipolo*, a square of monumental dimensions, is the *Colleoni Monument*, an equestrian statue by Verrocchio (1436-1488). Facing the square is the church of San Zanipolo, or Giovanni e Paolo, and the *School of San Marco*, now the Civic Hospital. The marble facade of the latter is the work of P. Lombardo, while the curved pediments are to be attributed to M. Coducci. The Gothic church of *San Zanipolo* was erected by the Dominicans in the 13-15th cent.; the Gothic-Renaissance portal is by B. Bon; the interior is divided into a nave and two aisles, and houses a valuable collection of paintings by G. B. Piazzetta, G. Bellini, Lotto, Vivarini, Veronese, tombs of Doges, and objects connected with

the life of the city. The church of *Santa Maria dei Miracoli*, an early Renaissance masterpiece, is the work of P. Lombardo, and completely faced with marble of different colours; it contains paintings by P. M. Pennacchi (1464-1516). *San Giovanni Crisostomo* is the work of Coducci. The church of the *Santi Apostoli*, with the Corner Chapel, is attributed to Coducci. The *Galleria Franchetti* is housed in the Cà' d'Oro, and has a collection of paintings, sculpture, furniture, and miscellaneous objects; the paintings are mainly by Venetian artists, while the sculpture includes busts by T. Lombardo, by Vittoria, and small bronzes by Bernini. The Gothic church of *San Zaccaria* was completely altered by Coducci; it has a multi-storeyed facade faced with marble. The interior consists of a nave and two aisles, together with a Gothic apse and side chapels, and contains a Madonna with Saints by G. Bellini, paintings by Tintoretto, and a chapel with valuable frescoes by A. del Castagno (1420-1457). The *School of San Giorgio degli Schiavoni* is famous for its series of paintings by Carpaccio (c. 1465-1526), depicting scenes from the lives of St. George, St. Jerome, and St. Tryphon. The church of *San Giovanni in Bragora*, rebuilt in the 15th cent., contains valuable works of art, such as a Resurrection by Alvise Vivarini. The 12th cent. *Arsenal*, formerly the shipyard of the Republic, was enlarged and rebuilt; it is surrounded by crenellated walls, in which there is a great Renaissance gateway. The 18th cent. church of *Santa Maria della Pietà* rises on the Riva degli Schiavoni, and contains works by Tiepolo. *San Giorgio Maggiore* is built on the island facing St. Mark's. It is now the seat of the Cini Foundation, and though a masterpiece of Palladio's, was completed by Scamozzi. It has a classical facade with a pediment supported by columns. It contains two of Tintoretto's masterpieces, the Last Supper and the Shower of Manna, as well as works by Carpaccio and others. The *Redentore* on the island of the

Venice, Galleria dell' Accademia. Paolo Veronese, Banquet at the House of Levi.

Murano, San Donato, apse.
Torcello, Basilica of Santa Maria Assunta, interior.

Venice, Doge's Palace. Paolo Veronese, The Doge Sebastiano Venier giving thanks to the Virgin, detail.

Venice, Doge's Palace. Titian, The Doge Grimani
worshipping the Faith, detail.

Venice, Doge's Palace. Tintoretto, Ariadne, Venus
and Bacchus, detail.

Venice, Doge's Palace. Tintoretto, The Doge
Gerolamo Priuli, detail.

Giudecca, is also by Palladio. The *Chiesa degli Scalzi*, a Baroque work of Longhena's, has a chapel decorated with frescoes by Tiepolo. The 15th cent. church of *San Giobbe* has a doorway by P. Lombardo. The typically Venetian Gothic church of the *Madonna dell'Orto* has paintings by Tintoretto and Bellini. *San Francesco della Vigna* was designed by Sansovino, and contains many works of art. The Modern Art Gallery (*Galleria d'arte Moderna*) is housed in the Palazzo Pesaro; it contains works by Venetian artists from the 19th cent. to the present day, as well as an international art section. The *Peggy Guggenheim Collection* has many works of art from 1910 to the present day. The church of *San Stae*, which looks on to the Grand Canal, is a Baroque construction. Excursions: *MURANO*, famous centre of the Venetian glass industry, spread over five islets. The 12th cent. church of *Santi Maria e Donato* is in the Byzantine Romanesque style; it contains an excellent mosaic pavement. The 15th cent. church of *San Pietro Martire* contains works by G. Bellini, Tintoretto, and Veronese. *BURANO*, a fishing suburb, famous for its lace industry. The *Palazzo del Podestà* is a Gothic construction. *San Martino* was built in the 16th cent., and its facade has no doorway. *TORCELLO* was a rich, important island in the past, but is now almost deserted. The 7th cent. *Cattedrale* was rebuilt in the 11th with a bell-tower; the interior is divided into a nave and two aisles, and contains 12th cent. mosaics. The 11th cent. church of *Santa Fosca* has a central ground-plan, a portico, and an apse with two arches; the interior is in the form of a Greek cross. In the right side of the church is a bas-relief dated 1407. The *Museo Provinciale* contains a lot of excavated material, and a panel attributed to Veronese.

** **VENOSA** (Potenza). One of the most attractive little towns in Basilicata, situated between two valleys. The *Abbazia della Trinità* is one of the most characteristic monuments in southern Italy. It was built towards the middle of the 11th cent. on the site of an early Christian church, which had been built in its turn on the ruins of a pagan temple. It consists practically of two churches, the second being the continuation of the first. The facade has a harmonious 13th cent. doorway. The three apses at the bottom end of the church are stylishly modelled. Inside, there are important frescoes from various periods, the so-called pillar of friendship, and the tomb of Alberada, the only one in the area that has survived intact. The *Cattedrale*, consecrated to St. Andrew the Apostle, was built in the 15-16th cent., and has a facade with a single doorway, the work of Cola da Conza (lived in the 16th cent.). One reaches the Chapel of the Blessed Sacrament after passing under a majestic arch, erected in the first half of the 16th cent. Worth visiting are the *Catacombe Ebraiche* (Jewish

Catacombs), discovered in 1853, the ruins of the *Roman Amphitheatre*, the 15th cent. four-square *Castello*, and the *Chiesa del Purgatorio*, which has an interesting campanile and a painting of St. Philip Neri and the Madonna by Carlo Maratta (1625-1713). Walk to the *Tomb of Marcus Claudius Marcellus*, who died in 208 B.C.

* **VENTIMIGLIA** (Imperia). Cut in half by the river Roja. In the 11th cent. Romanesque *Cattedrale dell'Assunta* is a famous panel by Barnaba da Modena (lived in the second half of the 14th cent.), depicting the Madonna and Child. The *Civico Museo Archeologico* has a rich collection of objects found in the necropolis nearby. Particularly fine is the glass "patera" (dish) decorated with a Triton and the silver travel-set, the only one to have survived from antiquity. It is worth walking to the *Roman Theatre*, and to the archaeological area (*Zona Archeologica*).

* **VENZONE** (Udine). On the left bank of the Tagliamento, surrounded by mountains, with medieval houses and narrow streets. The Gothic *Duomo*, dedicated to St. Andrew the Apostle, is the finest work of Giovanni Griglio (lived in the 13-14th cent.). The sober facade has some interesting decorations. The church contains a baptismal font by Bernardino da Bissone (active in the early 16th cent.), and a Presentation in the Temple by Giulio Quaglia (1668-1751). The *Palazzo Comunale* was built in the Gothic style in the 14-15th cent., with an outer staircase leading to the upper floor. It contains an amusing, anonymous late 13th, or early 14th cent. fresco, depicting a fight on horse-back. Also interesting is the so-called *Rotonda*, which contains twenty-two mummies.

Venosa, Abbey of the Trinity, holy-water stoup.

** **VERCELLI.** Situated in the Po valley, on the right bank of the Sesia. The *Basilica di Sant'Andrea* is an example of early-13th cent. Cistercian Gothic architecture. The exterior is enlivened by the red bricks and the green of some of the stones, which produce unusual colour effects. The facade has three large, deeply moulded portals, and in the lunettes sculptures by Antelami (c. 1150-c. 1230). Flanking the facade are two, high, cusped bell-towers, with mullioned windows. The dome is tapered, and has unusual pendentives. On the left side of the church are the remnants of an abbey built in 1219, of which the cloister, chapter room and sacristy have survived. The *Cattedrale di Sant'Eusebio*, Bishop of Vercelli, 283-371), is an imposing building, which was begun by Pellegrino Tibaldi in 1572. The classical-looking facade has a large pronaos. Notice the remarkable huge statues of the twelve apostles. The 12th cent. Romanesque campanile is a sturdy, characteristic construction. The interior is characterized by movement, and contains many works of art, including numerous tombs of famous people. In the Cathedral Treasury are reliquaries, jewellery, ecclesiastical vestments and very valuable codexes. The *Museo Leone* is housed in the *Casa degli Alciati*, which dates from the 15-16th cent. It has a collection of objects illustrating the history of the district around the city, as well as that of the city itself, from pre-historic times to modern. The pavement mosaics, which may date from 1040, and the pieces of Roman marble are particularly interesting. The museum takes its name from its founder, the notary Camillo Leone (1830-1907). The *Museo Civico Francesco Borgogna* was founded by a lawyer, Antonio Borgogna (1822-1906), and its art gallery is considered the most important in Piedmont after the Galleria Sabauda in Turin. It contains works by all the major artists from Piedmont and the district around Vercelli and others by some of the most famous names in Italian art, especially from the 15th and 16th centuries. Vercelli has many monuments and is particularly rich in medieval works of art; it has a great number of archaeological, historical, and art collections.

* **VEROLANUOVA** (Brescia). The 17th cent. *Prepositurale di San Lorenzo* has two small bell-towers and a high dome. It contains two great paintings by Giambattista Tiepolo (1696-1770), the Shower of Manna and the Sacrifice of Melchizedek, a Nativity by Andrea Celesti (1637-1712) and other works of art. The *Chiesa della Disciplina* was built in the 15-16th cent., and contains the tomb of Nicolò Gambara, a condottiere who died in 1592. The *Palazzo Gambara* is 18th cent.

** **VEROLI** (Frosinone). On the southern slopes of the Monti Ernici, with important historical, especially medieval remains. The originally Romanesque *Cattedrale*, dedicated to St. Andrew the Apostle, has a facade of tra-

Vercelli, Sant'Andrea, lunette by Antelami.

vertine marble; it contains two fine paintings by Thaddeus Kuntz (c. 1731-1793), the Disciples of John the Baptist and the Martyrdom of St. Bartholomew. The church of *Santa Maria Salomè* was built for the first time in the early 13th cent., though the tripartite facade dates from the first half of the 18th. It has some fine paintings, such as a Madonna by Giuseppe Cesari, called Cavalier d'Arpino (1568-1640), a Dead Christ by Francesco Trevisani (1656-1746), and a S. Francesca Romana by Giacinto Brandi (1623-1691). The Romanesque church of *Sant'Erasmo* was built on the site of a monastery founded by St. Benedict, and retains the portico, the apses, and the bell-tower of the original construction. Many ruins have survived of the *Castello di San Leucio*. In the surrounding countryside may be seen remains of cyclopean walls (*Mura Ciclopiche*) where the acropolis of the ancient city of Aletrium once stood. From Veroli one can easily reach the important *Abbazia di Casamari*. Built in the Cistercian Gothic style, it forms a monumental group of buildings, which grew up in the late 11th cent., thanks to the initiative of some monks who had embraced the Benedictine rule. The basilica was consecrated in 1217 by Pope Honorius III, and flourished up to the early 15th cent., when it began a long period of decline. One passes through the abbot's house into the garden; this is laid out in front of the church and the main core of the monastery. The construction of the church was begun in 1203. It has a much-admired, deeply moulded central portal. The mystical interior is in the form of an Egyptian cross, and presents some interesting architectural contrasts, the predominant style being Gothic. The monastery has a museum, which contains material from the Stone, Bronze, and Iron Ages, findings from Cereatae Marianae (the town upon whose ruins the abbey is supposed to be built), as well as important paintings such as a St. Lawrence giving the possessions of the Church to the Poor, and a St. Lawrence Martyr, both by Giovanni Serodine (c. 1594-1631), a St. Ambrose by Giovanni Francesco Barbieri, called Guercino (1591-1666), a Madonna and Child with St. John the Baptist, perhaps by Raphael or one of his school (1483-1520), a Guardian Angel by Antiveduto Grammatica (c. 1571-1626), and a Madonna and Child by Francesco Solimena 1657-1747). From the museum one passes to the square cloister, with its beautifully harmonious arcade, and then to the Chapter house, which is connected to the refectory; the latter is divided into two aisles by cilindrical pillars. Excursion to *Prato Campoli*, where the fountains date from 1751.

*** **VERONA.** A very important agricultural and commercial city situated on the banks of the Adige, with many Roman and Renaissance

Verona, San Zeno.

monuments. The *Arena* occupies the eastern side of the characteristic Piazza Brà and is an important Roman amphitheatre of the 1st cent. Only four arches and three storeys of the outer arcade have survived, whereas the second is intact. The floor of the arena is a vast, elliptical space. In the centre of *Piazza delle Erbe*, which was rebuilt on the site of the ancient Roman forum, is the Colonna del Mercato; there is also a marble shrine dated 1500. Looking on to the square is the *Casa dei Mercanti*, a 14th cent. building with mullioned windows, the 17th cent. *Palazzo Maffei*, the *Torre del Gardello* and the *Torre Lamberti*. The *Piazza dei Signori* is surrounded by monumental buildings: the 12th cent. *Palazzo del Comune* or *della Ragione* has beautiful mullioned windows; the *Palazzo del Consiglio* has a doorway by Sanmicheli (1484-1559); the *Loggia del Consiglio* is a Venetian Renaissance structure, its facade consisting of a portico and a series of polychrome-faced windows. *Santa Maria Antica* is a small 12th cent. Romanesque church. The *Arche Scaligere* are tombs railed off in the form of chapels, and decorated with Gothic canopies. The church of *Santa Anastasia* was built by the Dominicans from the 13th to the 15th cent. The facade has a beautiful 14th cent. double door. The interior is divided by cylindrical pillars into a nave and two aisles and has an altar by Sanmicheli, a fresco by Altichiero (1320-1395), a fresco depicting St. George and the Dragon by Antonio Pisano, called Pisanello (1377-1458) and other Gothic panels. The church of *San Giorgetto* is near the Castelbarco Tomb, which is also Gothic.

The 12th cent. *Duomo* is preceded by a porch and flanked by a bell-tower, the work of Sanmicheli; it contains various works of art, including an Assumption by Titian (1477-1576). Of the medieval *Porta dei Borsari*, two archways surmounted by a pediment have survived. The *Palazzo Bevilacqua* and the *Palazzo Canossa* are both by Sanmicheli. The *Castelvecchio* was erected in 1354-1357 by Cangrande della Scala. Built in the form of a fortress, a keep was added to it a few years later. This brick construction consists of two parts: a rectangular part encompasses a courtyard, which was the parade ground, while another constituted the lord's residence, and is encircled by a double ring of walls. The castle houses the Civic Museum, which contains valuable works of the Venetian, and particularly Veronese school, from the 14th to the 18th cent. The three-arched *Ponte Scaligero* was reconstructed in its original form after the last war. The church of *San Zeno Maggiore* is one of the finest examples of Romanesque architecture. Begun in the 5th cent., it was rebuilt in the 12-13th cent. The facade has a large rose-window and a porch and is decorated with reliefs by Master Nicolò and a bronze door. The interior is divided into a nave and two aisles and has a raised sanctuary and a wooden ceiling; it contains a very beautiful triptych by Mantegna (1431-1506) and fine choir. The church of *San Bernardino* is built in the Gothic-Renaissance style: the facade has a beautiful Lombardesque portico and is preceded by a cloister; inside, there are paintings and a stylish chapel by Sanmicheli. In the church's convent (*Convento*) is

Verona, Museo Castelvecchio. Equestrian statue of Can Grande.

the Sala Morone decorated with frescoes by Domenico Morone (1422-1517) and his school. The *Porta Palio* was designed by Sanmicheli in a somewhat classical manner. Juliet's tomb (*Tomba di Giulietta*) is in the crypt of what was once a Romanesque church, with a beautiful adjoining cloister. The church of *San Fermo Maggiore* consists of two super-imposed buildings of the 12th and 13th centuries. The interior consists of an aisleless nave with a wooden ceiling, and contains a Crucifixion in the style of Altichiero, an altarpiece by Romanino (1485-1566), and a fresco by Pisanello. Only the lower part of the 12th cent. Gothic church of *Santa Maria in Organo* was faced with marble by Sanmicheli; the interior is richly decorated with frescoes by N. Giolfino (1476-1555), F. Caroto (1480-1546) and Domenico Ricci, called Brusasorci (1546-1605). Parts of the stage and auditorium of the 1st cent. *Roman Theatre* have survived. The *Museo Archeologico* has Etruscan, Greek and Roman bronzes and a rich collection of vases. The 6th cent. church of *Santo Stefano* was rebuilt in the 12th. The 16th cent. church of *San Giorgio in Braida* has a 17th cent. facade; the interior consists of an aisleless nave, and there are paintings by Tintoretto (1518-1594) and Veronese (1528-1588). Sanmicheli's *Porta di San Giorgio* has three archways. The *Palazzo Pompei* is another of Sanmicheli's masterpieces. The Gothic church of *Santi Nazaro e Celso* contains Venetian paintings of the Renaissance. *San Giovanni in Valle* is Romanesque.

* **VERRES** (Aosta) At the entrance to the Valle di Challant. The *Collegiata di S. Egidio* (1512) has a convent annexed to it. The architecture is Gothic, with pointed arches and cross-shaped windows. The village is overlooked by the *Castello di Verres*, a solid, square building erected in 1391 by Ibleto di Challant, and used as a fortress as well as a place of residence. The salons have monumental fireplaces and, in the courtyard, there is a wide external stairway linking the floors.

* **VERRONE** (Vercelli). The *Castello* is one of the most interesting in Piedmont, and consists of a group of buildings which enable one to understand how fortified residences were built in the plain. The Romanesque parish church of *San Lorenzo* is also interesting.

* **VETRALLA** (Viterbo). Large town with a medieval centre, situated on a plateau between two water-courses. The *Duomo*, built in the first half of the 18th cent., has a huge interior with an aisleless nave and Baroque decorations. One should notice the Immaculate Conception and St. Hippolytus by Domenico Maria Muratori (1661-1744), the Madonna of the Rosary, probably by Ludovico Mazzanti (c. 1679-1775), the painting of the Martyrdom of St. Andrew in the apse, also by Muratori, Saints John the Baptist, Gregory the Great, Lucy and

Mary Magdalen by Giacomo Triga (recorded 1710-1746), the Transfiguration by Marco Benefial (1648-1764) and, finally, a 12th cent. panel depicting the Madonna and Angels on one side and the Head of Christ on the other. The 11th cent. church of *San Francesco* is a successful Romanesque construction, with a sober facade and arcadings along its left side. The austere, basilican interior has damaged frescoes of the 15th, early 17th and 18th centuries. In the sanctuary is the tomb of Briobris, carried out in the early 15th cent. by Paolo da Gualdo Cattaneo, called Paolo Romano. The church of *Santi Filippo e Giacomo* contains a fresco of the Viterbo school, which dates from the late 15th or early 16th cent. and a fine tabernacle for the Holy Oil. Excursion to the prevalently rock-hewn *Etruscan Necropolis of Norchia*, which dates from the 5th-3rd cent. B.C.

** **VEZZOLANO** (Abbazia di Santa Maria di) (Town of Albugnano, province of Asti). It is considered one of the most important monuments in the region, and according to non-proven tradition, was built by Charlemagne. In the Middle Ages, when it housed the Augustinian Canons, it was a rich and active cultural centre. Information regarding the *Chiesa* goes back to 1095, and it is known that it was completed in 1189. The Romanesque facade is quite superb and has three blind arcadings. In the pulvins of the arch over the main portal are the symbols of the Evangelists Luke and Mark. The interior is in the early Gothic style, with traces of ultramontane influence, and contains interesting works of art, some from the 11th and 12th centuries. Worth noticing is the Gothic tabernacle and the terracotta triptych (c. 1430) depicting the Madonna and Child with a monk presenting Charlemagne to St. Augustine. On the jambs

of the central window in the main apse are two Romanesque reliefs depicting the Archangel Gabriel and the Virgin.

* **VIBOLDONE**, Abbey of, see Milan.

* **VIBO VALENTIA** (Catanzaro). Situated on a hill-side, with straight streets. The *Collegiata*, dedicated to S. Leone Luca, the town's patron

Vezzolano, Abbey.

saint, was rebuilt after an earthquake in the late 17th or early 18th cent., to a design by Francesco Antonio Curatoli (1670-1722). It has some works of art, including marble statues by Antonio Gagini (active 1541-1575) and Giacomo Gagini (1517-1598) and a marble group of the Madonna della Neve by Girolamo da Santacroce (1502-1537). The *Chiesa del Rosario* was rebuilt in the 18th cent., and contains the fine, Angevin-style Crispo Chapel. The 17th cent. *Chiesa degli Angeli* contains a painting of the Immaculate Conception, probably by Luca Giordano (1632-1705) and a wardrobe carved between 1663 and 1666 by Francesco Domenico di Gennaro. Trip to the *Ruins of Hipponion*, which, as far as is known, was the town's oldest name.

*** **VICENZA.** Situated in the plain, beneath the northern foothills of the Monti Berici, on both sides of the Bacchiglione, at its confluence with the Retrone. The *Basilica* or *Palazzo della Ragione*, Palladio's masterpiece, is the city's most important monument. The great architect took the already existing Gothic Palace of Domenico da Venezia (active towards the middle of the 15th cent.), and added on to it two superimposed storeys of open classical colonnades, insisting on the Serlian motif, or Venetian (Palladian) window. The twenty-three statues are by Giovanni Antonio Grazioli (lived in the 16-17th cent.), Agostino Rubini (active 1584-1595), Giovanni Battista Albanese (1573-1630), Francesco Albanese (recorded 1567-1611), and Bartolomeo Muzzini (active in the 16-17th cent.). The very tall, slender, 12th cent. *Torre di Piazza* has a niche above a mock doorway, with statues of the Madonna Crowned in glory and Saints Stephen and Lawrence, by Giovanni Battista Albanese. The *Loggia del Capitaniato* or *Loggia Bernarda* is a powerful expression of Palladio's art, frescoed by Titian (1477-1576) and Paris Bordone (1500-1571). The lower part of the *Monte di Pietà* is 15th cent., the upper 16th; its exterior was once decorated with frescoes (now destroyed) by Giovan Battista Zelotti (1526-1578). The 15th cent. church of *Santa Maria dei Servi*, begun by Giampiero Cermison in the Romanesque-Gothic style, has an aristocratic Renaissance portal, carried out in 1531 by Giovanni da Pedemuro (1495-1550) and Girolamo Pittoni (1504-c. 1550). It contains an altarpiece depicting the Madonna enthroned with Saints Sebastian and Roch by Benedetto Montagna (c. 1481-1558). In the *Casa Pigafetta*, which dates from the second half of the 15th cent., there is a typical blending of Gothic and Renaissance forms. *Corso Palladio* is the city's most important street, and is lined with fine palaces and beautiful churches. The *Palazzo del Comune*, formerly *Trissino*, is a masterpiece by Vincenzo Scamozzi (1552-1616); inside is the Town Council Hall and the Marriage Hall, with stuccoes by Giovanni Battista Barbarini

(lived in the 17th cent.) and frescoes by Louis Dorigny (lived in the 18th cent.). The *Porta Castello*, the remains of an 11th cent. city gateway, is dominated by a big Scaliger tower, the remains of a castle. The *Basilica dei Santi Felice e Fortunato*, perhaps of Constantinian origin, has been destroyed, rebuilt, and altered many times in the course of time. The interior is divided into a nave and two aisles, and contains two paintings representing the Massacre of five Innocents by Giulio Carpioni (1611-1674), a Madonna by Antonino di Nicolò da Venezia (recorded 1429-1458), and other works of art. The *Duomo* is of early Christian origin, but was remodelled later; the Gothic facade is by Domenico da Venezia. Inside the Gothic interior is a huge polyptych of the Death of the Virgin, the Crucifixion, Apostles, Evangelists and Saints by Lorenzo Veneziano (recorded 1356-1372). The high altar, richly decorated with marble, is the work of Giovanni da Pedemuro and Girolamo Pittoni. The church of *Santa Chiara*, or *San Bernardino*, dates from 1451, but apart from the Renaissance portal, is still predominantly Gothic; it contains paintings by Giulio Carpioni and Alessandro Maganza (c. 1556-1640). The *Oratorio di San Nicolò da Tolentino* was built in the early 16th cent. and remodelled in the first half of the 17th: its facade is by Carlo Butiron (active in the second half of the 17th cent.), and inside is a vigorous painting of the Trinity by Francesco Maffei (1600-1660). The 15th cent. *Palazzo da Schio*, also known as the Ca' d'Oro, is a masterpiece of Gothic architecture. The 13th cent. church of *Santa Corona* has a gabled facade. Its Romanesque-inspired interior has many interesting features, such as the Renaissance chancel by Lorenzo da Bologna (active 1479-1489), the Rosary Chapel by Giovanni Battista Albanese, the Barbaran Chapel by Lorenzo da Bologna, and the Thiene Chapel. In the left aisle is the altar of St. John the Baptist, with the Baptism of Christ, one of the finest masterpieces of Giovanni Bellini (c. 1430-1516). To the left of the chancel is the Chapel of the Holy Thorn, where a relic from the crown of thorns is kept in a precious Gothic reliquary; on one of the walls is a painting of the Adoration of the Magi by Paolo Caliari, called Veronese (1528-1588). The facade of Palladio's house (*Casa del Palladio*) may have been designed by the architect himself. The *Palazzo Chiericati* is by Palladio: it houses a civic museum, which has a rich collection of pre-historic and Longobard objects, and an art gallery, whose most precious works include a Crucifixion by Hans Memling (c. 1440-1494), a Madonna and Child enthroned with Saints by Bartolomeo Montagna (c. 1450-1523), a Lamentation over the dead Christ by Giovanni Buonconsiglio, called Marescalco (c. 1470-1537), a Madonna and Child with Saints by Paolo Veronese, St. Augustine healing the Plague-stricken by Jacopo Ro-

Vicenza, La Rotunda.
Vicenza, Olympic Theatre, interior.

busti, called Tintoretto (1518-1594), the Three Ages of Man by Anthony van Dyck (1599-1641), the Immaculate Conception by Giovan Battista Tiepolo (1696-1770), St. Francis receiving the Stigmata by Giovan Battista Piazzetta (1682-1754), and Time revealing Truth by Giovan Battista Tiepolo. The *Teatro Olimpico*, Andrea Palladio's last work, was completed in 1584 by Vincenzo Scamozzi. The late-Gothic church of *San Pietro* was remodelled in the 15th cent., and contains some notable paintings, including an Adoration of the Shepherds by Francesco Maffei. The facade of the 14th cent. church of *San Giuliano* has four Corinthian pilasters; the church contains works of art, including the statues of the Redeemer and four Saints on the high altar by Orazio Marinali (1643-1720). Other interesting buildings include the *Palazzo Valmarana*, now *Braga*, by Andrea Palladio; the church of *San Lorenzo*, built in the second half of the 13th cent., which has an imposing moulded portal, and an altar by the Poianas, an elaborate 16th cent. work; the church of *San Rocco*, perhaps designed by Lorenzo da Bologna; the church of *Santa Maria del Carmine* (1373); the 15th cent. church of *San Marco degli Scalzi*, remodelled in the first half of the 18th; the *Palazzo Iseppo da Porto*, now *Festa*, begun in 1552 by Andrea Palladio; the church of *Santo Stefano*, rebuilt between the 17th and 18th centuries, which contains a Madonna and Child enthroned with Saints George, Lucy and angel musician by Jacopo Palma the Elder (c. 1480-1528), and the *Palazzo Thiene*, perhaps the work of Lorenzo da Bologna. In the immediate neighbourhood is the famous *Basilica di Monte Berico*, which one reaches by climbing an avenue, lined by horse-chestnut trees on one side and by a colonnade of a hundred and fifty arches on the other, which symbolise the beads of the rosary. Inside the church is a Pietà, Bartolomeo Montagna's masterpiece, and in the refectory a painting of the Supper of St. Gregory the Great by Veronese. The *Villa Valmarana* was built in the second half of the 17th cent., and contains valuable frescoes by Giovan Battista Tiepolo and his son, Gian Domenico Tiepolo (1727-1804). The *Rotonda* is one of Andrea Palladio's most admired works and has been the model for many villas.

* VICOFORTE DI MONDOVÌ, Sanctuary, see Mondovì.

* VIESTE (Foggia).

The easternmost town of the Gargano; the inhabited part forms an ancient, picturesque, fortified centre. The *Cattedrale*, dedicated to Santa Maria Oreta, was built in very ancient times, perhaps on the ruins of a pagan temple, but has since been remodelled several times; it is flanked by a Baroque bell-tower. It contains a 16th cent., painted wood statue of Santa Maria Oreta, a marble bas-relief of the Deposition from the Neapolitan school of the same century and a panel of the Madonna and Child with Saints, signed by Michele Manchellis in 1581. The *Castello*, built in the second half of the 13th cent. by Frederick II, and completely remodelled in the 16th and 17th centuries, rises out of the living rock of a promontory. Its battlements command a fine view of the archipelago of the Tremiti islands.

* VIETRI SUL MARE (Salerno).

Situated in a magnificent position, where the coast of Amalfi begins, and with an expanse of luxuriant vegetation behind it. The parish church of *San Giovanni Battista* was built in 1732, and its dome is composed of maiolica tiles; it contains a 16th cent. polyptych of the Madonna and Child with Saints John and Andrew. The *Torre Crestarella*, overlooking the sea, once served as a fortification. Walk to the *Grotte di San Cesareo*, deep erosions, in one of which are the remains of a little church erected near the cave where the saint lived.

** VIGEVANO (Pavia).

An industrial town, with important Renaissance buildings. The *Duomo*, dedicated to St. Ambrose, was built on the site of a previous edifice to a design by Antonio da Lonate (active in the first half of the 16th cent.). It is flanked by a grandiose campanile, and contains important works of art, including a fresco of the Glory of St. Ambrose by Vitale Sala (1803-1835), the Baptism of Christ by Ferdinando Porta (1689-1767), Christ, the Madonna and St. John the Baptist by Bernardino Gatti, called Solaro (c. 1495-1575), as well as the Cathedral Treasury

Vigevano, Piazza Ducale.
Vigevano, Piazza Ducale.

Verona, Museo Castelvecchio. Gerolamo dai Libri, Nativity, detail.

Verona, San Zeno. Door panel (Stefano Lagerino, King enthroned and Stories of the Burning Furnace).

Vicenza, Villa Valmarana. Gian Domenico Tiepolo, "The New World", detail.
Volterra, Duomo. Deposition.

Museum, with its numerous sacred vases, gold and silver objects, and tapestries. The *Piazza Ducale* was laid out according to the wishes of Ludovico il Moro, and may have been designed by Leonardo da Vinci (1452-1519). It is dominated by the grandiose Castle Tower, which was designed by Donato Bramante (1444-1514). The *Castello Sforzesco*, built in the 14th and 15th centuries, and completed by Lodovico il Moro, also required the collaboration of Bramante. There are various buildings inside, such as the Falconiera (falcon-house), the Keep or Ducal Palace, and the Palazzo delle Dame (Ladies' Palace). The *Museo Civico* has an archaeological section with prehistoric material, and an art gallery, with works by local painters. The church of *San Pietro Martire* (1363) was designed by Bartolino da Novara in the Gothic style, and contains a few works of art. The church of *Santa Maria del Popolo* was designed by Giovanni Ruggeri (lived in the 17-18th centuries); it contains paintings of the Marriage of the Virgin and the Presentation in the Temple by Federico Bianchi (1590-1650).

* **VIGNANELLO** (Viterbo). Built on tufa rock, its houses and streets are typical of the region of Latium. The *Castello Ruspoli*, formerly Marescotti, is a sturdy, grey stone building which dominates the town; the fosse that encircles it was completely reconstructed in the second half of the 16th cent. In the huge, aisleless interior of the *Collegiata di Santa Maria*, which dates from the early 18th cent., is a Madonna and Child, probably by Annibale Carracci (1560-1609), and a much-admired Baroque organ. In the church of *San Sebastiano* is a damaged painting of the Coronation of Mary by Cristoforo Roncalli, called Pomarancio (c. 1570-1630).

* **VIGNOLA** (Modena). An important town for market garden products, situated on the left side of the Panaro. In the parish church, (*Parrocchiale*), rebuilt in 1687, and completed in the last century, a Martyrdom of Saints Nazarius and Celsus by Adeodato Malatesta (1806-1709), and a Madonna with Saints by Francesco Stringa (1635-1709). The *Rocca* is a grandiose, towered construction, built in the 14-15th centuries; it contains many 15th cent. decorations, as well as frescoes, mainly from the same century.

* **VIGO DI CADORE** (Belluno). A summer holiday resort, situated in a pleasant position. The little church of *Sant'Orsola* was built in 1344-1345, and contains 14th and 15th cent. frescoes. In the parish church of *San Martino* (1559), a Sacred Family with Saints Roch and Sebastian, Christ driving the merchants from the Temple, and Jesus among Children, works by Tommaso Da Rin (1838-1922). In the church of the *Madonna della Difesa* (1512), 16th cent.

frescoes, and two paintings of the Last Supper and the Marriage of Cana by Nicola Grassi (c. 1682-1748). Scenes from the life of St. Margaret, frescoed by various artists of the 14th and 15th centuries, decorate the interior of the 14th cent. church of *Santa Margherita*.

* **VILLA BASILICA** (Lucca). The 13th cent. Romanesque *Pieve* contains a Crucifixion by Berlinghiero Berlinghieri (recorded 1235-1274), and remains of bas-reliefs from an ancient ambo. Walk to San Gennaro, to the interesting Romanesque church of *San Gennaro*, which has a wonderful ambo, carried out in 1162 by a certain Master Filippo, with the symbols of the Evangelists.

* **VILLAFRANCA DI VERONA** (Verona). Industrial town south-east of Verona, built to a rectangular plan. Of the *Serraglio*, an imposing military construction, begun in 1345 by Mastino II and completed by Cangrande II, Lord of Verona, to keep back the incursions of Mantua, three castles (one of which known as the *Castello Scaligero*), the bridge over the Mincio, and other ruins have survived. It was at the *Villa Gandini Morelli-Bugna* that the armistice between Emperor Napoleon III and Franz Joseph of Austria was signed on 8 July, 1859.

* **VILLAMAR** (Cagliari). A notable agricultural town, situated among low hills. The little church of *San Pietro* is a modest, but very well-preserved example of Sardinian Romanesque architecture in the second half of the 13th cent. The asymmetrical facade is balanced by a disproportionate bell gable, which gives the town its character. The late-Gothic parish church (*Parrocchiale*) has a 16th cent. bell-tower; behind the high altar is an altarpiece representing the Crucifixion and Saints, in the centre of which is a wooden statue of the Madonna and Child, the work of P. Cavaro (recorded 1518-1537).

* **VIPITENO** (Bolzano). Situated on the right bank of the Isarco, in a verdant hollow, with 16th and 17th cent. houses. In the 15th cent. Gothic *Parrocchiale*, dedicated to Santa Maria in Vibitin, is an Assumption and other frescoes by Adam Josef Mölk (c. 1714-1794), and a wooden statue of St. George by Pietr Vischer (active in the early 16th cent.). The church of *Santa Elisabetta* dates from the early 18th cent., and the ceiling was decorated with a fresco of the Glorification of St. Elisabeth by Mattia Günther in 1730. In the 16th cent. late-Gothic *Palazzo Comunale* are paintings in distemper by Giovanni Multscher, called Giovanni da Ulma (c. 1400-1467), and artistic furnishings. One should also notice the crenellated *Casa dei Principi*, where the princes used to pass the night when travelling, and the church of the *Spirito Santo*, or *dell'Ospedale Vecchio*, first

built in the 15th cent., which contains frescoes by Giovanni da Brunico (active in the 15th cent.).

* **VISSO** (Macerata). Situated in the upper reaches of the Nera valley. The Romanesque-Gothic *Collegiata di Santa Maria* has a magnificent, deeply moulded portal, and a campanile with mullioned openings. The interior, remodelled in the 17th cent., consists of an aisleless nave, and contains works of the Renaissance, frescoes of the Umbrian school and a painting by G. B. Pellegrini (1675-1741); the Gothic Baptistery Chapel has two aisles, and contains a beautiful baptismal font, as well as 14th cent. tombs. The 14th cent. church of *Sant'Agostino* has a Gothic doorway. *Piazza Capuzi* is encircled by houses and small Renaissance palaces. The medieval tower (*Torre medievale*) was once part of a fortress (*Rocca*). The Gothic church of *San Francesco* has a doorway with a pointed arch; it contains a 15th cent. polyptych and a precious tabernacle.

*** **VITERBO.** Built upon undulating terrain, on the slopes of the Ciminian mountains. It is important both artistically, because of the abundance of its medieval remains, and as an agricultural town. The *Palazzo Comunale* was begun in 1460 and completed in the 16th cent. It has a large porch supported by solid columns, and a fine courtyard, where the colonnade has five bays, and in the middle of which is a 17th cent. fountain designed by Filippo Caparozzi (active in the 17th cent.). The ceiling of the Cappella del Comune is decorated with frescoes by Filippo Caparozzi and Mario Ganassini (active in the early 17th cent.). The Sala della Madonna contains a fresco of the Madonna by Giovanni Francesco d'Avanza-rano, called Fantastico (lived in the 15th cent.), and beautiful frescoes by an anonymous 16th cent. painter, illustrating the Miracles of the Madonna della Quercia. The Sala Regia, or Erculea, is decorated with frescoes by Baldassare Croce (1558-1628). Also interesting is the Marriage Hall, whose walls are decorated with paintings by Domenico Corvi (1721-1803), the former Council Hall and the Sala dell'Aurora. The *Palazzo Chigi* is a large 15th cent. building built in an austere Renaissance style, and flanked by a medieval tower. It contains a much admired fresco of the Madonna and Child by Antonio da Viterbo, called Pastura (recorded 1478-1509). The *Palazzo Farnese*, built in the early 15th cent., has a small architraved porch; the small courtyard is austere in style, the staircase steep, and there are also galleries. The 12th cent. Romanesque *Cattedrale*, dedicated to St. Lawrence, was probably built on the site of a temple dedicated to Hercules, but, was considerably altered in the second half of the 16th cent. A campanile, rebuilt in Gothic style in the second half of the 14th cent., towers above it. The nave and two aisles of the basilisan interior are divided by massive columns surmounted by precious capitals. The font in the baptistery is by Francesco da Ancona (lived in the 15th cent.). The church itself contains a fine fresco of the Marriage of St. Catherine and other Saints by anonymous artists working about the middle of the 15th cent., paintings by Lodovico Mazzanti (c. 1679-1775), a small, but beautiful panel depicting the Madonna and Child by Benvenuto di Giovanni (1436-1518), a St. Lawrence distributing Holy Communion by Marco Benefial (1684-1764), a painting of St. Lawrence by Giovanni Francesco Romanelli (1610-1662), a precious 12th cent. panel de-

Viterbo, Papal Palace and Duomo.

picting the Madonna della Carbonara, and a Christ Blessing between Saints and donor by Gerolamo da Cremona (lived in the 15th cent.). *Palazzo Papale*, one of Viterbo's most admired buildings, is reached by climbing a broad flight of steps. It was built towards the middle of the 13th cent. to provide lodging for the Popes during their frequent stays in the town. The seven interlaced arches of the loggia form a graceful piece of fretwork. The 12th cent. Romanesque church of *Santa Maria Nuova* has a charming facade, the doorway being surmounted by a head of Jove. The basilican interior contains a fresco of Christ on the Cross with the Madonna and Saints John, Anthony Abbot, Ambrose and Devotus by Francesco d'Antonio, called Balletta (active (1441-1449), a precious 14th cent. fresco of Christ with Saints, and a fresco of St. Jerome between Saints Lawrence and John the Baptist by Antonio da Viterbo. In the medieval quarter of the town, *Piazza San Pellegrino* is the best example of this kind of 13th cent. square in Italy. It opens up into the Via del Pellegrino, where we find the *Palazzo degli Alessandri*, an austere building with a large balcony beneath a large round arch, the *Fontana di Pianoscarano*, around which are grouped small, characteristic, partly medieval houses, and the 13th cent. *Porta San Pietro*, flanked by a crenellated palace. The 9th cent. Romanesque church of *San Sisto* occupies the site of an earlier pagan temple: its basilican interior is divided into a nave and two aisles, where there are some works of art, such as a huge panel with a gold background, depicting the Madonna and Child with various Saints, by Neri di Bicci (1419-1491). The *Fontana Grande*, the prototype of similar fountains in the region of Latium, consists of a large basin in the form of a Greek cross raised upon a flight of steps. A column rises out of the basin, providing the support for two smaller, super-imposed basins, and culminating in a pinnacle. It was begun in 1206 by Bertoldo and Pietro di Giovanni, and completed in 1279. The 11th cent. Romanesque church of *San Giovanni in Zoccoli* has an austere interior, divided into a nave and two aisles and contains a precious polyptych centred around the image of the Madonna and Child, the work of Francesco d'Antonio. In the Gothic Mazzatosta Chapel in the church of *Santa Maria della Verità* are superb frescoes by Lorenzo da Viterbo (recorded 1437-1476); they were seriously damaged by bombing in the Second World War, but were later recomposed perfectly on canvas, the fragments being put together piece by piece. On the ground floor of the *Museo Civico* are various archaeological collections. On the first floor is an art gallery, with many works of art, the most important being a small precious panel depicting the Madonna and Child by Vitale da Bologna (recorded 1330-1359), and a Pietà by Sebastiano del Piombo (c. 1485-1547),

regarded as one of the masterpieces of 16th cent. Roman painting. In the Gothic church of *San Francesco* (1236) is the tomb of Hadrian V, a stylish work decorated with Cosmatesque mosaics, perhaps by Pietro Vassalletto (recorded 1154-1186), or Arnolfo di Cambio (c. 1240-1302). The 14th cent. church of *Santa Maria della Salute* is a small Gothic construction, the facade embellished with a chequered band, and the portal (1320) decorated with precious bas-reliefs. In the immediate neighbourhood of the town is the unpretentious church of *Santa Maria del Paradiso*, which provides access to a 13th cent. convent with a Romanesque-Gothic cloister. Within the district of the town is the church of *Santa Maria della Quercia*, a perfect Renaissance building constructed between 1470 and 1525, with a severe, smooth ashlar facade, which has three doorways: the finest is the middle one, the work of Giovanni di Bernardino da Viterbo (lived in the 15-16th cent.), while the other two are by Domenico di Jacopo da Firenzuola (active in the early 16th cent.). Inside the basilican interior is a wonderful lacunar ceiling by Giovanni di Pietro, called Pazera (active in the first half of the 16th cent.), a marble tabernacle by Andrea Bregno (1418-1503), and a tondo of the Madonna della Quercia by Monaldo da Viterbo, called Truffetta (active in the early 16th cent.).

* **VITTORIA** (Ragusa). Situated on the edge of a plateau overlooking the river Ippari, a pleasant town with an 18th cent. appearance. The 18th cent. *Chiesa Madre*, dedicated to St. John, is one of the town's most important buildings, and its artistic merits include, above all, a much admired Baroque altar. The *Teatro Comunale* is a good example of neo-Classical architecture, its facade having two orders of columns. One should also see the lively, multi-linear facade of the church of the *Madonna delle Grazie*, which dates from the middle of the 18th cent.

* **VITTORIO VENETO** (Treviso). At the foot of the Pre-Alps, the result of the fusion of the two communes of Céneda and Serravalle. The 18th cent. *Cattedrale*, dedicated to the Assunta and the Bishop Saint Titian, has a 13th cent. Romanesque campanile, marble altars taken from the Venetian churches that were suppressed in the early 19th cent., and some interesting paintings. The *Loggia Cenedese* is a fine building, possibly designed by Jacopo Tatti, called Sansovino (1486-1570). It is not known whether the *Castle of San Martino* is of Longobard origin or foundation. The church of *San Lorenzo* was built in the first half of the 15th cent., and contains a cycle of frescoes of the same period. In the former Palazzo Comunale of Serravalle, or Loggia Serravallese (1462), is the *Museo del Cenedese*, with important collections of archaeological material, sculpture and paintings. In the church

of *San Giovanni Battista* (1357) is an altarpiece depicting the Baptism of Christ by Francesco da Milano (active in the first half of the 16th cent.), and large canvases by Agostino Ridolfi (1646-1727). The *Duomo*, dedicated to Santa Maria Nova, was rebuilt in the late 18th cent., and contains an altarpiece depicting the Madonna and Child with Saints Andrew and Peter by Titian (1490?-1576). In the ancient *Pieve di Bigonzo*, or church of *Sant'Andrea di Bigonzo*, are paintings by Francesco da Milano (active in the first half of the 16th cent.), Francesco Frigimelica (died 1621), and other artists.

* **VIZZINI** (Catania). Situated in a picturesque position on a mountain-spur. In the right side of the Baroque *Chiesa Matrice*, dedicated to St. Gregory, are Gothic remains and a large 15th cent. Catalan Gothic doorway; inside, the basilican interior contains a Martyrdom of St. Lawrence and the Madonna of Mercy by Filippo Paladino (c. 1544-1614). The church of *San Giovanni Battista*, which has a massive bell-tower, is decorated inside with beautiful stucco work. In the church of the Capuchins (*Chiesa dei Cappuccini*) is a Deposition by Filippo Paladino. In the church of *Santa Maria di Gesù* is a statue of the Madonna and Child by Antonello Gagini (1478-1536); called the White Madonna, it is an object of worship. Also interesting is the fine *Palazzo Municipale*, designed by Corrado Mazza (lived in the 19th cent.).

* **VOGHERA** (Pavia). The most important town on the southern side of the Po in the province of Pavia, situated on the left bank of the Staffora. The *Collegiata di San Lorenzo* was rebuilt in 1605 to a design by Mario Corbetta (lived in the 16-17th cent.), though the facade was added in the second half of the 19th cent. It contains an anonymous fresco of Our Lady of Succour (1496), and some Baroque altars. In the chancel of the church of *San Rocco* is a painting of St. Anne by Paolo Borroni (1749-1819). The entrance to the 14th cent. *Castello* consists of a large rectangular tower.

* **VOLTAGGIO** (Alessandria). A summer health resort situated at the confluence of the Rio Morsone, which is crossed by a bridge with two different-sized arches. The ruins of the *Castello* should be visited. There are some valuable paintings in the *Convento dei Cappuccini*. An excursion to the Gorzente lakes is well worthwhile.

** **VOLTERRA** (Pisa). A small, medieval-looking town, with remains of the Etruscan civilisation, situated above the watershed formed by the rivers Era and Cecina, and commanding wonderful views of the surrounding countryside. *Piazza dei Priori* has retained its

medieval aspect, and is surrounded by austere palaces, which rise where the houses of the Belforti, Topi, Allegretti, Afficanti, Magalotti and Maltragi once stood. Here too, is the Torre del Podestà, surmounted by the figure of a boar, which the people call "the little pig". The *Palazzo dei Priori*, a large stone parallelepiped, was begun in 1208, and completed in 1254: the Council Chamber contains a fresco in the form of a triptych by Jacopo di Cione, called Orcagna (recorded 1365-1398), and a huge canvas depicting the Marriage of Cana painted in the early 17th cent. by Donato Mascagni, on the second floor is an art gallery, with paintings by local and Sienese masters. The construction of the *Cathedral* began in the early 12th cent. The interior is in the form of a Latin cross, with a nave and two aisles, and contains, among other works, the tomb of St. Octavian, carried out in 1522 by Raffaele Cioli da Settignano and a much restored 13th cent. pulpit. The *Casa-torre Castellucci*, formerly Buomparenti, dates from the 13th cent. The *Etruscan Arch* has Etruscan jambs on the outside, while the archivolt was rebuilt in Roman times. The restored *Etruscan Walls of Santa Chiara* are still interesting. *Le Balze* is the name of a deep ravine formed by the erosion of the sandy strata that cover the layers of marly clay; the views from the top of it are magnificent, especially at sunset. The *Museo Etrusco* is extraordinarily rich in archaeological material, the main part of its collection consisting of six hundred cinerary urns. The *Biblioteca Guarnacci* contains thirty thousand volumes, five hundred manuscripts, and two hundred and thirty-three incunabola.

Volterra, Duomo, pulpit.

Many other monuments are worth a visit, such as the 15th cent. church of *San Girolamo*, the 14th cent. *Torri Cafferecci*, the *Fortezza*, one of the strongest fortresses built in the Renaissance, the Romanesque *Badia*, begun in 1030, and the medieval *Porta Fiorentina*.

* **VOLTRI** (Genoa). An industrial suburb, situated at the mouth of the Leiro. The church of *Santi Nicolò ed Erasmo* was designed and built in 1652 by Giovanni Battista Ghiso, though the dome was added in the early 18th cent. It contains some fair works of art, including an Addolorata by Domenico Piola (1627-1703), a St. Lucy and St. Charles Borromeo by Giovanni Andrea Ansaldo (1584-1638), and frescoes by Giovanni Andrea Carlone, called Genovese (1590-1630). The *Villa Brignole Sale Galliera* has a park of three hundred thousand sq. m., through which run avenues eighteen km. long. Walk to the *Sanctuary of Nostra Signora delle Grazie*, built in the late 12th cent but considerably altered in later times. The black and white striped interior contains some interesting works of art, including a Christ and the Adultress by Francesco Floriani (re-corded 1534-1593), a Madonna and Child with Saints by Luca Cambiaso (1527-1585), the much venerated Madonna and Child offering His mother a rose by Corrado Odone (16th cent.) and, in the crypt, the tombs of the Brignole Sale family, generous benefactors of the city of Genoa, who enriched it with important works of art. Excursion to the *Santuario di Nostra Signora dell'Acquasanta*, built in the 17-18th cent.

* **ZANICA** (Bergamo). Agricultural and industrial town. In the 18th cent. parish church (*Parrocchiale*) are paintings of the Crucifixion and Saints by Giampaolo Cavagna (1556-1627); in the sacristy, a painting of St. Anthony of Padua by Camillo Procaccini (c. 1551-1629), and a Nativity by Gerard Van Honthorst, called Gherardo dalle Notti (1590-1656).

* **ZUGLIO** (Udine). Little village, corresponding to the Roman Julium Carnicum forum of the 1st cent. B.C. It is the centre of an archaeological area, still only partly explored. The *Scavi Romani* consist mainly of the ruins of a forum and a basilica.

LIST OF PLACES

AGRIGENTO
Canicattì
Licata
Naro
Rivera
Sciacca

ALESSANDRIA
Acqui Terme
Bosco Marengo
Casale Monferrato
Gavi
Novi Ligure
Serravalle Scrivia
Tortona

ANCONA
Arcevia
Castelfidardo
Chiaravalle
Cupramontana
Fabriano
Falconara Marittima
Filottrano
Iesi
Loreto
Numana
Osimo
San Vittore delle Chiuse
Sassoferrato
Senigallia

AOSTA
Bard
Cogne
Fénis
Great St. Bernard Pass
Issogne
Pont-Saint-Martin
Ussel
Verres

AREZZO
Anghiari
Bibbiena
Camaldoli
Castiglione Fiorentino
Cortona
Gropina
La Verna
Lucignano
Monte San Savino
Montevarchi
Pieve di Santo Stefano
Poppi
Pratovecchio
San Giovanni Valdarno
Sansepolcro
Stia

ASCOLI PICENO
Amandola
Cupra Marittima
Fermo
Grottammare
Montefiore dell'Aso
Montegiorgio
Monterubbiano
Offida
Porto San Giorgio
Ripatransone
Sant'Elpidio a Mare

ASTI
Vezzolano

AVELLINO
Ariano Irpino
Bagnoli Irpino
Mercogliano
Mirabella Eclano
Montevergine
Sant'Angelo dei Lombardi
Solofra

BARI
Acquaviva delle Fonti
Alberobello
Altamura
Andria
Barletta
Bisceglie
Bitetto
Bitonto
Canne della Battaglia
Canosa di Puglia
Castel del Monte
Castellana Grotte
Conversano
Corato
Gioia del Colle
Giovinazzo
Gravina di Puglia
Locorotondo
Minervino Murge
Modugno
Mola di Bari
Molfetta
Monopoli
Palo del Colle
Polignano a Mare
Putignano
Rutigliano
Ruvo di Puglia
Trani

BELLUNO
Agordo
Auronzo di Cadore
Calalzo di Cadore
Cortina d'Ampezzo
Feltre
Lentiai
Pieve di Cadore
San Vito di Cadore
Valle di Cadore
Vigo di Cadore

BENEVENTO
Airola
Cerreto Sannita
Cusano Mutri
Guardia Sanframondi
San Bartolomeo in Galdo
San Salvatore Telesino
Sant'Agata dei Goti

BERGAMO
Albino
Almenno San Bartolomeo
Almenno San Salvatore
Alzano Lombardo
Ardesio
Brignano Gera d'Adda
Caravaggio
Clusone
Cologno al Serio
Gandino
Lovere
Martinengo
Ponteranica
Pontida
Romano di Lombardia
Trescore Balneario
Treviglio
Urgnano
Zanica

BOLOGNA
Budrio
Castel San Pietro Terme
Imola
Lizzano in Belvedere
Marzabotto
Medicina
Porretta Terme
San Giovanni in Persiceto

BOLZANO
Bressanone
Brunico
Burgusio
Chiusa
Malles Venosta
Merano
Naturno
Nova Ponente
San Candido
Terlano
Vipiteno

BRESCIA
Bovegno
Breno
Capo di Ponte
Chiari
Cividate Camuno
Desenzano del Garda
Edolo
Gardone Riviera
Gargnano
Gavardo
Lonato

Montichiari
Montirone
Palazzolo sull'Oglio
Pisogne
Pralboino
Quinzano d'Oglio
Salò
Toscolano Maderno
Verolanuova

BRINDISI
Fasano
Francavilla Fontana
Mesagne
Oria
Ostuni
San Vito dei Normanni

CAGLIARI
Abbasanta
Ales
Barumini
Carbonia
Dolianova
Domusnovas
Iglesias
Monastir
Nora
Oristano
Quartu Sant'Elena
Sanluri
Sante Lussurgiu
Senorbì
Sestu
Tharros
Uta
Villamar

CALTANISSETTA
Gela
Milena

CAMPOBASSO
Larino
Termoli

CASERTA
Alife
Aversa
Caiazzo
Calvi Risorta
Capua
Carinola
Caserta Vecchia
Maddaloni
Piedimonte d'Alife
Roccamonfina
Santa Maria Capua Vetere
Sessa Aurunca
Teano

CATANIA
Acireale
Adrano
Caltagirone

Paternò
Randazzo
Vizzini

CATANZARO
Crotone
Nicastro
Pizzo
Santa Severina
Serra San Bruno
Squillace
Taverna
Tropea
Vibo Valentia

CHIETI
Fossacesia
Guardiagrele
Lanciano
Ortona
Vasto

COMO
Bellagio
Campione d'Italia
Civate
Colico
Galliano
Gravedona
Lenno
Torno

COSENZA
Acri
Altomonte
Amantea
Castrovillari
Morano Calabro
Paola
Rossano
San Demetrio Corone

CREMONA
Castelleone
Crema
Piadena
Pizzighettone
Soncino
Soresina

CUNEO
Alba
Bene Vagienna
Bra
Cherasco
Dronero
Fossano
Manta
Mondovì
Racconigi
Saluzzo
Savigliano
Staffarda

ENNA
Agira
Calascibetta
Nicosia
Piazza Armerina

FERRARA
Cento
Copparo
Pomposa

FLORENZ
Bagno a Ripoli
Borgo San Lorenzo
Castelfiorentino
Cercina
Certaldo
Empoli
Fiesole
Figline Valdarno
Fucecchio
Galluzzo
Greve
Impruneta
Lastra a Signa
Montelupo Fiorentino
Peretola
Poggio a Caiano
Pontassieve
Prato
Rifredi
Rosano
Rovezzano
San Casciano in Val di Pesa
San Donnino
San Godenzo
Scandicci
Scarperia
Sesto Fiorentino
Settignano
Tavernelle Val di Pesa
Uzzano

FOGGIA
Ascoli Satriano
Bovino
Cerignola
Lucera
Manfredonia
Monte Sant'Angelo
San Giovanni Rotondo
San Severo
Siponto
Tremiti
Troia
Vieste

FORLÌ
Bagno di Romagna
Castrocaro Terme
Cesena
Civitella di Romagna
Forlimpopoli
Galeata
Predappio

Rimini
Santarcangelo di Romagna
Sarsina
Savignano sul Rubicone

FROSINONE
Alatri
Anagni
Aquino
Arpino
Casamari
Cassino
Collepardo
Ferentino
Fiuggi
Sora
Veroli

GENOA
Camogli San Fruttuoso
Chiavari
Lavagna
Nervi
Pegli
Rapallo
San Pier d'Arena
Sestri Levante
Sestri Ponente
Voltri

GORIZIA
Grado
Monfalcone

GROSSETO
Arcidosso
Magliano in Toscana
Massa Marittima
Orbetello
Pitigliano
Roccalbegna
Santa Fiora

IMPERIA
Sanremo
Taggia
Ventimiglia

ISERNIA
Agnone
San Vincenzo al Volturno
Venafro

L'AQUILA
Albe
Alfedena
Bazzano
Bominaco
Castel di Sangro
Celano
Corfinio
Fossa
Luco dei Marsi
Paganica
Pescocostanzo

Prata d'Ansidonia
Rosciolo
Scanno
Sulmona
Tagliacozzo

LA SPEZIA
Lerici
Levanto
Luni
Portovenere
Sarzana

LATINA
Cori
Fondi
Formia
Gaeta
Minturno
Norma
Priverno
Sermoneta
Sezze
Sperlonga
Terracina

LECCE
Carpignano Salentino
Casarano
Copertino
Galatina
Galatone
Gallipoli
Maglie
Nardò
Otranto
Patù
Rudiae
San Pietro in Lama
Santa Cesarea Terme
Santa Maria di Leuca
Soleto

LEGHORN
Piombino
Populonia
Portoferraio

LUCCA
Altopascio
Barga
Camaiore
Castiglione di Garfagnana
Coreglia Antelminelli
Gallicano
Pietrasanta
Seravezza
Villa Basilica

MACERATA
Camerino
Chiaravalle di Fiastra
Cingoli
Civitanova Marche
Corridonia

417

Matelica
Montecassiano
Montecosaro
Montelupone
Monte San Giusto
Potenza Picena
Recanati
San Ginesio
San Severino Marche
Sarnano
Tolentino
Treia
Urbisaglia
Ussita
Visso

MANTUA
Asola
Castiglione delle Stiviere
Goito
Ostiglia
Revere
Sabbioneta
San Benedetto Po

MASSA - CARRARA
Carrara
Massa
Pontremoli

MATERA
Irsina
Metaponto
Pisticci
Policoro
Tricarico
Tursi

MESSINA
Castroreale
Eolie
Milazzo
Patti
Taormina

MILAN
Abbiategrasso
Agliate
Cassano d'Adda
Legnano
Lodi
Melegnano
Monza
Ospedaletto Lodigiano
San Colombano al Lambro
Sant'Angelo Lodigiano
Trezzo sull'Adda
Vaprio d'Adda

MODENA
Carpi
Castelfranco Emilia
Fanano
Finale Emilia
Fiumalbo

Frassinoro
Guiglia
Mirandola
Nonantola
Sassuolo
Vignola

NAPLES
Acerra
Afragola
Bacoli
Capri
Cimitile
Cuma
Ercolano | Herculaneum
Frattamaggiore
Gragnano
Marigliano
Nola
Pomigliano d'Arco
Pompeji
Pozzuoli
Sorrento

NOVARA
Ameno
Arona
Baceno
Cannobio
Domodossola
Orta San Giulio
Pallanza
Stresa

NUORO
Bosa
Laconi
Macomer
Oliena
Orgosolo
Orosei
Orune
Ottana
Serri
Silanus
Urzulei

PADUA
Abano Terme
Arquà Petrarca
Battaglia Terme
Camposampiero
Cittadella
Este
Monselice
Montagnana
Montegrotto Terme
Ospedaletto Euganeo
Piazzola sul Brenta
Piombino Dese
Praglia
Teolo
Torreglia

PALERMO
Bagheria
Caccamo
Castelbuono
Cefalù
Monreale
Petralia Soprana
Petralia Sottana
Termini Imerese
Ustica

PARMA
Berceto
Busseto
Collecchio
Fidenza
Fontanellato
Fornovo di Taro
Salsomaggiore Terme
Soragna
Torrechiara

PAVIA
Belgioioso
Broni
Casteggio
Cecima
Certosa di Pavia
Chignolo Po
Lomello
Mortara
Robbio
Vigevano
Voghera

PERUGIA
Assisi
Bastia
Bettona
Bevagna
Campello sul Clitunno
Cascia
Castel Ritaldi
Castiglione del Lago
Cerreto di Spoleto
Città della Pieve
Città di Castello
Corciano
Deruta
Foligno
Giano dell'Umbria
Gualdo Tadino
Gubbio
Magione
Montefalco
Monteleone di Spoleto
Nocera Umbra
Norcia
Passignano sul Trasimeno
Sant'Anatolia di Marco
Sassovivo
Scheggino
Sigillo
Spello
Spoleto

Todi
Trevi
Umbertide
Vallo di Nera

PESARO AND URBINO
Cagli
Fano
Fossombrone
Gradara
Novafeltria
Pergola
San Leo
San Lorenzo in Campo
Sant'Angelo in Vado
Urbania

PESCARA
Città Sant'Angelo
Penne
Pianella
Popoli
Rosciano
Torre de' Passeri

PIACENZA
Alseno
Bobbio
Castell'Arquato
Cortemaggiore
Fiorenzuola d'Arda
Velleia

PISA
Calci
Cascina
Pontedera
San Miniato
Santa Maria Monte
Volterra

PISTOIA
Cutigliano
Pescia
San Marcello Pistoiese

PORDENONE
Codroipo
Sacile
San Vito al Tagliamento
Sesto al Reghena
Spilimbergo

POTENZA
Acerenza
Barile
Lagonegro
Lagopesole
Lauria
Melfi
Muro Lucano
Palazzo San Gervasio
Picerno
Rapolla

Rionero in Vulture
Venosa

RAGUSA
Comiso
Modica
Scicli
Vittoria

RAVENNA
Bagnacavallo
Brisighella
Cervia
Faenza
Lugo

REGGIO CALABRIA
Gerace
Locri
Palmi
Seminara
Stilo

REGGIO EMILIA
Castellarano
Ciano d'Enza
Correggio
Gualtieri
Guastalla
Rubiera
San Polo d'Enza
Scandiano

RIETI
Amatrice
Farfa
Leonessa

ROME
Albano Laziale
Anguillara Sabazia
Ariccia
Bracciano
Castel Gandolfo
Cerveteri
Civitavecchia
Frascati
Genazzano
Grottaferrata
Nemi
Nettuno
Ostia Antica
Palestrina
Rocca di Papa
Santa Marinella
Santa Severa
Segni
Subiaco
Tivoli
Trevignano Romano
Veio
Velletri

ROVIGO
Adria

Badia Polesine
Fratta Polesine
Lendinara
Loreo

SALERNO
Amalfi
Ascea
Atrani
Cava de' Tirreni
Eboli
Maiori
Mercato San Severino
Minori
Nocera Superiore
Padula
Paestum
Pertosa
Polla
Positano
Ravello
Sala Consilina
Scala
Teggiano
Vietri sul Mare

SAN MARINO

SASSARI
Alghero
Ardara
Bornova
Calangianus
Castelsardo
Codrongianus
Monte d'Accoddi
Olbia
Ozieri
Porto Torres
Sant'Antioco di Bisarcio
Sedini
Thiesi
Torralba

SAVONA
Alassio
Albenga
Finale Ligure
Laigueglia
Noli
Pietra Ligure
Vado Ligure
Varazze

SIENA
Abbadia San Salvatore
Asciano
Buonconvento
Castiglione d'Orcia
Chianciano
Chiusi
Colle di Val d'Elsa
Montalcino
Monte Oliveto
Montepulciano

Monteriggioni
Pienza
Poggibonsi
San Galgano
San Gimignano
San Quirico d'Orcia
Sinalunga

SONDRIO
Bormio
Chiavenna
Morbegno
Teglio

SYRACUSE
Augusta
Floridia
Lentini
Noto
Palazzolo Acreide

TARANTO
Castellaneta
Grottaglie
Manduria
Martina Franca
Massafra
Mottola

TERAMO
Atri
Notaresco
Roseto degli Abruzzi
Santa Maria di Ronzano

TERNI
Acquasparta
Alviano
Amelia
Arrone
Ferentillo
Ficulle
Giove
Lugnano in Teverina
Monteleone d'Orvieto
Narni
Orvieto
San Gemini

TRAPANI
Alcamo
Castelvetrano
Erice
Marsala
Mazara del Vallo
Salemi
Segesta
Selinunte

TRENT
Ala
Arco
Cavalese
Pinzolo
Riva

Rovereto
Sanzeno

TREVISO
Asolo
Castelfranco Veneto
Conegliano
Farra di Soligo
Follina
Maser
Montebelluna
Motta di Livenza
Oderzo
Possagno
Valdobbiadene
Vittorio Veneto

TRIESTE

TURIN
Alpignano
Avigliana
Carignano
Chieri
Chivasso
Ciriè
Ivrea
Moncalieri
Montanaro
Novalesa
Ozegna
Pecetto Torinese
Pinerolo
Rivoli
Sacra di San Michele
San Benigno Canavese
San Vito
Stupinigi
Superga
Susa

UDINE
Aquileia
Cividale del Friuli
Gemona del Friuli
Latisana
Palmanova
San Daniele del Friuli
Tolmezzo
Venzone
Zuglio

VARESE
Angera
Castel Seprio
Castiglione Olona
Luino
Saronno
Somma Lombardo

VENICE
Caorle
Chioggia

Dolo
Mestre
Oriago
Portogruaro
Stra

VERCELLI
Biella
Cossato
Crescentino
Gattinara
Oropa
Varallo Sesia
Verrone

VERONA
Badia Calavena
Bardolino
Bovolone
Caldiero
Garda
Illasi
Legnago
Malcesine
Monteforte d'Alpone
Peschiera del Garda
San Michele Extra
Sirmione
Soave
Torri del Benaco
Villafranca di Verona

VICENZA
Arzignano
Asiago
Bassano del Grappa
Lonedo
Lonigo
Marostica
Montecchio Maggiore
Noventa Vicentina
Thiene
Valdagno

VITERBO
Acquapendente
Bagnaia
Bolsena
Bomarzo
Capodimonte
Caprarola
Civita Castellana
Montalto di Castro
Montefiascone
Nepi
Orte
Ronciglione
Soriano nel Cimino
Sutri
Tarquinia
Tuscania
Vetralla
Vignanello

Acceptus: 67, 198, 335.
Acclozzamorra Leonello: 85.
Acquaviva Antonio: 35.
Actis Pietro Antonio da Ro-
dallo: 193.
Adeodato: 253.
Agabiti Pietro Paolo: 93, 143,
317.
Agnolo di Ventura: 28, 174.
Agostino di Duccio: 10, 20, 128,
238, 239, 240, 257, 268*, 273,
358.
Agostino di Giovanni: 28.
Agresti Livio: 205.
Albanese Francesco: 404.
Albanese Giovanni Battista: 404.
Albani Francesco: 348.
Alberti Cherubino: 292.
Alberti Cristoforo: 236.
Alberti Giovanni: 292.
Alberti Giuseppe: 84, 274, 367.
Alberti Leon Battista: 122, 165,
272, 280.
Albertolli Giocondo: 43.
Aldi Pietro: 253.
Aleandri Ireneo: 161.
Alessandri Filippo: 367.
Alessandri Marco: 45.
Alessandro di Jales: 59.
Alessandro Padovano: 336.
Alessi Andrea: 364.
Alessi Galeazzo: 136, 181, 184,
234, 237, 307, 381.
Alessio d'Elia: 70.
Alfani Domenico: 93, 106.
Alfano da Termoli: 40, 264.
Alfieri Benedetto: 70.
Algardi Alessandro: 10.
Alibrandi Girolamo: 189.
Aliense (Antonio Vassillacchi):
212, 240, 297.
Allegretti Carlo: 29, 213.
Allio Tommaso: 9.
Allori Cristoforo: 248.
Altamura Saverio: 18, 45.
Altichiero: 402, 403.
Alunno (Niccolò di Liberatore):
19, 42, 46, 106, 127, 141, 161,
194, 207, 315, 343.
Alvino Enrico: 85.
Amadeo Giovanni Antonio: 46,
81, 86, 103, 236, 316, 345.
Amalteo Pomponio: 43, 94, 99,
134, 201, 213, 258, 259, 299,
315, 358, 373.
Ambrogio da Milano: 342, 357.
Ambrosi Pietro di Giovanni: 355.
Amendola Giambattista: 12.

Amico di Bartolomeo: 77.
Amico Giovanni Biagio: 16, 154.
Ammannati Bartolomeo: 122,
159, 324.
Ammannati Giovanni: 216.
Amoretti Gaetano: 144.
Amorosi Antonio: 271.
Anastasi Giovanni: 323.
Andrea da Firenze (Andrea Buo-
naiuti): 202.
Andrea da Salerno: 35, 41, 45,
84, 297, 319, 336.
Andrea d'Aste: 38.
Andrea del Brescianino: 252.
Andrea del Castagno: 121, 395.
Andrea del Sarto: 38, 159, 197,
248, 253.
Andrea di Bartolo di Fredi: 372,
374.
Andrea di Giovanni da Orvieto:
163.
Andrea Pisano: 120, 121, 125*,
143, 216, 249*, 251.
Andrea Vicentino: 95, 153.
Anelli Franco: 78.
Angeli Marino: 374.
Angelo da Copertino: 100.
Angelo da Orvieto: 94, 142.
Angelo di Chirico: 83, 189.
Angelo di Pietro: 102.
Angelucci Camillo di Gaspare:
85.
Ansaldo Giovanni Andrea: 307,
413.
Anselmi Giorgio: 14, 80, 153.
Anselmi Michelangelo: 59.
Ansuino da Forlì: 224.
Antelami Benedetto: 103, 128,
233, 400*.
Antinori Giovanni: 197.
Antonelli Alessandro: 212, 360.
Antonello da Messina: 46, 84,
178, 222*, 228, 236, 243, 263,
335, 336, 358.
Antonello da Palermo: 336.
Antoniazzo Romano: 55, 69, 96,
127, 194, 206, 271, 274, 289,
346, 357, 382.
Antonibi Bernardino di Luca:
240.
Antonini Antonio: 110.
Antonino da Carinola: 71.
Antonino di Nicolò da Venezia:
404.
Antonio da Alatri: 14.
Antonio da Fabriano: 93, 109,
141, 149*, 168*, 174.
Antonio da Faenza: 196, 211.

Antonio da Foligno (Pier An-
tonio Mezzastris): 194, 205.
Antonio da Lodi: 91.
Antonio da Lonate: 406.
Antonio da Osteno: 25.
Antonio di Cristoforo da Cagli:
60.
Antonio di Ghino: 140.
Antonio di Girolamo Lombar-
do: 156.
Antonio di Guido Alberti da
Ferrara: 211.
Antonio di Sebola: 262.
Apollodoro of Damascus: 21,
276.
Appiani Andrea: 19, 19*, 200.
Appiani Francesco: 20.
Aprile Gaspare: 54.
Aprili Pietro: 173.
Arcangelo di Cola: 47, 64*, 218,
218*.
Arcimboldi Giuseppe: 88*.
Arcuccio Angelillo: 36, 309.
Argenta (Giovanni Battista A-
leotti): 233.
Arienti Carlo: 59.
Arnolfo di Cambio: 121, 122,
125, 216, 218, 232*, 239, 280,
411.
Arrigo Fiammingo: 93.
Arrigoni (Giovanni Laurentini):
273.
Asconi Francesco da Sant'Ippo-
lito: 129.
Asioli Luigi: 101.
Aspertini Amico: 159.
Avallone Giuseppe da Salerno:
201.
Azzalini Tito: 96.
Azzurri Francesco: 306.

Baburen Dirk: 84.
Baccari Francesco Antonio: 29,
153.
Baccari Giacomo: 153.
Baccio d'Agnolo (Bartolomeo
d'Agnolo Baglioni): 305.
Baccio da Montelupo (Baccio
Sinibaldi): 97, 306.
Baciocchi (Cesare Pronti): 262.
Badalocchi Sisto: 141.
Bagnacavallo (Bartolomeo Ra-
menghi): 38.
Bagnadore Pier Maria: 57.
Bagnasco Nicolò: 67, 206.
Balbi Alessandro: 271.
Balbi Filippo: 97.
Baldi Lazzaro: 321.

Balducci Giovanni: 163, 245.
Balducci Matteo: 142.
Balestra Antonio: 53, 80, 367.
Balletta (Francesco d'Antonio): 411.
Balmet Luigi: 363.
Balzaretti Giuseppe: 156.
Bambaia (Agostino Busti): 345.
Bandini Giovanni: 155.
Barabani Pietro: 189.
Barabino Nicolò: 307.
Baratta Giovanni di Isidoro: 78.
Barbagelata Giovanni: 382.
Barbalonga (Antonio Alberti): 98.
Barbantini Nino: 192.
Barbarini Giovanni Battista: 404.
Barbieri Giuseppe: 62.
Barchi Ludovico: 343.
Barili Antonio: 307
Barisano da Trani: 186*, 191, 363.
Barna da Siena: 300, 301*, 302*.
Barnaba da Modena: 15, 399.
Barocci Ambrogio: 375.
Baroccio (Federico Fiori): 60, 80, 197, 237, 306, 323, 374.
Baroni Gaspare Antonio di Cavalcabò: 290.
Baronzio Giovanni: 358, 374.
Barotto (Domenico di Antonio): 30.
Bartolino da Novara: 116, 201, 409.
Bartolo di Fredi: 80, 160, 193, 245, 303.
Bartolomeo (Baccio della Porta): 47, 158, 159, 253.
Bartolomeo da Mattiolo: 238.
Bartolomeo della Cisterna: 373.
Bartolomeo di Giacomo: 91.
Bartolomeo di Tomaso da Foligno: 72.
Baschenis Evaristo: 46, 49*.
Baschenis Simone: 247.
Baschiera Nicolò: 169.
Baseggio Sante: 291.
Basile Francesco: 343.
Bassano family: 42.
Bassano Francesco the Elder: 31, 42, 293, 386.
Bassano Francesco the Younger: 17, 29, 46, 57, 170, 376, 386.
Bassano Jacopo: 43, 46, 93, 112, 159, 170.
Bassano Leandro: 42, 201.
Bassi Martino: 86.
Bastianini Lazzaro: 191.
Bastianino (Sebastiano Filippi): 116, 117, 144, 153.
Batoni Pompeo Girolamo: 90, 103, 226, 350.
Battagio Giovanni di Domenico: 103.
Battaglia Antonino: 83.

Battaglia Matteo: 263.
Battista da Como: 306.
Battista del Moro: 156.
Battistello (Giovanni Battista Caracciolo): 45, 208.
Baviera Giacomo: 323.
Bazzani Cesare: 241.
Bazzani Giuseppe: 138, 170, 271.
Beato Angelico (Giovanni da Fiesole): 86, 102, 119, 122, 128, 132, 216, 238, 251.
Beaumont Claude François: 104, 146, 347.
Beccafumi Domenico: 85, 233.
Beccaruzzi Francesco: 99.
Becker: 112.
Begarelli Antonio: 143.
Bellini Filippo: 143, 163, 269.
Bellini Gentile: 387*.
Bellini Giovanni da Giambellino: 46, 202, 236, 240, 273, 291, 369, 374, 395, 399, 404.
Bellini Jacopo: 46, 57, 158.
Bellotto Bernardo: 29, 46.
Beltrami Luca: 182, 340.
Bellunello Andrea: 315.
Belvedere Andrea: 225.
Bembo Benedetto: 88*, 362.
Bembo Bonifacio: 104.
Benaschi Giovanni Battista: 271.
Benato Sante: 224.
Bencivegna Rosario: 319.
Bencivegna Venanzio: 319.
Benedetti Cristoforo: 26.
Benedetti Sebastiano: 26.
Benedetti Teodoro: 57.
Benedetto da Maiano: 110, 121, 122, 125, 202, 238, 252, 300, 320.
Benedetto da Rovezzano: 38, 343.
Benefial Marco: 120, 403, 410.
Benini Sigismondo: 244.
Benso Giulio: 325.
Benti Donato: 246, 323.
Benti Jacopo: 323.
Benvenuti Pietro: 86.
Benvenuto di Giovanni: 334, 334*, 410.
Benzi B.: 362.
Beretta Carlo: 215.
Bergamasco Guglielmo or d'Alzano: 369.
Bergamasco (Giovanni Battista Castello): 136.
Berger Pierre de Chambéry: 25.
Bergmann Ermanno: 101.
Bergognone (Ambrogio da Fossano): 28, 46, 86, 150*, 155, 175, 183, 187, 235.
Berlinghieri Berlinghiero: 409.
Berlinghieri Bonaventura: 241.
Bernabei Alessandro: 234.
Bernabei Pier Antonio: 234.
Bernardino da Bissone: 25, 399.

Bernardino de Ronchius: 320.
Bernardino di Nanni dell'Eugenia: 142.
Bernero Giovanni Battista: 71.
Bernich Ettore: 292.
Bernini Gian Lorenzo: 28, 78, 127, 206, 253, 271, 283, 286, 288*, 289, 342, 356, 395.
Bernini Pietro: 19, 200, 253.
Berrettaro Bartolomeo: 253.
Bertanza Andrea: 133, 297.
Berti Bellardino: 89.
Bertini Domenico: 234.
Berto di Giovanni: 237.
Bertoia (Giacomo Zanguidi): 69.
Bertola Giuseppe Ignazio: 345.
Bertoldo di Giovanni: 411.
Bertucci Giovanni Battista: 298.
Bertucci Giovanni Battista junior: 161.
Bettera Giovanni Maria: 27, 133.
Bevignato da Perugia: 142, 216.
Bevilacqua Giovanni Ambrogio: 340.
Bezzuoli Giuseppe: 54.
Biagio delle Lame: 109.
Bianchi Federico: 409.
Bianchi Ferrari Francesco: 189.
Bianchi Giacomo: 128.
Bianchi Giovanni Domenico: 11.
Bianchi Pasquale: 164.
Bianchi Saverio: 259.
Bianco Bartolomeo: 135.
Bibiena Ferdinando: 234.
Bicci di Lorenzo: 47, 109, 118, 119, 241, 357, 376.
Bigianelli Guido: 251.
Bistolfi Leonardo: 193.
Bitino da Faenza: 273.
Blandamonte Placido: 10.
Blasco Michele: 320.
Bo Ludovico: 345.
Boccaccino Boccaccio: 103.
Boccaccino Francesco: 104, 340.
Boccalini Giovanni: 156.
Boccati Giovanni: 232*.
Boetto Giovenale: 190.
Boito Camillo: 223.
Boltraffio Giovanni Antonio: 185*.
Bon Bartolomeo: 106, 385, 391.
Bonaiuto Natale: 62.
Bonanno da Barletta: 22.
Bonanno Pisano: 191, 248, 251.
Bonanno Rinaldo: 20, 323.
Bonechi Matteo: 119.
Bonfigli Benedetto: 100, 238.
Bonfini Desiderio: 274.
Bongiovanni Giacomo: 263.
Boni Giacomo Antonio: 135.
Bonifacio Veronese (Bonifacio De' Pitati): 67.
Boniforti Francesco: 163.
Bonino da Campione: 9, 181*.
Bonito Giuseppe: 41, 75, 225.

Bono Antonio: 105.
Bono da Ferrara: 224.
Bonomi Carlo: 117.
Bonomi Lucio: 274.
Bontulli Paolo: 260.
Bordone Paris: 13, 40, 112, 184, 298, 368, 379, 404.
Borghese Ippolito: 160, 334.
Borgognone (Jacques Curtois): 321.
Borremans William: 10, 16, 60, 62, 65, 82, 103, 107, 207, 244, 336.
Borromini Francesco: 130, 283, 286, 289.
Borroni Gian Angelo: 244.
Borroni Paolo: 412.
Bortolan Rosa: 379.
Bortoloni Mattia: 130, 247.
Bosco Antonio: 236.
Boscoli Andrea: 115, 163, 303, 312.
Boscoli Giovanni: 233.
Bottani Giuseppe: 215.
Botticelli (Sandro di Mariano Filipepi): 125*, 159, 272, 375.
Botticini Francesco: 299.
Botticini Raffaello: 107.
Bottiglieri Matteo: 69, 294.
Boulanger Jean: 318.
Braccesco Carlo: 154.
Bracci L.: 274.
Bracci Pietro: 288*.
Bramante Donato: 9, 37, 96, 134, 158, 182, 183, 208, 234, 280, 283, 286, 409.
Bramantino (Bartolomeo Suardi): 182*, 184.
Brandani Federico: 375.
Brandi Giacinto: 110, 130, 401.
Brandimarte Benedetto: 65.
Brea Ludovico: 319, 348.
Breglia Nicola: 208.
Bregno Andrea: 280, 364, 411.
Bregno Lorenzo: 89.
Briosco Benedetto: 86, 103.
Briotti Pietro Andrea: 96.
Bronzino (Agnolo di Cosimo): 97.
Bronzino (Alessandro Allori): 178.
Brunelleschi Filippo: 81, 119, 121, 122, 125, 148.
Bruni Achille: 173.
Brunori Federico: 143.
Brusasorci (Domenico Ricci): 14, 26, 55, 290, 367, 379, 403.
Brusasorci (Felice Ricci): 62, 306.
Brusinelli Antonio: 367.
Brustolon Andrea: 43, 112, 130.
Bucci Giovan Angelo: 242.
Bucciano Tommaso: 75.
Buffelli Placido: 71, 152, 164, 205.
Buglioni Benedetto: 240, 252.

Bugnato (Antonio Zanetti): 381.
Buonaiuti Bernardo: 326.
Buonamici Gian Francesco: 265, 311.
Buono Silvestro: 36.
Buontalenti Bernardo: 122, 196, 272.
Buratti Girolamo: 31.
Buscheto: 248.
Busi (Giovanni Cariani): 46.
Bussola Dionigi: 215.
Buti Michele: 26.
Butinone Bernardino: 70, 182, 368, 368*.
Butiron Carlo: 404.

Caccavello Annibale: 208.
Cadorin Guido: 42, 53, 138.
Caffi Ippolito: 178.
Cagnacci Guido: 128, 128*, 273, 311.
Cagnola Luigi: 182, 376.
Cailina Paolo the Younger: 107.
Calcagni Antonio di Bernardino: 156, 158, 269.
Caldara Domenico: 126.
Calderari Giovanni Maria: 258.
Calderari Ottone: 356.
Calderini Guglielmo: 318.
Calegari Antonio: 199.
Caliari Benedetto: 214.
Caliari Giovanni: 196.
Calimodio Giovanni Battista: 200.
Calliano Antonio Raffaele: 75.
Callot Jacques: 30, 129.
Calvaert Denijs: 259.
Camarda Francesco: 13.
Cambiaso Luca: 136, 307, 382, 413.
Cammarano Giuseppe: 75.
Campagnola Domenico: 354.
Campanaro Gherardo: 243.
Campi Antonio: 103.
Campi Bernardino: 70, 103, 104, 155, 253, 293, 299, 369.
Campi Giulio: 48, 340.
Campi Vincenzo: 104.
Campigli Massimo: 101.
Campilli Bernardino: 343.
Campolongo Domenico: 224.
Camporese Pietro the Elder: 346.
Camuccini Vincenzo: 350.
Canaletto (Giovanni Antonio Canal): 391.
Candi Giovanni: 43.
Caniana Giovan Battista: 98, 289.
Caniglia Giovanni: 263.
Canonica Pietro: 17, 91, 190.
Canova Antonio: 28, 31, 42, 117, 124*, 128, 260, 260*, 271, 289, 369, 372.
Cantalamessa Papotti Nicola: 30.
Cantarini Simone: 65, 110, 111, 174, 374, 375.

Cantone Pier Francesco: 135.
Cantoni Gaetano: 145.
Cantoni Simone: 99.
Canzio Michele: 135, 236.
Caparozzi Filippo: 410.
Capodieci Francesco: 177.
Capodivacca Bartolomeo: 196.
Caporali Bartolomeo: 42, 100, 234.
Cappellini Gabriele: 46.
Capponi Mattia: 105.
Capra Giuseppe: 244.
Capriolo Domenico: 201.
Capula Giovanni: 61.
Carattoli Pietro: 237.
Caravaggio (Michelangelo Merisi): 90, 168*, 178, 227, 280, 325, 336, 372.
Cardillo Francesco: 81.
Cardolo Pasquale: 36.
Carducci Achille: 152.
Carducci Michelangelo: 341.
Caregaro Negrini Antonio: 320.
Carella Domenico: 78, 129, 171.
Carenzio Belisario: 45.
Carlo da Camerino: 374, 378*.
Carlone Giovanni Andrea: 32.
Carlone Giovanni Battista: 307.
Carlone Taddeo: 137.
Carloni Francesco: 92.
Carnelivani Matteo: 227.
Caroto Francesco: 403.
Carpaccio Benedetto: 369.
Carpaccio Vittore: 91, 117, 372, 388*, 390*, 395.
Carpinoni Domenico: 95.
Carpioni Giulio: 356, 404.
Carrà Carlo: 101.
Carracci family: 52.
Carracci Annibale: 409.
Carracci Lodovico: 111.
Carrera Andrea: 109.
Carriera Rosalba: 199, 291, 369.
Cartorio Gregorio: 236.
Cascini Antonio: 147.
Cascini Salvatore: 147, 148.
Cascio Vincenzo: 294.
Cascione Giovanni Battista: 98.
Casella Francesco: 358.
Casnedi Raffaele: 161.
Cassani Lorenzo: 76.
Cassioli Giuseppe: 305.
Castellani Leonardo: 18.
Castellano Giuseppe: 45.
Castelli Giovanni: 40.
Castello Bernardo: 307.
Castello Valerio: 136*.
Castiglioni Giannino: 138.
Castracchini Gregorio: 215.
Catalano Gian Domenico: 132.
Cataldi Amleto: 309.
Catello Vincenzo: 349.
Catena Vincenzo: 84.
Cattaneo Sante: 68, 252.
Caula Sigismondo: 119.

Cavagna Giampaolo: 17, 96, 158, 368, 413.
Cavalcanti Andrea: 241.
Cavaliere d'Arpino (Giuseppe Cesari): 28, 38, 76, 89, 126, 163, 245, 401.
Cavallari Francesco Saverio: 14, 322.
Cavalli Alberto: 293.
Cavallini Pietro: 112, 202, 237, 280, 346.
Cavaro Michele: 61, 317.
Cavaro Pietro: 215, 262, 409.
Cavazzola (Paolo Morando): 37.
Cavedoni Giacomo: 70, 71.
Cavenaghi Luigi: 70, 290.
Ceccarini Sebastiano: 111, 318.
Ceccolo di Giovanni: 32.
Cefaly Andrea: 207.
Celesti Andrea: 57, 133, 156, 226, 263, 376, 400.
Cellini Benvenuto: 123*.
Cellino di Nese: 251, 252.
Cenatempo Girolamo: 147.
Cerano: 185*.
Ceresa Carlo: 27.
Cernison Giampiero: 404.
Cerulli Vincenzo: 354.
Cervi Bernardino: 188.
Cesare da Sesto: 155.
Cesarei Pierino: 310.
Cesari Bernardino: 245.
Cesarino del Roscetto: 26.
Chaneval Alvisio: 103.
Chiapetta Spirito Maria: 72.
Chiarella Gabriele: 294.
Chiarini Giovanni: 91.
Chiarottini Francesco: 258.
Chirus Clemente: 36.
Cialdieri Girolamo di Bartolomeo: 375.
Ciampelli Agostino: 306.
Ciancio di Pierfrancesco: 237.
Ciani Guglielmo: 141.
Cicognani Carlo: 231*.
Cidonio Narciso: 98.
Ciesa Gerolamo: 379.
Cignani Carlo: 81, 128, 374.
Cignaroli Giambettino: 14, 46, 90, 103, 156, 234, 274, 298, 367.
Cignaroli Giandomenico: 220.
Cigoli (Ludovico Cardi): 193.
Cimabue: 28, 32, 251.
Cima da Conegliano (Giambattista Cima): 99, 109, 134, 233, 326, 369.
Cino Giuseppe: 152.
Cioli Raffaele da Settignano: 412.
Cioni Giovanni: 294.
Ciotti Francesco: 108.
Cipolla Fabio: 148.
Cipriani Sebastiano: 271.
Ciuffagni Bernardo: 272.
Civerchio Vincenzo: 103, 226.
Civetta (Henry de Bles): 178.

Civiletti Benedetto: 189.
Civitali Matteo: 158, 159, 160.
Clemente Stefano Maria: 236.
Clementi Prospero: 165.
Clodio Ludovico: 66.
Coberger Wenceslas: 244.
Cocari Nicolò di Giovanni: 364.
Coccetti Liborio: 206.
Coccorante Leonardo: 45.
Coda Bartolomeo: 89.
Coducci Mauro: 385, 391, 395.
Coghietti Francesco: 318.
Cola da Conza: 399.
Cola dell'Amatrice (Nicola Filotesio): 29, 30, 31, 147, 153, 209, 375.
Cola di Matteuccio da Caprarola: 342, 357.
Cola di Pietro da Camerino: 379.
Coleberti Pietro: 324.
Colelli Francesco: 207.
Colimodio Giovanni Battista: 200.
Collino Filippo: 347.
Collino Ignazio: 347.
Colombo Giacomo: 107, 160, 347.
Coluzio Michele: 151.
Colyn de Coter: 178.
Comascan Masters: 140, 178, 348.
Conca Sebastiano: 60, 76, 83, 93, 130, 131, 163, 215, 228, 321, 340, 346.
Condivi Ascanio: 274.
Contini Giovanni Battista: 76, 83.
Coppo di Marcovaldo: 333.
Coppola Andrea: 72, 132.
Coppola Vincenzo: 45.
Corbetta Mario: 412.
Cordova Emanuele: 16.
Corenzio Belisario: 45, 160, 208, 244, 294.
Cornacchini Agostino: 347.
Cornienti Cherubino: 201.
Coronelli Vincenzo: 236.
Corradi Pier Antonio: 135.
Corradini Giovanni Battista: 82.
Corrado Teutonico: 26.
Correggio (Antonio Allegri): 231*, 233.
Corsi Domenico: 355.
Corvi Domenico: 323, 410.
Cosenza Giuseppe: 309.
Cosma di Jacopo di Lorenzo: 96.
Cosmati Masters: 346.
Costa Andrea: 269.
Costa Lorenzo the Elder: 46, 169.
Cotignola (Francesco Zaganelli): 234.
Courtois Antonio: 321.
Cozza Francesco: 190.
Cozzarelli Guidoccio: 334.
Cozzi Giuseppe: 103.

Cozzi Marco di Giampietro: 342.
Craffonara Giuseppe: 14, 274.
Crespi Daniele: 86, 243.
Cresseri Gaetano: 252.
Crevola Giuseppe: 138.
Criscuolo Giovanni Filippo: 130.
Cristadoro Matteo: 62.
Cristofali Adriano: 55, 306.
Cristoforo da Bressanone: 58.
Cristoforo da Milano: 373.
Cristoforo di Bindoccio: 246.
Crivelli Carlo: 21, 23*, 29, 101, 163, 195, 195*, 374.
Crivelli Taddeo: 189.
Crivelli Vittore: 105, 259, 274, 312.
Croce Baldassarre: 410.
Cronaca (Simone del Pollaiolo): 122.
Crosato Giovanni Battista: 362.
Cunaci Andrea da Mesegne: 310.
Curatoli Antonio: 404.
Curia Francesco: 14.

Dalle Masegne Jacobello: 240, 385.
Dalle Masegne Pier Paolo: 240, 385.
Dalle Vacche Filippo: 297.
Damiani Felice: 158, 357.
Damiani Pietro: 29.
Dandini Pietro: 246.
D'Anna Alessandro: 10.
D'Anna Vito: 60, 98, 205, 211, 263, 354.
Danti Ignazio: 54.
Danti Vincenzo: 237.
Darenu da Palermo: 228.
Da Rin Tommaso: 36, 409.
De Aria Michele: 319.
De Aria Giovanni: 319.
De Belarducci Nicola: 71.
De Blasio da Napoli: 171.
De Carolis Adolfo: 195.
De Caulis Pietro: 201.
De Chirico Giorgio: 101.
Decker Cornelius: 30.
Deddi Francesco: 128.
De Dominici Antonio: 75.
De Ferrari Orazio: 325.
De Fonduti Agostino: 79.
Delai Giacomo: 92.
De Lera Bernardino: 104.
Del Gaizo Giovanni: 83.
Delitio Andrea: 34*, 35.
Della Gamba Crescenzo: 75.
Della Gatta Bartolomeo: 81, 159.
Della Porta Antonio (Antonio Tamagnino): 297.
Della Porta Giacomo: 129, 283, 382.
Della Porta Giovanni Battista: 293.
Della Quercia Jacopo: 51, 116, 158, 251, 296*, 326, 330.

Della Robbia family: 39, 47, 52, 81, 93, 193, 195, 197, 198, 246, 258, 272, 309, 344.
Della Robbia Ambrogio: 196, 260.
Della Robbia Andrea: 22, 132, 147, 148, 159, 252, 344, 364.
Della Robbia Giovanni: 26, 118, 139, 198, 304.
Della Robbia Luca: 121, 122, 145, 159, 236, 252, 291.
Della Robbia Mattia: 105, 274.
De Luca Domenico: 105.
De Magistris Giovanni Francesco: 101.
De Magistris Giuseppe: 316.
De Magistris Simone: 109, 142, 213, 218, 303.
De Maio: 176.
De Martini Gaetano: 45.
De Matteis Paolo: 41, 45, 141, 142, 191, 324, 349.
De Min Giovanni: 36.
De Mura Francesco: 14, 41, 45, 126, 191, 309, 353.
De' Muti Feliciano: 127.
De Nittis Giuseppe: 41.
De Passeri Andrea: 340.
De' Pieri Antonio: 379.
De Pisis Filippo: 101.
De Rosis Giovanni: 152.
De Russi Francesco: 189.
De Saliba Antonello: 84, 187, 263, 343, 349.
De Sanctis Francesco: 286.
De Simone Antonio: 75.
De Simone Nicolò: 45.
De Stauris Rinaldo: 340.
De' Veris Filippolo: 66, 66*.
De' Veris Franco: 66, 66*.
De Vita Francesco: 358.
De Vivo Tommaso: 75.
Devò Luigi: 30.
De Wobreck Simone: 60, 108, 336.
Diamante Giuseppe: 16.
Diana Giacinto: 10, 45, 139, 147, 207.
Diodato Romano: 354.
Diotisalvi: 251.
Di Robilant Nicolis: 236.
Diziani Gaspare: 43, 94.
Diziani Giuseppe: 94, 95.
Dolci Carlo: 346.
Dolci Lucio: 374.
Domenichino (Domenico Zampieri): 40, 55, 111, 141, 199, 306, 348.
Domenico da Martina: 141.
Domenico da Venezia: 404.
Domenico del Tasso: 237, 238.
Domenico di Bartolo: 332*.
Domenico di Giacomo da Leonessa: 112.
Domenico di Jacopo da Firenzuola: 411.

Domenico Veneziano: 326.
Domi Baccio: 248.
Dominic of Paris: 116.
Domiziano Domiziani: 109.
Donatello (Donato de' Bardi): 119, 121, 122*, 123*, 125, 132, 223, 224*, 241, 248, 262, 319*.
Donatello Jacopo: 330.
Donati Alessio da Offida: 198.
Donatus de Aretio: 55.
Doni Dono: 32, 47.
Donnini Girolamo: 111.
Dorigny Ludovico: 97, 373.
Dorigny Louis: 404.
Dossi Battista: 110.
Dosso Dossi (Giovanni Luteri): 59, 110, 186*, 188.
Dotti Carlo Francesco: 52, 175.
Dottori Gerardo: 46.
Drudo da Trevio: 115.
Duccio da Boninsegna: 123*, 193, 238, 329*, 330, 331*.
Dufourny Leone: 228.
Dupré Amalia: 13.
Dupré Giovanni: 13.
Du Quesnoy Francesco: 155.
Dürer Albrecht: 46, 92, 129, 132.

Egidiucci Cruciano: 341.
Elmo Serafino: 131, 152.
Enrico da Campione: 173.
Episcopio (Giustino de' Salvolini): 374.
Ercole Orfeo da Fano: 115.
Erlin Corrado: 52.
Ernesto da Utrecht: 119.
Eusebio da San Giorgio: 174.
Eustathios: 71.

Faccini Pietro: 142.
Fagnoni Raffaello: 61.
Falcone Giovanni Angelo: 135.
Falconetto Giovanni Maria: 339, 367.
Falconieri Carlo: 319.
Fancelli Giovanni: 133.
Fancelli Luca: 169.
Fancelli Pietro: 110.
Fanelli Pier Simone: 93.
Fantastici Agostino: 193.
Fantastico (Giovanni Francesco d'Avanzarano): 410.
Fantino (Ascensidonio Spacca): 47.
Fantoni Andrea: 19, 27, 46, 96, 133.
Fanzago Cosimo: 76, 242, 245, 324.
Farelli Giacomo: 35.
Farinati Paolo: 133, 156, 242, 306, 339.
Fasolo Bernardino di Lorenzo: 76.
Fasolo Giovanni Antonio: 356.
Fedeli Domenico Antonio: 347.

Federighi Antonio: 326.
Felice Giuseppe: 294.
Felici Giovanni Maria: 67.
Ferdinando del Cairo: 56.
Ferraiolo A.: 320.
Ferramola Floriano: 262.
Ferrara Francesco: 41.
Ferrari Defendente: 47, 49*, 93, 274, 294.
Ferrari Gaudenzio: 67, 99, 182, 184, 187, 201, 212, 215, 316, 340, 365*, 379, 381.
Ferrari Luca: 42.
Ferraro Antonino: 80.
Ferraro Orazio: 80, 320.
Ferrari da Faenza: 38, 357.
Ferrero Gabriele: 90.
Ferret Eugene: 308.
Ferri Pietro Antonio: 369.
Ferrucci Andrea: 118, 252.
Ferrucci Francesco di Simone: 128, 236, 239, 272, 375.
Festa Felice: 16.
Fetti Domenico: 101, 168*, 170.
Fiamberti Tommaso: 128.
Filarete (Antonio Averulino): 182, 184.
Filiberti Giuseppe: 243.
Filippi Camillo: 117.
Filippi Cesare: 117.
Filippi Giovanni Maria: 26.
Filippo da Campello: 355.
Filocamo Antonio: 10.
Filotico Vincenzo: 164.
Finelli Carlo: 347.
Finoglia Paolo Domenico: 14, 100, 191.
Fiorenzo di Giuliano: 72.
Fiorenzo di Lorenzo: 47, 106.
Fischetti Odoardo: 189.
Fischietti Fedele: 75.
Florestano di Fausto: 199.
Floriani Francesco: 373, 413.
Floriani Pompeo: 219.
Foggia Michele: 253.
Foggini Giovanni Battista: 155, 252.
Fogolino Marcello: 258, 367.
Folchetti Stefano: 303, 316.
Foler Antonio: 212.
Fontana Carlo: 125, 195, 271, 283, 286.
Fontana Domenico: 70, 201.
Fontana Giovanni: 129, 372.
Fontana Girolamo: 129.
Fontana Lavinia: 144.
Fontana Luigi: 195, 196.
Fontebasso Francesco: 358, 373.
Foppa Vincenzo: 46, 57, 170, 183, 185*, 235, 319, 326.
Fornaretto Mantovano: 293.
Fornovo Giovanni Battista: 234.
Fortiguerra Nicolò da Siena: 61.
Fosco Andrea: 148.
Fracanzano Cesare: 41, 261.

Fracanzano Francesco: 190, 261.
Franceschini Marcantonio: 144.
Francesco d'Alessandro: 16.
Francesco da Ancona: 410.
Francesco da Castello: 215.
Francesco da Milano: 379, 412.
Francesco da Rimini: 374.
Francesco da Schicci: 291.
Francesco da Sebenico: 189.
Francesco da Tolentino: 358.
Francesco da Volterra: 142.
Francesco del Brina: 119.
Francesco del Cossa: 52, 117*.
Francesco di Antonio: 379.
Francesco di Gentile da Fabriano: 41.
Francesco di Giovanni: 29.
Francesco di Pietro: 102.
Francesco di Rinaldo: 326.
Francesco di Ser Cenni: 303.
Francesco di Vito: 202.
Francesco Domenico di Gennaro: 404.
Francesco Gaetano: 147.
Francia (Francesco Raibolini): 89, 304.
Freri Antonello: 82.
Frey Sixtus of Nurimberg: 367.
Frigimelica Francesco: 43, 153, 193, 412.
Frigimelica Girolamo: 291, 344.
Fuga Ferdinando: 226.
Furini Francesco: 107.

Gabbiani Giuseppe: 41.
Gabriele Feltrensis: 127.
Gabriello Onofrio: 263.
Gaddi Agnolo di Taddeo: 119, 262, 306, 325.
Gaddi Taddeo: 251, 258.
Gadio Bartolomeo: 340.
Gaetano d'Agostino: 208.
Gagini Antonello: 10, 16, 20, 60, 77, 80, 81, 83, 109, 171, 178, 189, 200, 207, 211, 226, 227, 228, 230, 263, 323, 335, 412.
Gagini Antonio: 109, 175, 320, 404.
Gagini Domenico: 242, 294, 335, 336.
Gagini Fazio: 84.
Gagini Giacomo: 263, 320, 404.
Gagini Giuseppe: 62.
Gagini Nibilio: 62, 107.
Gagini Vincenzo: 206, 263.
Gagliardelli Giovanni Francesco: 274, 347.
Gagliardi Pietro: 350.
Gagliardi Rosario: 189, 211, 263, 321.
Gaidano Paolo: 70.
Galasto di Como: 289.
Galeone Giovanni: 349.
Galilei Alessandro: 283.
Galliari Bernardino: 368.

Gallo Francesco: 128, 190.
Gallo Giovanni: 224.
Gamba Paolo: 148.
Gambara Lattanzio: 57, 199.
Ganassini Mario: 410.
Gaudini Antonio: 54, 133.
Gandolfi Gaetano: 158.
Gandolfi Ubaldo: 175, 318.
Gandolfino d'Asti: 318.
Gardona Gian Battista da Ligornetto: 358.
Gargalli Piero di Bartolo: 291.
Garofalo (Benvenuto Tisi): 78, 100, 117, 291.
Garola Paolo: 195.
Gasparino di Antonio: 238, 239.
Gasparo da Cairano: 297.
Gastaldi Andrea: 90.
Gattapone Matteo (Matteo di Giovannello): 142, 343.
Gatti Annibale: 306.
Gavazzeni Giovanni: 340.
Gemignani Alessandro: 242.
Gemignani Giacinto: 28, 160.
Genga Bartolomeo: 240.
Genga Girolamo: 240, 323, 374.
Gennari Cesare: 59.
Gennari Ercole: 219.
Gennari Giovanni Battista: 219.
Gennaro d'Amore: 245.
Genovese Gaetano: 75.
Genovese (Giovanni Andrea Carlone): 307, 413.
Genovesino (Luigi Miradori): 79, 104, 201, 340, 341.
Gentile da Fabriano: 216, 374, 382.
Gentile di Aversa: 36.
Gentileschi Artemisia: 261.
Gentileschi (Orazio Lomi): 112.
Genuino Giovanni Bernardino: 132.
Genuino Vespasiano: 132.
Gerini Niccolò di Pietro: 251.
Gerino da Pistoia: 118.
Gerolamo da Cremona: 411.
Gherardi Antonio: 271.
Gherardi Cristoforo: 269.
Gherardini Alessandro: 38, 78.
Gherardini Tommaso: 119.
Gherardo delle Notti (Gerard van Honthorst): 18, 413.
Ghezzi Giuseppe: 289.
Ghiberti Lorenzo: 121, 311, 327*, 330.
Ghioldi Giovanni Battista: 156.
Ghirlandaio (Domenico Bigordi): 94, 122, 123*, 205, 273, 299, 300, 301*, 306.
Ghirlandaio Michele: 198.
Ghirlandaio (Ridolfo del): 22, 97, 132, 199, 272.
Ghiso Giovanni Battista: 413.
Giacolone Giuseppe: 62.
Giacomo (fra): 262.

Giacomo da Campli: 274.
Giacomo da Recanati: 193.
Giacomo da Vicenza: 367.
Giacomo di Giovanni: 343.
Giacomo di Servadio: 237.
Giambono Michele: 138, 326.
Giandomenico da Carrara: 341.
Gian Jacopo dell'Acaja: 151, 152.
Giannicola di Paolo: 237.
Giaquinto Corrado: 189, 362.
Gigante Giacinto: 45.
Gigli Pier Matteo: 310.
Giolfino Bartolomeo: 339.
Giolfino Nicolò II: 403.
Giordano Aniello: 245.
Giordano da Monte Sant'Angelo: 198.
Giordano Domenico: 187.
Giordano Luca: 13, 43, 45, 92, 102, 130, 170, 225, 260, 262, 291, 294, 308, 325, 404.
Giorgio da Milano: 76, 354.
Giorgio Fiorentino (Giorgio Marchesi): 144.
Giorgione (Giorgio Barbarelli): 73*, 78, 393*.
Giosafatti Giuseppe: 30, 31.
Giosafatti Lazzaro: 29, 31, 213.
Giotto (Giovanni di Bondone): 32, 34*, 52, 121, 122, 125, 187, 194, 202, 224, 253, 256, 306, 357.
Giovanelli Orazio: 84, 211.
Giovanello di Benvenuto: 237.
Giovannelli Benedetto: 329.
Giovanni Angelo d'Amato: 35, 370.
Giovanni Antonio da Pesaro: 93, 317.
Giovanni Battista Antonino: 309.
Giovanni Battista da Lugano: 376.
Giovanni Bernardo: 339.
Giovanni da Brunico: 410.
Giovanni da Campione: 46.
Giovanni da Casalbore: 370.
Giovanni da Corfù: 189.
Giovanni da Gaeta: 127, 130.
Giovanni da Judenburg: 211.
Giovanni d'Alemagna: 93.
Giovanni da Milano: 201.
Giovanni da Modena: 51.
Giovanni da Montalparo: 116.
Giovanni da Nola: 36, 45, 102.
Giovanni da Pedemuro: 404.
Giovanni da Pistoia: 27.
Giovanni da Rimini: 110*, 336.
Giovanni da San Giovanni (Giovanni Mannozzi): 119, 319.
Giovanni d'Asciano: 300.
Giovanni da Sebenico: 189.
Giovanni da Sulmona: 338*.
Giovanni da Udine: 299, 342, 372, 373.

Giovanni da Ulma (Giovanni Multscher): 409.
Giovanni da Verona: 155, 197.
Giovanni del Biondo: 299.
Giovanni d'Enrico: 379*, 380*, 381*.
Giovanni d'Enrico d'Alemagna: 355.
Giovanni del Ponte: 262, 290.
Giovanni di Agostino: 253.
Giovanni di Balduccio: 181*, 183, 236, 299.
Giovanni di Bernardino da Viterbo: 411.
Giovanni di Betto: 240.
Giovanni di fra Giovanni Angelo Montorsoli: 177.
Giovanni di Gian Pietro da Venezia: 368.
Giovanni di Giliacco: 357.
Giovanni di Guittone: 350.
Giovanni di Marco: 89.
Giovanni di Nicola: 127.
Giovanni di Paolo: 80, 331*, 332*.
Giovanni di Santuccio da Fiorenzuola di Spoleto: 357.
Giovanni di Simone: 251.
Giovanni di Uguccione da Orvieto: 216.
Giovanni Francesco da Tolmezzo: 134.
Giovanni Maria da Treviso: 336.
Giovanni Pisano: 135, 135*, 222*, 224, 237, 248, 249*, 251, 252, 253, 328*, 329.
Giovanni Siracusano: 81.
Giovenone Giuseppe the Elder: 93.
Girolamo da Carpi (Girolamo Sellari): 100, 117.
Girolamo da Santacroce: 160, 362, 404.
Girolamo da Treviso: 368.
Girolamo da Vicenza: 147, 379.
Girolamo dei Libri: 196, 407*.
Girolamo di Benevento: 10, 198.
Girolamo di Giovanni: 64*, 65, 66, 314*, 316.
Giroldo da Lugano: 174.
Girondi Raffaele: 41.
Giuffré Antonino: 187, 349.
Giuliano da Maiano: 201, 202, 237, 269, 280, 300, 319.
Giuliano da Rimini: 358.
Giuliano di Simone: 80.
Giuliari Bartolomeo: 196.
Giulio Pierino d'Amelia: 372.
Giulio Romano (Giulio Pippi): 169, 170, 206, 220, 298.
Giuseppe d'Annibale: 131.
Giuseppe di Lauro: 129.
Giusto d'Alemagna: 136.
Giusto de' Menabuoi: 187, 222*, 224.

Glantschnigg Ulric: 53.
Goro di Gregorio: 168, 174, 177, 178.
Gossaert Jean: 291.
Gozzoli Benozzo: 122, 194, 216, 301*, 303, 324, 355.
Graegorius de Aretio: 55.
Graffeo Giacomo: 354.
Grammatica Antiveduto: 401.
Grano Antonino: 226.
Grasmair Giovanni Giorgio Domenico: 59.
Grassi Giovanni: 151.
Grassi Giovanni Battista: 134, 373.
Grassi Nicola: 358, 409.
Grassi O.: 283.
Grassi Pasquale: 152.
Graziani Ercole the Younger: 95, 175, 297.
Grazioli Giovanni Antonio: 404.
Grechetto (Giovanni Benedetto Castiglione): 136.
Greco Gennaro: 45.
Greco Giuseppe: 220.
Greppi Giovanni: 138.
Gricci Giuseppe: 306.
Griglio Giovanni: 134, 399.
Grigoletti Michelangelo: 36, 259, 367, 373.
Grimaldi Francesco: 151, 202.
Grossi Francesco: 138.
Gruamonte: 252.
Guadagnini Antonio: 27, 252.
Gualandi Giuseppe: 155.
Gualtieri Gualtiero: 156.
Gualtiero d'Alemagna (Walter of Munich): 147.
Guardassoni Alessandro: 59, 259.
Guardi Andrea: 247.
Guardi Francesco: 46, 84, 110, 181, 391.
Guariento di Arpo: 42, 221*.
Guarini Francesco da Solofra: 139, 207, 339.
Guarini Giovanni: 202.
Guarini Guarino: 359, 360.
Guarino Felice: 340.
Guarino Giovanni Tommaso: 252, 339.
Gubleyras Giuseppe: 272.
Guercino (Giovanni Francesco Barbieri): 17, 21, 29, 45, 50*, 52, 85, 111, 119, 128, 174, 218, 241, 243, 271, 304, 306, 343, 358, 401.
Guerra Achille: 83.
Guerra Gaspare: 274.
Guerrieri Giovanni Francesco; 317, 374.
Guerrini Giacomo: 104.
Guerrini Giovanni Francesco: 110.
Guglielmo del Sale: 224.
Guglielmo di Pisa (Guglielmo

Agnelli): 247, 252.
Guidaccio da Imola (Antonio Checci): 144.
Guidetto da Como: 262.
Guidi Domenico: 316.
Guido da Como: 252.
Guinaccia Deodato: 134.
Gunther Mattia: 409.
Guttuso Renato: 45.
Guzzardi Giuseppe: 12.

Haller Francesco: 52.
Harris William: 322.
Hellweger Franz: 59.
Henrici Carl: 9, 52.
Hill Francis: 75.
Holbein Hans the Younger: 233.
Hovic Gaspare: 190, 254.
Hugford Ignazio: 54.
Hyschilos: 96.

Iacometti Pietro Paolo: 218.
Iacometti Tarquinio: 156, 218.
Iannelli Filippo: 81.
Idolorico: 101.
Ierace Francesco: 83, 269.
Imparato Girolamo: 131, 353.
Indivini Domenico di Antonello: 308.
Inigo Jones: 154.
Innocenzo da Imola: 110.
Innocenzo da Petralia: 240.
Isabello Pietro: 19, 45, 46, 257.
Italia Angelo: 16, 82, 83.

Jacobelli Silvestro: 85.
Jacobello del Fiore: 354.
Jacobello di Bonomo: 311.
Jacopo da Empoli: 45.
Jacopo da Leonessa: 196.
Jacopo da Montagnana (Jacopo Parisati): 9, 43.
Jacopo da Varagine: 28.
Jacopo del Casentino: 132, 320.
Jacopo del Sellaio: 304.
Jacopo di Chimenti: 248.
Jacopo di Grondolo: 110.
Jacopo di Lorenzo: 96.
Jacopo Siculo (Jacopo Santori): 29, 154.
Jappelli Giuseppe: 224.
Jaquerio Giacomo: 112, 165, 274.
Jean Boulogne: 52, 97, 248, 272, 357.
Justus of Ghent: 65, 375.
Juvarra Filippo: 43, 99, 345, 347, 358, 359, 360.

Kessler Stefano: 92, 176.
Klocker Giovanni: 52.
Knoller Martino: 164, 176.
Kuntz Thaddens: 401.

La Barbera Vincenzo: 60.
Labisi Paolo: 211.

Lagerino Stefano: 407.
Lama Giovanni Battista: 151.
Lama Giovanni Bernardo: 176, 294.
Lamberti Simone: 234*.
Lambertini Michele di Matteo: 209.
Lampi Francesco: 84.
Lampi Giovanni Battista the Elder: 52, 315, 367.
La Naia Angelo: 12.
Landini Taddeo: 38.
Landolina Giovanni Battista: 210.
Landulfo Pompeo: 131.
Lanfranco Giovanni: 12, 163, 261, 306, 343.
Lanino Bernardino: 103, 133.
Lanzani Bernardino: 48.
Laparelli Francesco: 373.
Lapiccola Nicola: 318.
Lapis Gaetano: 60, 143.
Lattanzio di Niccolò Alunno: 79, 127.
Laurana Francesco: 22, 60, 178, 201, 211, 226, 227, 228, 294, 320, 336.
Laurana Luciano: 240, 323, 374.
Laureti Tommaso: 52.
Lazzarelli Giulio: 218, 274.
Lazzarini Antonio: 379.
Lazzarini Giovanni Andrea: 93, 271, 318.
Lazzarini Gregorio: 153, 259.
Leonardo da Bressanone: 52.
Leonardo da Teramo: 347.
Leonardo da Vinci: 92, 183, 235, 379, 409.
Leonardo di Giovanni: 252.
Leone di Matteo: 238.
Leoni Leone: 142, 142*.
Leopardi Alessandro: 20, 223.
Letizia Oronzo: 152.
Liberi Pietro: 156, 293.
Lierni Giovanni Pietro: 354.
Ligari Giovanni Pietro: 90, 200, 340, 340*.
Ligorio Pirro: 356, 356*.
Ligozzi Jacopo: 47, 244, 248.
Lilli Andrea: 21, 312, 323.
Lippi Filippino: 78, 122, 159, 317.
Lippi Filippo: 261*, 262, 319, 342.
Lisippo: 336.
Lodovico di Antonibo: 238.
Lo Forte Salvatore: 211.
Lojacono Francesco: 13.
Lombardo Antonio: 193, 368.
Lombardo Aurelio: 157*, 158.
Lombardo Cristoforo: 86.
Lombardo Giacomo: 156.
Lombardo Girolamo: 158.
Lombardo Paolo: 156.
Lombardo Pietro: 94, 156, 265, 368, 386, 391, 395, 399.

Lombardo Tullio: 112, 261, 265, 368, 395.
Lomi Aurelio: 251.
Lo Monaco Sebastiano: 263.
Longhena Baldassarre: 42, 91, 156, 230, 385, 386, 392, 399.
Longhi Alessandro: 344, 369, 391.
Longhi Alessio: 367.
Longhi Barbara: 89.
Longhi Francesco: 81.
Longhi Luca: 128, 261.
Longhi Pietro: 369.
Longo Antonio: 84.
Longo Jacobino: 236.
Lonis Giuseppe Antonio: 323.
Lopez Francesco Palomino: 200.
Lorenzetti Ambrogio: 174, 274*, 275, 329, 330, 334.
Lorenzetti Pietro: 28, 34*, 80, 102, 326, 333.
Lorenzetti Ugolino da Siena: 159.
Lorenzi Francesco: 144.
Lorenzo da Bologna: 404, 406.
Lorenzo da Viterbo: 86, 411.
Lorenzo di Alessandro: 101, 174, 308, 315, 364, 374.
Lorenzo di Credi: 197, 252.
Lorenzo Veneziano: 158, 336, 404.
Loreti Giovanni Battista: 110.
Loreto di Ciccio: 319.
Loschi Bernardino: 71.
Loth Karl: 369.
Lotto Lorenzo: 21, 31, 45, 46, 93, 143, 158, 198, 257, 269, 269*, 366*, 367, 369, 395.
Lovati Angelo: 59.
Lovati Bernardino: 59.
Lo Verde Giacomo: 60, 227.
Loverini Ponziano: 252, 367.
Luca di Tommé: 160, 271, 275.
Lucchese (Pietro Ricchi): 274.
Lucini Giovanni Battista: 103.
Luini Bernardino: 92, 99, 153, 161, 187, 218, 314*, 316.
Lupo (Defendente di Antonio): 30.
Lurago Rocco: 134.
Lusso Andrea: 61, 321.
Lutz Giovanni: 52.
Luzzo Lorenzo: 112.

Maccari Mino: 45.
Maccaruzzi Bernardo: 178.
Macrino d'Alba: 15, 365*.
Maderno Carlo: 78, 129, 283, 289.
Maestro del Cassone Adimari: 304.
Maestro dell'Osservanza: 33*.
Maestro di Celle Macra: 295*.
Maestro di S. Giovanni di Capestrano: 150.
Maestro di Varlungo: 344.

Maffei Francesco: 56, 57, 78, 404, 406.
Maffei Girolamo: 143.
Maganza Alessandro: 147, 297, 356, 404.
Maggiotto Domenico: 153.
Maggiotto Francesco: 42.
Magnani Giovanni Battista: 233.
Magnani Piero: 350.
Magnasco Alessandro: 30, 42, 58, 90, 104, 369.
Maieski Sebastiano: 174.
Mainardi Andrea: 341.
Mainas Antioco: 262.
Maitani Lorenzo: 216, 221*, 239.
Malatesta Adeodato: 126, 409.
Malatesta Giuseppe: 110.
Malatesta Novello: 89.
Maldarelli Federico: 155.
Malinconico Nicola: 45, 76, 132, 201.
Malosso (Giovanni Battista Trotti): 103, 297, 340, 341.
Mameli Giovanni: 61.
Manchellis Michele: 406.
Mancinelli Giuseppe: 18.
Mancini Domenico: 153.
Mancini Francesco: 110, 163, 311, 374.
Mancini Nicodemo: 319.
Mancino Giuliano: 108, 109, 320.
Manenti Ascanio: 271.
Manenti Vincenzo: 272, 346.
Manetti Antonio: 121, 122.
Manieri Mauro: 59, 151.
Mansueti Giovanni: 375.
Mantegna Andrea: 46, 101, 165, 167*, 169, 170, 221*, 223, 224, 269, 402.
Manzi Gilberto: 101.
Manzini Giusto d'Andrea: 236.
Manzoni Giacomo: 354.
Marabitti Ignazio: 65, 175, 335, 336, 354, 364.
Maragliano Antonio Maria: 90.
Maraldo da Monte Sant'Angelo: 198.
Maratta Carlo: 45, 98, 158, 227, 316, 346, 374, 399.
Marcantonio di Antoniazzo Romano (Marcantonio Aquili): 205, 271.
Marcello di Gherardo di San Marcello: 25.
Marchesi Girolamo da Cotignola: 143.
Marchesi Pompeo: 316.
Marchesi Salvatore: 13.
Marchesini Alessandro: 53.
Marchesini Francesco: 187.
Marchetti Antonio: 90, 199.
Marchisi Antonio: 368.
Marcillat Guglielmo: 102.
Marco Costanzo: 335, 336.
Marco Pino (Marco da Siena):

36, 39, 45, 81, 139, 191, 292.
Marconi Giovanni Battista: 138.
Marescalco (Giovanni Buonconsiglio): 192, 404.
Margaritone d'Arezzo: 21, 80, 197.
Marghinotti Giovanni: 223, 317.
Mari Giovanni Antonio: 271.
Mariani Camillo: 247.
Mariani Cesare: 354.
Marinali Orazio: 78, 406.
Marini Benedetto: 243.
Marino di Marco Cedrino: 19.
Marino Giovanni Battista: 16, 62, 336.
Mario di Bartolomeo: 262.
Marocchetti Carlo: 241.
Maroni Gian Carlo: 133.
Martelli Francesco: 223.
Martinelli Carlo: 349.
Martinenghi Giuseppe: 72.
Martini Arturo: 101, 379.
Martini Francesco di Giorgio: 60, 102, 129, 143, 238, 241, 305, 332*, 334, 374, 375.
Martini Giovanni: 259.
Martini Simone: 32, 34*, 140, 251, 299, 326, 328*, 330.
Martino di Bartolomeo: 334.
Martinuzzi Napoleone: 138.
Marullo Giuseppe: 69, 82.
Marvuglia Venanzio: 192, 228.
Masaccio (Tommaso Guidi or Tommaso di Ser Giovanni): 122, 202, 251, 304.
Masazza di Valdondona: 360.
Mascagni Donato: 412.
Maso di Banco: 125.
Maso di Bartolomeo: 252, 375.
Masolino da Panicale (Tommaso di Cristoforo Fini): 74*, 81, 81*, 107*, 122, 132, 202, 279, 357.
Massabò Leonardo: 145.
Massari Giorgio: 226.
Massari Lucio: 79.
Mastelletta (Giovanni Andrea Donducci): 59.
Master Andrea: 271.
Master Atto: 126.
Master Binello: 47.
Master Filippo: 409.
Master Gallo: 196.
Master Giovanni: 290.
Master Guglielmo: 316.
Master Martino: 290.
Master Nicolò: 402.
Master of Castelsardo: 61.
Master of the Coronation of Eboli: 107.
Master of the Cross of Piazza Armerina: 244.
Master of the Gardner Annunciation: 355.
Master of the Madonna della Misericordia: 20.
Master of the Madonna di Alvito: 14.
Master of the Madonna of Straus: 379.
Master of the polyptych of Trapani: 364.
Master of the vault-panels: 32.
Master Pietro De Maria: 318.
Master Rodolfo: 47.
Master Sarolo da Muro Lucano: 264.
Masters of Campione: 66.
Masucci Domenico: 75.
Masucci Natale: 62, 364.
Mates Juan: 63*.
Matteo da Campione: 200.
Matteo da Gualdo: 141, 207, 334.
Matteo de' Pasti: 273.
Matteo di Giovanni: 33*, 59.
Mazza Antonio: 211.
Mazza Corrado: 412.
Mazzanti Ludovico: 403, 410.
Mazzola Giovanni Battista: 82, 177, 336.
Mazzoni Angelo: 138.
Mazzoni Guido: 59, 142, 202.
Mazzoni Sebastiano: 291.
Melanzio Francesco: 194.
Melchiorre da Montalbano: 264, 310, 353.
Mellin Carlo: 202.
Melozzo da Forlì: 128, 158, 194.
Memling Hans: 404.
Memmi Lippo: 80, 216, 303, 333, 334.
Menetto da San Marino: 306.
Menga Evangelisto: 41, 100.
Mengoni Giuseppe: 181.
Mengs Antonio Raffaele: 41.
Menzocchi Francesco: 128.
Mercurio Antonio: 108.
Merlini Orlando: 375.
Messeni Angelo: 40.
Messina Gabriele: 16.
Messina Vincenzo: 16.
Mezzastris Bernardino: 194.
Miani Pietro: 95.
Miazzi Giovanni: 42, 320, 379.
Michelangelo Buonarroti: 96, 101, 117, 121, 122, 123*, 125, 182, 280, 283, 286, 289, 325.
Michele da Firenze: 12.
Michele da Salisburgo: 367.
Michele Fiammingo (Michele Desubleo): 318.
Michelozzi Michelozzo: 121, 122, 126, 145, 183, 262.
Michetti Francesco Paolo: 241.
Miliani Michelangelo: 110.
Mino da Fiesole: 118, 125, 240.
Mino di Neri del Pellicciaio: 330.
Minuccio di Rinaldo: 326.
Mirabella Mario: 13.
Mirone: 14.
Mochi Francesco: 243, 243*.
Molk Adam: 409.
Molin Domenico: 290.
Molinari Angelo Giovanni: 318.
Molinari Luigi D'Andorno: 236.
Monacelli Oreste: 306.
Monaco Ambrogio: 109.
Moncalvo (Guglielmo Caccia): 90, 104, 201.
Mondo Domenico: 75.
Monocolo (Pietro d'Asaro): 67.
Montagna Bartolomeo: 86, 261, 404, 406.
Montagna Benedetto: 404.
Montanini Martino: 349.
Montemezzano Francesco: 153, 156.
Monteverde Giulio: 13.
Monti Claudio: 75.
Monti Francesco: 68, 104.
Monti Gaetano Matteo: 90.
Monti Innocenzo Cristoforo: 187.
Monti Nicola: 115, 116.
Montorsoli Giovanni Angelo: 177, 178.
Moor Antonio: 163.
Morani Vincenzo: 83.
Moranzone Andrea: 134.
Morazzone (Pier Francesco Mazzucchelli): 58, 99, 201, 212, 243, 380*, 381.
Morbiducci Publio: 141.
Morelli Cosimo: 129, 161, 163.
Morelli Domenico: 18, 102.
Moretti Gaetano: 90.
Moretto da Brescia (Alessandro Bonvicino): 46, 56, 57, 156, 158, 184, 261.
Morganti Pompeo: 119.
Moriggia Giovanni: 70.
Morlaiter Giovanni Maria: 42, 226.
Morone Domenico: 158, 403.
Morone Francesco: 339.
Moroni Giovanni Battista: 16, 17, 46, 49*, 289, 367.
Mosca Bernardo da Pescocostanzo: 147.
Mozzillo Angelo: 12, 208.
Mozzoni Guido: 188.
Muller David: 324.
Muratori Domenico Maria: 403.
Murillo Bartolomeo Stefano: 135.
Muru Giovanni: 24*, 27.
Muttoni Bernardino the Younger: 242.
Muttoni Francesco: 156.
Muttoni Pietro (Pietro della Vecchia): 9.
Muziano Girolamo: 158.
Muzzini Bartolomeo: 404.

Naccherino Michelangelo: 19, 81.
Nanni di Bartolo: 358.

Napoli Tommaso Maria: 37.
Napolitano (Abramo Breughel): 225.
Nardini Girolamo: 93.
Narvesa Gaspare: 259.
Nasini Antonio: 174.
Nasini Francesco: 9, 140.
Nasini Giuseppe: 9.
Nazzari Bartolomeo: 344.
Nebbia Cesare: 343.
Negro de' Negri: 243.
Negro Gaspare: 373.
Nelli Ottaviano: 127, 142, 143, 149*, 194, 346.
Neri di Bicci: 38, 109, 119, 241, 253, 353, 411.
Nerucci Raniero: 158.
Netti Francesco: 18.
Niccoli Lattanzio: 271.
Niccolini Antonio: 202.
Niccolò dell'Arca: 79.
Nicodemo di Guardiagrele: 244.
Nicola da Guardiagrele: 142, 147, 354.
Nicola da Léquile: 131.
Nicola da Monteforte: 45.
Nicola d'Ancona: 269.
Nicola di Angelo: 130.
Nicola di Antonio di Pantaleone Pasquali: 147.
Nicola Pisano: 51, 158, 237, 251, 327*, 329.
Nicolò da Siena: 72.
Nicolò dell'Abate: 307.
Nicolò di Bartolomeo: 264.
Nicolò di Pietro Paolo: 368.
Nicolò Lionello: 373.
Nino Pisano: 100, 122, 215, 249*, 251, 363.
Nono Andrea: 103.
Novelli Paolo: 84, 192, 225, 227, 263.
Novelli Pietro: 84, 192, 225, 227, 263.
Novelli Pietro Antonio: 95.
Novelli Sebastiano: 243.
Novello Giovan Battista: 224.
Nucci Avanzino: 110.
Nucci Benedetto: 143.
Nucci Virgilio: 142.
Nuvolone Giuseppe: 68, 90.
Nuvolone Panfilo: 59, 201.
Nuzi Allegretto: 109, 113*.

Oberty Luigi: 126.
Oddi Muzio: 109, 371.
Oderisi Roberto: 107, 353.
Oderisio da Benevento: 370.
Odone Corrado: 413.
Oliva Domenico Simone: 370.
Olivieri Giovanni: 224.
Olivieri Leonardo: 171.
Omiccioli Giovanni: 45.
Oppido Giovanni Donato di Matera: 174, 175.

Oravia Giovanni: 358.
Orbetto (Alessandro Turchi): 14, 37, 66, 69, 274.
Orcagna (Andrea di Cione): 122, 216.
Orcagna (Jacopo di Cione): 290, 412.
Orlandino Teodosio: 103.
Orlando Pietro: 109.
Orsini Giorgio: 21, 22.
Orsolino Giovanni: 135.
Ortega Giovanni Battista: 353.
Ottoni Lorenzo: 271.

Pacecco (Francesco De Rosa): 45, 174.
Pacelli Giuseppe: 164.
Pacher Federico: 52, 58.
Pacher Michele: 53.
Paciotto Francesco: 243.
Padovanino (Alessandro Varotari): 16, 42, 138, 230, 254, 261, 315.
Paganelli Domenico: 110.
Paganelli Giuseppe: 206.
Pagani Giovanni: 115.
Pagani Lattanzio: 198.
Pagani Vincenzo: 29, 31, 116, 141, 259, 303, 364.
Pagano di Parma: 198, 199.
Pagano Giuseppe: 349.
Paglia Antonio: 54.
Paglia Francesco: 68, 133.
Paglia Nicola: 59.
Paladino Filippo: 65, 107, 154, 189, 244, 412.
Palizzi Filippo: 382.
Palladino Leterio: 187.
Palladio Andrea: 56, 112, 130, 156, 173, 192, 214, 247, 324, 373, 399, 404, 406.
Pallavicini Giacomo: 340.
Palma Andrea: 335.
Palma Jacopo the Elder: 46, 56, 320, 395, 406.
Palma Jacopo the Younger: 13, 28, 29, 39, 43, 78, 93, 94, 95, 99, 106, 111, 133, 138, 153, 191, 192, 201, 213, 220, 260, 261, 271, 289, 291, 297, 306, 308, 362, 374, 379, 395.
Palmezzano Marco: 59, 81, 110, 128, 174.
Palmieri Giuseppe: 201.
Palumbo Francesco: 85.
Panbianchi Giampietro di Colorno: 243.
Pandolfi Giovanni Giacomo: 272.
Panettera Giovanni: 84.
Panfilo da Spoleto: 19.
Pantaleone: 220.
Pantaleone da Amalfi: 198.
Paolo da Cailina the Younger: 57.
Paolo da Visso: 30, 33*.
Paolo di Gregorio: 142.

Paolo Romano (Paolo da Gualdo Cattaneo): 403.
Paolo Uccello: 121, 375.
Paolo Veneziano: 91, 297, 363, 369.
Papacello (Tommaso Bernabei): 102.
Paparo Emanuele: 253.
Pardo Vito: 77.
Parisi Nicola: 126.
Parmigianino (Francesco Mazzola): 52, 124*, 158, 231*, 233, 234.
Parodi Giovanni Battista: 136.
Parrucchetti Ludovico: 236.
Pascucci Francesco: 321.
Pasetti Carlo: 116.
Pasqualino (Pasquale De' Rossi): 110.
Pasquino di Matteo da Montepulciano: 262.
Passaglia Augusto: 159.
Passari Ascanio: 26.
Passeri Andrea: 200.
Passeri Giovanni Battista: 115.
Passignano (Domenico Cresti): 111.
Pastore Jacopo: 208.
Pastura (Antonio da Viterbo): 350, 372, 410, 411.
Pastura (Antonio Massaro): 364.
Patalano Gaetano: 152.
Patania Giuseppe: 16.
Patini Teofilo: 101.
Patricolo Giuseppe: 227.
Paul: 115.
Pauri Giuseppe: 158.
Pazera (Giovanni di Pietro): 411.
Pellegrini Giambattista: 70, 200, 410.
Pellegrino Pellegrini (Pellegrino Tibaldi): 21, 85, 139, 155, 178, 212, 312, 316, 381, 400.
Pellegrini Sebastiano di Francesco: 205.
Pellegrino: 325.
Pellegrino da Fanano: 111.
Pellegrino da San Daniele: 95, 299, 342, 373.
Pellizzi Domenico: 271.
Penna Cesare: 151.
Pennacchi P.: 395.
Pennino Leonardo: 84.
Pennisi Antonio: 83.
Peranda Sante: 71, 99, 187.
Peretti Lorenzo: 106.
Perin del Vaga (Pietro Buonaccorsi): 86, 274.
Perini Francesco di Amelia: 20.
Peroni Giuseppe: 234.
Perricci Ignazio da Monopoli: 191.
Persico Paolo: 75.
Persico Saverio: 28, 139.
Persio Altobello: 174.

Persio Domizio di Matera: 174.
Perugino (Pietro di Cristoforo Vannucci): 46, 47, 54, 80, 86, 93, 100, 111, 194, 196, 238, 240, 308, 330.
Peruzzi Baldassarre: 71, 152, 283.
Peruzzini Domenico: 374.
Peruzzini Giovanni: 143.
Pesenti Pietro: 292, 293.
Petondi Gregorio: 135.
Petrini Francesco: 147.
Petrini Giuseppe Antonio: 200.
Petruccioli Cola: 341.
Piacentini Marcello: 53, 56.
Pialorsi family: 54.
Piazza Albertino: 155.
Piazza Callisto: 56, 95, 103, 107, 155, 261.
Piazza Martino: 155.
Piazzetta Giovanni Battista: 41, 42, 156, 291, 392, 395, 406.
Picàno Giuseppe: 12.
Picchi Giorgio: 374.
Piccio (Giovanni Carnovali): 17.
Pier Francesco Fiorentino: 86, 142.
Piergentili Francesco da Cascia: 72.
Piermarini Giuseppe: 76, 170, 178, 181, 182, 200.
Piero della Francesca: 27*, 28, 238, 308, 313*, 374, 378*.
Pieroni Alessandro: 154, 155.
Pietro Alemanno: 29, 198, 274, 303, 354.
Pietro da Borghetto: 243.
Pietro da Cagnano: 243.
Pietro da Cortona: 36, 53, 78, 102, 129, 321, 323.
Pietro da Montepulciano: 163, 218.
Pierre d'Agincourt: 41, 165, 214.
Pietro da Rimini: 38, 358.
Pietro de Bontade: 227.
Pietro di Giovanni: 411.
Pietro di Vannini: 20.
Pilacorte Giovanni Antonio: 258, 341.
Pintorno Giovanni Francesco: 207.
Pinturicchio (Bernardino di Betto): 102, 280, 287*, 289, 308, 324, 330, 341*, 342, 357*.
Piola Domenico: 136, 147, 325, 413.
Piperno Donato: 45.
Pippo di Antonio Fiorentino: 342.
Pirez Alvaro: 299.
Pisanello (Antonio Pisano): 46, 167*, 170, 402, 403.
Pistocchi Giuseppe: 110.
Pittoni Giovan Battista: 57, 199, 200, 356.
Pittoni Girolamo: 404.

Pizzafuoco (Francesco Dattaro): 104.
Platania Giacinto: 234.
Poletti Luigi: 90, 311.
Polidoro da Caravaggio: 45, 62.
Polidoro da Lanciano: 191.
Polinari Andrea: 357.
Pollack Leopold: 99, 181.
Pollaiolo Antonio: 181, 253.
Pomarancio (Cristoforo Roncalli): 101, 158, 260, 308, 312, 409.
Pomarancio (Niccolò Circignani): 20, 93, 324.
Pompei Alessandro: 144.
Pontelli Baccio: 66, 141, 206, 218, 280, 323, 375.
Pontormo (Jacopo Carrucci): 132, 254, 272.
Ponzello Domenico: 135, 307.
Ponzi Domenico: 138.
Poppi (Francesco Morandini): 97, 258, 306.
Pordenone (Giovanni de' Sacchis): 19, 99, 101, 103, 127, 132, 243, 258, 259, 299, 341, 342, 372.
Porretta Eugenio: 347.
Porrina Pietro Paolo da Casole: 333.
Porta Andrea: 144.
Porta Carlo: 78.
Porta Ferdinando: 406.
Porta Orazio: 160.
Portalone Giovanni: 320.
Postiglione Raffaele: 75.
Postiglione Salvatore: 208.
Pourbus Frans, the Younger: 167*, 170
Pourbus Pieter: 80.
Pozzo Andrea: 52, 160, 190, 283.
Prata Francesco: 70.
Prestinari Michele: 215.
Preti Francesco Maria: 78, 344.
Preti Mattia: 41, 55, 83, 101, 131, 202, 321, 353.
Previati Gaetano: 103.
Previtali Andrea: 17, 46.
Primario Gogliardo: 202.
Prina Giuseppe: 54.
Prinzi Giuseppe: 263.
Probst Agostino Luigi: 58.
Procaccini Camillo: 58, 70, 80, 243, 271, 368, 413.
Procaccini Giulio Cesare: 133, 201, 257.
Provenzani Domenico: 205.
Provost Jean: 243.
Puccio di Paolo: 240.
Puig Michele di Bolotana: 163.
Puligo Domenico: 22.
Puppin Valentino: 320.

Quadrio Giovanni Battista: 96.
Quadrio Girolamo: 18.
Quaglia Giulio: 95, 399.

Quaresima Francesco: 60.
Quarini Mario Ludovico: 298.
Quattrini Enrico: 263.
Quentin Massys: 130.
Querici Dario: 263.

Raffaellino (Raffaello del Colle): 311, 374.
Raffaellino da Reggio (Raffaellino Motta): 38, 69.
Raffaellino del Garbo: 253.
Raffaello da Montelupo: 241.
Ragazzi Giovanni Battista: 189.
Ragazzini Giovanni Battista: 111.
Raggi Antonio: 78.
Ragozzino Gennaro: 187.
Raguzzini Filippo: 45.
Raimondo da Francavilla: 164.
Rainaldi Carlo: 289.
Rainaldi Girolamo: 69, 116, 283.
Rainaldo: 35, 248.
Ramazzani Ercole: 119, 174, 207, 305.
Ramegialli Giovanni Pietro: 200.
Ranghieri Giovanni Battista: 52.
Raphael (Raffaello Sanzio da Urbino): 46, 61, 93, 130, 142, 151, 238, 243, 280, 283, 286, 321, 325, 368, 375, 401.
Rapous Vittorio Amedeo: 236.
Ratti Carlo Giuseppe: 206.
Raverti M.: 391.
Rebolino Gennaro: 83.
Regolia Michele: 254.
Rembrandt Harmenszoon van Rijn: 129, 159.
Reni Guido: 13, 30, 69, 78, 92, 119, 129, 158, 159, 271, 354.
Revelli Salvatore: 348.
Ricca Michele: 13.
Riccardi Gabriele: 151.
Riccardo da Lentini: 82.
Ricci Alessandro: 115.
Ricci Camillo: 141.
Ricci Giovanni: 128.
Ricci Marco: 43, 369.
Ricci Sebastiano: 41, 43, 96, 347, 356, 367.
Riccio (Andrea Briosco): 223.
Richini Francesco Maria: 184.
Riccomanni Francesco: 316.
Riccomanni Leonardo: 316.
Rico Andrea da Candia: 40.
Ridolfi Agostino: 412.
Ridolfi Claudio: 26, 237, 374, 375, 379.
Rizzo Antonio: 269, 369.
Rizzo Pietro: 107.
Roberto: 159, 167*.
Roberto di Oderisio: 364.
Rocco di Tommaso da Vicenza: 66, 237, 341, 368.
Rodari Tommaso: 99, 200.
Rodelgrimo di Monte Sant'Angelo: 198, 199.

Rodin Auguste: 110.
Romanelli Giovanni Francesco: 271, 410.
Romanino (Girolamo Romani): 31, 56, 57, 103, 189, 251, 261, 297, 367, 403.
Romano A.: 274.
Romano Gian Cristoforo: 86, 104.
Romualdo: 67.
Roos Filippo Pietro: 271.
Rosa Carlo: 40, 189.
Rosa Salvatore: 225, 275.
Rosai Ottone: 101.
Rosselli Bernardo di Girolamo: 234.
Rosselli Cosimo: 159.
Rosselli Domenico da Rovezzaño: 129, 309.
Rosselli Matteo: 246.
Rossellino Antonio: 110, 128, 202, 252.
Rossellino Bernardo: 122, 125, 240, 245, 280, 333.
Rossello di Jacopo Franchi: 118.
Rossetti Biagio: 117.
Rossi Domenico: 373, 386.
Rossi Epifanio: 62.
Rossi Gino: 101.
Rossi Mariano: 75, 320.
Rossi Nicola Maria: 245.
Rossi Pier Maria: 362.
Rossi Tommaso: 320.
Rosso Francesco: 16.
Rosso Giuseppe: 16.
Rosso Medardo: 243.
Rovisi Valentino: 84.
Rubens Peter Paul: 10, 92, 116, 135, 168*, 169, 325, 391.
Rubini Agostino: 404.
Ruggeri Giovanni: 58, 409.
Ruggero de Fragenis: 382.
Rustici Lorenzo: 326.
Ruther Carlo: 147.
Ruzzolone Pietro: 12, 84, 354.

Sabatini Carlo: 242.
Saccaccini Saccaccino: 126.
Saccardo Pietro: 220.
Sacchi Andrea: 38, 65, 271.
Sacchi Gaspare: 144.
Sacchi Pietro Francesco: 154.
Sacco Gennaro: 202.
Sacconi Giuseppe: 96.
Sada Carlo: 104.
Sagrera Guillèn: 201.
Sala Alessandro: 252.
Sala Vitale: 405.
Salimbeni Jacopo: 303, 308, 375.
Salimbeni Lorenzo: 302*, 303, 308, 314*, 375.
Salimbeni Ventura: 275.
Salmeggia (Enea Talpino): 16.
Salomone Gaetano: 75.
Salvi Niccolò: 286.

Sanfelice Ferdinando: 160, 205, 208.
Sangallo Antonio the Elder: 198, 206.
Sangallo Antonio the Younger: 68, 76, 93, 96, 127, 158, 198, 206, 217, 239, 283, 286.
Sangallo, Francesco da: 118, 132.
Sangallo, Giovanni da: 254.
Sangallo, Giuliano da: 102, 125, 141, 254, 262.
Sangiorgio Abbondio: 90.
San Martino da Napoli: 236.
Sanmartino Giuseppe: 203.
Sanmicheli Matteo: 71, 90, 297, 298.
Sanmicheli Michele: 152, 156, 192, 195, 223, 306, 391, 402, 403.
Sano di Matteo: 326.
Sano di Pietro: 10, 96, 193, 307, 334, 372.
Sansone (Giuseppe Marchesi): 79.
Sansovino Andrea (Andrea Contucci): 116, 198.
Sansovino Jacopo (Jacopo Tatti): 56, 111, 223, 385, 386, 391, 392, 399, 411.
Santacroce Federico: 22.
Santafede Fabrizio: 67, 245, 260.
Santi Giovanni: 60, 63*, 375.
Santi di Tito: 325.
Sanz Giovanni Antonio: 98.
Saraceni Carlo: 130.
Sarnelli Antonio: 70, 200.
Sarti Antonio: 105, 143, 218.
Sartori Antonio Giuseppe: 290.
Sartorio Giuseppe: 143.
Sarzana (Domenico Fiasella): 154, 307, 325.
Sassetta (Stefano di Giovanni): 101, 102, 140, 140*, 326.
Sassoferrato (Giovanni Battista Salvi): 30, 60, 195, 372.
Savoldo Gerolamo: 50*.
Savonanzi Emilio: 65, 323.
Scacco Cristoforo: 69.
Scalvini Pietro: 95, 199.
Scalza Ippolito: 118, 197, 218.
Scamozzi Vincenzo: 78, 106, 156, 192, 230, 293, 385, 386, 395, 404, 406.
Scapitta Giovanni Battista: 71.
Scaramuzzino B.: 324.
Scarpagnino (Antonio Abbondi): 386, 391, 395.
Scarpari Giovan Battista: 12.
Scarsella Ippolito: 100.
Schauer Valentino: 58.
Schiaffino Francesco: 136, 206.
Schiavi Domenico: 246.
Schiavi Giuseppe Antonio: 144.
Schiavone (Andrea Meldolla): 43.
Schopf Giuseppe: 52, 58.
Sciacca Tommaso: 153, 175.

Scilla Agostino: 62, 335.
Sciuti Giuseppe: 10, 83, 263.
Scoccianti Andrea: 105.
Scolari Aldo: 192.
Sebastiani Sebastiano da Camerino: 156.
Sebastiano da Osteno: 25.
Sebastiano del Piombo (Sebastiano Luciani): 93, 233, 283, 411.
Sebastiano Pisano: 139.
Secante Sebastiano: 134.
Secanti Secante: 95.
Segna di Bonaventura: 74*, 81.
Segusini Giuseppe: 13.
Semeghini Pio: 101.
Semini Francesco: 206.
Senisio Angelo: 192.
Serafini Paolo: 41.
Serafini Serafino: 186*, 188.
Seregni Vincenzo: 316.
Sermoneta (Girolamo Sicciolante): 372.
Serodine Giovanni: 401.
Serpotta Giacomo: 13, 16, 60, 77, 227, 354.
Serra Antonio: 306.
Sicurtà Luigi: 80.
Signorelli Luca: 26, 81, 89, 93, 94, 102, 158, 160, 197, 216, 218, 326, 326*, 373, 375.
Silvani Gherardo: 59, 326.
Silvestro dell'Aquila: 147, 154, 354.
Simone da Corleone: 228.
Simonelli Giuseppe: 36.
Simonetti Domenico: 212.
Siragusa Federico: 354.
Sirani Elisabetta: 78, 306.
Smiriglio Mariano: 294.
Sodo (Giovanni Pace): 22.
Sodoma (Giovanni Antonio Bazzi): 29, 197, 283, 307, 330, 334, 337*, 346.
Sogliani Giovanni Antonio: 22.
Solari Cristoforo: 99.
Solari Giovanni: 86.
Solari Guiniforte: 86.
Solari Pietro Antonio: 182.
Solario Andrea: 381.
Solario Antonio: 93, 116.
Solaro (Bernardino Gatti): 406.
Solimena Angelo: 294, 297, 339.
Solimena Francesco: 36, 41, 45, 69, 147, 152, 164, 205, 294, 297, 325, 339, 401.
Solosmeo Antonio: 258.
Sommavilla Goffredo: 246.
Sorbilli Giuseppe: 36.
Sorri Pietro: 258.
Sozi Bino: 373.
Sozio Alberto: 338*, 343.
Sozzi Olivio: 12, 67, 83.
Sozzo (Giuseppe Albino): 370.
Sozzo di Rustichino: 140.

Spadafora Giuseppe: 60.
Spadarino (Giovanni Antonio Galli): 21.
Spadino Giovan Paolo: 271.
Spagna (Giovanni di Pietro): 79, 194, 320, 343, 357.
Spagnoletto (Giuseppe Ribera): 207.
Spagnolo (Giuseppe Maria Crespi): 59, 102, 119.
Spani Bartolomeo: 271.
Spani Francesco: 291.
Spani Prospero (Prospero Logari): 271.
Spanzotti Giovanni Martino: 146, 365*.
Spazzi Lorenzo: 99.
Specchi Alessandro: 286.
Speranza Giovanni Battista: 126.
Spinelli Bartolomeo da Busseto: 243.
Spinello Aretino: 198.
Spotorno Domenico: 16.
Stagi Stagio: 323.
Stanziani Luigi: 130.
Stanzione Massimo: 10, 225, 364.
Starace Girolamo: 75.
Stefano da Carpi (Giuseppe Solieri): 319.
Stefano da Putignano di Apulia: 254.
Stefano da Verona (Stefano da Zevi): 144.
Stefano di Martino: 13.
Stella Fermo: 20, 200.
Stocchi Achille: 41.
Stocinger Giovanni: 52.
Stolz Michael: 59.
Stomer Mattia: 45, 60, 227.
Storer Johann Christophorus: 133.
Stradivari Antonio: 104.
Strafella Gianserio: 100, 151.
Stringa Francesco: 409.
Strozzi Bernardo: 154.
Sunter Jacopo: 58.

Tabacchetti Nicola (Nicholas Wespin): 381.
Tacca Pietro: 154*, 155, 262.
Tacconi Francesco: 362.
Taddeo di Bartolo: 26, 97, 197, 215, 248, 251, 303*.
Talenti Francesco: 121.
Tamagni Vincenzo: 29, 253.
Tanadei Francesco: 236.
Tantillo Bartolomeo: 77.
Tantino Giovanni d'Ariano di Puglia: 174.
Tauzio da Varallo (Antonio d'Errico): 106, 113*, 204*, 212, 379*, 380*, 381, 383*.
Tarabusi Andrea: 189.
Tarchi Ugo; 62.

Taricco Sebastiano: 55.
Tassi Agostino: 38.
Taucher Cristoforo: 138.
Tavarone Lazzaro: 325.
Tedici Filippo: 252.
Tempesta Antonio: 38, 68, 345.
Tenerani Pietro: 248.
Terzuolo (Mariotto di Paolo Sensi): 237.
Tessari Girolamo: 261.
Testa Giuseppe: 175.
Testone Gaspare: 320.
Theodoli Girolamo: 318.
Theofilaktos: 71.
Tiarini Alessandro: 78, 158, 212, 243, 259, 271.
Tiberio di Assisi: 47, 79, 194.
Tiepolo Gian Domenico: 46, 106, 325, 373, 392, 406, 408*.
Tiepolo Giovanni Battista: 41, 46, 58, 109, 109*, 129, 212, 224, 291, 325, 344, 345, 369, 372, 373, 377*, 378*, 392, 394*, 395, 399, 400, 406.
Tino da Camaino: 83, 202, 248.
Tintoretto Domenico: 40.
Tintoretto (Jacopo Robusti): 12, 19, 57, 115, 163, 170, 236, 306, 376, 385, 386, 391, 392, 395, 398*, 399, 403, 406.
Tiso Oronzo: 58, 72, 151, 152.
Titian (Tiziano Vecellio): 21, 46, 57, 99, 246, 364, 368, 369, 375, 382, 385, 386, 392, 398*, 402, 404, 412.
Todeschini Giulio: 106.
Todeschino (Giacomo Francesco Cipper): 45.
Todos Pietro: 319.
Tolentino Francesco: 208.
Tomaiuoli Giuseppe: 187.
Tomaso da Villaco: 52.
Tominz Giuseppe: 138.
Tommaso da Modena: 189, 369.
Tommaso di Andrea da Pontedera: 251.
Tommaso Pisano: 251.
Torelli Felice: 89.
Torner Martin: 27.
Torreggiani Alfonso: 57, 175.
Torresani Alessandro: 205.
Torresani Bartolomeo: 205, 271.
Torresani Lorenzo: 272.
Torriani Orazio: 244.
Torricelli Giuseppe: 54.
Toschini Giovanni: 143.
Toselli Ottavio: 59.
Tosi Giuseppe: 374.
Traiano da Palestrina: 382.
Traini Francesco: 223, 251.
Tramello Alessio: 243.
Trécourt Jacques: 90.
Treglia Matteo: 61.
Trevisani Francesco: 52, 55, 259, 289, 401.

Tribolo (Niccolò Pericoli): 122, 272.
Triga Giacomo: 403.
Trivisonno Amedeo: 145.
Troger Paolo: 52, 58, 84.
Trotti Euclide: 54.
Truffetta (Monaldo da Viterbo): 411.
Tuccari Giovanni: 82.
Tura Cosmé: 46, 114*, 116, 117, 188*.
Turbino Antonio: 199.
Turri Teofilo: 274.
Tuscanus: 243.
Tuzi Vanni: 210.

Ugolino da Siena: 160.
Ugolino di Neri: 299.
Umile da Petralia: 98, 228, 254, 294.
Unterberger Cristopher: 58, 84, 143, 374.
Unterberger Francesco Sebaldo: 84, 211.
Unterberger Michelangelo: 58, 84.
Urbani Ludovico: 269.
Urbano da Cortona: 334.
Urbino Carlo: 103.

Vaccarini Giovanni Battista: 82, 83.
Vaccaro Andrea: 22, 40, 45, 130, 353.
Vaccaro Domenico Antonio: 142, 170.
Vaccaro Francesco: 62.
Vaccaro Giuseppe: 62.
Vaccaro Nicola: 41.
Vago Pietro: 243.
Valadier Giuseppe: 101, 286, 315.
Valenti Francesco: 177.
Valorsa Cipriano: 200.
Van Aelsi Pieter: 367.
Van den Heeke Francis: 375.
Van der Goes Hugo: 65.
Van der Stokt Vrancke: 64*.
Van Dyck Anthony: 135, 170, 227, 345, 364, 406.
Van Dyck Daniel: 42.
Van Loo Charles: 317.
Vanni Francesco: 26, 159, 334.
Vannone Andrea: 135, 136.
Vannucci Nicola: 357.
Van Oostsanen Jacob Cornelisz: 178.
Van Pitloo Antonio: 45.
Vanvitelli Carlo: 72, 75, 176.
Vanvitelli Luigi: 14, 21, 72, 73*, 75, 130, 158, 163, 241, 280, 283, 335.
Varlé Gioacchino: 115.
Varotari Dario: 261.
Vasari Giorgio: 28, 30, 40, 65, 93, 94, 122, 130, 198, 248, 251, 272, 300.

Vassalletto Pietro: 21, 411.
Vasta Pietro Paolo: 10.
Vecchietta (Lorenzo di Pietro): 80, 81, 245, 326.
Vecelli Francesco: 369.
Vecellio Cesare: 153.
Vecellio Francesco: 315.
Vecellio Marco: 369.
Vecellio Orazio: 61.
Velasquez Giuseppe: 12, 60, 77, 207, 211, 263.
Vellani Francesco: 188.
Venturi Ghino: 138.
Venusti Marcello: 274.
Venuta Domenico: 38.
Venzano Luigi: 325.
Vergelli Tiburzio da Camerino: 65, 156, 158.
Verla Francesco: 320.
Vermexio Giovanni: 336.
Veronese (Paolo Caliari): 40, 78, 95, 148, 172*, 173, 191, 192, 223, 273, 385, 386, 392, 394*, 395, 395*, 397*, 399, 403, 404, 406.
Verrio Antonio: 152.
Verrocchio (Andrea di Cione): 123*, 251, 252, 374, 395.
Vetraio (Gianfranco Bembo): 104.
Vetri Paolo: 102.
Viani A. Maria: 165.
Viani Domenico Maria: 144.
Vici Andrea: 111, 129, 218.
Vigarani Gaspare: 271.
Vignali Jacopo: 272.
Vigni Corrado: 355.
Vignola (Jacopo Barozzi): 38, 59, 68, 69, 101, 209, 234, 243, 272, 283, 289, 341.
Villareale Valerio: 14, 75.

Vincenzo d'Annibale: 131.
Vincenzo da Pavia (Vincenzo degli Azani): 13, 226.
Vischer Pieter: 409.
Visconti Giovanni Maria: 239.
Vitale da Bologna: 95, 256, 373, 411.
Vitale Filippo: 170.
Vitali Alessandro: 115.
Vitali Candido: 85.
Vitali Giovanni Battista: 156.
Vitaliano Gioacchino: 227.
Viti Timoteo; 129, 142, 143, 375.
Vitoni Ventura: 253.
Vittone Bernardo Antonio: 55, 90, 193, 236, 298.
Vittoria Alessandro: 96, 386, 395.
Vittozzi Ascanio: 190, 358, 360.
Vivarini Alvise: 41, 375, 395.
Vivarini Antonio: 40, 42, 46, 93, 101, 132, 218, 291, 395.
Vivarini Bartolomeo: 17, 31, 40, 42, 69, 175, 200, 218, 254, 391, 395.
Viviani Antonio: 111.
Viviani Lodovico: 374.
Viviani Ottavio: 158.
Viviani Santi: 250*.
Volaire Pierre Jacques: 45.
Volpe Vincenzo: 199.
Volterrano (Baldassarre France-schini): 272.
Voltolini Luigi: 339.

Wenter Marini Giorgio: 291.
Wicar Giovanni Battista: 55.
Wiligelmo: 188, 188*.

Zaccagni Bernardino: 234.
Zaccagni Giovanni Francesco: 234.

Zalone: 85, 85*.
Zambelli Damiano: 240.
Zambelli Stefano: 240.
Zamberlan Francesco: 291.
Zampa Giacomo: 161.
Zancani Montuoro Paola: 225.
Zanchi Antonio: 109, 153, 192.
Zanchi Giuseppe: 101.
Zaniberti Filippo: 37.
Zannino di Pietro: 271.
Zanotti Bianco Umberto: 225.
Zavattari (brothers): 220.
Zeiller Francesco Antonio: 101.
Zelli Costantino di Jacopo: 350.
Zelotti Gian Battista; 156, 196, 261, 356, 404.
Zenale Bernardino: 70, 368, 368*.
Zeni Bartolomeo: 247.
Zenone da Campione: 341.
Zenon Veronese (Zeno Donato): 106, 297.
Zimatore Carmelo: 343.
Zimbalo Francesco Antonio: 151, 152.
Zingarello (Pietro Negroni): 14, 82, 103.
Zingarello (Giuseppe Zimbalo): 151, 152.
Zocchi Gabriele: 244.
Zondini Francesco: 89.
Zoppo di Gangi (Giuseppe Sa-lerno): 107, 242.
Zuccarelli Francesco: 344, 345.
Zuccari Federico: 11, 68, 69, 111, 346, 375.
Zuccari Taddeo: 11, 68, 69, 306, 346.
Zucchi Matteo: 106.
Zugno Francesco: 130.
Zullo Pietro: 177.
Zurlango Antonio: 56.

PHOTOGRAPHIC CREDITS
Photographs are by Sergio Anelli, Bruno Balestrini and from Electa Editrice archives.